Curtiss Fighter Aircraft 1917-1948

Curtiss Fighter Aircraft

A Photographic History 1917-1948

Francis H. Dean and Dan Hagedorn

Schiffer Military History
Atglen, PA

Book design by Ian Robertson.

Library of Congress Control Number: 2006931885

Printed in China.
ISBN: 978-0-7643-2580-9

We are interested in hearing from authors with book ideas on related topics.

Published by Schiffer Publishing Ltd.
4880 Lower Valley Road
Atglen, PA 19310
Phone: (610) 593-1777
FAX: (610) 593-2002
E-mail: Info@schifferbooks.com.
Visit our web site at: www.schifferbooks.com
Please write for a free catalog.
This book may be purchased from the publisher.
Please include $3.95 postage.
Try your bookstore first.

In Europe, Schiffer books are distributed by:
Bushwood Books
6 Marksbury Avenue
Kew Gardens
Surrey TW9 4JF, England
Phone: 44 (0) 20 8392-8585
FAX: 44 (0) 20 8392-9876
E-mail: Info@bushwoodbooks.co.uk.
Visit our website at: www.bushwoodbooks.co.uk
Free postage in the UK. Europe: air mail at cost.
Try your bookstore first.

Contents

Introduction and Acknowledgments

"Diz" Dean was, for me, the best kind of friend. He spoke airplane very fluently indeed, and it is a signal honor for the undersigned to have been entrusted by his sweetheart and wife, Evelyn, and son Bob, to complete this, his labor of love.

Fellow aviation historian Ted Young himself, with Lou Eltscher, both great chroniclers of the Curtiss-Wright epic, upon review of a draft of this work, asked exactly what I thought Diz had in mind when he started it all. Clearly, as an engineer of the first order, he wanted to detail the aircraft described herein from that perspective. Not a single word of his content has been changed. It is all here, and it will not take the reader long to comprehend the words and performance data that are his great contribution. He was determined to present to students of Curtiss aircraft, and posterity in general, the best information available on this subject—and often found the data published and attributed as sacred, questionable.

There have been a number of outstanding contributions to the history of Curtiss and Curtiss-Wright aircraft. Page Shamburger and Joe Christy co-authored ***The Curtiss Hawks*** (Wolverine Press, Kalamazoo, MI, Library of Congress 79-173429) in 1972, and for overall coverage, with the data and first-hand interviews with many of the pilots and engineers still alive at that time, it remains one of the very best treatments of this class of warplanes extant. Then, in 1979, the late, great historian Peter M. Bowers gave us ***Curtiss Aircraft 1907-1947*** (Putnam & Co., Ltd, London, ISBN 0-370-10029-8). These two standards were followed by Diz Dean's own ***America's Hundred Thousand*** from Schiffer in 1997 (ISBN 0-7643-0072-5), which has an outstanding section on the P-40 series and, over the span of years, numerous other smaller monographs and journal articles devoted, in particular to the *Hawk* and P-40 series. One of the best of these has been the two-volume ***P-40 Warhawk in Detail*** by Bert Kinzey (Squadron/Signal Publications, Carrollton, TX, 1999, ISBN 1-888974-15-X etc).

No single work, however, has been devoted to the scout, pursuit, and fighter aircraft that were spawned by Curtiss engineering during its meteoric, barely four decades of existence. This volume was designed to fill that void.

All of the previous works cited, that dealt with various aspects of Curtiss aircraft, suffered from three specific shortcomings, at least insofar as your scribes have been able to determine. These were not the fault of the authors in question but, rather, due to the simple logistics of the resources available. The so-called Sarah Clark Collection at the National Archives at College Park (Records Group 342) had not been opened for public review. The Curtiss-Wright Corporate Archive Collection held by the National Air and Space Museum's Archives had not been processed to completion and opened, and the records of the U.S. Air Force Historical Research Agency at Maxwell Air Force Base, Alabama, had not been completely indexed or opened. Diz was aware of these resources, but ran out of time before he could avail himself of the enormous resources of data that these three repositories held. The undersigned deliberately decided to do so, and the resulting wealth of data presented herein, much of it for the first time, has been the result. The Curtiss-Wright Corporate Archive alone, some 330 cubic feet in size, which was examined page-by-page, box-by-box, was nothing short of a revelation in many instances.

A few words about the designations of Curtiss and Curtiss-Wright aircraft contained herein, and about the several Annexes.

The section headings and aircraft designations presented herein are *precisely as they were documented on primary source Curtiss, Curtiss-Wright, or customer documents*. This may require reconsideration of some very long-standing and deeply rooted accounts of Curtiss and Curtiss-Wright aircraft. We have, for instance, included as an Annex a complete reproduction of the document that Peter M. Bowers used as the basis for his own presentation of both Curtiss and associated end-user designations. We felt it was important to do this so that the reader can gain a measure of understanding of how this document originated (well after the fact), and how it compares with the data contained in this volume. Although Pete spoke to the provenance of this document in the opening pages of his classic book, his words have been largely overlooked, and the greater text and resulting headings accepted as gospel. Other Annexes have been included that, it is hoped, will facilitate further research by students of aviation history. These Annex additions are purely the responsibility of the undersigned and, although Diz had commenced some notes along this line, he was unable to complete them.

Some readers will also observe that some Curtiss aircraft that have been included in other works on this manufacturer under the extremely broad "fighter" genre have been omitted from this work, while others, not usually so connected, have been added. Notable amongst these, to some readers, will be the nearly complete absence of any of the notable Curtiss racing aircraft of the 1920s, in particular. Diz Dean made a conscious decision not to include these aircraft, although they may arguably have had "pursuit" or fighter connections, on the grounds that, without exception, they were not armament capable. In other instances, co-author Hagedorn has expanded the content relating, in particular, to aircraft produced by the Curtiss-Wright St. Louis factory. This is justified on the grounds that the aircraft included specific mention in sales literature and Curtiss-Wright Export Corporation documents to "fighter" variants or capabilities, even though they were often employed in a more "general purposes" role.

In a work of this magnitude, a very large number of people had involvement at many levels. Unfortunately, Diz had not assembled a listing of the sources he had engaged, but it is hoped that this summary, prepared by the undersigned, will acknowledge most, if not all, of the friends that have combined their resources, talent, and energy to make this book a reality.

First and foremost, once again to Diz himself, his lovely Evelyn, and son Bob, for entrusting the undersigned with this duty of honor. I sincerely hope that the result will please them, and do justice to his memory and vision.

To my colleagues at the National Air and Space Museum, where I have the high privilege of spending my waking hours, my profound thanks to my fellow staffers Dana Bell, Phil Edwards, Marilyn Graskowiak, Kate Igoe, Allan Janus, Mark Kahn, Kristine Kaske-Martin, Melissa Keiser, Brian Nicklas, David Schwartz, Paul Silbermann, Mark Taylor, Barbara Weitbrecht, Patricia Williams, and the great Larry Wilson. Each, in his or her own unique way and area of specialization, has contributed to this work. They constitute, collectively, a hidden national treasure for aviation historians, and seldom receive recognition for their sterling efforts.

Staff members of the National Archives at College Park, especially Kate in the Still Pictures Branch and Dave Giordano in Military Textual Reference, guided the undersigned through the often labyrinthine holdings of that national treasure trove. An enormous amount of work still remains to be done, however, and students of Curtiss history should take heart. Many answers reside therein.

Other aviation museums and their dedicated staff members were also extremely helpful, and include the great aero-historian Ray Wagner, Pam Gay (Archivist and Librarian), Alan Renga, and the staff of the San Diego Aerospace Museum, and Dennis Parks and Katherine Williams at the Museum of Flight in Seattle, who were especially important in identifying the spectacular color imagery that was added, at the eleventh hour, to this work. Piotr C. Zliwowski of the Warsaw Rising Museum verified the identity of one of the few remaining genuine *Hawk* export aircraft. Mr. Louis S. Casey, one of the great officers of the formative years of the National Air Museum and National Air and Space Museum, led the undersigned to the Holly Grail after a 35 year search, the so-called Curtiss Billing Book, which enabled verification of many of the delivery statistics presented herein for the first time. For that singular effort, thanks must be extended to previously unheralded Curtiss accountants Louis Kessler and Ethel McNaughton.

Special thanks are due to a number of long-suffering specialists, without whom the quality of this work would have been very different. These include James P. Rybarczyk, who prepared the special maps and assignment summaries for all P-36, YP-37, and P-40 aircraft in the Army Air Corps inventory as of December 7, 1941. Joe Weathers did an enormous amount of dark room work for Diz, and many of the illustrations in this volume can be traced to his exquisite skills. Harm J. Hazewinkel, the great historian of Dutch aviation, contributed previously unpublished details and photos of Dutch use of Curtiss and Curtiss-Wright aircraft, as did Portuguese historian Mario Canongia Lopes on the *Mohawks* used by the airmen of his nation. John W. (Jack) Connor and Jessie Hendershot, former Pratt & Whitney employees, came through with little-known shots of the "Super P-36" through the efforts of Bruce van der Mark, and David Zwolak assisted with the little-known Ernest Udet *Hawks*. Former Senior NASM Curator and friend Robert C. Mikesh led the undersigned to Shorzoe Abe, noted historian of Japanese aviation, and Ted Young, co-author of ***What Ever Happened to Curtiss-Wright?***, reviewed the draft of this manuscript, and made very important suggestions and modifications. Tuncay Deniz provided exceptional assistance on the little-known details of Turkish Air Force *Hawks*. Fellow enthusiasts, historians, and authors that provided unique insights and photos to this project have included Roger Besecker, W. Yip, Philippe Listemann (of the French *Aéro ...ditions)*, Leif Hellström (one of the most tenacious aero-historians I know), William B. Johnson, M. L. Shetle, Jr., Lennart Andersson, William Green, Colin A. Owers, Jim Halley (OBE), James V. Sanders of ***Small Air Forces Observer***, and Clarence Fu. Dave Ostrowski, editor of the wonderful quarterly ***Skyways***, dedicated to the aviation history of the 1920s and 1930s, was invariably supportive, and a priceless friend through it all. Roland Rohlfs provided priceless images of the earliest Curtiss scout designs that have for so long confounded historians. Brazilian artist and aviation historian Rudnei Dias DaCunha also donated his beautiful drawings of Brazilian Air Force P-40s to this work, which have never been presented in an English-language publication before. Amaru Tincopa of Peru provided some extremely rare photos of Peruvian aircraft not otherwise obtainable anywhere, and Cato Guhnfeldt and Per Bugge provided extremely rare images of Norwegian *Hawks*.

Last but by no means least, to my sweetheart Kathleen, who has endured the lonely hours listening to me pecking on this instrument of the devil in the den, and who always seemed to know when I needed a break or a hug, or a cup of nectar.

Dan Hagedorn
Fairfax, VA, February 2006

1

The First Curtiss Scouts and Pursuits

As the war in Europe escalated in 1914, and held every promise of continuing on for some time, the exponential demand for ever more capable aeroplanes by the warring powers spurred an industry into existence. Ironically, the European demands for new and better types for combat were directed towards their own home infrastructure, and the British, in particular, relied upon U.S. sources, of whom Curtiss was the chief beneficiary, for primarily training, unarmed reconnaissance, and slow patrol flying boat types.

It is perhaps not surprising, therefore, that U.S. development of what were commonly termed "scouts" during the interim period lagged behind the very rapid evolution of such types pouring forth from the factory doors of European designers. By 1915 the French had fielded the Nieuport 11 *Bèbè* in modest numbers, while the British had mounted, in squadron strength, both the Bristol *Scout D* series and Royal Aircraft Factory F.E.2b pushers, to counter the so-called "Fokker Scourge" of the German Fokker E.IIIs.

Inspired by designer B. D. Thomas, who had worked with Sopwith in England before coming to Curtiss, the Model S (retrospectively called the S-1) was allegedly a 1914 product, but probably didn't fly until this November 21, 1916, image with Victor Carlstrom at the controls. The rudder and vertical stabilizer were almost certainly inadequate. *(via Peter M. Bowers)*

By the close of 1916 the French had produced the Nieuport 17 and SPAD S.VII, the British the Sopwith *Pup* and Bristol F.2B *Fighter,* and the Central Powers were sending to combat units the classic Albatros D.II and Halberstadt D.II. The United States, meanwhile, was floundering about in uncertainty, and only dimly aware that it might become embroiled in the conflict in the not-so-distant future. As an indirect consequence, a combination of exceptionally poor intelligence on the part of U.S. agencies and industrial concentration on preparing for and fulfilling comparatively huge orders for non-combat types had combined to place U.S. development of "scout" type aircraft woefully far behind European technology.

While it may appear that the Curtiss S series benefited from European experience up to the time the first of the series appeared in 1916, they probably owed more to the preceding JN trainer series than to any deep analysis of the latest developments in France and Britain.

Thus Curtiss, by 1916 the largest aircraft manufacturer in the United States, entered into the development of "scout" aircraft hesitantly, and on a rather low priority basis, and probably would not have gone that far had it not been encouraged by relatively modest U.S. Army and Navy development contracts. One of the great fighter aircraft producers of the first half of the 20th century, the products of which became literally legendary, had arrived at the threshold of this epoch with virtually no experience in designing or building single-seat, combat aircraft.

The Curtiss S-1 to S-6 Series

The first Curtiss airplane design that could possibly be labeled a fighter type was the Model S-3 of 1917. Such a label was, even at that, a stretch, since the basic aircraft had no armament, and the airplane was defined as a scout, although many aircraft so defined were retrospectively described by the modern term 'fighter.' A small, neat, single seat triplane, the S-3 had been preceded in the Curtiss family by a 1914 Model S-1 *Scout* (initially as simply the Model S *Scout*, and later, occasionally, as *Baby Scout*) biplane. The S-1 had been designed as the smallest airplane that could be built using the Curtiss OX or OXX-3 type engine of 90 to 100 horsepower, and had a wingspan of only 20 feet. Apparently, it was tested only with a Curtiss OX-2 90hp V-8 engine. Only one was built, and very little is known about its testing or subsequent existence, although some components were apparently used to fashion the following S-2. The aircraft was not sold, and was apparently retained by Curtiss and faded into obscurity.

The single S-2 *Scout (Tubing)*[1] biplane, also sometimes cited as the *Wireless Scout*—again a private venture with no military sales—had an upper wing of increased span (21 feet, 10 inches, although the span of the lower wing was reduced from 18 to 11 feet, three inches) and was "wireless," because no external wires were used for wing cellule bracing. A single wide I-type strut was employed outboard on each side between biplane wings. It also employed an OX-2 engine of 90hp and, surprisingly for such a small aircraft, had an endurance of 3.58 hours. It was flown for the first time on August 8, 1916, by Victor Carlstrom, and it was credited with turning in a speed of 119mph, very creditable for the day.

The next variation in the series, the S-3[2], differed in being a triplane with narrow two foot chord wings each of 25 foot span and, in the final variant, gaps between wings of 30 inches. An early S-3 version had the middle wing sections attached, at their inboard ends, to the wide chord cabane struts from fuselage to top wing in an apparently poor structural arrangement. Later (some time after February 15, 1917) a change was made to make the inboard ends of

Redesigned with a new, larger upper wing, extra set of diagonal interplane struts, and much larger rudder and vertical fin, the S-1 flown by Carl Betts at Newport News, Virginia, for Army observers, by which time it was being cited as the *Baby Speed Scout*. This configuration has never been illustrated before. *(via Peter M. Bowers)*

One of the fastest aircraft in the U.S. as of its first flight August 8, 1916, the S-2, although frequently cited as having been built up from the S-1, in actuality shared very few features. Surprisingly, it was said to have an endurance of more than three hours. The rudder was almost certainly inadequate. (*Dean Collection*)

A very dapper Glenn H. Curtiss himself, right, listens to test pilot Victor Carlstrom comment on the tight cockpit of the Curtiss S-3, complete with "E" type spinner and very large prop blades, probably before the first flight late in 1916. The S-3 owed much to the S-1 fuselage. (*Curtiss via Johnson*)

the middle wing attach directly to the fuselage upper longerons in a more structurally efficient manner. The wing gap was thus reduced to the 30 inches noted. The top wing had no dihedral, while the lowest wing was sloped up at 4.5 degrees. The wing system had no sweepback, a stagger of 9.5 degrees, and an incidence of 3.5 degrees. Total wing surface area was 142.66 square feet, equally distributed, yielding a wing loading at design gross weight of 9.25 pounds per square foot. Wing bracing, both cabane and outboard, was of the single strut I-type, but wire bracing was also employed. Ailerons were fitted on each of the three wings, and tied to work together. Wing structure was wood with fabric covering, as were fuselage and tail surfaces. The fixed tail down landing gear was conventional, with fairing between gear struts, and used a wheel size of 26 by 3 inches.

The S-3 power plant was a water-cooled Curtiss OXX-3[3] eight cylinder upright "V" type rated at 100hp at 1400rpm driving a two blade fixed pitch propeller. Engine bore and stroke were 4.25 and 5.0 inches, respectively. Fuel tank capacity was 25 gallons, and engine oil capacity 4.0 gallons. Specific fuel and oil consumptions of the OXX engine were nominally 0.60 and .03 pounds per horsepower per hour, respectively. In a very clean arrangement, an annular engine water cooling radiator was located just behind the propeller with cooling air fed through an open-nosed propeller over the hub, making a snub nose. This arrangement was later called an E-type spinner.

Empty weight of the S-3 was only 970 pounds. Adding a useful load of 350 pounds, comprised of 155 pounds of fuel, 30 pounds of oil, and a rather light pilot weight of 165 pounds (no parachute!), the gross weight came to 1320 pounds.

Standard items of fixed equipment included a tachometer, gas and oil gages, and a complete set of tools.

The Curtiss Aeroplane Company had the following comments about the S-3 in their 1917 brochure:

This photo of an S-3, with the middle wing joining the fuselage longerons at the base of the cabane struts, has never been published before, and also reveals a much smaller rudder than on the definitive version. Test pilot Roland Rohlfs remembered it as an S-1, but it is clearly an S-3 variant. (*Roland Rohlfs*)

Although the U.S. had not yet entered the war, the advent of the triplane scout had been followed keenly, as both the Allies and Central Powers in Europe fielded variants in large numbers. Mating a 100hp Curtiss OXX-3 with a good airframe could have given the U.S. its first competitive fighter. *(Dean Collection)*

"The Curtiss Triplane Speed Scout is essentially a one man machine designed for speed and great climbing ability. Inasmuch as its safety in war, like that of the torpedo boat destroyer in the Navy, depends on its ability to dart here and there, with a swiftness that precludes successful pursuit, this little craft is so compacted in size, and so intensely powered as to be able to make the maximum speed of 115 mph, yet it will fly at the slow speed of 55 mph.

Under normal conditions, it is able to leave the ground in less than 300 ft., and it has frequently in tests, been made to climb 9,000 ft. in 10 minutes.

Due to its small size it rapidly becomes imperceptible to the eye after it has been in the air a few minutes. At 5,000 ft. it is barely a dot; at 10,000 ft. it is out of sight to the average human eye.

It has a total wing spread of 25 ft., an overall length of 19.5 ft., and stands less than 9 ft. high. It differs quite materially in general construction from any of the other Curtiss models, not only in its triplane wing design, but the style of struts, bracing, and general assembly. The entire fuselage is covered, and even the propeller is fitted with a truncated streamlined hood which assists in cutting down the wind head-resistance.

Victor Carlstrom, the well known aviator, says it is one of the nimblest machines he has ever handled. He easily attained an altitude of 16,500 feet with it on its second trial flight.

Equipped with wireless (radio) it can be a wonderful aerial observation post, and for military reconnaissance and fast scouting work, promises to excel any other machine so far produced."

This glowing company account noted a scouting mission, with no guns mounted; thus, it could not be called an air-to-air fighter. However, a Curtiss letter dated February 15, 1917, listed 10 changes that a Captain Clark of the Army Air Service requested, and these included (No.7):

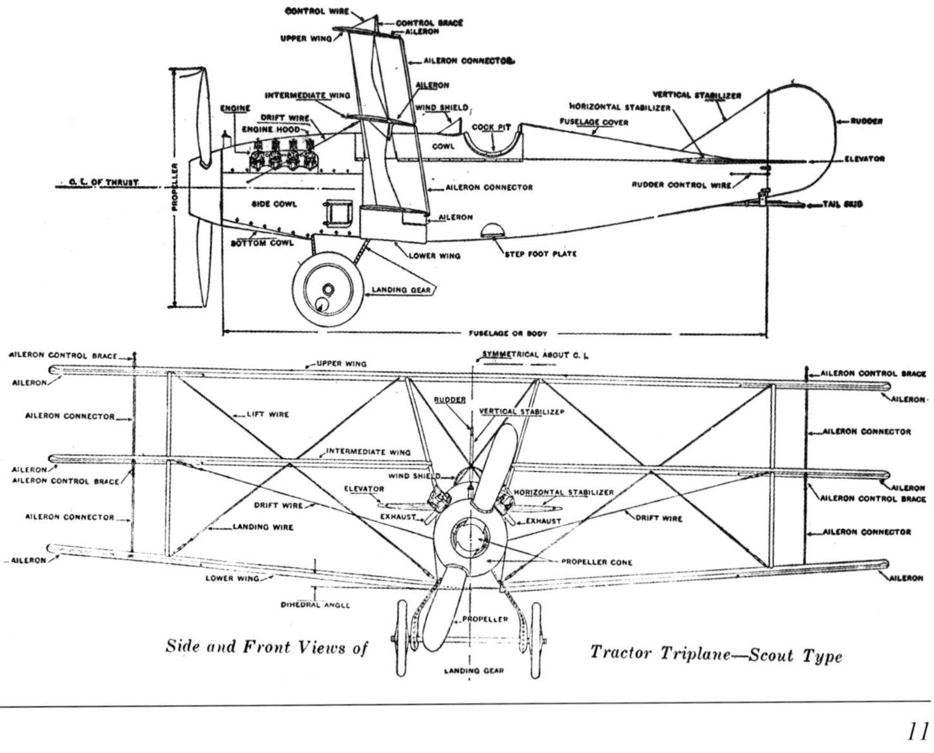

The only known schematic for the Curtiss S-3 appeared in a U.S. Army Air Service publication as a model for naming aircraft components current at that time. Oddly, it was not in the configuration accepted by the Air Service. *(U.S. Army Air Service)*

Delivered in mid-1917, four Curtiss S-3s were used only as trainers, although mounting at least a gun was mentioned as early as February of that year. Here, S.C.322 is shown in the final configuration in Virginia. (*NARA*)

"*...method of operating the gun decided upon was one in which a handle was grasped and pulled backward.*"

The four aircraft purchased by the Army Signal Corps on Contract No.5947, (see footnote 3) November 20, 1916, and delivered in mid-1917 (S.C. serial numbers 322 to 325) were used only as trainers, and the propeller spinner was omitted. The first of these was delivered in June 1917, followed by the other three in July, at Hampton, VA, where the Army received an urgent telegram from Curtiss advising that they wanted to "*...send a mechanic to install extra braces to strengthen the beams of the upper wing panel.*" One of these, S.C.324, was reported "*...broken in sand blowing tests at Hampton, Langley Field, and should be taken up on records as unserviceable*" as of July 8, 1918. It is significant that the four aircraft ordered by the Army were identified on the contract as simply Curtiss *Pursuits*.

With the exception of the triplane wings, a fad possibly initiated by the German Fokker Dr I triplane, the S-3 set the pattern in configuration for subsequent Curtiss pursuit/fighter planes.

It is worth noting that Curtiss prepared a special promotional flyer describing the S-3 in Spanish, which may rank as one of the first attempts to interest Latin American prospects in the Curtiss line of new-build aircraft. Interestingly, the S-3 was described in Spanish, accurately, as the *Explorador Veloz*.

Curtiss continued their S-series of scouts with S-4 (built for the U.S. Navy as Bureau of Aeronautics Number A-149 on Requisition CR-49, and formally designated by the Navy as the Curtiss *Triplane Tractor Speed Scout*; it was delivered to the Navy at Miami, FL, November 26, 1917, where it was lost on February 21, 1918, when the central pontoon collapsed on landing with a total of 3:40 hours on the airframe), S-5 (also built for the Navy, as A-150 on Requisition CR-49, it was delivered to Miami April 17, 1918, and was also formally designated as a *Triplane Tractor Speed Scout*, and survived to be placed in storage at the Naval Storehouse at Gloucester, NJ, June 28, 1918), and S–6 designs. The S-4 seaplane was a triplane tested by pilot Roland Rohlfs on November 4, 1917, using a single main seaplane float and wingtip floats. The S-5, cited in some Curtiss documents as the *OX Fighter* (significant in that it is the first known use of the term "fighter" associated with a Curtiss design) was similar, except it was fitted with twin floats having flat bottoms instead of a "V" shape. Rohlfs remembered it would not plane on the water, and had to be jerked into the air. The S-6 with the OXX-2 engine (cited in some Curtiss documents as the *Tractor Land*, only one of 12 ordered on Contract 6814[4] dated March 10,

Curtiss wired Army officials in Virginia in August 1917 to advise them that they were sending mechanics to add additional bracing to the upper wings of the four S-3s, but this did not happen in time to save this example, bearing the new national insignia in all four wing positions. (*NARA*)

Built for the Navy, the Curtiss S-4 (A149) was cited in Navy records as a *Triplane Tractor Speed Scout*, and was delivered to Miami November 26, 1917. It was lost there February 21, 1918, when the central float collapsed on landing. It has been cited erroneously in many accounts as having had twin floats. (*via Colin A. Owers*)

The first Curtiss "scout" series aircraft armed as a fighter, the S-6 incorporated major changes in the series that had commenced with the S-3. Still a triplane, the middle wing was now merged with the fuselage in a more structurally efficient manner, and two machine guns were fixed rather precariously to fire above the prop arc. (*Roland Rohlfs*)

Appearing ready for combat, Curtiss test pilot Roland Rohlfs poses in the armed S-6. This view shows good detail of the rather flimsy gun installation, and the complex cabane structure of the armed S-6. (*Roland Rohlfs*)

1917, was actually delivered, Signal Corps S.C.492) was a new landplane design with twin forward firing machine guns awkwardly supported on its cabane struts so as to fire above the propeller arc, and thus avoid a synchronization requirement. It was the first U.S. design to be so equipped as standard from the outset. Whether the guns were test fired is not known, but at least an attempt was made to mount weapons on an S- series design. The S-6 was the last known aircraft of the series, and is really the qualifying design for calling the S-type a Curtiss "fighter." The single example accepted by the Army was demonstrated by Curtiss at Dayton on December 27, 1917, along with the Model X-1 training triplane, and the Signal Corps formally accepted both on January 7, 1918.

Not previously reported, however, was the Curtiss S-8 *Biplane Scout*, apparently a design only, intended to mount a 275hp engine of unspecified type. The specifications, which were calculated to include a top speed of 140mph, were dated July 14, 1917. This design, of course, suggests that a type S-7 may have also been contemplated, but no documentation of this has been located.

The Curtiss GS-1 and GS-2

Again, Curtiss produced two types of scout aircraft—these for the U.S. Navy—which could not strictly be called fighter aircraft, because they were not armed. They are included because they had the general configuration of a fighter, and if they had been successful might have been developed into fighters. These planes were the single place GS-1 and GS-2 seaplanes. One GS-1 *Speed Scout*, Navy

The first Curtiss GS-1, the so-called *Speed Scout* for the U.S. Navy (A-868), was fitted with a rotary *Gnome* engine. The single main float had shock absorbers on the rear support struts and pin joints on the front support struts. It crashed during landing tests April 1, 1918, while being flown by Roland Rohlfs, who claimed it was due to the very strong torque reaction of the rotary engine. (*Roland Rohlfs*)

The Navy contracted for five Curtiss GS-2s in November 1917, and these are shown still under construction in the Curtiss shops as of February 15, 1918. All were accepted by the Navy by the end of March. They differed considerably from the single GS-1, mainly in their biplane configuration, and the unusual conical covering over the Gnome radial engines. If they were to be armed, no record has survived as to how this was to be accomplished. (*via Peter M. Bowers*)

Bureau of Aeronautics Number A-868, was procured under Contract 33603, and delivered to the Navy at Miami January 18, 1918: five GS-2 *Speed Scout* aircraft, Navy A-445 through A-449, were built under Contract 687W of November 22, 1917.

Early Curtiss test pilot Roland Rohlfs, who tested both aircraft types, provided the following information on these little-known aircraft in a letter of April 22, 1970:

"The GS-'s were Gnome Scouts having of course Gnome motors. The GS-1 and GS-2 were for the Navy. The GS-1 triplane was unique in that it had a shock absorbing pontoon hinging at the front, and its wings were covered with bakelite (this was a first). The use of shock absorbers was to see if they could compensate for a flat bottomed pontoon in rough water. We had no chance to prove this because it was cracked up on its first flight after we delivered it. Its color was olive drab throughout. I believe that the tail surfaces were also covered with bakelite. It was a tricky plane to land because of the heavy torque if the motor was applied while landing. That is what cracked it up.

The GS-2 biplane was all gray in color. The first flight proved that the water balance was tail heavy and the motor cowl came loose. We called it "The Swiss Cheese Wonder" because of the many holes in the tail post to lighten the structure.

Both aircraft were designed and built on Buffalo, NY. I do not know who designed them. It could have been the Navy. Performance was poor in each case, underpowered. I do not know what happened to the GS-2. I tested both in the Niagara River. I can only guess at the horsepower of the motors, but I think they were 110 HP each."

The Navy Aircraft History Cards for these aircraft in fact cited the engines as 100hp Gnomes. Exactly why the single GS-1 was issued an out-of-sequence Navy Bureau Number is unknown, although it was accepted by the Navy ahead of the GS-2s. It was damaged beyond repair April 1, 1918, while being tested, when it was forced to land due to engine trouble. The five GS-2s were accepted by the Navy between February and March 1918. A-445 and A-446 were assigned to Miami in February, and A-445 was wrecked there February 16th. A-446 survived to be stored at the Naval Storehouse at Gloucester, NJ, and was sold to an unknown buyer June 9, 1920, after accumulating 19 hours, 50 minutes of flying time. It had been damaged beyond repair, however, at Miami on July 6,

Test pilot Roland Rohlfs said that the GS-2 was tail-heavy, despite attempts to lighten the empennage, and was underpowered, as well. Of the five acquired, two went to Miami and three, with the end of the war, apparently never flew at all; two of these were sold surplus. Thus, the example shown here must be either A-445 or A-446 at Miami underway. (*Roland Rohlfs*)

Test pilot Roland Rohlf said that the GS-2s were tail-heavy, and this image seems to bear that out, while at the same time showing very good detail of the unusual strut arrangement on the main float, and diminutive size of the little scout. *(Roland Rohlfs)*

1918, when it turned over on landing, so apparently was sold as salvage only. A-447 was apparently never flown at all, going directly into storage at Gloucester, then to the Naval Aircraft Factory May 22, 1920, until sold to A. E. Carter of Sommerville, MA, August 10, 1920. A-448 was initially assigned to Anacostia Naval Air Station, DC, May 23, 1918, but passed to storage at Gloucester October 18th with no flight time recorded. The final aircraft (A-449), completed in May 1918, also went to storage at Gloucester in August, but was at the Naval Aircraft Factory by May 22, 1920, and was the last of these early aircraft still on the Navy inventory, not being formally stricken until November 9, 1923.

It is worth noting that the GS aircraft were the only Curtiss types designed from the outset to mount rotary engines.

The Curtiss Bristol *Fighter*

The English Bristol *Fighter*, produced starting in 1917 by the British and Colonial Aeroplane Company as the F.2B, was known affectionately as the "*Brisfit*," or "*Biff*." A two seat, double-bay biplane, the Bristol *Fighter*, after a slow start, became a great success, and was considered by many to have been the best all-around Allied fighter of World War I. The arrangement of pilot ahead and gunner close behind in a back-to-back arrangement seemed a quite efficient arrangement for air fighting.

Tested in January 1918 with a *Liberty 12* engine, the Curtiss-built Bristol *Fighter* rendered "dubious results." Although this image has been published and identified as A.S.34232, U.S. Army designation USAO-1—supposedly first off the line at the new Curtiss plant at Elmwood, near Buffalo—this was more likely the second example, A.S.34233. The *Liberty* and other added equipment were too much for the airframe. *(via Peter M. Bowers)*

This fighter biplane had a wingspan of 39 feet, 3 inches, and a length of 25 feet, 10 inches.

Both wings were spaced vertically away from the fuselage to give an aerodynamically efficient gap between wings of 64.5 inches, with the upper wing separated by conventional cabane struts, and the lower wing separated by struts from the fuselage bottom by several inches.

Though at times powered by various engines, the usual power plant was the 190hp Rolls Royce *Falcon*, a twelve cylinder water cooled "V" type later up rated to as high as 275hp. With the lower powered engine the aircraft gross weight was about 2780 pounds, and high speed was 120 mph. Construction was conventional, with wood framing and fabric covering. The horizontal tail assembly included a variable incidence stabilizer. Armament was a single forward firing fixed gun, and twin guns on a flexible mount for the rear seat man.

At war's end Britain had produced no fewer than 3,101 Bristol *Fighters*, with many employed all over the British Empire and in foreign service for years after the end of World War I.

Because of its success on the western front in the war the F.2B was selected by the Bolling Commission during wartime for mass license manufacture in the U.S. The U.S. program to produce an Americanized version was certainly a very confused one, and served as a good example of the frustration encountered in American attempts to be a primary source of aerial fighting machines for the Allied war effort of World War I. In June 1917 the U.S. Bolling Commission was sent to Europe to search for appropriate aircraft to produce. On August 1, 1917, General Pershing sent word that the F.2B, equipped with a 200hp Hispano Suiza engine, was the plane to build.

A sample British-built F.2B, to be used as a pattern aircraft, arrived in Washington, DC, on September 5, 1917, and got to Curtiss in November. The American desire was to make use of the then-new U.S. designed *Liberty* engine in a 12 cylinder version, and a set of design drawings to retrofit this engine type in the F.2B was made up by the U.S. Army Air Service. The Curtiss Aeroplane Company had been selected to produce the Bristol *Fighter* using the *Liberty* 12 engine, with American armament and other equipment. Curtiss engineers quickly decided the *Liberty* 12 engine was too much for the F.2B structure, and attempted a lot of redesign work, to the point where the aircraft was quite different from the original design set down by the Army. These aircraft received the U.S. designation USAO-1, which was, significantly, an Observation classification, not a fighter. The first contract (No.20203) for 1,000 aircraft was issued November 3, 1917, but this was cancelled and replaced by Order 20285, with serials in the S.C.25809 to 29058 blocks. This, too, was cancelled, and replaced once again with Contract 20387, with the total ordered doubled to 2,000, and the serials to have been S.C.34232 to 36231.

The first *Liberty* 12 powered aircraft was completed in late January 1918, and in early March was flight tested with "*...dubious results*," and the flight ended in a forced landing. Structural strengthening, plus more guns, ammunition, and fuel capacity had increased gross weight to almost 4,000 pounds. The plane was initially designed for a gross weight of 2,940 pounds, including all necessary equipment. The new aircraft, as built and test flown by Curtiss, weighed 700-800 pounds more than the Army design staff, led by Lt.Col. V. E. Clark, had calculated.

A second prototype aircraft was built up in a few days, and crashed when some fabric came off the upper wing. By late July 1918, 25 aircraft of the contract had been delivered, with 22 more assembled in the Curtiss shops, and about 90 aircraft sets of parts had been fabricated. Of these, apparently only 27[5] were actually accepted by the Army, and the fate of the remainder was strange, to say the least (see below). It had become clear that the *Liberty* 12 engine was simply too heavy and powerful for the airframe. The whole program was finally brought to an end by a third accident in July 1918 that killed both pilot and observer. The verdict was that "*...the plane as presently constructed was unsafe, overloaded, and had no military value, and was not acceptable*." Certainly nothing said could be more damning. The grand 2,000 plane program was ended with 27 planes produced at a staggering cost of $6.4 million. Curtiss was then supposed to build the British designed, Royal Aircraft Factory SE-5A fighter.

To this point, most of the facts laid down have been fairly well established. What has not been previously reported is that, as late as May 12, 1919, the Air Service test establishment at Wilbur Wright Field, Fairfield, Ohio, still had in their possession what they offi-

The complete absence of any markings whatsoever on this Curtiss-built Bristol *Fighter* is, at best, curious. The mating of a proven British design with the U.S. engine was highly successful on the deHavilland D.H.4 series, but the USAO-1 program was a very costly failure. (*via Peter M. Bowers*)

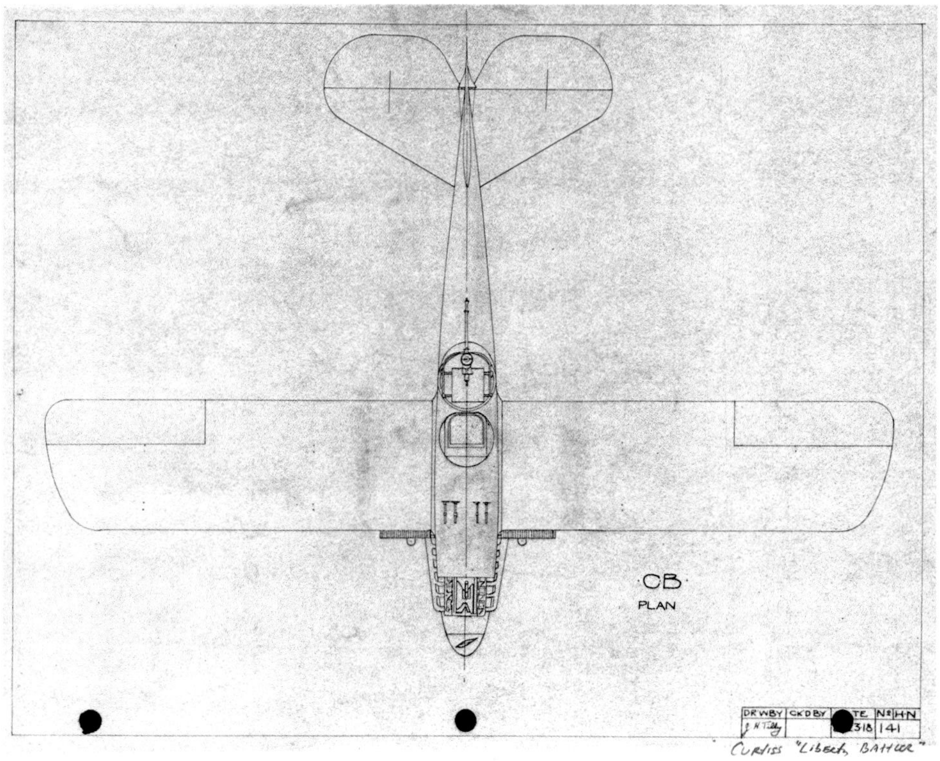

Never published before, these Curtiss May 22, 1918, drawings of the CB *Battler* reveal several hitherto undocumented features. First, the aircraft included provision for four forward-firing guns over the engine cowl, and second, while the crew enjoyed supreme visibility above and around the aircraft (but certainly not downward, in the case of the pilot), they had no protection from the wind at all, aside from a very small windscreen for the pilot. (*Curtiss*)

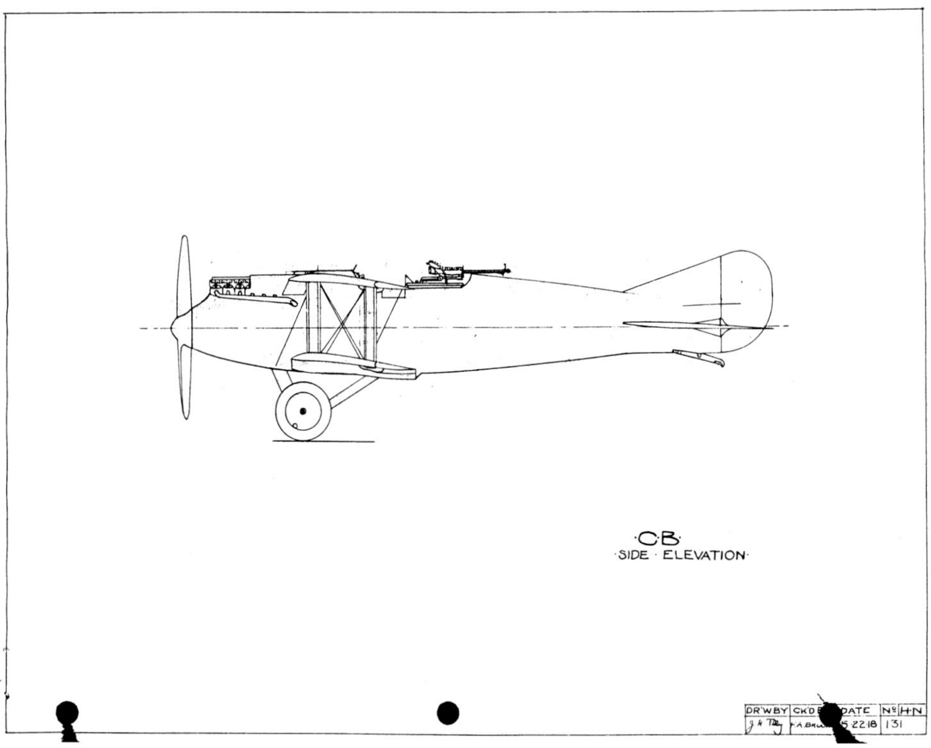

cially reported as a "*Bastard Bristol*," which they rather oddly described as "...*a combination of Bristol and DH-4 and which has no standard classification*." They further stated that it was an "FA-2 No.2174 [this was probably the Bristol Sequence Number (2174) for an F.2B, *authors*], Field No. P-30," and that it had been languishing there since at least November 26, 1918. They also reported that they had shipped 15 Curtiss-built Bristol aircraft *to Curtiss* (with three more to follow)[6] around October 5, 1918, and that they had received one "*genuine*" Bristol *Fighter*, British serial C949 (MSN 3361), on July 9, 1918.

Exactly why these aircraft, of the 27 actually accepted by the Army, were returned to Curtiss at this late date is unknown and, further, it is unclear what Curtiss intended to do with them, if anything. They could account for the unconfirmed reports of Bristol *Fighters* appearing in the hands of private citizens between the end of the war and the start of Federal regulation of aircraft in 1927.

Finally, there had been thoughts of using the smaller *Liberty* 8 cylinder version in the Curtiss-built F.2Bs, but that never happened. Had it been done, the program might have been more successful.[7]

The Curtiss CB *Battler*

With the demise of the Curtiss Bristol *Fighter* program after the failed attempt to modify the type to utilize the *Liberty* 12 engine, Curtiss made an effort to design a new aircraft suited more for that engine, but to perform the same duties as the Bristol.

This design was the CB—the Curtiss *Battler*, or the Curtiss *Battleplane*[8] of 1918. A two-seat, double bay biplane like the Bristol *Fighter*, the CB design was noteworthy for having a plywood monocoque fuselage, with the *Liberty* 12 engine driving a two blade propeller nicely faired with a spinner. An unusual location of cooling radiators for the water cooled engine placed them inboard under the upper wing, where they were alleged to have had a rather unfortunate effect on airflow.

However, the most unusual aspect of the aircraft was the narrow gap, or vertical distance between biplane wings, much contrary to the arrangement of the successful Bristol *Fighter*. Quite clearly the structures people must have won the day over the aerodynamicists (if there were any), since the wing gap was clearly inadequate aerodynamically. While the design gave the rear gunner an exceptional field of fire, it seriously restricted the downward view of the pilot, to the extent that small windows had to be built into the forward fuselage sides for him to see during landings.

The single CB prototype two-place fighter crashed during testing, apparently during May 1918. According to one account, quoted by historian Hal Andrews from a long-time Curtiss engineer, the aircraft was lost during a flight test when it stalled in a steep turn following a low-altitude, high-speed pass. The pilot was fatally injured. This rather strange design's most important contribution was that the type of fuselage construction was brought forward by Curtiss in other designs, such as the civil *Oriole* aircraft.

Although the CB *Battler* carried USAAS style rudder markings, it has been cited by most historians as a private venture. The aircraft was apparently ordered by the Army, however, as A.S.34632. This never before published view shows that the upper decking of the fuselage was crudely painted a dark color, possibly to reduce glare for the crew, who were very exposed for an aircraft of that time. The prop in this view was clearly not the one in use at the time of its loss on the first flight. (*via Peter M. Bowers*)

Apparently ordered by the Army and built as a Curtiss-inspired hedge against the doomed Bristol *Fighter* program, the CB *Battler* crashed on its first flight, killing the pilot. Compare the obviously pointed tip of the very short prop blade visible here with the over-head view. Aerodynamically, the gap between the wings was very poor for a good biplane wing cellule design. (*via Peter M. Bowers*)

Although frequently quoted as having been a private venture by Curtiss, there is evidence that the single aircraft was included in the Air Service Contract 20387 issued to Curtiss for 2,000 USAO-1s, and it probably was issued serial S.C.34632.

Known weights and dimensions included an empty weight of 3,575 pounds, a span of 39 feet, four inches, and a fuselage length of 27 feet, one inch.

The Curtiss License-Built R.A.F. SE-5A

The Curtiss Aeroplane Company was associated in a rather oblique fashion with the successful British Royal Aircraft Factory SE-5 fighter design. SE-5 stood for Scouting Experimental, fifth design. A trim looking single seat biplane, the aircraft had a good combat record during World War I.

The SE-5 airframe was a conventional wooden structure with fabric covering. The constant chord wings of 26 foot eight inch span were in a single bay configuration with a significant stagger. Ailerons were fitted on both upper and lower wings. The fuselage was somewhat boxy, with a flat cooling radiator set just behind the propeller, and the landing gear was conventional. The horizontal tail was fitted with a variable incidence stabilizer.

In England, the SE-5's first flight took place in December 1916. The prototype was equipped with a 150hp Hispano Suiza engine. Armament comprised a Vickers .303 caliber machine gun in the fuselage, forward of the cockpit, and a Lewis gun of the same caliber on the center section of the upper wing. The prototype crashed, but the aircraft went into production, with first deliveries to a British squadron in March 1917. The American Expeditionary Force obtained 38 SE-5A fighters with 210hp Hispano engines while in Europe and equipped one operational squadron, but World War I ended in November 1918 before it got into action.

In the United States Curtiss, in June 1918, obtained Army Contracts No.21290 and 4038, issued June 8th and August 1, 1918, to license build 1,054 SE-5s using a Hispano engine manufactured by

Had the First World War continued, Curtiss stood to become the premier contractor for the U.S. Army, with very large numbers of Bristol *Fighters* and 1,000 British-designed Royal Aircraft Factory SE-5A fighters to be built under license. One of the best fighters of the war, with the armistice, Curtiss in fact built only one (S.C.43153), seen here, with a Martin-built Hispano engine, although they apparently assembled as many as 50 others, which were later modified to SE-5E standard by Eberhardt. (*via Peter M. Bowers*)

the Wright Martin Company. Parts to build SE-5A aircraft were imported from England by Curtiss to get started during the 1918 summer. Curtiss assembled 56 fighters from these parts in late 1918 and early 1919 and, apparently, the Army tested the one-and-only[9] Curtiss built example (S.C.43153) around September 17, 1918. In addition to the Curtiss assembled aircraft, during the early 1920s the Eberhardt Steel Products Company modified 50 aircraft as the SE-5E version, and it appears that these were in fact the survivors of the aircraft assembled by Curtiss. These had reportedly been flown by the Army prior to this conversion, bearing their original British serial numbers and markings. Some sources claim that these aircraft were assembled from spare parts, but available evidence seems to contradict this.

In the end, Curtiss had only a peripheral association with the SE-5 fighter, but did gain experience in producing this type of aircraft. The Curtiss built SE-5A had a high speed of 122 mph at sea level, and a service ceiling of 20,400 feet. It could climb to 6,500 feet in eight minutes. With a useful load of 574 pounds, including a fuel capacity of 210 pounds of gasoline, adding to an empty weight of 1,486 pounds, the gross weight came to 2,060 pounds. This all-up weight gave a wing loading of 8.34 psf., and a power loading of 11.4 pounds per horse power. At high speed the SE-5A could fly 1.33 miles per pound of fuel for a total of 280 miles.

Aside from the modified Bristol *Fighter*, the SE-5A was the closest the Curtiss Aeroplane Company came to manufacturing a fighter of foreign design. They had received two U.S. Army Contracts (Numbers 1812 and 20035) to produce a total of not less than 3,000 French SPAD XIIIs on September 19th and October 8, 1917, but that contract was cancelled without any of that type produced. These aircraft would have received Army serials S.C.5376 through 8375 if they had been built. Another order (Number 20204 dated November 3, 1917, for 1,500 SPAD XIIIs) replaced the earlier two, but this, too, was cancelled on November 26th, but was replaced with yet another order (Contract 20285) that was also cancelled.

Ironically, had these contracts for the SE-5A and SPAD XIIIs been completed as laid down, placing such large numbers of capable fighters in the service of the U.S. Army would have almost certainly spelled doom for any Curtiss fighter designs for years to come, and this history would have been very different indeed, perhaps even nonexistent.

The Curtiss *Liberty Fighter* HA, HA-1, and HA-2

The first purpose-built Curtiss fighter intended for Navy use was the Model HA.[10] The Navy had issued a requirement specification for a two-place seaplane fighter. However, the actual design of the HA was attributed to Captain B. L. Smith of the U.S. Marine Corps, and Curtiss merely received a contract (No.33830) to build the prototype at Garden City. It was envisioned for use in gaining air control over the Calais-Dunkirk area in France, where the U.S. Navy had considerable responsibilities during the war. German seaplane fighters were interfering with Allied operations in the area, and the Navy wanted a *Dunkirk Fighter*, as the type came to be unofficially known, to counter these raids. The specification called for good speed and climb rate, and armament of two forward firing Marlin .30 caliber machine guns, along with dual flexible Lewis guns in the rear position. The engine to be used was the new *Liberty* 12 then under development, putting out about 330 horsepower.

Curtiss proposed their Model HA, and received the Navy Secretary's authorization to proceed with the fighter project on December 17, 1917. There were eventually three development aircraft involved. The first example was assigned Navy Bureau of Aeronautics serial number A-2278, and it was acquired on Contract 33830.

After a fast design and fabrication phase, the initial HA fighter was ready for a first flight on March 21, 1918, at Port Washington, Long Island, near the Curtiss Garden City plant, newly opened the previous January. The Curtiss test pilot was Roland Rohlfs, and the rear seat observer was Captain B.L. Smith, U.S. Marine Corps, the designer.

The original configuration of the Curtiss HA, unofficially labeled the *Dunkirk Fighter*, included a most interesting four-bladed prop, complete with large spinner, a very different vertical fin and rudder, and a large radiator immediately behind the prop, and without the cooling louvers so prominent later in the design. This photo was probably taken immediately prior to the first flight on March 21, 1918. (*via Peter M. Bowers*)

The Curtiss HA-1 (also cited at this time as Experiment 506), Navy A-4110, underway at Rockaway December 23, 1918, in full period U.S. national insignia. The pilot appears to be standing in the cockpit in order to clear the view ahead. Note the kite balloon at far right. (*Curtiss via Jack Satterfield*)

The prototype aircraft was a double bay biplane mounted on a single main float and two wingtip floats. Initial wingspan was 36 feet, with aircraft length 30 feet, nine inches, and height 10 feet, seven inches. Wing area totaled 490 square feet. Wing gap varied from 55.5 inches at the fuselage to 70 inches at the wingtips. Wing chord was constant at 72 inches. Main float dimensions were 20 feet long, 24 inches wide, and 30 inches high. Empty weight was 2,638 pounds, useful load 962 pounds, and gross weight 3,396 (less crew) pounds, giving a wing loading of 7.35 psf, and a power loading of 10.0 pounds per horse power.

The first flight, apparently on March 21, 1918, was close to a disaster, with the aircraft gyrating wildly, and Rohlfs was barely able to land the plane. The wing had been located improperly. A second flight was made on June 15th in which the first HA was, again, badly damaged when it porpoised uncontrollably in spite of efforts to control same. It was declared a wreck, and formally stricken from the Navy list on September 17, 1918.

Using both salvageable and new parts, a second prototype, dubbed the HA-1,[11] was built up at Garden City with very significant modifications. The wings were properly located, tail area was significantly increased, and the whole fuselage nose was redesigned, with the cooling radiator now placed directly behind the propeller. The more awkward placement of the early prototype radiator along with the bulbous spinner was deleted. The Navy was very unhappy about the positioning of the two synchronized Marlin guns on the aircraft, which it described in no uncertain terms as "*very unsuitable*," as they had been placed directly over the exhaust pipes, with the ammunition box projecting down between two of the pipes!

Bad luck still dogged the new HA, however. In a test flight at Rockaway, with Rohlfs again piloting, the engine overheated and the plane caught fire. The plane was landed in the water, with pilot and observer quickly evacuating. This HA was consumed by fire. It was sent to the Naval Aircraft Factory for repairs July 31, 1919, but apparently saw no further use, and was stricken from the inventory May 16, 1921.

Curtiss and the Navy were not ready to give up, however, and later in May 1918 a third aircraft, designated HA-2 by Curtiss, made an appearance. The wing area of 490 square feet was kept, but span

The HA-1 was a state-of-the-art aircraft as of the end of 1918, and was amongst the aircraft proudly displayed by the maker at an annual indoor aviation show. Here, it has a two-bladed prop, but a three-bladed prop is leaning against the platform near the aircraft. This aircraft was later damaged by fire, but survived as late as May 16, 1921, on records. (*Gordon S. Williams Collection Ac6005, Museum of Flight*)

The solitary Curtiss HA-2, Navy serial A-4111, in its element. The Navy cited this aircraft on records as the *Experimental Fighter Seaplane*. It is seen here at Hampton Roads in its final year of service, 1922. (*NASM via Peter M. Bowers*)

was increased to 42 feet, and gross weight went up to 4,012 pounds, resulting in a wing loading of 8.19psf and power loading of 11.14 pounds per horse power, using the same *Liberty* engine. Empty weight was 2,950 pounds, giving a useful load to gross weight ratio of 0.265.

The high speed of the later HA-2 was about 126 mph at sea level, and the aircraft took about 10 minutes to climb to 7,100 feet, while "average" speed was given as 123.3mph. The configuration was changed in the third aircraft by raising the upper wing so as to be supported by cabane struts in conventional fashion; engine cowling contours and radiator shape were again changed, and a three bladed propeller was fitted. Propellers tried on the HA models varied from a 9 foot, two inch diameter two blade, a three blade of 8 foot, six inch diameter, to a four blade type used off and on. The two bladed prop proved best.

By the time the HA seaplane fighter was developed into a working configuration the war was over, and the Navy was no longer interested in the design. With further modifications three civil HA types were sold to the U.S. Postal Service after the war. Surviving Curtiss records indicate that Manufacturers Serial Numbers (MSN) 10006 through 10010 were assigned, apparently retrospectively, to these five aircraft, which seems to suggest that the first aircraft, when rebuilt as the HA-1, was assigned the same number. The last aircraft (Navy A-4111) was also tested at Rockaway. It spent nearly all of its service life at NAS Hampton Roads, where it was being reconditioned by August 1922. It suffered an accident at, of all places, the Army's Selfridge Field, MI, October 8, 1922, where it was damaged beyond repair when it sank shortly after leaving the runway. It was finally stricken from the inventory February 3, 1923, having been listed for sale for $300.

Curtiss JN-4HG and JN-6HP Pursuit

Although seldom regarded as anything but a trainer, the Army in fact ordered numbers of both JN-4H and JN-6H *Jenny* aircraft specifically for gunnery, bombing, observation—and pursuit training purposes. By August 2, 1918, Curtiss had turned over 125 JN-4HG aircraft specifically configured as "pursuit" aircraft (19 by July 12th, 29 more by July 19th, 45 additional by July 26th, and nine more by August 2nd—the order was complete by July 29th). Similarly, the Army order (No.21036) for JN-6H aircraft included 126 specifically identified as JN-6HP "pursuit" variants, and this portion of the total order had been completed by July 27, 1918.

Undoubtedly, these aircraft were not "pursuit" aircraft in the strictest sense of the term, but rather trainers intended to aid in the preparation of pilots being prepared for this form of combat assignment. Exactly how they may have differed from standard JN-4H and JN-6H aircraft remains unknown, and they are included here only because they had the designator "pursuit" attached to them.

The Curtiss Model 18-T

In 1918 Charles B. Kirkham, a veteran aircraft engine man, was Curtiss' Chief Motor Designer. Glen Curtiss wanted a new engine that would be competitive with the two foremost American inline aircraft engines being produced at the time, the *Liberty* 12 and the Wright-produced Hispano Suiza. Kirkham set to work, and came up with the Curtiss-Kirkham K-12, a revolutionary design with cooling features allowing development of full power for sustained periods without overheating.

The new K-12, V-1145 developed 400-425hp at 650-680 pounds weight with only 4.66 square feet of frontal area, compared to the *Liberty* with 400hp at 850 pounds weight and 5.16 square feet, and the Wright-Hispano V-1127 with 300hp at 625 pounds weight and 4.75 square feet of frontal area. The new K-12 did have its troubles, however, the biggest of which was the reduction gearing required between engine crankshaft and propeller speeds. Various gear arrangements were tried, including spur, helical, and herringbone, without complete success. But the K-12 was the most advanced engine of the period from a technology standpoint at the time.

Clearly a new fighter aircraft was needed to take advantage of this new K-12 engine, and the Curtiss people at Garden City[12] came

One of the two Navy Curtiss 18-T *Kirkham Fighters* taken July 6, 1918, at Garden City, even before flight testing had commenced. Note that the wings are unswept. The port side forward firing gun trough can just be seen between the prop blades, and the aircraft appears devoid of any markings. (*Curtiss via Cradle of Aviation Museum*)

up with the Model 18-T. Two aircraft were ordered by the Navy on March 30, 1918, under Contract 37372 at $55,400 each, less government furnished equipment, and these informally took on the name *Wasp* at some point.[13] These gained Navy Bureau of Aeronautics serial numbers A-3325 and A-3326. Initially, they were identified by the Navy as Curtiss *Trainer Triplanes* but, later, A-3325 was noted as a Curtiss 18T-2, while A-3326 was given as a Curtiss 18T-1. These "dash" numbers have been variously explained, but appear most likely to have been associated with the reconfiguration of the wings. The triplane configuration had been selected, in the first place, because it was felt that a shorter wing span, with three lifting surfaces, would enhance maneuverability. Initially the wings were unswept, which caused excessive tail heaviness. The aircraft flew for the first time in this configuration on July 5, 1918. The -1 was added to the basic designation after an alternative set of five degree swept wings, with longer span, became available on what became the -2. The rudder shape, which had originally been rounded, was quartered at the upper and lower trailing edges on A-3325.

Initial Navy tests of the so-called *Kirkham Fighter*[14] on September 1, 1918, were impressive in some respects, as the aircraft made 153.1mph against the wind over an official speed course, although "official climb" trials were noted as "impossible," as the radiators were too small, although the take off (in less than four seconds) was rated as outstanding. These trials were conducted at Garden City with Navy Lt. McCullough as the official observer, and the aircraft mounted full fuel and armament load, including two rear Lewis guns and two forward-firing Marlin guns with full ammunition containers. Evidently, the aircraft involved was A-3325.

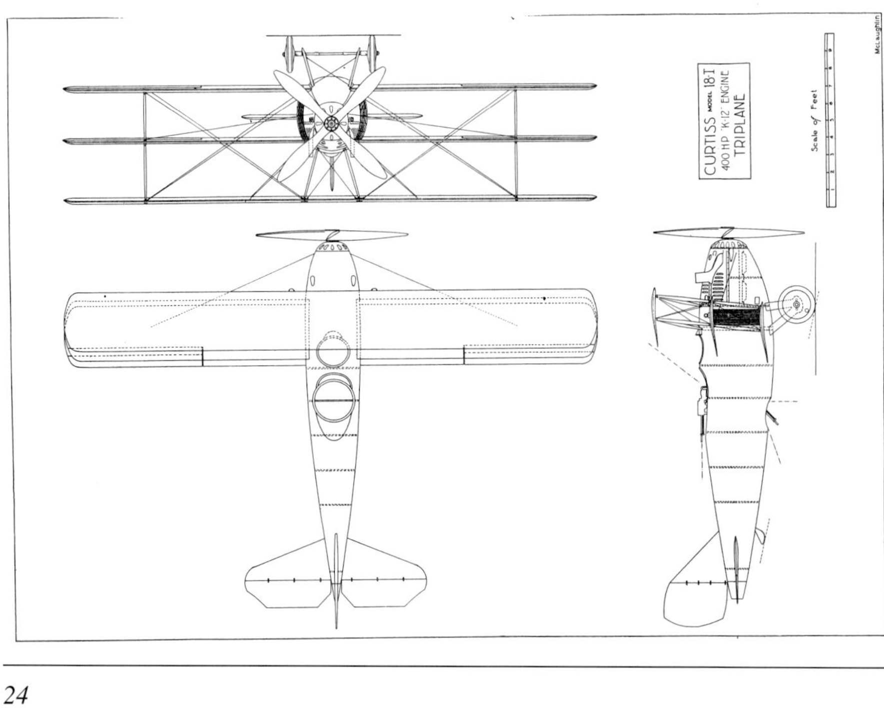

This three-view shows the original configuration of the two Navy Model 18-Ts, including the rarely shown ventral gun, original rudder configuration, and experimental form-fitting radiators. (*McLaughlin via Dean Collection*)

Taken December 4, 1919, and cited as Navy Experiment No.526, A-3325 had been converted to floats on November 28th. In this view the sweep of the wings is very dramatically portrayed, and the aircraft has been converted to a two-bay configuration. The aircraft was probably the most advanced aircraft in the U.S. at this time. *(Curtiss via Cradle of Aviation Museum)*

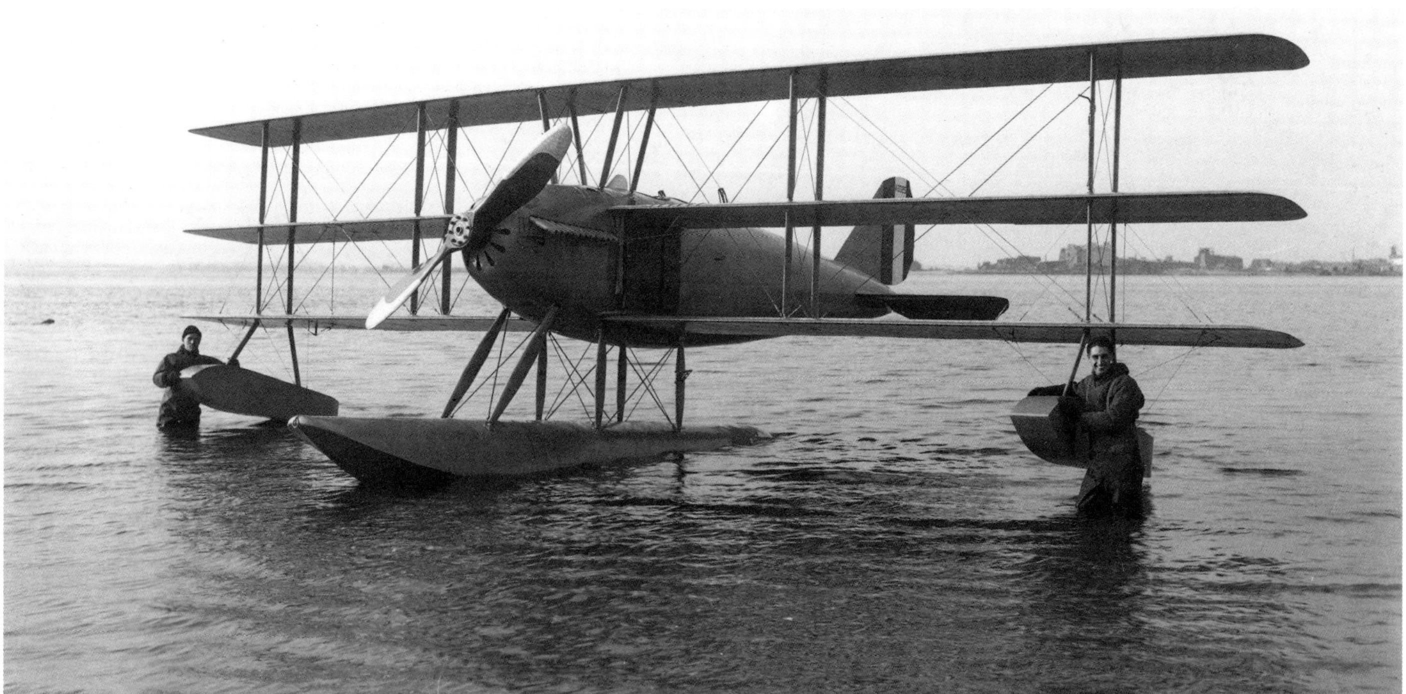

Taken the same day as the side view, this frontal view does not reveal the wing sweep, but does show the two-bay configuration to good advantage. *(Gordon S. William Collection AC643 via Museum of Flight)*

Navy Curtiss 18-T A-3325 was cited as the 18I-2 at one point. Here, with race number "5" and painted green in a single bay configuration, this aircraft had been entered in the 1922 Curtiss Marine Trophy Race, to be flown by Marine Lt. L. Sanderson. It was unable to start the race due to engine failure. The rear gunner's pit had been faired over, it bears a four-blade prop, and the engine has a tarp over it. The ventral fin is of interest. (*Dean Collection*)

The Navy loaned A-3326 to Curtiss on December 2, 1918, so that the company could exhibit the aircraft in Philadelphia.

The 18-T designed and built at Garden City was said to have been Glenn Curtiss' favorite design from that plant.[15] A two-seat, land triplane that could be adapted as a seaplane with a single main and tip floats, the basic 18-T had equispan wings measuring 31 feet, 11 inches, and equal chords of 42 inches for a wing area of 309 square feet, and wing loading of 9.4 psf at its gross weight of 2,901 pounds. Lower wing gap was three feet, and upper wings gap three feet, six inches. Initially the 18-T had no wing sweep, but shortly, a five degree sweep of all wings was incorporated to correct for an aft center of gravity location by moving the center of lift aft, as noted earlier.

Normal useful load of the 18-T was 1,076 pounds, comprised of 400 pounds of fuel, 45 pounds of oil, 330 pounds for pilot and passenger, and 301 pounds of equipment, including guns and ammunition. Empty weight was 1,825 pounds, giving a very good useful load to gross weight ratio of 0.361. Power loading was 7.25 pounds per horse power.

The 18-T was 23 feet, four inches long, with a fuselage constructed as a monocoque shell comprised of laminated birch and redwood veneer strips covering wooden formers. Surfaces were final-coated with linen, doped with light gray varnish. Engine cooling radiators were located alongside the fuselage between lower wings, allowing exceptionally clean fuselage nose contours. Wings were two-spar wooden framed and fabric covered, except the leading edges, which were covered by Spanish cedar. Ailerons were located on the two lower wings. Tail surfaces were wood framed, with fixed portions covered in Spanish cedar plywood, and moveable surfaces covered with fabric. The wheeled landing gear was conventional, with a tread of 4 feet 11 inches.

The armament consisted of two forward synchronized Marlin .30 caliber guns with 750 rounds of ammunition, firing through troughs on either side of the nose, and two rear flexible Lewis guns on a Scarff ring with 875 rounds of ammunition. A single fixed Lewis gun could be installed to fire downward from the belly of the aircraft as well.

The new K-12 twelve cylinder, water-cooled engine developed 400hp at 2,500rpm, and this power plant provided outstanding per-

Race No.4, U.S. Navy Curtiss 18-T A-3326, was also entered in the 1922 Curtiss Marine Trophy Race, and was allegedly painted yellow at the time. Flown by L. R. Irvine, it had to pull out of the event on the last lap due to an overheated engine and nearly out of fuel. The shadows from the exhaust stacks make the aircraft appear to have louvers on the engine cover. Note that the prop has been removed and that, unlike its sister ship, the race number is not outlined. (*via Peter M. Bowers*)

The U.S. Army Air Service ordered two Curtiss 18-T triplanes and two 18-Bs, which were biplane versions of essentially the same aircraft. Bearing McCook Field test number P-86, this is A.S. 40058.

formance for the period. In trials conducted on August 19, 1919, a high speed near sea level of 162 mph was attained with full military load. Maximum speed at 10,000 feet was 145 mph, and landing speed was 55 to 58 mph. A flight endurance of 1.75 hours could be attained. Later, on September 18, 1919, piloted by Curtiss test pilot Roland Rohlfs, the Curtiss *Wasp* triplane, equipped with longer wings extending to 40 feet, seven inches span in a double bay wing cellule arrangement as an 18T-2 version, set a new world's altitude record of 34,910 feet after earlier tries had to be abandoned due to the failure of the pilot's oxygen system. In addition, on September 19, 1919, a rate-of-climb record was set with an altitude of 20,100 feet attained in 10 minutes. One of the aircraft was also referred to, as of December 4, 1919, as the "Navy Experimental 526," and was pictured as such at Rockaway that date.

In spite of this fine demonstrated landplane performance, the Navy had no use for wheeled fighters, since there were no aircraft carriers. Interest was only in seaplanes at that time, so the 18-T type was converted to a seaplane of single main and tip float configuration.[16] In any case, as a result of final trials on September 20, 1919, the Navy recommended acceptance of the two aircraft, and in accordance with the Naval Board recommendation an 18-T was tested on floats in May 1920 using both two and four bladed propellers. High speed on floats was about 138 mph.

With this speed capability both Navy aircraft were entered as landplanes in the Pulitzer Trophy Race of 1920, but were modified by having the rear cockpit faired over. However, engine trouble forced both aircraft from the race. In 1922 the two aircraft entered the active U.S. Navy fighter aircraft inventory, but they were really only to be used for racing. Then both were entered as seaplanes in the Curtiss Marine Trophy Race of 1922, but again there was engine trouble, with Marine Lt. L. Sanderson (in A-3325, painted green and bearing Race Number 5) not being able to start the race, and Lt.

A most confusing photo, from an historical perspective. S.C.40054, according to Army records, was ordered and delivered as an 18-T triplane. Clearly, this excellent image shows her to have been a biplane, and with an entirely different exhaust system from the two other Model 18-Bs acquired. Had the war continued, this could well have been a contender for major production. (*Curtiss via Museum of Flight*)

Viewed from just aft of the rear gunner's position, looking forward, this view shows the surprisingly well equipped and spacious cockpit of an Army Curtiss 18-T. The aircraft could be equipped with up to five guns: two forward-firing, two for the rear gunner on a ring, and one ventral gun. (*U.S. Army, Wright Field, Dean Collection*)

R. Irvine (in A-3326, painted yellow and with Race Number 4) pulling out of the race in the last lap with a combination of an overheated engine and near fuel exhaustion.

It has often been reported that the final known public appearance of the two Navy aircraft came at the October 1923 St. Louis Air Meet. However, this is impossible, as A-3325 was totally wrecked at Selfridge Field, MI, in October 1922 (apparently having returned to a wheel undercarriage), and was stricken from the Navy inventory on March 24, 1923, with a total time on the airframe of 40:35. One of the Navy planes, confirmed as A-3326, however, adorned with orange fuselage and cream colored wings, did in fact crash at St. Louis on October 4th during a check flight prior to the Pulitzer Race, with the pilot managing to escape. The crank shaft had broken, and the pilot made a forced landing in a soft, plowed field, and the aircraft nosed over, completely wrecked.

It is seldom recognized that the Army also acquired two Curtiss 18-T aircraft. Ordered on the same contract as the 18Bs (see below), the first of these was S.C.40054 (it has initially been assigned S.C.40065, but this remained unused). The second was S.C. 40059. S.C. 40054 was delivered to the Army around January 20, 1919, and was cited on Army documents as the Curtiss *Triplane* Model 509, with no mention whatsoever of the "18-T' appellation. One of these was apparently tested to destruction, as an Army document dated April 17, 1919, referred to the fuselage failure of a "Curtiss Kirkham Triplane" during tests. However, by June 30, 1920, at least one of the aircraft was cited by the Army by the name *Wasp* [the only such reference, *authors*], with the rather curious statement that:

"*...the aircraft was never tested for climb by the Army. The aircraft was flown a few times at McCook by the factory pilot they sent to Wilbur Wright Field in September 1918, where Rohlf, the factory pilot, attempted a climb carrying recording instruments. The flight was a failure due to serious overheating. The aircraft was* not *flown by Army pilots.*"

One of the earliest of a long line of Curtiss export sales to Latin America was this solitary Curtiss-18-T for Bolivia, that nation's first genuine military aircraft. Pictured here October 29, 1919, it arrived in La Paz April 15, 1920, where U.S. pilot Donald Hudson took charge of it. It lasted a scant 35 days in Bolivian service, suffering an accident on May 20th. It had a larger rudder, different exhaust stack system, and no ports for forward firing guns. (*Curtiss via Hagedorn Collection*)

Curtiss Model 18B
One of the two Navy 18-T aircraft was tested on loan by the Army at McCook Field (A-3325),[17] and after an August 1918 order (Contract No.106) they took delivery in February 1919 of two 18B biplane versions of the aircraft called *Hornets*.[18] These received Army serials S.C.40058 and 40064. At that time one aircraft was static tested to destruction circa July 8, 1919, and this may have been McCook Field Number P-86 (which is known to have been S.C.40058 at one point), which was given, for some reason, as S.C.3488. However, P-86 is also cited as the aircraft in which Captain Jones and civilian George Buzane were killed circa July 14, 1919. It is possible that the McCook Field Number P-86 may have, in fact, been assigned to both aircraft.

These two aircraft were acquired, apparently, as a direct result of what were termed by the Army as Experiment 503 (Two-Seater Biplane Fighter)[19] and Experiment 505 (Two-Seater Triplane Fighter), as expressed in a letter to Curtiss dated June 15, 1918, by Lieutenant Colonel J. G. Vincent, Airplane Engineering Division at Dayton. The Experiment 503 was clearly the Model 18B, which was defined in an Army document dated August 13, 1918, as a "*...two seater fighter*" fitted with two Marlin machine guns firing via synchronized gear through the prop arch, and a Lewis gun on a U.S.A. gun ring in the rear pit, as well as another fitted to fire through a port in the lower fuselage, all with 500 rounds per gun. It was powered by what was described as a Curtiss D-3000 engine of 400hp at 2,250rpm. The document was signed by none other than Second Lieutenant Alexander Klemin.

The Army 18B biplane version employed the same fuselage as the Navy triplane, but incorporated double bay biplane wings of 37 feet, six inch span set in a conventional manner, and having a total wing area of 306 square feet. The same model Curtiss K-12 engine was employed.

With an empty weight of 1,690 pounds and useful load of 1,177 pounds, 318 pounds (53 gallons) of which was fuel, the normal gross weight of the 18B was 2,867 pounds, and maximum gross weight was 3,010 pounds. At normal gross the wing loading was thus 9.37psf, and power loading 7.17 pounds per horse power. In this case, the useful load to gross weight ratio was 0.41, an extremely high figure for that time.

The Army service record details of the 18B *Hornets* are obscure, and no more of the type were ordered by that service. Oddly, Curtiss records indicate only one *Hornet* acquired by the Army, given retrospectively as MSN 10001, while MSNs 10002 to 10005, totaling four aircraft, included one for Bolivia. This situation is further confused by a letter from Curtiss to the Airplane Engineering Division at Dayton dated August 5, 1918, in which confirmation of an Army order, Contract No.106, for "*...two Biplanes and two Triplanes*" is clearly stated.

In a letter to Curtiss dated November 11, 1918, the Air Service Chief of Engineering further confuses the issue by stating that "*...your telegram states that you intend to apply the first two-seater fighter around the Liberty-12 on an order for three machines obtained from the Post Office Department. The engine loaned to you for this ship is charged to Airplane Engineering Division and should not be delivered to the P.O. Dept. unless proper transfer is made,*" reflecting the highly personal and rather tedious processes of the time in aircraft procurement.

This is all rather confusing, as press reports of early 1920 clearly indicate that the 18-T that went to Bolivia in the care of U.S. pilot Donald Hudson arrived there on April 15, 1920, and was cited at the time as "*...the same machine as used by Roland Rohlfs in establishing a new world's altitude record on September 18, 1919.*"[20] Hudson subsequently, on May 19, 1920, used this aircraft to fly at more than 30,000 feet over Mt. Illimani, near La Paz. Unfortunately, the aircraft was lost the following day in an accident. Not only was the Bolivian aircraft the first post-war acquisition by the infant Bolivian air arm, it also represented the first of many Curtiss aircraft to reach that nation and other foreign nations in years to come.

Curtiss received a contract to construct 50 Orenco D fighters, commencing in November 1920. This anonymous example, photographed on June 18, 1921, has the standard box-type radiator located on the port side of the fuselage. They had balanced ailerons on the upper wings only. (*Curtiss*)

Curtiss Orenco D (L-44-2)

In 1918 ORENCO (Ordnance Engineering Co.) of Long Island, NY (later Baldwin, NY), produced four prototype fighters (S.C. 40107 to 40110) based on a design of the Army Engineering Division. These two-bay, single seat biplanes, the first delivered in January 1919, were reported on by at least one test pilot as having good flying qualities—better than the wartime SPAD and other types. Powered by a Wright-Hispano H eight cylinder V-type water cooled engine of 300hp, the ORENCO D prototypes had a wingspan of 30 feet, length of 21 feet, five and one-half inches, and a height of seven feet, nine inches. Total wing area was 261 square feet, so with a design gross weight of 2,432 pounds the wing loading was 9.3psf. Power loading was 8.1 pounds per horse power. With an empty weight of 1,776 pounds, the resulting useful load was 656 pounds, of which 330 pounds (55 gallons) was fuel, and the remaining 326 pounds was oil, pilot, and the armament of two .30 caliber forward firing machine guns and their ammunition.

The slab sided fuselage was a plywood covered wooden frame, and tapered to a horizontal knife edge at the tail end. The ORENCO prototypes, along with most production Curtiss built aircraft, had a rather neat cowl for the engine, and a nose radiator just behind the propeller, though some Curtiss machines were equipped with Lamblin or other design radiators mounted alongside the fuselage. The double bay wings were fabric covered over a wooden structure, as were the tail surfaces. The rudder was balanced, and the elevator and horizontal stabilizer were single piece. Ailerons were located on the upper wing only.

Prototype performance was quite good, with a top speed of 147mph at sea level and 142mph at 6,500 feet altitude. Cruise speed was 139mph, and the aircraft landed at 56mph. It could climb to 6,500 feet in 5.2 minutes, and service and absolute ceilings were 22,000 and 23,600 feet, respectively.

Curtiss made a few modifications in their 50 production design aircraft, not delivered until 1920 and 1921, with the first production plane flown early in November 1920. Contrary to many previously published accounts, Curtiss referred to these aircraft internally as Model L-44-2s, rather than "Model 26." The Hispano H engine was up-rated to 330hp, and upper wing span and wing area was increased to 32 feet, 11 and 5/8 inches, and 273 square feet, respectively. The upper wing ailerons were now balanced at the tip. A new engine mount was employed.

These aircraft were heavier and slower. Empty weight grew to 1,908 pounds, and useful load, including 318 pounds of fuel, was 912 pounds, making a normal gross weight of 2,920 pounds. Wing loading was now 10.3psf, and power loading was up to 8.55 pounds per horse power. Production aircraft speed dropped to 139.5mph at sea level, and 136mph at 6,500 feet, with cruising speed 133.5mph. At the higher wing loading the aircraft landed at 64.5mph. Service and absolute ceilings dropped to 18,450 and 20,250 feet, and climb performance required 6.9 minutes to attain 6,500 feet altitude. Armament stayed at two .30 caliber machine guns, but an option allowed provision for one .30 caliber and one .50 caliber. This option was the first instance of use of the .50 caliber weapon in an Army fighter type.

The service life of the Curtiss-built ORENCOs is obscure; some did go to the 1st Pursuit Group, but apparently they were not used extensively. One distinction involved the first pursuit type use of a turbo-supercharger test installation, but the aircraft was reported to have crashed soon after the modification was made. Records say that plane was surveyed in May 1922. Curtiss records referred to these aircraft as *Orenco Biplane Pursuits*, and they received Curtiss MSNs 10288 to 10387, indicating a total of 100 aircraft. However, only 50 were actually built for the Army as A.S.63281 to 63330 on Contract 269 issued June 16, 1920. It is interesting to note that the Army contract listed them as Orenco (rather than ORENCO) aircraft.

The third from last Orenco D built by Curtiss, A.S. 63328 shows the semi-circular French design Lamblin radiators mounted on the port-side of the fuselage. The single piece elevators are shown to good advantage in this view. (*Curtiss via M. Copp*)

2

Post World War I Fighter Designs

Curtiss PN-1 *Nighthawk*

Certainly the earliest U.S. Army Air Service (USAAS) attempt at a pursuit aircraft for night fighting work, the Curtiss PN-1 was designated under the new system started postwar in September 1919. PN meant Pursuit, Night work. However, as of April 1921 the aircraft was cited in Air Service documents as the Curtiss *Night Pursuit Airplane, Type II.*

Two aircraft were ordered in 1920, and assigned Curtiss MSNs 10281 and 10285. They were single seat biplanes. The first plane was very unusual, in having thick section wings tapered in both planform and thickness, and doubtless copied by the Air Service Engineering Division from German Fokker designs. Indeed, correspondence in the National Archives between McCook Field and Curtiss explicitly suggested that Curtiss make use of some "*...Fokker wings available*" in the construction of this aircraft. Strictly speaking, the aircraft were not designed by Curtiss at all, but rather by the Engineering Division of the Air Service, with Curtiss merely the contractor executing the design. Ailerons were located on the overhung upper wing only, and roll-over bumpers projected below the fully cantilevered lower wing. Tail surfaces and landing gear were conventional for the period. The fuselage basic structure was of welded steel tubing. The aircraft power plant was a six cylinder version of the *Liberty*, the L-285 of 220hp. In the first aircraft, the straight-up *Liberty* was neatly cowled and drove a two-bladed propeller with the hub enclosed in a large propeller spinner.

Static testing performed at McCook Field, Ohio, in November 1920 indicated the cantilever wing arrangement was not structurally suitable, and the first incarnation of the PN-1 was not flown with that wing system. In addition, the cantilever wings were heavy, and aircraft gross weight was 2,785 pounds. It appears that, since

The first Curtiss fighter to be associated with a "popular" name, the Curtiss PN-1 *Nighthawk* owed much to the Curtiss-built Orenco D and, in fact, shared the same Curtiss internal design number, L-44-2. This is the original configuration of the design, with full cantilever wings, slightly tapered, and owing more than a little to Fokker concepts. The significance of the devices under the lower wings are unknown, but may have been flare mounts. This aircraft is not believed to have flown as such. (*Curtiss via Peter M. Bowers*)

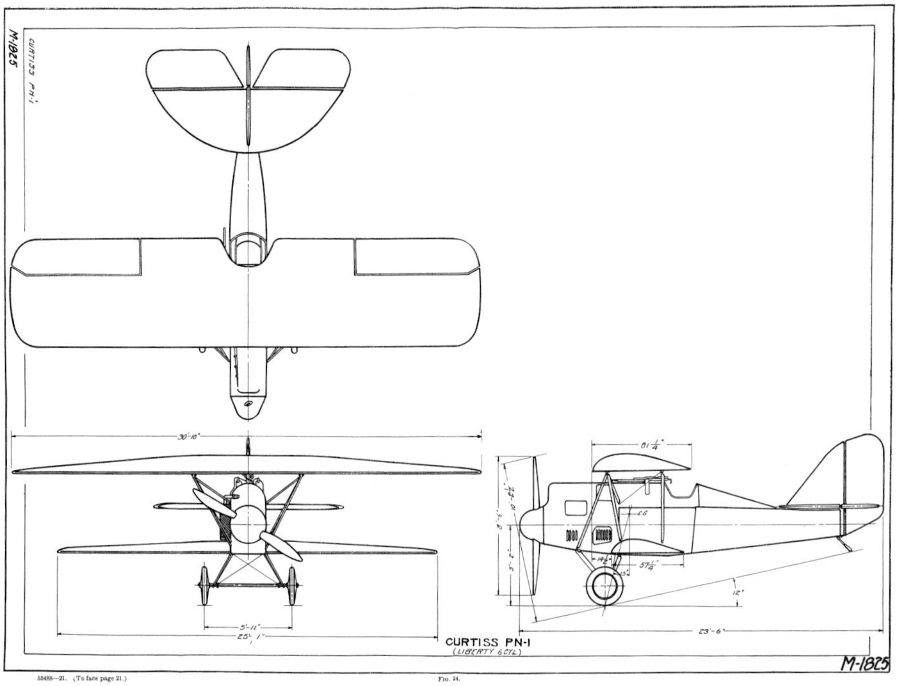

The original configuration of the PN-1 *Nighthawk* included installation of the radiator on the starboard (right) side of the fuselage. The aircraft was apparently a mix of Engineering Division, Curtiss, and Fokker ideas, and with a *Liberty Six* engine, would probably have been underpowered in this configuration. (*USAAS*)

this aircraft was not flown as such, that the Army did not accept it, and thus no Air Service serial number was assigned.[21] It was apparently tested to destruction, however, as it was noted as having suffered spar failure during tests on February 4, 1921. This was almost certainly the aircraft referred to as the Curtiss *Night Pursuit Airplane, Type II*, and may in fact have never been assigned the designation PN-1. In spite of the fact that the airframe was obviously tested to destruction, the aircraft was noted as having been fitted with two synchronized machine guns at some point (mounted on the top of the cowling, just ahead of the cockpit, and apparently consisting of Marlin guns), as well as cartridge boxes, feed and ejection chutes, and a type XVIII bomb rack. It is not clear what utility a bomb rack on an aircraft designed for night fighting might have had! Other equipment consisted of an air speed indicator, altimeter, compass, clock, oil and fuel pressure gauges, tachometer, inclinometer, lateral indicator, water temperature gauge, and an S.C.R.59 radio telephone set. The aircraft was unusually well equipped for the time.

The PN-1 design was then revised to incorporate a new, thinner overhanging upper wing with balanced ailerons, conventional interplane "N"-struts, and revised cabane struts, and the faired engine cowling and propeller spinner were done away with. This revised aircraft, assigned Army serial A.S.63276 and McCook Field Test Number P-198,[22] was delivered for tests in August 1921.[23] It had a span of 30 feet, 10 inches, length of 23 feet, six inches, and a height of 10 feet, three inches. Wing area was an even 300 square

Painted black overall, aside from the national insignia and serial number (A.S.63276), the second PN-1 was dramatically revised from the original concept, and also wore McCook Field test number P-198 on the rudder. Now it had untapered, strut braced wings and balanced ailerons. Note the position lights on the upper side of each lower wing, one of the very earliest applications. The aircraft remained in the inventory from 1921 until January 1926. (*USAAC 1276 via Peter M. Bowers*)

feet, and at a light gross weight of 2,311 pounds the resulting wing loading was 7.7 pounds per square foot. With the 220hp *Liberty* 6, power loading was 10.5 pounds per horse power. At an empty weight of 1,631 pounds useful load became 661 pounds, of which 318 pounds (53 gallons) was fuel, leaving an allocation of 351 pounds for engine oil, pilot, and armament, the latter consisting of two fixed forward firing .30 caliber machine guns in the fuselage.

Performance of the PN-1 was unexceptional, with a sea level high speed of only 108mph, service and absolute ceilings of 23,900 and 25,600 feet, respectively, climb performance taking 5.5 minutes to 6,500 feet, and a range at high speed of 255 miles.

To reflect its mission as a night pursuit, the PN-1 was painted black. The Army issued very specific painting instructions for this, the very first U.S. night fighter, on June 19, 1920. They stated that:

"*...the colors of the Curtiss Night Pursuit airplanes will include: all fabric covered fuselages are to be covered with black pigmented dope. Exposed wood parts are to be covered with dull black pigment. Exposed metal parts, not in stress, are to be a dull black pigment. This applies to such parts as cowlings.*"

Lower wingtip lights were provided, as well as a long engine exhaust pipe along one side beyond the cockpit, this apparently an attempt to hide exhaust flame, as well as to protect the pilot from exhaust fumes.

Though there was no production for Curtiss, the Army held on to a single PN-1 until it was finally stricken from the active rolls on January 14, 1926. The first attempt at a night fighting plane was no success. A second aircraft, A.S.63277, was apparently not built.

Curtiss TS-1

Early in the 1920s, the U.S. Navy had an urgent need for a new fighter airplane to serve aboard their first aircraft carrier, the U.S.S.

Curtiss entered the history books as the manufacturer of the first U.S. carrier-based fighter, the little Navy-designed TS-1. Since carriers were still experimental, all Navy operational aircraft of the day were also required to adapt to floats for water operations. Twin floats did not work well in rough water, however, so later, most designs had a single main float and small wingtip floats. A-6248 was delivered July 27, 1922, and served with both the USS *Wright* and *Langley* for experimental purposes. Ironically, this aircraft may still exist, as it ditched in the Potomac River off the *Langley* July 10, 1924, and was not recovered. (*U.S. Navy*)

Langley. The ship was a conversion of the Navy collier *Jupiter*, slated to be re-commissioned as a carrier in March 1922.

The new fighter was to be designed by the Navy Bureau of Aeronautics, formed in 1921 out of the Aeronautical Section of the Navy Bureau of Construction and Repair, and was much later to be re-named the Naval Air Systems Command.

In March 1921 the Navy appointed Rex B. Beisel, at age 28 one of the first certified aeronautical engineers, as project engineer heading the design of the new fighter. Beisel had graduated from the University of Washington in 1916, and soon after joined the

A rare view of VF-1 Curtiss TS-1 aircraft aboard the U.S. Navy's first aircraft carrier, the USS *Langley*, late in 1922. The aircraft at left is a Boeing FB-5, using a Curtiss water-cooled engine. The TS-1 had a maximum speed of 131mph wheel equipped, with a service ceiling of over 14,000 feet. (*U.S. Navy*)

An exceptionally small and compact aircraft, this aircraft, bearing only the number "5" on the fuselage, may have been A-6249, which was sent to the NACA at Langley, VA, in November 1923, where it was configured for catapult tests. Note the unusually thick lower mid-section, lack of a spreader bar on the undercarriage, and odd attachments to the interplane struts. (*Cradle of Aviation Museum*)

Bureau. He much later was to be well known in conjunction with the design of the classic World War II era Vought F4U-1 *Corsair* fighter. In the meantime, he was one of the principle engineers involved in the design of the Curtiss F7C, F8C, and entire *Hawk* fighter series—contributions that are seldom recognized.

The Navy fighter destined for the *Langley* was designated the TS-1,[24] this standing for Tractor, Single seat, and the Navy put out bid requests to industry for construction of TS-1s. They also decided to let the Naval Aircraft Factory in Philadelphia build a few aircraft of this design to validate costs.

At the same time, the Lawrance Aero Engine Company of New York had worked out a promising new aircooled radial engine design with nine cylinders in a single row developing 220hp for a weight of 442 pounds. On January 7, 1922, the Model J-1, as the new engine was designated, completed successfully a 50 hour test stand run qualifying it for test installation in a prototype aircraft. This engine had the advantage of eliminating a heavy and vulnerable water cooling system, and was the forerunner of the later aircooled engine trend in the Navy, and of many Wright and Pratt & Whitney radial piston engines. Wright Aeronautical Corporation took over the Lawrance Engine Company, and the J-1 was the predecessor of the Wright *Whirlwind* engine series.

With a bid of $9,569 each for the first 11 aircraft and $9,975 for the remainder (less Government Furnished Equipment, or GFE), the Curtiss Aeroplane and Motor Company won a contract (No.54109) for 34[25] aircraft, and the NAF was assigned the job of building five. The Curtiss built aircraft were delivered in two distinct batches: Navy Bureau of Aeronautics serial numbers A-6248 to 6270 (23 aircraft) and A-6305 to A-6315 (11 aircraft). In July 1922 Curtiss delivered their first TS for test at Anacostia Naval Air Station, DC.

Designed to operate on either wheels or wooden, NAF-designed twin floats, the TS-1 was a compact single-bay biplane to minimize space requirements aboard the carrier. Basically of steel tube and wood construction covered with fabric, the little fighter was characterized by a unique diagonal metal interplane strut system employed in a manner to minimize external wire bracing. To assure sufficient wing gap for efficient wing cellule performance, and to

This TS-1 (A-6307) is unusual, in having a propspinner on its Lawrence J-1 engine. It was accepted on June 4, 1923, and was stricken December 23, 1925, with 298:31 total time after an accident on October 30th. (*A. J. Bibee Collection, Museum of Flight*)

provide a short landing gear, both upper and lower wings were strut-braced off the fuselage in an unusual fashion. A fattened lower wing center section made up the fuel tank fairing. Two .30 caliber fixed machine guns were installed under a cowling forward of the cockpit. The main landing gear was equipped with multiple hooks to catch the longitudinal deck arresting wires on the *Langley*, though some aircraft were equipped with the rear, arrestor tail hook as well later on.

Late in 1922 the TS-1s started carrier suitability tests as Squadron VF-1 aboard *Langley*. The first aircraft was delivered to the ship on December 9, 1922, and the last aircraft came aboard on October 8, 1923. Tests were also made of the twin float seaplane variant.

In addition, tests were conducted to compare TS-1 wings with USA-27 versus N-15 airfoil sections, and the former design was accepted as standard.

When operated from land airfields the TS-1s were considered susceptible to ground looping, but flight characteristics were generally satisfactory.

The diminutive fighter had essentially equispan wings with a span of only 25 feet (the lower wing was 5/16 inch longer), and constant chords of 4 feet, nine inches. Wing gap was 5 feet, six inches, and there was no stagger, incidence, or sweepback. The lower wing alone had 3 degrees of dihedral. Total wing area was 227.88 square feet; horizontal tail area totaled 27.8 square feet, and vertical tail 10.3 square feet. Aircraft length and height were 22 feet one and 3/16 inches, and 8 feet 11 and 15/16 inches, respectively.

The structural factor of safety at low speed (high angle of attack) was 7.

A landplane empty weight of 1,239.5 pounds (consisting of 612 pounds of structure, 573 pounds of powerplant, and 54.5 pounds of fixed equipment), plus a useful load of 692 pounds (comprised of a 180 pound pilot, 300 pounds of fuel, 38 pounds of oil, 38 pounds of equipment, and 136 pounds of armament) totaled to a gross weight of 1,931.5 pounds, thus giving a wing loading of 8.46psf.

In the production TS-1 the Lawrance J-1 radial engine was rated at 230hp maximum at 1,800rpm, giving a power loading for the aircraft of 8.4 pounds per horse power. The engine drove a two-bladed wood propeller of 7 feet, 10 inches diameter. Basic fuel consumption was 0.5 pounds per horsepower, per hour, and oil consumption 0.026 pounds per horsepower per hour. Fuel and oil capacities were 50 and 5 gallons, respectively.

Performance of the wheeled TS-1 was modest, with a high speed of 131mph and low speed of 50mph. Sea level rate of climb was 1,280 feet per minute, and it took five minutes to climb to 5,400 feet, while service and absolute ceilings were 14,400 and 16,000 feet, respectively. Endurance at high speed came to 2.6 hours.

In the twin float configuration TS-1 length and height increased to 24 feet, 10 inches, and 9 feet, seven inches. Empty weight increased about 200 pounds to 1,443.3 pounds because of the floats, with the gross weight going up to 2,135.3 pounds, and wing and power loading increasing to 9.35psf and 9.27 pounds per horse power.

At least one Curtiss TS-1 was fitted with streamlined blisters over the cylinders, probably to aid cooling. Note the ports for the two guns on top of the cowling, seldom pictured. (*Naval Aircraft Factory 31890*)

Seaplane TS-1 performance dropped to a high speed of 121mph and low speed of 53mph, initial climb rate to 980 feet per minute, and service and absolute ceilings dropped to 13,500 and 15,100 feet.

All performance figures were the result of actual flight testing. Reports of VF-1 Squadron operations were quite favorable, and the J-1 engine gave a minimum of trouble. These aircraft served until 1929-30. In June 1923 at San Diego, CA, a TS-1 seaplane set a World Speed Record for Class "C" at a speed of 122mph for 100 kilometers. In early 1925 VF-1 went on twin floats as scouts aboard most all of the fleet battleships, and they were also used aboard large destroyers. They could not be catapulted, however. Sea operations were limited, since the fighting ships had to employ a crane to hoist the TS-1s into the water and out. In addition, twin floats did not work well in rough seas. At least one (A-6249) was assigned to the NACA at Langley Field, VA, by November 1, 1923, from Hampton Roads, where it was reconfigured for catapult tests and, interestingly, for both engine supercharger work and pontoon pressure distribution tests. Although it was assigned the NACA number '15,' it is not clear if this was painted on the aircraft.

In mid-1926 the Navy still had over 20 TS-1s, but replacements were at hand. Sixteen aircraft were stored at Pensacola in November 1927 and later disposed of, though one was rescued to survive at the National Museum of Naval Aviation. By 1929 remaining aircraft were in the reserves, and the last three (A-6305, A-6311, and A-6312) were stricken from the inventory May 29, 1930. The first U.S. carrier fighter plane had seen its day.

The five NAF-built cost comparison aircraft of standard design were completed in 1923, and four more came forth as special racing planes, but the Curtiss Aeroplane and Motor Company was not directly involved in those efforts, though they did sponsor the Curtiss Marine Trophy Races.

An interesting experiment took place in 1923 and 1924 when a comparison was made between wood and metal construction of what was basically the same fighter design. The experiment was conducted as a cooperative endeavor between the Navy, Curtiss, and Charles Ward Hall, the latter a leading advocate of metal construction. Essentially, the Curtiss F4C-1 was a TS-1 made of metal instead of wood. (*Curtiss*)

Curtiss F4C-1

In 1922 and 1923 the U.S. Navy became interested in the potential advantages of metal structures for aircraft to replace the then-current methods of construction. The Curtiss Aeroplane and Motor Company of Garden City, Long Island, NY, was awarded a contract to design and produce two copies of a new experimental fighter using the maximum amount of aluminum construction, and based on the Navy TS-1 design to the maximum extent possible.

A leading advocate of metal aircraft structures, Charles Ward Hall, was called upon by Curtiss to head the design team. The experimental planes were labeled Curtiss design L-410-1,[26] and designated by the Navy as F4C-1 in their new system as the fourth Curtiss fighter design for the Navy. The first three designs were paper designations only for past Curtiss racer airplanes. One of the two F4C-1s was to be used for flight testing, and the other as a static structural test article. This seems to be supported by the fact that Curtiss documents list only one MSN for an F4C-1 (10501). The Navy, however, assigned Bureau of Aeronautics serial numbers A-6689 and A-6690 to the two aircraft built on Contract 57525. A-6689, after being briefly assigned to Anacostia, the Naval Aircraft Factory, and Hampton Roads, VA, was transferred on May 7, 1926, to Langley Field, VA, where it was apparently examined by the NACA. It was stricken from the Navy inventory October 28, 1927, with no recorded flight time. Another F4C-1 (A-6690) was also at the NACA briefly in 1927.

By April 1923 Hall had completed all design specifications, and after fabrication initial testing was started at Curtiss Field, Mineola, Long Island, NY, in early September 1924. The plane was quite revolutionary in American design practice for the time. In the words of the Curtiss company in 1924:

"The F4C-1 light pursuit plane was designed and built in a collaboration by Mr. Charles Ward Hall and Curtiss Aeroplane and Motor Company Inc. for the U.S. Navy, and embodied Mr. Hall's interesting metal construction. The plane follows closely the lines of the Curtiss-Navy TS Fighter of 1922, but by the use of metal construction a savings in weight of nearly 300 pounds was accomplished, which is remarkable for a small plane.

The machine is a single seater, single bay tractor biplane powered by a Wright J-3 200 HP radial air cooled motor. The entire structure is of duraluminum, covered with cloth.

Of chief interest is the wing construction. The wings are all of duraluminum, covered with cloth. The ribs are duraluminum stampings forged in a die. The spars, of which there are two for each wing, are made with multiple tube flanges and Warren truss webs. Each flange is composed of two or more duraluminum tubes laid side by side and riveted together by long rivets at the points of attachment of the web members. The web members are also dural tubes with their ends flattened so as to pass between the flange tubes at the rivet points. It is thus possible to reduce the number of flange tubes at points of low stress, from four to two, by simply discontinuing the outer tubes.

Curtiss F4C-1 A-6689 as she appeared, almost brand new, on September 23, 1924. The relationship to the TS-1 is obvious, though there were differences. The lower wing was connected to the fuselage. The TS-1 carried 612 pounds of structural weight, while the F4C-1 had only 377. In spite of the advantages, it took some time for the Navy to adopt all-metal construction. The single flyable F4C-1 joined a TS-1 squadron. It served until October 28, 1927, last assigned to the NACA. (*Curtiss*)

The fuselage is a Warren truss of duraluminum tubing joined by machined duraluminum fittings. A patented tube end has been used which gives 100 % of the tube strength both in tension and compression. The tail surfaces are of duraluminum construction, the same dies having been used for stamping the tail ribs for the most part as the wing ribs. The landing gear is of the wide tread horizontal axle type, especially adapted to deck landings, although the layout of the machine is such that a split axle landing gear or single or double floats could be fitted as an alternate arrangement.

The small overall dimensions of the plane, its light weight, absence of adjusting wires, and extremely accessible air cooled motor make it particularly suitable for naval ship-board use."

On the second flight, test loaded to a gross weight of 1,656 pounds, a high speed of about 130mph was achieved, and the aircraft was reported by the pilot, Lt. Cudihy[27] of the Navy, to handle well and have very good stability. In addition, the F4C-1 was evaluated as both stronger and lighter than the TS-1.

The wingspan of the F4C-1, for both wings, was 25 feet, with length and height 18 feet four inches, and 8 feet four and 1/2 inches. Wings chord was 44.25 inches and gap 54 inches. There was no stagger, incidence angle, or sweep. The lower wing only had 3 degrees of dihedral. Total wing area was 172.7 square feet, so at the normal gross weight of 1,703 pounds, wing loading was 9.87psf. Wing airfoil sections were USA 27. Horizontal and vertical tail areas were 21.4 and 9.4 square feet, respectively, and the tail arm, Center of Gravity (CG) to elevator hinge, was approximately 12 feet.

The engine of the F4C-1 was a Wright J-3[28] (with no oil cooler) rated at 205hp at 1,750rpm, driving a two-blade Curtiss Reed EX-32921 dural propeller of 8 feet seven and 1/2 inch diameter and 7 feet, 11.75 inch pitch, propeller number Ex-32921. Nominal fuel consumption came to 0.53 pounds per horse power per hour, with oil consumption .025 pounds per horse power per hour. Capacities were 52 gallons of fuel and 5 gallons of oil.

The aircraft empty weight totaled 1,029 pounds, composed of 377 pounds of structure, including a 164.5 pound fuselage (194 pounds less than that of the TS-1), 609 pounds of powerplant, and 43 pounds of fixed equipment. The useful load was 674 pounds, composed of a 180 pound pilot, 335 pounds of fuel and oil, and 122 pounds of ordnance (two fixed forward firing synchronized .30 caliber 1917 pattern Marlin machine guns with 250 rounds per gun). At 205hp the power loading was 8.31 pounds per horse power.

Normal high speed at design gross weight was 125mph, and landing speed 55mph. Initial climb rate was 1,520 feet per minute, and it took 8.35 minutes to attain 10,000 feet, and 10 minutes to 11,000 feet. Service and absolute ceilings were 19,900 feet and 21,200 feet. All the performance data was based on Curtiss tests of late September 1924. Maximum range was estimated at 525 miles, and range at high speed 350 miles.

It is worth noting that, besides the pair of Marlin .30 caliber machine guns, the detailed specification also called for a pigeon box with two birds!

Though there were many merits in the metal construction, costs at that time were considered relatively high, and the metal workmanship and finish was not considered completely satisfactory. Indeed, the officers who evaluated the aircraft rated it as "*...fair for gunnery, excellent for landing,*" and noted that they could "*...not stall the plane with power off, and will not spin easily, otherwise handles very similar to TS.*" The actual wording of their overall impression was that "*...the workmanship and finish on this plane is not considered first class.*"

The F4C-1 never went into production, but the single flight test aircraft went into regular service with VF-1 on the USS *Langley* by December 14, 1926, for further evaluation, and remained there until September 1, 1927, when it was transferred to the California Institute of Technology at Pasadena.

Curtiss Pursuit Airplane, Experimental, TYPE I

In September 1922 Curtiss advised the Army Air Service that it was developing, at its own expense, a new pursuit aircraft built around their D-12 engine.

By April 10, 1923, the Army had become sufficiently intrigued by the reports of this design to bear the expense of sending an of-

The true granddaddy of them all, and arguably the first of the classic *Hawk* line, this private venture, the so-called Curtiss Pursuit Airplane, Experimental, Type I, was pictured here on January 19, 1923—four months before the Army finally took an interest. The Army PW-8s that followed were direct descendants. (*Curtiss*)

Leaning casually against the prop of the first prototype of the new Curtiss XPW-8 Army pursuit (although marked as a PW-8, and with test number P-295 as of May 22, 1923) is Lt. Russell Maughan, flanked by his ground crew. The new PW-8 with double-bay wings featured skin cooling radiators on the upper wing, and the new Curtiss D-12 water cooled engine. Note the small access door marked "Mag." for access to the magneto, just near the aft end of the exhaust stacks. (*Curtiss*)

ficer, D. C. Maier, from McCook Field to the Curtiss factory on Long Island to examine and test the aircraft first hand.

Maier returned a detailed report on April 10th, on which he identified the aircraft as the Curtiss Pursuit Airplane, Experimental, Type I. This was almost certainly the aircraft that became the so-called prototype of the PW-8 series that followed, and was probably acquired by the Air Service as XPW-8 A.S.23-1201.

Maier noted a number of interesting things in his report, which focused on the armament installation. He observed that the pilot's instruments were located on the right side of the cockpit, were well arranged, and offered no interference with the guns.

By May 21st this aircraft had in fact been acquired by the Army, and was thereafter cited as a Curtiss Pursuit - Type I -PW-8.

Curtiss PW-8 *Pursuit* Series

The first dedicated U.S. Army pursuit ship, as they were then called, of basic Curtiss design was their Model L-18, or the PW-8 *Pursuit*[29] as designated by the Army. In the Army system of the time this label meant Pursuit, Water-cooled engine, eighth design. The PW-8 was derived from the Curtiss Pursuit Airplane, Experimental, Type I, described just previously.

The PW-8 was a single seat, double bay, straight winged biplane with two major distinctions: a Curtiss D-12 engine, and wing "skin cooling" radiators. Both of these features had been used in the famous record breaking Curtiss landplane and seaplane military racing aircraft with success and, it was felt, were applicable to a new pursuit aircraft.

Unsuccessful in two earlier attempts with one of the XPW-8s, Lt. Russell Maughan achieved fame in January 1924 by piloting A.S.24-204 on the "Dawn to Dusk, Coast to Coast" flight, a distance of 2,607 miles in 22 hours with five stops. Starting on Long Island and arriving in San Francisco, the aircraft had lengthened exhaust pipes, and wore McCook/Wright Field test number P-361, as well as a more or less standard Army scheme for the day. (*Curtiss*)

After the "Dawn to Dusk" flight was a success, the Army painted the historic aircraft in a special color scheme, complete with appropriate emblem on the fuselage. Often published as the way it appeared during the flight, the aircraft is far too "clean" in this post-flight view. (*USAF*)

During late World War One, Charles B. Kirkham, the Chief Motor Engineer at Curtiss Aeroplane and Motor Company, Inc., of New York, undertook the design of a new liquid cooled engine with some then radical features. Kirkham's new K-12 engine, first mounted on the Model 18T and 18-B described earlier, featured low frontal area combined with minimum weight and maximum power and efficiency. The engine employed wet cylinder sleeve design in direct contact with coolant such that full engine power could be developed without overheating. The Curtiss-Kirkham K-12 gave 420hp for 650 pounds weight with a 1,145 cubic inch displacement, and a frontal area of 4.66 square feet. By comparison, the *Liberty* engine provided 400 horsepower for 850 pounds with 1,649 cubic inches, and frontal area of 5.16 square feet, and the Wright Hispano engine 325hp at 625 pounds, 1,127 cubic inches, and 4.75 square feet. Clearly the K-12 was the superior engine, though there were problems, especially with the reduction gear set required between engine and propeller because the K-12 was a high speed engine.

When Kirkham resigned, a new Chief Engineer, Arthur Nutt, only 24 years old, took over and corrected many of the K-12's problems. One result was to de-rate the engine to lower speed and power, and eliminate reduction gearing, but with improvements increasing torque to again raise the power. The engine thus redesigned became the Curtiss CD-12, meaning Curtiss Direct Drive 12 cylinder engine. It later became the Curtiss D-12, and was at its best when used with a Reed forged aluminum propeller that was still efficient at the higher rotational speeds, because thinner airfoil sections could be used than with a wood propeller.

This aircraft is actually the prototype PW-8 (A.S.23-1201 - note that incredibly complex landing gear!), converted to a fake Corp Observation two-seater as the CO-X, specifically to compete in a September 1923 Pulitzer Air Race in St. Louis for observation planes. The Navy complained that the Army had entered a "ringer," and the CO-X was disqualified! Note that it bears no service markings, and was probably being funded for this effort by Curtiss directly. (*USAF 164915AC via M. Sheppard*)

The second feature of the PW-8 turned out to be, at best, a mixed blessing; this was use of the Curtiss-patented wing radiators. Made up of thin corrugated brass panels in strips, the radiator system covered both top and bottom surfaces of most of the upper wing in five sections formed in halves around the wing section contour by means of hinge pins. In all there were 220 square feet of cooling surface. Engine cooling water entered the radiator leading edge through a front header, flowed aft through the corrugations to the trailing edge header, and then back to the engine. The system was quite satisfactory for a racer, but presented a great deal of vulnerable area in a pursuit plane!

The emergence of the D-12 engine was a seminal event in the history of Curtiss fighters and, for all intents and purposes, was the genesis of a dynasty. What is not generally known is that, on September 15, 1922, Curtiss had advised the Army that it was building, at its own expense, an Army pursuit ship around the D-12 that may almost certainly be regarded as the prototype PW-8, and this was almost certainly the Curtiss Pursuit, Type I, described earlier. Curtiss wanted the Army to loan them, for the purposes of this development, amongst other items, one .50 and one .30 caliber Browning machine gun, as well as a set of Mark XVIII bomb racks, and an SCR 59 radio telephone set. Perhaps to the astonishment of all concerned, the Army agreed and provided the equipment, thus contributing in this manner, for the first time, to a long standing relationship with Curtiss designed fighters. The Curtiss Company in 1924 had this to say about the PW-8:

"This machine, which was designed and built in 1923, and put into production early in 1924, is one of the standard service machines of the US Army. It is a development of the original Curtiss 1922 pursuit plane. The outstanding achievement of the machine to date was the Atlantic to Pacific flight of Lt. R. L. Maughan between dawn and dusk of June 20th. This flight covered 2,700 miles in 17

This PW-8 (A.S. 24-202, and McCook Field test number P-358) was employed as an early turbo-supercharger test bed. Although the installation of the turbo was crude, the 150.4mph high speed at sea level was improved to 174.3mph at 25,000 feet and 160mph at 30,350 feet service ceiling. Empty weight remained about 270 pounds over a standard PW-8. (*USAF*)

hours and 52 minutes flying time, with but five stops, and is probably the most severe service test ever given a pursuit ship. The PW-8 is a two bay biplane designed around the Curtiss D-12 motor. The wooden structure wings are of multi-spar planked spruce veneer construction developed for the Curtiss racing planes. The fuselage is a welded steel tube (tin coated) truss braced with wire and cloth covered. Most of the internal bracing is of duraluminum. The tail surfaces and ailerons are of steel, cloth covered, the former being externally braced. The landing gear is of the split axle type sprung upon rubber compression discs.

The powerplant is characterized by wing radiators, a water cooled oil cooler, and hand-starting crank.

Aside from the generally excellent performance attained by the machine, it is well liked on account of its maneuverability and its freedom from the more common maintenance difficulties. The squadron of PW-8 planes which attended the Dayton races performed throughout with uniform reliability, and created a very favorable impression"

A total of 29 PW-8 aircraft were built, including three XPW-8 prototypes (Curtiss MSNs 10493 to 10495, USAAS serials 23-1201 to 23-1203),[30] 25 U.S. Army production PW-8 aircraft (Curtiss MSNs 10503 to 10528, USAAS serials 24-201 to 24-225), and one plane, often cited as a PW-8 variant, but in fact something of a hybrid, was exported to Japan in 1930 (Curtiss MSN 10660, q.v.). The initial PW-8 prototype design, Curtiss L-18-1, was given a go ahead in May 1922 to meet Army requirements, with the Curtiss group headed by William Gilmore. First flight took place in January 1923. It was sold to the Army Air Service in April 1923. Curtiss obtained a contract for two more prototypes at the same time. The first aircraft, XPW-8 23-1201, could be distinguished by a slightly indented engine cowl between cylinders, a rather odd split axle landing gear and, while being evaluated at McCook Field, got the number P-295 by May 22, 1923.

Wingspan, length, and height were 32 feet, 22 feet, nine and 15/16 inches, and 9 feet, respectively. The structural factor of safety at high angle of attack was 8.5. Wing airfoil sections were Curtiss C-27 (C-62 on the XPW-8s), upper and lower wing chords were five feet and four feet, wing gap was four feet, six and 3/4 inches, stagger two feet, 10 inches, and there was no incidence or sweepback. Wing area totaled 265.3 square feet. Horizontal and vertical tail areas were 24.6 and 12.7 square feet, respectively.

The empty weight of Serial 23-1201 was 1,887 pounds, with 104 pounds of cooling water, and was composed of 761 pounds of structure, 1,067 pounds of powerplant, and 59 pounds of fixed equipment weight. Useful load comprising a 180 pound pilot, 430 pounds

Another view of the turbo-supercharged PW-8 shows an intercooler radiator sort of "patched on" under the forward fuselage. The turbo-supercharger was mounted on the starboard side of the powerplant section, and port-side exhaust was piped across the front to the turbine. This was one of the very earliest turbo installations. (*USAF*)

The second prototype PW-8 (A.S.23-1202), also bearing McCook Field number P-333 as of February 4, 1924. Note the ailerons on both wings. The nature of the small device just aft of the cockpit on the fuselage side is unknown. This aircraft was washed out June 30, 1926, at Selfridge Field. (*USAF Wright Field 20482*)

of fuel and oil, 120 pounds of equipment, and 197 pounds of armament (two fixed guns and ammunition) came to 927 pounds. Then gross weight was 2,799 pounds (first article) and 3,151 pounds (second article), giving a wing loading of 10.5psf, and a useful load to gross weight ratio of .329—quite good for the time.

The low compression version of the D-12 engine was rated 417hp at 2,200rpm, giving a power loading of 6.67 pounds per horse power. Full throttle fuel and oil consumption came to 0.53 and .015 pounds per horse power, per hour, with fuel and oil capacities at 77 gallons and eight gallons, respectively. The D-12 drove a Curtiss two blade wood Curtiss X-9048 propeller on the prototype, designed for the climb condition, and of eight feet, two inches diameter.

Performance with the low compression engine, by test, included a high speed of 159 mph at sea level, a 62 mph landing speed, an initial climb rate of 2,060 feet per minute, a full throttle endurance of 2.83 hours, and service and absolute ceilings respectively of 21,800 feet and 23,350 feet.

Using a high compression D-12 engine developing 460hp at 2,300rpm, and fuel consisting of 50% aviation gasoline and 50% Benzol with a full throttle fuel consumption of 0.58 pounds per horse power, per hour, along with a two blade seven foot, 10 inch diameter wood two-blade propeller, the serial 23-1201 machine had a sea level high speed of 170 mph, sea level climb rate of 2,500 feet per minute, a full throttle endurance at 10,000 feet of 2.8 hours, and service and absolute ceilings of 27,150 feet and 28,600 feet. With the high compression engine the aircraft could be used for air racing.

XPW-8 23-1201 was used by Army Lt. Maughan in two unsuccessful cross country (the so-called "Dawn-to-Dusk") flight attempts in 1923, once on July 9th, and a second time July 19th. On

Photos of PW-8s in squadron service are comparatively rare. This otherwise anonymous 1st Pursuit Group aircraft bears unit number "55," and no evidence of her Air Service serial. (*Cradle of Aviation Museum*)

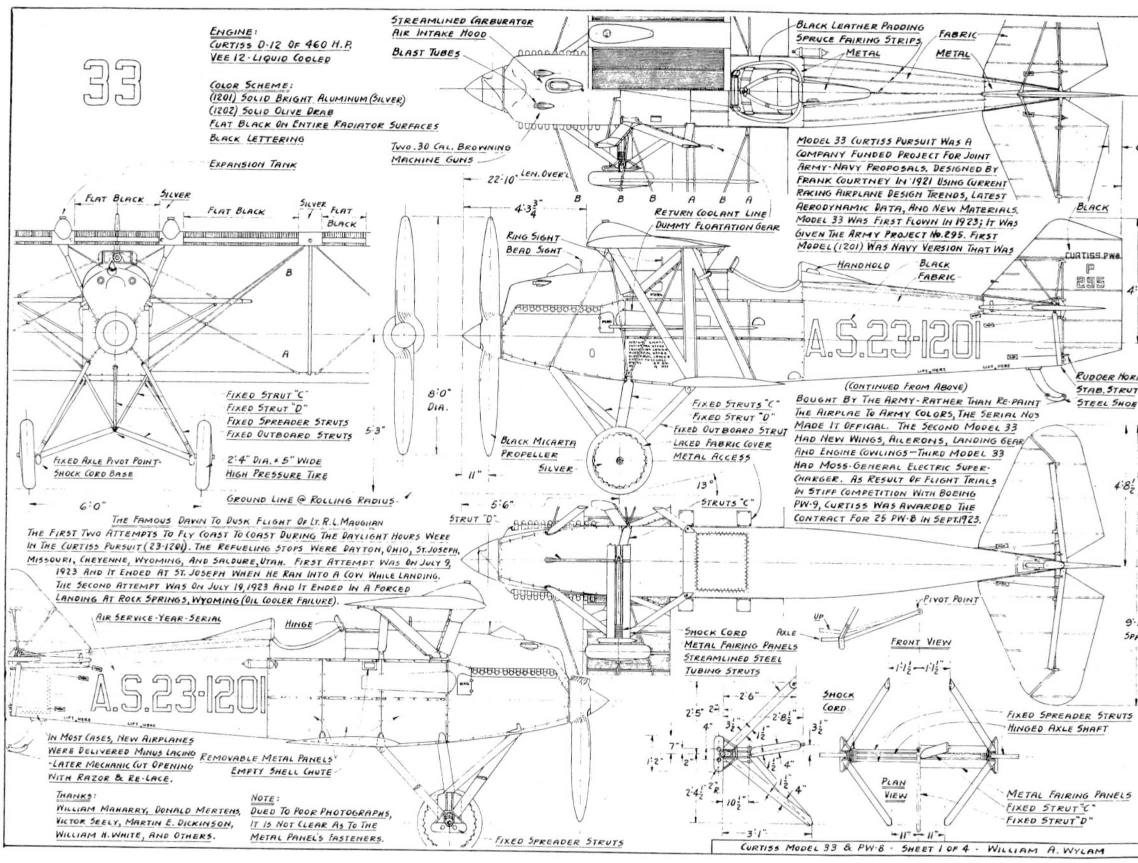

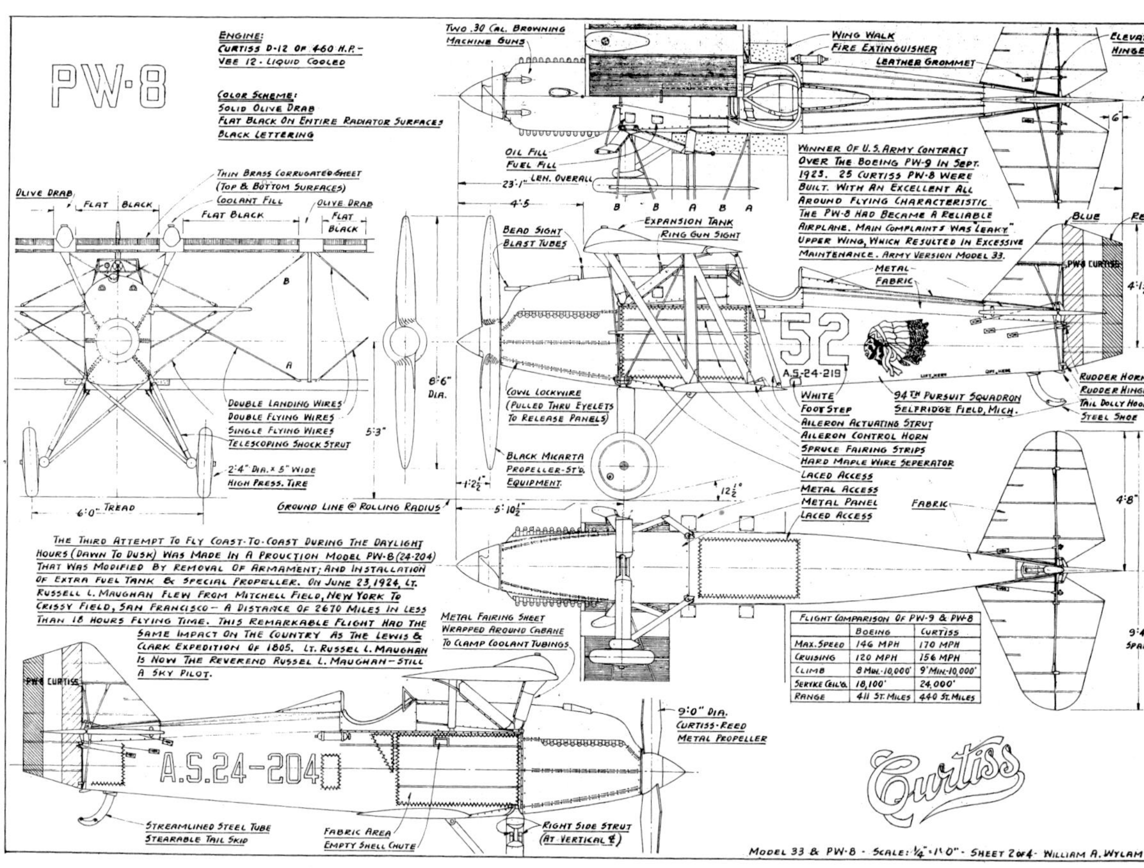

(Courtesy William A. Wylam)

July 11, 1923, the Chief of the Air Service authorized work to make the PW-8 into a two place aircraft to compete as a CO-X model entered into Event #3 of the 1923 Pulitzer Air Races at St. Louis, Missouri, for Corps Observation aircraft types.[31] In September new wing fittings were made, and on September 24, 1923, the aircraft model designation was officially changed to CO-X, meaning Corps Observation Experimental. On September 25, 1923, the CO-X, with the high compression D-12 engine and Curtiss high speed propeller EX-29048-A, was flown on a speed course at a high speed of 168mph at 2,360rpm to test the cooling system. Two days later, a higher capacity oil tank (the one for the transcontinental flight) was installed to improve cooling, and a Curtiss-Reed forged duraluminum propeller was installed. On September 28, 1923, Army Lt. Brookley piloted the CO-X to St. Louis. Three days later the St. Louis Air Board, after hearing protests from the Navy, disallowed the use of the CO-X in the observation plane race, since it was a modified pursuit plane, rather than a true observation type, spelling the end of the CO-X. This aircraft was finally surveyed and disposed of at McCook Field February 21, 1925.

The second XPW-8 prototype (A.S.23-1202), Curtiss design L-18-2, was different in several ways from the first, and was to form the basis for the 25 production aircraft. The landing gear struts were simplified. Still a double bay biplane of 32 foot span, the skin cooling system wing radiator area was increased, the airfoil section changed to a C-62 design, the factor of safety at high angle of attack increased to 12, length went to 23 feet, one inch, and the height was increased an inch. Upper wing chord was revised to five feet, six inches, thus increasing wing area to 279.3 square feet. Ailerons were now on both wings, with a total area of 20.3 square feet. Vertical tail area increased to 13.55 square feet, and wing gap increased to slightly over 55 inches.

On A.S.23-1202 (the second article, McCook Field number P-333 by February 4, 1924) empty weight increased to 2,185 pounds, including 123 pounds of water, 857 pounds of structure (reflecting the higher safety factor), 1,245 pounds of powerplant, and 83 pounds of fixed equipment. The useful load comprised a 180 pound pilot, 510 pounds of fuel and oil, 50 pounds of equipment, and 230 pounds of armament, totaling 970 pounds. Empty weight and useful load came to a gross weight of 3,155 pounds, well over that of the first prototype, giving a wing loading of 11.33psf. Useful load to gross weight ratio was 0.307.

The L-18-2 prototype used the low compression D-12 engine of 420hp at 2,200rpm. Fuel and oil capacity and consumption rates were the same as the first aircraft. A Curtiss wood propeller (EX29048) of seven feet, 10 inch diameter and designed for high speed was now employed.

Additional aileron area improved roll rate, and test pilots seemed to like this second prototype even more than the first. Tests were conducted against the competing Boeing PW-9, and the XPW-8 A.S.23-1202 was judged sufficiently successful to garner an order for 25 similar production aircraft as 24-201 to 24-225 on September 25, 1923. These pursuits were delivered from Curtiss in the three month period starting June 14, 1924, and went mainly to the Army's 1st Pursuit Group. The final aircraft in the batch was delivered August 14, 1924. Meanwhile, the second XPW-8 (A.S.23-1202) suffered a forced landing April 19, 1924, and later crashed again; it was repaired both times by Curtiss. During the course of these repairs, a center section core radiator was installed in place of the wing radiators, but was not found satisfactory. It was finally surveyed and disposed of at Selfridge Field, MI, June 30, 1926.

It is seldom noted that the third XPW-8 (A.S.23-1203) was not completed as such, thus accounting for a complete lack of photos of the aircraft. It was reworked into the XPW-8A on Change Order No.899 before delivery from Curtiss.

Actual performance of these L-18-2/PW-8 machines with the low compression D-12 engine included a high speed capability of

PW-8 A.S.23-1203, the third prototype (Curtiss Model L-18-3), was actually completed as an XPW-8A, and involved a major design revision. It obviously had only single bay wings of shorter overall span, and a radiator in the wing upper center section only. This was found to be inadequate, however. It mounted a Curtiss V-1150, 435hp engine. After barely a month as a PW-8A, it was converted to an XPW-8B January 31, 1925. It was lost on June 1, 1925, when Lt. Frank Hunter crashed while engaged in mock combat at McCook Field with a total time of only 67:33. (*via Peter m. Bowers*)

171mph at sea level and a 63mph landing speed, a climb rate at sea level of 1,830fpm, a full throttle endurance of 2.75 hours at 10,000 feet, and service and absolute ceilings of 20,350 and 21,500 feet, respectively—these numbers gained using the same engine and wood propeller as in the second prototype. Fuel consumption was 0.53 pounds per horse power, per hour.

Equipped with a high compression D-12 of 460hp at 2,300rpm, and using a metal Curtiss-Reed propeller,[32] also of seven feet, 10 inch diameter, it was estimated the gross weight would be 3,167 pounds, and performance would be as follows: High speed 177mph at sea level, 174mph at 5,000 feet, 169mph at 10,000 feet, and 160mph at 15,000 feet; a sea level full throttle endurance of 1.7 hours; and climb in 10 minutes to 13,600 feet. Estimated service and absolute ceilings were 21,000 and 22,000 feet, respectively.

Of the production aircraft, the first (24-201) served as a production test batch aircraft with the McCook Field number P-357, as did the second and fourth, as P-358 (A.S.24-202, fitted with a supercharger by July 19, 1924) and P-361 (which was the famous "Daylight Coast-to-Coast"" aircraft of June 23, 1924). Several production PW-8s were tested on skis. In February 1925 ski equipped PW-8s of the 1st Pursuit Group operated during winter maneuvers in Michigan. The quite awkward patch-on of turbo system components on P-358, including an under slung intercooler, was strictly for research and test purposes.

On this aircraft, a low compression (5.3:1) D-12 was rated at 391hp at 2,125rpm, based on its output at 20,000 feet altitude using aviation gas, and driving an Engineering Division X-48349 two-blade propeller of nine feet diameter and seven feet, 4.3 inch pitch.

Aircraft empty weight with the turbo installation was 2,456 pounds with 109 pounds of water. Useful load came to 1,020 pounds, including a 180 pound pilot, 503 pounds of fuel and oil, and armament of 337 pounds. Thus, gross weight was 3,457 pounds, a 321 pound increase over the basic model. The wing and power loadings were 12.4psf and 8.89 pounds per horse power.

The supercharger certainly improved altitude performance according to McCook Field Report 2615 dated September 26, 1925. High speeds were 150.4mph at sea level, 158.5mph at 5,000 feet, 164.9 mph at 10,000 feet, 174mph 20,000 feet, 174.3mph at 25,000 feet, and 160mph at 30,350 feet. Landing speed, however, went up to 69.5mph. Climb rates were 1,310 feet per minute at sea level, 1,238 feet per minute at 5,000 feet, 1,174 feet per minute at 10,000 feet, 1,007 feet per minute at 20,000 feet, and 756 feet per minute at 25,000 feet. Climb times were 3.9 minutes to 5,000 feet, 8.0 minutes to 10,000 feet, 17.1 minutes to 20,000 feet, and 22.7 minutes to 25,000 feet. Full throttle endurance at 20,000 feet was 2.0 hours, with range 348 miles. Ceilings for the turbo supercharged model were 30,350 feet service and 30,650 absolute.

Another rather spectacular event for the time took place on June 23, 1924, when PW-8 24-204,[33] the fourth production model, piloted by Army Lt. Maughan flew coast-to-coast in daylight (dubbed by the press as "The Dawn to Dusk Flight") starting at Mitchell Field, Long Island, NY, and ending at San Francisco—2,607 miles in about 22 hours with five refueling stops. The flight was the third attempt for Maughan after two failures. In this third flight Maughan took off from Mitchell at 3 AM EST, and arrived at McCook Field, Dayton, Ohio, four hours later. It took an hour there to take on gas, have a gas line repaired, and to install larger wheels for the next landing at a muddy field at St. Joseph, Missouri, where another refueling took place and Maughan ate lunch. He then flew to Cheyenne, Wyoming, just after 2PM, and was in the air just after 3 PM to proceed to Salduro, Utah, where he again refueled in about 30 minutes. Airborne again just before 6 PM, he proceeded to San Francisco, arriving safely at 9:44PM.

The coast-to-coast PW-8 had fuel capacity increased to 167 gallons (consisting of a 75 gallon main tank, a 47 gallon rear tank, and a 45 gallon top tank), and oil increased to one gallon. A new Curtiss-Reed metal propeller (EX-32919) of eight feet, eight inches diameter and seven feet, nine and 3/4 inch pitch was fitted.

The third prototype PW-8 (A.S.23-1203) at yet another interim stage in its life as the XPW-8A, with a new tunnel radiator, but the constant chord, single bay wings are retained. After tests opposite the Boeing PW-9, which had wings that were tapered, and with maneuverability rated higher, the Curtiss crew adopted the same taper and, as the saying goes, the rest was history. The significance of the white "71" on the rear fuselage and under the starboard wing is unknown (*Wright Field 23805*)

Empty weight was 2,300 pounds, and useful load 1,304 pounds, giving a gross weight of 3,604 pounds, and a wing loading of 12.87psf. Performance-wise, high speed was 171mph, and landing speed a rather sporty 71mph. Sea level rate of climb came to 1,700fpm. Full throttle endurance with the increased fuel load was 4.5 hours at 10,000 feet. Service and absolute ceilings were 17,400 feet and 18,400 feet, respectively.

The third XPW-8 prototype aircraft, as noted earlier, was actually completed as the XPW-8A,[34] Curtiss Model L-18-3 and Army A.S.23-1203, and was a major design revision in configuration. Delivered by Curtiss September 4, 1924, the biplane had single bay straight wings of shorter span. Because the Army and Curtiss had second thoughts about the skin cooling wing radiators requiring so much precision to prevent leaks, and presenting so much combat vulnerable area, a new design radiator was first incorporated in just the center section of the upper wing. Tests of this aircraft at McCook Field as P-364 soon showed this radiator design to be inadequate in cooling and disturbing to wing airflow. With this failure Curtiss decided they had to use a tunnel radiator underneath the engine as in the competitor Boeing XPW-9, and the XPW-8A was so equipped in October 1924 by Curtiss. A tunnel water cooled oil cooler was also used. The characteristics of this aircraft included span of the single bay equi-span wings with ailerons, both at 30 feet. Airfoil sections were C-62. Upper wing chord was 66 inches, and lower wing chord 48 inches. Gap was 53 inches, and stagger 36 inches. There was no dihedral on the upper wing, but the lower wing had 1.5 degrees. Total wing area came to 253.6 square feet, including a total aileron area of 16.2 square feet. Horizontal tail area was 32.5 square feet, and vertical tail 13.35 square feet. High angle of attack factor of safety was 12.0 It also differed from the XPW-8s in having a new design split axle undercarriage with rubber discs in place of shock absorber cord.

The XPW-8A was powered by the low compression D-12 of 440hp at 2,240rpm, with nominal fuel consumption of 0.52 pounds per horse power, per hour, and oil consumption of .015 pounds per horse power, per hour. Internal fuel capacity was 54 gallons, with an auxiliary tank capacity of 13.6 gallons. Oil capacity was 5.2 gallons. The engine drove a metal Curtiss-Reed X-32937 two blade propeller of eight feet, six inches diameter, and pitch of seven feet, nine inches.

The empty weight of 1,986 pounds of this trim looking pursuit consisted of 810 pounds of structure, 1,123 pounds of powerplant, and 53 pounds of fixed equipment. Useful load comprised a 180 pound pilot, 366 pounds of fuel and oil, 210 pounds of ordnance, and 59 pounds of equipment totaling 814 pounds. Adding empty weight and useful load, the gross weight totaled 2,819 pounds. Wing loading became 11.05psf.

The XPW-8A's maximum speed, by Army test of November 7, 1924, with the new tunnel radiator, was 178mph at sea level, and landing speed was 65.6mph. Initial climb capability was 1,925 feet per minute, and the pursuit could get to 12,000 feet in 10 minutes. Service and absolute ceilings were 22,250 and 23,400 feet.

The XPW-8A, marked as McCook Field P-364 with tunnel radiator, was used for racing, and in racing configuration placed third in the 1924 Pulitzer Trophy Race piloted by Lt. Rex Stoner. As a racer the plane used a high compression D-12 engine rated at 460hp at 2,300rpm, and used a 50-50 mixture of aviation gasoline and Benzol, reducing power loading from 6.67 to 6.09 pounds per horse power. Fuel consumption was 0.58 pounds per horse power, per hour. Fifty gallons of fuel and five gallons of oil were carried. The same Curtiss-Reed dural propeller was used. Weights hardly changed from those above. The high speed of the racer was 183mph, sea level climb rate 1,775fpm, full throttle endurance 1.25 hours, and service ceiling 25,000 feet.

During tests of the XPW-8A against the Boeing XPW-9 in late 1924, designer Bill Gilmore of Curtiss recognized that the tapered Boeing wings were superior in performance to the constant chord wings of the XPW-8A, particularly in maneuverability, and ordered Curtiss engineers to copy the Boeing design. Although it may be a folk legend, Curtiss engineer George Page was reported to have redesigned the wings based solely on photos he was given of the XPW-9. In any event, the P-364[35] prototype shortly reappeared by January 2, 1925, as the XPW-8B with tapered Clark Y wings of 31 feet, six inch span, and 250 square feet area. These tapered wings,

This view of the XPW-8A hides the upper wing center section radiator, and the aircraft, at this point was probably the shapeliest Curtiss fighter to date. Unfortunately, the center section radiator didn't work. The untapered wing was also about to go. (*Curtiss*)

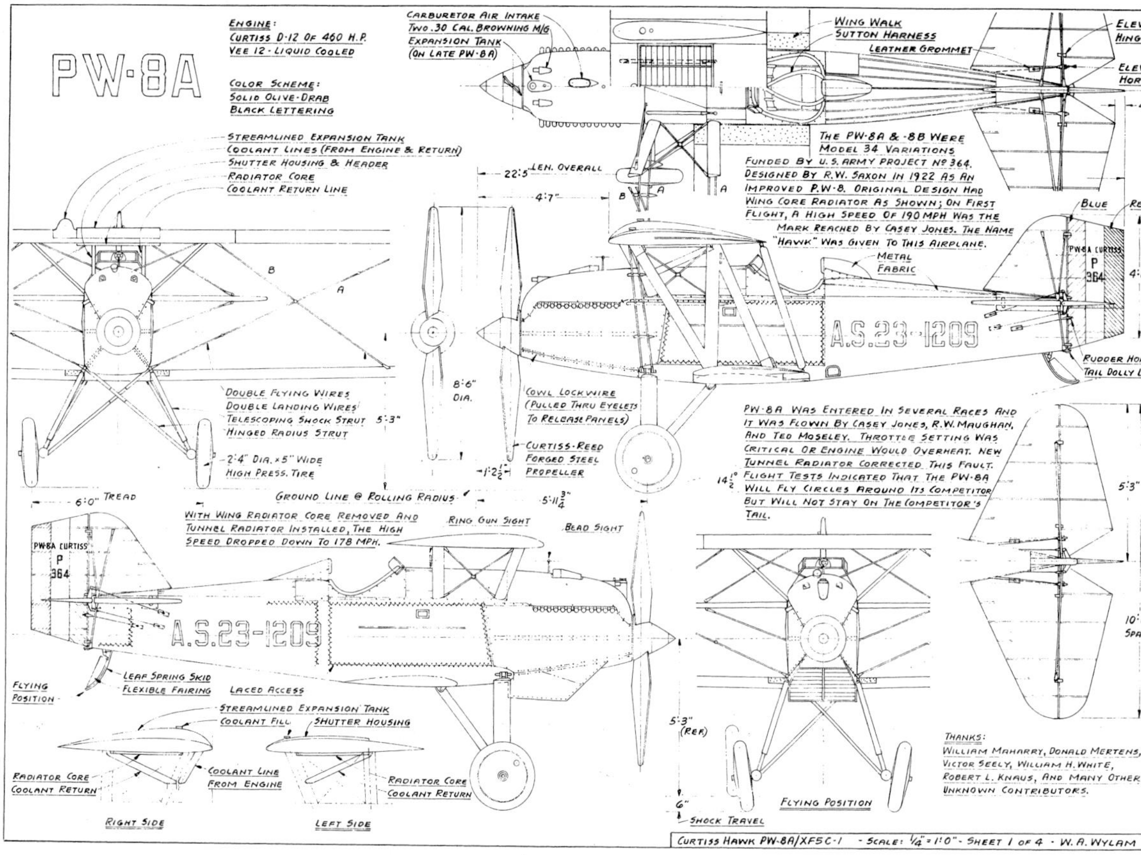

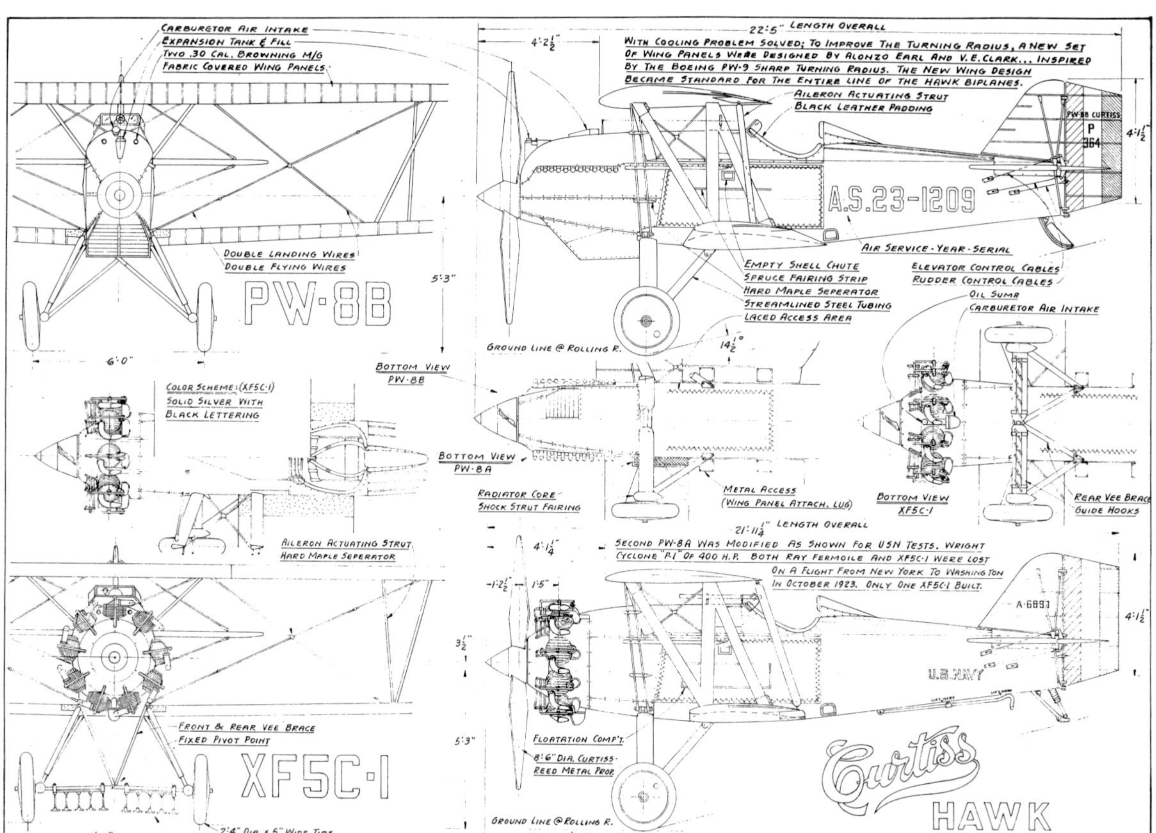

(Courtesy William A. Wylam)

One of the original three prototype XPW-8s, then as the XPW-8A, became the XPW-8B around January 1925, now with tapered Clark "Y" wings of 31 feet, six inch span, and a D-12 engine. Even though still marked as PW-8A, it was effectively the XPW-8B when photographed. The aircraft served in this configuration for a brief six months, being surveyed at McCook Field on June 1, 1925. The boom under the port upper wing was to get a sensor out into relatively undisturbed air in front of the aircraft for test purposes. *(via Peter M. Bowers)*

allegedly inspired by the Boeing XPW-9 design, stayed as a permanent fixture on future Curtiss biplane *Hawks*. For the XPW-8B version, length was 22 feet, two inches, and height eight feet, six inches. Empty weight came to 2,032 pounds, normal useful load to 770 pounds and maximum 894 pounds, and normal and maximum gross weights were 2,801.5 pounds and 2,926 pounds. Internal fuel capacity was 50 gallons, with an external detachable tank adding another 50 gallons.

The Curtiss D-12 engine in the XPW-8B was rated at 435-440hp at 2,300rpm, and gave the pursuit a high speed of 167mph at sea level (162mph with the external tank aboard), and 163mph at 5,000 feet. Landing speed was 61mph. Initial climb rate was 1,800fpm, and it took 7.3 minutes to reach 10,000 feet. Endurance at full throttle was one hour and 35 minutes. Service and absolute ceilings were 21,400 and 22,600 feet, respectively. This aircraft satisfied Army requirements, and provided the basis for the new P-1 series *Hawk*. Though it has been claimed that the name *Hawk* was never applied to the PW-8 aircraft, the Curtiss Company Characteristics Sheet, prepared in January 1926 calls out the supercharged test version of the PW-8 as *Hawk*. But since the Army, in March 1925, had decided to order P-1 *Hawks* nearly a year before the date on the company data sheet, it may have been just a retrospective error by a Curtiss employee. The XPW-8B was surveyed and disposed of at McCook Field, Ohio, June 1, 1925.

3

Birth of the Biplane *Hawks*

As noted above, the first Curtiss built aircraft to gain the popular name *Hawk* was the PW-8 equipped with a supercharger in January 1926, and the general appearance and dimensions of the PW-8 series certainly confirm that they served as the genesis for what followed.

But the *Hawk* dynasty of aircraft, from this point on, and nearly throughout the wartime *Tomahawk*, *Kittyhawk*, and *Warhawk* series, firmly established the Curtiss connection with world class, single-seat combat aircraft—even while at the same time designing and producing an amazing array of reconnaissance, observation, bombardment, training, and civil aircraft nearly without peer.

The cross-weave of Army, Navy, and export aircraft has been the subject of scrutiny by numerous students of the subject, and taken together, constitute a unique, almost unbroken study in the evolution of "engineering stretch" and carefully considered, progressive development.

The narrative, as follows, attempts to place these designs in more or less chronological order, although this is often difficult to follow, as Curtiss labored to cope with orders from Army, Navy, and export customers at the same time—a practice that they learned to become comfortable with and the prevailing norm, even when monumental demands were placed on the firm as yet another world war appeared on the horizon.

Our account, appropriately, commences with the P-1, the first strictly "pursuit" design acquired by the United States Army Air Service, in a series that continues under the "F" for "Fighter" designator to this day.

Curtiss P-1, P-1A, P-1B, P-1C, XP-17, and P-2 *HAWK*

With the appearance of the XPW-8B pursuit, with its tapered wings and under slung radiator, the configuration for future Curtiss *Hawks* with liquid cooled engines was set.

Curtiss, on the basis of XPW-8B performance, received a contract for 15 production type XPW-8B aircraft. Because of a designation system change in May 1924 these aircraft were labeled, instead, Army types P-1[36] and P-2, the basic difference being the en-

The very first Curtiss P-1 *Hawk* was A.S.25-410, the serial number barely visible on the rear fuselage in this photo taken in early August 1925 just after delivery. (*Signal Corps No.27772 via C. Mandrake*)

A.S.25-410, the first P-1, served in numerous roles, including that of a racer and engine test bed. Here it is seen wearing a race number in addition to McCook/Wright Field number P-400, and fitted with an inverted, aircooled *Liberty 12* engine of 410hp. It averaged 172.6mph in a race at Kansas City, but the inverted *Liberty* engine was not put into production. (*via M. Copp*)

gine employed, a modified rudder, and additional wing center section strut. The Curtiss design was L-18-5. Ten of this number (A.S.25-410 to 25-419) were to be P-1s with the 435hp D-12 (V-1150-1) engine, and five were to be P-2s (A.S.25-420 to 25-424)[37] with the higher powered V-1400 engine.

The Curtiss Company had the following to say about these new aircraft at the time:

"The Curtiss Hawk pursuit plane in its present form has been adopted as the standard pursuit machine of the U.S. Army Air Service, and is being purchased in quantities to replace the previous types. This machine is the result of four years of intensive development by the Curtiss organization in close cooperation with the military services, and is probably the finest pursuit plane in service today.

The Hawk is a single bay tractor biplane with a pronounced wing stagger which affords the pilot exceptionally good vision.

The wings are tapered in planform, and are of the conventional two spar type with cloth covering, the upper wing having a greater span and chord than the lower. Interplane struts are of the N-type using streamline steel tubing, and the wires are of streamline section.

All tail surfaces, as well as ailerons, are of metal construction, fabric covered. The ailerons are operated through a positive push-pull linkage, adjustable to permit of various degrees of differential or synchronous aileron motion. The tail controls are cable operated, with a differential motion incorporated in the elevator controls. The differential control of elevators and ailerons provides excellent control at all speeds, and avoids excessive stick loads.

An excellent study of the details of a standard P-1 and Navy F6C-1 engine compartment as of July 2, 1925. Note the unusual Curtiss logo on the metal prop. (*Dean Collection*)

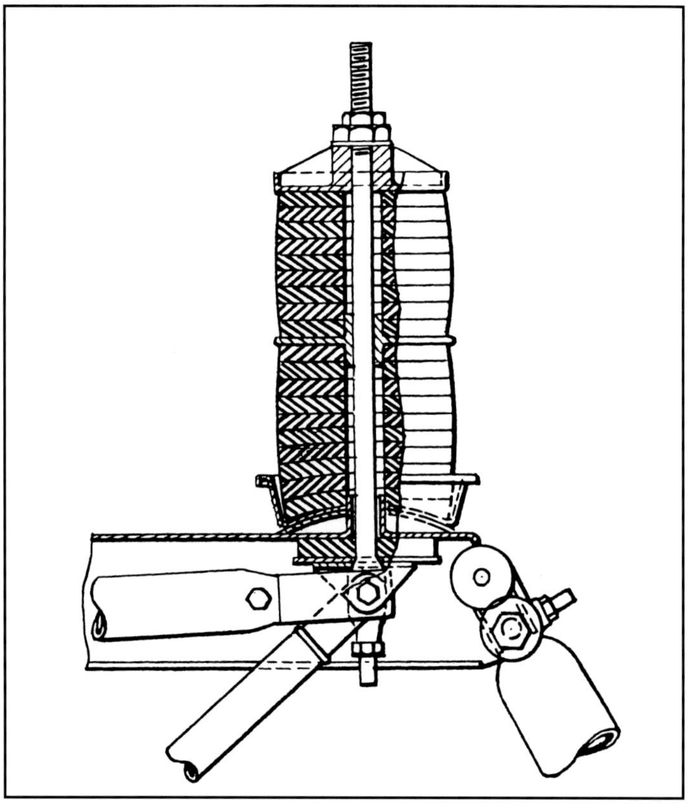

Close-up study of the landing gear shock absorber unit fitted to both the P-1 and F6C-1 *Hawks*. (*Courtesy Cradle of Aviation Museum*)

The fuselage is a welded steel tube, Pratt type truss, cloth covered. The landing gear is of the usual Curtiss split-axle type using rubber compression discs housed within the fuselage. The tailskid is also of the compression disc type, and is steerable, a feature that provides excellent ground control.

The powerplant consists of either the 430hp Curtiss D-12 motor (used in the P-1), or the 500hp V-1400 motor (used in the P-2). Both motors fit on the same motor mount which, in accordance with the usual Curtiss practice, is a detachable welded steel unit. The water and oil systems, incorporating a tunnel radiator and Curtiss oil temperature regulator, have been so refined that the Hawk, in freezing weather, can be started, warmed up, and flown in half the time usually required.

The gasoline tank is 'leak proof', and an auxiliary droppable gasoline tank of 50 gallons capacity can be hung under the fuselage for use in long distance flights. A Curtiss Reed duraluminum propeller is used.

The armament consists of two fixed Browning machine guns, firing through the propeller disc, and provision is made for carrying bombs to be used in ground attack. The equipment includes the regulation Army parachute and oxygen equipment."

The first P-1 got to the Army August 3, 1925, with the final article delivered on January 11, 1926. Compared to the XPW-8B, it had an extra cabane strut, and a new vertical tail with a balanced rudder. McCook Field testing started August 17, 1925, with aircraft Serial 25-410 and McCook Number P-400. By September 1926 it was being used to test an inverted *Liberty* 12. Still later, it was

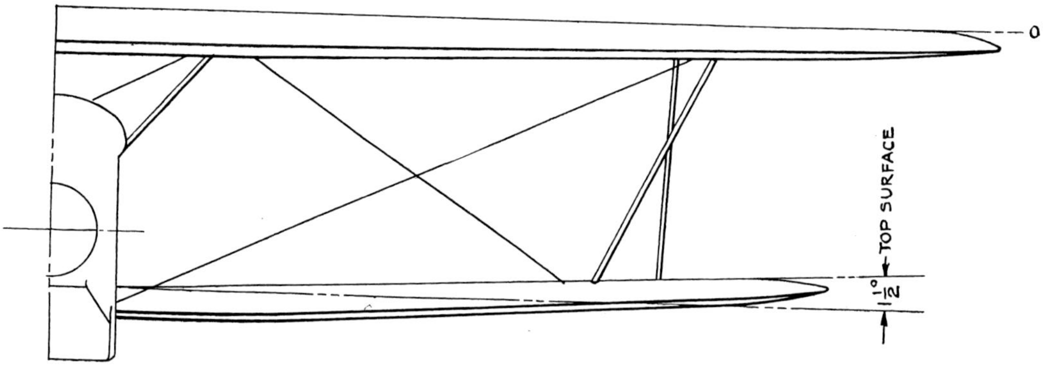

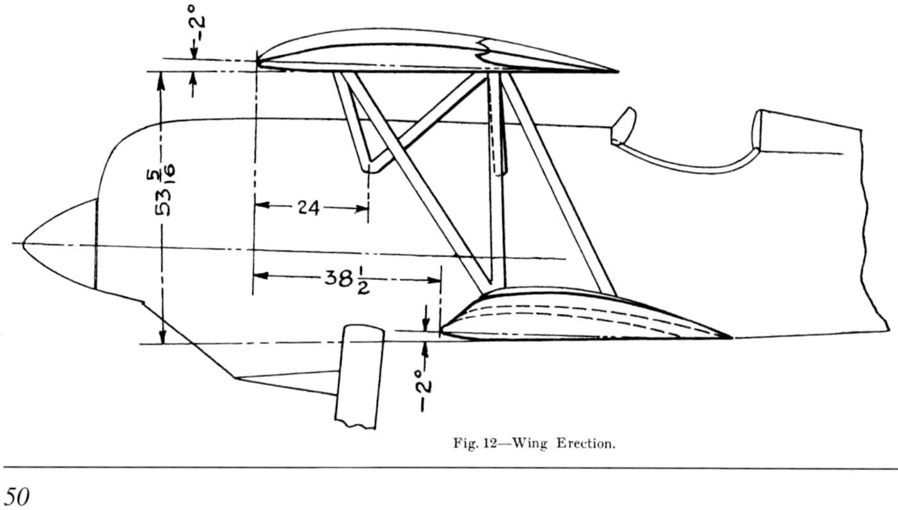

Fig. 12—Wing Erection.

This excerpt from an erection and maintenance manual for the Curtiss P-1 *Hawk* series reveals the wing erection and rigging measurements for proper installation. Note the flex allowed in the lower wing panel. (*Courtesy Cradle of Aviation Museum*)

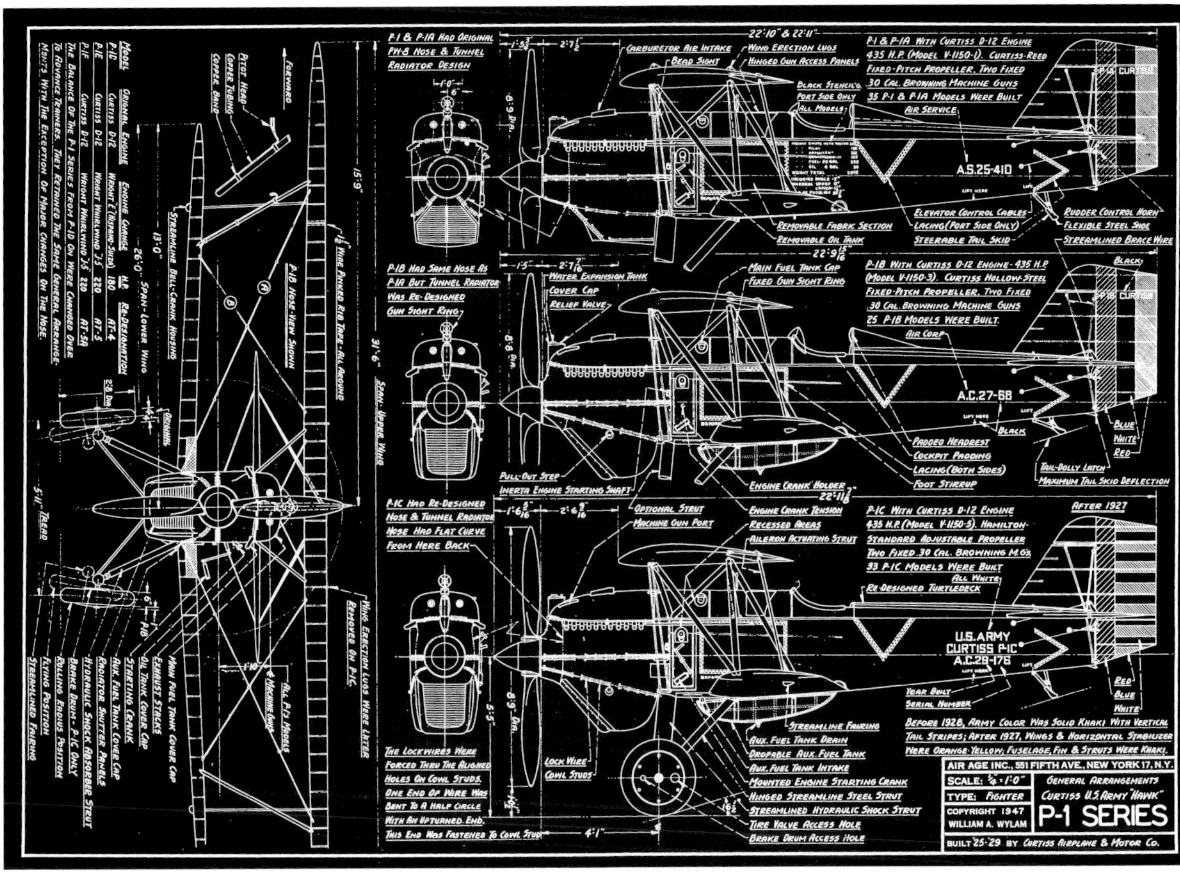

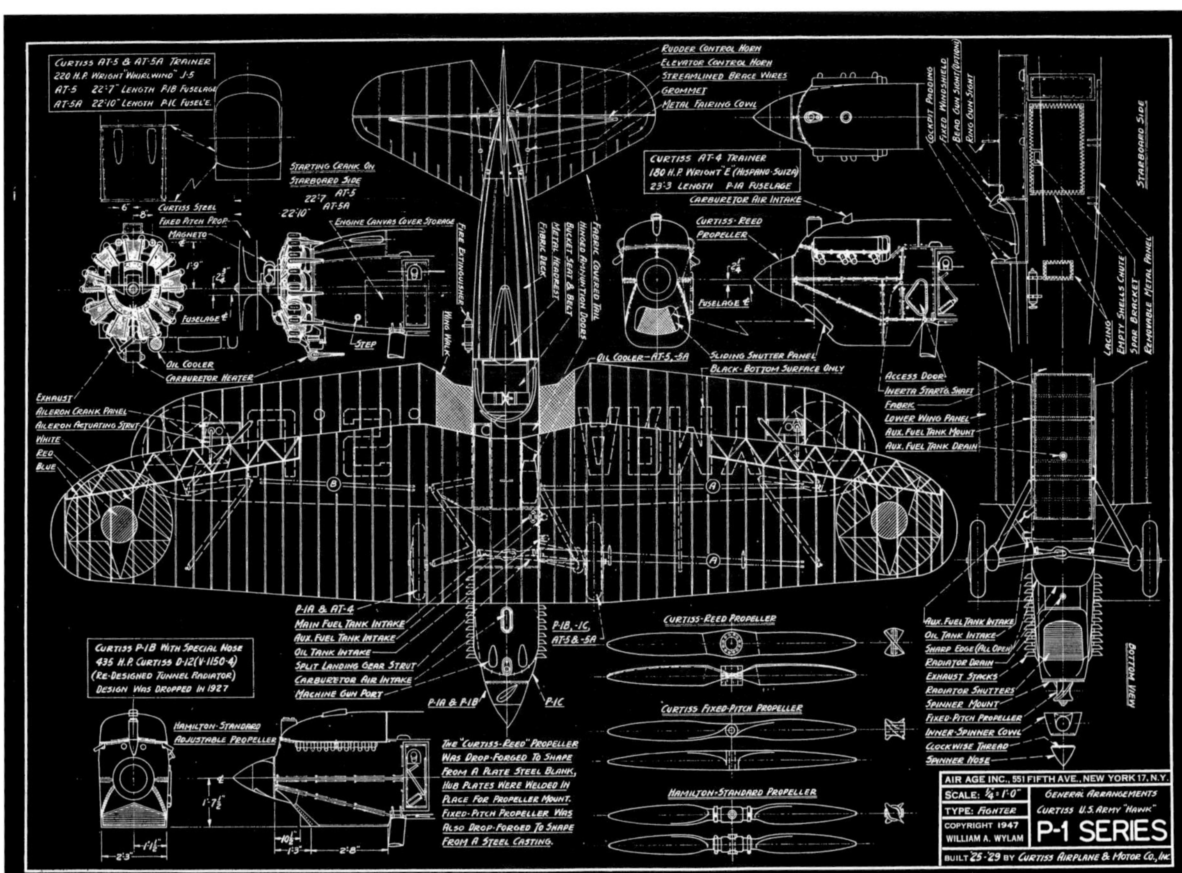

(Courtesy William A. Wylam)

Along with the original P-1s, 25 P-1A *Hawks* were ordered and entered service with the Army in 1926. They were little different from the P-1. In fact, Curtiss used the same characteristics sheets to describe them. This P-1A is missing the forward section of the prop spinner, and was apparently assigned to the 17th Pursuit Squadron when photographed. (*U.S. Army*)

tested with a V-1470 engine and redesignated as the XP-17 (q.v.). Though the aircraft was criticized by some as not much of an advance over the Boeing PW-9, it was judged somewhat more maneuverable. One pilot commented years later that the *Hawks* were sturdy, easily maintained machines, and that the Curtiss engines were exceptionally reliable, with these characteristics being demonstrated many times. Before the Army testing, Curtiss flight tests were conducted on August 6 and 7, 1925, and the performance data reflected below resulted for the P-1.

The Curtiss data sheets make no differentiation between P-1 and P-1A models, 25 of the latter (MSN 10613 to 10637 and A.S.26-276 to 26-300) being produced April 5 through October 5, 1926. Wing span was 31 feet, six inches, length 22 feet five and 1/2 inches, and height eight feet, 10 1/2 inches. Wing geometric mean chords for upper and lower wings were 62 inches and 49.5 inches, gap at the fuselage was 53.5 inches, and leading edge stagger 38.5 inches. Wing incidence was -2 degrees for both, lower wing dihedral 1.5 degrees, and sweep was zero. Wing area came to 250 square feet, with horizontal and vertical tail areas 32.5 and 13.32 square feet, respectively. Tapered Clark Y airfoil sections were used. The high angle of attack factor of safety was 12.0.

Empty weight, including 116 pounds of water, was 2,041 pounds, comprised of 817.5 pounds of structure, 1,151.9 pounds of powerplant, and 71.6 pounds of fixed equipment. Useful load was 800 pounds—a 180 pound pilot, 325 pounds of fuel and oil, and 295 pounds of armament and equipment. Thus, the gross weight totaled 2,841 pounds, making the wing loading 11.37psf, and the useful load to gross weight ratio 0.28—not too spectacular.

The P-1 and P-1A engine, a D-12 (V-1150-1), was rated at 435hp at 2,300rpm, with full throttle fuel consumption of 232 pounds per hour. Fuel capacity was 50 gallons internal and 50 gallons in an external under-fuselage tank. The cooling system type is noted as a "tunnel radiator." A Curtiss-Reed X-32973-84 dural propeller was installed.

Performance of the P-1 and P-1A from Curtiss tests noted a 161mph high speed at sea level (but it was noted a velocity of 170mph was obtained over a one kilometer course, but was believed to be three miles too high!).[38] High speed at 15,000 feet was

This otherwise anonymous Army P-1A was painted in spurious camouflage and WW1 era national markings, marked on the rudder as a "SPAD XIII," and used in the classic movie *Wings* as one of the combatants. (*San Diego Aerospace Museum*)

154.5mph, and landing speed 58.7mph. Sea level climb rate was measured at 1,810fpm, and time to achieve 15,000 feet was 14 minutes, with 10 minutes of climb getting to 12,350 feet. Service and absolute ceilings were 20,250 and 21,350 feet. The P-1As used EX-33061-78 propellers, and the P-1As differed from the basic P-1 in a number of minor ways. The fuselage was lengthened by two inches in the cockpit and one inch in the fuel tank bay, and they had a 3-way fuel system valve. The radiator support brackets had been redesigned, as were the pilot's seat, cockpit cowling, and the cowling under the main fuel tank. They also had a standard bomb release handle, increased vertical travel of the landing gear, guards for the stabilizer control chains, a different oil system, and a fuel tank without a rubber cover. They were originally fitted with 28x4 inch tires, but these were later changed to 30x5 inch wheels.

The first P-1, Serial 25-410, had a long life as a racer and engine test bed. A P-1 competed in the last (1925) Pulitzer Trophy Race, taking third place behind two Curtiss R3C-1 racers at 170mph average for 124 miles. It finished ahead of three PW-8s.

Fitted with an inverted aircooled *Liberty* engine of 410hp, the aircraft was entered in the Kansas City Rotary Club Race for military planes. It was disqualified for cutting a pylon, but averaged 172.6mph. In June 1930, as noted, the Army converted 25-410 as an XP-17 model using a 480-550hp Wright V-12 (V-1640-3)[39] inverted aircooled *Tornado* engine for tests. Visibility was good, but engine troubles discontinued the project. The plane was finally scrapped as an XP-17 in March 1932. The XP-17 had empty and gross weights of 2,204 and 2,994 pounds, yielding a useful load of 790 pounds. High speed was 164.7mph at sea level, cruising speed 130mph, and landing speed 62mph, and the XP-17 was capable of service and absolute ceilings of 21,400 feet and 22,800 feet, respectively.

Selfridge Field in Michigan got most of the P-1A *Hawks* (most were assigned to either the 17th, 27th, or 94th Pursuit Squadrons), with others going to Kelly Field, Texas, with the 43rd School Squadron. A few got to Langley or Wright Field for tests. All were wrecked or surveyed by 1930 or 1931. One (25-411) was detailed to NACA Langley in July 1929 for unspecified tests, while 26-280 was redesignated as an XP-1A for various tests (and not a prototype, as has often been suggested).

In addition to the 10 P-1s and 25 P-1As, Curtiss constructed five P-2 models, all delivered between November 23, 1925, and January 11, 1926. The difference was installation of a Curtiss V-1400 engine of greater power (530hp at 2,300rpm) fitted on the same engine mount. Dimensions and areas were the same as the P-1 and P-1A. There were some fuel system changes. The V-1400 was, of course, developed from the basic D-12 engine, the first examples having been specifically built for use on aircraft flown during the 1925 Pulitzer Races. Although of smaller overall dimensions and lower weight, the engine had larger cylinders and developed more power than the D-12.

P-2 empty weight with 110 pounds of water was 2,013.5 pounds, which included 817.5 pounds of structure, 1,124.4 pounds of powerplant (less than the D-12!), and 71.6 pounds of equipment. The useful load of 794.5 pounds included a 180 pound pilot, 325 pounds of fuel and oil, and 289.5 pounds of equipment, including armament. Gross weight was thus 3,255 pounds.

The Curtiss V-1400 engine was rated at 530hp at 2,300rpm, or 90hp more than the D-12. Because of this greater power, Curtiss' original estimate for the P-2 high speed was 180mph at sea level, but this estimate was later revised downward to 173.5mph. The Air Corps credited it with 170mph. At 15,000 feet speed was noted as 172mph. Initial climb rate was considerably improved to 2,550fpm, as was time to climb to 15,000 feet, which was only nine minutes, compared to the 14 minutes of the P-1. Climb for 10 minutes achieved 16,000 feet. Service and absolute ceilings went up to 21,800 and 22,980 feet.

All the P-2s except the first went to Selfridge Field for the 1st Pursuit Group. The V-1400 engine installation did not work out so well, however, so three P-2 aircraft (A.C.25-421, -422, and -424) were modified with D-12 engines as P-1As, and one airframe, A.C.25-423, was revised into the XP-6 pursuit model with a Curtiss *Conqueror* engine. The first P-2 (A.S.25-420) became a turbo supercharger test bed aircraft as XP-2, McCook Field test number P-431, by April 12, 1926, with a Curtiss D-12F engine. A data sheet for that version has not been found, so details are not available. However, this XP-2 was, in 1927, considered the fastest pursuit plane in the world at 20,000 feet. The plane stayed as an XP-2, and was wrecked in March 1932. It is worth noting that oleo brakes were also installed on 25-420 and 25-424, one of the earliest known applications of brakes to a U.S. fighter.

The P-1s and P-2s were very similar to the XPW-8B, as noted, but incorporated the following major changes: they had larger fuselage bracing wires; remotely controlled booster magnetos; elevator and rudder control cables that ran through separate pulleys; a redesigned engine section which enabled either the P-1 or P-2 to be fitted with either the D-12 or V-1400 engine; redesigned expansion tanks and fuel system; and crash-proof main fuel tanks. The P-2s had EX-32993-98 propellers.

Another new *Hawk* version was ordered from Curtiss in August 1926. This was the P-1B, and 25 of these (MSNs 10693 to 10717 and A.C.27-63 to 27-87[40]) were delivered to the USAAC starting October 28, 1927, and continuing through January 24, 1928, though one article was held back until March, 1928. None of these aircraft were much modified from the P-1A configuration. Changes from earlier *Hawks* included a larger wheel size (32x6), radiator modifications, a redesigned cowling, a two-inch longer fuselage, slightly larger tail surfaces, controls changes, the addition of standard airways flares, and a longer control stick as standard equipment. They mounted EX-33075-78 props on V-1150-3 engines.

A.C.27-71 was equipped with a Heinrich Prestone radiator, and later with an enclosed cockpit.

Most P-1Bs went to the 17th, 27th, and 94th Pursuit Squadrons at Selfridge Field, Michigan, with a couple going to the 43rd School Squadron at Kelly, Bolling Field, Washington, DC (three planes), and Wright Field (A.C.27-68, 27-82, 27-87, and 27-80 as P-457, P-460 to 462, respectively). About 13 of the aircraft were wrecked in service in the period 1927-1932; the rest were surveyed in 1931-1933, the last being XP-1B P-523 in February 1933 at Wright Field.

These diagrams were issued to assist Army mechanics in distinguishing the components that differed between the standard P-1A and P-1B as of March 1929. (*U.S. Army*)

Two P-1Bs were redesignated as XP-1Bs for test work (27-71 and 27-73), and the latter was at one point fitted with wing guns, the first U.S. fighter to be so equipped. It is not clear which of these two wore McCook/Wright Field Number P-523. One, temporarily named *Flying Comet*, was fitted with fireworks and associated racks, and flown over Niagara Falls, New York, in July 1931. One source claims that eight of the survivors were sold to China, but this is believed to be an error, for nine essentially identical new-build aircraft that went to Chile. Curtiss data for the P-1B *Hawk* follows:

Empty weight was 2,170 pounds (904 pounds of structure, 1,175 pounds of powerplant, and 91 pounds of fixed equipment). Useful load was 782 pounds with a 180 pound pilot, 325 pounds of fuel and oil, 55 pounds of equipment, and 222 pounds of armament, the latter being two fixed guns and ammunition. All this totaled to a gross weight of 2,952 pounds, an increase of 111 pounds over the P-1A, this in empty weight. The wing loading increased to 11.7psf, and the useful load to gross weight ratio went down to 0.26.

P-1B performance changed slightly. With a Curtiss D-12D of 435hp at 2,300rpm, high speeds were 157.4mph at sea level, 162mph at 5,000 feet, 157mph at 10,000 feet, and 149mph at 15,000 feet. Stall speed was 59.2mph. Cruise speed was 132mph at 1,800rpm. Sea level rate of climb was 1,720 feet per minute, and climb times were 3.3 minutes to 5,000 feet, 7.9 minutes to 10,000 feet, and 14.9 minutes to 15,000 feet. Endurance at full throttle was 1.31 hours, while at 1,800rpm (cruise) it was 2.57 hours, and ranges were 216 miles at full throttle and 339 miles at 1,800rpm (cruise) setting. Climbing altitude achieved in 10 minutes was 11,950 feet, and service and absolute ceilings were 20,500 feet and 21,800 feet.

The next and final Army D-12 *Hawk* order was for the P-1C version in October 1928, the largest at 33 aircraft (MSNs 11181 to 11213, A.C.29-227 to 29-259) with V-1150-5 engines. There was little in the way of design changes—wheels were larger (30x5 inch) and wheel brakes were added, and the last two aircraft delivered had oleo landing gear. A.C.29-238 was equipped with a Prestone cooling system and Heinrich radiators. These aircraft were delivered by Curtiss between January and April 1929. About 21 were sent to Selfridge Field for the 17th, 27th, and 94th Pursuit Squadrons, and most others went to the 43rd School Squadron at Kelly Field. One aircraft went to Wright Field for tests,[41] and a couple arrived at Chanute Field in Illinois. All were either wrecked or salvaged in the 1929 to 1934 period except one aircraft, which lasted into 1936 as a ZP-1C (the "Z" prefix indicated obsolete). The P-1C aircraft were worked hard during their careers, and there were lots of repairable wrecks during these lean years of the depression. One P-1C *Hawk* was converted to an XP-6B long range aircraft, and another was utilized for test work on engine cooling systems. This P-1C, serial A.C.29-227, and Wright Field XP-537 with a Curtiss D-12E engine, was for some unknown reason equipped with a skin cooling system and tested circa July 3, 1929, the only case of skin cooling applied to a tapered wing *Hawk*. Another P-1C (29-238), the 12th example built, while fitted with so-called Heinrich radiators circa February 20, 1930, and a V-1150E powerplant, was cited as type XP-1C. This radiator radically changed the distinctive nose configuration of the aircraft, all but eliminating the "chin."

Curtiss Export D-12 Powered *Hawks*

D-12 engine powered *Hawks* were also exported to Latin America. In 1926 Curtiss officials asked the Army to give Lt. James Doolittle a leave of absence to demonstrate the P-1 type *Hawk* in South America, and they agreed. A pursuit[42] was shipped to Santiago, Chile, where Doolittle flew the aircraft in competition with aircraft from other countries, and came out ahead. In the course of his visit with the hospitable Chileans, Doolittle managed to break both ankles under what may be termed unusual circumstances, but completed

In 1926, Curtiss asked the Army to allow famed aviator Jimmy Doolittle to demonstrate their new D-12 powered *Hawk* in Latin America, and they agreed. Here Doolittle (at left) poses with two Curtiss officials with a doped aluminum *Hawk*, the one used for most of his demonstrations, devoid of any markings, other than the Curtiss logo on the fuselage (behind Doolittle) and "Curtiss Hawk" on the rudder. (*Hagedorn Collection*)

Although numerous sources claim that Bolivia bought D-12 powered *Hawks*, this did not happen. However, it was not due to any lack of trying by Jimmy Doolittle, who ably demonstrated both his *Hawk* and a D-12 powered *Falcon* at lofty La Paz in 1926. Here the *Hawk* (left center) is flanked on the left by a Bolivian Breguet Bre 19, and on the right by the D-12 *Falcon*, while two Bolivian Caudron C 59s are on the right. Reportedly, the *Hawk* and *Falcon* were painted bright red for this demonstration, not only to add luster to their appearance, but to help locate them if they had gone down in the Andes during the flight from Chile. (*Hagedorn Collection*)

his demonstration flights with casts on both legs, which impressed the Chileans immensely. He later flew to La Paz, Bolivia, putting on a very spirited demonstration there, but since the Bolivians were on very bad terms with Chile no aircraft orders were obtained. The next flight was southeast to Buenos Aires, Argentina, broken ankles and all. There, Doolittle performed the first outside loop in his demonstrator D-12 *Hawk* on May 25, 1927. Later he returned to the U.S. for a stay in Walter Reed Army Hospital, and a long period of recuperation.

As a result of this demonstration tour, in 1926-1927 Chile purchased nine aircraft (MSN 11172 to 11180 on Sales Order K8650, Contract P.O.244) of the basic P-1A design when it was still a first-line U.S. pursuit plane, and the first two of these were on hand by February 12, 1927, the other seven being shipped in March and April. The *Hawk* proved out well enough in Chilean service that nine additional planes of the P-1B[43] standard were ordered by Chile in 1927, and at year's end they were 95 percent released, according to Curtiss company data. Characteristics and performance of these D-12 export *Hawks* were similar to those of the U.S. Army types. Eight of these were ordered in 1928 on the initial batch, complete with two guns and two A-3 bomb racks each for $187,008, followed by a ninth machine, similarly equipped, in 1929 for $20,000.

In fact, *Coronel* Marmaduke Grove of the Chilean Army had entered into a contract with Curtiss on January 6, 1926, for the delivery of 14 P-1s. Lawrence Leon represented Curtiss in this, the first large foreign order for Curtiss fighters. They were priced at $28,000 in gold each, and Curtiss had agreed to ship the first five within 60 days of signing, with the remainder following at the rate of three every 30 days. Chile reneged on this contract on February 12, 1926, however, citing "*...reasons of legislative order*," when in fact the order had been placed under the aegis of the "old" Constitution. An arrangement was reached, however, and the nine aircraft followed, accompanied by William H. McMullen, who not only supervised their erection and testing, but gave preliminary instruction on the aircraft to Chilean pilots. The Chilean aircraft were serialed simply "1" to "18," and by March 20, 1930, 12 of them were in service with *Grupo 1* (described as a "Mixed Aviation Group"). By October 15, 1937, 15 of the *Hawks* remained on Chilean strength and, of these, *Grupo I "Los Condores"* at Iquique had nine, one was assigned to *Grupo II* along with other types at Quintero, *Grupo III* at Marquihue had four (plus other types), and *Grupo IV "Halcones"* at Magallanes had one. Incredibly, Chile's *Hawks* remained on the Order of Battle as late as July 1, 1939.

Due to the spectacular flight demonstration by Jimmy Doolittle, Chile bought nine D-12 powered P-1A *Hawks* for her Army aviation element. Here is the very first example, unusual in having the national insignia on the fuselage, with a Chilean pilot. (*via Pedro Turina*)

One of the first nine Chilean P-1As—probably No.7—on the right, flanked by a Chilean D-12 *Falcon* and crews. The entire rudder of Chilean service aircraft was painted deep blue, with a large white star centered. By this time, the national insignia on the fuselage was a three-colored roundel with a white star in the center. (*Rino Poletti via Pedro Turina*)

Chile also acquired nine P-1Bs, which differed from the earlier P-1As in having an improved D-12D engine and longer range. Here, the very last aircraft (No.18) bears full Chilean markings. The attachments for a belly slip fuel tank can just be seen. Oddly, Curtiss records do not account for the order for the nine P-1Bs. (*via Pedro Turina*)

The so-called *Japanese Hawk*, a rather mysterious and poorly understood export aircraft. Pictured here prior to delivery on March 14, 1930, bearing what was apparently a spurious U.S. civil Identification Mark (72K), the ultimate fate of this aircraft remains an open question. (*Curtiss*)

The Japanese *Hawk*

As noted earlier, Curtiss company records also confirm that a single *Hawk*, often cited as a PW-8 variant, was purchased by the Mitsubishi manufacturing consortium of Japan in 1925, in that country's continual effort to keep abreast of the latest U.S. designs. Cited as the *Japan Hawk*, it wore the temporary U.S. Department of Commerce Identified Aircraft number -72K during testing at Buffalo. However, the date of 1925 appears highly suspect, since the U.S. Department of Commerce did not commence issuing numbers until 1927, and numbers with suffixes in the "K" series until somewhat later still. Some sources claim that this aircraft did not appear in Japan, in fact, until 1930, and that it was assembled there by Mitsubishi.

In fact, the aircraft was known by Curtiss as the Design L-18-30, and cited as the *Japanese P-6 Hawk*, equipped with a high compression *Conqueror* engine. Known Curtiss photos of the instrument panel are dated March 4, 1930, confirming that this aircraft appeared rather late on the scene. Curtiss-Wright Export Corporation documents also confirm that it was purchased during 1930, at a cost of $40,000, complete with two guns and two A-3 bomb racks. Apparently, a spare Curtiss V-1570 *Conqueror*, valued at $8,500, was purchased as well. A U.S. Military Intelligence Division (M.I.D.) Report dated June 30, 1930, advised that U.S. Army Air Corps 1st Lieutenant Wallace Evans Whitson had arrived in Japan on leave from his assignment in the Philippines on June 6th to serve as the demonstration pilot on the aircraft, in the hire of Curtiss. By June 30th, he had demonstrated the aircraft at Kagamigahara and Tachikawa. At the latter place, at the close of his demonstration, he suffered engine failure when two bearings burned out, no doubt as a result of what were described as his stunning aerobatics display. This necessitated shipment of a new engine from the U.S. before the demonstrations could be continued. Whitson was able to land "dead stick," which apparently amazed the Japanese observers. Whitson told the U.S. Attaché that it was his understanding that Mitsubishi had not only bought the aircraft but, as well, the rights to manufacture it in Japan which, if true, has not been previously reported. It appears never to have gained a pre-war Japanese civil registration, and therefore must be assumed to have gone to the Army or Navy at some point. The ultimate fate of this unique aircraft remains unknown.

Noted Japanese aero-historian Shorzoe Abe related for this account that there was even more than this to the Japanese *Hawk* saga. The Mitsubishi company had dispatched Jiro Horikoshi to Germany early in June 1929, where he was to study the fundamental technology of the flying boat that Mitsubishi wanted to add to its product menu. After studying the technology of large, all-metal flying boats at Junkers in Dessau for about three months, he moved on to England to study a new subject, biplane fighters. Towards the end of 1929 he received new orders from Mitsubishi advising that the flying boat project had been cancelled, and that he was to travel on to Buffalo, NY, and join Taizo Soda, Mitsubishi's 1st Airframe Tooling Section manager, and study the P-6 series *Hawks*.

This apparently was incident to the failure of the Mitsubishi designed Type 10 Carrier Fighter, which had been bested by the Nakajima, which delivered the Type 91 to the Imperial Japanese Army, and the A1N and A2N to the Imperial Japanese Navy. Being determined to make up for the repeated losses, Mitsubishi did in fact seek a production license for the P-6 series *Hawk*, as Mitsubishi very much wanted to win fighter business from the Japanese Army. Horikoshi arrived in New York December 31, 1929, and stayed at Curtiss until the fall of 1930, but apparently did most of his work at the Garden City offices. He was apparently impressed by what he saw, and learned much about American systems for design and manufacturing as a result. There can be little doubt that the Japanese *Hawk* was exported to Japan as a direct result of this visit, and possibly as a pattern aircraft for license production.

According to the memoirs of Major General Issaku Imagawa, who as of 1930 was a noted all-round Army pilot and Director of the Air Evaluation Department at Fussa (Yokota) while still a Colonel, the Japanese *Hawk* surprised Japanese Army pilots by its clear superiority over the Type Ko Model 4 (Nieuport-Delage 29C), which was then the first-line Japanese Army fighter. He recalled that the *Hawk* was one of the best aircraft he had flown to that time.

Clearly, Mitsubishi never entered into license production of the *Hawk*, but, in a note of irony, Horikoshi was subsequently appointed Chief Designer of the *7-Shi* carrier fighter which, in his own words, "*...was based chiefly on my experience and knowledge of fighters gained by contact with the P-6.*" The *7-Shi* fighter, of course, became the *Zeke* of WWII fame, more commonly known as the A6M series *Zero*.

The *Doolittle Demonstrator*

The fate of the so-called *Doolittle Demonstrator* has, until now, been obscure. Clearly, the aircraft never returned to the U.S., as it simply cannot be accounted for. Apparently the aircraft remained in Chile, consigned to the so-called Curtiss "factory" at Los Cerrillos aerodrome, near Santiago, where it served as a sort of company exhibit.

When neighboring Peru entered into hostilities with Colombia over the Leticia region in 1933, Peru hastily cast about for capable aircraft—and found that not only the former Curtiss D-12 *Falcon* demonstrator, but MSN 10876, Doolittle's demonstrator, were still available in Chile. Still owned by the Curtiss Wright Export Corp., in New York, the Peruvians paid $18,000 each for these rather tired aircraft, and they were flight delivered to Lima around the first of April 1933, but not without behind-the-scenes intrigue. In later testimony to the U.S. Congressional Investigation into the Munitions Industry, they quoted from a letter from J. V. van Wagner to C. W. Webster of the Curtiss-Wright Export Corp. dated March 15, 1933. It is quoted herewith in full, as it sheds considerable insight into the machinations that often accompanied the marketing of aircraft overseas:

"*We cabled you on the 13th that the Peruvian Ambassador demanded immediate action with regard to the delivery of the* Hawk *and* Falcon, *and the following day received your cable 'O.K. delivery.' From this message we understood that the $36,000 held by the Chase National Bank had been placed to your credit without restrictions. Now, the whole trouble is in getting permission to fly the ships out of the country* [Chile]. *Since the money was first depos-*

Mixed in with the Army's contract for P-1s and P-1As was a modification for five aircraft designated as P-2s, delivered between November 1925 and January 1926. The primary difference was the installation of a Curtiss V-1400 engine of 530hp, a change not readily apparent to the casual eye. To add to the confusion, some of the surviving P-2s later got D-12s. Note the severe twist in the upper blade of the Curtiss Reed metal prop. (*Curtiss*)

As with so many of the early Army pursuit aircraft, the first P-2 was labeled with a McCook Field test number (XP-431), and equipped for a time with this General Electric turbo-supercharger as a test bed. (*U.S. Army*)

ited in New York, Pancho [the Curtiss representative in Chile], *has come along almost every day to say that he expected authorization the following day, and we are now in just the same fix as we were then. The Peruvian Ambassador came out to the factory* [the so-called Curtiss 'factory' in Chile] *on Monday and took up a very furious attitude over the business, saying that he had complied with his part of the contract and that it was up to us to deliver the goods. It seems quite evident that Pancho has been bluffing the Ambassador all along by saying that as soon as the money was paid the ships would fly away, little thinking of the difficulties to be met in trying to do so. With the present action taken by the Chilean Foreign Minister to foment peace in South America, he cannot possibly give his consent to allow war materiel to leave Chile, especially to a country engaged in warfare. Consequently, we are stuck in the mud. Pancho has just left the factory for the Ministry in an endeavor and as a last resort to obtain permission to ship the machines by steamer to Callao and the Peruvian Ambassador has offered to pay all expenses to be incurred in boxing and freight. This will not hide the fact that the planes are intended for Peru and will become known by everybody sooner or later. So we really think the Minister will not offer any kind of facilities. We are at a loss to imagine what to do further, as we have thought out every possible way of getting the machines out of the country, even going so far as trying to get permission to fly them to the U.S. Pancho sold the ships, placed at the factory ready for flight, so he says, so what more can we do? He has requested us to cable you to place the $3,000 on each ship to his credit in the National City Bank, but we have deemed it necessary to wait until something definite has been arranged getting the planes away before doing so. If the ships cannot leave the factory (we have specific instructions from the authorities that under no circumstances must they leave the hangar) we may even be asked by the Peruvian Ambassador to refund the $36,000 and consider the contract rescinded.*"

By March 30th, Webster was able to write to van Wagner, expressing his relief that "*...the* Hawk *and* Falcon *got away safely and with official permission,*" but with the admonition to ensure that he should "*...please refrain in all your letters sent to this office from mentioning the name of Orsini,*" who was apparently the official who "greased" this most unusual transaction to completion.

Peru apparently tried to acquire at least two more D-12 powered *Hawks*, to be assembled from parts still on hand at the Chilean factory, but it remains unclear if this order was consummated, in view of the obvious Chilean political position on the matter. The

This Curtiss photo shows a brand new P-1B fresh out of the doors of the Garden City factory, one of 25. Changes from earlier P-1s were minor, mainly involving slight powerplant revisions and larger wheels. Weight increased a bit over 100 pounds compared to the P-1A. The Air Corps had not yet adopted the new rudder stripes. (*Curtiss*)

Starting with the Air Corps Act of 1926, new rudder stripes were adopted by the service, and an era of extremely colorful Army aviation commenced. A.C.27-78 is unusual, in having the wheel covers removed and "F.A.D." (for Fairfield Air Depot) on the fuselage ahead of the designation. It was only at Fairfield slightly more than a month in 1931, and spent nearly all of its service life at Chanute Field, where it passed to Class 25 in August 1932. *(via Jack Satterfield)*

solitary Peruvian D-12 *Hawk* was coded either C-1-04 or C-1-B, and survived as late as July 22, 1936, when it was crashed at Playa de Villa, killing pilot *Tte.* Jose Luscas Raguz Veran.

Curtiss J-4 *Pursuit*

On March 22, 1926, the Curtiss design team published the description of a Wright J-4 powered *Tractor Biplane, Pursuit Trainer*, which was essentially identical to the P-1, but with the omission of the single .50 caliber gun, leaving but one .30 caliber weapon aboard for training. This design probably evolved into the AT-4 (q.v.).

Curtiss R-1454 *Pursuit Ship*

On March 30, 1926, Curtiss described this proposal mounting an air-cooled 400hp R-1454 engine, and based on actual tests of a P-1 at McCook Field, and predicted a high speed of 159mph. It remained a proposal only.

Curtiss *Pursuit Ship (Wright Simoon)*

On April 2, 1926, the design team once again proposed what amounted to a P-1 airframe equipped with a 350hp, air-cooled Wright *Simoon* engine, which they postulated would attain a maximum speed of 149mph. It, too, remained only a proposal.

Curtiss *Pursuit Ship (R-1300 MOTOR)*

On May 12, 1926, yet another variant of the basic P-1 airframe was proposed, mounting an air-cooled 420hp R-1300 engine. It was calculated to be capable of a maximum speed of 161mph. The same proposal was also modified to mount twin pontoons, probably for marketing to the Navy and export markets and, with these, was estimated to be capable of 146mph. Neither design was proceeded with.

This P-1B (AC27-71), cited in the press and Air Corps records as *The Flying Comet*, had special racks beneath each lower wing panel holding flares, and performed at Niagara Falls at night in July 1931 to the enjoyment of all. Delivered in December 1926, it was designated as an XP-6B in January 1930 with a V-1150E engine. It also sports a most unusual, streamlined radiator under the nose, which has eluded documentation. *(via David W. Ostrowski)*

The 12th P-1C (A.C.29-238) was fitted with Heinrich radiators and a V-1150E engine in February 1930 and, later, this V-1570 engine, and redesignated as XP-1C. It also sported McCook/Wright Field number XP-579. *(via Peter M. Bowers)*

Curtiss Design L-113 (O-1 Modified)
This proposal, dated August 3, 1926, was for a two-seat observation and fighter training aircraft, based on the O-1 observation aircraft, but mounting a Wright J-5 engine. It was calculated to be capable of 120mph maximum. It was not further developed.

Curtiss Navy Fighter EX-36251 and EX-36252
Yet another Curtiss proposal, dated August 31, 1926, called for a single-seat Navy fighter fitted with a 410hp Pratt & Whitney *Wasp* engine. Basically dimensionally similar to the P-1, it was calculated to be capable of a top speed of 166mph but, instead of the standard Clark "Y" airfoil, was to have incorporated a C-72 type with a total wing area of 242 square feet, including ailerons. A virtually identical proposal of the same date (EX-36252) featured a fuselage lengthened by four feet to 24 feet, 11 inches, a heavier empty weight (1,979 pounds, up from 1,719), and a top speed of 160mph. See the section on the F7C-1 for a full technical description of these.

Curtiss XAT-4, AT-4, P-1D, P-1E, AT-5, AT-5A, and P-1F *Hawks*
An idea was put forth at the end of March 1927 by Curtiss, apparently at the behest of the Army Air Corps, which suggested that the Army could meet the need for advanced training aircraft by using the already designed airframes of pursuit planes in combination with lower power engines, thus effecting savings in fuel, and negating the requirement to sponsor new trainer aircraft designs, all leading to cost savings for a cash strapped service. The idea had been first applied to the Curtiss *Hawk* in 1926, however. A Curtiss

Bearing the insignia of the 43rd School Squadron at Kelly Field, TX, this P-1C has had its standard aircraft information on the rear fuselage painted over, but has a larger Roman numeral "I" on the vertical fin. Note the mud guards over the main wheels, fairly standard on aircraft assigned to training and field duty. *(Robert Cavanaugh)*

This P-1C, the serial number of which has eroded on the rear fuselage, bears a number of interesting markings features, including a highly polished prop spinner, two-color wheel covers and, most unusual, a shield on the engine cover advising that the pilot was Lt. Olsen. The insignia under the cockpit appears to be that of the 17th Pursuit Squadron. (*Ahti Petrija*)

data sheet of June 17, 1926, describes a Wright Hispano E-2 "Pursuit" (AT-4, Curtiss design L-18-8) for the use of "pursuit training." Length was 22 feet, two inches. With 100 pounds of cooling water, the empty weight was 1,847 pounds, consisting of 833 pounds of structure, 850 pounds of powerplant, and 164 pounds of fixed equipment, and useful load was 637 pounds (180 pound pilot, 325 pounds of fuel and oil, 31 pounds of equipment, and 101 pounds of armament). The total gross weight was thus 2,484 pounds, giving a wing loading of 9.95psf.

The Wright E-2 water-cooled engine with under slung radiator provided 204hp at 1,800rpm, and at full throttle consumed 100 pounds of fuel per hour. The power loading was naturally high at 12.43 pounds per horse power.

Of course, performance was down compared to the standard single-seat fighter on which it was based. Sea level high speed was 132.8mph at 1,020rpm, with landing speed 54.6mph. Cruise speed at 1,500rpm was 108.5mph. Climb rate at sea level was a low 920fpm, with climb times of 6.5 minutes to 5,000 feet and 16.5 minutes to 10,000 feet. Endurance came to 2.97 hours at sea level at full throttle, and at 1,500rpm cruise length was 4.5 hours. Cruise range was 490 miles. Service and absolute ceilings were only 15,150 and 17,000 feet.

Although it did not gain an "X" prefix for experimental tests, this P-1C (A.C.29-227) had McCook/Wright Field Number XP-537, and was fitted with both a *Liberty L12-A* in February 1929 and a Curtiss D-12E, as seen here, by July 1929. The absence of the distinctive radiator under the nose gives the aircraft an appearance reminiscent of the contemporary British Hawker *Fury* fighter. It was wrecked at Cleveland, OH, September 1, 1929, while being flown by none other than 1Lt James H. Doolittle, with but 73 hours total time. (*via David W. Ostrowski*)

In June 1930, the Air Corps modified none other than the very first P-1 (A.C.25-410) to the rather odd looking XP-17, with an inverted Wright V-12 *Tornado* engine of between 480 and 550hp. It was scrapped in March 1932 after many difficulties with this installation. (*Dean Collection*)

In fact, the first aircraft was XAT-4, U.S. Army Air Corps serial A.C.26-296, a P-1A converted with the Wright Hispano E 180hp engine. This aircraft spent much of its service life at McCook Field as their number P-444, which it had gained by July 26, 1926, having been delivered to the Air Corps on July 1st. The XAT-4 was reconverted back to standard P-1A configuration on July 23, 1928.

The first AT-4 built as such (Advanced Training, 4th model) was finished at Garden City on June 9, 1926, after Curtiss received what was for the time a large order of 40 airplanes (these received Curtiss MSNs 10718 to 10752 and Air Corps serials A.C.27-88 to 27-97 and 27-213 to 27-237). Strangely, however, the remaining AT-4s were not delivered until commencing April 7, 1927, to the 43rd School Squadron at Kelly Field, Texas, for advanced trainer use, with the final article accepted June 25th. The production aircraft were very similar to that described above, though tail surfaces were enlarged slightly. The Wright E engine had a compression ratio of 5.5, and fuel and oil consumption figures at full throttle of 108 and 3.8 pounds per hour. Fuel and oil tank capacities were 50 gallons and four gallons, respectively. The cooling radiator was of the under slung type with a cartridge core. The propeller was a Standard Steel type per drawing 1519 of nine feet diameter, and pitch of 13.5 degrees at the 48 inch radius station.

Official performance of the advanced AT-4 version from Engineering Division Report #2746 included the following: High speed 132.5mph at sea level, 130mph at 5,000 feet, 125mph at 10,000 feet, and 113mph at 15,000 feet. Stalling speed was 58.5mph. Cruising speed at 1,560rpm was 107mph at sea level, 105mph at 5,000 feet, 101mph at 10,000 feet, and 91mph at 15,000 feet. Climb rates came to 1,070fpm at sea level, 690fpm at 5,000 feet, 430fpm at 10,000 feet, and 170fpm at 15,000 feet, and climb times were 6.2 minutes to 500 feet, 15.2 minutes to 10,000 feet, and 33.2 minutes to 15,000 feet. Endurance amounted to 2.7 hours at sea level at full throttle, and 5.0 hours at 1,560rpm cruise at sea level. At full throttle range was 362 miles, and at cruise 535 miles. Service and absolute ceilings were 17,700 feet and 19,500 feet.

Clearly the above performance was very poor, and it was decided to re-engine these AT-4 *Hawk* airframes. Five were kept as trainers, and the rest re-engined as full fledged pursuits, redesignated as P-1Ds using Curtiss D-12 engines. The five trainers were modified to use Wright J-5 radial engines (R-790), and redesignated as AT-5s (Curtiss MSNs 10753 to 10757, Air Corps serials A.C. 27-238 to 27-242).[44] The first conversion was delivered July 11, 1927, and the last September 1st. Further confusing the picture, all of the AT-5s were later converted to P-1E configuration by installing D-12 series engines. Curtiss had proposed, in March 1926, a Wright J-4 powered pursuit trainer, with the radial engine putting out 210hp at 1,800rpm, and gross weight and sea level high speed of 2,240 pounds and 132mph. The company later, in January 1927, proposed a "*J-5 Hawk*" as a Pursuit Training Fighter, this model

Converted from a standard P-1A, A.C.26-296 was the XAT-4 with a converted Wright Hispano E engine of 180hp. It spent much of its service life at McCook/Wright Field as P-444, which it adopted in July 1926, but was converted back to a standard P-1A in July 1928. (*Hagedorn Collection*)

A standard production AT-4, one of 35 *Hawk* trainers for the Army, as it appeared shortly after rollout on June 10, 1926. In service, AT-4s did not retain the prop spinner, and had a less expensive wooden prop installed. Nearly all of the surviving AT-4s were reconfigured as P-1D pursuits with Curtiss D-12 engines later. Difficult to distinguish, their chief recognition feature was the four exhaust stacks on either side of the engine. (*Curtiss*)

being labeled as an "AT-5 Proposal," and powered by a Wright J-5B aircooled radial engine of 220hp at 1800rpm.

In July 1927 the Army, still apparently convinced of the worth of the idea of using pursuit airframes with lower power engines as advanced trainers, ordered 31 Curtiss AT-5A aircraft (Curtiss MSNs 10962 to 10992, Air Corps serials A.C.28-42 to 28-72). The company delivered these between June 11 and September 26, 1928, with assignment, again, to the 43rd School Squadron at Kelly Field. Three went to Bolling Field in Washington, DC, and four to Langley Field, Virginia. At least one was tested with a Wright J-5BA engine in October 1928, with test number P-517. One was also detailed to NACA at Langley, VA (AC28-66), in August 1928, where it was equipped with a NACA cowling by November. The work performed on this aircraft resulted in NACA Langley being awarded the Collier Trophy in 1929, a little known footnote to the otherwise confusing lineage of these "advanced trainers."

These advanced trainers were powered by Wright J-5B Whirlwind nine cylinder radial aircooled engines (R-790) of 225hp at 2,000rpm, and fuel consumption at full throttle was 115 pounds per hour, and at cruise 89 pounds per hour. The planes incorporated

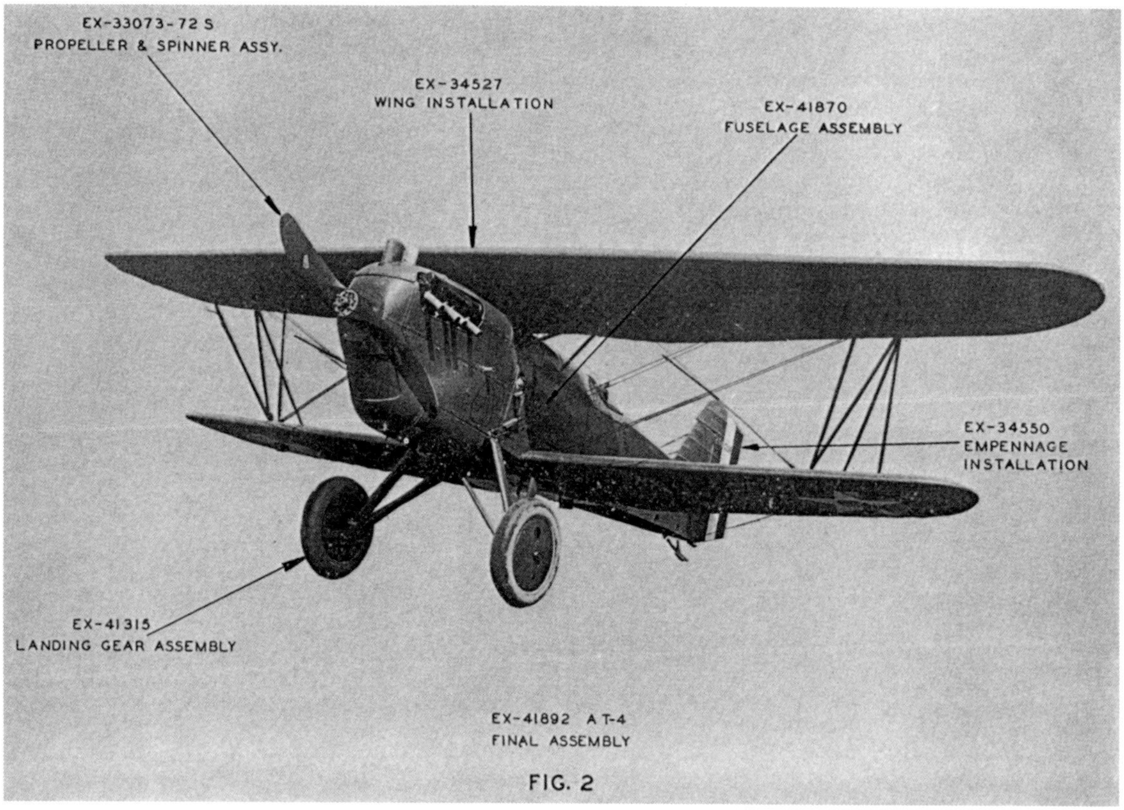

FIG. 2

This March 1929 diagram, provided to Army depots to facilitate erection and maintenance, provides a more definitive idea of what a standard AT-4 looked like. Note the radiator doors closed under the nose, and the wooden prop without a spinner. Otherwise, the aircraft was virtually indistinguishable from standard P-1 series aircraft. (*Courtesy Cradle of Aviation Museum*)

One of only five of the 40 AT-4s converted to an aircooled Wright *Whirlwind* J-5 radial engine as type AT-5. These provided a bit more power than the Wright E-2. The AT-5s became P-1Es with D-12 engines later on. A.C.27-239, shown here, had been the XAT-5 between November 1927 and May 1928, and became a P-1E September 30, 1929. (*Dean Collection*)

wiring the same as the P-1B pursuit plus ammeter, voltmeter, generator, control box, and storage battery. Typically a Curtiss Reed R type propeller of eight feet, nine inch diameter was installed. Empty weight was composed of 903 pounds of airframe, 836 pounds of powerplant, and 91 pounds of fixed equipment, totaling a 1,830 pound empty weight. Useful load was 644-671 pounds, giving a gross weight of 2,474 to 2,481 pounds, and a wing loading of 9.8 to 9.9psf.

Curtiss Flight Test Report 3055 showed the following performance for an AT-5A trainer: Sea level high speed was 121.9mph at 1,980rpm, cruising speed at 0.8 maximum rpms was 103.5mph, and landing speed 54.8mph. Sea level climb rate was 1,070fpm at 1,710rpm. Full throttle endurance, and at cruise, were 2.61 and 4.35 hours, respectively, and the ranges at those conditions were 338 miles and 450 miles. Service and absolute ceilings were 15,260 feet and 17,340 feet.

By 1928 it had been decided that these AT-5A aircraft could better serve the Army as D-12 powered pursuits, particularly since tactical squadrons were being depleted of earlier P-1 types due to crashes and surveys. During that year, of the total of 31 AT-5As acquired, only six remained in service: one (as a P-1F) at Wright Field, and five AT-5As at Kelly Field, TX. By 1930 these modified aircraft, redesignated as P-1F pursuits with the higher powered D-12 engines, were leaving the inventory as newer types replaced them.

Curtiss P-5 (XP-502) *Superhawk*

To meet the continuing desire of the Army to develop the turbo supercharged engine type of pursuit plane for excellent high altitude performance, the service let a contract to Curtiss dated May 14, 1927, for five D-12-F (V-1150-3 or -4) powered biplane *Hawks* equipped with General Electric Model F-2 turbo superchargers. These aircraft were given Curtiss designation L-18-7 and Army P-5. They were essentially P-1 type airframes with the supercharged engine installation, a cockpit heater fed from the engine exhaust manifold, a special pilot oxygen system, a larger diameter propeller to absorb altitude engine power, and as a result longer landing gear to effect proper ground clearance, with the gear having unusual shock absorbers right at the wheels. The cockpit could be equipped with a flexible cover around the pilot's shoulders to keep heat inside against the cold of very high altitude.

This Curtiss photo shows a brand new AT-5A fitted with a Wright *Whirlwind* nine-cylinder radial ready for delivery. When later converted to pursuit power, the survivors were redesignated as P-1Fs. A.C.28-72 was so converted September 14, 1929, having flown only 143 hours as an AT-5A, all of its service having been at either Langley Field or Kelly Field. (*Curtiss*)

Sometimes cited as the *Superhawk*, the one-off P-5 was yet another attempt to obtain service data on a turbo-supercharged D-12F engine. Only five of these were ordered in May 1927, and they actually had Curtiss serial numbers issued ahead of the AT-5As. This aircraft, the first one, was initially designated as XP-5, and later had a D-12P engine. It was destroyed by fire January 26, 1929. (*Curtiss*)

The five *Superhawks*[45] (Curtiss MSN 10957 to 10961, in order just ahead of the AT-5As, and with Air Corps serials A.C.27-327 to 27-331) were delivered January 19 through June 17, 1928, with the initial aircraft going to the Army Air Corps Materiel Division at Wright Field, Ohio, as an XP-5 P-502 for testing. By January 11, 1929, this aircraft, given as XP-502, was fitted with a Curtiss D-12P engine. The second P-5 was wrecked shortly after delivery, on February 15, 1928, and a third (A.C.27-329) crashed three months later on May 25, 1928, while stationed at Mitchel Field, Long Island, New York. A third loss came on January 26, 1929, when A.C.27-327 was destroyed by fire. The other two P-5s went to Selfridge Field, Michigan, with the 1st Pursuit Group, 94th Pursuit Squadron, and served until 1932.

When the turbo supercharger was working the aircraft was quite a barn burner for the time. The engine was the beefed up D-12F at 435hp of 2,300rpm. Like all the *Hawks*, span was 31 feet six inches, and wing area 252 square feet. Length and height were 23 feet, eight inches and nine feet, three inches, the greater height due to the longer landing gear required. They mounted 070717 props and, while delivered with oleo controlled brakes, these were later changed to toe operated mechanical controls.

Empty weight was 2,520 pounds, and useful load 828 to 840 pounds, adding to a gross weight of 3,349 to 3,360 pounds. As with the other P-1 type *Hawks*, normal fuel was 50 gallons internal, with an extra 50 gallons in an external tank when required.

High speed at sea level was only 142mph; however, the altitude power available through use of the turbo supercharger provided a 166mph high speed at 25,000 feet. Normal cruise and landing speeds were 117mph and 62mph, respectively. Initial climb rate was 1,110fpm, and the P-5 could get to 10,000 and 15,000 feet in 8.4 minutes and 12.4 minutes, respectively. Endurance was 1.31 hours at sea level at high speed. The supercharged engine allowed the P-5 to reach service and absolute ceilings of 31,900 feet and 32,500 feet, respectively, about 10,000 feet above the basic P-1 aircraft.

These aircraft were a small but important step in the early development of the turbo supercharged pursuit aircraft for the Army.

Curtiss P-3 and XP-21 *Hawk*

As early as 1923, McCook Field Army engineers were working up specifications for a new aircooled radial engine based on an earlier design by Wright. The specification was issued on August 15, 1923. It was to be a nine cylinder, single row type developing 390-400hp with a 1,454 cubic inch displacement. Curtiss won a development contract after a November 13, 1923, bid for the R-1454 engine, and proceeded with development. The first engine was delivered in September 1924. A P-1A *Hawk* airframe (A.C.26-300) was slated to take the engine. A preliminary estimated characteristic sheet for an "*R-1454 Pursuit Ship*" dated March 30, 1926 (based on actual McCook Field P-1 aircraft testing on January 23, 1925, noted ear-

At first glance the P-5, from this perspective, looked much like the others in the P-1 series. But a larger prop necessitated a longer undercarriage and increased ground clearance, and the pilot was provided with oxygen and heat for high altitudes. The engine exhaust manifold was obviously different, and there was an odd fairing under the inboard lower wing. (*Curtiss*)

One of the earlier P-1As (A.S.26-300) became the so-called *R-1454 Pursuit* and, later, was finally designated as the XP-3—but apparently was never flown as such. It was re-engined as the XP-3A on October 29, 1927. This aircraft became the XP-21 on October 24, 1930. (*U.S. Army*)

A former P-1A, the *R-1454 Pursuit* and then the XP-3, A.S.26-300 morphed once again into the XP-3A with the highly successful Pratt & Whitney R-1340 *Wasp* engine, pretty much duplicating the Navy F6C-4. This image shows an early attempt at installation of a long-chord cowling, and bears McCook/Wright Field number XP-451. (*Curtiss*)

lier), described the aircraft as follows: Length 21 feet, nine inches. Powerplant, one Curtiss R-1454 rated at 400hp at 1,650rpm with fuel and oil consumption 220 and 12 pounds per hour, respectively, at full throttle. Oil capacity was 6.5 gallons. The propeller assumed was a Curtiss Reed dural unit of 10 feet diameter and nine feet pitch.

Empty weight of 1,916 pounds involved 840 pounds of structure, 990 pounds of powerplant, and 86 pounds of fixed equipment. Useful load consisted of a 180 pound pilot, 325 pounds of fuel and oil, and 283 pounds of equipment totaling 788 pounds, giving an estimated gross weight of 2,704 pounds.

Performance of the *R-1454 Pursuit* (later to become the XP-3, and which had originally been built as a P-1A, modified to the XP-3 on Deviation W-401 issued on October 6, 1925) was estimated at a sea level high speed of 159mph, cruising speed at 1,400rpm of 131mph, and landing speed 57mph. Estimates of sea level climb rate and endurance at full throttle were 1,780fpm and 1.36 hours, with full throttle range predicted to be 218 miles. The estimate for climb altitude attained in 10 minutes was 12,500 feet, and for service and absolute ceilings 20,200 and 21,500 feet.

But these estimates were never to be proven out. The Curtiss data sheet for what was now the XP-3 aircraft with the R-1454 engine rated at 390hp at 1,700rpm, dated September 29, 1927, simply says: "*Ship was never flown. No further data on the machine is available.*" Apparently the engine was installed and photos taken of the plane, and a decision made not to fly it. The Curtiss engine effort had seemed half-hearted, and together the company and the Army decided to abandon the project, particularly since the new R-1340 *Wasp* engine from Pratt and Whitney in the same power class had appeared and was successful. The XP-3 was basically the same as the P-1A, except for the change in engine, mount, cowling, and the lowering of the oil tank.

The P-1A airframe (26-300) was soon to be fitted with this new Pratt & Whitney nine cylinder radial engine as the XP-3A on October 29, 1927 (Project Number XP-524, tested at McCook as P-451),[46] a definitely successful project. A Report for 1927 of the Garden City Chief Engineer, dated January 3, 1928, noted that the "*...XP-3A,* [was a] *Wasp in a P-1. Order has been placed for five additional aircraft for service test.*" Unit cost was $11,175, and all five were delivered between October 5 and 30, 1928, as P-3As,

The Army ordered five *Wasp* powered P-3 types for service testing, and these were delivered in the fall of 1928. The first of these (A.C.28-189) was held back from squadron use for further testing as the second XP-3A. It was flown as a racer in the Thompson Trophy Race at Cleveland in 1929 and was, in this configuration, the stuff of pulp magazine covers. It was converted as one of two XP-21s later and, still later, to P-1F configuration! It wasn't dropped from the inventory until July 1936, as a ZP-1F. (*U.S. Army*)

Air Corps serial 28-191 was one of five P-3As acquired with Pratt & Whitney engines. This one is fresh from the factory on October 6, 1928, and has an external fuel tank. Later, cowl rings were added around the cylinders on some. Note the stenciled servicing details on the fuselage forward of the pilot. This aircraft survived in service, at Chanute Field, until August 1933, by which time it had amassed 826 hours total time. (*Curtiss*)

Curtiss MSNs 10993 to 10997, and Air Corps serials A.C.28-189 to 28-193.

The initial aircraft (A.C.28-189) was to be used for test purposes as a second XP-3A,[47] but the other four went to either the 57th Service Squadron or the 94th Pursuit Squadron at Selfridge Field, Michigan. Two aircraft were washed out within two months of delivery, so there could really be little in the way of service testing. These P-3A aircraft were Curtiss Design L-18-24. The initial plane of the five (A.C.28-189) was fitted with another NACA engine cowling combined with a large propeller spinner, entered the 1929 Thompson Race at Cleveland, Ohio, and placed second at an average speed of 186.8mph piloted by Lt. R. Breen. It was beaten only by a Travel Air *Mystery* monoplane at 194.9mph. Later, in 1931 the same aircraft was re-engined with a 300hp Pratt & Whitney R-985-1 *Wasp Junior* as the second of two XP-21[48] aircraft. The plane ended up reconverted to a D-12 powered P-1F, and was finally surveyed in 1934.

The five P-3As were first delivered with no engine cowlings at all, but were later fitted with short-chord ring cowls. Specifications for the aircraft without an engine ring cowl follow: Span, length, and height were 31 feet, seven inches, 22 feet, five inches, and eight feet, nine inches. Wing area was 252 square feet. Powered with the Pratt & Whitney R-1340-3 *Wasp* of 410hp their empty weight was 1,956 pounds, useful load 832 pounds, and gross weight 2,788 pounds. Fuel capacity was the typical *Hawk* 50 gallons internal and 50 external, if required.

Performance for the no-cowl P-3A saw high speeds of 153mph at sea level, 151mph at 5,000 feet, 148mph at 10,000 feet, and cruise speed was 122mph. Landing speed came in at 59mph. The plane could climb to 1,742 feet in one minute, and to 5,000 feet in 3.2 minutes. Service and absolute ceilings were 23,000 feet and 24,400 feet, respectively.

The second XP-3A (A.C.28-189), with a venturi engine cowl and propeller spinner and entered as a racer, had a beefed up R-

Stepping back a bit in time, the U.S. Navy was also sold on the Curtiss Model L-18-5 with the D-12 engine, and ordered seven as F6C-1s. A-6968 was the first of these, pictured here on August 7, 1925—at almost precisely the same time that the Army got its first P-1s. They were very similar, and the F6C-1s were not equipped to operate from carriers. This aircraft flew in the September 1927 National Air Races as the XF6C-5 with a Pratt & Whitney *Hornet* engine. (*Curtiss*)

The F6C-1 *Hawks* for the Navy, although not carrier capable, could all be fitted with twin-float seaplanes, which cost only about 10mph in high speed. Early, pre-aircraft carrier fighters were required to have this capability. A-6970 has always been cited as having been converted to F6C-3 configuration later, but there is no evidence of this in Navy records. (*Curtiss*)

1340 radial engine of 450hp. Length and height were 22 feet, six inches and eight feet, seven inches. Empty weight was 2,107 pounds, useful load the same 832 pounds, and gross weight added to 2,939 pounds. It competed as such in the 1929 Cleveland races.

With the cowl and spinner streamlining, maximum speed was up to 190mph at sea level and 188mph at 5,000 feet, with normal cruise speed of 152mph and landing speed of 60mph. Climb capability came to 2,290 feet in the first minute, and 10,000 feet could be reached in 5.34 minutes. Ceilings were 28,100 feet service and 29,400 feet absolute. P-3A armament was comprised of one .30 caliber and one .50 caliber fixed forward firing Browning machine guns. P-3As A.C.28-102 and 28-193 collided in flight at 3,000 feet on December 11, 1928, and were completely destroyed, while 28-190 and 28-191 continued on in flying condition as late as December 1930. A.C.28-189 was later reworked into the XP-21 (q.v.).

The Army never did make a substantial buy of Curtiss *Hawks* powered by radial aircooled engines as did the Navy, preferring to stick with the Curtiss D-12 engine, and later the *Conqueror*-powered pursuit planes. Curtiss was never happy to see the Pratt & Whitney engine intrude on their Army business, and the very few P-3s were the only Army aircooled engine biplane Curtiss *Hawks* of the P-1 type.

Curtiss F6C-1, F6C-2, and F6C-3 (D-12 Powered) *Hawks*

In March 1925 the U.S. Navy ordered their initial D-12 engine powered *Hawk* fighters. The first of nine aircraft was delivered on August 7, 1925, and was taken on by Squadron VF-2. Curtiss released the following announcement at the time for the *Hawk* land and seaplane F6C-1 and F6C-2 variants:

"The U.S. Navy has recently adopted the Curtiss Hawk, equipped as an interchangeable seaplane and deck landing aeroplane. The deck landing type is identical with the Army P-1 type, with the exception of the landing gear which has been rede-

Photos of Navy and Marine Corps F6C-1s are seldom published in squadron markings, but this example (A-6972), the fifth example built, clearly served with VF-4M late in 1925. (*A.J. Bibbee Collection, Museum of Flight*)

The Navy F6C-1s of the 1920s were exceptionally well maintained, as evidenced by this close-up view of a period gun camera in place on the starboard lower inner wing of a VF-2 aircraft in April 1926. (*National Archives RG80-G 405498*)

signed for the special service required. In the seaplane the landing gear has been replaced by twin floats similar in appearance to the Curtiss racer floats. The performance of this seaplane is especially good."

In spite of the company statement, there was in actuality very little use of these aircraft as seaplanes, except for tests and racing purposes. The Navy F6C-1 (Curtiss design L-18-5), of which there were only seven (commencing Curtiss MSN 10553 and Navy Bureau of Aeronautics serial numbers A-6968 to A-6972, and A-6975 to A-6976) had wheeled landing gear suitable only for airfield landings; there were no carrier hooks installed. The other two fighters—Navy F6C-2s (A-6973 and 6974) and Curtiss design L-18-6—had the wheeled gear with a multi-hooked crossbar to catch the longitudinal deck arresting gear wires of the carrier USS *Langley*.[49]

The Navy also acquired two F6C-2 *Hawks* which, unlike the F6C-1s, had a multi-hooked spreader bar between the main landing gear struts to catch the longitudinal deck arresting gear on the USS *Langley*, and were thus carrier capable. These two aircraft, A-6973 and A-6974 (shown here), had been ordered as F6C-1s. (*Curtiss*)

The F6C-1 type on twin floats competed in the May 14, 1926, Curtiss Marine Trophy Race piloted by Lt. Jeter, and also in the November 1926 Schneider Trophy Race at Hampton Roads, Virginia, piloted by Lt. Tomlinson. Three of the F6C-1s logically went to the land based Marine Corps. Two F6C-1s (A-6970 and A-6972) were converted to an F6C-3 configuration.[50] The first F6C-1 (A-6968) was later used as an engine test bed for the 525hp Pratt & Whitney R-1690 *Hornet* engine as the XF6C-5 model, this modification having been performed at the Naval Aircraft Factory around July 20, 1927.

Four of the F6C-1 aircraft (BuA A-6973, A-6974, A-6975, and A-6976) were converted to F6C-2 configuration, involving rear fuselage strengthening and modification of landing gear to a cross axle type, so as to mount hooks for the carrier arresting wires. Navy Squadron VF-2 used the aircraft aboard *Langley* commencing in December 1925. In August 1928 two F6C-2 *Hawks* were aboard the USS *Lexington*. The F6C-2 aircraft were capable of carrying small bombs, and this type pioneered in dive bombing techniques. On October 22, 1927, F6C-2s dive bombed the fleet in what was deemed a successful surprise attack.

The three Marine F6C-1 aircraft were employed by that service from late 1928; two remained until 1931. Navy F6C-1s were out of the fleet by March 1931.

It is interesting to note that Curtiss very nearly enjoyed export success with the F6C-1 as well. Curtiss Export Corporation president C. W. Webster reported to the company on February 23, 1927, that:

"*...the Chilean Navy is in the market for some F6Cs and have requested us to supply a set of pontoons for a demonstration, the Chilean Army to loan them one of the P-1A Hawks, which have the pontoon fittings attached.*"

The first F6C-3 (A-7128) poses at the factory September 2, 1926, prior to going to the fleet five days later. The F6C-3 differed from the F6C-2s in having a strengthened fuselage and revised landing gear assembly, including oleo shock absorbers, plus a small radiator. F6C-3s mounted only .30 caliber guns. It was wrecked at Anacostia NAS April 13, 1927. (*Curtiss*)

He urged the plant to rush a set of pontoons to him as soon as possible, along with a company pilot versed in float operation, but nothing more came of the proposal. He also reported, in the same communication, that the Brazilian Navy was interested in the F6C as well, although he confessed that the Brazilians had been put off by the fact that the company had demonstrated the *Hawk* exhaustively in Chile, Bolivia, Argentina, and even Uruguay, but had neglected to do so in Brazil. As it happened, British and French interests were much more on top of the matter, and managed to ship demonstrators to Brazil that resulted in almost immediate orders of major proportions, and Curtiss frankly lost a golden opportunity.[51]

The F6C-2 landplane had the following characteristics, according to a Curtiss data sheet of February 20, 1926. Span and length were 31 feet, six inches, and 22 feet, five and 1/2 inches. Geometric mean wing chords were 62 inches upper and 49.5 inches lower. Wing gap was 53.5 inches measured at the fuselage, and leading edge stagger was 38.5 inches. Wing incidences for both upper and lower were -2 degrees; lower wing dihedral was 1.5 degrees. There was no wing sweepback. Total wing area amounted to 250 square feet, with total horizontal and vertical tail areas 32.5 and 15.54 square feet, respectively. The wing airfoil section was a tapered Clark Y.

This F6C-3 (A-7138) was aircraft number 3 of Bombing Squadron 1 (VB-1B), the famous *Red Rippers*. The F6C-3 did have, contrary to the information in many publications over the years, provision for an 8.5 pound bomb rack support installation. This aircraft passed to the Aviation Mechanics School at Great Lakes in September 1931, where it ended its days. (*U.S. Navy*)

This F6C-3 (A-7144) was specially revised with *Prestone* coolers built into the sides of the fuselage by the Naval Aircraft Factory in October 1929, and competed in the 1929 Pulitzer Race at the Cleveland Air Races as such. It was stricken from the Navy inventory in December 1931 with 848 hours total time. (*via Peter M. Bowers*)

The F6C-2 powerplant was a Curtiss D-12 rated at 440hp at 2,250rpm. Full throttle fuel consumption was 232 pounds per hour. Fuel capacity was 50 gallons internal plus 50 gallons external. The propeller was a dural Curtiss Reed type, and the cooling system employed a tunnel radiator configuration.

With 116 pounds of cooling water the F6C-2 empty weight came to 2,090 pounds, consisting of 852.3 pounds of structure, 1,151.9 pounds of powerplant, and 85.8 pounds of fixed equipment. The useful load, consisting of a 180 pound pilot, 325 pounds of fuel and oil, and 238.8 pounds of equipment (including two machine guns and their ammunition) added to 743.8 pounds. The gross weight was thus 2,834 pounds, giving a wing loading of 11.34psf. Power loading was 6.44 pounds per horse power, and the useful load to gross weight ratio was 0.262.

The F6C-2 landplane high speed was originally estimated at 170mph at sea level, but was later pencil marked in at 165mph; at 15,000 feet it was 154.5mph. Landing speed came in at 58.7mph. Initial climb rate was 1,800fpm, and times to climb to 10,000 feet and 15,000 feet were 7.4 and 14 minutes, respectively. Climb for 10 minutes got the F6C-2 to 12,350 feet. Service and absolute ceilings were 21,000 and 22,150 feet. A note at the bottom of the Curtiss data sheet stated:

"*The F6C-2 landplane is similar to the F6C-1 landplane, except that the landing gear, instead of being the conventional split type, is adapted for deck landing.*"

It is also noted that the F6C-2 was built in 1925.

The seaplane version of the F6C-2 Hawk had an overall length of 25 feet, five inches, and a height of 10 feet, eight and 1/2 inches. Empty weight with 116 pounds of water was 2,519 pounds (with 1,281 pounds of structure, 428 pounds more than the landplane version, 1,152 pounds of powerplant, and 86 pounds of fixed equipment). Useful load was 744 pounds—the same as the landplane. Gross weight totaled 3,263 pounds, making the wing loading 13.05psf, and power loading 7.41 pounds per horse power. Useful load to gross weight ratio was down to 0.228.

Performance estimates by Curtiss for the F6C-2 seaplane were: High speeds 159mph and 138.7mph at sea level and 15,000 feet, respectively, with cruise speed 128mph and landing speed 65.4mph. Sea level climb rate was 1,600fpm, and at 15,000 feet only 360fpm. Climb altitude attained in 10 minutes was 10,850 feet. With 50 gallons of fuel internally full throttle endurance came to 1.25 hours, and at cruise speed 2.22 hours. Ranges at full throttle and cruise were 200 miles and 290 miles. The service and absolute ceilings were 18,100 feet and 19,300 feet.

Thus far the Navy had not acquired enough D-12 powered *Hawks* for real squadron use, though VF-2 had used some F6C-1s and F6C-2s; however, an order for a new batch of 35 F6C-3 aircraft (Curtiss Design L-18-9, MSNs 10556 to 10590 and Navy A-7128 through A-7162) provided squadron quantities, with the initial F6C-3 airplane delivered in January 1927. F6C-3 A-7136 served as the XF6C-3 for testing purposes. Commissioned at the same time as the start of new aircraft deliveries, Fighting Squadron VF-5, the *Red Rippers*,[52] received 18 F6C-3s, this model having a further strengthened fuselage and arrestor gear for carrier operations, oleo shock absorbers, a smaller radiator, and conversion kits for twin float installation. Their aircraft went to Hampton Roads, Virginia, for the carriers *Lexington* and *Saratoga* Detachments. In the summer of 1928 the *Rippers* had 17 F6C-3s aboard. For a short while in 1928 some aircraft operated on twin floats. The F6C-3 was a pioneer in early Navy dive bombing experiments, having racks for light bombs added. By early 1929 the aircraft had been replaced by later types.

The F6C-3 was also operated by the Marines, and that service had eight aircraft in late 1927, seven in late 1929, and ten by June 1930. All were scrapped by 1932.

At least one F6C-3 (A-7162, the last aircraft in this series) was detailed to NACA Langley between January 11 and February 21, 1928, for a detailed maneuverability investigation, but then returned to NAS Hampton Roads. The aircraft was modified while at NACA to hold test recording instrumentation by removing the fuel tank and installing a smaller tank, thus allowing room for the instruments.

The type also had a racing career. Aircraft A-7147 was extensively modified for racing. It won the Curtiss Marine Trophy Race on floats in 1928, 1929, and 1930, with the latter race held May 31st at Anacostia NAS, DC. For this race the plane was specially lightened and the fuselage re-faired extensively. The race was won by Capt. A. H. Page, USMC, at a 164mph average speed over the 100 mile course. The earlier 1929 race was won by Lt. W. Tomlinson on May 25th, averaging 162.5mph. Other F6C-3 landplanes took third and fourth place at the last Pulitzer Race in the 1929 Cleveland Air Races, one believed to be A-7144 specially revised with *Prestone* coolers built into the sides of the fuselage between the wings.

As a standard landplane the F6C-3 had the usual span of 31 feet, six inches, length of 22 feet, 10 inches, and a height of 10 feet, eight inches. Wing area was 252 square feet. It was D-12 powered with 435hp at 3,200rpm, with a compression ratio of 5.3 and full throttle fuel consumption of 226 pounds per hour, and 115 pounds per hour at 1760rpm. Oil consumption was 8.6 pounds per hour. Internal fuel capacity was the usual 50 gallons. The propeller was a Curtiss Reed R type EX-33061-78S of 8 feet, eight inches diameter and six feet, six inches pitch. The radiator was of the under slung cartridge core type.

F6C-3 landplane empty weight was 2,161 pounds, useful load 802 pounds, and normal gross weight 2,963 pounds, giving a wing loading of 11.76psf and power loading of 6.81 pounds per horse power. Useful load to gross weight ratio was 0.27.

Maximum speed was 154mph at sea level, and landing speed 59mph. The airplane could climb to 5,000 feet in 3.5 minutes. Normal range was 351 miles, and with the 50 gallon external tank fitted 655 miles. Service ceiling was 20,300 feet.

Equipped as a twin float seaplane in normal configuration, length was 25 feet, five inches, and height 10 feet, nine and 1/8 inches.

A Curtiss data sheet of April 29, 1927, based on Navy Performance Data SH-3B from the Bureau of Aeronautics, gives empty weight of 2,524 pounds, composed of 1,262 pounds of structure, 1,181 pounds of powerplant, and 81 pounds of fixed equipment. The useful load was 812 pounds, consisting of a 200 pound pilot, 331 pounds of fuel and oil, 74 pounds of equipment, and 207 pounds of armament. The gross weight was therefore 3,336 pounds, or 373 pounds greater than the landplane version.

The seaplane high speed was, surprisingly perhaps, listed at 157mph at sea level, and 154, 149, and 139mph at 5,000, 10,000, and 15,000 feet altitudes, with normal cruise at 1,760rpm at 126mph. Sea level climb rate was recorded at 1,590fpm, with climb times

Late in their service careers, Navy F6C-3s with D-12 engines that had not met with disaster in one way or another were assigned as squadron hacks when later designs replaced them in front line service. Here, 7145 is marked as number 4 of Utility Squadron 4 (VJ-4). They were very popular for building up pilot flight time. It had previously served with VF-5. Delivered in November 1926, it was stricken in April 1932 as worn out. *(U.S. Navy)*

This F6C-3 (A-7146) was assigned to VF-1M at Quantico, though there were hardly enough of the aircraft surviving to form a complete squadron. The "F" for "Fighter" was circled to differentiate it from a Navy aircraft, though the rather prominent USMC insignia would seem to have conveyed ownership well enough! The pilot;s name, Lt. W. O. Brice, was on the fuselage just ahead of the cockpit. Note the apparent white sidewall tires. This aircraft was assigned as of August 1931 to Maxwell Field, AL—an Army field—for the specific use of a Marine officer attached to the Air Corps. It was stricken from the inventory June 16, 1932. *(U.S. Navy via J. Schrier, Jr.)*

5.7, 8.5, and 17.1 minutes to 5,000, 10,000, and 15,000 feet. Endurance at full throttle came to 1.3 hours, and for cruise at 1760rpm 2.6 hours. Ranges at full throttle and 1,760rpm cruise condition were 208 and 329 miles, respectively. Service and absolute ceilings were 18,900 feet and 20,200 feet. The plane could climb to 11,000 feet in 10 minutes.

Curtiss Radial Engined Proposals and the F6C-4 *Hawk*

For some time, the U.S. Navy had been interested in aircooled radial engines for their aircraft. These engine types had the advantages of being lighter and more reliable without the complication of a potentially leaky water cooling system like the D-12 and earlier liquid cooled engines. The Navy had been the sponsor of several radial development efforts, two of which were failures, and

The new F6C-4 *Hawk* looked the same aft of that big round engine with bare cylinders hanging out. That meant drag, but on the other hand, there was no cowling drag of a liquid cooling radiator, either. Best of all, there was no chance of cooling fluid leaking! A-7393 was the first of 31, delivered in March 1927, and spent nearly its entire service life of 115.2 hours at Anacostia NAS, being stricken as damaged beyond repair on July 22, 1927. *(Curtiss)*

An excellent close-up study of the rather straightforward—and fairly rigid—undercarriage assembly on one of the 31 F6C-4s as it appeared in February 1927. Note the circular cowling fasteners and the auxiliary fuel tank plumbing. *(U.S. Navy)*

one a resounding success. The two "failures" were Wright engines, though one would go on to be successful much later, and the success was from Pratt & Whitney. All three engines had been studied by Curtiss as potential installations for their *Hawk* fighter in the late 1920s. The Curtiss Aeroplane and Motor Company, Inc. had their own radial engine development failure in the Army-sponsored R-1454 of the earlier 1920s.

Wright Aeronautical Corp. was developing a nine cylinder radial aircooled engine of 1,200 cubic inch displacement called the *Simoon* for the Navy starting in 1924. Rated at 350hp at 1,900rpm, the *Simoon* was studied for the *Hawk* fighter application, as noted briefly earlier. In estimates dated April 4, 1926, using P-1 Hawk test data from the McCook Field Summary Sheet of January 23, 1925, the *Simoon Hawk* with a nine foot diameter Curtiss Reed propeller had an estimated empty weight of 1,797 pounds, a useful load of 788 pounds, and therefore a gross weight of 2,585 pounds. The powerplant part of empty weight was calculated at 871 pounds.

Simoon Hawk performance was estimated at a high speed of 149mph at sea level, cruising and landing speeds of 125mph and 55.6mph, climb rate of 1,500fpm at sea level, full throttle endurance and range of 1.55 hours and 230 miles, and service and absolute ceilings of 19,300 feet and 20,700 feet.

The Wright *Simoon* engine development was discontinued, and the engine never got into a *Hawk*, nor into production.

Another Wright engine, the R-1300, was being developed under Navy and Army sponsorship, and was just 100 cubic inches greater in displacement than the *Simoon*. A nine cylinder aircooled radial, the R-1300 was rated at 420hp at 1900rpm, and was studied for potential installation in a Curtiss *Hawk* biplane.

Curtiss data sheets for a proposal to the Navy dated May 12, 1926, show characteristics of an aircraft somewhat similar to the *Hawk*, but with some fundamental differences, and for both landplane and twin float seaplane variants.

Dimensions and areas of the studied aircraft, noted as Navy Proposal #1, with the R-1300 engine included a wing span of 30 feet, down from the 31 feet, six inch span of the standard *Hawk*, with wings of either Clark Y or Curtiss C-72 airfoil sections. The wing area was 227.4 square feet instead of the normal *Hawk* 250 square feet. Wing chords were less as well. Clearly a different wing cellule from the Hawk was envisioned.

Empty weights were 1,897 pounds for a landplane and 2,225 pounds for a seaplane version, and gross weights 2,705 pounds landplane and 3,033 pounds seaplane. High speeds were estimated at 161mph at sea level landplane and 146mph seaplane, but it was noted that if the R-1300 engine rating were increased to 475hp at 2,200rpm these numbers would increase to 169mph and 152mph, respectively. Performance seemed to change little from the standard *Hawk*. There remains no picture to show what this version might have looked like. Also, there was no mention of wing taper.

The Navy radial aircooled engined *Hawk* that got into hardware, and was produced in some quantity (for those days), was the Navy F6C-4, Curtiss model L-18-14, powered with the new Pratt & Whitney R-1340 *Wasp* engine.

An F6C-1 (Bureau Number A-6968) was converted to take this engine for testing by the Naval Aircraft Factory. A Curtiss Characteristics Sheet dated April 27, 1927, gives the following notes: "*F6C-4 Hawk, First article built at Garden City on July 28, 1926,*" and "*Performance based on Navy Performance Data SH-3B Navy Bu-*

The U.S. Marine Corps operated a few F6C-4s starting in 1927, and retained some as late as 1932. This well-worn article shows signs of hard use. High speed was 162mph at sea level. Delivered in April 1927, A-7394 was stricken from the inventory November 29, 1932, with 1037 hours total time at San Diego. *(USMC)*

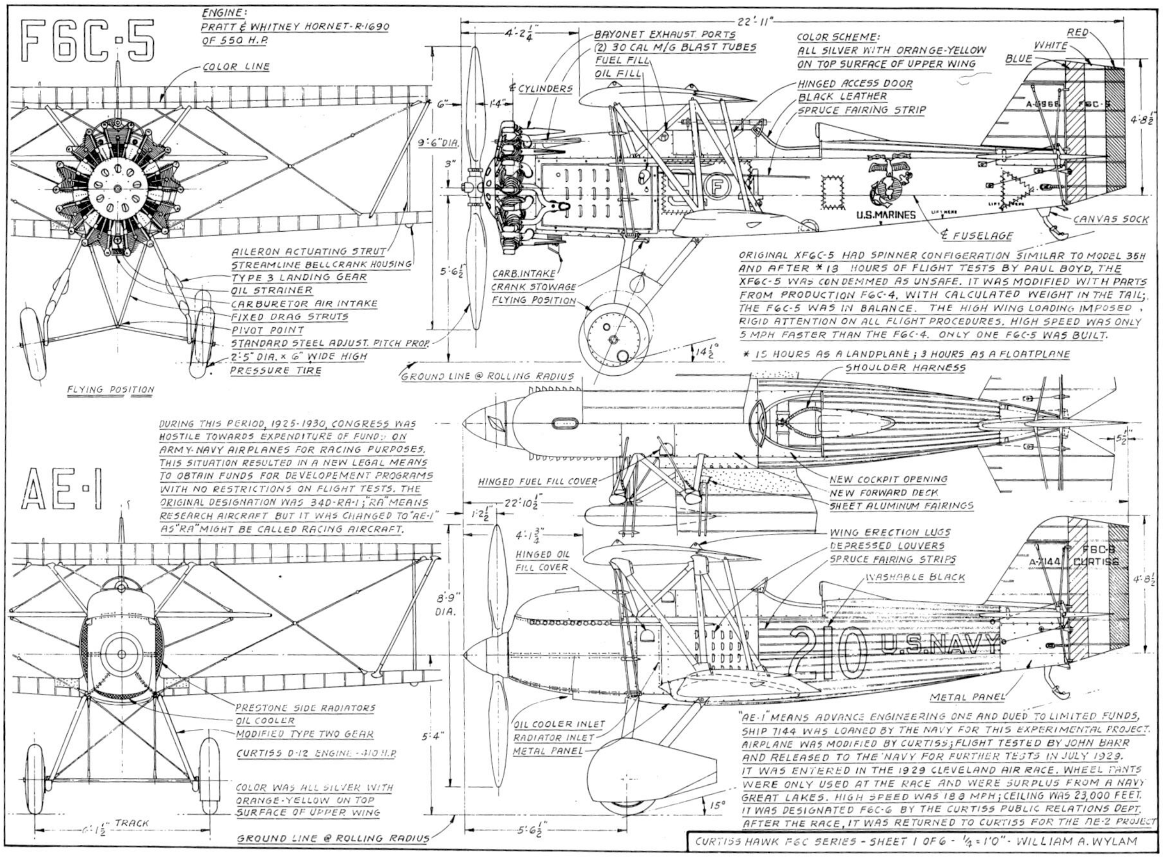

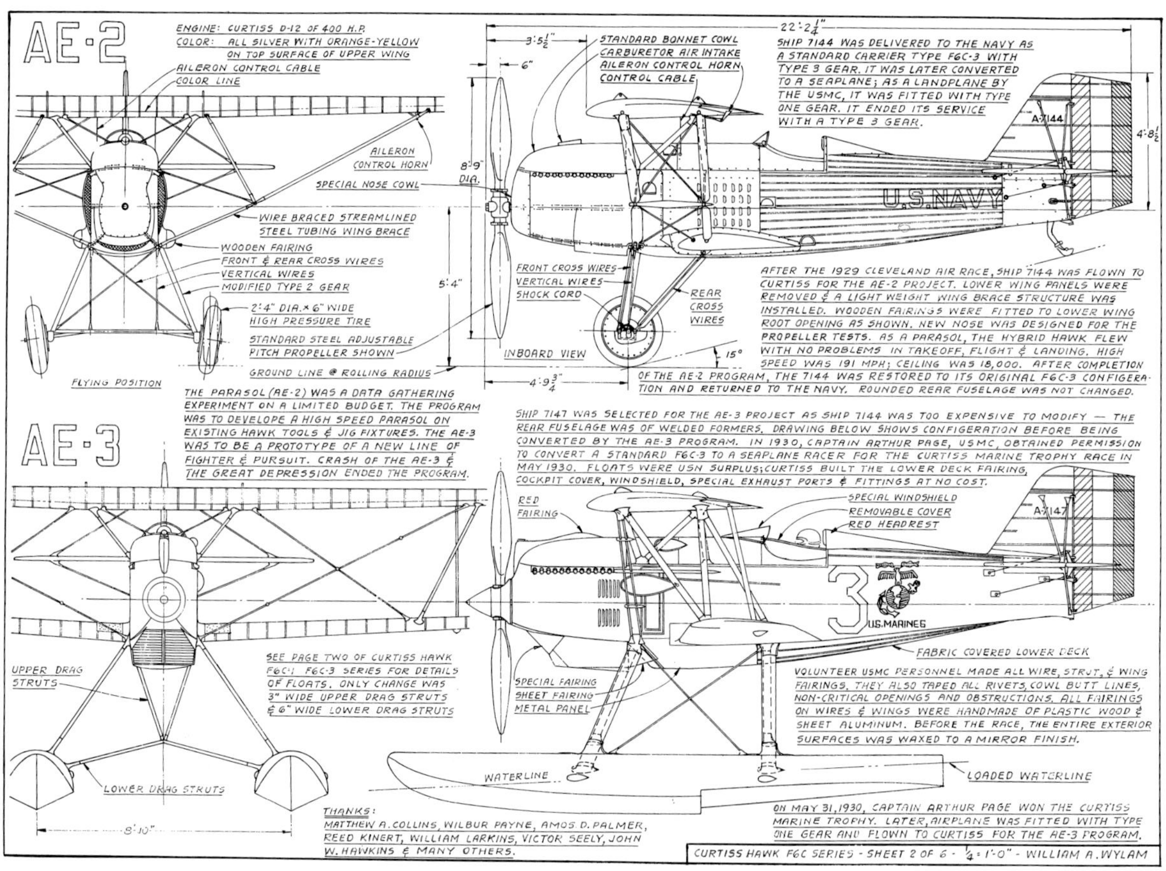

(Courtesy William A. Wylam)

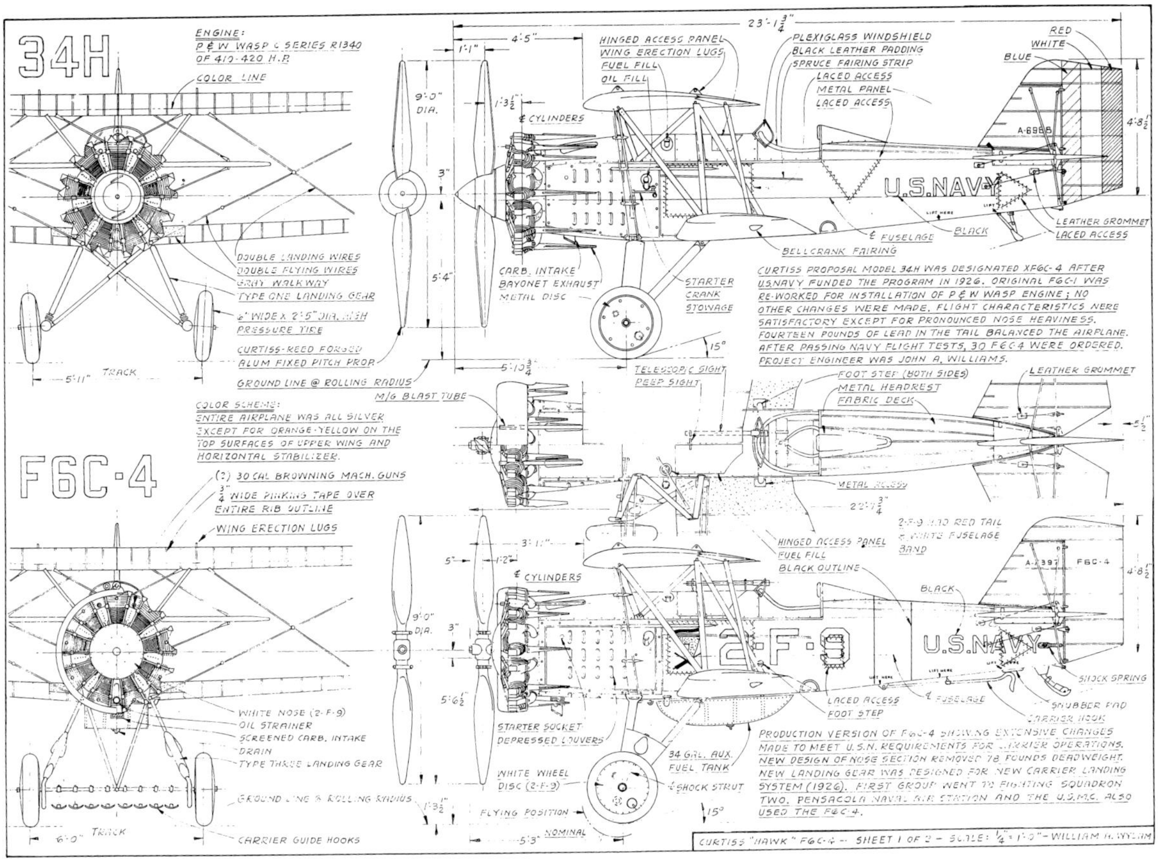

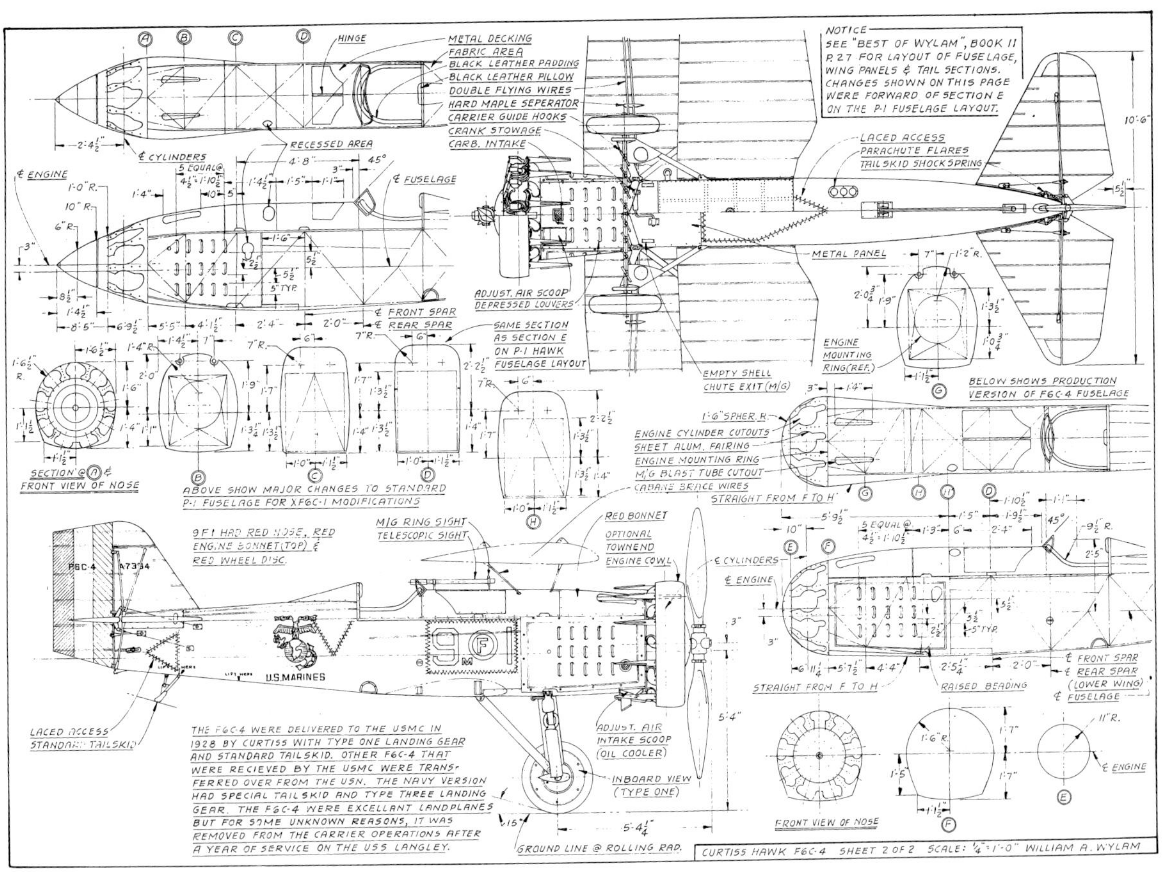

(Courtesy William A. Wylam)

The chief of Marine Corps aviation, Colonel Brainard (for whom the airfield at Hartford, CT, was named) sits in full flying togs on the wheel of this F6C-4. With tail skids still in use, the aircraft could be moved about easily via the wheeled dolly under the tail. A-7395 served a turn at Quantico, Pensacola, San Diego (with VF-2B), and finally with the Marines at San Diego. It was wrecked on August 12, 1930. *(USMC)*

reau of Aeronautics." Another note says "*This ship was rebuilt from F6C-1 #18, and had the regular land type undercarriage which is cleaner aerodynamically than the production F6C-4 deck landing gear.*"

The characteristics for this XF6C-4 were span, length, and height: 31 feet, six inches, 22 feet, five and 19/32 inches, and nine feet, one and 1/2 inches. Upper and lower average wing chord 52.6 inches and 49.4 inches. Gap was 51.1 inches. Wing stagger at the wing leading edge at the fuselage was 38.5 inches. Wing area was 252 square feet. Horizontal and vertical tail areas were 32.9 and 15.5 square feet, respectively.

The Pratt & Whitney *Wasp* aircooled radial engine was rated at 435hp at 1950rpm, and fuel consumption was 250 pounds per hour at full throttle. Internal fuel capacity was 50 gallons, and oil capacity 4 gallons. The XF6C-4 propeller was a Curtiss Reed R type EX-33025-9 of eight feet, eight inches in diameter and eight feet, three inches pitch.

Empty weight was 1,838 pounds (851 pounds of structure, 904 pounds of powerplant, and 83 pounds of fixed equipment), and 731 pounds of useful load (180 pound pilot, 325 pounds of fuel and oil, 183 pounds of armament, and 43 pounds of equipment), adding up to a gross weight of 2,569 pounds. The wing loading was 10.2psf, and power loading was 5.9 pounds per horse power. Useful load to gross weight ratio was 0.285.

The XF6C-4 performance figures consisted of a high speed of 162mph at sea level, 159.5mph at 5,000 feet, 156mph at 10,000 feet, and 150mph at 15,000 feet. Cruise speed at 1,560rpm at sea level was 129.6mph, and stall speed was 55.2mph. Rate of climb at sea level was 2,140fpm. Times to climb were 2.6 minutes to 5,000 feet, 6.1 minutes to 10,000 feet, and 10.9 minutes to 15,000 feet. Altitude achieved in 10 minutes was 14,265 feet. Endurances were 1.17 hours at full throttle, and 2.3 hours at 1,560rpm. Range at full throttle was 190 miles, and at 1,560rpm, 298 miles. Service and absolute ceilings were 23,170 feet and 24,300 feet.

The purchase of 31 F6C-4 (Curtiss MSNs 10661 to 10691 and Navy BuA Numbers 7393 to 7423) aircraft in 1926 was made from Curtiss subject to successful testing of the XF6C-4 described above. Tests at Anacostia NAS, DC, showed good all around performance. Production aircraft were to be similar to earlier F6C- types, except for the new engine, a Hamilton ground-adjustable pitch propeller, and some wing and aft fuselage structural redesign. The F6C-4s took the first production *Wasp* engines. The prototype XF6C-4 (A-6968) was flown from Pratt & Whitney at Hartford, Connecticut, to San Diego, California, starting October 1926. There it was flown by service pilots, together with the *Wasp* powered Boeing XF2B-1 against service Navy fighters with liquid cooled engines, outclass-

The major fleet use of production F6C-4s was by VF-2B aboard the USS *Langley* in the 1929-1930 period. This *Hawk* (A-7403), as noted, was based when photographed at NAS Anacostia, the Naval aviation test base at the time. With dark paint on the forward fuselage, unsightly exhaust stains were not as apparent. *(U.S. Navy)*

When an aircraft posed for a formal portrait at NAS Anacostia, it was common for a sign to be displayed. This aircraft was the first F6C-4 modified to employ the Pratt & Whitney *Hornet* engine, more powerful than the *Wasp* at 525hp, as the XF6C-5. To get the center of gravity properly located, 40 pounds of lead shot was needed as ballast in the tail. High speed increased to 173mph at sea level. (*U.S. Navy*)

ing them. It was later flown to Boeing in Seattle, and then back east. This *Hawk* was well liked, and considered maneuverable and easy to fly, with particularly good low speed lateral control, and generally good overall performance. The XF6C-4 then became the XF6C-5 (q.v.).

Production F6C-4 aircraft went to Navy Fighting Squadron VF-2B and served aboard the carrier *Langley* in late 1929 into early 1930; 19 were on board in December 1929. Some aircraft went to Pensacola NAS, Florida, to advanced fighter training Squadron VN4D8, with 26 on hand in the 1928 summer, and 11 still there in 1930.

One F6C-4 (BuA 7398) was converted at the Naval Aircraft Factory circa November 22, 1932, to take an in-line SGV *Ranger* engine, giving a very strange configuration indeed. This same aircraft was tested briefly by the NACA at Langley between July 23 and September 30, 1927, but was then returned to VF-3B at NAS Hampton Roads. A standard F6C-4 (A-7406) was also detailed to NACA in 1927 for maneuverability investigations, as well as for detailed measurements of pressure distribution on the tail surfaces, and was coded 3-FS-2 at the time. The same aircraft returned to NACA between August 2 and October 11, 1932, for tests on the drag and torque of a Hamilton controllable pitch propeller in terminal velocity dives, which must have been most entertaining to have witnessed.

The USMC obtained four aircraft in September 1927, and eight were with the Corps in September 1930 to late 1932. They were replaced in early 1933 by Boeing F4B-4 fighters. Serial A-7394 was surplused in 1930 by the U.S. Marine Corps. One of the Marine aircraft (A-7394) was also detailed to NACA in 1928 from Quantico, where it was used for maneuverability and landing gear tests. The latter involved tests measuring the difference between rubber-cord and rubber-disc shock absorbers. The aircraft was also used for tests of a one-way radio for communication to the pilot.

Curtiss XF6C-5 *Hawk*

The original test aircraft, F6C-4 A-6968 (built originally as the first F6C-1) was modified again in July 1927 to take the new Pratt & Whitney *Hornet* engine for test purposes, and was redesignated XF6C-5. It was tested as both a landplane and on floats.

The Curtiss data sheet of December 1, 1927, for the XF6C-5 conversion gives the following notes: "*F6C-4 with Hornet (Hawk) Navy fighter built at Garden City July 26, 1927, originally F6C-4 #1.*" The data sheet was based on "*...Estimate Charts and Navy Performance for F6C-4.*" A further notation stated:

"*Balance can be shifted to 30.5 percent Mean Aerodynamic Chord by addition of 40 pounds of shot (ballast) in after part of fuselage, making total weight 2838 pounds. The ship was re-built from F6C-4 #1 which was re-built from F6C-1 #18, and has regular land type undercarriage.*"

Dimensions and areas of the XF6C-5 were nearly identical to the F6C-4. The engine was the Pratt & Whitney R-1690 *Hornet*, rated at 525hp at 1,900rpm at sea level. Full throttle fuel consumption was 289 pounds per hour, and at 1,520rpm, 134 pounds per hour. Fuel and oil capacities were 50 gallons and 4 gallons. The propeller was a Standard Steel adjustable type of nine feet, six inches diameter, with pitch set at 22 degrees at the 42 inch radius station.

Empty weight of the XF6C-5 landplane was 2,067 pounds. Useful load consisted of a 180 pound pilot, 325 pounds of fuel and oil, 43.2 pounds of equipment, and 182.9 pounds of armament. Gross weight without lead shot ballast was 2,798 pounds. Wing loading was 11.1psf, and power loading 5.3 pounds per horse power.

Performance was summarized as: high speeds 173mph at sea level, 169mph at 5,000 feet, 167mph at 10,000 feet, 161mph at 15,000 feet, and 149mph at 20,000 feet. Sea level cruise speed at 1,520rpm was 138mph, and stall speed 57.7mph. Sea level climb rate was 2,440fpm, and times to climb were 2.3 minutes to 5,000 feet, 5.3 minutes to 10,000 feet, 9.5 minutes to 15,000 feet, and 15.9 minutes to 20,000 feet. Endurances were 1.0 hours at sea level full throttle, and 2.2 hours at sea level at 1,520rpm, and ranges at sea level 173 miles at full throttle, and 304 miles at 1,520rpm cruise. Climb for 10 minutes got the XF6C-5 to 15,500 feet. Service and absolute ceilings were 24,100 feet and 25,100 feet.

The aircraft was assigned to Marine Squadron VF-9M after testing at Anacostia in November 1927. It was also tested with various landing gear arrangements. It was stricken from the inventory April 6, 1928, as a total wreck after catching fire, with a total time of 323:09.

With nearly everything modified, except perhaps the empennage, the XF6C-6 poses for its first photo, its slick single-leg landing gear struts ending in a set of fancy wheel pants. To keep the huge 750hp *Conqueror* engine installation very clean, a skin cooling radiator system was used on the tapered wing. A-7147 had started life as an F6C-3 and, by the time she was stricken in September 1930, had suffered four serious accidents—all at Quantico. (*Curtiss*)

Curtiss XF6C-6 *Hawk*

Though not really a fighter at all, but rather an aircraft specially and extensively modified for racing, the XF6C-6 was actually the redesignated basic F6C-3 BuA number A-7147 airframe. After winning the 1930 Marine Trophy Race this aircraft was groomed for the 1930 summer Thompson Trophy Race at the National Air Races in Chicago, with Captain Page of the USMC as pilot. The modifications were to be major, with the aim of achieving 247-250mph speed capability based on Curtiss estimates. Power would be increased to 740-750hp using a special Curtiss *Conqueror* engine, the wing airfoil sections changed to Curtiss C-72, wing skin cooling radiators employed, new racing landing gear fitted, the lower wing omitted to make the craft a high wing monoplane, and the fuselage completely refaired. Curtiss estimated cost for the modifications was slightly over $15,000!

As it turned out the original upper wing was retained, but was covered with skin type radiators.

Unfortunately, after leading the race for 17 laps the XF6C-6 veered off course, half circled the field at 200 feet altitude, and then dived down and crashed. Captain Page died in a hospital that night. Investigation led to the belief that Page was overcome from carbon monoxide poisoning due to engine exhaust. The crash ended participation of the services in air racing for many years to come.

A-7403 again, appearing very different from the standard F6C-4 configuration, although retaining that designation. In this guise, the aircraft was used to test a tight cowling over a radial engine, a harbinger of things to come. Note also that the forward fuselage had been considerably modified so as to blend nicely with the cowl. No results of these tests have surfaced. Delivered in April 1927, she was stricken after a forced landing on September 29, 1932, with 574 hours total time. (*Wright*)

The same aircraft (A-7403) again—and although marked as an F6C-4 on the rudder, this was in fact the elusive XF6C-7 fitted with a Ranger V-770-SG engine by the Naval Aircraft Factory as of July 25, 1932. (*National Archives*)

The prototype Curtiss XF7C-1 *Seahawk* (A-7653) reveals the slightly swept upper wing, and a less than lovely undercarriage—with no evidence of an arrestor hook for carrier use. Performance resulted in a contract for 17 production aircraft, however, and this aircraft was exhaustively tested starting in February 1927. (*M. Copp*)

Curtiss XF6C-7 *Hawk*

This variant was a modification of F6C-4 A-7403 to test another aircooled engine in the early 1930s. The Naval Aircraft Factory in Philadelphia modified this aircraft to use the Ranger V-770-SG, 12 cylinder inverted "V" engine—rated at 450hp maximum—in a test bed installation by July 25, 1932. Navy interest had to stem from the fact that the engine combined the unique combination of low frontal area and air cooling. The engine was in an early development stage, and nothing came in the way of production from the installation. Apparently, although officially cited as type XF6C-7, the aircraft was still marked on its rudder as type F6C-4, even after the installation was complete.

Curtiss XF7C-1 and F7C-1 *Seahawk*

The Curtiss *Seahawk*, designated F7C-1 by the Navy and L-115 by the company, was a Pratt & Whitney *Wasp* powered single place fighter designed from scratch as either a wheeled carrier aircraft or a battleship catapult type single float seaplane. Its competition was the Boeing F3B-1 type. An excerpt from the Curtiss Garden City Chief Engineer's report for the year 1927 states:

"The F7C-1 won first place in performance, but was higher priced by 30-40 percent, and therefore rated even with the competition. A contract was received for 17 additional aircraft. As of December 28, 1927 one of the major engineering jobs was XF7C-1 and F7C-1 (17 aircraft)."

Curtiss preliminary characteristics sheets of August 31, 1926, define two aircraft: the first a single seat Navy Tractor Biplane Class VF (fighter) landplane EX-36251, and the second a Class VF seaplane EX-36252, the performance estimates being from charts. These were preliminary proposals leading to the definition of the XF7C-1.

For the landplane span, length, and height were 30 feet, eight inches, 20 feet, 11 inches, and nine feet even. Wing chords were 59 inches upper wing and 48 inches lower. Wing gap was 56 inches, and stagger at the leading edge 43 inches. Incidence was -1 degree for both wings. There was no dihedral, but upper wing sweepback was seven degrees. Total wing area came to 242 square feet. Horizontal and vertical tail areas were 32.9 square feet and 15.5 square feet. Wing airfoil sections were the Curtiss C-72, and the high angle of attack structural load factor was 12.

Another view of XF7C-1 A-7653, now fitted with a long-chord engine cowl for tests. This aircraft remained at Anacostia for numerous tests, with short deployments to Hampton Roads and Langley Field, VA, and late in service was redesignated as a straight F7C-1. She was stricken in May 1932. (*M. Copp*)

With floats and a big Pratt & Whitney R-1340 engine, complete with huge prop spinner, the XF7C-1 looks like a completely different aircraft, afloat here near Anacostia. (*via Peter M. Bowers*)

The powerplant was a *Wasp* radial of 410hp at 1,900rpm with a compression ratio of 5.25:1, and full throttle fuel consumption of 185 pounds per hour. Fuel and oil capacities were 80 gallons and 8 gallons, respectively. The propeller was a Curtiss Reed dural type of nine feet diameter and seven feet, nine inch pitch.

Empty weight was 1,719 pounds, consisting of 736 pounds of airframe, 895 pounds of powerplant, and 88 pounds of fixed equipment, with useful load totaling 749 pounds, including a 200 pound pilot, 331 pounds of fuel and oil, 23 pounds of equipment, and 195 pounds of armament. Gross weight was 2,468 pounds, giving a wing loading of 10.2psf and a power loading of 6.0 pounds per horse power. Useful load to gross weight ratio was 0.303.

Performance estimates showed a sea level high speed of 166mph, cruising speed at 1,600rpm at 139mph, and a landing speed of 53.6mph. Sea level climb rate was estimated at 2,120fpm, and altitude achieved in 10 minutes was 14,200 feet. Times to climb were 2.7 minutes to 5,000 feet, 6.2 minutes to 10,000 feet, and 11 minutes to 15,000 feet. Endurance and range figures at full throttle were 2.6 hours and 430 miles, respectively. Service and absolute ceilings estimated out at 22,900 and 24,000 feet.

The estimates for the EX-36252 seaplane version differed as follows: length 24 feet, 11 inches, height 10 feet, one and 1/4 inches. Seaplane weights were 1,979 pounds empty, consisting of 996 pounds of structure, and the rest the same as the landplane. Gross weight was 2,729 pounds. Sea level high speed was 160mph estimated, cruising speed 131mph, and landing speed 56.5mph. Sea level climb rate was 1,720fpm, and times to climb were estimated as 3.4 minutes to 5,000 feet, 7.8 minutes to 10,000 feet, and 15.1 minutes to 15,000 feet. Full throttle range went down to 405 miles, and service and absolute ceilings to 20,100 feet and 21,400 feet relative to the landplane version.

The prototype XF7C-1—Bureau Number presented as 7653—now designated as simply F7C-1 attached to a utility squadron, but with a modern carrier arresting hook suitable for lateral arrests on the latest carriers. As it turned out, this was the solitary F7C-1 ever fitted with a hook. (*U.S. Navy*)

A factory fresh, production F7C-1 *Seahawk* (A-7654), the first ready for delivery to the Fleet from the Curtiss Garden City plant in November 1928. The prop spinner is gone, and the landing gear has been redesigned. There is no carrier arrestor hook; the F7C-1s were destined to be used only as "land Hawks" by the Marines. A-7654 was one of the longest serving, being stricken in January 1933. (*Curtiss*)

With a Navy contract in hand, Curtiss started construction of an experimental prototype XF7C-1 (Curtiss MSN 10692 and Navy serial A-7653) in 1926, and the first flight took place on February 28, 1927. With a large propeller spinner, the prototype had a slightly swept upper wing and a straight lower wing. On June 30, 1927, the Navy purchased the XF7C-1 at a cost of $72,456, and the prototype reached Anacostia NAS, DC, on August 28, 1927, for Navy testing. The data below is from the Curtiss characteristics sheet based on Navy performance tests (NA5A-11) of the landplane.

For the XF7C-1, span, length, and height were 30 feet, eight inches, 22 feet, seven and 1/4 inches, and nine feet, eight and 1/2 inches. Wing chords were 59 inches and 48 inches, wing gap 56.7 inches, and both wings incidence -1 degrees. Upper wing sweepback was 7 degrees, and total wing area was 242 square feet. Horizontal and vertical tail areas were 28.59 and 14.71 square feet. The powerplant was the Pratt & Whitney *Wasp* giving 447hp at 2,000rpm. Empty weight came to 2,049 pounds. Adding a useful load of 755 pounds gave a gross weight of 2,804 pounds.

The third production F7C-1 (A-7655) reveals the external fuel tank under the fuselage. The external wall of the internal tank defined the outer skin line in that area. The balanced rudder of the XF7C-1 was retained. It was stricken in August 1931 following a collision. (*Curtiss*)

The measured performance consisted of a high speed at sea level of 155.5mph, and cruising speed at 1,400rpm of 101mph, with a stall speed of 58mph. Sea level climb rate was 1,860fpm, and climb for 10 minutes got the plane to 12,750 feet. Endurance at full throttle at sea level was 1.54 hours, and at 1,400rpm cruise, 3.5 hours. Range at full throttle at sea level was 239 miles, and at 1,400rpm, 355 miles. Service and absolute ceilings were 22,100 feet and 23,400 feet.

Modifications recommended after test included a revised landing gear and a new propeller. After their incorporation, 16[53] production aircraft were ordered at a unit cost of $17,000. The first three production aircraft were tested again, resulting in removal of the propeller spinner, and a change to an oleo-type landing gear. Tests were also made in seaplane configuration. The XF7C-1 was later revised to F7C-1 configuration, but remained the only aircraft to keep carrier compatibility. Along the way the XF7C-1 was also tested, in 1929, with a wide chord NACA type engine cowling by Squadron VX1D5 at Norfolk NAS, Virginia. This may have coincided with the detail of the aircraft, between December 7, 1928, and August 18, 1930, to the NACA at Langley, where it also underwent tests with various cowlings, including the NACA-developed Variable Angle Cowling.

F7C-1 aircraft were used for some other interesting tests. The second production aircraft (A-7655) was checked out in December 1928 with Reed tandem type two blade propellers.

An F7C-1 aircraft equipped with single main and wingtip floats won the Curtiss Marine Trophy Race of 1929 piloted by Lt. Boyden at 142.9mph. However, a Navy document dated May 29, 1929, which commented on this race rather bluntly, stated that:

"*...the speed of 175mph accredited this job last Saturday in the Curtiss Marine Trophy Race, was all wet. The actual speed was 162.52mph. This job was cowled at NACA and is being returned to them to complete their flight tests. This plane was put over the speed course at Anacostia before being sent to NACA and did 150.8mph. Its speed over the course as it now stands is 165.8mph. All this increase is not due to the venture cowling. Some of the Navy pilots think this cowling is O.K. for pursuit, but Lt. Al Williams says NO! After sitting in the cockpit of the F7C-1, I am inclined to believe that Al is right. Williams is strong for Prestone cooling.*"

Another view of the slat-equipped F7C-1 test ship, A-7656. The slats were automatic, in that they popped automatically as the wing angle of attack increased. Hopefully, they would not pop asymmetrically. (*Curtiss*)

Another series of tests were performed on F7C-1 A-7656, shown here with the upper wing equipped with Handley-Page automatic slots, as pointed out by the Curtiss test pilot standing on the wheel. The Navy and Curtiss had an agreement with Handley-Page of England, and Curtiss made liberal use of slat equipped aircraft designs. (*Curtiss*)

The third production aircraft (A-7656) was modified to test upper wing leading edge slots, one of the first such developments in the U.S.

The F7C-1 was the first Curtiss type to use integral fuel tanks on each side of the fuselage outboard of the primary structure, where they formed the outer skin line of the aircraft. In addition, one aircraft was used for tests of auxiliary fuel tanks.

Though intended for such use originally, the *Seahawks* never got to sea aboard a carrier; they were turned over to the Marine Corps which, by January 1928, had received five aircraft, the first having gone to Squadron VF-5M on the 28th. Seven or eight were on hand from 1929 to late 1932, four were left in February 1933, and all were out of the inventory by 1934, having been replaced by Boeing F4B-4s. During their service some of the F7C-1s had short chord ring engine cowls added.

Construction of the F7C-1 fuselage was made up of steel and dural tubing, with the forward section and sections above the upper longerons covered in dural sheet, and the aft section fabric covered. The wings consisted of a spruce structural frame with fabric covering. Tail surfaces were fabric covered.

Currently the National Museum of Naval Aviation at Pensacola, Florida, has a beautifully restored F7C-1 (A-7667).

Curtiss XP-10

Responding to an Army requirement for a new pursuit aircraft having good maneuverability, good pilot visibility, and having its high speed at altitude, Curtiss proposed their L-119 design, and obtained a development contract on June 18, 1928, for a single prototype machine.

The Curtiss XP-10 for the Army (A.C.28-387) was something of an anomaly in the Curtiss pursuit line. It had no relationship whatsoever to the biplane *Hawk* line, though P-6 *Hawks* were ordered the same year, and both were powered with *Conqueror* engines. (*Curtiss*)

The agreed upon cost was $50,000 on Contract W535-ac-1333. The aircraft was given the designation XP-10, and Army Serial number 28-387 (Curtiss MSN is, oddly, not accounted for in Curtiss documents). The first flight took place in May 1930. For those days the time between contract signing and prototype first flight was unusually long.

The Curtiss aircraft that emerged was distinctly different from those of the usual *Hawk* line; there was no resemblance at all, except it was also a single seat single bay wing biplane using a Curtiss *Conqueror* engine. This may account for the fact that no mention of the then-current popular name *Hawk* has been found associated with the XP-10. An unusual feature had the upper wing gulled off the fuselage with no cabane struts, and to achieve the desired wing gap the lower wing was also set low off the fuselage and faired in. The other unusual feature was the use of skin cooling radiators on both surfaces of the upper wing inboard, a feature already found to be unsuited and undesirable for a pursuit aircraft after experience with the Curtiss PW-8, and eliminated in the P-1/P-6 series.

The fuselage structure was made up of steel tubing. Contours were filled out with formers and fairing strips, and the frame covered with fabric. Wing structure was of wood, with wood skinning of thin plywood sheets.

The powerplant was a geared supercharged Curtiss *Conqueror* SV-1570-15 of 600hp water-cooled via skin radiators, and driving a two bladed propeller. Nose lines were exceptionally clean.

Characteristics of the XP-10 were as follows: span, length, and height were 33 feet, 24 feet, six inches, and eight feet, eight inches. Wing area was 269.8.square feet. Empty weight was 3,040 pounds, useful load 935 pounds, and gross weight 3,975 pounds. Wing load-

Seldom viewed from the frontal aspect, the Curtiss XP-10 was the stuff of pulp fiction. This May 3, 1930, image seems to show a ground-adjustable metal prop. (*Curtiss via H. Therall*)

Although ordered with Fiscal Year 1928 funding (hence the serial number A.C.28-387), the XP-10 apparently did not fly for the first time until April 1930—an extremely long gestation for the time. It spent its entire, brief service life of but 10 hours at Wright Field, and later passed to Class 25 at Chanute Field in October 1931. (*Curtiss*)

Decorated with the "Snow Owl" insignia of the 17th Pursuit Squadron, the Curtiss XP-6, formerly a P-2 procured as A.S.25-423 (note shadow of "P-2" in the vertical stripe of the rudder insignia), the aircraft was modified for racing purposes with a V-1520 high-compression *Conqueror* engine which, with special fuels, up-rated the engine to 730hp at 2,600rpm. That was a lot of power for the P-2 airframe. (*Curtiss*)

ing was thus 14.73psf, and power loading 6.63 pounds per horse power, with a useful load to gross weight ratio of 0.235—on the low side.

The aircraft was tested only a few hours by the Army (total time appears to have been no more than nine hours), and was found to be lacking, primarily with troubles encountered with the skin cooling system, a lesson learned once and, now, a second time. As was intended, pilot visibility was reported as generally good, but the XP-10 performance was little better than the then-current operational pursuits, or those to soon come into service.

Maximum speed was variously reported as 173mph at sea level and 191mph at sea level, and 215mph at 12,000 feet. Initial climb rate was 1650fpm. Normal range calculated at 461 miles, and service ceiling was 26,500 feet. Armament consisted of the standard two fixed synchronized .30 caliber machine guns.

The very different XP-10 was disposed of in October 1931 to Class 25 status at Chanute Field, and Curtiss continued with their development of more conventional *Hawk* variants.

Curtiss XP-6 *Hawk Racer*, XP-488, and XP-6A *Hawk*

Starting in the mid-1920s, Curtiss had under development a new liquid cooled "V" type 12 cylinder engine as a larger and more powerful growth of their D-12 (V-1150) and V-1400 types. Known as the *Conqueror*, and originally of 1,550 cubic inches displacement (later V-1520), the engine was at first rated at 600hp.

To demonstrate the worthiness of this new engine it was decided to re-engine P-2 *Hawk* A.S.25-423 with the *Conqueror*, and race it at the National Air Races held at Spokane, Washington, in September 1927. The modified racer was designated XP-6 by the Army. The undated Curtiss characteristics sheet for the XP-6 calls it a *Hawk Racer* with use to be "*racing at Spokane, 1927*." Oddly, Army records show the XP-6 as delivered December 6, 1927, suggesting that the aircraft was still Curtiss property at the time of the race.

Wing geometry was that of the P-2, with Clark Y airfoils, 31 feet, six inches span, and 252 square feet wing area, and length with the new engine was 22 feet, five and 19/32 inches.

The powerplant was a V-1550 *Conqueror* high compression model rated for racing at 730hp at 2,600rpm. A tunnel radiator was used with water cooling. Empty weight of the XP-6 with 125 pounds of water came to 2,234 pounds, comprised of 867 pounds of structure, 1,286 pounds of powerplant, and 81 pounds of fixed equipment. Useful load was 777 pounds, and consisted of a 180 pound pilot, 325 pounds of fuel and oil, 50 pounds of equipment and, somewhat strangely for a racing aircraft, 222 pounds of armament. All this totaled to a gross weight of 3,011 pounds. The wing loading was 12.0psf, and power loading 4.12 pounds per horse power. Useful load to gross weight ratio was 0.258.

The Curtiss characteristics sheet lists high speed at 191mph; cruising speed at 0.8 maximum RPM was 153mph, and landing speed 60mph. The estimate (only) of sea level climb rate was a classy 3,200fpm, and climb in 10 minutes attained 18,500 feet. Full throttle endurance at sea level was 0.86 hours. The estimated service and absolute ceilings were 25,400 feet and 26,200 feet. Army figures differed, however, showing a sea level high speed of 176.2mph, service ceiling of 23,110 feet, and absolute ceiling of 24,200 feet. The XP-6 utilized an EX-33073-87 prop.

At the Spokane National Air Races the *Conqueror* powered XP-6, flown by Army Lt. Lyon, placed second on the race, averaging 189.6mph, being beaten only, ironically, by the Curtiss XP-6A. Later in September 1928 the aircraft went to Selfridge Field, Michigan, and was wrecked there, still designated as an XP-6, February 25, 1929, when it failed to pull out of a dive. It had been tested as Wright Field number P-494.

The aircraft placing first in the above mentioned Spokane Race (the XP-6A) was described in the 1927 Curtiss Report of the Chief Engineer dated January 3, 1928, as: "*XP-6A, an easy winner in the Spokane Races, a V-1550 engine in a PW-8A*."(In actuality, it was a remodeled P-1A airframe, A.S.26-295, using PW-8A constant chord wings with skin cooling on both upper and lower wings, and issued number XP-488 for tests circa October 27, 1927.) It was actually accepted by the Air Corps on October 19, 1927.

The Curtiss data sheet of October 5, 1927, for the XP-6A gives the following figures: span (not clear), length, and height (not given).

The XP-6A was very much a real racer than the XP-6, and it looked more the part with the beautifully clean nose lines. Powered with the same souped-up *Conqueror* engine, it was capable of 210mph. It had XPW-8A wings incorporating PW-8 surface radiators. (*U.S. Army*)

The second aircraft to bear the Army Air Corps designation XP-6A, and the cause of no end of confusion, was A.C.29-263. This was, in actuality, a standard P-6 used for development tests. It spent its entire service life, from October 3, 1928, until surveyed March 26, 1934, at Selfridge Field, MI. (*U.S. Army*)

Upper and lower wing chords 66 and 48 inches, respectively, wing gap 53 inches, stagger at leading edge 36 inches, lower wing dihedral 1.5 degrees, and wing area 253.6 square feet. Airfoil sections were Curtiss C-62. Horizontal and vertical tail areas were 32.5 square feet and 15.54 square feet.

The powerplant was a high compression (compression ratio 5.9) V-1570[54] Curtiss *Conqueror* rated at 600hp at 2,400rpm using the wing skin cooling radiator system. The only weight data provided is a gross weight of 3,204 pounds. Another source shows an empty weight of 2,350 pounds, which would mean a useful load of 854 pounds. Wing loading was 12.65psf, and power loading 4.4 pounds per HP.

The performance cited for the XP-6A, noted as based on speed trials at Mitchell Field, Long Island, was a high speed of 193.8mph at sea level, a cruising speed of 168mph, and a landing speed of 70.5mph, the last fairly high for the time, but excused for a racer type. A note says: "*This machine not a service type. Further flight test data not available.*"

This aircraft was the winner at the 1927 Spokane *Spokesman Review* Races, flying at an average speed of 201.2mph and piloted by Army Lt. Batten, beating the XP-6 and three Boeing FB-5s amongst others. It later crashed on August 13, 1928, and was surveyed.

Curtiss XP-6B (XP-590) *Hawk-Hoyt Special*

The last P-1C *Hawk* (A.C.29-259) was delivered in April 1929 as a regular D-12 powered pursuit, but shortly was modified and then redelivered July 18th as an XP-6B,[55] since a major modification included installation of a 600hp V-1570 Curtiss *Conqueror* engine, and so powered the plane was given a P-6 series designation. In addition, the fuselage was much modified to include additional internal fuel tankage for long range capability. The fuselage was fattened by the addition more fairing stringers around basic structure, and covered.

The plan was to make a spectacular demonstration of the ability of the *Conqueror* powered *Hawk* to fly long distances, and a trip from the U.S. east coast to Alaska was envisioned, piloted by Army Captain Ross G. Hoyt. The plane was soon to be called the "*Hawk-Hoyt Special*," or sometimes the "*Newlaska*."

Taking off from Mitchell Field, Long Island, on July 18, 1929, Hoyt got to Minneapolis in seven hours, and reached Edmonton, 1,100 miles away in Canada, before dawn for breakfast. Hoyt then flew to Whitehorse, Fairbanks, and finally to Nome, the latter reached in 38 hours elapsed time, and 34 hours, 10 minutes flying time. On the return trip he was forced to land at Valmont, British Columbia, on July 21st due to water condensation in the fuel tanks.

The Curtiss XP-6B, also known by the Wright Field test designation XP-590, and usually termed the *Hawk-Hoyt Special*, was A.C.29-259, delivered in April 1929 as a regular D-12 powered pursuit, but reconfigured with a 600hp V-1570 *Conqueror*. Captain Ross G. Hoyt made an epic flight to Alaska in 34 hours, 10 minutes flying time in July 1929. The designation XP-6B was not applied to the aircraft until *after* this flight, contrary to many published reports. (*Curtiss T-4684*)

Although bearing standard USAAC insignia, the fact that the *Hawk-Hoyt Special* had the Curtiss logo prominently displayed on the vertical fin, with no evidence of standard Air Corps lettering on the fuselage, strengthens the case that the aircraft may have been sponsored on its flight to Alaska by Curtiss directly. *(Curtiss)*

The XP-6B flipped over and sustained some damage in the landing. The aircraft was repaired, and served the Army until it was relegated to Class 25 in December 1931, still as an XP-6B. It is interesting to note that, according to Army documents, the designation XP-6B was not assigned until *after* the Alaska flight, and after the special instruments installed for the flight had been removed. The aircraft remained in the inventory as late as December 1930.

The XP-6B had a span of 31 feet, six inches, length of 23 feet, seven inches, and a height of eight feet, nine inches. Wing area was the standard 252 square feet, and the standard Clark Y tapered airfoil sections were used.

The powerplant was a 600hp Curtiss V-1570-1, and total internal fuel capacity was 250 gallons for long range flight, five times that of a standard *Hawk*.

Empty weight was 2,545 pounds, normal useful load 724 pounds, and normal gross weight 3,269 pounds. The overload gross weight for the start of a long range flight had to include a useful load, with 250 gallons of fuel, of about 1,800 pounds. The total weight therefore was about 4,345 pounds. Takeoff distance with full load was a little over 800 yards.

At normal gross weight the XP-6B's high speed was 178mph at sea level, and 175mph at 5,000 feet. Sea level cruise speed was 143.5mph, and landing speed 62.4mph. Climb to 5,000 feet took 2.7 minutes at normal gross weight. High speed endurance and cruise endurance at normal gross weight takeoff were 1.9 hours and 3.8 hours, respectively. Service and absolute ceilings were 22,600 feet and 23,800 feet.

Curtiss P-6 and P-6A *Hawks*

On October 3, 1928, on the basis of the performance of the XP-6 racer with the new *Conqueror* engine, the Army gave Curtiss an order for 11 P-6 *Hawk* pursuit aircraft, and then added two more P-6 types originally ordered as Hexagon engine powered XP-11 aircraft, for a total of 13 new planes. Army Air Corps serial numbers were 29-269 through 29-273 and 29-363 through 29-368.[56]

With the new Curtiss V-1570 *Conqueror* engine, after the two racing and long distance conversions used the engine as noted, 18 P-6s were produced by Curtiss in 1929 and 1930. Eight of these were revised to P-6As with Prestone cooling instead of water, and A.C. 29-260, although marked as a P-6, was one of those so converted. It was converted as the XP-6 at Wright Field November 1, 1929, then to P-6A December 1, 1930, XP-6A on January 31, 1931, and XP-6D on May 1, 1931! *(Curtiss via Roger Besecker)*

Another view of A.C.29-260 dated October 22, 1929, which tends to make the rather stout *Conqueror* engine appear more streamlined than it was. (*Curtiss T-5048 via R. E. Johnson*).

The P-6, designed under the leadership of Ted P. Wright of Curtiss, was basically similar to a P-1B *Hawk*, except it was *Conqueror* powered with the fuselage deepened and faired forward into the cooling radiator up front, and the fuselage guns were moved forward and cockpit instruments relocated.

These P-6 aircraft were delivered from October 1929 to December 1930. The first aircraft, Serial 29-269, was the experimental plane of the lot, and was given Wright Field number XP-580. The P-6 pursuits had water cooling systems, whereas the P-6As used the newer Prestone in their radiators. Prestone was a much more efficient cooling medium, having a higher boiling point and a lower freezing point, and better heat transfer qualities, with the result being a smaller cooler and less system fluid required. Sources differ as to the exact number of aircraft originally delivered with Prestone cooling. One source indicated only nine were originally so equipped and 11 delivered with water, however, a former Curtiss Garden City employee maintained 14 were delivered with Prestone cooled engines at $10,760 each, and the rest with water cooling at $9,300 each. In any case, all were eventually converted to a Prestone system except 29-261, which was wrecked in November 1929, and 29-260, which stayed at Wright Field.

This P-6 (A.C.29-269) was the first production example, and here bears the Fairfield Air Depot (F.A.D.) arrow, a "Prestone" emblem on the engine cowl, and was probably photographed very late in her service life. This angle vividly reveals the dramatic difference in the angles of the swept upper and lower wings. (*U.S. Army*)

Possibly also A.C.29-269, and bearing the same F.A.D. arrow and "Prestone" emblem, the aircraft here sports a three-blade prop and no spinner. Note what appear to be flare chutes below the mid-fuselage. (*U.S. Army*)

P-6 types went to the 17th, 27th, 36th, and 56th Pursuit Squadrons at Selfridge Field, and to the 37th Pursuit Squadron at Langley Field, with a couple going to Chanute Field, IL, as well.

The water-cooled P-6s were powered by a V-1570-17 *Conqueror* of 600hp. Internal fuel capacity was 50 gallons. Span and length were 31 feet, six inches and 23 feet, seven inches, and wing area was the typical *Hawk* 252 square feet. Normal gross weight was 3,150 pounds, making wing loading 12.5psf and power loading 5.25 pounds per horse power.

High speed was 178mph at sea level, 171mph at 5,000 feet, and 144mph at 20,000 feet. Full throttle sea level range was 260 miles. Climb at sea level came to 2,140fpm, and 10,000 feet could be reached in 6.6 minutes. Service and absolute ceilings were 22,700 feet and 24,000 feet.

The nine Prestone cooled P-6As used a Curtiss V-1570-A *Conqueror* engine rated 600hp at 2,400rpm. Fuel capacity was 50 gallons. Empty weight added to 2,389 pounds, and useful load was 783 pounds, giving a gross weight of 3,172 pounds, a wing loading of 12.59psf, a power loading of 5.29 pounds per horse power, and a useful load to gross weight ratio of 0.247. The P-6As used 0153689 type propellers.

Maximum speed was 178.6mph at sea level, 176.8mph at 5,000 feet, 173.5mph at 10,000 feet, and 154.8mph at 20,000 feet. Cruise and landing speeds were 154mph and 60mph. Sea level climb rate was 2,320fpm. Climb times were 2.8 minutes to 5,000 feet and 5.8 minutes to 10,000 feet. Service and absolute ceilings were 27,200 feet and 28,400 feet, respectively.

Of these P-6A Prestone cooled pursuits, one was wrecked in 1931, two each were wrecked in 1932 and 1933, and one each in 1934 and 1935. The remaining planes were converted to P-6D variants with turbo supercharged engines. P-6A A.C.29-263 was equipped with a V-1570C engine with a side type supercharger, while 29-262 went to Curtiss on Contract AC-3787 for reworking into the XP-22 airplane (q.v.). The following chart, derived from the actual Individual Aircraft History Cards, is presented in an effort to clarify, once and for all, the very confusing evolution of the P-6 series.

A.C.Serial	Accepted	Redesignated	Redesignated	Redesignated	Redesignated
29-260	10/3/28	XP-6 11/1/29	P-6A 12/1/30	XP-6A 1/31/31	XP-6D 5/1/31
29-261	10/3/28	w/o Selfridge 11/18/29			
29-262	10/3/28	P-6A 11/6/30	XP-22 5/4/31	P-6A 9/28/31	
29-263	10/3/28	P-6A 12/4/30			
29-264	10/3/28	P-6A 11/6/30			
29-265	10/3/28	P-6A 11/6/30	w/o in Michigan 2/1/32		
29-266	10/3/28	P-6A 11/6/30	P-6D 11/18/33	Survey Nov1934	
29-267	10/3/28	P-6A 11/6/30	Survey Selfridge 1/4/32		
29-268	10/3/28	P-6A 11/6/30	P-6D 12/18/32	Survey as ZP-6D 8/20/37	
29-269	10/3/28	P-6D 6/10/32	Survey Nov1937		
29-270	10/3/28	P-6D	37th Attack Squadron, Langley	Survey Oct1935	
29-271	10/3/28	w/o 9/3/31 Selfridge			
29-272	10/3/28	P-6D	Survey w/o Chanute 12/14/36		
29-273	10/3/28	P-6D	Survey with 1st School Squadron	As ZP-6D Apr1937	
29-363	10/3/28				
29-364	10/3/28	P-6D			
29-365	10/3/28	Wrecked			
29-365	10/3/28	P-6D	37th Attack Squadron, Langley	Survey Oct1935	
29-366	10/3/28	P-6D			
29-367	10/3/28	P-6D	Survey 9/1/37		
29-368	10/3/28	P-6D			

By 1928, Curtiss had finally decided to pursue export markets decisively and, with the combination of the *Hawk* airframe and the *Conqueror* engine, felt that they had a contender. This is the demonstrator that later gained the Department of Commerce number 9110. The sole markings on the aircraft are the Curtiss logo and the words "Oxygen" and "Flares" on access panels, and rather large letters near the wing root cautioning ground crews to *Disconnect Electrical Features & Air Speed Tubes* before fueling. (*Curtiss*)

Curtiss P-6 *Hawk* Export Variants

Curtiss had some minor success in the export trade with *Conqueror* powered *Hawks* of the P-6 water-cooled variety. In mid-1930 eight were exported to the Netherlands East Indies,[57] and one aircraft, with the temporarily civil Department of Commerce Identification Mark -72K, was purchased by Mitsubishi in Japan in 1930 for their study purposes, as noted in detail earlier.

The little-known Dutch aircraft were in fact acquired for use by the *Luchtvaart Afdeling* (LA, or Air Division) of the *Koninklijk Nederlands Indisch Leger* (KNIL, or Royal Netherlands Indies Army), the solitary previous experience of this obscure colonial air arm with fighter type aircraft having been six Fokker D-VIIs fitted with British-built Siddeley *Puma* engines acquired in 1922.

Although under pressure by 1928 to replace the aged Fokker fighters, of which only one remained, with domestically produced Fokker D-XVI fighters, in 1929 none other than Lt. James Doolittle, who seemed to be everywhere representing Curtiss (see *anon*), arrived at Andir Field, Bandung, on Java, to demonstrate the *Conqueror* powered *Hawk*. Subsequently, in spite of pressure to "buy

Another view of the *Conqueror* powered *Hawk* demonstrator, which was an extremely well traveled aircraft. Some sources state the aircraft was painted bright red, while others say it was olive drab. The latter is more likely—and more warlike, perhaps, in the eyes of potential customers. All access panels were neatly labeled. (*Curtiss*)

The first of the Dutch P-6s for the *Luchtvaart Afdeling* of the *Koninklijk Nederlands Indisch Leger* (Air Division of the Royal Netherlands Indies Army) at Andir, still in the basic overall green as shipped from the factory. (*Royal Netherlands Air Force*)

A trio of Dutch P-6s of the *1e Vliegtuig Atdeling* (No. 1 Squadron) at Andir, with C-317 showing red or blue "patrol" chevrons. The squadron had three flights, and each used either one, two, or three chevrons in red, white, or blue. (*Royal Netherlands Air Force*)

This Netherlands East Indies P-6 shares a hangar with a venerable Avro 504K. C.310 may have been one of the Aviolanda license-built aircraft, and appears to be undergoing heavy maintenance involving the fuel tank. (*Royal Netherlands Air Force*)

One of the six P-6s built under license by Aviolanda at Papendrecht, in the Netherlands, for the East Indies Army. The "color" that seems apparent on the upper main plane and horizontal tail surfaces was in fact doped silver, in an effort to reduce temperature inside the structure and the cockpit—and aid visibility if forced down in the jungle. (*Royal Netherlands Air Force*)

One of the last of the Dutch *Conqueror* powered P-6s at Andir (C.319). These aircraft served on well into 1938, and gave excellent service. (*Royal Netherlands Air Force*)

Dutch," an order was placed for eight P-6s equivalent to the "civilian" P-6 model that Doolittle had demonstrated. These aircraft were delivered in April 1930, and arrangements were made by Curtiss to have Lt. Blackburn of the U.S. Army Air Corps come to Java from Manila, in the Philippines, to test fly the new aircraft and check out the Dutch pilots on the type. The first Dutch pilot to fly a *Hawk* was Lt. Swartjes on May 7, 1930. The order totaled $184,080, and included two guns and two A-3 bomb racks for each aircraft.

The new aircraft were subsequently assigned to the *1e Vliegtuig Atdeling* (1-VA, or No.1 Squadron), which had dual interceptor and ground attack responsibilities and, in order to provide a reserve for this, the solitary unit of its kind in the service, funds were provided for an additional six aircraft in 1930, and these were in fact built under license for the LA by the Dutch firm Aviolanda. These were identical to the Curtiss-built P-6s, with the exception that the first example had wheel spats, although these were, in the event, removed in Java. These aircraft were finally delivered to Java in 1932, although the total cost of the aircraft far exceeded what they would have cost had they been acquired direct from Curtiss. The *Hawk* dependability in NEI service was outstanding, in spite of the fact that they had not been designed for prolonged operation in semi-tropical environments.

The Dutch *Hawks* served on with the LA until 1938 based at Kalidjati, when both flight and ground crews were needed to man the new fleet of modern Martin 139 bombers that had been acquired for defense of the territory from the U.S. The remaining aircraft were then scrapped, with the exception of their engines, which served on in Fokker C-V reconnaissance biplanes. The Dutch P-6s had averaged a total airframe life of some 496 hours.

None other than Lt. Jimmy Doolittle poses with the extremely well-traveled Curtiss *Conqueror* powered *Hawk I* demonstrator, marked with the U.S. Department of Commerce Identification Number 9110 as of March 15, 1930. This aircraft was demonstrated throughout Europe, and later returned to the U.S. under unusual circumstances. (*Curtiss*)

The well traveled *Hawk I* demonstrator eventually returned to the U.S., where it was flown at the National Air Races by Jess Bristow in spectacular red, white, and blue *Esso* markings marked as NX-9110, in the experimental category. Note the very long exhaust pipe, probably used for producing sky writing smoke. (*Curtiss*)

An effort was made to sell more using a company demonstrator *Hawk I* with a civil registration NX-9110 (initially as merely Identified Aircraft -9110, with no prefix as early as March 13, 1930), some of this work again done by pilot James Doolittle, who left the Army in 1930. No more sales were recorded, however, of the *Conqueror* powered *Hawk*, in spite of an extensive demonstration tour. This tour of Europe got under way on April 10, 1930, when Jimmie Doolittle, Capt. James Cannon, and Lt. James Parker sailed for Greece. The mission, planned by Curtiss-Wright Export Corp., was to demonstrate four aircraft types never before flown in Europe: the *Hawk I* (NX-9110, changed to NR-9110 later, a P-6 water-cooled engine type), *Falcon* observation, *Fledgling* trainer, and civil *Robin* in the hope of promoting sales of Curtiss-Wright products. The first demonstration was held late in April in Athens before high offi-

The rather portly trio of P-6S *Cuban Hawks* were completed and ready for delivery at the end of January 1930, and the first one poses here for the camera. The upper wing surfaces and horizontal tail surfaces were painted chrome yellow. The *Wasp* powered version was chosen to achieve commonality with a number of Vought *Corsairs* also operated by Cuba at the time. (*Curtiss T-5364*)

The second of at least three P-6S aircraft delivered to the *Cuerpo de Aviacion Ejercito de Cuba* (CAEC), No.16 shares the line here with a similarly powered Vought O2U-1A *Corsair* at Campo Columbia, near Havana. (*Captain George G. Farinas*)

cials. The mission then flew through the Balkan states, including demonstrations in Yugoslavia and Bulgaria, with a side trip to Turkey, and north to Poland and other countries on the Baltic. After visits to Norway and Sweden the planes were flown across Germany to Switzerland, the last country to be visited. The return to the U.S. was in early August.

NX-9110,[58] quoted as MSN 17 (which is an unexplained number in the Curtiss MSN sequence), was later flown at the National Air Races by pilot Jess Bristow, wearing "Esso" titles and a spectacular red, white, and blue color scheme, but was later reported lost at sea some time after 1938. As of 1933 it was registered to the Curtiss-Wright Export Corp. However, the story of this well traveled aircraft is rather more extensive than hitherto recorded. According to noted Dutch aviation historians Herman Dekker and Gerard Casius, after the sales tour NR-9110 was stored at the Aviolanda plant, where it apparently served as a pattern aircraft for the license-built aircraft described elsewhere in this account. By September 1934 a Dutch private pilot wrote to the civil aviation authorities in Holland asking if the aircraft would be eligible for civil licensure in that nation, apparently with a view towards buying it. Curiously, in October the Dutch authorities replied that the *Hawk's* tail surface construction did not comply with Dutch structural strength requirements for civil aircraft, and the citizen ended up purchasing a Beech 17 *Staggerwing* instead. Apparently, shipping the aircraft back to the U.S. was viewed as costing more than it was worth to the Curtiss-Wright Export Corp., which by that time had rather a lot on their plate in other overseas adventures. Exactly how and when the aircraft returned to the U.S., which it obviously did, remains something of a mystery.

The general characteristics of the water-cooled export *Hawk I* model were: span, length, and height 31 feet, six inches, 22 feet, and nine feet, one inch. Wing area was 252 square feet, and wings were the tapered type, with Clark Y airfoil sections. Empty weight was 2,542 pounds, useful load 834 pounds, and gross weight 3,376 pounds. Wing loading was 13.4psf, and power loading 5.36 pounds per horse power.

The powerplant was the Curtiss V-1570 *Conqueror* of 630hp. Fuel capacity was 50 gallons normal, with an overload capacity of 100 gallons.

The highest serial known assigned to a Cuban P-6S was No.18, suspected of being a fourth, replacement aircraft. The emblem on the fuselage shows a shield with a bell on the upper right, and a stylized, descending "CAEC" logo at the lower left, separated by a bar sinister. This photo clearly shows the chrome yellow upper wing surfaces and horizontal tail surfaces, and the fact that the star in the Cuban national insignia of the day pointed aft. (*Captain George G. Farinas*)

Performance included a high speed of 187mph at sea level, and cruise and stall speeds of 144mph and 61mph. Climb to 10,000 feet took 5.7 minutes, and service and absolute ceilings were 22,000 feet and 23,500 feet, respectively. Full throttle endurance at sea level was 1 hour and 40 minutes.

Another export P-6 type was the so-called P-6S *Cuban Hawk*, of which three[59] went to that country in early 1930. This version was the only P-6 type powered by a Pratt & Whitney *Wasp* R-1340 engine, this developing 450hp. Span, length, and height were, respectively, 31 feet, six inches, 22 feet 10 inches, and eight feet, six inches. Wing area was 252 square feet. Gross weight was 2,910 pounds, and fuel capacity was a maximum of 100 gallons.

This lower powered machine had a substantially lower top speed of 157mph at sea level. Initial climb was 1,820pfm, and climb to 12,500 feet took 10 minutes. Endurance at cruise speed was 2.54 hours. Service ceiling was 21,800 feet.

Delivered in January 1930, the Cuban P-6S aircraft were assigned *Cuerpo de Aviación Ejercito de Cuba (CAEC)* serial numbers 16 to 18 (although serials 10 and 15 have also been reported). At least one survived in Cuban service until September 1, 1937, and one had been lost to a crash by July 1, 1930. The purchase price for the trio was $61,200, including two guns and two A-3 bomb racks each.

Finally, one source claims that Curtiss documents reflected an application for an export license for two P-6 export variants for Persia, but no confirming Curtiss documents have been located, and no evidence has surfaced from intelligence or other sources to confirm what must have been, at best, a frustrated and little known export.

Curtiss *Pursuit* U.S. Civil Identified Aicraft NO.471

This aircraft has been inserted into this narrative purely in the interests of resolving confusion that has resulted, over the years, from its sudden appearance on the U.S. civil register February 2, 1929, with what, at the time, was Department of Commerce Identified Aircraft Number 471.

In actuality, it was not a Curtiss-built "pursuit" at all. Registered to E. E. Terrell and B. Larsen of Oakland, California, their application listed the aircraft as a Curtiss *Pursuit* built in 1918 with a Curtiss OX-5 90hp engine, and described as a two-place, open-cockpit biplane. They had purchased the aircraft from a C. Sanders, also of Oakland, on July 31, 1928. Since they could not provide the Department of Commerce with a Manufacturers Serial Number for the aircraft one was assigned, which was T.L.100, an obvious combination of the first initials of their last names, with the arbitrary number 100.

The aircraft is known to have been overhauled as of January 1, 1929, but was cancelled by the Department of Commerce May 7, 1930, after fruitless attempts by the Department to determine exactly what form of "pursuit" aircraft this actually was.

It was almost certainly a modified Curtiss JN-4 *Jenny*, numerous examples of which abounded at the time.

Curtiss *Hawk 1* and *1-A* Demonstrator (Designs L-18-38 and L-18-39, the *Gulfhawk*)

Although strictly speaking not a fighter *per se*, the one-off aircraft built in 1929, which came to be known as the *Gulfhawk*, was arguably one of the most well known of the entire *Hawk* line, and is included in this narrative since it was very much a part of the lineage.

This aircraft, which initially gained the U.S. Department of Commerce Restricted License NR-636E listed as a *Hawk 1*, is something of a mystery aircraft, and no known Curtiss Manufacturers Serial Number in the conventional series represented thus far has emerged. It was listed in Department of Commerce registration applications as MSN 1, built in April 1929, and registered owner was given as Alford ("Al") J. Williams of 237 Cathedral Avenue, Garden City, NY.

Williams, of course, was flying for the Gulf Oil Co. between 1929 and 1936, and this aircraft was intended to be his mount to demonstrate the dependability of Gulf oil products in aviation applications. Initially it was fitted with a*Conqueror* engine, and had

Although initially fitted with a *Conqueror* engine, the famous *Gulfhawk* of Al Williams was rebuilt following a crash, and fitted with a Wright *Cyclone*, pictured here bearing simply Department of Commerce Identification Number -982V. It was at this point that the aircraft was first cited as a *Hawk 1-A*. (*Curtiss T-5995*)

After Al Williams formally gained title to the aircraft from Gulf, his sponsor, he arranged to have the *Gulfhawk* re-engined with a British Bristol *Jupiter* engine, and fitted with a huge prop spinner. The contours of the fuselage were also changed, and the registration changed to the Restricted category as NR-982V. *(A.C.16514 via Cradle of Aviation Museum)*

After yet another accident, the *Gulfhawk* was once again extensively rebuilt and reconfigured, and again fitted with a 710hp R-1820F-3 *Cyclone*, complete with a racy cowl. This is the configuration remembered by most air show spectators of the day. *(Hagedorn Collection)*

The one-of-a-kind XP-6D was a conversion of an earlier P-6A (A.C.29-260), fitted with a rather ungainly turbo-supercharger arrangement on top of the V-1570-23 engine. (*Curtiss*)

additional fuel capacity fitted in the fuselage, similar to those installed in the Navy's *Helldivers*, for extended range.

After an accident, in which it suffered considerable damage, it was returned to Curtiss and extensively rebuilt, so much so that the Department of Commerce issued a new Restricted License for the aircraft, NR-982V—but still listed as MSN 1, though now identified as a *Hawk 1-A*, fitted with a 575hp Wright *Cyclone*. Williams did not officially gain title to the aircraft (on paper) until August 1931, however, so it must be assumed that Gulf was the registered owner till that time. After transfer of ownership, a 575hp Bliss *Jupiter* engine was installed, which was a U.S. derivative of the British Bristol *Jupiter*. Following yet another serious accident, NR-982V was once again rebuilt, and this time mounted a 710hp R-1820F-3 *Cyclone*, by which time the aircraft had been repainted and the prefix marks removed, rendering it as Identified Aircraft -982V. The saddle tanks were removed, and the fuselage skinned with lightweight alloy. By 1936 the engine had been removed and installed in Williams' new Grumman *Gulfhawk II*, and the remains of the *Gulfhawk 1-A* were donated to an aeronautical trade school. These were retrieved in 1958 by Frank Tallman, who then installed a 600hp Pratt & Whitney *Wasp* in the airframe. The airframe is now reportedly in the collection of the U.S. Marine Corps Air-Land Museum at Quantico, VA.

Curtiss P-6D *Hawk*

Stated simply, the P-6D *Hawks* were 11 P-6 and six P-6A aircraft with an F-2E side type turbo supercharged V-1570-C *Conqueror* engine. Most sources agree 13 aircraft were converted to P-6D configuration.[60] The first aircraft, serial A.C.29-260, was flying as an XP-6D at Wright Field in the spring of 1931, and the remaining conversions were accomplished at Fairfield Air Depot (F.A.D.) between February and April 1932. The principal value perceived for the P-6D was to obtain operational experience in a service squadron with the turbo supercharged power plants that gave these pursuit craft such excellent high altitude capability. Thus, a dozen con-

A fine close-up showing the "alien" looking turbo-supercharger installation on one of the 17 P-6Ds. No P-6D was built as such, all being conversions of either P-6 or P-6A airframes. The single operating unit (the 37th Pursuit Squadron) reported no end of difficulties with the installation. (*Wright Field No.40999*)

Photos of P-6Ds in full service markings are rather rare, since there were only 17 configured as such. Unit number "71" was assigned to the 37th Pursuit Squadron at Langley Field, VA. (*via Peter M. Bowers*)

versions to P-6D of 1932 were assigned to the 37th Pursuit Squadron of the 8th Pursuit Group at Langley Field, Virginia. This squadron was immediately equipped with the P-6D after its formation in September 1933. One aircraft (A.C.29-363) was wrecked near Langley a month after squadron formation. Service of the type was not a success. In a June 1932 letter, there was an attempt to kill the conversion program by Major Hugh Knerr, Chief of the Field Service Section, by citing difficulties with the V-1570 turbo supercharger installation. There were also difficulties with the plane's fuel system.

In spite of these difficulties, a notable flight was made in early 1932, however, by a P-6D piloted by Army Capt. Reuben Moffat from Wright Field, Dayton, Ohio, to Washington, DC, in one hour and 26 minutes, cruising at 25,000 feet and averaging 266mph.

The P-6D was heavier than the other *Hawks*, and thus there were some rather severe restrictions imposed so as not to overburden the structure. The XP-6D was later revised to a P-6A with no turbo, and eventually crashed in August 1936.

The XP-6D had a span of 31 feet, six inches, and a length of 23 feet, seven inches. Gross weight was 3,212 pounds, and maximum speed 183mph. The P-6Ds had the same dimensions, but mounted a three blade propeller in place of the two blade model of the XP-6D.

As with the X-model, the P-6D powerplant was the V-1570-23 *Conqueror* of 600hp, with a General Electric F-2 turbo supercharger. Fuel capacity was normally 50 gallons, with overload capacity of 100 gallons. Gross weight was 3,483 pounds, giving a wing loading of 13.82psf.

High speeds were 172mph at sea level, 190mph at 10,000 feet, and 197mph at 15,000 feet. Landing speed was 63mph. Sea level climb rate was 1,720fpm, and it took 8.7 minutes to attain a height of 15,000 feet. Service ceiling was a healthy 32,000 feet.

The XP-6D remained in airworthy condition with the Air Corps as late as January 1934.

Curtiss YP-11, YP-20 *Hawk*

Three *Hawk* types were ordered in 1929 with basic P-1C airframes, but slated to use the new 600hp Curtiss R-1640 *Chieftain* hexagon engine as Curtiss YP-11 pursuits. The *Chieftain* engine turned out to be a failure, so two of the three airframes (A.C.29-367 and -368) were finished as P-6 *Conqueror* powered *Hawks*, and delivered in October and November 1930. The third airframe (A.C.29-374) became the YP-20, at the expense of Curtiss, with a nine cylinder aircooled, single row radial Wright *Cyclone* SR-1820E-9 enclosed in a ring cowl, also company owned. It was delivered as such October 17, 1930. This single plane had flight controls revised from a P-6, tail changes, a three strut main landing gear fitted out with wheel pants, and a panted steerable tail wheel. On December 4, 1930, the YP-20, piloted by Harvey Ogden, flew the 400 miles from Wright field, Dayton, Ohio, to Washington, DC, in two hours and two minutes to provide a demonstration there for high officials.

The YP-20 was rated by tests about equal to a Boeing P-12 type in performance, but was considered less maneuverable, and to have poorer overall visibility. In addition, the Wright *Cyclone* engine installation was judged to not work out well. As a result the

Laid down originally as one of three YP-11s with *Chieftain* engines that were not proceeded with, one of these (A.C.29-374) became the handsome YP-20 instead. Incorporating nearly all of the classic features of a pulp fiction cover, especially noteworthy is the special brace just aft of the cowling ring to support the barrel of a .50 caliber gun, which was placed rather far forward. (*Curtiss*)

The spats worn by the single YP-20 were certainly amongst the largest made for any Curtiss fighter, but were a maintenance headache on dirt fields, as most were at the time. The YP-20 was also one of the first Curtiss fighters to have a streamlined tail wheel. Note that the guns over the cowling in this view are .30 caliber weapons, and the brace shown in the other photo is not evident here. Seldom noted, this aircraft was converted to a standard P-6E by Curtiss November 3, 1931, and was also briefly designated XP-6E twice. (*Curtiss*)

YP-20 was rejected, and the airframe used to define an XP-6E *Hawk* with a *Conquero*r engine.

Characteristics of the YP-20 *Hawk* follow: span, length, and height were 31 feet, six inches, 23 feet, nine inches, and nine feet, two inches. The basic Hawk wings of 252 square feet total area were incorporated. The Wright R-1820-9 engine was rated at 575hp. Empty weight was 2,477 pounds, useful load totaled 756 pounds (comprised of a 180 pound pilot, 300 pounds of normal fuel, 60 pounds of oil, 36 pounds of equipment, and 180 pounds of two gun armament), and normal gross weight was 3,233 pounds. Wing loading was thus 12.85psf, power loading 5.62 pounds per horse power, and the useful load to gross weight ratio was 0.234. Normal internal fuel capacity was 50 gallons; overload fuel capacity 103 gallons.

The YP-20 (the Y prefix was an Air Corps symbol denoting service test status) had a maximum speed of 187mph at sea level, and of 184mph at 5,000 feet, while cruising and landing speeds were 149mph and 61mph, respectively. Climb capability was 2,400 feet in the first minute and 5,000 feet in 2.3 minutes. Endurance came to 1.10 hours at maximum speed. Service and absolute ceilings were 26,700 feet and 27,800 feet, respectively.

Continuing the convoluted and incestuous between-the-wars practice of converting the few precious airframes for further development, the YP-20 was returned to Curtiss on Contract AC-3787 for reworking yet again into a high speed pursuit ship to be designated XP-22. However, the decision was made to conduct further tests with an engine having 12:5 to 1 indicator gearing. This change was therefore made by Curtiss, and the aircraft returned to the Engineering Division January 13, 1931, and apparently remained as the YP-20, since the actual XP-22 (see next) was a conversion of a P-6A.

Curtiss XP-22, Y1P-22, and P-6C *Hawk*

The XP-22 was a major redesign and a redesignation of P-6A A.C.29-262, but still made use of the Prestone cooled 600hp V-1570-C *Conqueror* engine. A note in Louis Kessler's Curtiss bill-

The single XP-22 was a redesign of P-6A A.C.29-262, and is pictured here as of April 17, 1931, with a most unusual cowl ring arrangement, with the radiator lodged in the lower section of the cowl. The guns were moved to the fuselage sides. Curtiss performed this transformation essentially at its own expense, charging the Army $1.00. It remained as the XP-22 a scant five months, being converted back to P-6A configuration September 28th. (*Curtiss T-6599*)

By May 8, 1931, the single XP-22 had been reconfigured once again, eliminating the odd cowl, and apparently deepening the radiator under the chin. Exactly where the guns were to have been ported in the fuselage sides is unclear. (*Curtiss T-6631*)

ing book says: "*US Army, May 3, 1931, XP-22, from P-6, $1.00*" (a cheap price to the Army!). A major portion of the test work on this aircraft concerned radiator configuration. Changes from a P-6A included use of a three bladed propeller, a single strut landing gear with wheel pants, and relocation of the two machine guns alongside the fuselage. One of the interesting test configurations was use of a ring cowl around the nose just behind the propeller, with a Prestone radiator lodged in the lower section of the cowl. Another was use of a radiator between and just ahead of the single landing gear struts under the fuselage. The XP-22 was approaching the configuration of the later P-6E *Hawk*, and had been completed as such by June 18, 1931. The A.C.29-262 airframe was later again revised back to the P-6A standard configuration, the cause of much confusion amongst Curtiss historians.

Curtiss was in a bad way in 1931 due to the deepening worldwide depression, and needed business. Boeing, with their P-12, had done much better in pursuit plane orders. The XP-22 was a very fast pursuit for the time, with a slightly over 200mph maximum speed, and to keep Curtiss in the pursuit aircraft business, the Army placed an order for 46 new aircraft in July 1931. An XP-6E prototype was made by combining YP-20 and XP-22 features. The YP-20 airframe was revised by incorporating the XP-22 *Conqueror* engine installation and single strut landing gear on the YP-20. At first this combination was labeled as type Y1P-22, but for procurement purposes was finally ordered as type P-6E. Another interim designation had been P-6C, and a project to acquire 46 of these was cancelled in favor of the P-6E. The XP-6E was serial A.C.29-374, once the YP-20, and later and finally the XP-6F. With the economics of the day it was often necessary to use the same airframe for many test purposes.

Curtiss P-6E (L-18-36) *Hawk*

To maintain two major sources for pursuit aircraft and assure competitive bidding, as well as continued development of the *Conqueror* engine as the only high powered liquid cooled engine available, the Army, on July 8, 1931, gave Curtiss a production contract for 46 P-6E aircraft. These incorporated the YP-20's fuselage, wings, and tail surfaces, and the XP-22's engine mount and landing gear.

According to the Curtiss billing book records, the Army order was broken out as follows: two were listed as "remodeled ships," the first as a P-6A delivered on September 28, 1931—no doubt the XP-22 redone to P-6A configuration—and the second as a P-6E

Continuing the confusing saga of the P-6 series, one of the first two aircraft to become P-6Es was none other than the former XP-20, handed over to the Army on November 2, 1931, as the solitary XP-6E. This image was taken two days later and, to all appearances, basically looks like a standard P-6E. (*Curtiss W-6947*)

Certainly one of the cleanest pursuit designs produced anywhere to that time, the XP-6E (A.C. 29-374) was also one of the first U.S. fighters to use a three-bladed prop routinely. (*Curtiss W-6949*)

delivered on November 2, 1931, this being the XP-20 reworked into XP-6E form. The charge to the Army for these aircraft was $1.00 for both on Contract 101/14400! On December 1, 1931, Curtiss started production delivery of the P-6E, with the first two priced at $12,307.85 each. Then, on January 8, 1932, the price rose to $12,362.68 each for aircraft delivered through P-6E #40, with this article delivered on February 25, 1932. Aircraft number 42 through 45 went for the same price, with the last delivered March 25, 1932. What happened with #41 is not clear. Aircraft #46 was not to be a P-6E, but was to be developed as the single XP-23. This mix of remodeled aircraft and conversions is why the total of aircraft on Order W535-ac-4434 came to only 45 aircraft (not 46), Curtiss MSNs 11567 to 11611,[61] and Army A.C.32-233 to 32-277. The final and 46th aircraft was instead converted into the XP-23 (q.v.) on Engineering Order W-3511, and acquired on Contract AC-4400 for $12,279.36 on April 16, 1932.

Of the total production run, no less than 33 aircraft were delivered to the 17th and 94th Pursuit Squadrons of the 1st Pursuit Group, stationed at Selfridge Field, Michigan, with the remainder to the 33rd and 37th Pursuit Squadrons at Langley Field, Virginia. Attrition was very high; fully 10 aircraft were wrecked in the first year of delivery (1932), and half that number bit the dust in the following year. Thus, one third of the P-6Es were lost in the first two years, and five more were gone in 1934.

The P-6E had the same wooden wing spar and rib construction with fabric covering as the P-6/P-6A. Ailerons—metal framed—were on the upper wing only. The fuselage was made up of chrome molybdenum steel tubing with welded joints, built in three sections riveted together just aft of the pilot's cockpit, and aft near the tail wheel with hollow steel rivets. The front section was tubular braced, with the three last bays wire braced. The cowl stiffeners and stringers were of dural. All cowling was 51S aluminum alloy. The side and belly of the fuselage was fabric covered from pilot's cockpit to the tail. There was baggage access in the upper fuselage deck aft of the cockpit. The main fuel tank of 50 gallons capacity was located aft of the firewall, and an auxiliary tank of 50 gallons capacity could be attached externally to the fuselage underside. There was a window in the cockpit floor to read the auxiliary tank fuel gage. The tail group structure was of steel tubing augmented by dural ribs, a leading edge member, and auxiliary spars. Covering was fabric.

An almost pastoral scene at a between-the-war Air Corps installation, these two service P-6Es bear the classic blue fuselage/yellow wings and control surfaces color scheme of the day. The operating unit is unknown, and there is no evidence of unit insignia. (*Pima Air and Space Museum 79-43-1*)

Bearing the insignia of the 33rd Pursuit Squadron, this P-6E seems to be in other than the classic blue/yellow color scheme of the 1930s. In fact, it is a trick of the film used. Note the masts for the radio antenna on the vertical fine and either outer upper wing. (*Pima Air and Space Museum 99.337-102*)

Unusual in having no unit insignia, No.41 shows the belly auxiliary fuel tank to good advantage. This was almost always installed in service. This winter image shows an aircraft with some hours on the airframe, probably late in her service life. (*Dean Collection*)

Tail surfaces were braced by stainless steel streamlined wires above, and flexible cable assemblies below the stabilizer. The stabilizer was adjustable by use of a cockpit hand crank.

The landing gear was a cantilever type with oleo shock absorbers located in the fuselage. Tread was 7 feet, one inch, and tire size was 8.5 x 10. Fairings were of dural.

Wing span was 31 feet, six inches, with length and height 23 feet, two inches and eight feet, 10 inches. Wing area was 261.7 square feet. (It should be noted this figure is greater than the previous *Hawk* wing figure, and it is believed in this case the area across the fuselage on the lower wing is being counted as opposed to earlier.) Wing airfoils were Clark Y. Upper wing and lower wing dihedral was 0 degrees and 1.5 degrees, respectively. Stagger was 30.5 inches, gap 32.5 inches, and incidence was -2 degrees for both wings. Other areas were: Stabilizer 17.2 square feet, elevators 12.6 square feet, vertical fin 5.1 square feet, and rudder 9.4 square feet.

The P-6E powerplant was a Curtiss V-1570-C 12 cylinder "V" type rated at 700hp at 2,400rpm, and Prestone cooled with a system of eight gallons capacity, with radiator size length nine and 1/4 inches, width 20 inches, and depth nine inches, with a frontal area of 1.29 square feet and empty weight of 44 pounds. The flow rate was 110 gallons per minute. There was no temperature adjustment. The propeller was three bladed and ground adjustable of seven feet, nine inches diameter, with pitch 18 degrees at the 42 inch radius station.

The following data is for Army serial number A.C.32-233, the first production example. In an Army report of April 19, 1932, weights were listed as: empty weight 2,743 pounds, useful load of 693 pounds (consisting of a 200 pound pilot, 300 pounds of fuel, 30 pounds of oil, 21 pounds of equipment, and 142 pounds of armament), adding up to a gross weight of 3,436 pounds. The wing loading was thus 13.13psf, the power loading 5.72 pounds per horse power, and a useful load to gross weight ratio of 0.20—not very good.

Most unusual in bearing no evidence of national or unit insignia, and being totally camouflaged, this P-6E participated in the 1935 war games with the 1st Pursuit Group at Selfridge Field, MI. It was probably no longer a first-line aircraft by this time. (*Fred Dickey, Jr. via Museum of Flight*)

The end of the line for most surviving P-6Es was as Class 26 ground instructional air frames at Air Corps technical schools, like No.5 shown here. Note the empennage components numbered to aid students in identifying parts. (*Gordon S. Williams AC 8030 via Museum of Flight*)

The report cited level flight speeds of 197.8mph at 2,400rpm at sea level, 191.5mph at 2,370rpm at 5,000 feet, 188mph at 2,320rpm at 10,000 feet, 180.5mph at 2,255rpm at 15,000 feet, 147mph at 2,160rpm at 20,000 feet, and 140mph at 2,010rpm at 23,900 feet. Climb figures were 2,460fpm at sea level, 1,940fpm at 5,000 feet, 1460fpm at 10,000 feet, 970fpm at 15,000 feet, 480fpm at 20,000 feet, and by definition, 100fpm at 23,900 feet. Climb times were 2.3 minutes to 5,000 feet, 5.2 minutes to 10,000 feet, 9.4 minutes to 15,000 feet, 16.5 minutes to 20,000 feet, and 32.6 minutes to 23,900 feet. Landing speed was 61mph. Service and absolute ceilings were 24,700 feet and 25,800 feet. The P-6Es used type 13299 propellers

The P-6E armament consisted of two fixed synchronized .30 caliber Colt Browning machine guns firing through troughs on the fuselage sides below the engine exhaust stack line with 600 rounds per gun. There were wing racks available for 244 pounds of bombs. The P-6E was slightly faster and more powerful than the contemporary Boeing P-12 type and could dive away from that aircraft, but was several hundred pounds heavier and less maneuverable. The tables were turned later in their career when Langley Field pilots would accept dogfights with local Navy pilots in Grumman F3F series fighters. The F3Fs were more powerful and faster, and could out-dive the P-6Es, but the Curtiss machines had the maneuverability edge.

As the 1930s wore on the P-6Es became weary, and were also gaining weight, which moved the longitudinal center of gravity aft, reducing stability, and structural strengthening became necessary. In 1934 a P-6E lost its wings in a dive, and the type was grounded until new wing fittings could be installed. By 1937, with the new monoplanes coming into service, the P-6Es remaining on strength were not considered worth the maintenance required for weary aircraft. By 1939 they were all turned over to civilian aviation training schools around the country as non-flying mechanics trainers. At least one P-6E has been saved and refurbished, and resides in the U.S. Air Force Museum in a tribute to a quite handsome biplane pursuit aircraft.

Curtiss-WRIGHT C-14-R *Osprey*

While the parent company in Buffalo was laboring to produce the continuing series of classic *Hawk* military, naval, and export single-seat fighter series, the Curtiss-Wright Corporation had acquired the Wichita based Travel Air Co., moved it to St. Louis, and established it as the Curtiss-Wright St. Louis Airplane Division.

First foreign customer for the general purpose Curtiss-Wright C-14-R *Osprey*, marketed as a two-place fighter, was the Government of Panama, which acquired either two or four, depending on sources. Capable of bearing one synchronized and one rear gun, this one had passed to the early Panama civil operator *Transportes Aéreos Gelebert* (*TAG*), and been disarmed by the time this photo was taken. (*Germinal Sarasqueta*)

Bearing the national roundel of Ecuador on the vertical tail surfaces, this Curtiss-Wright C-14-R *Osprey* (R-3), with crew aboard, shows the diminutive size of this light combat aircraft. With a 420hp engine, it was remarkably nimble. The headrest spine aft of the rear cockpit was removable to mount a flexible gun. (*via Francis H. Dean*)

The talent of this Golden Age manufacturer had been recognized by Curtiss, and the fact that they had produced a lengthy series of general aviation and light air transport types second only in numbers to Waco, even into the early Depression years, had not been missed.

On August 13, 1931, the St. Louis firm gained a coveted Approved Type Certificate, number 442, for what was described as the Curtiss-Wright (Travel Air) A-14-D *Sportsman*. Unfortunately, by this date, the very restricted market for high speed, three-seat biplanes for the general aviation market had all but evaporated, even though an improved version, the B-14-B *Speedwing*, gained ATC#485 on June 1, 1932. Altogether only nine A-14-Ds, two B-14-Bs, and one D-14-B were built, and of these, only six were registered in the U.S. to private or corporate owners, one other being sold to the Department of Commerce directly.

The engineers and managers in St. Louis were encouraged by the parent organization to develop the series for export as light military aircraft, as such sales were obviously one of the few remaining avenues towards survival.

The result was the Curtiss-Wright C-14-R *Osprey* which, for the purposes of this account, qualifies for inclusion, as the sales literature specifically identified it as a "*...two-place fighter, observation, attack and light bombing plane*."

The genius of this decision became obvious almost immediately. By November 1933, a scant 18 months after the B-14-B had gained its ATC, Curtiss-Wright (St. Louis) had built and exported to four nations not fewer than 33 of these very capable aircraft.

The aircraft was offered in any of five versions, differing only in engine selection. In sales literature, these were defined as the D-14-R, C-14-D-6 (with a Wright R-760ET of 235hp), C-14-D-7 (with 285hp R-760E-1), C-14-B-9 (with a 330hp R-975E), or the C-14-R, with a Wright 420hp R-975E.

The *Osprey* was not a large aircraft, and with a 420hp engine, was a fairly capable performer. Dimensions included wing spans of 31 feet (upper), 27 feet, nine inches (lower), length 23 feet, two inches, and height nine feet, six inches. The majority of those built featured the Wright J-6 series (R-975-E) nine cylinder, 420hp engine rated at 2,150rpm.

One of two standard C-14-R *Ospreys* acquired by Venezuela, these were very colorfully marked, with dark green fuselage and vertical fin, yellow wings and horizontal tail surfaces, and Venezuelan national insignia in six positions, with appropriate rudder stripes. Note the A-3 bomb racks under the starboard wing, and the forward-firing synchronized gun protruding from the cowling. (*Curtiss-Wright*)

By far the most important customer for the C-14-R *Osprey* was Bolivia, which was locked in the bitter Chaco War with Paraguay. She acquired no less than 20, many of which saw active combat—including air-to-air action as two-place fighters. (*Curtiss-Wright*)

The aircraft could operate on 80 octane fuel, and consumed 36 gallons per hour at best setting, and 20 gallons per hour at 85% maximum throttle. Empty, it weighed 2,081 pounds with both guns and two A-3 bomb racks installed, and had a useful load of 1,155 pounds, consisting of 516 pounds of fuel, 45 pounds of oil, two crew calculated at 340 pounds, 126 pounds of armament, 72 pounds of ammunition (500 rounds per gun), a 40-pound allowance for a radio (if installed), and 16 pounds for a camera, if installed. This resulted in a gross weight of 3,486 pounds.

Performance at gross weight, ironically, was not too bad, compared to single-seat fighters of the same vintage. High speed was 170mph, while it could cruise at 1,750rpm at 145mph, with a stall speed of 60mph. Rate of climb at sea level was 1,510fpm, and range at full throttle was 385 miles. Cruise range was a decent 580 miles. The service ceiling was 18,800 feet, with an absolute ceiling of 20,500 feet, and it could climb, fully loaded, to 10,900 feet in 10 minutes. The aircraft could also be ordered as a twin-float seaplane with Edo P-3277 floats, although so far as can be determined none were operated or ordered as such.

The first customer for an armed version was rather unusual. The Government of Panama had decided to create a small air arm for internal policing, mail, and communications, and at the gentle prodding of the Curtiss-Wright Export Corporation, ordered two examples of what were described as Travel Air (Curtiss-Wright) C-14-D *Speedwing Sportsmen 240s*.[62] Built in September 1931, these were probably MSNs C14D-2004 and 2005, and in Panamanian service were numbered "1" and "2," and christened *El Constitucion* and *Republica*. Capable of bearing armament, including one synchronized, forward-firing, and one free gun in the rear pit of .30 calibers, they also had two A-3 bomb racks. For all intents and purposes, these two aircraft served as the prototypes for all of the C-14-Rs that followed. The experiment in organizing and running this small service was not successful and was never properly funded, and on March 9, 1933, the Government leased the two aircraft to Eustacio Chichaco, who formed the *Empresa Chichaco-Estrada* for use in passenger and mail services in the Republic, one of the very first such enterprises in Panama. This apparently did not prosper, and one of the aircraft was apparently later exported to neighboring Costa Rica, the other having crashed.

One very similar *Speedwing Sportsman*, complete with two guns and two A-3 bomb racks, was also exported to Argentina in 1931, at a cost of $4,025, but the end user has remained a mystery. It is possible it may have been a demonstrator.

Ecuador ordered the first genuine C-14-Rs, and these two (C14R-2014 and 2015) were delivered August 15, 1932, at a cost of $15,500 each, marked as R-3 and R-4. These aircraft were painted white overall, with the exception of the three-color Ecuadorian national roundel, which was carried in all four wing positions and, unusually, on either side of the vertical fin and rudder. One of these suffered damage the day it was delivered and tested, and although repaired, was damaged again September 4, 1934. The other survived as late as August 5, 1939, when it too succumbed to a crash.

The next customer was Venezuela, which ordered two standard C-14-R *Ospreys* for $37,552.50 in 1932, and one additional, "stretched" version, known as the *Special Osprey*. This latter aircraft was C14R-2012, and the two standard aircraft were probably C14R-2013 and 2016. These were ready for shipment to Venezuela September 6, 1932, not far behind those for Ecuador. The Venezuelan aircraft were very striking in their overall olive drab paint scheme, with three-color rudders and Venezuelan national insignia in four wing positions, and on either side of the fuselage. They wore simple in-series serial numbers "1" to "3." One was lost at Maracay on October 4, 1932, immediately following delivery, with the loss of both crew members, and another was lost November 15, 1938. The *Special Osprey* was apparently flown exclusively by the Assistant Director of the *Escuela de Aviación Militar* at Maracay as of April 1937. Aside from being noticeably longer than the standard C-14-R, no other differences are known.

Colombia, embroiled in a territorial dispute with neighboring Peru over the Leticia region, was enticed into acquiring at least three C-14-R *Ospreys* as part of a package deal with the Curtiss-Wright Export Corp. These had arrived by December 1932, and received *Aviación Militar* serials 121, 122, and 123. They are believed to have been MSNs C14R 2017 to 2019. By February 1933 the U.S. Legation in Bogot· was reporting that the Colombians were pleased with the versatility of the C14Rs, and intended to order 10 more, but this apparently was shelved as the crisis with Peru ebbed. Meanwhile, one of the aircraft crashed at Girardot on February 8, 1933, killing pilot *Tte.* Guillermo Zarnosa, who was stunting the aircraft at low altitude. Another was lost the same day when *Mayor* Benjamin Mendez crashed into tall trees in fog flying from Caucay·. Since the Order of Battle for May 17, 1933, reflected three still on hand, either another aircraft was acquired, or the Mendez accident was repairable. One of the Colombian C-14-Rs survived as late as July 3, 1939, although it was being overhauled by that time. The Colombian order was valued at $52,958.04, and included two guns and bomb racks.

By far the major employer of the C-14-R was the *Cuerpo de Aviación* of Bolivia, which acquired not less than 20 examples between May 1933 and November 1934, and which were, numeri-

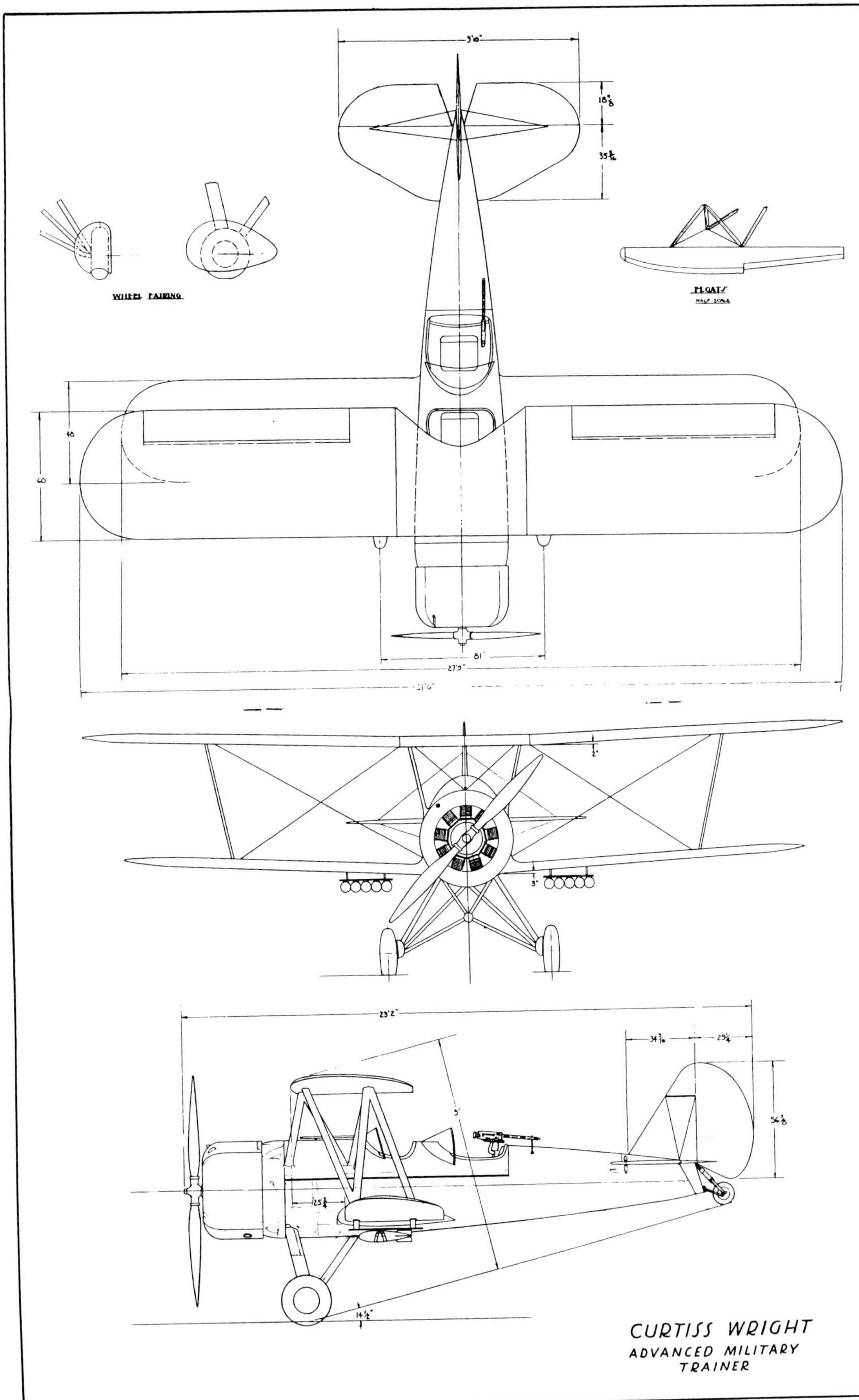

The C-14-R *Osprey* could be fitted with floats, wheel pants (so far as can be determined, never installed in military service), and up to 10 light bombs and two .30 caliber weapons. For the money, it was a very effective performer. (*Curtiss-Wright*)

cally, the most significant aircraft in the Bolivian arsenal during the Chaco War with neighboring Paraguay. Unlike the vast majority of fighter types produced by Curtiss and Curtiss-Wright during the inter-war years, these aircraft actually saw extensive combat service, including numerous engagements as two-seat fighters and interceptors.[63] The Bolivian aircraft received the serials 11, 13, 20, 22, 25, 30, 39, 45, 50, 60, 62, 64, 68, 78, 87, 91, 93, and 95, and two that were thrown into service and lost before they could have serials painted on. These apparently random numbers were issued as a form of disinformation, for the benefit of Paraguayan intelligence, to give the impression that there were more of the aircraft in service than were actually on hand. Bolivian C-14-Rs continued on the Bolivian Order of Battle in dwindling numbers, incredibly, as late as January 1955. At least six were lost in action or associated accidents in the combat zone of the Chaco. The Bolivian aircraft were acquired in increments of 12 (late 1932, for $222,000), four (1933, for $$59,944.97), and four more after February 1934.

The final customer for the C-14-R was tiny El Salvador, which bought three in late August 1933 (MSNs C14R-2033 to C14R-2035), gaining Salvadorian serials 19 to 21. Two of these survived in service by August 1940, and one as late as September 1942, the last report. This order was valued at $44,236.32, and included guns and bomb racks.

The final aircraft in the series appears to have been the solitary D-14-B (MSN D14B-2038) which, with a Wright R-975E engine, was tested at Robertson, MO, on April 7, 1936, against the U.S. Army Air Corps advanced training plane standard. Oddly, no U.S. civil registration is noted for this aircraft, nor its ultimate fate.

The perplexing "Curtiss-Wright Airplane Model Designations" listing, prepared in September 1945—cited elsewhere in this volume and presented in its entirety as an Annex, unabridged—also listed an intriguing aircraft identified as the Curtiss-Wright CW-17R *Osprey Pursuit*. Listed as powered by a 420hp Wright *Whirlwind* engine in 1932, it was listed as "metal," suggesting that it may have dispensed with some of the fabric covering of the C-14-R, but the list did not identify any as being built. It remains yet one more enigma of the St. Louis factory.

Curtiss Navy Design #115, Two-Place Fighter

In April 1932 Curtiss was studying a two-place fighter design for the Navy to be fitted with a Curtiss SGV-1800 engine.

It was described as a single-bay biplane, with a continuous upper wing with lower panels attached to fuselage stubs of only 12 square feet, with two metal frize type ailerons. The wing was to have had dural interior construction with cloth covering, and the lower wing was to accommodate Mk.31 bomb racks capable of carrying one 116 pound bomb each. The aircraft would have had standard Navy flotation gear and hoisting sling fittings with a NACA 2412 wing section.

The fuselage was to have been an all-metal monocoque construction with two cockpits, built in two sections, with built in gun mounts and arresting gear fittings

Curtiss, in the limited documentation available on this design, invariably compared it with the Army P-6E and O-39, with a tail group to have apparently been similar to the XF9C-1.

It apparently proceeded no further than a detail preliminary weight estimate dated April 14, 1932.

Curtiss XP-6F, XP-6G, and XP-6H *Hawk*

In another Army effort to explore the serviceability of the turbo supercharged inline engine, and further to assess the effect of a closed cabin installation on pilots, as well as protect them from the extreme cold of high altitudes, one P-6E (A.C.29-374, previously the YP-20 and the XP-6E) was returned again to Curtiss for the turbo supercharger and closed cabin installation. On March 17, 1933, the "new" plane appeared as an XP-6F.

The new version of the *Conqueror* engine was the 600hp V-1570-F with a General Electric F-2E turbo supercharger system mounted alongside. The cooling radiator was completely modified with less frontal area, but more cooling surface. The wheel pants

The Air Corps certainly got its money's worth from the P-6 series in terms of experimentation into ways to improve pursuit aircraft. This is the single XP-6F (A.C.29-374 which, yes, was also previously designated YP-20 and XP-6E), fitted with yet another turbo-supercharger installation and a canopy as of March 20, 1933—the first for a USAAC pursuit. (*Curtiss W-8041*)

The aircraft designated XP-6G was a standard P-6E (A.C.32-254), temporarily refitted with a V-1570-51 *Conqueror*. Aside from this and slight armament changes, it was difficult to distinguish from a P-6E. (*via Thorell Collin*)

Yet another conversion of a standard P-6E resulted in the XP-6H, A.C.32-233. This was an armament installation experiment, involving the installation of two .30 caliber guns in both the upper and lower wings for a total of six, including the normal synchronized pair. It was the most heavily armed Air Corps pursuit for some time to come. (*Dean Collection*)

were now open-sided to assure a more practical means of cleaning out dirt. A very basic cockpit canopy using rather simple single degree of curvature transparency panels was fitted.

Some XP-6F tests were accomplished in mid-1933, yielding the report that there was some longitudinal instability, but the aircraft was quite maneuverable. The canopy protected the pilot well in high altitude flying, but made the cockpit hot in warm weather down low because of inadequate ventilation. Tests were run only up to 18,000 feet before the work was discontinued due to persistent powerplant overheating. There was some thought to correct this problem, but the work was never carried through.

Wingspan was 31 feet, six inches, and length 23 feet, two inches, with height eight feet, 10 inches. The airframe was like the standard P-6E in terms of construction dimensions and areas.

The powerplant was a turbo supercharged V-1570-F *Conqueror* rated 600hp at 2400rpm at 6.25:1 compression ratio up to 15,000 feet and 674hp maximum at sea level. Gross weight was 3,842 pounds, about 400 pounds over a standard P-6E; wing loading was 14.7psf, and power loading 5.7 pounds per horse power.

The XP-6F's high speed was 194mph at sea level, 212mph at 10,000 feet, and 225mph at 15,000 feet. Climb at sea level was 1,400fpm, and climb times were 6.1 minutes to 10,000 feet and 10.1 minutes to 18,000 feet. The service ceiling was never determined. The aircraft utilized type S32B997 prop blades.

The aircraft was surveyed in October 1937 as an XP-6F.

The XP-6G was a standard P-6E (A.C.32-254) with a temporary refit of a V-1570-F (-51) *Conqueror* engine of 600hp. Gross weight was 3,450 pounds, and high speed 191.9mph. Identified as Curtiss Design L-18-36, the aircraft was delivered September 5, 1932, but the Flight Test Report was dated August 30, 1932. The most important change was the engine installation and a 16 inch core radiator, and the extension of the .50 caliber gun shell ejection

Detail view of the starboard (right) lower wing gun installation on the solitary XP-6H as of May 21, 1933. It had provision for 450 rounds. (*Wright Field 46740*)

chute to discharge under the wing by October 4, 1932. After tests the aircraft was assigned to Selfridge Field for further, extensive tests, and remained airworthy as late as January 2, 1934.

The XP-6H was a P-6E conversion (A.C.32-233) approved September 1932, and delivered on April 20, 1933, to Wright Field. The conversion price was $13,250. Wings were fitted incorporating machine gun installations additional to those already in the fuselage. Four new .30 caliber unsynchronized wing guns were installed, two in the upper wing each with 600 rounds per gun, and one in each lower wing with 450 rounds per gun.

It was soon found that this six gun installation was not practical in a machine of the P-6E type, and the project was discontinued. It is noteworthy that the XP-6H, probably with the six-gun armament, was also used to test the newly developed N-1 gun sight at Langley Field—itself a development of the German *Optische Anstalt Oigee* "*Eni*" gun sight, which had been acquired by Wright Field in February 1932 via the U.S. Military Attaché in Berlin. A second "*Eni*" unit was installed in a standard P-6E and tested at Selfridge Field, where it was reported as superior to the standard bar type sight then in standard use in the Air Corps. This basic sight evolved into the N-2 and N-2A sights.

The engine was aV-1570-C (-51) *Conqueror* model rated at 600hp. Dimensions were identical to the P-6E.

Gross weight was 3,850 pounds. High speed at sea level was 190mph with six guns and 191mph with four. Climb rate at sea level was 2,000fpm, and climb in 10 minutes achieved an altitude of 13,400 feet. Range at 85 percent of full throttle at sea level was 256 miles. Service and absolute ceilings were 22,800 feet and 24,000 feet, respectively.

At Langley Field, by January 1934 the XP-6H later went to Selfridge Field, and then March Field for further tests. The XP-6H ended up at a civilian technical training school in California still as an XP-6H, and survived until at least July 1939.

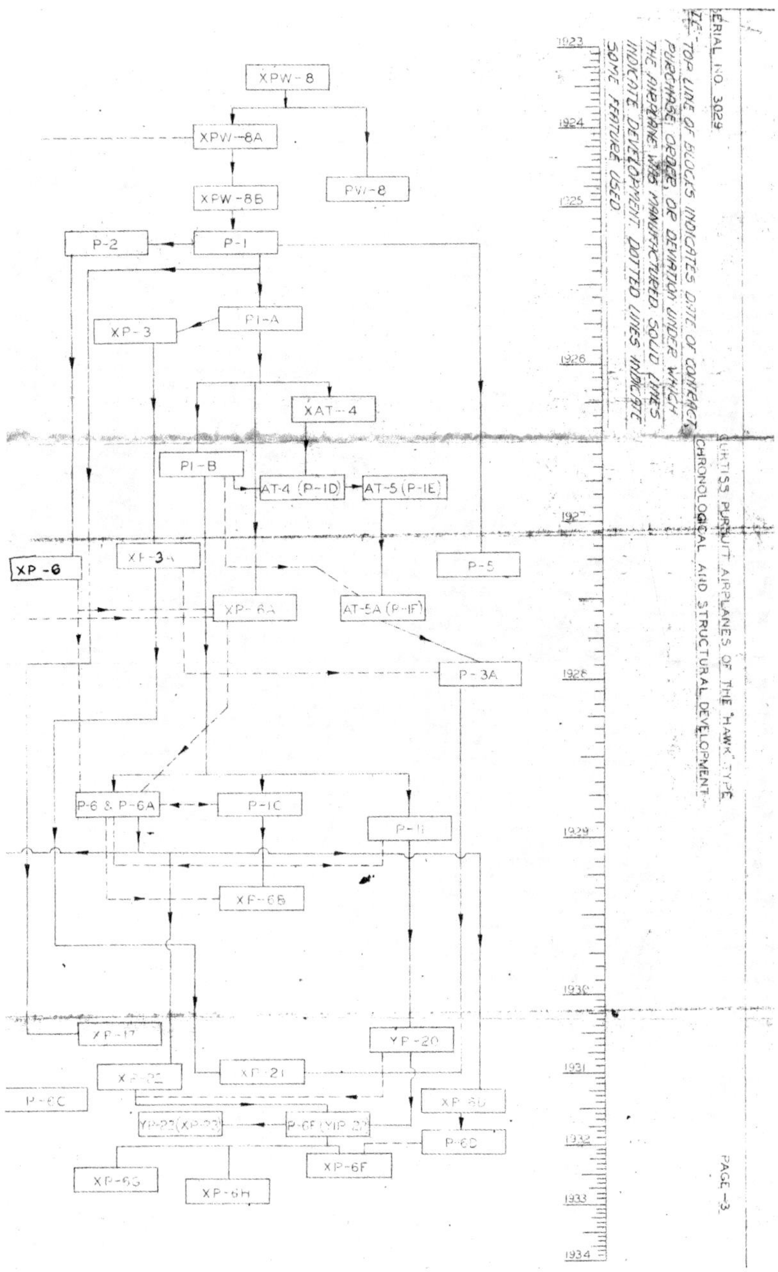

An Army prepared chart showing the evolution of the Curtiss family of fighters from the XPW-8 through the XP-6H. (*USAAC*)

Curtiss XP-23/YP-23 *Hawk*

The last aircraft on the 46 plane order W535-ac-4434, which had included the 45 P-6Es from the Army to Curtiss, was quite different from the others. This was the XP-23,[64] destined to be the final biplane pursuit type ever procured by the U.S. Army. Delivered on April 16, 1932, it is listed in company records priced at $12,279.36, and was MSN 11614 (A.C.32-278), assigned after the last P-6E, with the single XS3C-1 and YO-40 in between. This figure was, as usual, without equipment furnished by the government, known as GFE. The Curtiss XP-23 was designed in response to a Wright Field Board recommendation for a pursuit plane with high speed at altitude.

The resulting aircraft resembled previous Curtiss *Hawk* types only in the wing design, which used the same span and tapered Clark Y airfoil sections as previous *Hawks*. Wing framing was either of wood or metal, depending on which reference is believed; it was most probably wood. The rest of the airframe was of a brand new design, however, including fuselage, tail surfaces, and landing gear, these being of all metal construction.

Company data from the first of two preliminary Characteristics Sheets dated February 24, 1932, is as follows: XP-23 Tractor Biplane High Altitude Pursuit. Span, length, and height 31 feet, six inches, 23 feet, nine inches, and eight feet, nine inches. Upper wing chord 62.6 inches, wing gap 54.6 inches, stagger at leading edge 28.5 inches, upper and lower wing incidences -2 degrees, and upper and lower wing dihedral 1.5 and 0 degrees. Wing area was 252 square feet, and horizontal and vertical tail areas 30.1 and 13.7 square feet. The load factor at high angle of attack was 12.

The XP-23 powerplant was a Curtiss GIV-1570-C geared inverted engine with an F-2C General Electric turbo supercharged *Conqueror* having a 7:1 propeller gear reduction ratio, with actual rating of 600hp at 2,400rpm at 15,000 feet altitude, and a compression ratio of 6.1:1 using 80 octane gasoline. Fuel consumptions were 60 gallons per hour at full throttle and 36 gallons per hour at 88 percent RPM. Normal fuel and oil capacities were 78 gallons and 11 gallons. The propeller was a three bladed Hamilton Standard ground adjustable type of nine feet, six inch diameter. Prestone cooling was employed.

The predicted weights were as follows: Empty 3,142 pounds, useful load 890 pounds, consisting of a 200 pound pilot, 561 pounds of fuel and oil, 21 pounds of equipment, and 118 pounds of armament, with a resulting gross weight of 4,032 pounds. Wing loading was 16 pounds PSF, and power loading at 15,000 feet 6.2 pounds per horse power. The useful load to gross weight ratio was 0.22.

The estimated performance for the XP-23 was a high speed of 220mph at 15,000 feet. Cruising speed at 15,000 feet at 88 percent RPM was 192mph, and stalling speed at sea level 69mph. Climb rate at 15,000 feet was 1,660fpm. Endurance at 15,000 feet at full throttle, and at 88 percent RPM was 1.3 hours and 2.17 hours, respectively. Ranges were 292 miles at full throttle and 416 miles at 88 percent RPM at 15,000 feet. The estimates for service and absolute ceilings were approximately 32,000 and 33,000 feet, respectively.

A second Curtiss Company Characteristics Sheet is of interest as a variation of the same XP-23 aircraft proposed using a Curtiss Wright (apparently Curtiss) SGIV-1800 12 cylinder engine. It is possible, though not probable, that the XP-23 aircraft was later modified to use this engine as the YP-23. The engine specified was an inverted "V" type with propeller reduction gearing, and a geared mechanical supercharger, no doubt single stage. The Army had initially supported this V-1800 development, but became dissatisfied with the design, and cut off funds in 1932. The engine was intended to replace the Curtiss *Conqueror*. The U.S. Navy had also supported the development of the V-1800 up until the decision was made to

Actually included on the order for the 46 P-6Es as the last aircraft, the elegant XP-23 was destined to be the last biplane fighter ordered by the USAAC. A.C.32-278 bared the wings of the P-6E, but the fuselage was completely different, as evidenced by this April 12, 1932, image. It was formally handed over to the Army four days later, hence no stenciling on the fuselage as yet. (*Curtiss W-7268*)

Left and Opposite: The XP-23 was originally configured to mount the 600hp, turbo-supercharged GIV-1570-C geared engine, as shown on the first of these three-views. Another Army drawing, however, shows it without a visible turn-supercharger installation, and with the SGIV-1800, but this is not believed to have actually been mounted. (*USAAC*)

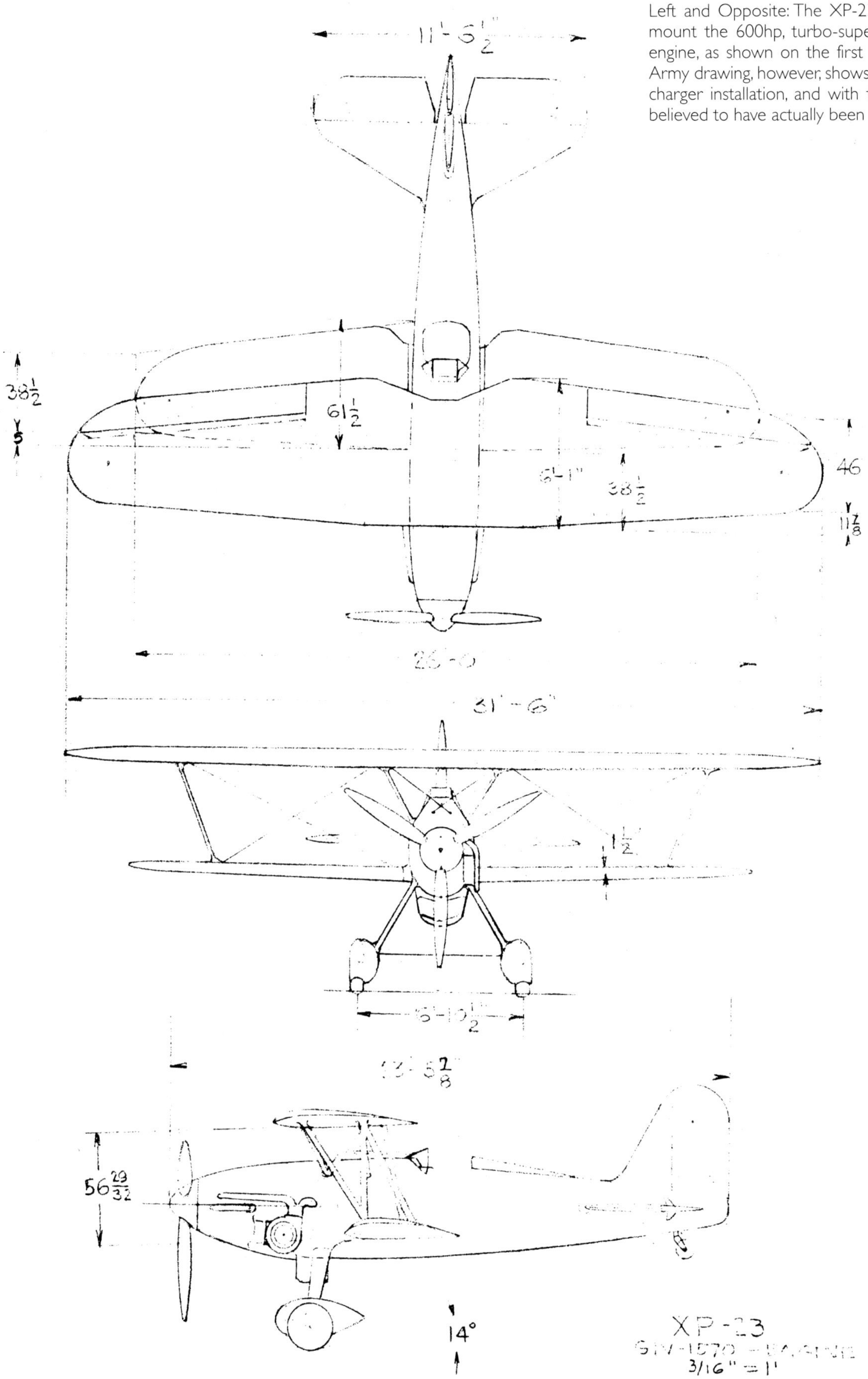

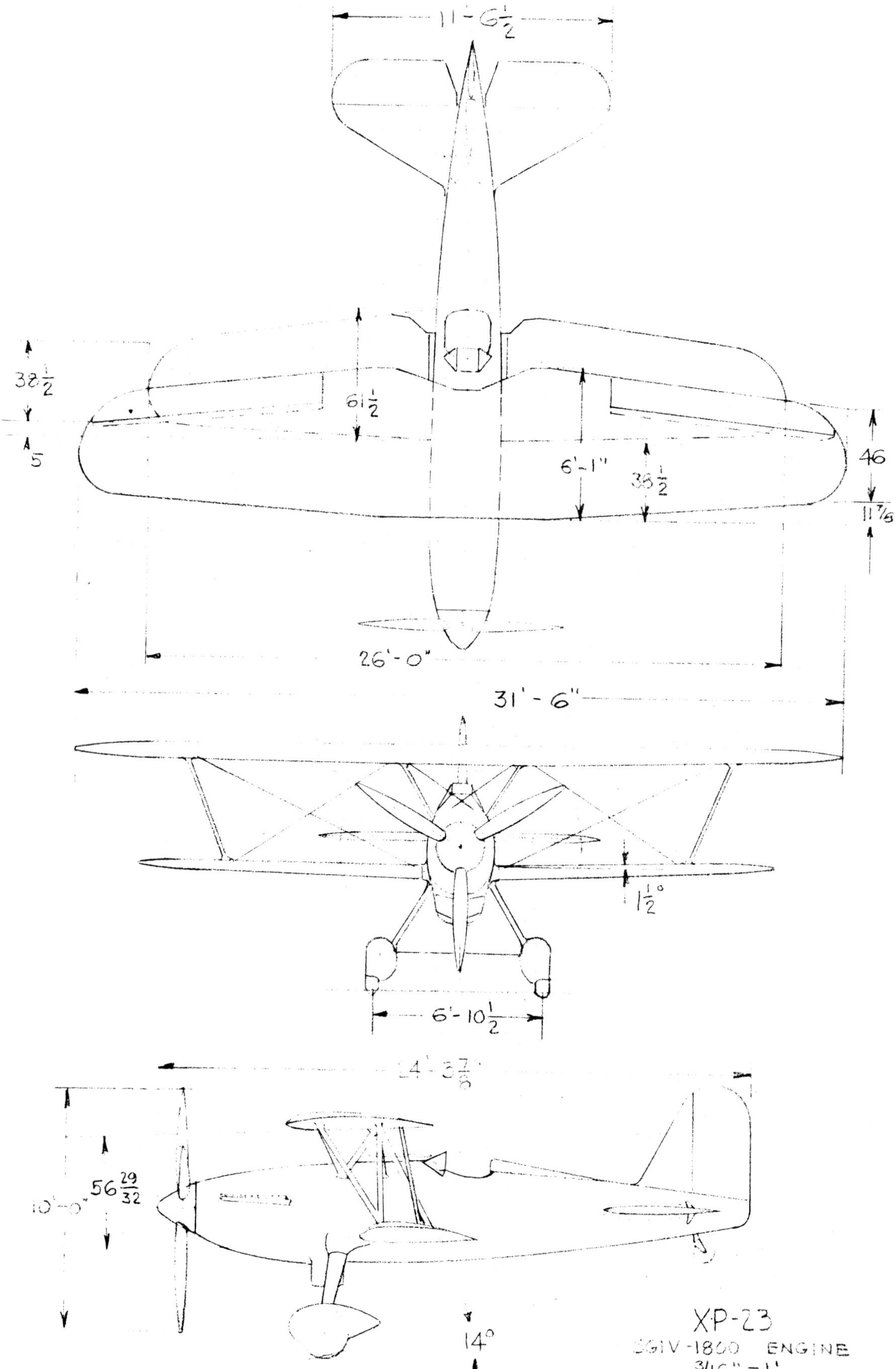
11'-6 1/2
38 1/2
61 1/2
5
6'-1"
38 1/2
46
11 7/8
26'-0"
31'-6"
1 1/2°
6'-10 1/2
24'-3 7/8
10'-0"
56 29/32
14°
XP-23
GIV-1800 ENGINE
3/16" = 1'

Cited in some period publications as the YP-23 *Hawk Special*, but never cited as such in any known Army or Curtiss documents, requires careful examination to differentiate it from the XP-23 configuration. The complete removal of the under-slung radiator is the key difference. (*Real Photographs A-5306*)

go all the way with aircooled radial engines. The V-1800 successfully completed its testing in 1934 at 800hp. After U.S. military support was dropped the engine was licensed to Russia, where the rating was subsequently raised to 900hp.

The estimated differences of the XP-23/YP-23[65] with the V-1800 engine were recorded as: Length 23 feet, 11 inches. In February 1932 the GIV-1800 had a rating of 700hp at 2,400rpm (propeller reduction gearing was 7:5) at 12,000 feet, fuel consumption at full throttle was 65 gallons per hour, and at 88 percent RPM 39 gallons per hour. The three bladed Hamilton Standard propeller was 10 feet in diameter. In the Curtiss Company material there is a note saying "*...wing may have to be moved to give proper balance*."

Estimated empty weight was 3,227 pounds, useful load 890 pounds, and gross weight 4,117 pounds.

Performance estimates at 12,000 feet were a 234mph maximum speed and a 199mph cruise speed. Other items were generally similar to the earlier figures given.

The XP-23 had an all metal monocoque fuselage and an oleo unit in the undercarriage. Some interesting aspects included the *Conqueror* reduction gearing, allowing a clean set of basic nose lines, the installation of a machine gun along each side of the pilot's cockpit firing through long blast tubes below the engine exhaust level, and both a main and a reserve fuel tank between firewall and cockpit. The tail surfaces were all metal monocoque structures. The main landing gear legs ended in open sided wheel pants, and oleo shock units were local just inboard of the pants.

The tests with the turbo supercharger were followed by testing with an unsupercharged Curtiss GIV-1570-23 *Conqueror* of 600hp with propeller reduction gearing driving a two blade propeller. Without the side-mounted supercharger the aircraft nose lines were much cleaner, but high speed was reduced to 200mph at 15,000 feet.

The aircraft was further tested with the under slung Prestone radiator completely removed to assess the drag change. The YP-23 was flown for a few minutes with engine cooling achieved by filling the main fuel tank with cooling water, pumping it through the engine, and then dumping it overboard while running the engine from the reserve fuel tank.

The day of the Army biplane pursuit was over, however, and the beautiful YP-23 was not to be produced. The aircraft was dismantled, and the wings were used to build the Navy XF11C-1 fighter (q.v.).

As noted earlier, the aircraft was eventually reworked on P.O.32-6538 by installing a cabin and type F-2E supercharger, at which point it became the YP-23. The cabin was later installed on the XF-6F (q.v.). The aircraft otherwise remained airworthy as late as January 2, 1934.

4

Navy *Helldivers*

Curtiss XF8C-1, F8C-1, XF8C-2, F8C-3 (OC-1 and OC-2) *Helldiver*
The U.S. Marine Corps had been using U.S. built variants of the de Havilland DH-4 two-seat aircraft with some success in their Central American and Caribbean operations. The services needed replacements for these aging aircraft, and ordered Curtiss *Falcons* in 1927 using Pratt & Whitney *Wasp* engines as observation and attack aircraft. By the spring of 1928, six XF8C-1/F8C-1 and 21 F8C-3 two-seat *Falcons* had been ordered from Curtiss by the Navy. Though the aircraft were designated as fighters, they certainly were not, and the Navy soon recognized that fact by redesignating the F8C-1 and F8C-3 aircraft as OC-1 and OC-2 observation types. It is interesting to note that the Curtiss order list does not reflect any mention of the XF8C-1 or F8C-1 designations, giving MSNs 10929 to 10955 (BuA 7671, 7672 and BuA 7945 to 7948) as a mix of the OC-1 and OC-2 aircraft noted.

The Navy did feel, however, that a useful two seat fighter and light bomber aircraft could be produced, and at the same time the XF8C-1 was ordered a new design for this new type was included. The first mention of this comes from the T. P. Wright Papers Report of the Garden City Chief Engineer for 1927 dated January 3, 1928: "*XF8C-2 Specifications and preliminary drawings now being prepared*," and listed the F8C-2 (MSN 10956 and Navy BuA 7673) under Major Engineering Jobs.

Ordered in March 1928, the Navy XF8C-2, Curtiss Design L-117-1, was a more compact and lighter aircraft than the *Falcon*, though not much increased in performance. It was first flown in November 1928. The plane was a dive-bombing pioneer, able to carry one 500 pound and two 100 pound bombs in addition to two fixed and two flexible machine guns, with the fixed .30 caliber guns mounted in the upper wing center section outside the propeller disc.

Photos of aircraft actually marked as F8C-1s are rare, as the aircraft retained this designation only briefly. This Marine example (A-7945) is the first F8C-1, delivered in January 1928, and was photographed on March 29, 1928. It served with both VO-8M and VJ-7M, and was stricken in January 1934 as an OC-1 with over 1621 hours. (*A. J. Bibee Collection, Museum of Flight*)

Although bearing the same root designation as the production F8C-1s and F8C-3s, the single XF8C-2 (A-7673) was actually a completely different and much lighter design. Inexplicably, the Bureau of Aeronautics serial number was far removed from its F8C relatives, and was delivered in April 1929. Note the hooks on the undercarriage assembly for carrier arresting. (*Cradle of Aviation Museum*)

In April and May 1929 a series of flights were made with the XF8C-2 at Anacostia NAS, with both Marine Corps officers and NCOs in the gunner's cockpit as observers, several of whom had only recently returned from combat in Nicaragua, where they had been rear gunners on earlier types. All stated that the rear cockpit of the XF8C-2 was far superior to anything they had used previously.

The following data are from the Curtiss Characteristics Sheet for an F8C-2 of December 3, 1927, with Navy data of March 1933 for XF8C-2 directly following in parentheses. Wing airfoil section Clark Y (C-72), Factor of safety at high angle of attack 10. Span, length, and height were 32 feet (32 feet), 25 feet, 11 inches (25 feet, 11 inches), and 10 feet, 1.5 inches (10 feet, 6 inches). Wing chord 64 inches (64 inches) for both upper and lower wings, wing gap 62 inches (64 inches), stagger at leading edge 48 inches (49 inches), wing incidence for both upper and lower -1 degree (-1 degree), dihedral 0 degrees (0 degrees), and upper wing sweep 12 degrees. Wing total area was 309 (308) square feet, and horizontal and vertical tail areas were 38.5 (39.7) and 16.2 (17.3) square feet, respectively.

The powerplant was an aircooled Pratt & Whitney (R-1340B) *Wasp* of 425hp (450hp) at 1,900rpm (2,100rpm), with fuel consumption at full throttle 225 pounds per hour, and at economical RPM 84.5 pounds per hour. Fuel capacity was 85 (86) gallons total and 55 gallons normal, and oil capacity 7.5 (6.5) gallons total and 4.5 gallons normal. The propeller was a two blade Curtiss Reed R type (Design 3792) of nine feet, three inches (nine feet even) diameter and 87 inch pitch (16.5 degrees at the 42 inch radius station).

Aircraft empty weight was 2,055 (2,229) pounds, made up of 1,010 pounds of structure, 905 pounds of powerplant, and 140 pounds of fixed equipment. Useful load was 1,085 (1,118) pounds, consisting of 360 (400) pounds of crew, 365 (364) pounds of fuel and oil, 75 pounds of equipment (no radio), and 285 (272) pounds of armament. Gross weight totaled 3,140 (3,347) pounds. Wing loading was 10.2psf (10.9psf), power loading 7.4 (7.5) pounds per horse

The original XF8C-2 crashed during tests in December 1928 and, apparently, some components were used by Curtiss to build a "new" XF8C-2 (with the same Navy Bureau of Aeronautics serial number) with a different engine and NACA cowl. It is pictured here on April 12, 1929, and may have in fact been officially designated as the XF8C-2A. (*Curtiss T-4398*)

Owing more to the Army Air Corps Curtiss *Falcon* series than to a dedicated fighter design, all production F8C-1s and F8C-3s—like A-7966, pictured here on November 27, 1928—were operated by the U.S. Marine Corps. This is a VO-8M aircraft (*A. J. Bibee Collection, Museum of Flight*)

power, and the useful load to gross weight ratio was 0.346 (0.334), very good (Overload gross weight was 3,549 pounds.).

F8C-2 predicted performance in the Curtiss data, and presumably actual performance in the Navy case was: high speed 151.5mph (144.9mph) at sea level, 149mph (143mph) at 5,000 feet, 145mph at 10,000 feet, and 138mph (130mph at 15,000 feet. Cruising speed at most economical RPM was only 80.3mph, and landing speed 55.5mph (Stall speed 55.7mph).

Sea level climb rate was 1,745fpm, and in 10 minutes 12,200 feet were gained. (4.0 minutes to 5,000 feet, and 18.5 minutes to 15,000 feet). Endurances were 1.47 hours at full throttle and 3.9 hours at most economical RPM. Range at full throttle was 223 miles, and at most economical RPM 313 miles. Service and absolute ceilings were 21,100 (20,800) and 22,400 feet. (Takeoff run with no wind was 305 feet and with a 25 knot wind 81 feet.)

Another Curtiss characteristics sheet of the same date as above for a *Wasp* powered F8C-2 gave fuel capacity as 90 gallons normal and 110 gallons total, and 6.5 gallons of oil normal and 10 gallons total. Empty weight was 2,128 pounds (1,067 pounds of structure, 921 pounds of powerplant, and 140 pounds of fixed equipment). Useful load was composed of 400 pounds of crew, 590 pounds of fuel and oil, 76 pounds of fixed equipment, and 286 pounds of payload, totaling 1,362 pounds. The aircraft gross weight was 3,480 pounds. Speeds were listed as 151mph at sea level, 147mph at 5,000 feet, 142.5mph at 10,000 feet, and 133.5mph at 15,000 feet. Sea level stall speed was 57.5mph. Rate of climb at sea level was 1,575fpm. Endurance figures at full throttle at sea level were 2.4 hours, and at economical RPM 6.4 hours. The equivalent ranges were 360 miles and 509 miles. Service and absolute ceilings were 19,800 feet and 21,200 feet.

The first XF8C-2 crashed in December 1928 during dive bombing tests. Some sources have indicated an empennage failure, but a former Curtiss employee has indicated that during dive flight tests a wing strut failed, and the pilot jumped out. As a result, Curtiss was forced to build a second considerably strengthened ship.[66] In the summer of 1929 the new aircraft tested a new long chord engine cowl that extended well aft past the exhaust stacks, with those sticking out through the cowl. Apparently, Curtiss reissued the same MSN to this second example, perhaps using components of the first XF8C-2.

The XF8C-2 *Helldiver* had a steel tubing fuselage structure filled out with formers and stringers, and this was fabric covered aft of the forward cockpit. The external skin line forward was formed by side fuel tank outer walls. Aluminum alloy skins covered the engine compartment. The wings were framed in wood and fabric covered. Tail surfaces were fabric covered over aluminum frames.

Curtiss XF8C-4 and F8C-4 *Helldiver*

Following successful testing of the XF8C-4 *Helldiver* prototype (BuA 8314), the U.S. Navy decided to follow through on their thinking that a two seat fighter would be useful, particularly if it could double as a dive bomber with a 500 pound bomb, thus the name *Helldiver*. The -4 model was a heavier beefed up version of the -2 with full operational equipment, including bomb racks, a new tail skid, and an increase in fuel capacity. In June 1929 Curtiss obtained a Navy order for one XF8C-4 and 27 F8C-4 (MSN 11260 to 11286, BuA 8421 to 8445, and accounting for only 25) production aircraft. The XF8C-4 first flew in August 1929. The X model cost the Navy $31,218, and the production F8C-4 aircraft $16,500 each. The XF8C-4 was delivered in January 1930, and the first of the production lot on May 1, 1930.

The production *Helldivers* went aboard carrier USS *Saratoga* in the summer of 1930 with VF-1B, the *High Hat* Squadron.

The F8C-4 characteristics from Curtiss data are shown with Navy characteristics data following in parentheses. Span, length, and height were 32 feet, 25 feet, 11 inches, and 10 feet, 10 inches. Wing area was 308 (317.8) square feet (Wing airfoils C-72, wing stagger 49 inches, upper wing sweep 12 degrees, both wings chord 64 inches, gap 64 inches, dihedral 0 degrees, and horizontal and vertical tail areas 42.3 and 17.2 square feet, respectively.).

Often confused by the casual observer with period Vought *Corsair* variants, the XF8C-4 *Helldiver* prototype (A-8314) poses with engine running on a rainy day. Accepted in April 1930, it remained at Quantico until stricken December 17, 1930, with only 93 hours on the airframe, having been rather severely bent in tests. (*Dean Collection*)

Most sources cite Curtiss as having built 27 production F8C-4s for the Navy, but only 25 can be accounted for in Curtiss records. A-8425, the fifth production example, poses for the camera on August 12, 1930, the day she was delivered. Note the cover aft of the rear pit, which housed life jackets, etc, in the event of ditching. Starting with the second example most had engine cowl rings, but this one is missing hers for some reason. The aircraft later served for 17 months with VF-1B, and survived until May 2, 1936, when she was stricken as obsolete. (*Curtiss 3926B*)

Empty weight was 2,513 (2,513) pounds, normal useful load 1,270 (1,270) pounds, consisting of 400 pounds of crew, 516 (480) pounds of fuel, 45 (49) pounds of oil, 35 (75) pounds of equipment, and 274 (266) pounds of armament. Fighter gross weight was 3,783 pounds. As a bomber the useful load was 1,770 pounds, and normal gross weight was 4,238 pounds. Wing loading was 12.28psf, and power loading 8.41 pounds per horse power. Normal useful load to gross weight ratio was 0.336.

The F8C-4 was powered by a Pratt & Whitney R-1340-88 *Wasp* engine of 450hp at 2,100rpm at sea level. Normal internal fuel capacity was 86 gallons, with the option of adding a 50 gallon external belly fuel tank in the fighter version. Oil capacity was 10.5 gallons. (The propeller was a two blade model of nine feet diameter, Design 3792, with pitch of 15.5 degrees at the 42 inch radius station.)

Armament consisted of two .30 caliber Browning machine guns in the upper wing center section firing above the propeller arc, and one or two flexible .303 caliber Lewis machine guns on a Curtiss Type 1 Flexible Gun mounting[67] at the rear cockpit. Used in both the F8C-4 and F8C-5, this unit weighed 21 pounds, and was suitable for two-seat fighters and ground attack, as well as bomber aircraft where 180° of transverse fire was considered sufficient. The angle of fire could cover half of a sphere. The mount included a seat for riding forward and rearward, back rest when riding forward, rings for a safety belt when operating the mount, also serving as a support for the gunner's back in various positions of the mount, and latch for securing the Lewis gun when not manned, as well as foot braces, which were required when operating the mount. Provision was made for carriage of a single 500 pound bomb under the fuselage, or two 116 pound bombs under the wings in the bomber version. Airframe construction was basically the same as in the XF8C-2.

High speed of the F8C-4 was 137mph at sea level, and 145mph (134mph) at 6,000 (5,000) feet. Cruise speed was 116mph at 6,000 feet, and landing speed was 59mph (stalling speed 59.2mph). Rate of climb was 1,030fpm at 6,000 feet, and 5,000 feet could be gained in six minutes. Normal range was 455 (455) miles at 6,000 feet, and maximum range 722 (722) miles. Service ceiling was 15,000 (15,000) feet as a bomber. (Takeoff distance, no wind, was 436 feet, in a 15 knot wind 232 feet, and in a 25 knot wind 130 feet!

The dramatic sweep on the upper main plane, and slight stagger of the lower wings, is only apparent in this side view of the XF8C-4. The basic idea was to make the two-seat fighter more durable by enabling it to also perform a dive-bombing mission. It was essentially a beefed up version of the XF8C-2. (*Dean Collection*)

All of the production F8C-4s went to the Navy, going aboard USS *Saratoga* with VF-1B during the summer and fall of 1930. The unit insignia on BuA 8432 (note the "A-" prefix has been deleted) appears to be a black disc, but is in fact a Reserve unit insignia. During peace time, usually only one of the two wing guns was fitted for training. This aircraft wasn't stricken until June 30, 1937. (*Dean Collection*)

Endurance at maximum speed at design gross weight was 1.84 hours.)

After fleet introduction of the F8C-4 a lesson was soon learned. The larger and heavier two-seat fighter could not keep up with or maneuver with the faster and more agile single seat Navy fighters, and in formation flying the larger craft set the speed of the formation. High speed was 30 to 40 mph slower than the single seat aircraft. Why the Navy had to learn this fact the hard way is not known.

In June 1931, all remaining F8C-4 aircraft were sent to Reserve units. None served with the Marine Corps. A total of 20 aircraft were still in the Reserves in 1934, and a single aircraft remained in the reserves at NRAB Glenview, California, until 1937.

Curtiss F8C-5 *Helldiver*

The next *Helldiver* was the F8C-5, much like the F8C-4, but using an exhaust collector ring along with a ring cowl around the engine cylinders, improved engine compartment cooling louvers, and a pneumatic tail wheel, but no carrier arrestor gear.

The first nine F8C-5s were ordered with the F8C-4s at a cost of $10,500 each in June 1929. A total of 63[68] aircraft were obtained

Most F8C-4s were passed to Naval Reserve units, including BuA 8442, pictured here with the New York Naval Reserve Air Base insignia. Note the brightly painted empennage and sectionalized cowl colors. (*Roger Besecker No.2268*)

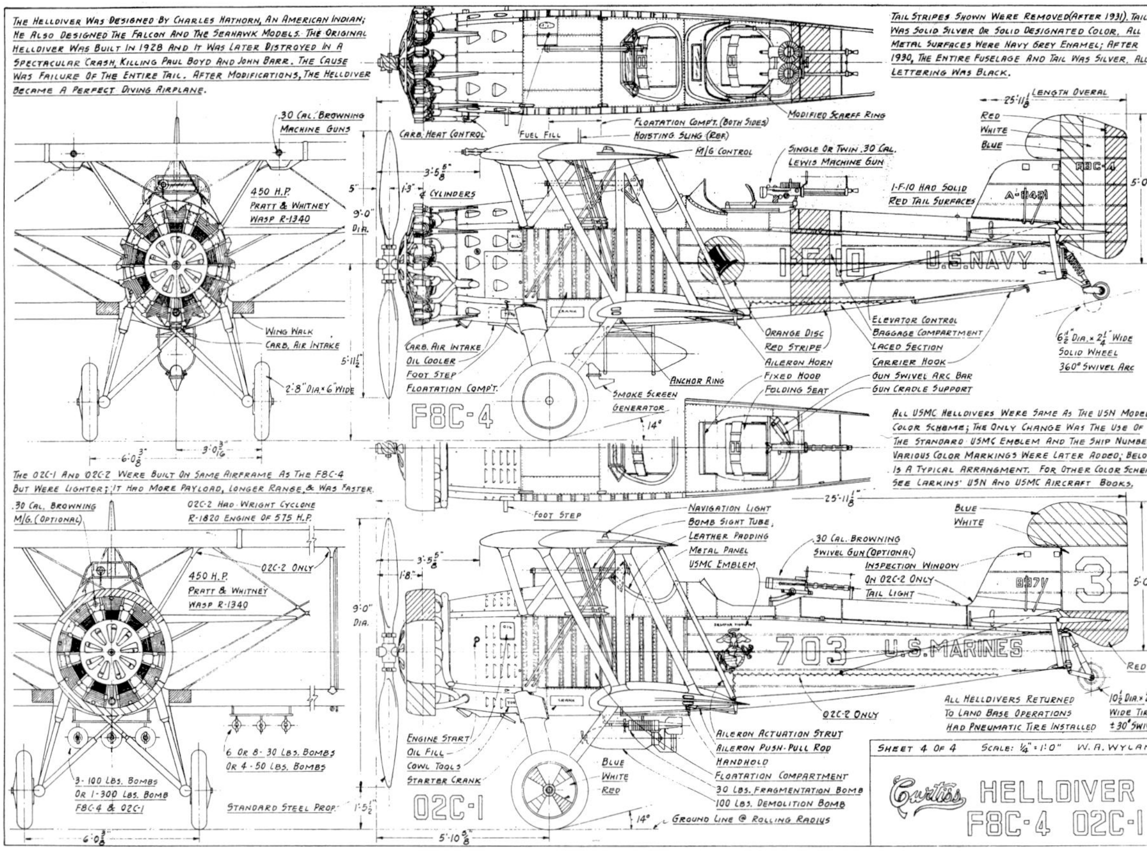

(William A, Wylam)

Despite the disadvantages of the design as a "fighter," the Navy continued to acquire surprising numbers of two-seat aircraft in this category, possibly as a means of circumventing Congressional restrictions on funding for less glamorous multi-purpose aircraft. F8C-5 A-8589 was the first of the second batch of nine aircraft, and is completely devoid of armament and arrestor equipment. None were ever operated on carriers. This aircraft was redesignated as an O2C-1, and lasted in service until September 1935, when she was stricken for lack of funds to overhaul her. (*Dean Collection*)

A-8589 again, in virtually the same pose, but this time equipped with a partial canopy cover for the pilot only. (*Dean Collection*)

from Curtiss, with the remainder ordered in June 1930. The first deliveries of the -5 came in September 1930, and continued into 1931. Of the total, 18 were contracted as F8C-5s (MSN 11287 to 11304), after which they, and all subsequent planes, were redesignated as O2C-1 observation aircraft (MSN 11452 to 11524). It had been recognized that the *Helldiver* was not a fighter after the experience with the F8C-4s.

Two F8C-5s were modified as XF8C-6s to test wing high lift devices, with both leading edge slats and trailing edge flaps installed. They were subsequently restored to standard F8C-5s and, later, O2C-1 configuration.

The first 27 aircraft went to the Marines, and operated with the active squadrons VO-6M and VO-7M. In September 1930 these aircraft were being operated as Marine fighters. By mid-1931 28 aircraft were active with the USMC, and 22 stayed through 1933. The number was reduced to 15 by mid-1935, 7 in early 1936, and only one O2C-1 was left by the start of 1937. A total of 55 Navy O2C-1s served at Naval Reserve Air Stations in 1934, and six were left by mid-1937. No F8C-5/O2C-1 aircraft ever served with the fleet at sea.

The F8C-5 had essentially the same dimensions as the F8C-4, and weights were little different. Empty weight was 2,520 pounds, useful load 1,437 pounds, and normal gross weight 3,957 pounds. Wing loading was thus 12.85psf, and useful load to gross weight ratio 0.36, rather good for the period.

This *Helldiver* was powered by a Pratt & Whitney R-1340C *Wasp* radial engine of 450hp. Fuel capacity was 120 gallons.

Performance was similar to earlier models, with high speed 140mph at sea level, and 142.5mph at 6,000 feet. Cruise and landing speeds were 110mph and 63mph, respectively. Ceiling was 18,200 feet, range 560 miles, and maximum endurance at best cruise speed 7.6 hours.

Armament, when fitted, consisted of the same two .30 caliber machine guns in the upper wing center section, and a single or twin flexible .30 caliber installation mounted at the rear seat location.

Most surviving F8C-5s were redesignated, eventually, into the O2C-1 category for two-seat observation aircraft, a role for which they were much more suitable. Here, BuA 8589 bears the markings of Naval Reserve Air Base Seattle. (*Dean Collection*)

The so-called F8C-7 "*Cyclone Command*," with a special color scheme and snazzy cockpit cover for transporting the Secretary of the Navy (A-8845), appeared on December 10, 1930. The aircraft did in fact retain wing gun capability, so it could honestly be described as a "fighter" at this point. (*Dean Collection*)

Curtiss *Helldivers* with *Cyclone* Engines
XF8C-7 (XF8C-8), O2C-1, O2C-2, (XF10C-1) XS3C-1 *Helldivers*

There were four *Helldiver* aircraft put out by Curtiss that were unusual, being powered by nine cylinder Wright R-1820 *Cyclone* radial engines rated at 575hp. These were individually distinctive, and will be so treated. The Navy serial numbers were A-8845, 8847, 8848, and 8849.

XF8C-7 *Helldiver* A-8845 (MSN 11305) was a special deluxe version, initially a Curtiss owned company demonstrator, ostensibly to show what a high powered Wright *Cyclone* powered example could do performance-wise. It was introduced at Curtiss Garden City in the summer of 1930, and on November 6, 1930, was purchased by the Navy as a command transport. The aircraft was used, in dark blue "command" finish, as a special transport for David S. Ingalls, Assistant Secretary of the Navy for Aeronautics. Cyclone powered with a ring cowl and full wheel pants on both main and tail wheels, and fully enclosed cockpits for both pilot and high level passenger, the XF8C-7 was a pretty fancy aircraft, but hardly set up for fighting. Specifications follow, with Curtiss data followed by Navy data in parentheses: Span, length, and height 32 feet, 26 (26) feet, and 11 (11) feet. Wing area 308 (308) square feet. (Wing gap 64 inches, incidence -1 degree, dihedral 0 degrees, stagger 48 inches, sweepback 12 degrees.) (Vertical and horizontal tail areas were 17.3 and 39.7 square feet.)

The R-1820E (F) *Cyclone* engine was rated at 575hp (575hp) maximum at 1,900rpm and 648hp normal at sea level. (Fuel capacity was 120 gallons; engine oil capacity was 10.5 gallons.) (The propeller was a Design 5868 two blade type of nine feet, nine inches diameter, with pitch of 20.7 degrees at the 42 inch radius station.)

Empty weight was 2,958 (2,958) pounds, useful load 1,317 pounds, (1,316 pounds composed of crew 200 pounds, passenger 200 pounds, fuel 720 pounds, oil 75 pounds, armament 0 pounds, and equipment 121 pounds), and a gross weight of 4,275 (4,274) pounds. Wing loading was 13.9psf, and power loading 7.5 pounds per horse power.

Maximum speed was 178.5mph (178.5mph) at sea level, 176mph at 5,000 feet, and 162mph at 15,000 feet. Landing speed was 63mph. Climb was 1,840fpm at sea level. Climb times were

BuA 8945 late in her career, gussied up with stylish wheel pants, rarely seen, and by this point redesignated as O2C-1. Configured as such, despite their limited operational capabilities, they did much to spark the popular imagination during the lean depression years. (*Dean Collection*)

Rarely illustrated, Curtiss described this aircraft as the XF8C-7 *Cyclone Military Helldiver*, and at this point it was very much Curtiss property, and wore Department of Commerce Identification Number 983V. It was subsequently sold to the Navy as A-8845 in late November 1930, where its odyssey was very confusing, as described in the text. It was stricken in May 1934 as "worn out," and was used for barrier crash tests as an O2C-2. (*Curtiss T-6315*)

Navy Bureau of Aeronautics Serial Number 8847, although often cited as having been designated as one of the three XF8C-8s, never carried this designation. It was delivered as an O2C-2, and assigned to VF-6B in January 1931. It was wrecked as such, killing both crew, and was rebuilt and redesignated as the solitary XS3C-1, as seen here. It crashed again February 25, 1932, not quite a month after this photo was taken. (*Curtiss W-7115*)

Although described by many sources as having been designated XF8C-8, this O2C-2 *Helldiver* (BuA 8848) is not reflected with this designation on its History Card. Acquired in January 1931, it was assigned to fighter units (VF-3B, VF-6B, and VF-1B), but ended its service with a scouting unit (VS-1F at Pensacola) in February 1934 with only 393 hours total time. (*Curtiss T-6485 via Peter M. Bowers*)

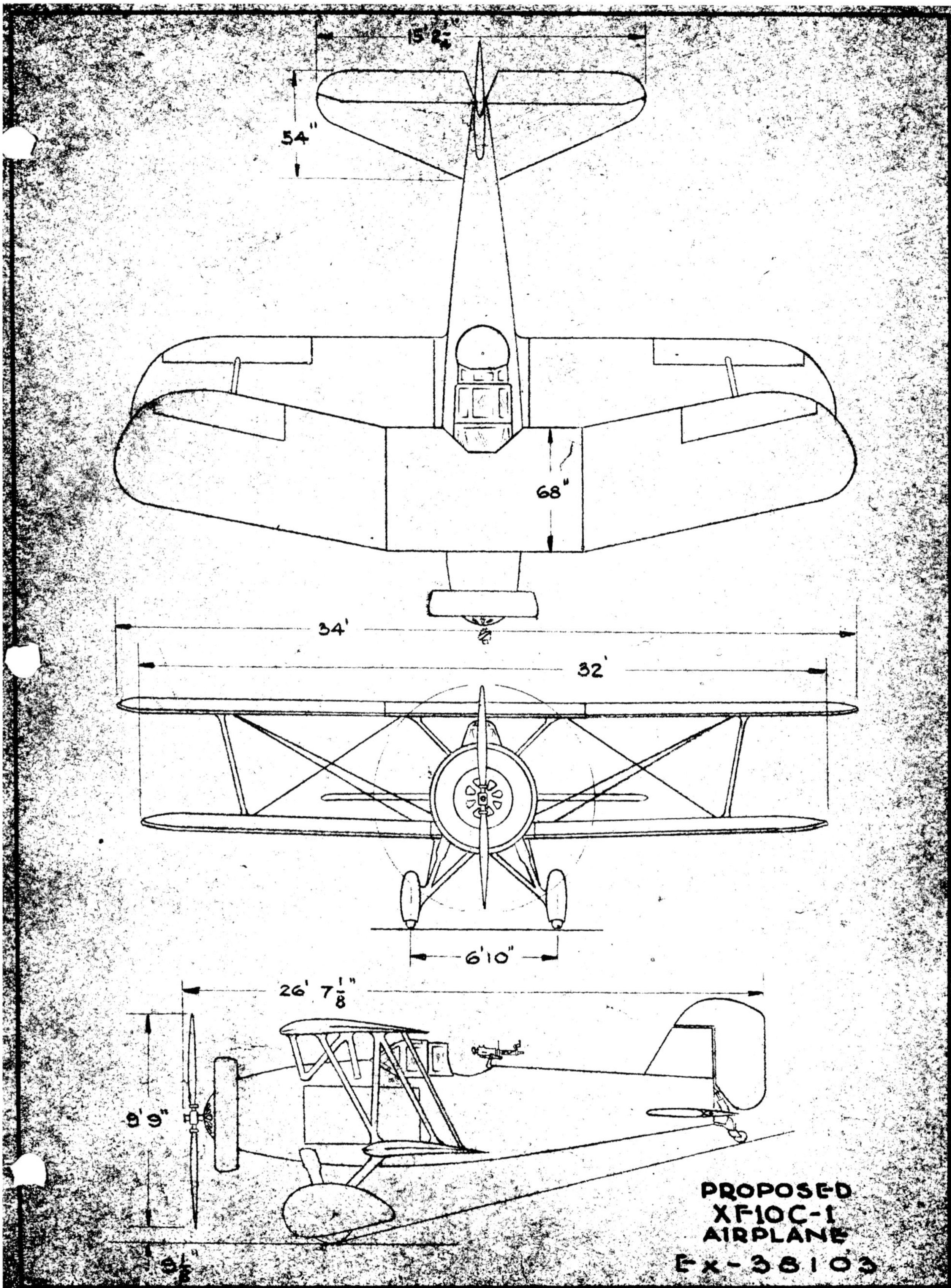

Although many sources have cited the designation XF10C-1 as having been briefly assigned to BuA 8847—just before XS3C-1—the solitary evidence found was this Curtiss Proposal (Ex-38103), and it is not believed to have actually been used. (*Curtiss*)

Also often cited in many publications as an XF8C-8, BuA 8849 was described only as an O2C-2 on its History Card. Delivered in January 1931, it served with VF-3B and VF-1B at San Diego before going to the Naval Aircraft Factory, where it was fitted with an R-1510 engine seen here. It was lost on July 14, 1933, when it caught fire in flight. This photo was taken June 8, 1933. (*Naval Aircraft Factory via Peter M. Bowers*)

3.2 minutes to 5,000 feet, 7.2 minutes to 10,000 feet, and 10 minutes to 12,500 feet. The service ceiling was 20,800 feet. (Takeoff distance in zero wind was 456 feet; with a 25 knot wind, 150 feet).

There was, in fact, provision for two .30 caliber guns in the upper wing, but none were installed. Since this aircraft was not really a fighter, some sources state that it was redesignated in March 1931 as an XO2C-1 observation plane, but in 1933 it was again labeled an XF8C-7, though still used as a staff transport at Anacostia NAS, before ending service life in May 1934 as "worn out," and ending its days in barrier crash tests. The Navy Aircraft History Card for A-8845, however, makes no mention of the designation X02C-1 whatsoever.

Cyclone powered *Helldiver* A-8847 (MSN 11612) was another aircraft starting as a company owned machine. The initial version could be identified by a civil Department of Commerce Identification Number -983V on the rudder. It was to go through a confusing welter of designations. Tested in December 1930, it was originally considered (by Curtiss at least) as the first Navy XF8C-7 two-seat fighter, and was shown armed with two fixed guns in the upper wing, and a single flexible machine gun for the rear seat man. Subsequent to purchase for $27,433 by the Navy with Fiscal 1931 funds it got an O2C-2 observation plane designation, and the History Card for A-8847 makes no mention whatsoever of the designation XF8C-7. It had a ring cowl, large wheel pants, including one over the tail wheel, a fully enclosed front cockpit, and a partially enclosed gunner's cockpit. This aircraft crashed during tests, and according to Curtiss company billing records, was sent back to the factory, where Curtiss charged the Navy under S.O.3053 $8,000 "*...for fuselage in replacement for crash-delivered 2/14/32.*" Flying again in early 1932, the plane is alleged to have been given the XF10C-1 fighter designation (apparently on paper only), and then the designation of this plane was changed to an XS3C-1 scout. It was much revised, with two open cockpits, a single strut landing gear—again with panted wheels—and revised tail surfaces. Your scribes could find no evidence that this aircraft actually was assigned the designation XF10C-1, which was Curtiss Proposal Ex-38103 only.

As an XS3C-1, this *Helldiver* had a span, length, and height of 32 feet, 26 feet, four inches, and 10 feet, two inches, respectively, with the same 308 square feet of wing area. Powered with a 650hp *Cyclone* R-1820E engine, empty weight was 3,387 pounds, useful load 1,572 pounds, and gross weight 4,959 pounds. That made wing loading 16.1psf, power loading 7.63 pounds per horse power, and the useful load to gross weight ratio 0.317.

The XS3C-1 performance figures were maximum, and stalling speeds 178mph at sea level and 64mph. Climb capability was 1,680fpm at sea level, and attainment of 10,000 feet took 10 minutes. Service ceiling was 20,000 feet.

The XS3C-1 type was never put into production, but the Navy's interest in two seat fighters had not yet waned. After Curtiss testing, the rebuilt plane was delivered to the Navy in February 1932, but again soon after crashed during diving tests.

The two *Helldiver* aircraft A-8848 and A-8849 may have been temporarily designated in the fighter category as XF8C-8s by the Navy, but the History Cards make no mention of this whatsoever. Both were formally designated as O2C-2 observation planes, although A-8849 was assigned to VF-3B, VF-6B, VF-1B and, later, VJ-1F between January 1931 and January 1932. These were almost certainly MSN 11307 and 11308.

5

Sparrow-Hawks

Curtiss XF9C-1 and XF9C-2 *Sparrow-Hawk Dirigible*

On original Curtiss documents, the "popular name" for the first of these enigmatic biplane fighters is given as shown above. More often during the intervening years, however, the fame gained by the Curtiss F9C- *Sparrowhawks* (as they have been more frequently, albeit inaccurately coined) was seemingly out of all reasonable proportion to their numbers. But as the only dirigible hook-on fighters ever used by the Navy—or any other service—they were certainly interesting.

Basically, the F9C series fighters were designed "outside the box" by Curtiss to meet the highly unusual requirements of Navy Specification No.96, dated May 10, 1930. This called for a nimble, rather small single-seat fighter intended to be operated from a series of huge Navy rigid airships, which commenced with the *USS Akron* and *Macon*—the only such "parasite" arrangement in aviation history to actually reach operational status. In retrospect, the entire concept might appear ill conceived, and fraught with obvious hazards, involving, as it did, "trapeze" like hook-ups and departures, on-board billeting, and downright splendid piloting skills. However, as of 1930 the defense policy of the United States, and the reasonable capabilities of potential enemies, made such an enterprise not only attractive, but logical, as well. The huge airships were viewed, by some very vocal and well placed proponents, as far ranging scouts for the conventional surface fleet of the Navy, which had primary responsibility at the time for the defense of both coasts of the nation. The F9Cs were intended to provide the dirigibles with at least some form of practical defense against enemy carrier-based or ship-borne aircraft, as well as yet additional scouting range. The popular fascination with the highly visible dirigibles, and a seemingly inordinate fascination in the F9C series in the aviation press of the day, led to an almost inevitable legend surrounding the aircraft, with few in the general populace having anything like a clear understanding of their actual numbers and genuine capabilities—let alone liabilities.

In fact, there were only a total of eight aircraft produced, the first an XF9C-1 prototype (Curtiss MNS 11525, Navy BuA 8731), six F9C-2 "production" aircraft (MSN 11616 to 11621 on Navy Contract 24021, BuA 9056 to 9061), and a single XF9C-2[69] that started out as a company owned plane as early as November 1931 (MSN 11670, operated by Curtiss as X-986M,[70] but sold to the Navy on Contract 11670 as BuA 9264). One aircraft has been preserved at the National Air and Space Museum in Washington, DC, apparently a mix of parts from the first production machine and the XF9C-2.

Certainly unique in aviation history, the XF9C-1 (BuA 8731) was the first of a small batch of fighters designed to operate from large rigid airships. It was, necessarily, a small aircraft, with a wing span of barely 25 feet, six inches on the upper wings. This aircraft was the last one built at Garden City, Long Island, and was handed over to the Navy March 27, 1931. It was stricken as of "no further use" January 8, 1935. (*Dean Collection*)

Winner of a competition with Fokker and Berliner-Joyce offerings against Bureau of Aeronautics Design Specification #96 of May 10, 1930, for a small carrier based fighter, the initial XF9C-1 was ordered from Curtiss at Garden City, Long Island, on June 30, 1930, for $40,217.21, and was ready for Navy testing in late March 1931 after a first flight on February 12, 1931. It was flown to Anacostia NAS on March 27th, and demonstrated there by a Curtiss pilot on April 3rd. The XF9C-1 was the final aircraft built at the Garden City plant and, although the major part of the construction was done there, final assembly actually was completed at the new Buffalo plant.

The project engineers for the aircraft were Arthur Butler and Rolf Zurwelle and, once the drawings were released to the shop, Zurwelle was put in charge of the floor changes. Ralph Damon, the Shop Superintendent at the time, was also instrumental in solving many of the manufacturing problems that were experienced with what was described at the time as the first all-metal, monocoque fuselage made in the United States.

The aircraft was a very compact, single bay, single seat biplane using a Wright *Whirlwind* aircooled radial engine. Wing structure was all metal, with fabric covering aft of the front spar location. The fuselage and empennage were of aluminum alloy. The prototype had a balanced rudder, high pressure tires, a small hard rubber tail wheel, and a fully faired, fixed cantilever landing gear. A distinguishing feature was the upper wing tied directly to the fuselage.

Specifications for the XF9C-1 follow. Curtiss data is followed by Navy figures directly afterward in parentheses. Where there is nothing in parentheses the numbers are the same. Spans, length, and height were 25 feet, six inches upper, 23 feet, four inches lower, 19 feet, five inches, and 7 feet, one inch. Wing area 172.9 (172.8) square feet (Wing stagger 25 inches, upper and lower wing chords four feet, eight inches and three feet, four inches, wing gap three feet, six and 3/4 inches). Wing airfoils were Clark CYH. The design load factor was 12. There was no airship hook on this first aircraft, but a carrier arrestor hook was fitted.

The powerplant was a Wright R-972C (-22) with a supercharger blower having a gear ratio of 10.15:1, and a compression ratio of 6:1. The engine developed 421hp (420hp) at 2,310rpm at sea level, and the propeller was a two blade, Hamilton metal, ground adjustable type, design 4651 (5462), of eight feet diameter, and blades were set at 18.1 (18.5) degrees at the 42 inch radius station. Fuel capacity was 59 gallons (Oil capacity five gallons).

XF9C-1 empty weight was 1,836 pounds, useful load 666 (659) pounds, and normal gross weight 2,502 (2,474) pounds (Maximum gross weight 2,572 pounds.). (Useful load consisted of crew 180 pounds, fuel 258 pounds, oil 26 pounds, armament 163 pounds, and equipment 32 pounds.)

The wing loading was 14.47psf, and power loading 5.94 pounds per horse power. Useful load to gross weight ratio was 0.266, not very impressive.

Armament consisted of two .30 caliber Browning M-2 fixed machine guns with 600 rounds per gun, synchronized, firing through the inside of the cowl ring over the engine.

Performance was as follows: Maximum speed 176.5mph at sea level, 160mph at 10,000 feet, and 152mph at 16,000 feet. Stall speed was 60mph. Sea level climb was 2,150fpm. (Climb to 5,000 feet 2.6 minutes, to 15,000 feet 11.7 minutes.) Climb in 10 minutes to 13,800 feet. Climb to 24,000 feet 53 minutes. Ceiling was 24,200 feet. Normal and maximum ranges were 396 miles and 536 miles, but range at high speed was 204 miles and endurance 1.16 hours. (Take off run with zero wind was 362 feet; with a 25 knot wind, 115 feet.)

Navy Anacostia testing as a carrier fighter was completed on May 18, 1931, and on June 10th the *Sparrowhawk* prototype was flown to Hampton Roads for arresting gear tests. There were several criticisms: The hook needed relocation to alleviate too much tail rise and too little propeller to deck clearance, and changes were

Strictly speaking a three-point landing, but probably much to the chagrin of the pilot, who now confronts his worst fears—a Yeoman with a clipboard! This aircraft was undergoing a series of tests at the NACA as of this date, June 16, 1931. *(NMUSAF)*

needed to improve pilot vision; the Navy wanted the upper wing raised four inches. There were many other minor criticisms, but generally the aircraft was rated well.

The XF9C-1 was subsequently equipped in March 1932 with an experimental airship hook-on gear over the upper wing, and was otherwise modified to the later production aircraft configuration with open panted landing gear and low pressure tires. It then joined the *Akron* airship unit (and later the *Macon* unit) until withdrawn to the Naval Aircraft Factory in Philadelphia in 1933. This first *Sparrowhawk* was scrapped at the end of 1934.

The XF9C-2 aircraft, first marked with civil Department of Commerce experimental registration NX-968M as a company owned aircraft, incorporated most all of the Navy recommended changes for the XF9C-1 prototype, including a four inch raising of the upper wing. Painted blue and silver with cantilever strut full panted landing gear, it had the broad fin and an unbalanced rudder, but was never equipped with an airship hook. It was purchased by the Navy for $30,000, assigned serial BuA 9264, and delivered on January 10, 1933, to the North Island Naval Air Station in California, according to Curtiss company billing records. It was assigned to the USS *Akron* unit but, as noted, never had a hook installed. This aircraft, unpainted, was at Anacostia NAS from 1934 to 1935. It was to be flown to Norfolk, Virginia, in late 1936 for overhaul. Some parts of this aircraft were apparently put into production aircraft 9056, which has been saved and restored by the NASM, and which is now on loan to the National Museum of Naval Aviation at Pensacola.

The Curtiss Characteristics Sheet for the XF9C-2 Carrier Fighter, with wire braced landing gear and without airship hook, dated February 29, 1932, provides the following details:

Span, length, and height were 25 feet, six inches, 19 feet, five inches, and seven feet, six inches, respectively. Upper and lower wing chords were 56 inches and 40 inches, and wing gap was 46.75 inches mean. Stagger was 25 inches. Wing incidence and sweepback were 0 degrees, and upper wing dihedral was three degrees. Wing area totaled 173 square feet, and horizontal and vertical tail areas were 23.3 and 12.4 square feet. Wing airfoils were Clark YH, and load factor at high angle of attack was 12.

The powerplant was a Wright R-975E *Whirlwind* aircooled radial with supercharger gear ratio of 10.5 to 1, and a direct propeller drive rated at 420hp at 2,200rpm, but actual power was 440hp at 2,200rpm. Compression ratio was six to one. 87 octane fuel was used. Full throttle fuel consumption was 40.5 gallons per hour, and at 80 percent RPM, 20 gallons per hour. Fuel capacity was 43 gallons normal and 60 gallons maximum. Oil capacity was 3.5 gallons normal and 4.8 gallons maximum. The propeller was a Hamilton Standard two bladed model of eight feet, six inches diameter.

Aircraft empty weight was 1,985 pounds, with a useful load of 661 pounds (consisting of a 180 pound pilot, 284 pounds of fuel and oil, 52 pounds of equipment, which included a life raft but no radio, and 145 pounds of armament, which consisted of two .30 caliber fixed guns and ammunition.) The total gave a gross weight of 2,646 pounds. Thus, wing loading was 15.3 psf, and power loading 6.0 pounds per horse power. Useful load to gross weight ratio was 0.25.

An exceptional view of the Curtiss XF9C-2, dated September 29, 1931, bearing Department of Commerce Identified Aircraft Number 986M. The aircraft had been completed a month earlier. Still owned by Curtiss, it wears U.S. National Insignia and the Navy designation on the rudder. It later became BuA 9264 in January 1933. It is seldom noted that the aircraft was "modernized" to straight F9C-2 configuration. It was stricken in August 1937 with but 254 hours in Navy service. (*Curtiss W-6890*)

The same aircraft, now bearing only designation F9C-2 and still owned by Curtiss, but now wearing Experimental License X986M as it appeared on July 18, 1932. Note that brace wires have been added between the main gear struts and the wing root of the upper wings, with additional stiffening wires between the main gear. The colors of the aircraft were probably gloss blue and yellow wings. *(Curtiss W-7533)*

Curtiss estimated performance included a high speed at sea level of 182mph and stall speed of 66mph at sea level. Cruising speed at 0.8 of maximum RPM was 141mph at sea level. Sea level climb rate was 1,850fpm. Full throttle endurance at sea level and 0.8 maximum RPM were 1.06 hours and 2.15 hours, and the equivalent ranges were 193 miles and 303 miles. Service and absolute ceilings were 22,700 feet and 24,000 feet, respectively.

Curtiss F9C-2 *Sparrowhawk*

As noted above, there were a total of only six "production" F9C-2 fighters, Navy serials BuA 9056 through 9061. Their design was based on the XF9C-1, plus the changes recommended by the Navy on that aircraft. Ordered October 12, 1931, the aircraft were delivered, according to Curtiss billing book records, between May 2, 1932, and September 12, 1932, at a unit cost varying between $27,356 for #1 aircraft and $23,561 for #6 aircraft.

The first of the batch (BuA 9056) functioned as the Navy flight test "X" model, and was also the one to test design innovations, including modified landing gear. It was later brought to production configuration. This aircraft was first delivered by air to Anacostia NAS on May 2, 1932. The Curtiss piloted demonstrations, including dives, started May 10th. All known flight maneuvers were demonstrated except outside loops. On May 13, 1932, the aircraft again demonstrated aerobatics and terminal velocity dives at the Naval Proving Ground, Dahlgren, Virginia. Two tail spins of 10 turns each way were performed. The recovery from the left spin required one full turn. In accordance with the contract, four test dives were performed from 14,000 or 15,000 feet, with pullouts starting from 6,500 to 8,000 feet. About 1,200 feet were lost in pullouts. The maximum speed at the start of the dive pullouts was 275mph, and the maximum "g" encountered was 9.5.

Arresting gear testing at Hampton Roads, Virginia, took place between June 14th and 30th. The first USS *Akron* dirigible hook-on took place on June 29, 1932, and Navy testing was completed on July 11th.

The F9C-2 differed from the XF9C-1 in having a split axle, tripod landing gear with low pressure tires and open sided wheel pants, and installation of the airship hook, making the aircraft directionally unstable. Vertical tail area was added on the production aircraft. An upper wing raised four inches was also incorporated, and rudder balance was removed. Landing gear length was increased six inches, and propeller diameter was increased to eight

A good profile study of F9C-2 BuA 9056, with the trapeze gear rather spoiling the otherwise elegant lines of the diminutive fighter. This aircraft was delivered at Anacostia NAS May 3, 1932, and served mainly with the USS *Akron*, although it was also with the *Macon* in June 1933. Remarkably, it survived on the Navy inventory until October 20, 1939, when stricken finally as obsolete with 676 hours total time. It is now in the collections of the National Air and Space Museum *(Dean Collection)*

Bearing nearly full markings as used while operating aboard the USS *Akron*, F9C-2 BuA 9058 poses at a civilian airfield. It was one of the aircraft lost at sea with the USS *Macon* February 20, 1935. (*Dean Collection*)

feet, six inches. However, the F9C-2 was considered deficient in visibility for carrier operations.

All six aircraft were manufactured in Buffalo, New York, and delivered to the dirigible unit in 1932, but none were with *Akron* when she crashed on April 4, 1933. The planes then went to the USS *Macon* unit. In 1934 small fins were added on the landing gear pants as carrier arresting wire stops. In airfield operations, the aircraft type was a ground looper. Also during 1934, operations from the airship were undertaken with the landing gear removed, and an extra belly fuel tank installed. These operations were quite successful, and the planes acted as scouts for the airship.

With the crash of the *Macon* on February 12, 1935, four of the F9C-2 *Sparrowhawks* were lost. Two aircraft were then left in the inventory. They were later redesignated as XF9C-2s, and had the airship hooks removed, since there were no more airships for them to operate from. One of these aircraft was scrapped in 1936, and the other saved as a museum piece, as noted.

The Curtiss Characteristics Sheet dated February 24, 1932, for an F9C-2 Carrier-to-Airship Fighter gives data as follows, and is followed in parentheses by Navy data of the same time period: span, length, and height 25 feet, six inches, 19 feet, five inches (20 feet one and 1/2 inches), and 10 feet, five inches (10 feet 11.5 inches.) Wing chords 56 inches upper and 40 inches lower, gap 46.75 inches mean, stagger 25 inches, and upper wing dihedral 3 degrees. Wing, horizontal tail, and vertical tail areas were 173 (185.4) square feet, 23.3 square feet, and 13.1 square feet, respectively. Wing airfoils were still Clark YH contour.

The powerplant was a Wright R-975E3 (-22) rated at 440hp (400hp) at 2,200rpm with a 10.5:1 supercharger gear ratio and a direct propeller drive. (The propeller was a two-blade Design 5678 type of eight feet, six inch diameter, and pitch of 19.7 degrees at the 42 inch radius station). Engine compression ratio was 6.0, 87 octane fuel was used, and fuel consumption at full throttle and 80 percent RPM were 40.5 and 20 gallons per hour, respectively. Fuel capacities were 43 gallons normal and 60 gallons maximum, with oil capacities 3.5 gallons and 4.8 gallons.

Empty weight of the F9C-2 was 2,056 (2,089) pounds useful load, consisting of a 180 pound pilot, 284 (286) pounds of fuel and oil, 52 (57) pounds of equipment, and 145 (141) pounds of armament—this being two .30 caliber machine guns and ammunition—totaled 661 (662) pounds, making a total gross weight of 2,717 (2,776) pounds. (Overload gross weight was 3,103 pounds with wing loading of 15.0psf and power loading of 6.9 pounds per horse power.)

The Curtiss estimated performance (with Navy actual performance in parentheses) was: high speed at sea level 178mph (176.5mph), (173mph at 5,000 feet, and 152mph at 15,000 feet), cruising speed 139mph, and stall speed 66mph (64.9mph). Sea level climb rate was 1,800fpm (1,700fpm); endurance at full throttle and 80 percent RPM were 1.06 and 2.15 hours. The ranges at these conditions were 169 and 300 miles. Service and absolute ceilings were 21,700 feet (19,200 feet) and 23,000 feet.

A later Navy characteristics sheet of September 1, 1934, gives the following characteristics for the F9C-2 fighter: span 25 feet, six inches upper, 23 feet, four inches lower wing, length 20 feet, one and 1/2 inches, and height 10 feet 11.5 inches. Wing chords were: upper, four feet, eight inches, and lower, three feet, four inches. Incidence 0 degrees, dihedral 2.5 degrees upper and -0.5 degrees lower, wing stagger 25 inches, sweepback 0 degrees, airfoil sections Clark YH. Wing area was 185.4 square feet, horizontal tail area 27.6 square feet, and vertical tail area 15.6 square feet.

Powerplant was the Wright R-975-22 rated at 400hp at 2,200rpm at sea level, but test rated horse power was actually 438. Propeller was Design number 5678, two blade ground adjustable type of eight feet, six inches diameter, and 19.7 degrees pitch at the 42 inch radius station. Normal fuel was 60 gallons and maximum fuel 90 gallons. Oil capacity was 4.8 gallons.

Empty weight was 2,114 pounds, useful load 662 pounds, consisting of a 180 pound pilot, 258 pounds of fuel, 28 pounds of oil, 141 pounds of armament, and 57 pounds of equipment. Gross weight came to 2,776 pounds normal and 3,103 pounds overload. Normal gross weight wing loading was 15psf, and power loading 6.9 pounds per horse power. Normal load useful load to gross weight ratio was 0.238.

Maximum speeds were 176.5mph at sea level, 173mph at 5,000 feet, and 152mph at 15,000 feet. Stalling speed at normal load was 64.9mph. Times to climb were 3.5 minutes to 5,000 feet and 16.6 minutes to 15,000 feet. Service ceiling was 19,200 feet. Endurance

19 November 83

SPARROW HAWK alternate landing gear.

This ubit was built and tested by company and Naval Pilots at the Buffalo air base.

This single strut gear was made of swaged steel tubing. The landing load was absorbed by rubber disks of correct durometer. The sketch shows that the disks were in compression during landing. The assembly of the disk system was slightly staggered to permit the load arms to clear each other.

In this design the wheel treads were increased about 35% to improve ground handling and to stop looping.

On landing there was atendency for the plane to bounce a little. We designed shock absorbers which seemed to solve the problem. The gear was of lighter weight and much easier to remove and replace. Why it was not used was not known to me as by that time I had left the company.

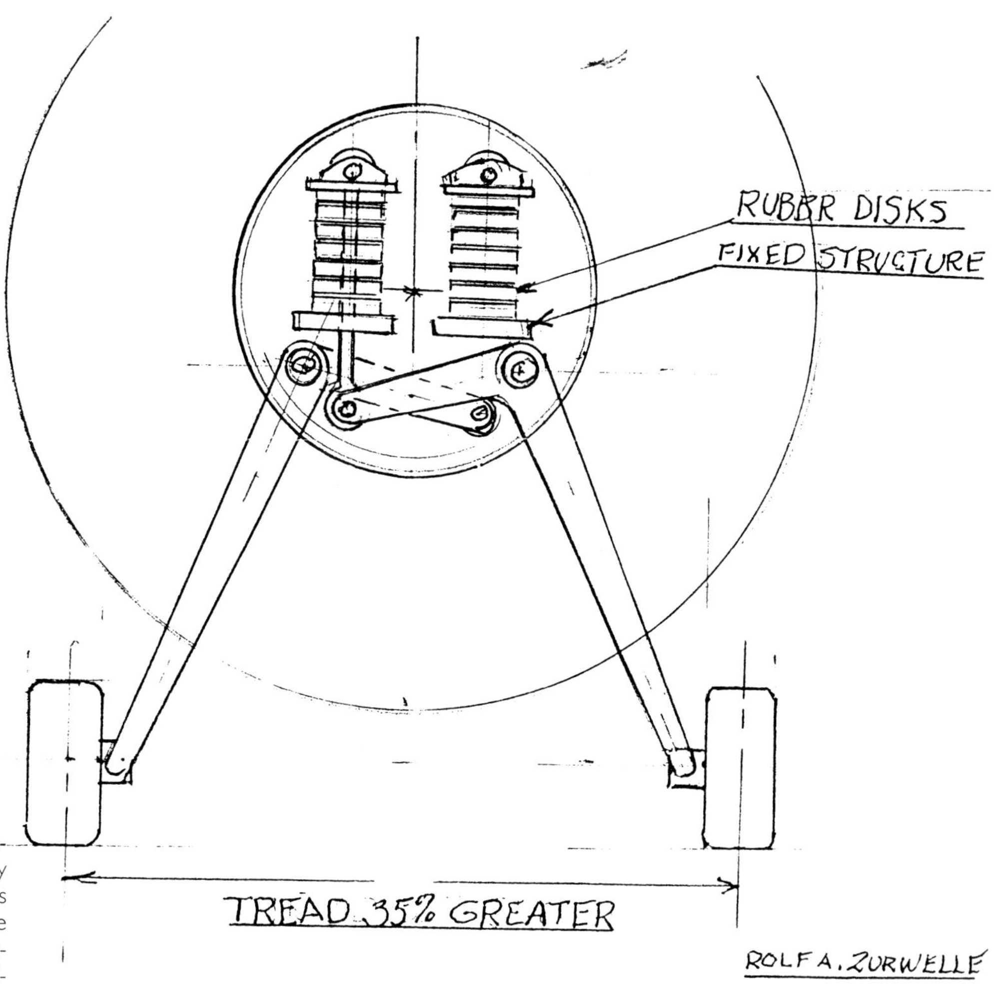

Details of an alternate landing gear installation designed, built, and tested by both Navy and Curtiss pilots at Buffalo. The intention was to eliminate the rather pronounced bounce that the standard F9C-2 landing gear provided, even at the hands of the most experienced pilots. (*Curtiss*)

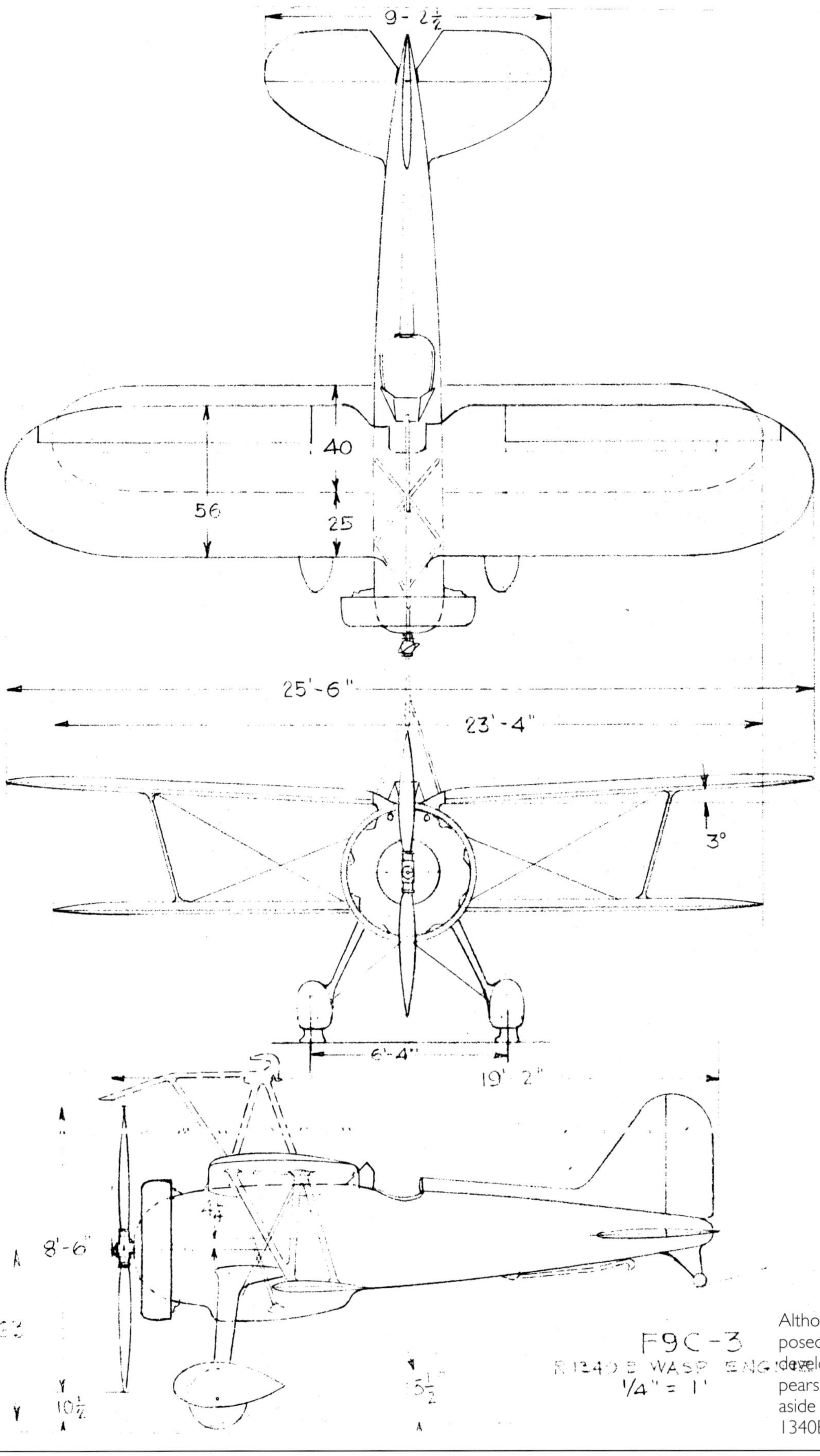

Although no known drawings of the proposed F9C-4 carrier fighter are known, a development—the proposed F9C-3—appears to have differed little from the F9C-2, aside from employing a Pratt & Whitney R-1340E *Wasp* of 500hp. (*Dean Collection*)

at normal load was 1.01 hours at maximum speed, 2.34 hours at 75 percent of maximum speed, and 3.41 hours at 60 percent of maximum speed. Range with normal load was 366 miles, and with overload 719 miles. Takeoff run with zero wind was 427 feet, with 15 knot wind 242 feet, and with 25 knot wind 147 feet.

It is interesting to note that Curtiss, in exploring the possibility of additional Navy business, did some analysis of potential follow-on versions of the *Sparrowhawk* fighter. These were labeled F9C-3 and F9C-4, implying at least some Navy interest and sanction.

Whereas the F9C-2 was noted as a "Carrier to Airship fighter," the studied F9C-3 and F9C-4 models were labeled as "Carrier Fighter." However, extant three-view drawings do show the airship hook in dotted lines.

The F9C-3 was envisioned as powered by the Pratt & Whitney *Wasp* engine variously rated at 500hp at 2,200rpm at 6,000 feet, 500hp at 2,200rpm at 11,000 feet, 600hp at 2,200rpm at 6,000 feet, and 500hp at 2,200rpm at 7,600 feet, all using the same useful load as the F9C-2. The engines all had mechanically geared superchargers, no doubt single stage. The estimated maximum speeds of the four variants above at the altitudes noted were 200mph, 211mph, 216mph, and 204mph. There was no airship hook since there were no airships!

An F9C-4 was studied using the twin-row, 14 cylinder Wright R-1510 *Whirlwind* 14 engine rated in various configurations at 525 or 600hp at 2,200rpm at 6,000 feet. It was noted, however, not unreasonably, that "*No data is given because proper balance with this engine is impossible*."

One final episode in the F9C chronicles was related to the Smithsonian's Dr. Paul Garber in November 1983 by engineer Rolf Zurwelle. It seems that famed Naval aviator Al Williams was intrigued by the aircraft and, one day, decided to try one of the aircraft on, literally. The Curtiss staff tried to explain to Williams that he was much too large a man to get into the very small cockpit, but he insisted, and had soon levered himself into the aircraft. After looking over the controls, the pilot view from the cockpit, and exchanging details with the staff, he complained at length about how small the cockpit was, and how he could hardly move the controls. Finally, when he tried to exit the aircraft, he could not even begin to do so. The Curtiss staff had to quickly improvise a sling under his arms, and pulled him out using a block and tackle, much to his embarrassment.

6

More Biplane *Hawks* and *Goshawks* for the Navy

Curtiss XF11C-1 Goshawk

One of two prototype, single seat biplanes built as fighters and light dive bombers by Curtiss, the XF11C-1 was distinguished by an open cockpit, a two-row, 14 cylinder cowled Wright *Twin Whirlwind* R-1510 engine, open panted single leg landing gear with large diameter wheels, and a three blade propeller.

It was first flown as a Curtiss private venture on March 25, 1932.[71] On April 16, 1932, the Navy bought the aircraft under Contract 26572 (MSN 11669), and Navy BuA 9269 was assigned. This plane was then tested at Anacostia NAS. The XF11C-1 was designed to carry a 500 pound bomb under the fuselage using a swing-release mechanism to clear the propeller when dive bombing. As an alternative to the 500 pound bomb, four 116 pound bombs could be carried.

Precisely why Curtiss invested in this classic Navy series as a private venture probably has more to do with the ongoing depression and the day-to-day realities of Navy procurement that were operative at the time than any other factors. Curtiss, for its part, wanted to promote their new, 600hp Wright R-1510, twin-row *Whirlwind 14* engine, mated with the stout undercarriage of the XF6C-6 and the Army's successful P-6E. The Navy, on the other hand, was strapped for funding for yet another experimental type, and probably left Curtiss with the impression that if they would build it, "we would come." Basically, that is what happened and, in the process, Curtiss seized the opportunity to use the basic airframe for the highly successful export *Hawk Type I*, *II*, *III*, and *IV* series that followed. Additionally, a new contender for the precious few Navy and Army contracts of the day, Boeing, with its P-12 and F4B series, undoubtedly encouraged Curtiss to spend some of its own money and take a calculated risk on eventual Navy procurement of a radial-engined fighter that they very much desired to standardize upon.

First built and flown as a Curtiss private venture as early as May 1933, the Navy tested the aircraft that became the XF11C-1 in July 1933 (BuA 9219) with a number of propeller and cowl arrangements. Here, it has a single bladed prop and a narrow chord cowl. (*Dean Collection*)

In support of this contention, although formally ordered in April 1932, the Curtiss Engineering Annual Report for 1933 indicated that the XF11C-1 was still undergoing development at the Wright Aeronautical plant, where cooling tests on the two row Wright *Twin Whirlwind* engine were taking place, experimental work that would ultimately benefit not only the Navy, but Curtiss and Wright, as well.

Curtiss had made proposals for three variations of the XF11C-1 with different versions of the *Twin Whirlwind* engine, these recorded on Characteristics Sheets dated February 24, 1932, for two variants of a Carrier Fighter and a dedicated Dive Bomber. The economies being imposed on the services at the time dictated that they had to get as much "stretch" out of aircraft procurement as possible, and Curtiss had not missed this central point. The engine versions were the plain R-1510, unsupercharged, and with direct propeller drive, rated 525hp at 6,000 feet, the SR-1510 supercharged, and direct propeller drive model, rated at 600hp at 8,000 feet, and the GR-1510 with a 4:3 propeller gear reduction rated at 525hp at 6,000 feet. It is believed the supercharged direct propeller drive model engine was selected for the XF11C-1.

The Curtiss estimates on the Characteristics Sheets were as follows: span, length, and height were 31 feet, six inches, 22 feet, six and 1/2 inches, and nine feet, 11 inches. Mean wing chords were 62.5 inches upper and 49.4 inches lower, wing gap was 56 29/32 inches, stagger at leading edge 38.5 inches, incidence of both

Pictured as configured on September 25, 1933, the XF11C-1 had a modified forward fuselage, a tight fitting, long chord cowl, and a three-bladed prop. (*Curtiss W-8547*)

wings -2 degrees, lower wing dihedral -2 degrees. Wings were tapered with no sweepback. Wing area was 252 square feet, horizontal tail area 30.1 square feet, and vertical tail area 13.7 square feet. The wing sections were Clark Y, and the high angle of attack load factor was 12.

The powerplant was the supercharged SR-1510 engine rated at 600hp at 2,200rpm at 8,000 feet. Compression ratio was 6.1:1. Fuel was 87 octane, and fuel consumptions at full throttle and at 0.8 maximum RPM were 57 gallons per hour and 28 gallons per hour, respectively. Fuel capacity was 65 gallons normal and 110 gallons maximum with an external tank. Oil capacity was five gallons normal and nine gallons maximum. The engine drove a three bladed ground adjustable Hamilton Standard propeller of eight feet, eight inches diameter.

Weights of the XF11C-1 as a fighter were estimated as follows: empty weight 2,886 pounds, useful load 869 pounds (consisting of a 200 pound pilot, 428 pounds of fuel and oil, 88 pounds of equipment, and 153 pounds of armament), making up a gross weight of 3,755 pounds. In this case wing loading was 14.9psf, and power loading 6.26 pounds per horse power. Useful load to gross weight ratio was 0.231.

Weights as a bomber were defined as: empty weight 2,886 pounds, and useful load 1,382 pounds (with armament increased to 555 pounds), giving a gross weight of 4,268 pounds.

Performance estimates were: high speed 201mph at 8,000 feet, cruise speed 157mph, and landing speed at sea level 66mph. Endurances at full throttle and at 0.8 maximum RPM were respectively 1.14 hours and 2.32 hours. Ranges at those two conditions were 230 and 365 miles. Service and absolute ceilings were estimated to be 26,400 and 27,400 feet, respectively.

Navy figures at that time were somewhat different. Wing area was cited as 262 square feet (this was either a typographical error, or the fuselage area between lower wings was being counted), and empty and gross weights were 3,290 pounds and 4,368 pounds, with a 1,078 pound useful load. High speed was 203mph, climb to 5,000 feet took 8.2 minutes, range was 530 miles, and service ceiling was 23,800 feet.

After testing, the XF11C-1 was sent back to Curtiss in Buffalo, New York, later in 1933, and used by the Inspector of Naval Aircraft there into 1934, at which time it was redesignated as an XBFC-1 bomber fighter. It was in storage for awhile, then assigned to the Inspector of Naval Aircraft at Wright Aeronautical Corp. at

Intended from the outset as both a fighter and dive bomber, the Navy redesignated the XF11C-1 as the XBFC-1 in 1934. By this time, it had still a different cowling. The nature of the dark colored modifications to the lower forward fuselage are unknown. Incredibly, it survived in the inventory until declared obsolete March 10, 1939. (*Dean Collection*)

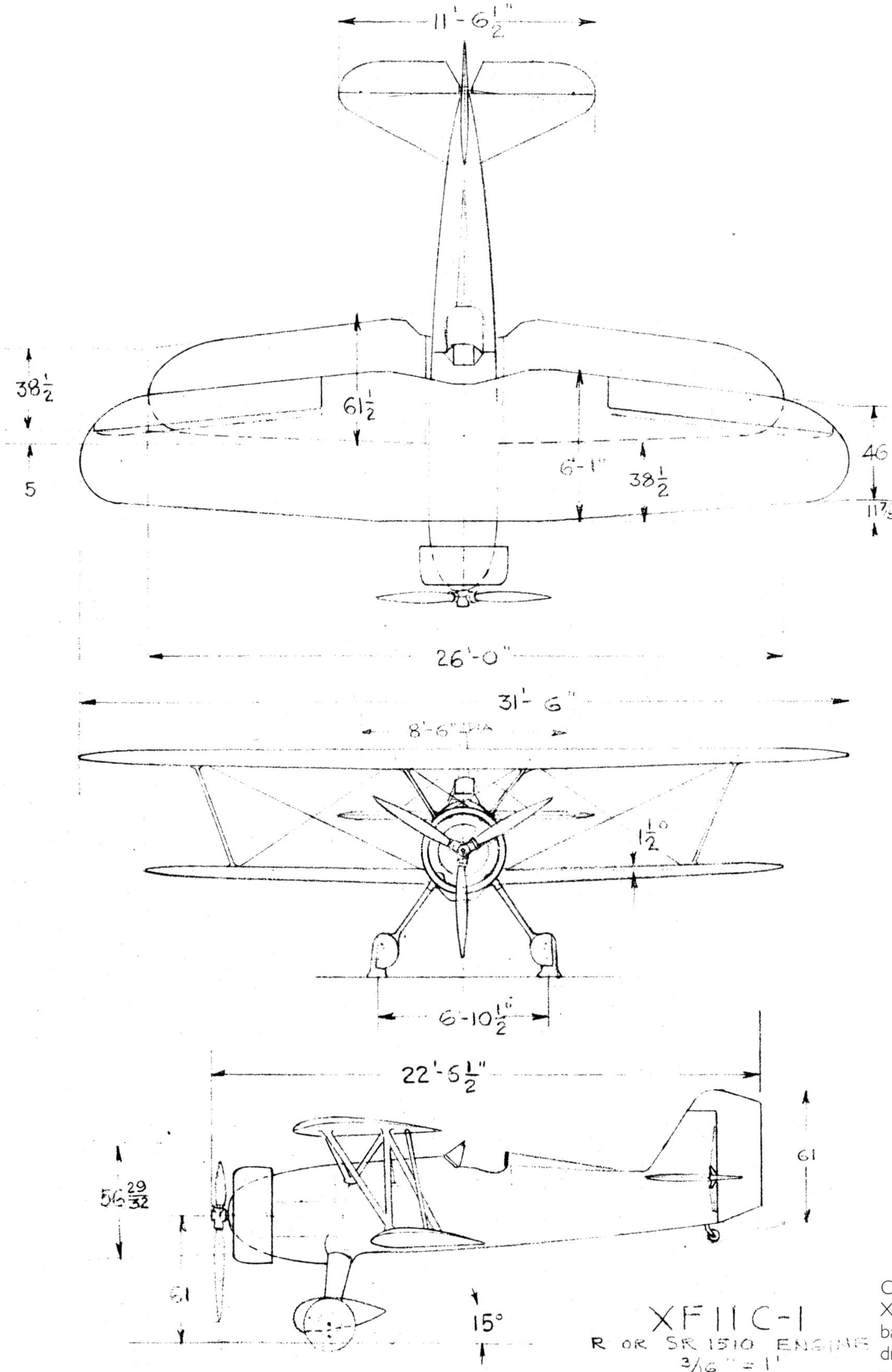

Curtiss made good use of the XF11C-1 airframe to test out their basic Wright R-1510 engine. This drawing of the aircraft shows the proposed SR-1510 installation, with yet another cowling arrangement, with a rather short chord. (*Curtiss*)

Patterson, New Jersey, until 1936. The plane then went to the NACA at Langley Field, Virginia, on January 13, 1936, to be used as a test bed for various engine cowling arrangements designed to help cool two row radial engines. It was also used to test nose-slot cowlings and the field of view from the cockpit. It stayed in this test role until at least March 3, 1939, when it returned to Navy custody. The Wright R-1510 *Twin Whirlwind* engine was not a success like its competitor, the Pratt & Whitney R-1535 *Twin Wasp Junior*. This fact did not help the fortunes of the XF11C-1.

In March 1933 Navy Characteristics for the XF11C-1 were: span, length, and height 31 feet, six inches, 26 feet even, and nine feet, 11.5 inches. Wing area was 252 square feet using Clark Y airfoils. Chords at root were 6 feet even, upper, and five feet, one and 1/2 inches lower. Wing gap was four feet, eight and 19/32 inches, stagger 38.5 inches, sweepback 0 degrees, and dihedral 0 degrees upper, 1.5 degrees lower. Horizontal tail area was 31.9 square feet, and vertical tail area was 14.1 square feet.

Powerplant was a Wright R-1510-98 rated at 600hp at 2,100rpm at sea level driving a three bladed Design number 3792 propeller of eight feet, six inches diameter, with pitch of 21.5 degrees at the 42 inch radius station. Fuel tank capacity was 94 gallons, and oil tank capacity 9 gallons.

Empty weight was 3,003 pounds, and useful load was 1,396 pounds, consisting of a 200 pound pilot, 390 pounds of fuel, 38 pounds of oil, 673 pounds of armament (including bombs), 49 pounds of equipment, and a 46 pound radio, giving a gross weight of 4,399 pounds, which in turn gave a wing loading of 17.5psf and power loading of 7.3 pounds per horse power. Useful load to gross weight ratio was thus 0.317.

High speed was 176.8mph, while stalling speed at normal load was 66.9mph. Service ceiling was 16,600 feet. Takeoff run was 521 feet with zero wind and 187 feet with a 25 knot headwind.

Mounting a single-row, nine cylinder Wright *Cyclone*, and with a much narrower cowl, is the single XF11C-2 (BuA 9213, not marked on the aircraft in this view dated March 25, 1932, since it had not yet been accepted by the Navy). Accepted in early May 1932, the aircraft was so badly damaged in August that it was stricken. It served, however, as essentially the prototype for the highly successful export derivatives that followed. (*Curtiss W-7243*)

Curtiss XF11C-2 *Goshawk*

The single XF11C-2 fighter prototype differed from the XF11C-1 principally in being powered by a single row, nine cylinder Wright *Cyclone* radial engine. Oddly, Curtiss records, usually religious about listing the popular name for each variant produced, do not list the name *Hawk* with the XF11C-2, although logically it certainly should have been. It was also distinguished from the -1 in having smaller, fatter low pressure tires, longer landing gear, and a two bladed propeller. The engine cowl was larger in diameter and narrower in chord to suit the *Cyclone* installation. It was set up to accept a belly auxiliary fuel tank between the landing gear legs.

The XF11C-2 (MSN 11615) was first flown as a Curtiss-owned aircraft on March 25, 1932, at Buffalo, New York. It was later bought on Navy contract 26480 dated April 16, 1932, the same date as the contract for the XF11C-1, and assigned BuA serial 9213. Like the XF11C-1, it apparently was owned and flown by Curtiss prior to actual acceptance by the Navy, although under what authority is not known, as there are no known civil experimental registrations applied to the type.

The XF11C-2 was tested first with an SR-1820E supercharged *Cyclone* with a two blade propeller, then with an SR-1820F supercharged engine with a three bladed propeller, and later with the "F" series engine and a two blade propeller.

The Curtiss Characteristics Sheet of February 22, 1932, for a "Carrier Fighter and Dive Bomber" gave the following estimates for the E and F engine variants with a two bladed propeller: span, length, and height 31 feet, six inches, 22 feet, four inches, and nine feet, 11 inches. Wing upper and lower geometric mean chords were 62.6 inches and 49.4 inches. Wing gap was 56 29/32 inches, and stagger at the leading edge 38.5 inches. Wing incidences were both -2 degrees, and lower wing dihedral 1.5 degrees. The wing airfoil sections were Clark Y tapered. Wing area was 252 square feet, and horizontal and vertical tail areas were 30.1 and 13.7 square feet. The design load factor at high angle of attack was 12.

Construction of the fuselage was of welded steel tubing with formers and stringers covered with fabric, except for aluminum skins above the upper longerons and around the engine compartment. Horizontal and vertical tail surfaces had a combination of steel and aluminum framing with fabric covering, except dural sheet was used at the stabilizer leading edges. Wings were made of two built up wood spars, built up wood ribs, and fabric covering, except sheet dural skin was used forward of the front spar. Ailerons were all metal.

As noted, the XF11C-2 had either a Cyclone SR-1820E or SR-1820F engine, the E supercharger gear ratio being 12.69:1. Both engines had a direct drive to the propeller. The "E" engine was rated at 575hp at 7,600 feet at 1,900rpm, and the "F" engine 600hp at 8,000 feet at 2,000rpm. Engine's compression ratio was 6.25:1, and fuel used was 87 octane. Fuel consumption at full throttle was 52.5 gallons per hour at 7,600 feet for the "E" engine, and 58 gallons per hour at 8,000 feet for the "F" version. At 0.8 of maximum RPM the respective fuel rates were 26.3 gallons per hour at 7,600 feet and 29 gallons per hour at 8,000 feet. Fuel capacity was 65 gallons normal and 110 gallons maximum with an external belly

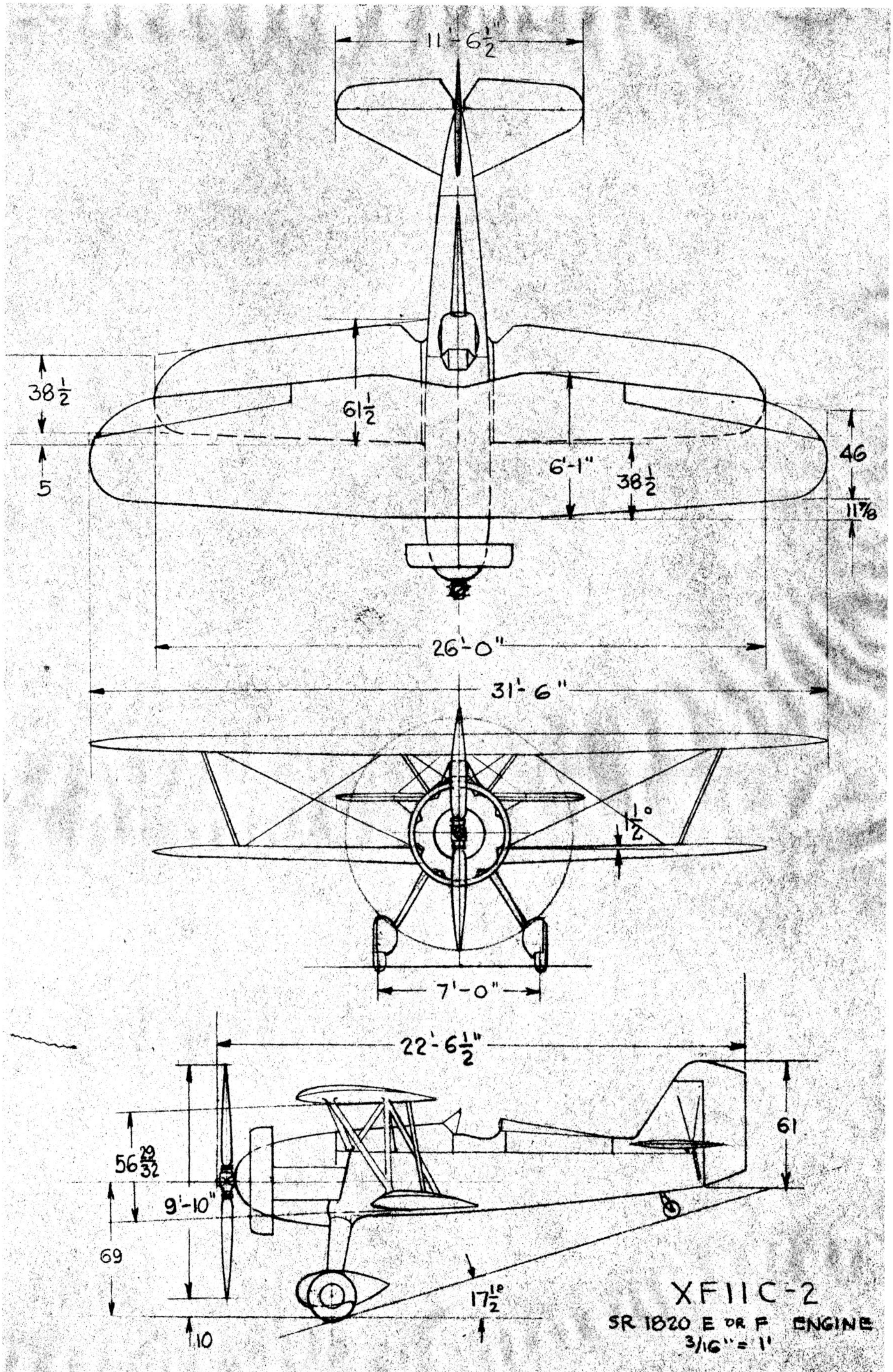

It is interesting to compare this drawing of the XF11C-2 with that for the XF11C-1. It differed principally in having smaller wheels, narrower cowl ring, and a higher stance, plus a hinged compartment on the upper decking just aft of the cockpit. *(Curtiss)*

tank. The propeller was a two blade Hamilton Standard type of either nine foot, 10 inch or nine foot, six inch diameter.

The XF11C-2 estimated weights were: empty weight 2,898 pounds, and fighter useful load 869 pounds, composed of a 200 pound pilot, 428 pounds of fuel and oil, 88 pounds of equipment, and 153 pounds of armament, making a fighter gross weight of 3,767 pounds. Bomber useful load items were the same, except armament (with a bomb) was 666 pounds, making useful load 1,382 pounds and bomber gross weight 4,280 pounds.

Estimated fighter performance with the R-1820E engine at 7,600 feet (with F engine in parentheses at 8,000 feet) was: high speed 196mph (198mph). Cruising speed at 0.8 maximum RPM was 153mph (154mph). Endurance at full throttle was 1.24 hours (1.12 hours), while endurance at 0.8 maximum RPM was 2.47 hours (2.14 hours). Full throttle range 243 miles (222 miles); range at 0.8 maximum RPM 378 miles (345 miles), service ceiling 26,100 feet (26,300 feet), and absolute ceiling 27,000 feet (27,400 feet).

Other data, no doubt Navy figures, gave the following for the XF11C-2 with Wright R-1820-78 engine rated 700hp at 8,000 feet: wing area 262 square feet. Empty weight 3,000 pounds, useful load normal 1,132 pounds, normal gross weight 4,132 pounds, and maximum gross weight 4,601 pounds, with fuel capacity 94 gallons. Maximum speed was 202mph at 8,000 feet, landing speed 65mph, climb 10,400 feet in 10 minutes, range at full throttle 303 miles, and service ceiling was 25,100 feet.

The XF11C-2 arrived at Anacostia NAS on May 2, 1932. It force landed twice that month, and was tested temporarily with a three bladed propeller. Curtiss and Navy tests were conducted through the spring and summer of 1932, including a dive test to a 10.2 G pullout, and carrier arrestor tests were made at Norfolk, where the aircraft, with its small wheels, overturned and was badly damaged on landing August 1, 1932. Serial 9213 was repaired, and larger 36x6 wheels were fitted. However, the aircraft was in fact stricken from the Navy inventory on August 25, 1932, with a total of only 74 hours on the aircraft.

Curtiss F11C-2 and BFC-2 *Goshawk*

On October 18, 1932, the Navy let Contract 28847 to Curtiss Aeroplane and Motor Co. Inc. for 28 production F11C-2 *Goshawk* carrier fighter-bombers. They were assigned Curtiss MSNs 11668 and 11675 to 11700, and Navy serials BuA 9265 to 9268, 9270 to 9282, and 9331 to 9340.[72] These had a slightly wider ring engine cowl, larger 36x6 main wheels inside open sided pants, and a tail wheel assembly moved aft with a shock absorber in a rudder lower cutout, leaving room for a carrier hook just forward. The first aircraft was apparently held for testing. According to the Curtiss Billing Book records 16 F11C-2s were delivered to the Navy between March 11 and April 11, 1933, at a unit price, no doubt without government furnished equipment (GFE), of $13,108.68. A second batch of 10 aircraft was delivered between April 13 and April 27, 1933, at the same price. One aircraft, serial 9269, was held at Curtiss for modification to an XF11C-3 with a retractable landing gear.

From the time they entered service, the F11C-2s underwent a number of significant changes. The initially fitted, low-pressure tires were notable failures in the carrier landing test program, and were replaced by 32 x 6 tires. The arrestor hook was also moved further aft, the initial 12-inch chord anti-drag ring became 18 inches, and the ailerons reverted to fabric covering. The most visible change was, of course, the aft turtledeck. The F11C-2 started with a P-6E style rear deck and a radio mast, but the headrest was increased in size, changed to a half-round shape, and for a time was even flat topped. The definitive version was a high-rise turtledeck (higher than the pilot's head) with a sliding half-canopy. The reason for these changes were simple: Navy pilots complained continuously of a cold draft on the back of the head and neck!

These planes were initially sent to the Navy's "*High Hat*" fighter squadron aboard the carrier USS *Saratoga*: at that time the squadron was designated VF-1B, and this squadron operated the *Goshawks* through most all their operational life, though under different squadron designations. This has led to some confusion amongst students of the subject, as the same unit successively became VF-1B, VB-2, and VB-3. The only other unit to fly the F11C-2 was assigned to the USS *Enterprise*, on which it, however, never landed nor took off.

From Curtiss characteristics data for the F11C-2: span, length, and height were 31 feet, six inches, 25 feet, and 10 feet, seven inches. Lower wing span was 26 feet, six inches. Wing area was 262 square feet (apparently counting the fuselage area between lower wings). Clark Y airfoil sections were used.

Nearly the definitive form of what shortly became a major export success, this U.S. Navy F11C-2 shows no evidence of her Bureau of Aeronautics serial number as of October 24, 1932, when photographed, and had probably not yet been turned over. (*Curtiss W-7791*)

Delivered to the Navy February 25, 1933, as an F11C-2, BuA 9265 was back and forth between Anacostia, Norfolk, and Curtiss in Buffalo, until finally assigned to San Diego to the Battle Force in January 1935 (and then NAS Seattle, for disposition only in November 1937) as a BFC-2. She was briefly assigned to VB-2B on the USS *Saratoga*. (*Dean Collection*)

The powerplant was a Wright R-1820-78 *Cyclone* rated at 715hp for takeoff at 1,950rpm at sea level. Compression ratio was 6.4:1; fuel was 87 octane, and fuel capacity 94 gallons internal, with an additional 52 gallons optional in an external tank.

Empty weight was 3,111 pounds, normal useful load 1,009 pounds, and normal gross weight 4,120 pounds. Maximum useful load and maximum resulting gross weight was 1,527 pounds and 4,638 pounds.

Performance data included maximum speed 205mph (fighter), 198mph (bomber), and landing speed 65mph. Service ceiling 24,300 feet (fighter), and absolute ceiling (fighter) 25,100 feet. Climb to 5,000 feet required 2.6 minutes (fighter). Range at maximum speed 303 miles, maximum range 628 miles, and endurance at maximum speed 1.5 hours.

Navy data on the F11C-2 in September 1933 was as follows: span, length, and height 31 feet, six inches, 26 feet lower wing, 25 feet, and 10 feet seven and 1/2 inches. Airfoils were Clark Y, upper and lower wing root chords 6 feet, one inch and 5 feet, one and 1/2 inches. Wing gap four feet, eight and 29/32 inches, stagger 38.5 inches, angle of incidence -2 degrees, upper wing dihedral 0 degrees, lower wing dihedral 1.5 degrees, sweepback 0 degrees, and airfoils Clark Y. Horizontal tail area 30.1 square feet, vertical tail area 13.2 square feet.

F11C-2 power plant was the Wright R-1820-78, rated at 600hp at 1,950rpm at 8,000 feet, driving a two blade Design 5868 propeller of nine feet, 10 inches diameter and 22.6 degrees pitch at the 42 inch radius station. Normal internal fuel capacity was 94 gallons. Overload fuel capacity 146 gallons. Oil capacity was 10.5 gallons.

Empty weight was 3,000 pounds, normal useful load 1,083 pounds (Pilot 200 pounds, fuel 564 pounds, oil 60 pounds, armament 160 pounds, equipment 52 pounds, and radio 47 pounds), giving a normal gross weight of 4,083 pounds, wing loading of 15.6psf, and a power loading of 6.8 pounds per horse power. Useful load to gross weight ratio was 0.265. Overload gross weight was 4,471 pounds.

High speed was 192mph at sea level, 202mph at 8,000 feet, and 197mph at 15,100 feet. Stall speed at normal gross weight was 64.4mph. Times to climb were 2.5 minutes to 5,000 feet, and 10 minutes to 15,000 feet. Service ceiling topped out at 25,100 feet.

Endurance at normal load at maximum speed was 1.57 hours, at 90 percent maximum speed 2.23 hours, at 75 percent maximum speed 3.29 hours, and at 60 percent maximum speed 4.6 hours. Takeoff distance with no wind was 530 feet; with a 25 knot wind, 180 feet.

In March 1934, the Navy officially recognized the type's light dive bombing capability by redesignating the planes from F11C-2 to BFC-2 for "bomber fighter." Modifications were made in the cockpit and turtledeck areas. The aft upper fuselage was raised to enclose stowage space for a life raft aft of the headrest. In addition, a short sliding semi-canopy was installed to provide partial protec-

After barely a year of service as F11C-2s, all surviving aircraft were reclassified as essentially fighter-bombers as BFC-2s in February 1934. Here, BuA 9274 shows full operational markings, and rather unusually configured wheel pants. Note also that the cowl is a solid color. This aircraft was assigned to VT-1B in May 1933, VB-2B on the *Saratoga* in December 1934, VB-6 on the *Enterprise* in May 1938, and was stricken at Norfolk June 10, 1938, as worn out with 1,098:30 total time. (*Dean Collection*)

This view of BFC-2 BuA 9338 shows the double ring-and-bead gun sight arrangement just ahead of the windscreen and full unit operational markings. She was assigned to VB-2B and VB-3 on the USS *Saratoga*, and VB-6 on the *Enterprise* between March 1934 and February 1938. She was one of the very few Navy Curtiss fighters to be stationed overseas, going to Coco Solo Naval Air Station in the Canal Zone in July 1938, and was stricken there in May 1940. (*Dean Collection*)

tion for the pilot, though photo evidence shows that this canopy section was not always used.

In January 1928 11 BFC-2 aircraft were transferred from the *High Hats* to Squadron VB-6, but the assignment lasted only into May 1938. One BFC-2 was at the Naval Aircraft Factory in Philadelphia for tests in 1934-5. Two aircraft were at Wright Aeronautical Corp. in 1934, used by the Inspector of Naval Aircraft there, and one was still assigned there in 1935. In June 1938, BFC-2s were assigned strictly for utility duty: two at NRAB Seattle, four at Pearl Harbor, and three at Norfolk, Virginia. At the end of 1938 10 aircraft were left, including five in Hawaii and three stored in the Panama Canal Zone at Coco Solo NAS.

After three years of restoration, a BFC-2 *Goshawk* (BuA 9332) now resides in the National Museum of Naval Aviation at Pensacola, Florida.

The Navy data for the BFC-2 changeover to bomber fighter of September 1, 1934, is as follows (this for the bomber):

Dimensions and areas and powerplant data were the same as that for F11C-2. Empty weight 3,000 pounds, useful load 1,601 pounds, consisting of a 200 pound pilot, 564 pounds of fuel, 60 pounds of oil, and 679 pounds of armament (including a 500 pound bomb, 52 pounds of equipment, and 46 pounds of radio) for a gross weight of 4,601 pounds, giving a wing loading of 18.3psf and power loading of 7.7 pounds per horse power. Useful load to gross weight ratio was 0.348.

High speed was 194.5mph at 8,000 feet, and 182mph at 15,000 feet. Stalling speed was 68.4mph. Time to climb to 5,000 feet was 4.0 minutes, and to 15,000 feet 15.1 minutes. Service ceiling was 20,000 feet. Endurance at normal load was 1.57 hours at maximum speed, 2.23 hours at 90 percent of maximum speed, 3.32 hours at 75 percent of maximum speed, and 4.4 hours at 60 percent of maximum speed. Range at economical speed was 518 miles. Takeoff distance with no wind was 672 feet, and with a 25 knot headwind 249 feet.

Actually the last of the second batch of F11C-2s, BuA 9269 was held at Curtiss at the Navy's request for modifications that included installation of a hand operated, retractable landing gear assembly. Pictured here barely four months old on September 12, 1933, the vestigial cockpit enclosure, stout radio mast, bulging belly, and fully cowled engine make it appear a much more robust aircraft. It was later redesignated as the XBF2C-1, but crashed at Norfolk in September 1934. (*Curtiss W-8516*)

7

Those Curtiss *Hawk* Export Aircraft

Curtiss, via the subsidiary, and very energetic Curtiss-Wright Export Corp., had better sales in the export market than with the U.S. military in the early 1930s, and these very substantial sales almost certainly saved the company when the U.S. was caught in the deepening economic depression of those times. A prime export product were the aircraft built in what has commonly been cited as the *Hawk II* series, in either landplane or seaplane form, the latter sometimes called the *Seahawk*.

To say that these aircraft have been misunderstood and victim of repeated misinformation would be a radical understatement. As it actually happened, they were frequently tailored to the specific requirements of the foreign customer, and the designations that Curtiss assigned them were not, in point of fact, as straightforward as nearly every previously published account would have us believe.

What follows, in production order, is the first coherent description of at least 20 separate orders for these exotic aircraft, based entirely on original Curtiss records, and using the descriptors that the company used in its own internal documentation.

Most of these aircraft were externally similar to the U.S. Navy XF11C-2, but this similarity has been rather exaggerated, as will be seen. Most of the land based variants had smaller, panted but open-sided landing gear wheels, and two basic variants of the large diameter, single-row, nine cylinder Wright *Cyclone*. Nearly all of them could mount a newly contoured, flattened slipper type belly auxiliary fuel tank of 50 gallon capacity, which blended in very well with the underside. Between 1932 and 1934, when most were built and delivered, they were very much "state-of-the-art" warplanes, and amongst the most modern fighting machines anywhere.

Perhaps because of the arms trafficking investigations of the U.S. Congress during the 1930s, these classic Curtiss biplane fighters completely missed participation in one of the central military aeronautical events of the between-the-wars years, the Spanish Civil War. It has been suggested, in fact, that the projected sale of *Hawk Type Is* to Mexico, which winked at arms transfers sympathetic to the Spanish Republican loyalist element, may have been intended for transshipment to the warring factions. Indeed, the popular press of the day, perhaps accustomed to seeing Curtiss aircraft turning up in hot spots, frequently reported Soviet supplied Polikarpov I-15 *Chato* and *Super-Chato* fighters as "Curtiss" types. These very reports have led many historians, over the years, to search in vain for Curtiss fighters in Spain, when there were none whatsoever.

Although customized to order, most of the export *Hawk Type Is* and *Type IIs* as landplanes had similar overall measurements. Span, length, and height were, typically, 31 feet, six inches, 22 feet, four inches, and nine feet, nine inches. The span of the lower wings was 26.5 feet, while total wing area was 252 square feet. The *Type I* export *Hawks* appeared essentially the same as the *Type II* externally, and differed mainly in that the latter had two main fuselage fuel tanks totaling 94 gallons, whereas the former had only a single 50 gallon tank. When Curtiss first developed the *Type II*, they briefly referred to it as the *Type I Export Hawk with SR-1820F-53 Engine*.

Curtiss performance characteristics for the assorted aircraft included under this heading have never been reliably reported. Not surprisingly, they varied slightly depending on engine and equipment choices, but those for the *Hawk Type I*, *Hawk Type II*, and *II-A* landplane and seaplane variants (the latter in parenthesis) are included here.

Following are the characteristics for the *Hawk Type I* landplane and seaplane (in parenthesis):

Overall length was 22 feet, four and 1/2 inches (25 feet, seven and 1/2 inches), while overall height was nine feet, eight and 1/2 inches (12 feet, six inches). Wing span for both was 31 feet, six inches, with a resulting wing area of 262 square feet, indicating that the wings for both *Type Is* and *IIs* were virtually identical. With the nine cylinder Wright SR-1820-F *Cyclone* rated at 575hp at 1,950rpm in the landplane and SR-1820F-2 rated at 600hp in the seaplane variant, maximum speeds at 7,540 feet were 198mph (182mph), and stalling speed 60.5mph (62mph), while cruise speed was 154mph (140mph). Range with internal fuel was 291 miles (259 miles), but this could be augmented in some aircraft as an option, by the addition of a slip tank to 578 miles (518 miles). Service ceiling was 28,600 feet (26,000 feet), and absolute ceiling 29,600 feet (27,000 feet). Gross weight was 3,416 pounds (3,780

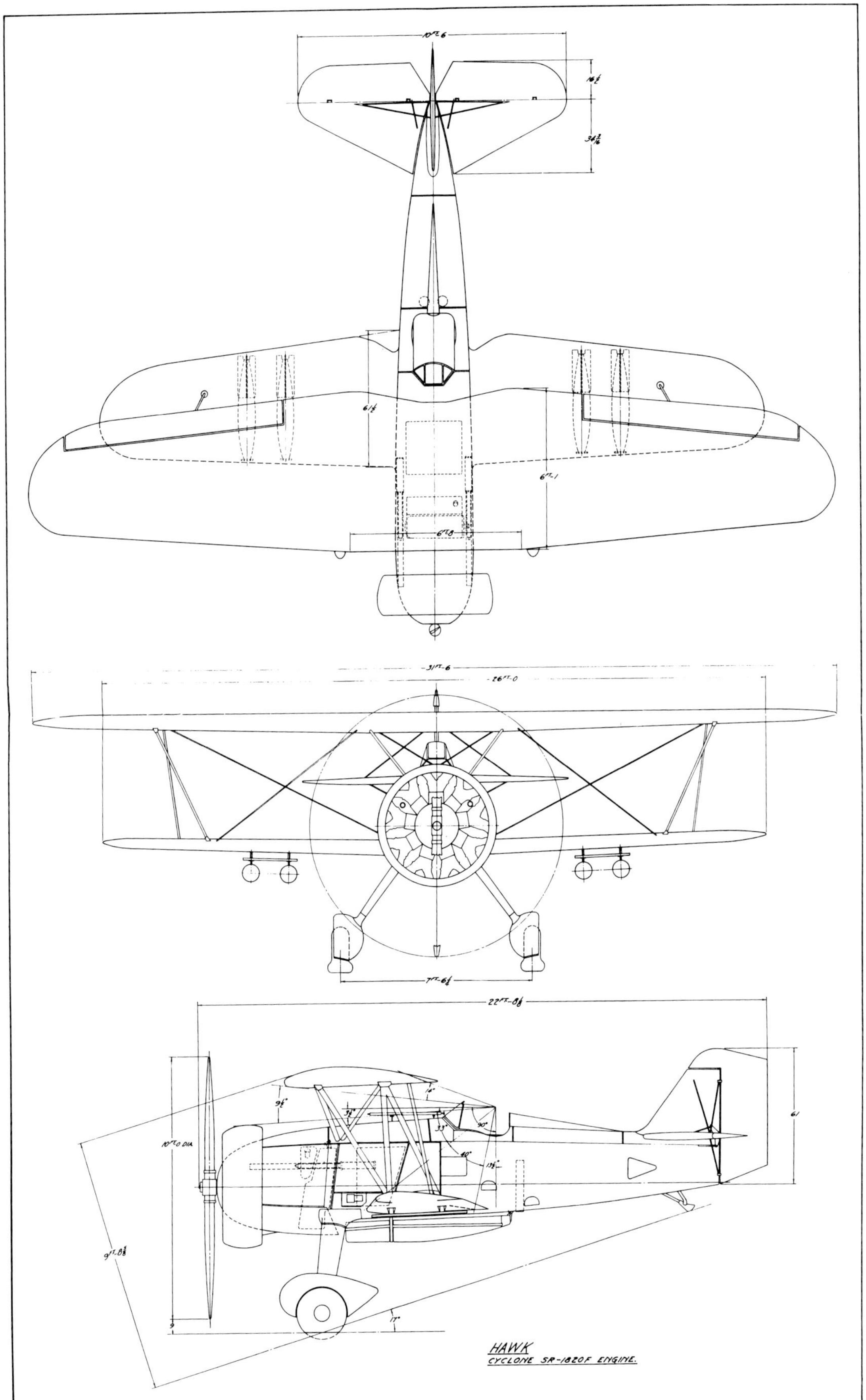

Cited nearly universally in all manner of publications as type Curtiss *Hawk II*, the highly versatile series of export aircraft with this basic configuration are now known to have included *Hawk I*, *Hawk IA*, *Hawk II*, and *Hawk IIA* variants, depending on customer specifications. This drawing shows the Wright *Cyclone* SR-1820F installation, making this essentially a *Hawk I* variant. (*Curtiss*)

pounds), and empty weight 2,723 pounds (3,094 pounds), with an internal fuel capacity of 50 gallons in both variants. This could be augmented to 100 gallons with the slip tank.

Figures for the *Hawk Type II* and *II-A* varied slightly from the *Type Is*, although many sources have cited them as being identical. Figures for the landplane and seaplane variants (in parenthesis) were:

Overall length was 22 feet, seven inches (25 feet, 11 inches), while overall height was nine feet, eight and 5/8 inches (12 feet, six inches). Wing span for both variants was 31 feet, six inches, and wing area was constant at 262 square feet. With the nine cylinder Wright SR-1820-F2 *Cyclone* rated at 712hp at 1,950 rpm, the maximum speed at 3,300 feet was given as 202mph (185.5mph), and stalling speed at 61.5mph (64.5mph), which was really quite impressive. Cruise speed at 3,300 feet was 172mph (158mph), while cruising range with internal fuel was 400 miles (365 miles), which could be stretched to 610 miles (560 miles) with auxiliary belly tanks. Service ceiling was 29,500 feet (24,000 feet), and absolute ceiling 30,500 feet (25,000). Normal gross weight was 3,863 pounds (4,248 pounds), and empty weight 2,895 pounds (3,280 pounds). Normal internal fuel capacity was 94 gallons for both variants, which could be increased to 144 gallons with the auxiliary slip tank.

Curtiss *Hawk I* (Landplane Design 35-A, Turkey)

The first export sales success for the classic Wright R-1820F-2 *Cyclone* powered *Hawk* series came from Turkey on Sales Order No.105 (Curtiss-Wright Export Corp. Order #2126) for 18 aircraft. These were assigned Curtiss MSNs 11635 to 11652 and, in keeping with the relatively new Curtiss practice, type serial numbers H-1 to H-18, and the order was valued at $324,000. No guns or bomb racks were included in this sale.

The Turks had ordered 12 French Gourdou-Leseurre GL-32T fighters in 1931 but, due to the depression and financial difficulties experienced at the time by the French firm, the order had to be cancelled. As luck would have it, Turkey had only recently hosted a Curtiss demonstration team with both *Hawk* fighters and *Fledgling* trainers, and the timing was providential.

These aircraft were delivered to Turkey as kits between August 30 and September 20, 1932. Although appearing externally similar to most subsequent aircraft in this series, they did in fact differ in detail. The first aircraft (H-1) was priced at $12,000 even, with the following seven priced at $11,825 each. They had Eclipse Series XI hand, inertial starters, 12-inch chord ring cowls, and were fitted with two .30 caliber machine guns, as well as an A-3 bomb rack under each lower wing panel, capable of accommodating up to four 116 pound bombs. They could be fitted with 50 gallon auxiliary belly fuel tanks, additional to the standard main fuselage tank of the same capacity. As with most *Hawk* series aircraft, the wings were Clark Y airfoil, but there was provision for landing light installation on the lower wings. The first aircraft on the order was also fitted with an Eclipse M-B radio generator to power a Radio Marine radio. When delivered, the aircraft were doped aluminum overall, with Turkish national insignia on the rudder, four wing positions, and on the fuselage, and all instruments were in Turkish, with metric unit increments.

The Turkish aircraft were, as of February 23, 1932, cited in Curtiss documents as the Design L-18-38, one of the few confirmed

The first foreign customer for the Model 35-A (L-18-38) *Hawk I* was Turkey, which bought 18, delivered in the fall of 1932. Here, one of the first is being prepared for testing at Buffalo with Turkish national insignia. Note that the belly auxiliary slip tank is more streamlined than previous incarnations. (*Curtiss*)

Introduction of the powerful *Hawk Is* into Turkish service was not without incident. Here, the first example, Manufacturers Serial Number H-1—the very first export *Hawk I*, to have been assigned to the Turkish 53rd Fighter Company—was wrecked early in her service. (*via Tuncay Deniz*)

In addition to the 18 *Hawk Is* delivered by Curtiss, Turkey also assembled six lots totalling 40 more aircraft in their *Kayseri Tayyare Fabrikasi'* (*KTF*), and Number 24 was the 18th of these. Note that the KTF serial number (1524) appears near the top of the vertical fin with their logo. (*via Tuncay Deniz*)

The fifth Turkish *Hawk I* (Number 5), complete with under wing A-3 bomb racks. Note also that the aircraft has position lights on the wing tips. The characters on the vertical fin indicate that this is the second (No.2) aircraft donated to the Turkish Air Force by Abdurrahman Naci Demirag, brother of a famous Turkish businessman of the time. (*via Tuncay Deniz*)

In an effort to get more performance from their aircraft, the Turks modified the final 15 aircraft to mount 700hp SR-1820F-s with three-bladed props. This created an unexpected problem with the synchronized guns, however, and so the two forward guns were moved to the inboard sides of the wheel spats. In this camouflaged example the guns have been removed, but the spats are obviously larger than normal. Note also the landing lights and the Supermarine *Spitfires* in the background! (*via Tuncay Deniz*)

references to anything but the Design 35-A nomenclature, and one of the last vestiges of the earlier internal system. The first aircraft on the contract was tested exhaustively at Buffalo by August 5, 1932, all on one day, accumulating some 10 hours of flight time. Amongst other things, the test report had a rather protracted discussion of the relative horsepower of the Navy XF11C-2's R-1820E, as compared to the R-1820F to be installed in the Turkish aircraft. The report contained some rather frank language. For instance, it stated that:

"*...with regard to drag, items favorable to the Turkish Hawk are that it does not have the radio mast and arresting hook which were present on the XF11C-2. The belly tank, which serves to fair the fuselage back to the engine cowl, may help and may not. Compared to the 'E' engine, the 'F' looks very unfavorable from the standpoint of drag and propeller interference. On the 'F' engine, the prop is several inches closer to the cylinders than on the 'E' or the 'Hornet,' but no closer than on the 'Wasp.' The baffle system certainly looks very bad. The space inside the engine cowl ring is almost completely choked up, and the effectiveness of the ring is probably impaired by vanes attached to it.*"

On the plus side, the engineers noted that they would have no problem meeting the stall, take-off, and landing run guarantees, and they felt sure they could meet the service ceiling, absolute ceiling, and rate-of-climb to 5,000 meters (which, they noted, was probably the most important guarantee of all). However, in the overload condition, they admitted that there was no way they could expect to meet the net specified ceilings or time to 5,000 meters without a "*...considerable increase in power.*" They concluded that their chief concern were the "F" engine, and the drag produced by the baffles in the cowl.

The first six Turkish *Hawks* were assembled by the Kayseri Aircraft Factory (KTF) under the supervision of Turkish engineer Hikmet Anter, aided by Curtiss representatives named Kuhn, Grot, and Pordi, and issued to the newly formed 53rd Fighter Company on November 21, 1933, KTF Assembly Numbers 1501 to 1506. Although the Curtiss Sales Order accounted for only 18 aircraft, 24 kits (probably consisting of 18 whole aircraft and sufficient spares to erect six additional aircraft) were delivered. After the first six were completed, KTF assembled four more lots of two (No.1507-1508), five (1509-1513), three (1514-1516), and eight aircraft (1517-1524).

Although of marginal quality, this mass takeoff image of five Turkish Air Force *Hawk Is* includes three of the last batch of 10 that had been modified to include three-bladed props, camouflage, and guns in the wheel spats. These are just visible on the two aircraft on the right in the image. This modification was unique in Curtiss fighter history, with the solitary exception of the Curtiss-Wright 19R. (*via Tuncay Deniz*)

Previously unreported is the fact that the KTF then produced two additional batches of seven (No.1525-1531) aircraft in 1934, and 15 aircraft (No.1532-1546) in 1938-39. This latter batch was modernized aircraft with 700hp Wright SR-1820F-3s with three-bladed, Hamilton-Standard steel props, although a few apparently had two-blade props. The three-bladed props, however, caused the Turks problems with the synchronization of the Colt-Browning guns, and apparently had not been vetted with Curtiss before production. The solution to this was radical. The guns were removed from the fuselages and remounted, somehow, to the *inboard* sides of each main landing gear spat, creating an astonishing and unique appearance. The KTF built aircraft were equipped, for the most part, with tail skids rather than wheels, but in later service, as the aircraft went to depot maintenance, these were replaced with steerable tail wheels.

The Turkish Air Force got excellent service from its fleet of *Hawks,* and at least 10 remained in service as late as April 16, 1945.

Curtiss *Hawk I* (Seaplane Design 35-A, Colombia)

Close on the heels of the Turkish order, Sales Order No.110 covered four float-equipped aircraft for the *Aviación Militar Colombiana* with Curtiss MSNs 11653 to 11656, and within-series serial SH-1 to SH-4. These aircraft were priced at $15,700 each. These aircraft were, as of November 7, 1932, cited in Curtiss documents as Project L-18-39 aircraft.

These aircraft, aside from the floats, were virtually identical in equipment to the Turkish aircraft, but had no provision for landing lights, nor any radio equipment. They, too, were doped aluminum overall as of delivery and, aside from Colombian national insignia, had U.S. English language instruments and cockpit lettering.

Oddly, a supplementary order for two additional aircraft was appended to Sales Order 112 (the first Bolivian order) for two more aircraft for Colombia, possibly as a diversion. These received MSNs 11657 and 11658 and in-series serials SH-5 and SH-6, and were delivered on December 27, 1932, and January 9, 1933, respectively. These may have been attrition replacements, as, of the known first six aircraft, only five received Colombian serial numbers (801 through 805). The first aircraft (801) was apparently wrecked (possibly on February 15, 1933) and later rebuilt as 801a.

Although clearly issued in-series serials in the "SH" series, indicating *Sea Hawk* or *Seahawk* configuration, these aircraft are never cited as such in Curtiss records, nor are any of the "SH" prefixed aircraft, and thus this appellation must be regarded as a popular descriptor.

The first Colombian seaplane *Hawk* was extensively flight tested on October 27, 1932. The pilot observed that the aircraft had "*...good control on the water and could be maneuvered by means of the water rudders very satisfactorily in as high as a 17mph wind up, down, or cross-wind.*" Take off was noted as "very good," requiring only an incredible eight seconds in a normal fuel and overload condition, and experienced "*...practically no planning.*" During a speed test at full throttle across Grand Island (north of Buffalo), the highest calibrated airspeed achieved was 189.56mph, although with additional passes it averaged out to 185.13mph.

Unfortunately, due to the "*...very urgent demand for immediate delivery of*" these first four airplanes, Curtiss never had adequate time to investigate the longitudinal stability of the aircraft in flight. In a report dated April 27, 1933, and as a result of input from the field in Colombian operating conditions, they concluded that the design was "*...definitely unstable longitudinally and that this was caused largely by the airfoil section strut between the floats.*" The subsequent investigation, and fix on all other float equipped *Hawks* built, centered around the means of fairing the strut so as to have little or no effect on stability. It was also found prudent to modify the auxiliary ventral fin to address these issues (see illustrations).

Curtiss *Hawk I* (Landplane Design 35-A, Cuba)

Almost always cited, in error, as *Hawk IIs,* the four aircraft ordered for the *Cuerpo de Aviación, Ejercito de Cuba* on Sales Order 111 were designated by Curtiss as *Hawk I* variants.

The second foreign customer for Model 35-A *Hawk Is* was Colombia, which was hastily arming for a conflict with Peru in the remote Leticia trapezium. These aircraft were the first Curtiss fighters to actually see combat operations. They were also the first Model 35-As to be fitted with floats, as seen here in this factory photo. The Colombian national insignia on the rudder has been primed, but not applied. Note the beaching gear and pair of A-3 bomb racks under each lower wing panel. (*Curtiss 7911*)

The first Colombian order for *Hawk Is* involved four aircraft, supplemented quickly by two more, in November and December 1932. These were shipped to Cartagena, where they were assembled by Curtiss crews and had Colombian serials 801 to 805, one having been lost during tests. Note that the floats on this example have already been camouflaged with splotches of green and brown paint for jungle conditions. (*Hagedorn Collection*)

Delivered on January 12, 1933, at a cost of $103,300 for the package, these aircraft received Curtiss MSNs 11663 to 11666 and in-series serials H-19 to H-22. These aircraft were almost identical to the first four Colombian aircraft noted above, but were land planes. The solitary difference was that they were delivered with welded chassis, which were interchangeable with the forged type. The Cuban aircraft were priced at $12,600 each, and received *CAEC* serials 19 to 22. The last one known (s/n 21) crashed in January 1939, but was apparently repaired, as a photo is known taken in November 1943, although by then the individual serial number had been deleted.

Curtiss *Hawk I* (Landplane Design 35-A, Bolivia)

Deep in the throes of expanding her military aviation component to deal with the widening war with Paraguay, Bolivia ordered an initial batch of four *Hawk Is* on Sales Order 112 (Curtiss-Wright Export Corp. Order 2469), and these were delivered on December 19, 1932. They were issued MSNs 11659 to 11662 and in-series serials H-23 to H-26. These were priced at $12,950 each, although the

FIG C

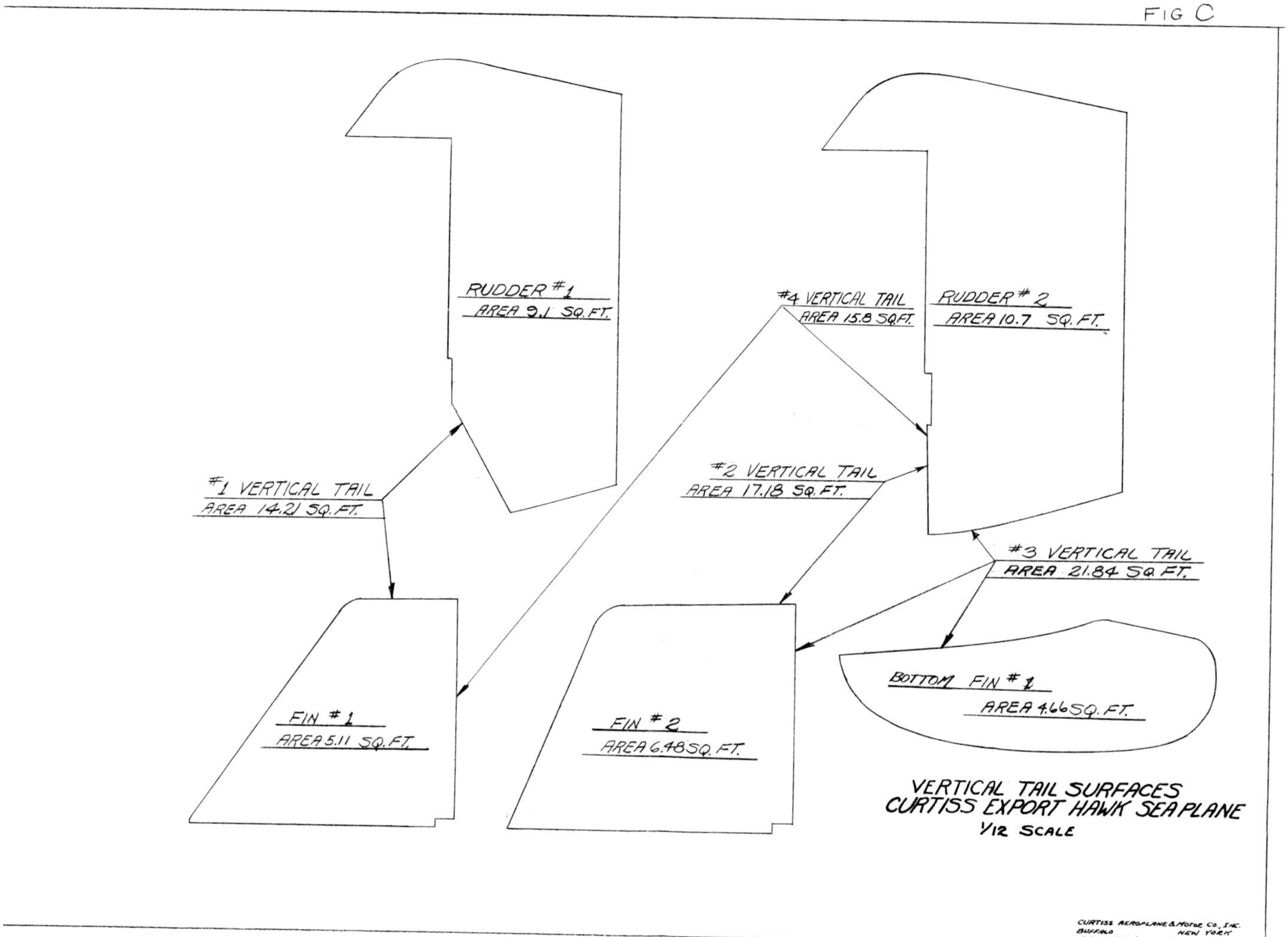

7-8-33 5220-25

Seldom noted, except through very close examination of existing photos, shortly after delivery, Colombian and U.S. mercenary pilots reported back to Curtiss that the seaplane *Hawk Is* lacked directional stability on the water. Curtiss immediately put into effect a "fix," dated April 27, 1933, for the vertical fin, the rudder, and the ventral bottom fin. These were fitted to all subsequent export seaplane variants and, ironically, also benefited the *Hawks* being flown on floats by their Peruvian opponents. (*Curtiss*)

The next foreign customer for the state-of-the-art Model 35-A *Hawk I* was the *Cuerpo de Aviación, Ejercito de Cuba* (CAEC), which acquired four on Sale Order 111 in January 1933. Pictured here at Buffalo just prior to flight delivery, the pilots are bundled up in unaccustomed winter togs. These gained Cuban serials 19 to 22 and, like their Colombian cousins, also saw limited action in several internal incidents. (*Curtiss via Robert J. Pickett*)

total deal, with spares, was valued at $50,000—which may have included the costs of doing business, *soborno*.

These aircraft had the Wright SR-1820F-3 *Cyclone* and 7.65mm guns, in addition to the A-3 bomb rack under each lower wing panel. When delivered, they were doped aluminum overall, aside from Bolivian national insignia on the rudder and six standard positions, and had Spanish language, metric instruments. They received Bolivian serials 30, 32, 34, and 36. Of these, s/n 30 was wrecked December 26, 1934, as was s/n 32 on an unknown date, but was rebuilt as s/n 48 by September 1937.

Curtiss *Hawk Type I* (Seaplane Design 35-A, Peru)

At almost precisely the same time that Curtiss was providing *Hawks* to Colombia, she accepted an order (S.O. 113, Curtiss-Wright Export Order No.2496) in the amount of $88,200 from Peru, with whom Colombia was at war in what became known as the Leticia Incident.

Assigned MSNs 11671 to 11673, three aircraft also gained in-series serials SH-7 to SH-9 and were, of course, twin-float equipped to operate in the rivers of eastern Peru. These were delivered to Peru on January 9 and 10, 1933, at $13,180 each.

The engines of these three aircraft were cited simply as R-1820Fs, but they were otherwise identical to their opposite number on the Colombian side of the conflict.

When delivered, they were most colorful, as they left the factory with light blue (No.23) fuselages, natural aluminum floats, and Army No.4 yellow wings, with Peruvian red/white/red rudder stripes and national insignia roundels in four wing positions. Although their instruments were marked with English lettering, they were in metric units.

Originally coded by the Peruvians as simply 1/1VF-1 to 1/1VF-3, these aircraft later gained unit codes when assigned to the *4° Escuadron*, and became 1-C-13, 1-C-18, and one other, with the Roman numeral "IV" placed over the central "C" in the code on each of the fuselage sides.

All three were initially fitted with floats, but the Peruvians complained that, so equipped, the aircraft lost too much power operating at the headwaters of the Amazon region (although this apparently proved no problem for the similarly equipped Colombian air arm). The first loss occurred in short order when 1/1VF-3 crashed, apparently during familiarization training, before ever reaching the war zone. A second (1/1VF-2) was lost after its first mission in the

The quartet of Cuban *Hawk I* fighters did not get their individual serial numbers until after delivery. They were otherwise fully marked, however, with chrome yellow upper wing surfaces and horizontal tail surfaces, and full Cuban national insignia on four wing positions and the rudder. Note that the Cuban national insignia at the time had the five point star point aft. (*Curtiss W-7909 via Stephen J. Hudek*)

After delivery to *Campo Columbia*, near Havana, the four Cuban *Hawk Is* had serials 19 to 22 applied to both sides of the fuselage, and on the upper starboard and lower left wing panels. Hitherto unreported, they also sported a unique service shield on the vertical fin, as shown here on No.22. (*Captain George G. Farinas*)

Never illustrated in color before, No.21 was the Cuban *Hawk I* flown by CAEC chief Len Povey at Miami, where he demonstrated the "Cuban Eight" and night aerobatics with flares. Note that the colors are blue, white, red, chrome yellow, and blue again, and that the CAEC "shield" is on the vertical fin, as well. (*via Jay Miller*)

Len Povey standing next to No.21, showing details of the special insignia painted on his *Hawk I* during the demonstrations at Miami. (*via Nick J. Waters*)

The last of the four Cuban *Hawk Is* as it appeared at *Campo Columbia*, near Havana, in November 1943. Believed to have been the personal mount of the officer commanding the Air Corps, it was highly polished, retaining the chrome yellow wings and horizontal tail surfaces, but had no individual aircraft serial number whatsoever. (*Bachmann via Peter M. Bowers*)

Engaged at the time in a life-or-death struggle with neighboring Paraguay in the Chaco War, Bolivia also invested in Model 35-A *Hawk I* fighter-bombers, acquiring an initial batch of four in December 1932. Three of these, including serial numbers 34, 30, and the other (unidentified foremost), are seen here in the theater of operations. They were unquestionably the most potent combat aircraft of the conflict. (*via Tony Sapienza*)

Engaged in a distant jungle border conflict with Colombia in the Leticia region, Peru also acquired three Model 35-A *Hawk Type I* float fighter-bombers in January 1933. In keeping with Peruvian practice at the time, these aircraft were exceptionally colorful, having blue fuselage, and yellow wings, vertical fin, and horizontal tail surfaces, in addition to the national colors of red/white/red rudder and roundels in four wing positions. Here 1/1-VF-1 prepares to launch, probably at San Ramon or Iquitos. (*via Sergio de la Puente*)

Nearly all of the aircraft that Peru was able to bring to bear during the 1933 Leticia Incident with Colombia were float-equipped, which brought with it both versatility and unforeseeable hazards. Here, *Hawk I* 1/1-VF-2 has been beached following a collision with obstacles in the water. (*via Sergio de la Puente*)

This post-war photo of two of the surviving Peruvian *Hawk Is*, in the center of a cluster of most unlikely stable mates (including a single Nieuport-Delage NiD-626C-1 in a dark color, two Fairey *Fox IIs*, and a trio of Hanriot H-438s, reveals that the unit codes on the blue fuselages had been change from black to white characters). Note the open air basketball court to the left! (*via Sergio de la Puente*)

Leticia district; it lost one of its floats in the process and was apparently written off. Thus, only 1/1VF-1 survived the action in the war zone. However, another aircraft, also equipped with floats, was lost May 22, 1934, at Iquitos due completely to "*...the carelessness of the pilot*" (*Tte.* Augusto Tello, who died in the crash), according to the U.S. Military Attaché, when he attempted a full-power take off on the Rio Perene, near San Ramón. The engine was recovered, and it seems it may have been used to rebuild the aircraft. However, yet another loss, on March 27, 1936, cost the life of pilot *Ensign* Guillermo Bolaños, which throws the entire question of exactly how many *Hawks* Peru actually acquired into question.

It is known that Peru had attempted to order a total of seven *Sea Hawks*, but only the three noted were confirmed as actually delivered, due to the sudden U.S. Congressional interest in the export activities of Curtiss. Once in Peru, the aircraft were erected and tested by the redoubtable Cliff Travis, together with mechanics Jack Jennings and a Mr. Jugielski at the Chilean port of Ancon.

Bearing all of the known losses in mind, as noted above, the U.S. Attaché reported that not less than *three* Peruvian Hawks of the *Escuadron de Caza* took part in a fly-past demonstration at Lima on September 23, 1937, suggesting that either the two aircraft that had crashed after the conflict had been repaired and restored to

Peru is known to have lost, or had seriously damaged, all three of the *Hawk Is* acquired in 1933 during the Leticia Incident. This post-war image, taken with codes known to be in use after 1937, clearly shows three aircraft intact, including 1-4-3 and 1-4-2, suggesting that the third was 1-4-1. This anomaly cannot be explained by available records. (*via Sergio de la Puente*)

Believed to be the so-called Design 35-A *Hawk Type I Shanghai Demonstrator* flown so ably in March 1933 by Lt. James Doolittle (serial number H-45/11674), this appears to be supported by the Chinese script on the forward fuselage, which seems to read "*City of Shanghai*." (*via Ted Young*)

airworthy status (the most likely scenario), or that two additional aircraft had been acquired (which cannot be substantiated from existing, known production). This is further supported by the fact that the Peruvian Order of Battle for July 1, 1940, clearly showed a total of three *Hawks* on strength, by then assigned to the *28er Escuadron de Instruccion* at the Central School at *Las Palmas*, coded as I-4-2, I-4-3, and one other, unknown. Although speculation, it is possible that two or three ex-Bolivian *Hawks* may have been acquired by Peru between September 1937 (when at least five Bolivian *Hawks* participated in the *III Conferencia Tecnica de Interamericana de Aviación*, the only time the aircraft were ever out of the country) and 1941. Bolivian strength returns do not account for some aircraft between these two years. However, the leading Bolivian aero historian, Lic. Ramiro Molina Alanes, could find no evidence of such a transaction.

During the Peruvian *Dia de Aviación* on September 23, 1942, one of the surviving *Sea Hawks* engaged in a mock dog fight with one of the Peruvian Caproni Ca 114 fighters and, according to the U.S. Air Attaché, "*...the Ca 114 handily outmaneuvered the Hawk*."

By December 18, 1943, the two surviving *Sea Hawks* had been withdrawn from service and assigned as ground instructional airframes to the NCO mechanics school at Callao. However, the Order of Battle for March 7, 1944, still counted both, but noted that they were in process of being decommissioned. One of the final codes known was 28-4-5 for a *Hawk* that was by then assigned to the *28° Escuadron*.

Curtiss *Hawk Type I* (Landplane Design 35-A, Canton China and Shanghai Demonstrator)

Sales Order No.116 covered 18[73] *Hawk Type Is* for the Kwangtung Government of Canton, China, MSNs 11707 to 11723, and within-series serials H-27 to H-44. These were delivered between March 15 and May 8, 1933. These apparently were issued Kwangtung Chinese serial numbers in a straight sequence of "1" to "18." It is important to note that this was a provincial air arm at this point, and not to be confused with the so-called "central" Nationalist Chinese regime of Chiang Kai-shek in Nanking. The survivors of these aircraft may have later been integrated into the Nationalist Air Force, but as might be expected, records on such transfers are scant. Most of them reportedly ended up serving with the Central Aviation School.

These aircraft carried two .30 caliber guns, plus the standard A-3 bomb racks and English language instrumentation and units. They had the Wright R-1820F-3 *Cyclone*.

One additional aircraft on S.O.116, and charged against Curtiss-Wright Export Corp. Order No.2765, was a single *Shanghai Demonstrator* (MSN 11674 and within-series serial H-45), and this aircraft was in fact destined for the Nanking government of Chiang Kai-shek, the Nationalist Chinese. This aircraft had an R-1820F-1 engine and, for the first time, mounted one .30 and one .50 caliber machine gun, in addition to the A-3 racks. It was painted olive drab (fuselage) with yellow wings and yellow empennage, and had English language instruments and units. It was actually delivered ahead

Taken November 22, 1934, during an air defense exercise of Nanchang, this quartet of Chinese Kwantung Air Force *Hawk Is* appear to be taking off in formation. Included are serial numbers 4, 9, 6, and 7, of which the foremost have colored bands around their rear fuselages. The Chinese *Hawk Is* were nearly all painted what was described by Curtiss as "olive drab" overall. (*via Ted Young*)

This lineup of Kwangtung Chinese *Hawk Is*, headed by No.12 at right, includes at least 10 aircraft at Canton. The fifth aircraft in line has Chinese characters on the vertical fin, although they are too distant to be read. At this time, many Chinese aircraft were named for cities and provinces, possibly due to donations for their purchase. They were painted olive drab, with the distinctive Chinese blue and white roundels in four positions, and rudder stripes.

This Kwangtung China *Hawk I* (No.16) also has Chinese characters on the forward fuselage, and they appear to read *Whang-p'u* (a harbor area across the river from Shanghai proper), or *Whampoa*, in the Canton area. Note that, in this instance, the stylized Curtiss *Hawk* logo at mid-fuselage has been moved forward and smaller than presented on other aircraft, and the engine has a tarp over it. (*via Ted Young*)

One of the Chinese *Hawk I* fighters receiving final attention from work crews at the CAMCO facility prior to delivery. Note the turtle deck propped open aft the cockpit, and the un-spatted undercarriage leg. (*San Diego Aerospace Museum*)

Bearing U.S. Department of Commerce Experimental License X-13263, this September 18, 1933, image shows the first aircraft to bear the *Hawk II* designation, in this instance Design 65-A, *Landplane Type II-A*. This aircraft had a combination engine mount, capable of taking one of four engine types. The longer-chord engine cowl is an obvious difference, and it had F11C-2 type ailerons and a retractable landing light, just visible in the lower left wing panel. After a number of apparently intentional evasions, this aircraft is believed to have ended up in Bolivia. Although it had a standard doped aluminum fuselage, the wings were chrome yellow. (*Curtiss W-8535*)

of the other 18 aircraft, on March 10, 1933, and was almost certainly the aircraft used by Lt. James Doolittle to wow the Chinese. This aircraft has been pictured in a lineup with the later production Chinese Nationalist *Hawk Type I* order with stylized Curtiss *Hawk* logo on the fuselage, and Chinese characters on either side of the forward fuselage.

Curtiss *Hawk Type II-A* (Landplane Design 65-A, Curtiss-Wright Demonstrator)

Equipped with a Wright R-1820F-3, this aircraft (MSN 11767, series serial DH-46) remains something of a mystery aircraft. Apparently "sold" to the Curtiss-Wright Export Corporation, on Sales Order 147 (originally S.O.121, amended to S.O.85027, and clearly out of sequence with all other Curtiss Sales Orders for this period), it was delivered to Curtiss-Wright on July 18, 1933. It was issued U.S. Department of Commerce Experimental License X-13263. It was armed typically, with two .30 caliber guns and two A-3 bomb racks, but featured an aluminum doped fuselage and yellow painted wings, and no insignia whatsoever.

It is interesting to note that, as of July 6, 1933, this unique aircraft had a combination engine mount, referred to as a "...*F11C-2 Double Bay Engine Mount*," capable of taking either the 650hp direct drive Wright R-1820F *Cyclone*, the 650hp GR-1820F, the 625hp R-1510, or the 680hp GR-1510 engine. It is not clear if it in fact ever was tested with all four engine variants. It did feature a four barrel type carburetor, and the ailerons were changed to F11C-2 type, and the upper wing panels were modified accordingly. A retractable landing light, made by the Indiana Lamp Corp., was installed in the lower left wing panel—certainly a key recognition factor. Additionally, the tail skid, common to all other *Cyclone* powered *Hawks*, was replaced by a tail wheel similar to that used on the F11C-2, except that it employed a 10 and 1/2 inch streamline wheel.

A note in the entry after the customer (Curtiss-Wright) noted "Chile," suggesting that it, like the so-called Norwegian aircraft

Following the extensive build-up of her air arm (the *Aviación Militar*) during the Leticia crisis with Peru, Colombia found herself with one of the largest and most modern air arms in Latin America. Here, a well-dressed Colombian trooper guards a lineup of not less than 14 *Hawk I* and *Hawk II* aircraft at Palanquero, all converted to wheel undercarriages, of which at least three were camouflaged, including the second in line. The first two aircraft are *Hawk IIs*, which are easily compared with the first, silver aircraft, which is a *Hawk I*. (*Hagedorn Collection*)

Colombia eventually acquired a total of not less than 28 *Hawk I* and *Hawk II* landplanes and floatplanes. Here, No.813 and 814, from the third batch of six Design 65 *Hawk IIs*, sit at anchor at Boca Grande, Cartagena, prior to departure for the interior, one camouflaged and the other doped aluminum. Note the shape of the ventral auxiliary fins. (*Hagedorn Collection*)

(MSN 11827), may have ended up in Bolivia. However, a note at the bottom of the Curtiss document stated that "*...plane #11767 under S.O.147 was released under S.O.122.*" Ironically, S.O.122 was a batch of six float-equipped *Falcon* attack seaplanes delivered to Colombia July 1 through 12, 1933; thus, it is entirely possible that this aircraft in fact ended up with the Colombian military. This appears doubtful, however, and may have been a Curtiss subterfuge to evade the widening arms export investigation then ongoing. This is because the U.S. Experimental License was renewed on three separate occasions, dated to expire, respectively, on October 24, 1933, February 1, 1934, and August 15, 1934. The Experimental License was finally cancelled around May 1934 when Curtiss advised the Department of Commerce that the aircraft had been "*...withdrawn from service for overhaul at the factory and, upon completion, was to be delivered to a foreign country.*" However, a final note stated that the aircraft was "*...delivered to Chile March 2, 1935.*" Since Chile absolutely did not acquire any *Cyclone* powered *Hawk* variants, despite statements to the contrary, this aircraft apparently ended up in Bolivia, probably not far ahead of U.S. customs officials.

Curtiss *Hawk Type II* (Seaplane Design 35-A, Colombia)

Curtiss S.O. 117 was initially identified in Curtiss records as a follow-on order from Colombia for five more *Hawk Type I* aircraft. However, this was changed to read *Hawk Type II* before delivery between March 14 and 24, 1933, although the rationale for this change of designation is unknown. It is the first confirmed use of the Roman numeral "II" nomenclature assigned to a *Hawk* series aircraft. The aircraft, aside from Colombian national insignia, were doped aluminum on delivery, and had English language instruments and units. These aircraft were MSN 11701 to 11705 (SH-10 to SH-14), and they received Colombian serials 806 to 810. They were priced at $13,250 each.

Although highly regarded and trusty mounts, the Colombian *Hawk Type IIs* were not without their problems. When equipped for dive bombing (usually with 122 pound bombs, standard with the Colombians, who adapted them to fit the A-3 racks designed for 116 pound weapons) the aircraft had a center of gravity location of 27.9% MAC with a normal fuel load, and 30.4% of MAC with both internal and auxiliary fuel tanks installed. These proved satis-

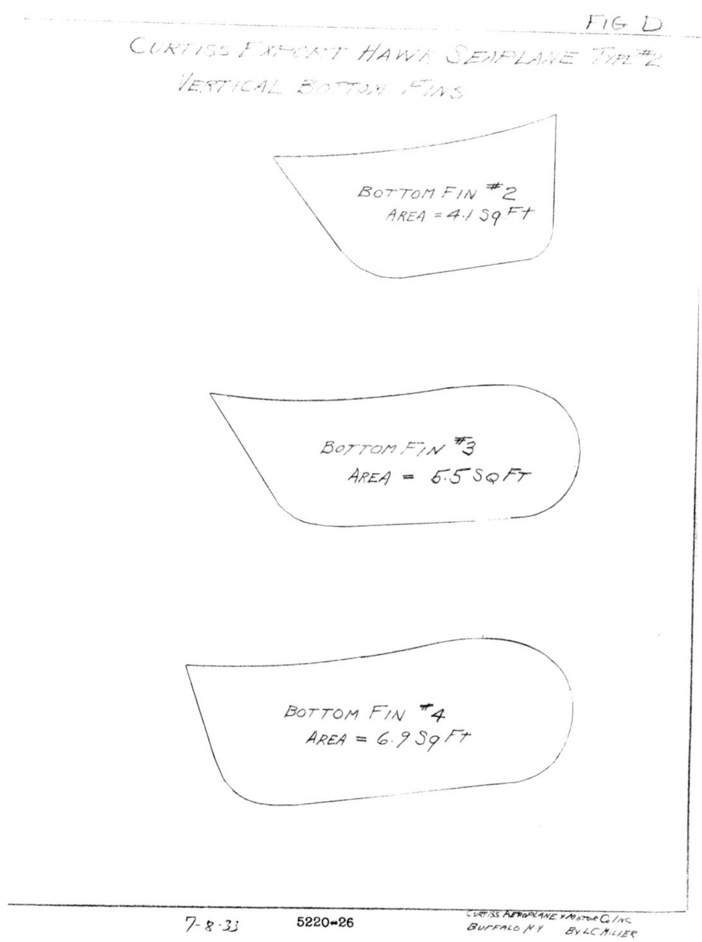

Field experience with the new Colombian *Hawk IIs* on floats quickly established that additional ventral fin area was needed to properly control the aircraft on and off the water. This July 8, 1933, set of drawings shows the evolution of these auxiliary "bottom fins," as described by L. C. Miller of Curtiss. (*Curtiss*)

Whether from enemy action or other causes, this Colombian Model 65 *Hawk II*, serial 813, has suffered extensive fabric damage to both upper and lower wings, rudder, and bottom fin. The floats are camouflaged, as is the *Hawk* in the background in this June 30, 1933, Cartagena photo. (*San Diego Aerospace Museum*)

factory for normal operations, as well as for "getting the tail down" when landing. However, as a fighter, flying with maximum useful load (but no bombs), the center of gravity was at the 21.2% MAC. In this condition, the aircraft definitely tended to be nose heavy. As a result, a ballast weight was designed and rushed to Colombia, along with strict instructions that it was to be carried at all times, both as a fighter and as a dive bomber. Ironically, the ballast took the shape of what were called "dummy flares."

Curtiss *Hawk Type I* (Landplane Design 35-A, Argentine License Production)

On May 2, 1933, Lawrence Leon, the Curtiss-Wright Export Corporation representative in Buenos Aires, Argentina, rushed back to the home factory with the news that he had all but concluded a deal with the Argentine Army to license-build not less than 40 *Hawk Type I* fighters at the Argentine *Fabrica Militar de Aviones (FMA)* at Cordoba, in addition to the rights to license manufacture *Cyclone* and *Whirlwind* engines.

The Argentines had apparently paid him $35,000 for the license rights, and Leon was returning to thc U.S. to arrange for the jigs and special tools that the *FMA* would require to complete this extraordinary order.

While the *FMA* did in fact subsequently license manufacture a number of Wright engines, nothing more was heard of the contract for *Hawk Type Is*, and lack of necessary funding may have been the cause.

Curtiss *Hawk Type II* (Seaplane Design 65, Colombia)

Pleased with the performance of the 11 *Hawk Type I* and *II* aircraft acquired, Colombia placed yet another follow-on order (S.O.121, Curtiss-Wright Export Corp. Order 3094) for six more aircraft with SR-1820F-2 engines rated at 712hp at 1,900rpm at 3,300 feet. These were significant, in that they were the first aircraft to be fitted with Eclipse Series XI electric starters, demanded as a direct result of the difficulties that the Colombian crews had experienced in starting their aircraft while on floats on the swollen rivers of the Amazon basin. They also had a significantly larger internal fuel capacity (94 gallons in the two separate fuselage tanks, as opposed to the standard 50), as well as provision for the 50 gallon belly slipper tank. Armament remained unchanged, and the aircraft, delivered between June 30 and July 3, 1933, were marked identically to the earlier Colombian aircraft. They also differed in that the floats and engines were moved forward some three inches, and a small ventral fin was added on the bottom of the fuselage at the aft end to improve longitudinal stability (see the earlier discussion). The aircraft employed Edo Design 4546 floats with water rudders installed. It is important to note that these aircraft were convertible to either float or wheel undercarriage.

It is interesting to note that, even with the floats, the maximum speed in level flight was determined to be 185.43mph at 1,970rpm at 1,900 feet with the auxiliary fuel tank installed (but no bombs).

These aircraft were MSNs 11754 to 11759, SH-15 to SH-20, priced at $12,980 each, and received Colombian serials 811 to 816.

Curtiss *Hawk Type I* (Landplane Design 35-A, China (Shanghai))

Like the Colombians, the Chinese Nationalists had been pleased with the demonstrator *Hawk Type I* noted earlier, and placed a follow-up order for 17 more.

These aircraft were issued Curtiss MSNs 11733 to 11749 and in-series serials H-47 to H-63, and were covered by Sales Order No.124 (Curtiss-Wright Export Corp. Contract #3130). These aircraft were delivered between June 18 and July 17, 1933, and billed at $11,850 each.

These aircraft, like the first batch, were powered by the slightly modified Wright SR-1820F-3, and had one Colt .30 caliber and one Colt .50 caliber machine gun, as well as the standard A-3 bomb racks under each outboard lower wing. They were fitted with C-3 type gun sights, and normally the .50 caliber gun had provision for 200 rounds and the .30 caliber for 600 rounds. However, in addi-

A most unlikely customer for Curtiss *Hawks* was Ernst Udet of Germany. Acquiring single examples of both the Design 35-A *Hawk Type I-A* and Design 65-A *Hawk Type II-A*, these were ostensibly used to refine his concepts of dive bombing. Incredibly, the *Hawk II-A* (D-IRIS) survived World War II, and is pictured here in the collection of the *Muzeum Lotnictwa Polskiego* in Krakow, where it is awaiting full restoration. (*David Zwolak*)

tion, they had an additional, single A-3 under the fuselage centerline that could accommodate an additional pair of 116 pound bombs, the only export *Hawk* variant to be so equipped. They also had an oxygen supply tank, valve and regulator, and a low pressure supply line for the pilot. These examples, aside from Chinese Nationalist insignia, were painted olive drab overall, and had English instrument markings and units. Known serials appear to have continued the straightforward two digit serial started with the initial deliveries.

Curtiss *Hawk Type I* (Landplane Design 35-A, Bolivia)

Bolivia placed an additional follow-up order for two more *Hawk Is* on Sales Order No.125, Curtiss-Wright Export Corp. Contract 3250. These were assigned MSNs 11768 and 11769 and series serials H-64 and H-65. These aircraft were identical in all other respects to the order received in December 1932. These aircraft were weighed at Buffalo on August 10, 1933, and delivered that same month. They received Bolivian serials 38 and 40. The later is one of the few Bolivian aircraft of the Chaco war to receive a personalized name, having *El Tigre-Hawk* painted on at some point while being flown by the Bolivian "ace" *Mayor* Rafael Pabon. These aircraft were also priced at $12,950 each.

Curtiss *Hawk Type I* (Landplane Design 35-A, China (Shanghai))

Yet another Chinese Nationalist order for 14 more *Hawk Type Is*, on Sales Order 126 (Curtiss-Wright Export Corp. #3334), resulted in deliveries between August 14 and September 1, 1933. These were

One of the last batch of six Design 65 *Hawk II* seaplane fighters acquired by Colombia, No.824 (Manufacturers Serial Number SH-31/11837) poses here at Palanquero with proud Colombian airmen after conversion to wheels. Note how far outboard the Colombian national insignia appears on the starboard lower wing. (*Museum of Flight PM10541*)

The final foreign customer for Design 65 *Hawk II* biplane fighter-bombers was the Royal Siamese Aeronautical Service, which acquired 12 in August and September 1934. Here, three pose for the camera at Don Muang aerodrome in 1938, complete with full national insignia and A-3 bomb racks. They were known in Siamese service as "Pursuit Type 9s," and most were assigned to the 2nd Squadron of the 1st Wing. (*via Ted Young*)

identical to those acquired in June and July 1933, and brought the total acquired to this point to an even 50 aircraft. These were MSN 11770 to 11783 (H-66 to H-79).

Curtiss *Hawk Type I-A* (Landplane Design 35-A, Udet (Germany))

One of the more surprising Curtiss export orders came from Ernst Udet in Germany, who acquired two aircraft. Both on Sales Order No.127, the first of these was a *Hawk Type I-A*, MSN 11784 (series serial H80).

This aircraft had an R-1820F-1 engine, and was delivered October 6, 1933, at a cost of $11,500. Although not fitted to the aircraft, two .30 caliber machine guns were in fact shipped separately for mounting, and the aircraft also had the standard A-3 racks under each lower wing panel.

It was doped aluminum overall when shipped, and had English markings on the instruments and U.S. units. It was issued the German civil registration D-IRIK.

Curtiss *Hawk Type I* (Landplane, Mexico)

The Curtiss-Wright Export Corp. came very close to closing an order for six *Hawk Type I* fighters for the Mexican Army in October and November 1934, quoting a unit price of $24,000 each. Incredibly, the entire deal floundered when the "middle man" in the deal, none other than *Ing.* Juan F. Azcárate, refused to budge on his demand that the company present the Government with a price of $26,000 each, allowing him a $2,000 per aircraft "commission" for facilitating the deal.

Curtiss *Hawk Type II-A* (Landplane Design 65-A, Udet (Germany))

Along with the earlier aircraft noted, and on the same Sales Order (amended to include No.9334 and Curtiss-Wright Export Corp. Contracts 3368 and 4372, invoiced together at $49,400), the Germans also acquired this exotic aircraft. MSN 11785 and series serial H-81, this aircraft mounted a Wright SR-1820-F3 rated at 708hp at 1,900rpm and 6,500 feet, and an 18 inch chord engine cowl. It also had a 94 gallon main fuselage fuel tank, and could mount as well the standard 50 gallon auxiliary slipper tank. Like the first aircraft, the two .30 caliber guns were shipped separately, and it also had provision for the under wing A-3 bomb racks. The supplementary Contract (No.9334) covered the parts needed to convert this aircraft to a floatplane. It initially received German civil registration D-3165, but was later changed to D-IRIS. Amazingly, this aircraft still survives, having apparently been evacuated from Berlin during WWII along with other historic aircraft to Poland. The fuselage was last reported in the possession of the *Muzeum Lotnictwa Polskiego* in Krakow in good condition. Oddly, although equipped differently than H-80, the cost was identical at $11,500.

Curtiss *Hawk Type II* (Seaplane Design 65, Colombia)

Adding to her growing fleet, Colombia placed yet another order with Curtiss (S.O.129) for six more *Hawks*, nearly eight months after their previous order. Given MSNs 11809 to 11814, these were in-series serial SH-21 to SH-26, and had R-1820F-2 engines. They were delivered between March 2 and 9, 1934, and gained Colombian serial numbers 817 to 822. They were priced at $13,325 each.

Curtiss *Hawk Type II* (Seaplane Design 65, Bolivia)

These three aircraft for Bolivia were seaplanes (all of the earlier Bolivian aircraft had been delivered with fixed landing gear only), and were delivered on Sales Order 131 (Curtiss-Wright Export Corp. Contract #3855) between June 18 and 27, 1934, at the very climax of the war with Paraguay. They were MSNs 11824 to 11826, SH-27 to SH-29. They had 94 gallon main fuselage tanks and 50 gallon auxiliary tanks, and were fitted with a Harrison C-3118 oil cooler, unique amongst all export *Hawks*. This equipment and the floats were probably dictated by the severe heat and dry conditions encountered in the Chaco region, where the only possible landing areas in many instances were shallow rivers and lakes. They also had 7.65mm machine guns and dual A-3 bomb racks under each lower wing panel. These aircraft received Bolivian serials 42, 44, and 46. They were billed at $14,015 each.

Curtiss *Hawk Type I* (Landplane Design 35-A, Bolivia)

Apparently as attrition replacements, Bolivia once again ordered two additional *Hawk Type Is*, on Sales Order 133 (Curtiss-Wright Export Corp. Contract 3887). These were MSN 11844 and 11845, series serials H-82 and H-83. They were delivered on July 18, 1934, nearly a full year after the last examples acquired. These aircraft were distinguishable from earlier Bolivian *Hawks* only in having 18 inch engine cowls, but cost a bit less at $12,400 each.

Curtiss *Hawk Type II* (Seaplane Design 65, Colombia)

Finding the float-equipped *Hawks* ideal for operation from temporary river bases, Colombia acquired one final order of six aircraft on Sales Order 135, and these were delivered between July 24 and 27, 1934. Assigned MSNs 11836 to 11841 and SH-30 to SH-35, they were the final float-equipped *Hawks* built. They were priced at $13,215 each. They were standard in every respect to the earlier batch. They were issued Colombian serials 823 to 828. Colombia had thus acquired a total of not less than 28 *Hawks*, making her the largest export operator in Latin America, and examples of the aircraft soldiered on as late as September 1946 in Colombian service.

A footnote of interest is that, in May 1934, the Colombians approached the Driggs Ordnance Engineering Company with a request that they investigate the possibility of arming some of the *Hawks* and *Falcons* the Colombians had acquired from Curtiss with 37mm cannon! The selected *Hawks* would have had one such weapon in the upper right wing, firing to clear the prop arc. Driggs observed that this would require an increase in the beam spacing and added reinforcement. A 30-round magazine was to be suspended below the upper wing, which of course, it was observed, would cause a blind spot for the pilot. When Driggs approached Curtiss with their solution to the Colombian request, their engineers were aghast and flatly "*...ruled out any such installation.*"

Curtiss *Hawk Type II-A* (Landplane Design 65-A, Norway)

This aircraft, MSN 11827, series serial H-84, was acquired on Sales Order 137 (Curtiss-Wright Export Corp. Contract 3999) by the Government of Norway for $13,353. However, before delivery, Curtiss records indicate that it was diverted to Chile, where it was delivered (probably at Arica) on July 27, 1934.[74] In fact, this aircraft was almost certainly destined for Bolivia.

Fitted with a Wright SR-1820F-3 and an 18 inch chord engine cowl, and the Harrison C-3118 oil cooler (like the earlier Bolivian *Hawk Type II* seaplanes—a device that would have hardly been necessary in Norway!). This may probably be regarded as the final aircraft to slip into war-torn Bolivia before the embargo and armistice. It was unique amongst all export *Hawks* in having an F11C-2 type radio antenna mounted at the time of export, although it is not known to have had a radio exported with it! There were no markings instructions for the aircraft at crating, and it was doped aluminum overall. While it had English lettering on the instruments, they were calibrated in metrics and, also non-standard, it had a Turn & Bank Indicator and a Rate of Climb Indicator installed.

Curtiss *Hawk Type II* (Landplane Design 65, Siam)

The final export order for U.S.-built *Hawks* of the series came from Siam (today Thailand), which acquired 12 on Sales Order No.138 (Curtiss-Wright Export Corp. Contract 4025). These were assigned MSNs 11847 to 11857 (H-85 to H-96), and were delivered between August 21 and September 6, 1934. The Siamese *Hawks* carried a price tag of $12,400 each. In Siamese service, the aircraft were referred to as "Pursuit Type 9s," and most, if not all, were assigned to the 2nd Squadron of the 1st Wing of the Royal Siamese Air Force.

These aircraft had Wright SR-1820F-3 engines, 18-inch chord engine cowls, 94 gallon main fuselage fuel tanks (with the option of the 50 gallon auxiliary tank), and were fitted with one 12.7mm Vickers machine gun on the right side of the fuselage and a 8mm Vickers on the left hand side. These British-built guns required gun mount adaptors not found on any other *Cyclone* powered Hawks, as well as special link boxes and new type blast tubes. They also had the two A-3 bomb racks for each lower wing capable of mounting four 110 pound bombs. Unlike most other *Hawks*, they were not convertible to seaplanes. The *Hawks* replaced a squadron of Nieuport-Delage NiD-29s.

The surviving aircraft of this batch may have been amongst the last *Hawk Type IIs* to see action, as a number engaged Vichy French aircraft in the Franco-Thai border war of November 1940-January 1941.

According to noted aero-historian Ted Young, a specialist in aviation in the orient, Siam had in fact approached Curtiss as early as 1929, expressing an interest in acquiring a variant of the P-6. This did not develop, however, and in April 1931, the company again offered them a fighter with a Wright *Cyclone* engine, but the government could not arrange the financing.

The Royal Siamese *Hawk IIs* may have been amongst the last of the breed to see action, as a number of those survived as late as the Franco-Thai border war of November 1940-January 1941. Here one of these aircraft, with at least two light bombs on the racks, poses with the 1st Squadron at Kong Bin Noi 4 in 1940. (*via Ted Young*)

Curtiss *Hawk Type I* (Landplane Design, Turkish Knock-Down Kits)

The final 10 *Hawk Type I* units to be manufactured were, essentially, 10 knock-down kits, on Sales Order No.7075, for Turkey, delivered October 1, 1937, with Wright R-1820F-52 *Cyclones* (see the earlier section on Turkish production).

Curtiss XF11C-3 *Goshawk*

Of the order for Curtiss F11C-2 aircraft, one (Navy serial BuA 9269) was held back for modification, as noted earlier. As an excerpt from a 1933 Curtiss company report on type development stated:

"*...the Hawk development continued, but with changes so substantial as to represent a new development. The wings were altered to metal construction, and a retractable landing gear* [was provided] *with a large screw used for retraction. The maximum speed of the F11C-2 of 204mph increases on XF11C-3 to 229mph at 8,000 feet.*"

The company further reported that "*...contract negotiation with the Navy was nearing completion at the end of 1933 for 27 F11C-3 500 pound dive bombers.*"

Interestingly, the 1933 Curtiss Annual Report also notes that "*...a proposal was made to the Army Air Corps in October-November 1933 for* [adoption of] *Navy Cyclone Hawks with retractable landing gear.*" The Curtiss proposal was obviously not taken up by the Army, and it remains unclear whether it received any more than on-paper consideration.

The prototype aircraft with retractable landing gear was labeled an XF11C-3 (it had been F11C-2 airframe Manufacturing Number 5), and was delivered to the Navy at Anacostia NAS May 27, 1933, at a cost of $21,597.95.

Curtiss characteristics data for the XF11C-3 were: span, length, and height 31 feet, six inches, 23 feet, and 10 feet, seven inches. Wing area was 252 square feet.

The powerplant was a Wright R-1820-80 *Cyclone* rated at 700hp at 8,000 feet driving a two blade Hamilton Standard metal, controllable pitch propeller. Fuel capacity was 98 gallons, with provision for an additional external 50 gallon tank under the belly.

Empty weight was 3,230 pounds, normal useful load 1,265 pounds, and normal gross weight was 4,995 pounds. Wing loading and power loading at normal gross weight were 17.16psf, and 6.42 pounds per horse power. Normal useful load to gross weight ratio was 0.281. Gross weight, with a 500 pound bomb, was 5,020 pounds.

Performance of the XF11C-3 was: high speed 229mph at 8,000 feet, landing speed 69mph, climb in 10 minutes to 11,600 feet, and service ceiling 26,000 feet.

A Navy data sheet of September 1, 1933, gives the following figures for the XF11C-3 prototype fighter: span (upper/lower wings), length, and height were cited as 31 feet, six inches, 26 feet even, 23 feet and 1/2 inches, and 10 feet, seven and 1/2 inches. Wing chords at root (upper/lower) were six feet, one inch, and five feet, one and 1/2 inch. Angle of incidence 0 degrees, dihedral 0 degrees and 1.5 degrees, wing stagger 38.5 inches, and sweepback 0 degrees. Wing area was 262 square feet. Wing airfoils were NACA 2212. Horizontal tail area measured 30.1 square feet, and vertical tail area 13.2 square feet.

The powerplant was Wright R-1820-80 rated at 645hp at 1,950rpm at 8,000 feet, driving a Design 6091-6 two blade controllable pitch Hamilton Standard propeller of nine feet, 10 inch diameter. Normal fuel capacity was 110 gallons, and maximum fuel and oil was 162 gallons and 13 gallons, respectively.

Empty weight was 3,280 pounds, and useful load 1,189 pounds (composed of a 200 pound pilot, 660 pounds of fuel, 68 pounds of

While engaged energetically in fulfilling a host of most welcome export orders for fixed-gear *Hawks* in 1932 and 1933, Curtiss had time to further develop the XF11C-3, noted earlier, which evolved into the U.S. Navy's BF2C-1 fighter-bomber. An order for 27 F11C-3s followed, but the designation was changed to BF2C-1 before delivery. BuA 9586, pictured here on September 13, 1934, just before delivery to Anacostia on October 7th, was the first aircraft. (*Curtiss S-F9138*)

Bearing the full markings ofVF-1B, Curtiss BF2C-1 BuA 9601 is shown about to me mated and balanced for her prop. The auxiliary fuel tank arrangement is shown to good advantage. She was also assigned to VB-5B on the USS *Ranger* in November 1934, and last served as a platform for vibration tests at the Naval Aircraft Factory until stricken August 31, 1937. (*Naval Aircraft Factory, via Dean Collection*)

oil, 161 pounds of armament, 53 pounds of equipment, and a 47 pound radio). Normal gross weight was 4,419 pounds, and overload gross weight 4,813 pounds. At normal gross weight wing loading was 16.9psf, and power loading 6.8 pounds per horse power. Normal useful load to gross weight ratio was 0.269.

Maximum speed was 216.3mph at 6,000 feet and 209mph at 15,000 feet, with stalling speed 67.1mph at normal load. Climb times were 3.4 minutes to 5,000 feet and 9.3 minutes to 15,000 feet. Service ceiling was 25,800 feet. Endurances were 1.7 hours at maximum speed, 2.42 hours at 90 percent maximum speed, 3.54 hours at 75 percent maximum speed, and 4.9 hours at 60 percent maximum speed. Range at most economical speed was 634 miles. The takeoff run in a no-wind situation was 490 feet and, in a 25 knot wind, 177 feet.

Curtiss submitted performance estimates for four proposals for Army Air Corps specifications to meet Air Corps Pursuit Circular 34-223 dated January 6, 1934. These were basically modifications of the BF2C-1 and developments of the F11C-2 and XF-11C-3, all of which would have had retractable undercarriages and controllable pitch props.

Curtiss BF2C-1 (Model L-21-8) *Goshawk*

On the basis of XF11C-3 testing, the Navy ordered 27 production F11C-3 aircraft on February 21, 1934, and the designation of these aircraft was changed to BF2C-1 shortly after on March 21, 1934, this to add a designation reflecting bombing as well as fighting capability. These were acquired on Sales Order No.128 (Contract 34906), and were issued MSNs 11895 to 11921, and U.S. Navy serials BuA 9586 to 9612.

The new wings were structurally framed in aluminum alloy rather than wood, and the landing gear retracted into pockets in the forward fuselage via a hand cranked mechanical system. Another extremely important new feature was use of a Hamilton Standard controllable blade pitch propeller.

The initial BF2C-1 delivery was made on October 7, 1934, to Navy Squadron VF-1B, a squadron that went aboard the then new aircraft carrier USS *Ranger* of the Atlantic fleet in November 1934. The final aircraft delivery was made on November 12, 1934.

Armament was two fixed, forward firing .30 caliber synchronized machine guns in the forward fuselage. There were wing racks for four 116 pound bombs, and a rack for one 450 pound bomb under the fuselage. These racks were moved 14 and 1/2 inches outboard on each lower wing compared to the original design.

It has been stated that the retractable landing gear of the BF2C-1 gave trouble in service, and this being a relatively new feature it was probably true; however, an even more severe problem was encountered. The nine cylinder R-1820 *Cyclone* engine was not the smoothest of aero engines, and at one of the normal operating settings, a natural frequency of the new metal wing structure was excited, making the whole aircraft vibrate uncomfortably, and hastening fatigue of metal parts. In addition, poor airflow characteristics around the lower forward fuselage between retracted landing gears required the addition of a semi-circular streamlined fairing below the forward belly area to smooth out airflow. In addition to these matters, one BF2C-1 crashed when the wing failed in a dive. The type was then grounded, and shortly afterwards, taken out of service in late 1935. By the middle of the next year none were left in the Fleet, and in mid-1937 only two of the type remained at the Naval Aircraft Factory in Philadelphia: one for vibration testing, and one for disposal. The BF2C-1 was therefore not a success in service. However, one aircraft (BuA 9586) was detailed to NACA at Langley, VA, between October 28, 1935, and sometime in December of that year for unspecified tests.

Characteristics and performance of the BF2C-1, according to Curtiss figures, were: span, length, and height 31 feet, six inches, 23 feet even, and 10 feet, 10 inches. Wing area was 262 square feet.

Empty weight was 3,370 pounds, useful load 1,190 pounds, and thus normal gross weight was 4,560 pounds, with a maximum gross weight of 6,089 pounds. Wing loading and power loading were 17.53psf and 6.51 pounds per horse power, respectively, while normal useful load to gross weight ratio was 0.260.

The powerplant was a Wright R-1820-04 *Cyclone* rated at 700hp at 1,950rpm at 8,000 feet driving a two blade controllable pitch Hamilton Standard propeller. Fuel capacity was 110 gallons internal and 50-60 gallons in an external tank.

Maximum speed as a fighter was 228.8mph at 8,000 feet, and as a bomber 210-219mph. Landing speed was 69mph. Initial climb rate was 2,150fpm, and it took 2.6 minutes to reach 5,000 feet. Service ceiling was 25,700 feet as a fighter and 22,400 feet as a bomber. Range at maximum speed was 344 miles, and endurance at that condition 1.53 hours. Normal cruise range was 797 miles, and maximum range was 1,054 miles.

Navy data of September 1, 1934, for the BF2C-1 follows: (The first number is for the fighter version, and the second number in parentheses is for the bomber.): span, upper/lower wing, length, and height: 31 feet, six inches, 26 feet even, 23 feet even, and 19 feet 10 and 1/2 inches. Wing area was 262 square feet, wing airfoil sections NACA 2212. Horizontal and vertical tail areas were 33.1 and 12.2 square feet, respectively. Wing chord of the upper/lower wings were 6 feet, one inch, and five feet, 7/16 inches. Wing angle of incidence was 0 degrees, wing dihedral, upper/lower 0 degrees/ 1.5 degrees. Wing stagger measured 42 and 11/16 inches, and sweepback was 0 degrees.

The powerplant was a Wright R-1820-04 rated at 700hp at 1,900rpm at 8,000 feet driving a two blade controllable pitch propeller Design 6091 of nine feet, 10 inches in diameter. Normal fuel capacity was 110 gallons; overload capacity 160 gallons total. Oil capacity was 13 gallons.

Empty weight was 3,332 pounds, useful load 1,228 (1,757) pounds, consisting of a 200 pound pilot, 660 pounds of fuel, 68 pounds of oil, and 209 (738) pounds of armament, 46 pounds of equipment, and a 45 pound radio. Normal gross weight was 4,560 (5,089) pounds, and overload gross weight 4,961 pounds Wing loading was 17.4psf for the fighter, and 19.5psf for the bomber. Power loading was 6.5 pounds per horse power for the fighter and 7.3 pounds per horse power for the bomber. Useful load to gross weight ratio was .269 for the fighter and .345 for the bomber.

Maximum speed was 228.8mph (219.8mph) at 8,000 feet, and 221mph (210mph) at 15,000 feet. Stall speed was 69.4mph (73.4mph). Times to climb were 2.7 (3.2) minutes to 5,000 feet, and 9.0 (11.1) minutes to 15,000 feet. Service ceiling was 25,700 feet (22,400 feet), and range at most economical cruising speed was 885 (626) miles.

Takeoff run, with no wind, was 513 (655) feet; with a 15 knot wind 304 (401) feet, and with a 25 knot wind 195 (265) feet.

Curtiss *Hawk III* (L-18-40, Design 68)

As seen, Curtiss had enjoyed a most profitable export market for the fixed-gear and float-equipped *Hawk Type I and II* series, and saw little reason why it should not exercise the retractable-gear development, known generally as the *Hawk III*, similarly. From a production standpoint, the *Hawk III* export models, patterned to a great extent on the Navy BF2C-1, were the most successful of all the *Hawk* types, and this was at a time of economic depression, not only for Curtiss, but for the whole nation. Unfortunately, most of the production was generated by an Asian war between China and Japan.

The most significant (and probably fortunate) difference between the *Hawk III* and the U.S. Navy BF2C-1 was use in the export model of the older wooden framed wing structure, instead of the newer aluminum construction that was found to be excited into severe vibration by the impulses of the nine cylinder Wright *Cyclone* engine. Another important factor was use of a three bladed propeller on *Hawk III* versus the two bladed model of the BF2C-1.

Wearing U.S. Department of Commerce Restricted Category License NR-14703, this was the so-called Design 68, *Hawk Type III South American Demonstrator.* Taken on October 9, 1934, after extensive marketing throughout Latin America, the aircraft was sold to the Argentine Army, and probably became No. 11 with them. (*Curtiss S-F9163*)

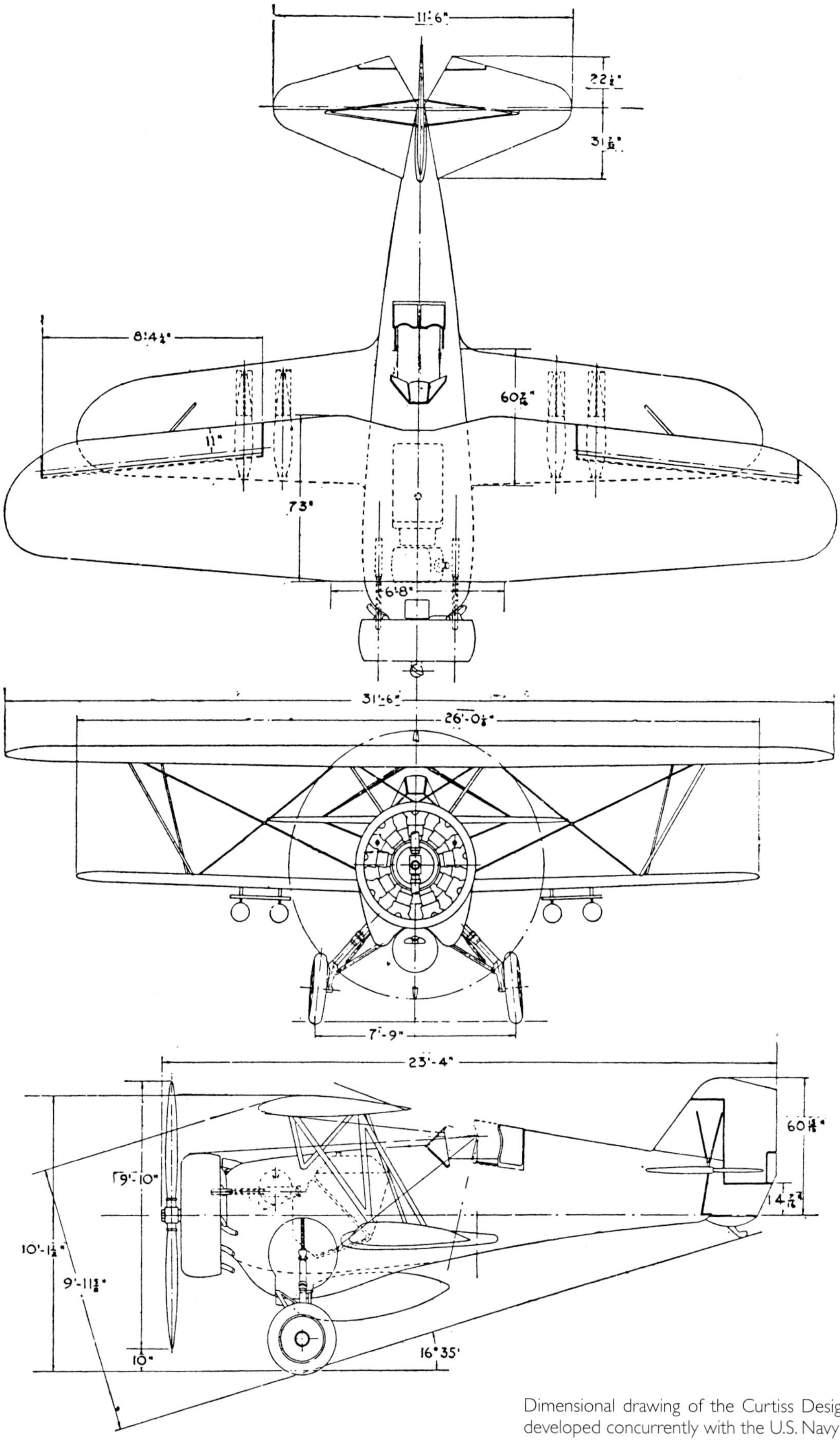

Dimensional drawing of the Curtiss Design 68, *Hawk Type III*, which was developed concurrently with the U.S. Navy XF11C-3 and BF2C-1. (*Curtiss*)

Dubbed the Design 68-A *Hawk Type III Turkey Demonstrator*, Manufacturers Serial Number 11924 gained Department of Commerce Restricted License NR-16Y by June 13, 1935, when photographed. It differed from the *South American Demonstrator* and U.S. Navy BF2C-1s in having a 750hp Wright SR-1820F-53 engine and a 22 inch chord cowl. Although many sources claim that the aircraft was sold to Turkey, it was in fact crashed there during sales efforts. (*Curtiss 9363*)

Three blade propellers were less subject to certain vibration characteristics than two bladed ones. The features of a manually mechanical retractable main landing gear and partly enclosed cockpit were retained. There was, however, an improved engine cowling, short stack exhausts, and a carburetor air intake heater.

A brief structural description of the *Hawk III* follows: Fuselage structure was of welded steel tubing, with sheet steel or forged attach fittings for major components. A welded steel tube engine mount was bolted on. Sheet steel bulkheads and formers were welded on. Fairing stringers were aluminum. Aluminum alloy sheet was used for cowlings forward of the cockpit and the aft turtledeck over the baggage compartment. A transparent, sliding "anti-draft shield" made of Pyrolin gave the pilot partial protection. With the exception of the turtledeck, the aft fuselage was fabric covered. The upper wing was one continuous panel, with hollow box spars of spruce and plywood. Ribs were built up of spruce and plywood. Lower wings construction was similar. Steel pins attached the lower panels to the fuselage. Double flying wires were provided. Dural sheet covered wing leading edges back to the front spar location. Ailerons were built up of dural. Wing panels and ailerons were cov-

Having had good experiences with the earlier *Hawk Type II*, the renamed Royal Thai Air Force ordered the first production Design 68-B *Hawk Type IIIs* in August 1935. Shown here bearing full Thai national markings, the first of an initial batch of 12 was Manufacturers Serial Number 12061, pictured here at Buffalo on August 28th. (*Curtiss S-F 9542*)

ered with cotton cloth. The tail surfaces were of mixed steel and dural construction with cotton cloth covering. Tabs were metal. The main landing gears were separate, and retracted by threaded screw and nut action with shock struts in the system. The retracting mechanism involved a cockpit hand crank, an endless chain and sprocket, and bevel gears. The tail wheel was a 360 degree swiveling unit controllable from the cockpit, and lockable in the fore-aft position.

Specifications and performance for *Hawk IIIs* varied in detail with the customer (each noted in a separate section following), but typically were as follows: span, length, and height were 31 feet, six inches, 23 feet, six inches, and nine feet 11 inches. Wing area was 252 square feet. (262 square feet of the fuselage area between lower wings was counted). Wing aspect ratio was 4.25. Airfoils were tapered Clark YH.

The powerplant was usually a Wright SR-1820-53 *Cyclone*, supercharged, rated at 750hp at 7,600 feet and 745hp at 2,100rpm at 11,500 feet, and driving a three blade ground adjustable propeller. Fuel capacity was 110 gallons internal, and a 50 gallon auxiliary under-fuselage external tank could be added. Oil capacity was 9 gallons.

Empty weight was 3,163-3,213 pounds (depending on customer equipment), useful load 1,067-1,193 pounds, and gross weight was 4,230-4,317-4,406 pounds.

Maximum speed was 204mph at sea level, 244mph at 10,000 feet, 240mph at 11,000 feet, and 237mph at 11,600 feet. Cruise speed was 204mph at 10,300 feet. Landing speed was 68mph. Sea level climb rate was 2,100-2,280fpm, and range was 572 miles at 204mph at 10,300 feet, with 110 gallons of fuel. Range with maximum fuel was 812 miles. Service ceiling was 25,800 feet.

Normal armament consisted of two .30 caliber fixed forward firing machine guns in the forward upper cowl, but many of the customers specified different calibers and arrangements. It is worth noting that the Curtiss report that described the *Hawk III* series (No.6024, dated September 23, 1935) described them as being "*...high performance, single place bomber fighters.*"

A total of 139 *Hawk III* export models were delivered to five different countries between early 1935 and mid-1938. Of the total, no less than 102[75] went to China. Detailed descriptions of each order follow.

Curtiss also proposed several variants on the basic *Hawk Type III* theme. One of these was the *Type 3A1 Landplane Hawk, Alternative H* of May 29, 1934, which was to have utilized an SR-1820F-3 rated at 730hp. Other variations included the *Type 3C Landplane Hawk* of September 11, 1934, with an SR-1820F-5 of 644hp, and the *Type C Landplane Hawk (Interceptor Type)* of September 14, 1934, also with an SR-1820F-5

Curtiss *Hawk Type III* (Design 68, South American Demonstrator)

The first *Hawk III* was Curtiss MSN 11894 (the serial immediately after the single U.S. Navy XF12C-1), and it was completed on October 9, 1934. On October 30, 1934, it was sold to the Curtiss-Wright Export Corp. on Sales Order 134[76] (Curtiss-Wright Export Co. Purchase Order 4601) for $17,615, and licensed commercially in the Restricted category with the Department of Commerce as NR-14703. It was completed October 16, 1934. This license was renewed three times, with expiration dates April 15, 1935, October 15, 1935, and April 15, 1936.

The aircraft was initially described by Curtiss as the *Type 3A3 Export Hawk Airplane*, and it was flight tested around November 15, 1934. It had a Series 11 hand and electric inertia starter generator and control box, flotation equipment, and an 18 point thermocouple. It was described as "*...similar to the BF2C-1*," except that it had Clark Y airfoils of wood construction (instead of the NACA 2212), no arresting gear, the lower aft portion of the fuselage cowl had been straightened, and the radio mast and antenna had been eliminated.

This first *Hawk Type III* was equipped with an SR-1820F-3 *Cyclone* rated at 780bhp at 2,100rpm at 7,000 feet, and had an 18 inch chord cowl ring around the engine. The aircraft was configured to mount either two 7.65mm machine guns or one .50 caliber gun and one 7.65mm gun (with a C-3 gun sight, and provisions for up to 1,200 rounds of ammunition), and there were two A-3 bomb racks, one under each lower wing, capable of mounting two 116

Nearly all surviving Royal Thai Air Force Curtiss *Hawk Type IIIs* were camouflaged by 1940, including this 2nd Fighter Squadron aircraft, running up with two light bombs on the inboard racks at Kong Bin Noi 4 in 1940. (*via Ted Young*)

Seldom pictured, the Royal Thai Air Force *Hawk Type IIIs* assigned to tactical units bore unit insignia—the triangle on the rear fuselage of this aircraft indicating that it belonged to the 3rd Fighter Squadron. Note the ring-and-bead gun sight, under wing bomb racks, and belly auxiliary fuel tank in place on this camouflaged example in 1940. (*via Ted Young*)

pound bombs each. It is interesting to note that Curtiss stressed that these racks were "*...horizontal bombing only, as they were not modified, and these racks were installed in the inboard position.*" For the first time, an export *Hawk* was fitted with flotation gear and, although this aircraft did not have a radio, a shelf for one was included in the fuselage. The instruments were marked in English, but all name plates were in Spanish. It had a fully steerable tail wheel and, aside from the black registration numbers, was doped aluminum overall.

Other differences between this aircraft and the XF12C-1, seldom noted, included the fact that the upper wing panel was moved forward one inch to a 43.5 inch stagger, the arrestor gear was obviously removed, there was no hoisting sling, and a hand-held fire extinguisher was added

This aircraft was demonstrated extensively in Latin America by Curtiss pilot J. Crosswell and, as a direct result, was sold to the Argentine Army on December 31, 1936, but only after the Army had already received a small production batch of *Hawk IIIs* (q.v.). The demonstrator gained Argentine Army serial number 11. It initially served with the production Model 68-C *Hawk IIIs* Argentina acquired (q.v.) with *Grupo 1 de Caza*, but in 1942 passed to the *3° Escuadrilla del Regimiento Aéreo 2*. It became an instructional airframe in 1943.

It is worth noting that, as early as May 29, 1934, Curtiss described a *Type III Landplane Hawk* with either the R-1820F-3 or the British-built Bristol *Mercury* engine. Incredibly, the maximum speed with either engine was calculated as precisely 241mph at 15,500 feet.

The last known surviving example of the breed, this Royal Thai Air Force *Hawk Type III* is displayed at the RTAF Museum in what are believed to be authentic camouflage. Note the unit insignia inside the blue diamond on the rear fuselage. (*Ray Wagner*)

Curtiss *Hawk Type III* (Design 68-A, Turkey Demonstrator)
Building on a highly successful sales relationship with the Turkish government, the Curtiss-Wright Export Corp. contracted on their Purchase Order 4516 for a single *Hawk Type III*, Curtiss Sales Order 145 (at a unit cost of $21,500), for a single demonstrator that differed in detail from the South American Demonstrator noted earlier.

Assigned Curtiss MSN 11924 (significantly, the serial just after the Curtiss Model 75 prototype), the chief difference was in the powerplant. The Turkey Demonstrator had a Wright SR-1820F-53, which was rated at 750hp at 2,100rpm at 11,000 feet. It also differed in having a 22 inch chord engine cowl ring, but the armament was listed as one 7.9mm Colt and one 12.5mm Colt with 500 and 200 rounds per gun, respectively. It was also equipped with a Very signal pistol (with 12 rounds), A-8 Airways Parachute Flares, an RCA Type AV radio, and an oxygen bottle and regulator, but the auxiliary fuel tank fittings were deleted. Like the South American aircraft, it was devoid of markings, and was doped aluminum overall. The aircraft had been approved for U.S. Department of Commerce Restricted License NR-16Y on March 1, 1935, and was sold by Curtiss to the Curtiss-Wright Export Corp. on April 5, 1935. It is known to have been demonstrated successfully in Turkey by Samuel D. Irwin. Although it has always been assumed that the aircraft was in fact sold to the Turks, the Curtiss representative in Turkey requested that the Department of Commerce cancel the Restricted License on June 3, 1935, as the aircraft had crashed.

As noted earlier, Turkey decided instead to produce more *Hawk Is* at their KTF facility, and no order for *Hawk Type IIIs* materialized.

Curtiss *Hawk Type III* (Design 68-B, Siam)
Returning yet again to another good customer, the first production order for *Hawk Type IIIs* came from the Government of Siam, which ordered 12 on Sales Order 148 (Curtiss-Wright Export Corp. P.O. 4819). These aircraft were MSNs 12061 to 12072. The first Siamese aircraft was weighed at Buffalo on August 18, 1935. They were turned over to Siamese custody between August 21 and September 19, 1935. They cost $17,800 each.

Like the Turkish Demonstrator, the Siamese aircraft had 750hp SR-1820F-53 engines, but 22 inch chord engine cowl rings, and the Siamese specified armament consisted of one 12.7mm Vickers gun on the right hand side and one 8mm Vickers on the port side, plus a slight modification, consisting of 12 small studs, which would allow installation of either British-built Vickers or Siamese modified Vickers guns in either location. The Siamese later regretted the use of the Vickers guns, as it significantly reduced the quantity of ammunition that could be carried. Two A-3 bomb racks, at the inboard location, were also fitted, although Curtiss once again stipulated that these were for horizontal bombing only. The aircraft were delivered with standard Siamese national insignia on the rudder and roundels on all four wing positions (but not, initially, on the fuselage), but were otherwise doped aluminum overall. One of the Siamese aircraft turned over onto its back in poor field conditions and ground looped around January 10, 1936, and the Siamese blamed the rather close-coupled undercarriage for this accident.

Curtiss *Hawk Type III* (Design 68-B, Siam)
Siamese authorities were so pleased with the first of their new *Hawk Type IIIs* that they almost immediately placed a follow-on order for 12 more aircraft on Sales Order 151 (Curtiss-Wright Export Corp. Purchase Order 5207, MSNs 12073 to 12084). The first of these aircraft was weighed at Buffalo, prior to shipment, on January 17, 1936, and they left on the delivery trip on January 23rd. Externally, these were virtually identical to the first 12, although there were slight differences. The 22 inch chord engine cowl ring was modified to include a new type top joint, making them easier to remove for servicing. They also had floor pads installed in the cockpits—a factory modification to match a local field modification that the Siamese had installed—that essentially blocked up the floors under the rudder pedals so that the Siamese pilots, all of rather short stature, could reach them!

It is seldom noted that Siam also acquired a license to manufacture *Hawk Type IIIs*, which were locally designated as the Type 10 Pursuit. In 1937 the Siamese shops at Bangsue, near Bangkok, commenced work on a batch of 25 aircraft, but experienced considerable difficulties in actual production. By 1939 work on an additional batch of 25 was laid down as well, even though by the middle of that year the shops had yet to turn out their first flyable example. Finally, with considerable help from Curtiss technicians, about a dozen were successfully completed in early 1940, and the remain-

Another good Curtiss customer, China acquired 29 complete sets of materials to assemble Design 68-C *Hawk Type IIIs* at CAMCO. This aircraft, photographed on April 19, 1938, is believed to have been the last such kit, assembled by Curtiss and photographed for the record. (*Curtiss S-F 10935*)

der of the first batch, started in 1937, later that same year. The Kingdom of Siam formally changed the name of the nation to the Kingdom of Thailand in June 1939.

The Siamese *Hawks* saw some action during the clash with the Vichy French forces in neighboring French Indochina in early 1941 and, of course, also engaged Japanese forces when they invaded the country later that year. The Siamese *Hawk IIIs* provided the bulk of the Thai fighter force in the late 1930s and well into World War II. At least one of the *Hawk IIIs* earned a most unusual footnote to history, as described in the *Small Air Forces Observer* No.59 of July 1991 by historian Christian Hotte. On the night of January 9, 1941, five French Loire 130.C flying boats of the *1/CBS (Commandement des Bases du Sud)* took off with orders to bomb the Thai airfield and supply dump at Ubon, 150km north-northeast of Siem Reap. Shortly after reaching their objective, the lumbering pusher flying boats were attacked by a solitary, camouflaged Thai *Hawk III*. Although the fighter made a number of firing passes at the flying boats, the French pilots were taking such violent evasive action that no hits were scored, and when the *Hawk* overshot in front of one of the Loire's, a forward gunner scored some hits on it, and the aircraft dived away into the darkness. Several days later, the French crew was credited with an air-to-air "kill," although the Thais have never admitted to this loss.

Thai *Hawk Type IIIs* served well into the post-war period as advanced trainers, although it is not clear exactly when the final example left the inventory.

One *Hawk Type III*, the solitary example still in existence, was preserved by the Royal Thai Air Force, but was relocated to the unique collection of the Royal Thai Air Force Museum upon its organization in the early 1960s.

Curtiss *Hawk Type III* (Design 68-C, China Demonstrator (Shanghai))

Yet another sustaining Curtiss customer, the Chinese Nationalist Government received special attention with the shipment of this aircraft on Sales Order 155 (Curtiss-Wright Export Corp. Contract 5475), MSN 12095, in March 1936, at a cost of $15,841.

Like the Siamese aircraft, it too had a SR-1820F-53 engine, and the same modified 22 inch chord cowl ring as the second batch of 12 Siamese aircraft. Armament was slightly different, consisting of one 7.9mm gun and one 12.7mm gun of unknown manufacture. However, in the case of this aircraft, the A-3 bomb racks under each lower wing had been specifically modified to allow dive-bombing, although the parts for this were only supplied after delivery to China. At that point the aircraft also ceased being cited as the China Demonstrator, and was noted as the "*...first production Shanghai airplane*."

This aircraft was painted olive drab overall, with aluminum interior, and with Chinese national insignia on the rudder, four wing positions and, oddly, forward fuselage, either side.

This first aircraft was followed, on Sales Order 156, by a Chinese order for not less than 59 production aircraft, MSNs 12096 to 12154 and Sales Order 156 (Modified by Curtiss-Wright Export Corp. Contract 5442, also given as 5710), which called for 11 more aircraft designated, for reasons that are unclear, as for China (Canton). These were assigned MSNs 12175 to 12185, but see the next section on the Argentine Army aircraft. These aircraft were to have one .30 caliber gun and one .50 caliber gun each, with A-3 racks in the outboard position, and modified to include provision for a fuselage center-line bomb rack for either a 500 or 600 pound bomb. They also had landing lights and, once in country, were to be fitted with Western Electric radios (although Curtiss noted that these would not fit the radio trays built into the aircraft). They were to be painted French Gray on all exterior surfaces, aluminum interiors, and semi-standard Chinese national markings. One unusual marking detail noted on at least two of the Chinese *Hawk IIIs* was that the large star national insignia was placed just above and forward of the main wheel receptacles on the extreme forward fuselage.

The 59 Shanghai aircraft were also fitted for one 7.92mm and one 12.7mm gun, plus the A-3 bomb racks in the outboard position, modified for dive-bombing. They were described as being painted "Khaki" on all external surfaces, aluminum interiors, with standard Chinese national insignia. Commencing around 1937, these aircraft were assigned four-digit Chinese serial numbers painted, usually in white, on both sides of the rear fuselage. The first two digits related to the squadron (e.g, 2101 to 2109 were assigned to the 21st Squadron). All of the *Hawk IIIs* were assigned to squadrons of the 4th Fighter Group, consisting of the 21st, 22nd, and 23rd Fighter Squadrons, and the 5th Group, consisting of the 24th, 25th, and 26th Fighter Squadrons. A few *Hawk IIIs*, assigned to the Group headquarters, carried special serial codes, such as IV-1 and IV-2.

Initially, the first batch of *Hawk Type III* aircraft sold to China are believed to have worn straight numeric serials from 1 to at least 59, including No.32 shown here. Like the earlier *Hawk Is*, these aircraft were painted olive drab overall. In the hands of a competent pilot, they could hold their own with the best the Japanese could field. (*Gordon S. Williams Collection AC 7909, Museum of Flight*)

The Chinese crews who were assigned to the *Hawks* were generally delighted with their mounts, and lost little time in engaging in contests with other Chinese units with different mounts. Aircraft 12105 suffered in such an event when, on August 4, 1936, while taking on a Chinese Fiat C.R.30, both reportedly at full throttle, the *Hawk* suffered a main bearing seizure in the engine—but only after winning the race! Another aircraft, probably MSN 12097, was washed out at Nanchang on August 20th when it ran out of fuel, when the Chinese pilot had apparently not been briefed on how to engage his auxiliary tank.

The first known aerial combat of the Sino-Japan War occurred on August 14, 1937, when 4th Group leader Kao Chi-hand, flying IV-1, shot down a Japanese Navy Type 96 bomber over Hangchow. Pilots of his Group downed two others, and August 14th is celebrated to this day as Air Force Day by the Taiwanese.

When the *Hawk IIIs* became outclassed the survivors were also transferred to aviation schools, and their serials changed to two-digit numbers. Known are 39 and 88.

After entry into service in quantity, Chinese Design 68-C *Hawk Type IIIs* eventually received four digit serial numbers, indicating unit of assignment and number-within-unit in white characters. Once again many of the aircraft were named, and Chinese characters can just be seen on the forward fuselage of this example. (*Dean Collection*)

Curtiss *Hawk Type III* (Design 68-C, Argentina)

Curtiss had been frustrated in its attempts to market its product line to the large and reasonably prosperous Latin American nation of Argentina.

The demonstrations of the *Hawk Type III*, the so-called South American Demonstrator, changed all of that, however, and an order for 10 aircraft resulted. Curtiss records regarding these aircraft are confusing, however. They are cited as having been built on Sales Order 156 and Curtiss-Wright Export Corp. Contract 5442, but this was the order for the 11 aircraft supposedly built for China (Canton) (see above).

The first production Argentine Army *Hawk Type III* was test flown at Buffalo by a Curtiss test pilot, while being observed by *Capt.* Dominguez of the Argentine Army, around May 8, 1936. Checks were made of high speed, climb, ceiling, and landing speed, compared to the guarantees made by Curtiss at contract time.

The Argentine Army aircraft were MSNs 12085 to 12094, and the first example was flown in Argentina on June 22, 1936; the cost per aircraft to Argentina was $15,103 each. These aircraft were almost identical to the Chinese aircraft, but were equipped with one .50 caliber Browning gun and one 7.65mm Browning, and the two A-3 racks on the lower wings were mounted in the outboard position, also modified for dive-bombing. They also were unique in having landing lights, and each had an RCA radio installed as standard. They were also unique in having a Pioneer Rate-of-Climb indicator amongst the instrumentation, and one of the 10 aircraft, for reasons unknown, had the standard altimeter replaced by a Sensitive Altimeter, and the Rate-of-Climb indicator replaced by an accelerometer—apparently for tests. At delivery, aside from standard Argentine Army national insignia on the rudder and roundels in six positions, the aircraft were doped aluminum overall. They received simple, straightforward serials 1 to 10.

The Argentine Army's experience with the *Hawks*, the first aircraft they had acquired with retractable undercarriages, was not without incident. One of the aircraft (No.9) shot a hole through one of the prop blades on August 25, 1937, raising concerns that the synchronization gear was faulty, as another, Argentine No.6, had trouble the same day. The Argentines also complained repeatedly that the hand-cranked retraction gear was too much to deal with. No.10 experienced a forced landing on September 1, 1936, and flipped over on its back. The pilot was unhurt, however, which immediately elevated the local opinion of the aircraft, but then it was learned that the pilot had exhausted his fuel and, in his exertions to get the gear down, had neglected to switch to his reserve.

This lineup of at least nine Chinese *Hawk Type IIIs* includes some with four digit serial number, and some with no serials at all. The nearest two aircraft do have Chinese characters on the forward fuselage, however, probably dedication names. The olive drab paint used on these aircraft was semi-gloss. (*Dean Collection*)

The aircraft received Argentine Army serials 1 to 10, but not in MSN order[77] (for instance, No.1 was MSN 12086, while No.3 was 12085, etc), and they were initially assigned to the *Grupo 1 de Caza*. Three (apparently s/n 7 to 9) were lost on the same day, October 26, 1937, during live fire exercises during Army maneuvers, as well as the single *Hawk IV*, with the loss of two pilots. The *Hawk IV* was reportedly blown out of the air when its own bomb, apparently incorrectly rigged, swung down and hit its own undercarriage in a dive bombing simulation. The objective was a series of targets on the ground, six meters apart, and the dive angle was reported between 80 and 90 degrees. Each aircraft was carrying two 50kg bombs of Federal (U.S.) design at the time, but actually built under license by the Naval Arsenal at Zarate. The explosion of the bomb on *Mayor* Capella's *Hawk IV* had sent shrapnel into *Teniente* Riviere's *Hawk III*, flying wing to the Major only six meters to one side, and striking him in the face. The other *Hawk III*, on the opposite side, had been literally riddled with shrapnel, but was repaired at Cordova. Another *Hawk III* was reported in intelligence documents destroyed on October 20, 1937, while practicing night landings at El Palomar, but this has eluded verification. The pilot survived, but an enlisted man driving a truck at an inopportune moment across the landing field was killed. By December 1941, when the U.S. entered WWII, the Army still had seven of the *Hawk IIIs* in service (s/n 1 to 5, 8, and 10), and formally requested U.S. assistance in obtaining spares for these and a host of other aircraft of U.S. origin that Argentina had acquired. The U.S. Department of State denied the request on the basis of the rather pro-Axis "neutrality" then being exhibited by the sitting Argentine government. In spite of this, the seven aircraft remained nominally on the Order of Battle as late as August 28, 1944, and, together with *Hawk 75-Os*, equipped the *2°Regimento de Caza* at the El Palomar air base near Buenos Aires. By that time, the survivors had been re-serialed as C-1, C-2, etc. Despite the wartime privations and lack of spares, this unit had been able to put 35 *Hawk 75-Os* and six of the *Hawk IIIs* in the air for a national parade on July 9, 1944. Most of these were apparently camouflaged after the start of World War II in 1939 in the then standard Argentine olive drab upper and light blue lower color scheme.

Incredibly, at least a few of the *Hawk IIIs* remained on the Argentine Air Order of Battle as late as April 1, 1950, although they last flew in 1947.

Curtiss *Hawk Type III* (Design 68-C, China (Canton))

Curtiss Sales Order 161 (Curtiss-Wright Export Corp. P.O. 5703), dated September 1937, covered 29 complete sets of material with which to build *Hawk Type IIIs* in China at the Central Aircraft Manufacturing Corporation (CAMCO) works, although the landing gear and associated retracting mechanisms were provided, complete, by the parent company. The order also included 11 sets of materials needed to make radio trays for the aircraft noted on S.O.156. The order included one complete set of paper Vandyke drawings, one set of blueprints, weight and balance reports, and sufficient structural analysis data to cover repairs to the aircraft. Curtiss assigned MSNs 12726 to 12755 to these aircraft which, as may be noted, actually totaled 30 (not 29) aircraft. The discrepancy cannot be reconciled. The 30th aircraft may have been the so-called *Canton China Demonstrator* delivered by the Curtiss-Wright Export Corp. in May

Although of marginal quality, this Chinese *Hawk Type III*, No.2509 of the 25th Fighter Squadron, was typical in having landing lights, A-3 bomb racks, the auxiliary fuel tank in place, and three bladed prop. The diminutive character of the Chinese pilot makes the aircraft appear rather larger than it in fact was. (*via Ray Wagner*)

Despite a concerted sales effort by Curtiss, the solitary Latin American customer for the Design 68-C *Hawk Type III* was the Argentine Army (not the Navy, as has so often been repeated), which acquired 10 in mid-1936. Here No.2, similar to the Chinese aircraft in most respects, poses for a photographer. The azure/white/azure Argentine roundel and rudder stripes—a very light blue—is almost washed out. *(Hagedorn Collection)*

1936 at $16,400. This may well have been the aircraft delivered to serve as a pattern aircraft, minus covering. However, the Curtiss Billing Book also notes these aircraft as on S.O.178 at $13,602.70 each "*...built from 7080 materials.*"

The Curtiss instruction booklet produced to aid the Chinese in the erection of the aircraft noted that, "*...under the adverse conditions existing, the construction of these airplanes must be accomplished on a high-production, emergency basis*," perhaps an understatement, considering the rate of Japanese advances into Chinese territory at the time.

The same instructional literature, however, did not speak of 29 or 30 aircraft but, rather, of not less than 60,[78] and stated that the actual construction should begin in December 1937. Incredibly, the packages Curtiss assembled for this process included all of the spruce parts needed, including beam flanges, cap strips, corner blocks, edge strips, and aileron braces. The package also included a brass bar (from which to cut special nuts, ferrules, fittings, and minor detail parts), steel sheet, streamline steel tubing, large diameter steel bars, ash lumber, spruce planking, birch plywood, internal tie rods, fuselage jigs, boring jigs, forgings, cork for the sidewalks, various aluminum components, instruments, props, and a huge array of miscellaneous parts. This was truly an extraordinary sale.

When hostilities with Japanese invading forces broke out in earnest, the Chinese *Hawks* were amongst the most numerous combat types in the inventory and, at least in the beginning, they were employed with some success, in the hands of the most experienced pilots. They saw action, in particular, around Shanghai in 1937, and were particularly effective against unescorted Japanese bombers raiding Nanking and other population centers. But the Japanese introduced the monoplane Mitsubishi A5M2b Navy Type 96 Carrier Fighter (later code-named

Claude by the Allies), and the nimble *Hawks* lost their edge, with many lost in combat and accidents. One Chinese pilot was a true *Hawk* admirer, even when pitted against the Mitsubishi monoplane. He is reported to have said that the Japanese fighter was good, but that "*...the Curtiss biplane could do wonders*" and was a "*...rugged machine*." After being credited with some 70 combat sorties in the type, he was finally shot down.

Of the license-assembled aircraft, a U.S. Military Intelligence Report (M.I.D.#252) dated September 29, 1937, reported that the CAMCO facility, then located near Shauchau (also given some times as Shiuchow, north of Canton), was turning out about one *Hawk* per week. By October 20th, a similar report stated that the Chinese Air Force had nine *Hawk IIIs* available for action at Canton, but that six of these were shot down in action with Japanese planes during the various raids, and that by the date of the report, only one of three survivors was still airworthy. He also observed that the Chinese pilots' aerial tactics:

> "*...left a good deal to be desired, but there was no lack of courage on the part of the pilots, who never hesitated to go up and engage hostile planes against great odds.*"

Yet another M.I.D. report, dated January 26, 1938, reported that, since the start of hostilities, a total of 13 Chinese *Hawk Type Is* and *IIIs* had crashed, but none in flames, and none were actually destroyed, and most of these had been shot down by Japanese fighters. His investigation into the direct cause of these losses revealed that, in nearly every case, the pilot was either wounded or died as a result of machine gun fire, and that only a comparatively few hits on the aircraft themselves were of any consequence. He urged that the Chinese lighten their aircraft by removing unnecessary oxygen equipment, etc, and that steel plate seats and back pads be installed as soon as possible. He further observed that, in the preceding two years, the CAMCO facility had turned out 26 *Hawks*, confirming that nearly all of the kits on Sales Order 161 had been put to good use.

Curtiss *Hawk IV* (Design NO.79, Argentine Demonstrator)
The final version of the Curtiss export biplane line was the *Hawk IV*, only a single example of which was built. It was like the *Hawk III*, with the major external difference being use of a fully enclosed cockpit in place of the earlier partially enclosed arrangement. The aircraft started life as a Curtiss company demonstrator with Restricted category civil registration NR-188M (MSN 12186), but was apparently aimed specifically at the Argentine Army or Navy market, as it is cited in company records as *The Argentine Demonstrator*. It was sold to the Curtiss-Wright Export Corp. on Contract 8310 on July 29, 1936, for $20,700, although FAA registration files show the sale date as November 10, 1936. The Restricted License was renewed three times, to expire on December 15, 1936, and June 15 and September 15, 1937. The aircraft was shipped to Argentina by boat and demonstrated there for the Corporation by Pete Brewster. It was flown only occasionally during the later part of 1937 at the Argentine Army's principal air field, *El Palomar*. It was not finally sold to the Argentine Army until September 24, 1937. The engine was sold separately. It is believed Curtiss sold a license to build the aircraft type in Argentina, but that country never produced any *Hawk IVs*.

Characteristics included: span, length, and height 31 feet, six inches, 23 feet, six inches, and 10 feet, 10 inches. Wing area was 262 square feet. Empty weight was 3,404 pounds, useful load 1,194 pounds, and gross weight 4,598 pounds.

The engine was a supercharged Wright *Cyclone* SR-1820F-56 rated at 745hp at 12,000 feet. Internal fuel capacity was 110 gallons.

The aircraft was the fastest of the export *Hawk* biplanes, with a top speed of 250 mph at 12,500 feet. Cruise speed was listed at 211mph, and landing speed 69mph. Normal range was 577 miles, and service and absolute ceilings were 29,700 feet and 30,300 feet, respectively.

The aircraft was delivered doped aluminum overall with no insignia. The aircraft had provisions for mounting one 7.65mm machine gun and one .50 caliber gun, and had provisions for one A-3 rack under each wing, although these were not mounted when delivered. It also had provisions for a radio (but none was installed at the time of delivery), and wing masts were provided. In Curtiss documents, it is described as being "*...similar to the airplanes built for Argentina under S.O.156*," with the major differences being the F-56 *Cyclone*, collector and shroud in place of the short exhaust stacks, the complete cabin enclosure and a redesigned windshield, and a new 22 inch chord engine ring cowl.

In Argentine service, the *Hawk IV* received the Army serial 12, and was assigned alongside the *Hawk IIIs* initially to the *Grupo 1 de Caza*. It was destined to have only a relatively brief service life, however, as it was wrecked while being flown by a *Mayor* Capella during maneuvers October 26, 1937, along with two *Hawk IIIs* (q.v.) during live fire training at the *Campo de Tiro y Bombardeo La Hullera*. Although the Major reportedly managed to open his chute when expelled from the aircraft, his injuries were such that he died shortly after reaching the ground.

Only one Curtiss Design 79 *Hawk IV* was built—Manufacturers Serial Number 12186, seen here bearing Department of Commerce Restricted License NR-188M in the summer of 1936. It was sold, eventually, to the Argentine Army in September 1937, along with a license to build them there, although this was never exercised, and became Argentine No. 12. (*Curtiss*)

8

Last of the 1930s Experiments

Curtiss XP-31 (XP-934) ***Swift***

The XP-31 was interesting as the first Curtiss attempt at a monoplane pursuit. The Army had issued a request for an aircraft designed for high speed at low altitude, and as an important pursuit plane contractor Curtiss was invited to compete. It was design transition time in the early 1930s, and clearly a monoplane configuration was in order. An agreement was reached that Curtiss would participate with an XP-934 design (MSN 11667, Curtiss Design L-22-1) with bailed GFE (Government Furnished Equipment), and a preliminary mockup inspection of the new configuration was conducted in November 1931.

The Curtiss aircraft was a low wing monoplane with fixed panted landing gear, and an enclosed cockpit with sliding canopy. The constant chord wing featured flaps and full span slots. There were no flying or landing wires; a "v"-strut system connected wing and landing gears. Construction was essentially all metal.

The Curtiss XP-934 proposal characteristics sheets dated February 24, 1932, defined the aircraft then under construction, as well as alternates being considered, all of which were powered by Curtiss or Wright engines, both inline and radial types. The following data was checked as being "OK" on March 7, 1932:

Alternate (a) The XP-934 low altitude pursuit powered with the propeller reduction geared inverted Curtiss GIV-1570 *Conqueror* liquid cooled engine rated at 670hp at 1,750rpm at sea level, with the note: "*Airplane as now being constructed.*"

Alternate (b) The XP-934 low altitude pursuit powered with the geared inverted Curtiss GIV-1800 *Super Conqueror* liquid cooled engine rated at 750hp at 1,750rpm at sea level. This was the engine, it will be recalled, that Curtiss intended to replace the V-1570, but for which program Navy and Army stopped funding, thus cutting off further Curtiss liquid cooled engine development in the early 1930s. The design was eventually sold to Russia.

Alternate (c) The XP-934 low altitude pursuit with the supercharged geared inverted Curtiss GIV-1800 liquid cooled engine rated at 1,100hp at 1,750rpm at sea level. A note here said: "*More definite*

A radical departure from anything that came before for Curtiss, the XP-934, which became the XP-31, was the stuff of pulp aero magazine covers. The first Curtiss shot at a pursuit monoplane, the aircraft was accepted by the Army February 28, 1933, as A.C.33-178, and spent her entire service life at Wright Field, aside her last three of 287 hours, while assigned to Edgewood Arsenal. This view, still as the XP-934, was dated October 10, 1932. It was surveyed December 10, 1936. (*Curtis W-7726*)

information on engine center of gravity may make this engine installation impractical."

Alternate (d) The XP-934 low altitude pursuit with the Wright SGR-1510 *Twin Whirlwind* double row aircooled radial engine rated at 600hp at 8,000 feet at 1,650rpm. Here the note was "*...balance satisfactory.*"

Alternate (e) The XP-934 Carrier Fighter (for the Navy!) with the Wright SGR-1510 *Twin Whirlwind* radial rated as noted above. Notes were: "*Navy useful load includes life raft but no radio; also includes flotation and arresting gear. Wings, landing gear, and fuselage weight increased to conform with Navy fighter design load conditions.*"

In alternate (a) span, length, and height were 36 feet, 25 feet, eight inches, and seven feet, eight inches, and wing chord 70 inches. Wing incidence and dihedral were 1.0 degrees and 4.0 degrees. Wing area was 180 square feet (somewhere along the line the wing area was increased to 203 square feet, though again this just may be counting the area across the fuselage). Horizontal and vertical tail areas were 28.8 and 12.6 square feet, respectively. The wing airfoil section was a C-80 with slots and flaps. High angle of attack load factor was 12.0.

The Curtiss GIV-1570-C powerplant had a 7:5 propeller reduction drive gear ratio, and was rated 600hp at 2,450rpm, but actual power capability was 670hp. Compression ratio was 6.1:1, and fuel was 80 octane. Fuel consumptions at full throttle and 87.5 percent RPM were 59 and 35.5 gallons per hour, respectively. Fuel capacity was 75 gallons normal and 150 gallons maximum with an external tank. Oil capacity was 6 gallons normal and 12 gallons maximum. The propeller was a two bladed Hamilton Standard type of nine feet, six inches diameter. Prestone cooling was used.

The empty weight was 3,239 pounds, useful load 814 pounds (a 200 pound pilot, 495 pounds of fuel and oil, and 119 pounds of armament), and gross weight was 4,053 pounds. It is interesting to note this predicted weight is less than 100 pounds, or only 2 percent less than the aircraft actual gross weight six months later at first flight with the *Conqueror* engine—a pretty good prediction. The actual weight thus came as no surprise to Curtiss engineers.

Predicted performance figures, based on wind tunnel tests, were overly optimistic, however. High speed at sea level was estimated at 250mph; cruising speed at 0.875 maximum RPM was 212mph at sea level. Climb rate was estimated at 2,220fpm at sea level. Climb for 10 minutes was 14,000 feet. Endurance at full throttle and 0.875 percent RPM was 1.27 hours and 2.11 hours at sea level, respectively, with the equivalent ranges 318 and 448 miles. Service and absolute ceilings were predicted to be 24,400 and 25,500 feet, respectively.

With the V-1800 inline engine rated at 750hp (GIV-1800) and 1,100hp (supercharged) with empty and gross weights estimated at 3,474 and 4,288 pounds the sea level, high speed were listed at 260mph and 296mph, again optimistic estimates no doubt, though never proven.

With the *Twin Whirlwind* radial aircooled engine, rated at 600hp at 2,200rpm at 8,000 feet, the empty weight and gross weight were 3,082 and 3,906 pounds, respectively, and high speed at 8,000 feet was listed at 252-254 mph.

At a mockup inspection in May 1932, the Army expressed the desire to install a radial engine in the XP-934. They were not happy with the *Conqueror*. Curtiss complied with a Pratt & Whitney SR-1340-G *Wasp* radial engine installation. Whether there was also a Wright R-1820 radial engine installation is somewhat doubtful. First flight took place July 20, 1932, after the *Wasp* installation, with W. Croswell at the controls, but performance was not good. In fact, the flight test program was not completed because this engine, with a 14-1 impeller, was grounded by order of Wright Field itself, and the aircraft was subsequently returned to Curtiss for the installation of a geared G1V-1570-F. Curtiss went to the *Conqueror* engine in August, and the aircraft was shipped to Wright Field for tests late in 1932.

Seldom illustrated, the XP-31 also tested a number of weapons installations, including a synchronized gun pod on either side of the fuselage abaft the cockpit. The stenciling for the Airspeed Drain and small venturi are noteworthy, as is the rather coarse finishing of the fuselage on this early all-metal structure. (*Curtiss*)

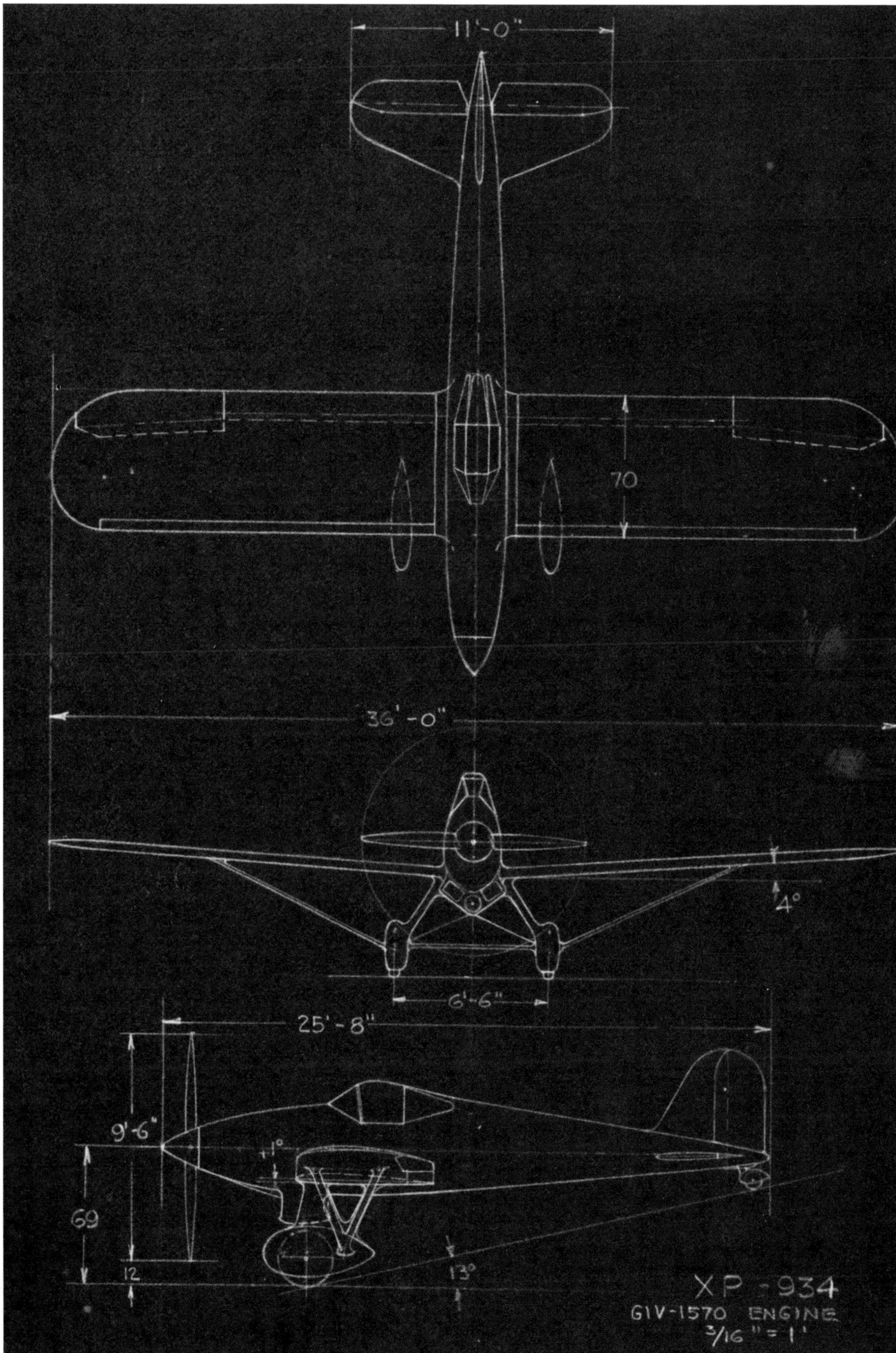
11'-0"
70
36'-0"
4°
6'-6"
25'-8"
9'-6"
+1°
69
12
13°
XP-934
GIV-1570 ENGINE
3/16" = 1'

The Army requirement was for a high speed of 240mph, and the Curtiss ship could not be coaxed over 215 mph. Two and three blade propellers and an alternate cooling radiator design were tested. The Army was quite complimentary about other aspects of performance, such as maneuverability, where flaps and automatic slots came into play at 15 mph above stall speed. The enclosed cabin and visibility were rated well.

The Army performance tests with the GIV-1570F engine of 600hp at 2,450rpm and two blade propeller showed: maximum speed 208mph, cruise speed 184mph, and landing speed 84.5mph without slots and flaps, and 80.5mph with them. Service and absolute ceilings were 24,400 feet and 25,600 feet. Empty and gross weights were 3,334 pounds and 4,143 pounds, respectively.

The XP-934 fuselage was of all metal semi-monocoque construction, and wings and fixed tail surfaces were also all metal, but externally braced. Control surfaces were cloth covered. The landing gear employed long stroke vertically mounted shock struts. Wheel size was 30x5 inches, and travel was 6.5 inches. The tail wheel was steerable.

Armament complement consisted of two .30 caliber machine guns with 1,000 rounds of ammunition mounted alongside the cockpit and firing through blast tubes. As an alternate, a .50 caliber gun could be mounted on the right side.

In March 1933 the Army formally accepted the Curtiss XP-934 and gave it an XP-31 designation and Air Corps serial number A.C. 33-178. It had lost the pursuit competition to the Boeing *Wasp* powered P-26. Curtiss had sold the basic airframe for $33,253, and charged $5,747 to install the SR-1340 *Wasp* engine, and retrofitted it later with a *Conqueror* for $40,000. The aircraft served as a utility hack until surveyed in December 1936, by which time it was designated as a ZXP-31, with a total time of 287 hours. Somewhere along the line it apparently acquired the name "*Swift*," which it was not.

Curtiss XF12C-1

The XF12C-1 aircraft from Curtiss (MSN 11669) was one of those caught up in the early 1930s Navy roles and missions conflict. Ordered as a fighter along with the Douglas XFD-1 and the Vought XF3U-1, the Curtiss offering was a non-responsive reply in April 1932 to Navy Bureau of Aeronautics Design Competition #113 for a two seat biplane fighter. In spite of the fact that Curtiss proposed a high parasol wing monoplane instead of a biplane like the other two competitors, the Navy, on June 30, 1932, ordered a single Curtiss XF12C-1 monoplane prototype, along with the two biplanes from Douglas and Vought.

The XF12C-1 (BuA9225) retained the fighter designation for only a relatively brief interval, from July to December 1933, when it became the XS4C-1. During that brief interval, however, it was subjected to a number of changes, including this truly ugly engine installation (but with a highly polished cowl!) showing the leading edge slats deployed. (*Dean Collection*)

The Curtiss aircraft, designed under the direction of Raymond Blaylock, had features not previously combined in one fighter, at least not by Curtiss. The machine was a radial engined parasol monoplane with its high, slightly swept wing mounted on cabane struts off the fuselage, and with outboard support supplied by long sloping struts down to the fuselage. In all, there were a total of 18 struts involved in the wing support system. The wing incorporated flaps and full span leading edge slats, and was manually foldable aft to decrease aircraft width for carrier stowage. The landing gear retracted into the forward fuselage generally like that of the XF11C-3/BF2C-1 biplane. Tandem cockpits were fully enclosed by a canopy. Armament comprised two forward firing synchronized .30 caliber machine guns in the front cowl, and a flexible .30 caliber gun aft. Light bombs could be carried hung off the outboard support struts. A ground adjustable two blade Hamilton Standard propeller was driven by a Wright *Twin Whirlwind*, 14 cylinder aircooled

The Navy, ambivalent in deciding for either monoplane or biplane fighters for carrier deployment, was a manifestation of the internal conflicts on this issue. Yet another departure from the then-current norm for Curtiss, which was busy building large numbers of export *Hawk I*, *II*, and *III* biplanes at the time of the XF12C-1's first flight in July 1933, the aircraft would win no beauty contests. This was the original configuration, as of October 25, 1933, with a rather complicated wing folding arrangement, and very odd fairing aft of the engine cowling. (*Curtiss W-8579*)

After being reclassified as the XS4C-1, the XF12C-1 was once again reclassified, after a June 14, 1934, accident and almost total rebuild by Curtiss, as the solitary XSBC-1. Here, with gear retracted and a large caliber bomb on the centerline, the aircraft cleaned up rather nicely. The aircraft existed in this configuration only briefly, as it crashed in September 1934 when a wing fold joint failed in a dive test and was destroyed. Incredibly, it was once again resurrected as the XSBC-3, and survived until 1944 at the Naval Aircraft Factory! *(via Peter M. Bowers)*

engine. The aircraft incorporated a carrier arrestor hook forward of the tail wheel and, as required, was equipped with flotation gear.

The XF12C-1 fuselage was an all metal semi-monocoque structure, and the wing an all metal aluminum alloy structure with stressed skin. Tail surfaces were cantilever and of metal structure. Flight control surfaces were fabric covered.

First flight took place in July 1933, and tests were continued by the contractor until the aircraft was sent to Anacostia NAS, DC, for Navy evaluation during October and November 1933.

As the Curtiss Chief Engineer, T. P. Wright said in his papers:

"*Curtiss delivered the XF12C-1 in response to the desire of the Navy for a two seat fighter, but at the time of its completion found that Navy interest centered around its availability for scouting and dive bombing. A contract change was obtained, and the plane was being modified early in 1934 for competition in this new field.*"

In December 1933 the aircraft was redefined as an XS4C-1 scouting type. Testing showed the climb rate to be slow, and maneuverability poor as a fighter. Very shortly, in January 1934, it was again redesignated as an XSBC-1 scout bomber. As T.P. Wright related in a report:

"*The ship thus resolved into the XSBC-1 500 pound bomb dive bomber and two seat scout with new wing features never before in combination. The engine was changed from an R-1510 to a Wright Cyclone just before demonstration trials at the same time provision was made for carrying a 500 pound bomb.*"

An excerpt from the Curtiss Billing book notes: "*XF12C-1 cracked up June 14, 1934.*" It crashed at the factory while under test, but shortly thereafter was rebuilt. Among other changes was an engine cowling revision to provide a better blend with the lower fuselage. The aircraft had two type M-8 parachute flares, and internal N-2 bomb rack vertical chutes for ten 25 pound bombs, as well as one five pound bomb rack on each side of the main fuel tank. Bombs were hung nose down, and pushed open spring-hinged doors on release. The aircraft could also carry two 100 pound or four 50 pound bombs externally on a P-1 type bomb rack mounted below the main fuel tank cradle. As an XSBC-1 it had the ability to carry a 500 pound bomb under the fuselage.

On the Curtiss estimated contracts list for 1934, the XSBC-1 was listed as unit price $20,000.

The XSBC-1 crashed again in September 1934 due to a failure in a wing fold joint during a dive test, and was totally destroyed. After this crash the high wing monoplane configuration was abandoned, and Curtiss went on to build a completely new XSBC-2 biplane in 1935, albeit with the very same serial number, BuA 9225.

The Curtiss and Navy specifications for the XF12C-1 aircraft follow. The initial numbers are those of Curtiss while the ones in parentheses are Navy figures.

Span, length, and height 41 feet, six inches, 29 feet, one inch (29 feet, one and 1/2 inches), and 12 feet, 11 inches (12 feet, 11.5 inches). Wing area was 272 square feet (wing chord 85 3/8 inches,

Perhaps spurred on by the experience with the XF12C-1, Curtiss designed yet another rather strange looking fighter in 1932, with the clear intent to demonstrate the advantages of a monoplane or biplane configuration on the same basic airframe. The result was the rather portly XF13C-1, BuA 9343. *(Dean Collection)*

Although possessing an earlier designation, the monoplane configuration of the basic design (the XF13C-1) did not fly until after the XF13C-2 biplane configuration (labeled as such by Curtiss in this December 9, 1933 view, but still marked as XF13C-1 on the rudder by the Navy!). Curtiss predicted that the biplane configuration would prove superior. *(Curtiss S-F8809)*

wing section NACA 0010, wing incidence 2.5 degrees, wing dihedral 2 degrees, wing sweep 12 degrees). (Horizontal and vertical tail areas were 48.6 and 21.3 square feet).

Powerplant was a Wright R-1510-92 *Twin Whirlwind* 14 cylinder radial rated 625hp at 6,000 feet driving a two blade (10 foot diameter) Hamilton Standard (Model 5704 29 degree pitch at the 42 inch radius station) ground adjustable propeller. Normal and maximum fuel capacities were 110 gallons and 170 gallons. (Oil capacity was 11 gallons.)

Empty weight was 3,884 pounds, useful load 1,577 pounds (consisting of a 400 pound crew, 660 pounds of fuel, 64 pounds of oil, 286 pounds of armament, 86 pounds of equipment, and an 81 pound radio), and gross weight was 5,461 pounds. (Overload gross weight was 5,840 pounds.) Normal wing loading was 20.08psf, power loading 8.74 pounds per horse power, and normal useful load to gross weight ratio was 0.289.

Performance consisted of maximum speed 217.4mph at 6,000 feet, and landing speed was 64mph at sea level (stall speed 64.1mph). Normal and maximum ranges were 738 miles and 1,079 miles, respectively. (Endurance at maximum speed and 60 percent of maximum speed was 1.79 hours and 5.65 hours, respectively.) Service ceiling was 22,500 feet. (Takeoff run was 810 feet with zero wind and 272 feet in a 25 knot relative wind.)

Curtiss XF13C-1, XF13C-2, and XF13C-3

In 1932 Curtiss designed a rather innovative aircraft with the idea of demonstrating differences between a monoplane and biplane configuration for a Navy fighter type.

Conceived as a high wing, strut braced monoplane with enclosed cockpit and retractable main landing gear, the aircraft was unusual in configuration for a fighter, and even more so when design provision was made on the same aircraft for the addition of a lower wing to make it a biplane.

The 1933 Annual Report of Curtiss Aeroplane and Motor Company to the Curtiss Wright Corporation noted the plane was equipped with a Wright R-1510 engine, was developed during the year, and was being flight tested by Curtiss prior to delivery to the Navy. In a later Curtiss report, it was described as a monoplane or biplane, with expectation the monoplane would be adopted, this with stressed metal skin, wing slats, flaps, and spoilers used for increased aileron effectiveness, along with a mechanical screw operated retractable landing gear.

The Navy ordered a prototype of this unusual aircraft on November 23, 1932, designated as XF13C-1 for the monoplane version, and XF13C-2 as a biplane. The first flight took place in December 1932 in biplane form.

The biplane wings were a separate set with fabric covering over metal structure. Slots and flaps were omitted on the biplane, and the lower wing spars connected to the fuselage at the same locations as the bracing struts of the monoplane. There was no biplane wing stagger.

Armament consisted of two forward firing synchronized machine guns, either two .30 caliber, or one .30 and one .50 caliber. In an effort to maximize pilot visibility in a configuration where the pilot's head was in line with the upper wing, Curtiss designers provided a large amount of transparency area. And in another effort to find a home for Wright's then-new *Twin Whirlwind*, 14 cylinder R-1510 engine, Curtiss specified that engine.

First flight of the monoplane XF13C-1 took place January 7, 1934, and after 34 hours of contractor testing it was delivered in this configuration to the Navy at Anacostia NAS in February 1934, and later to Dahlgren Naval Air Proving Ground, VA. Biplane wings

Rarely illustrated, Curtiss once again reconfigured the basic XF13C-1 and XF13C-2 airframe again to monoplane configuration as the XF13C-3. It is pictured here with special test instrumentation while at the N.A.C.A. between December 1936 and August 1937. Often described in error at the time as a two-place aircraft by some observers due to the extensive cockpit glazing (and very complex framing!), it was in fact always a single seater. *(NACA 12816)*

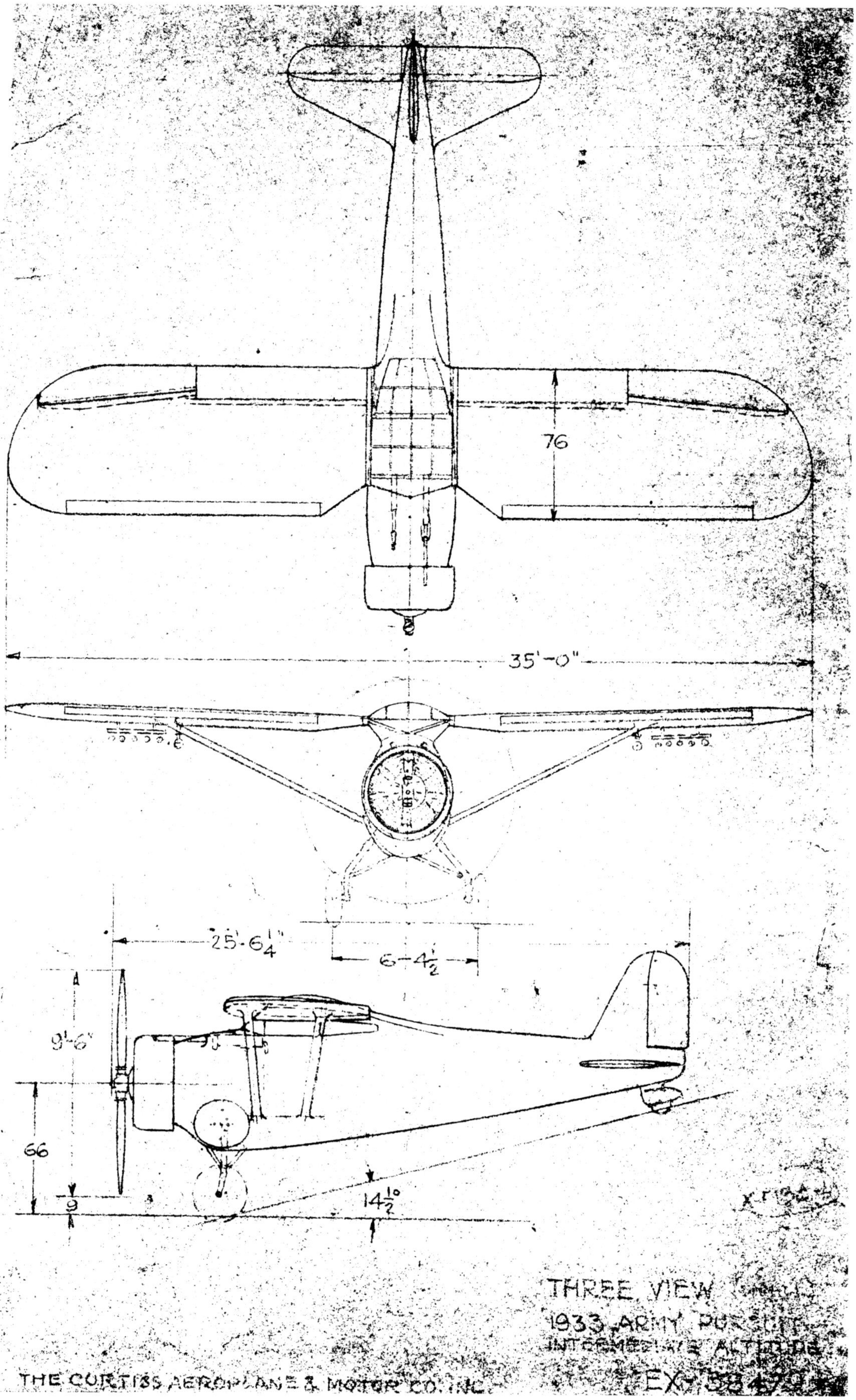

Seldom mentioned, Curtiss proposed an aircraft very similar to the XF13C-1 to the Army in 1933 described as an *Army Pursuit, Intermediate Altitude, Project EX-38479*. The bomb racks on the extreme outer wing panels are of interest, as is the rather less complex window glazing. (*Curtiss*)

were delivered shortly after. In June the Navy completed their preliminary evaluations, and the plane returned to Curtiss for minor changes. In July this Curtiss fighter was put aboard the carrier USS *Saratoga* for trials at sea—nominally assigned to VB-2B for this purpose—and this phase lasted until October 1934. It was then offloaded at Guantanamo Bay, Cuba NAS, and surface-shipped back to Norfolk. The next month the aircraft was flown to the Army Air Corps test center at Wright Field, Ohio, for an Army evaluation in November. Curtiss had proposed a monoplane version to the Army labeled as a 1933 Army Pursuit, Intermediate Altitude, Project EX-38479 per a drawing dated December 13, 1932, with one .50 caliber and one .30 caliber gun, along with the capability of hanging small bombs from racks just outboard of the sloped wing support struts. The Army was not favorably disposed, and rejected the configuration as not having military value. The plane was returned to Anacostia.

In February 1935, the XF13C-1/-2 was returned to Curtiss for conversion to a -3 monoplane variant. A new, more powerful version of the *Twin Whirlwind* engine had been installed, and the vertical tail height reduced slightly to better fit carrier hangar space restrictions. By May the new changes had been completed.

As an XF13C-3 monoplane, the aircraft was again sent to Anacostia for tests, and subsequently returned to Curtiss again for further modifications, including changes in the wing leading edge slats. The new Wright R-1510 engine was giving problems, and slowing down the program, however. It was also sent to NACA at Langley between December 18, 1936, and August 6, 1937, where it was subjected to abrupt vertical plane maneuvers and pitching accelerations.

Although the Navy had reported favorably on many aspects of the XF13C-1/-3 aircraft, it was now clear there was to be no production contract. In October 1935 the Curtiss fighter was turned over to the NACA at Langley Field, Virginia, for various experiments. These included landing load tests, as well as flight measurements of the motion of the aircraft during abrupt vertical plane maneuvers, with particular emphasis on pitching accelerations. By August 6, 1937, it was back in service with the Marine Corps at Quantico, Virginia, as a utility airplane with Squadron VMJ-1. At the end of 1938 the XF13C-3 was retired from the service, disassembled, and stored by NACA late that year.

The characteristics of the three variants of essentially the same airframe, Navy serial number BuA 9343 (and Curtiss MSN 29374) throughout its career, are recorded below:

Curtiss data for the XF13C-1 monoplane: span, length, and height 35 feet, 25 feet, eight and 1/2 inches, and 12 feet, nine inches. Wing area was 204.3 square feet. Wing chord was 76 inches. Slats and flaps were incorporated. The wing airfoil was the NACA 0010, dihedral 1.5 degrees. Wheel tread was six feet, four and 1/2 inches. Wheel size was 32x6.

Empty weight was 3,238 pounds, useful load 1,185 pounds, and gross weight 4,423 pounds. Wing loading was 21.6psf, and power loading 7.37 pounds per horse power. Useful load to gross weight ratio was 0.268.

The powerplant was a Wright SGR-1510 rated at 600hp at 10,000 feet driving a two blade, 10 foot diameter ground adjustable propeller. Fuel capacity was 110 gallons.

Maximum speed was 229.3mph at sea level, and 236mph at 10,000 feet. Landing speed was 67mph, and stall speed 61.5mph. Climb to 5,000 feet took 3.5 minutes. Service ceiling was 23,800 feet. Range at maximum speed was 284 miles; at cruise 864 miles, and endurance at maximum speed was 1.18 hours. Takeoff run was 617 feet, presumed at zero wind.

Equivalent Navy data for the XF13C-1 monoplane, as of February 12, 1934, was: span, length, and height 35 feet, 25 feet, eight and 1/2 inches, and eight feet, nine and 1/2 inches. Wing angle of incidence 2.5 degrees, dihedral 1.5 degrees, and sweep 0 degrees. Wing area was listed at 205 square feet. Airfoil sections were NACA 0010. Horizontal and vertical tail areas were 32.0 and 13.6 square feet, respectively.

Powerplant was Wright SGR-1510-A2, rated 600hp at 2,300rpm at 10,000 feet driving a Curtiss controllable pitch, two blade, 10 foot diameter propeller. Fuel capacity totaled 70 gallons, and oil capacity 5.6 gallons.

Empty weight was 3,241 pounds, and useful load 898 pounds, consisting of a 200 pound pilot, 420 pounds of fuel, 42 pounds of oil, 141 pounds of armament, and a 47 pound radio. Gross weight 4,141 pounds. Wing loading was 20.6psf, and power loading 7.0 pounds per HP. Useful load to gross weight ratio was 0.212.

Maximum speed was 238mph at 10,000 feet, and stall speed at normal load 64-65mph. Climb times were 3.2 minutes to 5,000 feet, and 10.3 minutes to 15,000 feet. Service ceiling was 28,000 feet (estimated). Endurance at maximum speed was 1.13 hours, at 75 percent maximum speed 2.58 hours, and at 60 percent of maximum speed 3.73 hours. Range at the most economical speed was 561 miles. Takeoff run with no wind was 711 feet, and against a 25 knot wind 273 feet.

A year later, on September 1, 1934, the Navy carried the following data for the XF13C-1: span., length, and height were given as 35 feet, 25 feet, eight and 1/2 inches, and 12 feet, nine inches. Wing chord six feet, four inches, wing dihedral 1.5 degrees, wing area 205 square feet, horizontal tail area 40.4 square feet, and vertical tail area 18.6 square feet. Wing airfoil was the NACA 0010.

Powerplant was a Wright XR-1510-94 with propeller reduction gear ratio of 4:3, rated at 600hp at 2,300rpm at 10,000 feet driving a two blade, fixed pitch propeller (Design 5074) of 10 feet diameter and 31 degree pitch at the 42 inch radius station. Fuel capacity was 110 gallons, and oil capacity 10 gallons.

Empty weight was 3,238 pounds, useful load 1,171 pounds, consisting of a 200 pound pilot, 660 pounds of fuel, 75 pounds of oil, 141 pounds of armament, 48 pounds of equipment, and a 47 pound radio. Gross weight was 4,409 pounds. Wing and power loadings were 21.5psf and 7.4 pounds per horse power, respectively, and the useful load to gross weight ratio was 0.266.

Maximum speed was 235.7mph at 10,000 feet and 228mph at 15,000 feet. Stall speed was 68mph. Times to climb were 3.5 minutes to 5,000 feet, and 11.5 minutes to 15,000 feet. Service ceiling was 23,800 feet, and endurances were 1.89 hours at maximum speed and 4.32 hours at 75 percent of maximum speed. Range at most economical speed was 847 miles.

For the XF13C-2 biplane version, Curtiss data was as follows: Upper wing span 35 feet, lower wing span 24 feet, three inches. Upper and lower wing chords were 70 inches and 48 inches. Dihedral was 1.5 degrees for both wings. Wing area was 281.7 square feet. There were no slats or flaps on the wings.

The powerplant and fuel capacity were the same as the -1 aircraft version.

Empty weight was 3,183 pounds, useful load 1,160 pounds, and gross weight 4,343 pounds. Wing loading and power loading were 15.42psf and 7.24 pounds per horse power, respectively, and the useful load to gross weight ratio was .267.

Maximum speed was 205.3mph at sea level, and 218mph at 10,000 feet. Landing speed was 68mph with stall speed 68 mph(!). Climb to 5,000 feet took 3.6 minutes. Service ceiling was 23,900 feet, and range at cruise speed 863 miles. The takeoff run was 504 feet.

The Navy figures as of September 1, 1934, for the XF13C-2 biplane were: data same as the XF13C-1 at the same date, except as follows: Airfoil sections were given as the NACA 2412. Lower wing span 24 feet, three inches. Upper and lower wing chords five feet, 10 inches and four feet, 10 inches, stagger 0. Total wing area was 281.7 square feet.

Empty weight 3,181 pounds, gross weight 4,352 pounds, wing loading 15.5psf, and power loading 7.3 pounds per horse power.

Maximum speed was 218mph at 10,000 feet and 211mph at 15,000 feet. Stalling speed at normal load was 68.4mph. Times to climb were 3.6 minutes to 5,000 feet, and 11.4 minutes to 15,000 feet. Service ceiling was 23,900 feet. Endurances were 1.89 hours at maximum speed and 4.36 hours at 75 percent maximum speed. Range at most economical speed 863 miles. Takeoff distances with no wind 732 feet, with 15 knot wind 430 feet, and against a 25 knot wind 271 feet.

For the XF13C-3 monoplane, Curtiss gave the following data: span, length, and height 35 feet, 26 feet, three inches, and 12 feet. Wing area was 204.3 square feet. Modified slots and flaps were incorporated.

Empty weight totaled 3,499 pounds, useful load 1,222 pounds, and gross weight 4,721 pounds. Wing and power loadings were 23.1psf and 6.74 pounds per horse power, with useful load to gross weight ratio 0.259.

The powerplant was a new version of the Wright *Twin Whirlwind*, the XSR-1510-12, supercharged direct drive type, rated at 700hp at 7,000 feet, and driving a two blade ground adjustable nine foot, six inch diameter propeller, though at the NACA a two blade constant speed variable pitch type propeller was tested. Fuel capacity was 110 gallons.

For performance, maximum speed was 232.9mph at 7,000 feet. Landing speed was 65mph. Climb time to 5,000 feet was 2.5 minutes. Range at cruise speed was 726 miles, and service ceiling 24,100 feet. Takeoff run was recorded as 232 feet.

The Curtiss/Navy XF13C- fighter experiment with monoplane versus biplane in the early 1930s, and the monoplane's apparently demonstrated superiority, still did not move the Navy from its biplane-oriented stance. It took a few more years.

Curtiss-Wright Model P-210 Single Place Pursuit

In late January 1935, the Curtiss-Wright Airplane Company of Robertson, MO, described a single place monoplane, designated as the P-210 (Project P210-Z1), intended to serve as a high-performance pursuit and fighting machine.

It was proposed to equip the aircraft with either a Wright SR-1820F-5 *Cyclone* of 640hp (at 12,000 feet and 1,950rpm) or the Wright SGR-1510C-2 double-row engine, which were predicted to promise excellent speed and climb characteristics, particularly at high altitudes. The basic structure was to have been an all-metal, stressed skin type for not only the fuselage, but the wings and tail surfaces, as well.

The wings and control surfaces were to be of full cantilever construction, with no exposed brace struts or wires whatsoever. The wings were to be tapered in both plan form and thickness, so as to produce the best wing from the standpoint of aerodynamic and structural efficiency. The landing gear was proposed to retract completely into the wings, leaving no exposed parts. The engine cowl would have been built to produce the least possible drag, and the contour around the cockpit was to be smoothly faired, with only a short fairing behind the cockpit.

Dimensions were proposed as a wing span of 34 feet, length of 24 feet, and height of eight feet, 11 and 1/2 inches, with a root wing chord of 100 inches and a tip chord of 50 inches.

With the SR-1820F-5, the high speed at sea level was calculated at 240mph, with 255mph at 12,600 feet and a stall speed of 63mph. Endurance was predicted at 3.27 hours, and an absolute ceiling of 32,500 feet was called for with a nine foot diameter Hamilton-Standard automatic prop. Gross weight would have been around 4,000 pounds.

Although this aircraft was obviously not developed, the characteristics appear to have helped form the thinking in St. Louis that resulted in the Curtiss-Wright Model 21 (q.v.).

9

The Model 75 Series and the P-36

Curtiss *Hawk* Model 75, 75-B, and Y1P-36

The Model 75 of 1935 was a turning point in Curtiss and U.S. fighter design. In the vanguard of aircraft technical progress for the period, it incorporated all of the advancements then favored, and was a great step forward past the company's mid-1932 XP-31 and the early 1934 XF13C-1 monoplanes. Indeed, it is difficult to believe that these three disparate designs were being developed at practically the same time.

Ultimately, the Model 75 and its developed versions saw exceptionally widespread service in nearly all theaters of the world war that soon erupted, and may lay claim to a number of nearly unique claims. Chief amongst these is that this fighter design probably served in more air forces than any other pre-World War II design. Additionally, the fortunes of the war put the *Hawk 75* in a truly unique situation, in which significant numbers were employed on not only neutral turf, but by both Allied and Axis nations, as well.

To start at the beginning, however, the U.S. Army Air Corps needed a replacement for their standard Boeing P-26 pursuit in standard front-line service in the mid-1930s, and wanted a 300mph, all-metal, cantilever monoplane with enclosed cockpit, retractable landing gear, and an engine producing near 1,000 horsepower as the next generation service fighter.

In order to meet this expectation, Curtiss needed engineers skilled in design of all metal cantilever and semi monocoque structures, and fortunately was able to lure a disgruntled Don Berlin away from Northrop, where he had been schooled in such structures. Berlin started work on the new Curtiss Design 75 on October 14, 1934, at a $6,000 annual salary. It was good timing. About two dozen engineers went to work, and prototype construction started

Earliest known photo of the original Curtiss Model 75, taken in Buffalo on May 5, 1935. Curtiss had arrived at the model number 75 rather casually, and there is little doubt that the marketing folks had something to do with the selection of an easily remembered number. (*Curtiss S-F9317*)

This is one of the earliest known photos of the original Model 75 after its first flight in April 1935. It had gained Department of Commerce Experimental Identification Number X-17Y for that and subsequent tests. Seldom noted are the machine gun troughs atop the engine cowling, the aircraft being slated for nothing more than two guns—standard 1920s and 1930s USAAC armament for fighters—even at this late date. (*Curtiss S-F9341*)

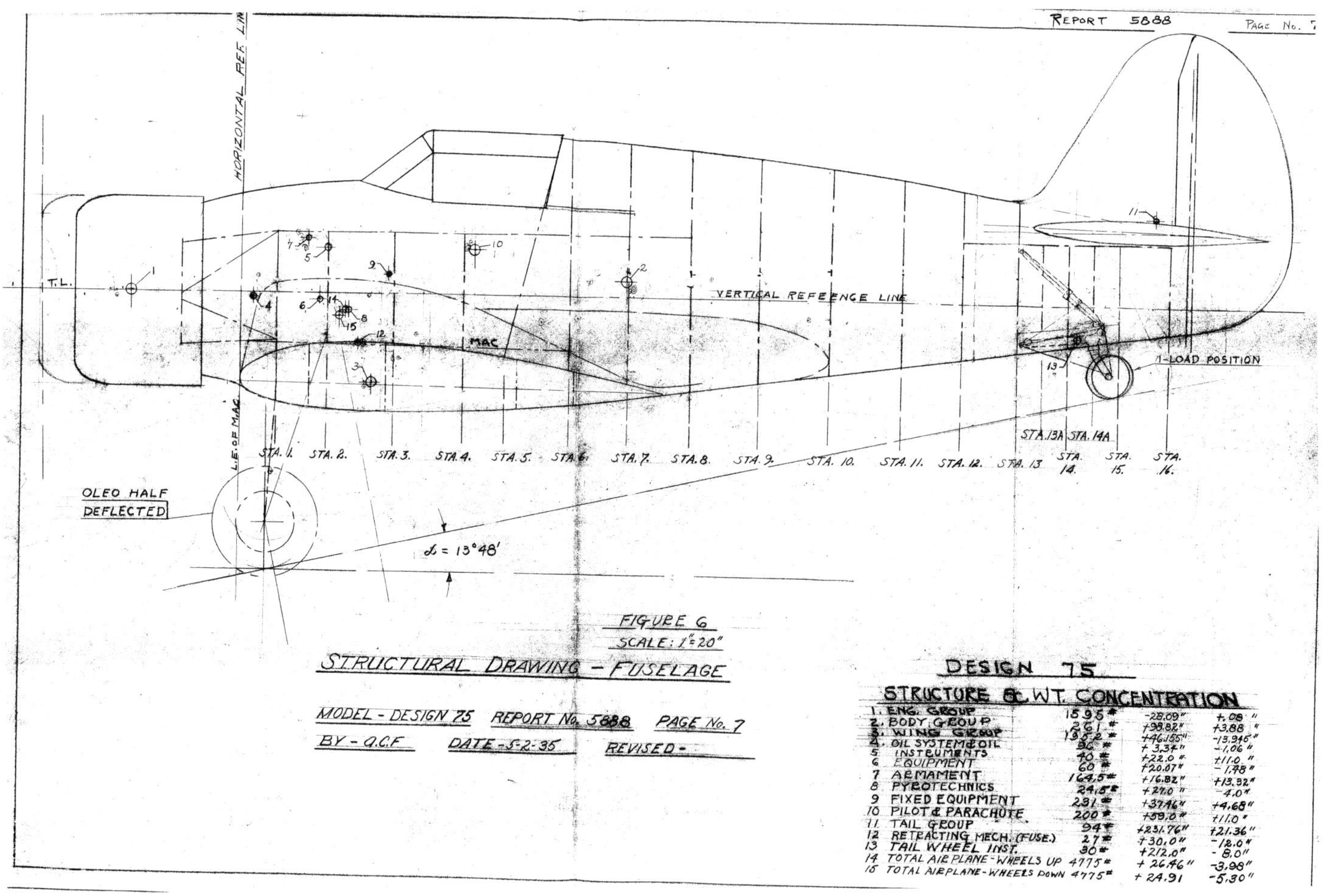

This Curtiss drawing, dated May 2, 1935, is the earliest known plan view for what must count as surely one of the seminal fighter aircraft designs of the first century of aviation. Note that the drawing accounts for two possible positions for the engine cowling, depending on the power plant selected. (*Curtiss Report 5888*)

The original prototype was reconfigured as the Model 75-B by April 1936 with a Wright XR-1820-39 single row engine, blue fuselage and chrome yellow wings, still as X-17Y. The two nose guns had been fully enclosed as well in the cowling, and the resulting aircraft gained an appearance very close to the definitive form. (*USAF 10727AC*)

in November 1934, since the Army wished to conduct a flying competition in the spring of 1935. First flight of the Model 75, MSN 11923, was in April 1935. Air Corps trials began May 27, 1935.

As it turned out, Curtiss was the only competitor with a viable prototype at hand, and the competition was postponed. However, this was not entirely a disappointment for Curtiss as, in the Flight Test Report for the first aircraft, dated June 4, 1935, it was observed that:

"*...the flight test reports on this airplane were incomplete due mainly to lack of time before necessary delivery and the results are therefore not as detailed as desired. Particularly with respect to longitudinal stability, it was not practicable to determine the most rearward c.g. at which the airplane would be stable with power on. The directional stability is undoubtedly excessive and improvement in rudder control is necessary. The aileron control is much more effective and lighter than the other controls. The elevator control may not be sufficient when the c.g. is moved forward and should be lightened. No maneuvers were attempted because of instability and lack of satisfactory control.*"

It is seldom noted that, in spite of the cancellation of the Army competition, Curtiss continued to intensively test the aircraft, and by October 16, 1935, it was back at Wright Field for unspecified demonstrations, where it suffered the loss of its canopy cover, with resulting damage to the aft fuselage and vertical fin.

The 75, since it was a civil, company owned prototype, was issued U.S. Department of Commerce experimental registration X-17Y. It was powered, initially, by a new design, twin row Wright SCR-1670-5 radial engine rated at 900hp, but the experimental engine gave trouble from the start, and was shortly replaced by a Pratt & Whitney R-1535 *Twin Wasp Junior*.

Characteristics of the Model 75 with the original *Twin Whirlwind* engine were: span, length, and height were 37 feet, 28 feet, three and 1/2 inches, and nine feet, one inch. Wing area was 236 square feet.

The powerplant was a Wright SCR-1670-G5 *Twin Whirlwind* rated at 900hp maximum.

Empty weight was 3,760 pounds, useful load 1,083 pounds, and gross weight 4,843 pounds. Wing loading and power loading were 15.93psf and 4.18 pounds per horse power, respectively. Useful load to gross weight ratio was 0.288. Armament consisted of two .30 caliber synchronized machine guns.

Maximum speed was 281mph at 10,000 feet, and cruising speed was 250mph. Service ceiling was 30,000 feet, and normal range 537 miles.

The *Twin Wasp Junior* engine installation also developed inadequate performance in August 1935. The major competitor was Seversky, whose entrant, later to become the P-35, was also having engine problems. With lack of competitors, and poor performance from both Curtiss and Seversky, the Army trials were again postponed until April 1936. That April, Curtiss came back with the Model 75-B modification, completely painted with an Army blue fuselage and chrome yellow wings, now using a Wright single row, nine cylinder XR-1820-39 (GR-1820-G2, but also given on some documents as an SGR-1820G-5 as of June 16, 1936) *Cyclone* rated at 850hp at 10,000 feet. Again this engine gave trouble, and the Model 75-B missed the performance guarantees, as did the Pratt & Whitney *Wasp* powered Seversky, but overall Seversky was the winner of the competition on points, and was awarded a production contract for 77 aircraft on June 16, 1936.[79]

The April 1936 competition was, in itself, a most interesting event. Responding to Circular Proposal (CP) 37-472 were, besides Curtiss and Seversky with its SEV-1XP, Vought with the V-141 and a hopelessly outclassed Consolidated entry, the PB-2A. The Board of Officers that convened to select the winners consisted of Lieutenant Colonels M. F. Harmon, Jr., A. H. Gilkeson, and Ralph Royce, and Majors R. G. Hoyt, H. H. George, Hez McClellan, and none other than C. L. Chennault. It is worth noting that economics had more than a little to do with the outcome, as Seversky somehow was able to come in with a unit price for its production P-35s of $31,728.27 as of the delivery date of the final example (August 30,

1938), while Curtiss, with the P-36, sent its last example to the Army on June 8, 1937, at a unit cost of $83,973.77! By the time of the delivery of the final Army P-36C (AC38-310) on May 4, 1939, however, the unit cost had dropped to $33,828.77. The Curtiss success in exporting their basic Model 75 series contributed, in no small part, to the affordability of the aircraft by the USAAC, while Seversky enjoyed only modest success with export derivates. However, initially, as was so often the case during the 1930s, as of 1937, the Model 75-A with retractable landing gear was not eligible for export, and it required nothing less than a letter from Curtiss to the U.S. Secretary of State, on October 28, 1936, to request permission to export the Model 75-B with fixed gear. However, alter consultations with the Army Air Corps, which had no objections, the Department of State granted Curtiss permission to export *fixed gear* Model 75s on December 19, 1936. An Air Corps Materiel Division memo of April 9, 1938, still restricted the P-36A with retractable gear from such sales, which very possibly delayed the flood of substantial orders that almost immediately followed the lifting of this restriction.

Specifications for the Curtiss 75-B prototype were: span, length, and height 37 feet, three and 1/2 inches, 28 feet, one inch, and nine feet. Wing airfoils were NACA 2215, tapering to NACA 2209. Wing area was 236 square feet.

Powerplant was a Wright XSGR-1820-39, rated at 850hp at 10,000 feet driving a three blade, Hamilton Standard constant speed variable pitch propeller. Normal fuel capacity was 133 gallons.

Empty weight was 4,049 pounds, useful load 1,025 pounds, and gross weight 5,074 pounds. Wing and power loadings were 21.5psf and 5.97 pounds per horse power, respectively. Useful load to gross weight ratio was 0.20.

Maximum speed was 285mph at 10,000 feet, and cruise speed 260mph. Landing speed was 66mph. Climb was 3.87 minutes to 10,000 feet. Service ceiling was 32,500 feet , and normal range 730 miles.

Armament consisted of the same two .30 caliber synchronized machine guns.

The 75-B,[80] as a company owned aircraft, was retained by Curtiss as a test plane, and was later much modified into the XP-37 pursuit (q.v.).

The Army, not fully convinced Seversky could come through on a P-35 production contract, very shortly, in July 1936, gave Curtiss an order (Contract W535-ac-9045) for three service test variants of the Model 75 defined by the company as 75-E, and the Army as Y1P-36, these with serial numbers 37-68 through 37-70, Curtiss MSNs 12240 to 12242. These three aircraft were very similar to the 75-B, except the Army specified use of the Pratt & Whitney *Twin Wasp* engine that had performed better than the others in the pursuit competition. They wished to combine this engine with an airframe having the especially good handling qualities of the Curtiss machine. At a cost of $70,000 each, Curtiss delivered the first two Y1P-36 pursuits to Wright Field, Ohio, on March 4th and March 7th, and the third aircraft to Selfridge Field in Michigan on April 3, 1937. Delivery was accepted by the Army on April 7, 1937.

The three Y1P-36s featured a retractable tail wheel and aft canopy changes to improve vision. After successful testing at Wright Field in the summer of 1937, the designation was changed from service test Y1P-36 to just P-36. These aircraft were used for experimental purposes, such as a test installation of the first dual rotation propeller, a Hamilton Standard model using two two-bladed sections, and also a four blade single rotation propeller. The Y1P-36 aircraft could be distinguished from later production P-36A aircraft in that the former had no engine cowl flaps. The Air Corps issued a limitation on diving speed for the Y1P-36s on June 8, 1937, however, instructing operators to paint a red line on the cover glass of each installed airspeed indicator, extending from the center and passing directly over the 390mph point on the dial, thus indicating the maximum permissible diving speed of the aircraft. This is the first known instance of an Air Corps aircraft having a "red line."

Armament of these aircraft consisted of two cowl machine guns as on the prototype X-17Y.

Construction of the Y1P-36 was all metal, with the exception of control surface covering, which was fabric. The wing was of three spar design, with bulb angle extrusions reinforcing the Alclad skins. The wing was built in only two main sections, joined at the aircraft centerline by bolted angle members. Wingtips were removable. The wing was equipped with all metal split, trailing edge flaps. The fuselage was built in two halves split on center, and was composed of Alclad formers, bulkheads, and stringer reinforced Alclad skins. Tail surfaces were aluminum alloy framing, with fixed surfaces skinned in Alclad. The landing gear was a Boeing design for which Curtiss paid a royalty. The wheels twisted 90 degrees as the gear retracted to lie flush in wells in the wing undersurface.

As a result of the rather protracted Air Corps fighter competitions of 1935-36, three developments of the Model 75-B (Curtiss Model 75-Es) were acquired by the USAAC for test as Y1P-36s. Here A.C.37-68, the first of these, poses for the camera on April 28, 1937. Note that the gun ports on the top of the engine cowl have been faired shut. (*Wright Field No.56927*)

This Y1P-36 (A.C.37-69, which actually bears the last two digits of its serial number on the vertical fin, a most unusual practice for the time), besides having the cowl guns and truncated blisters in place, also wears the Wright Field "arrow" emblem. The aircraft was exceptionally highly polished. *(Dean Collection)*

Specifications for the Y1P-36 were as follows: span, length, and height were 37 feet, three and 1/2 inches, 28 feet, two inches, and nine feet. Wing area was 236 square feet.

The powerplant was a Pratt & Whitney R-1830 *Twin Wasp*, 14 cylinder radial de-rated to 950hp for takeoff, but developing 1,050hp maximum, and 900hp at 12,000 feet driving a three blade Hamilton Standard constant speed variable pitch propeller. Fuel capacity was 100 gallons normal and 151 gallons maximum.

Empty weight was 4,389 pounds, useful load 1,071 pounds, normal gross weight 5,460 pounds, and maximum gross weight 5,960 pounds. Wing and power loadings were 23.14psf and 5.46 pounds per horse power, respectively. Useful load to normal gross weight ratio was 0.196, not so good.

Maximum speed was 294.5mph at 10,000 feet using 900hp. Cruise speed was 256mph at 10,000 feet using 600hp. Landing speed was 65mph. Climb capability was 3,145 feet in one minute, and 10,000 feet in 3.44 minutes. Service and absolute ceilings were 35,100 feet and 36,150 feet. Range on 150 gallons of fuel was 752 miles.

One other, rather mysterious *Hawk 75* aircraft is worthy of mention, and does not appear to fit neatly into this account, the reasons for which may become obvious.

By February 11, 1944, the Wright Aeronautical Corporation at Patterson, NJ, was using an unidentified *Hawk 75* for engine development trials. It had suffered an accident by that date, however, and Wright had asked the Army if they would loan them the parts needed to repair it to airworthy condition. These consisted of both wings, fuel tanks, and, if available "*...wings with landing gears, both left and right.*" The Army ended up selling the necessary parts to Wright Aeronautical by November 20, 1944. As this was clearly not an Army aircraft, it should have been wearing a Department of Commerce Experimental License. However, to date, this has not been identified.

Curtiss *Hawk* Models 75-A, P-75A, 75-C, 75-D, 75-E, 75-F, and 75-G

As noted, the basic Curtiss Model 75 was the original prototype, experimental registration X-17Y with retractable landing gear; the Model 75A was the export *Hawk/Mohawk* in various versions all with retractable gear, and also was applied to the company owned demonstrator bearing U.S. civil experimental marks NX-22028; the 75-B was the original prototype X-17Y re-engined with a Wright *Cyclone*, as noted earlier.

However, contrary to many previous accounts, the Model 75-A was actually the Curtiss design posted against U.S. Army Air Corps Pursuit Circular 35-464 dated January 15, 1935, based on Air Corps Type Specification X-603 of January 14th.

The Curtiss-owned Model 75-A received the Department of Commerce Experimental License NX-22028, and the company certainly made extensive use of the airframe—with the inevitable accident occasionally. Here, the airframe is being hoisted in a wintry setting after an undocumented accident that rather severely warped the port wing. *(Dean Collection)*

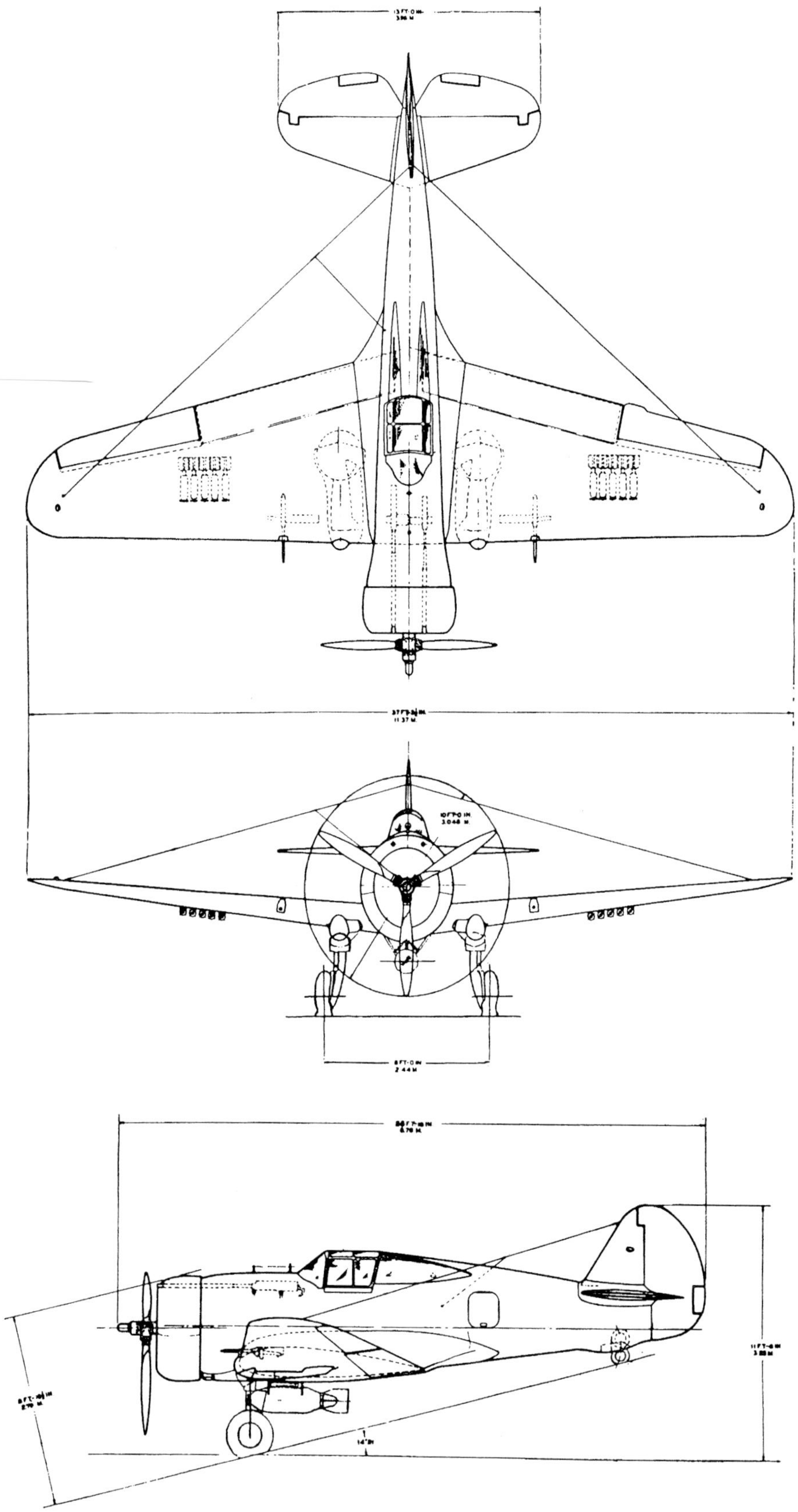

HAWK 75 A

Although Curtiss described designs with the in-house designations 75-A, P-75A, 75-C, 75-D, 75-E, 75-F, and 75-G, only the 75-A and 75-E (the latter as the Y1P-36s) reached construction. This Curtiss-originated drawing shows the basic 75-A layout and dimensions. (*Curtiss*)

Here, the Model 75-A (NX-22028) shares a hangar with a Grumman TBF-1 *Avenger*, a Vultee *Vengeance II* (in RAF markings, AF751), a Grumman F4F *Wildcat*, a North American B-25, and what appears to be a Republic P-43 on the left at the Wright hangar at Caldwell, NJ. NX-22028 by this time sported an anti-glare panel. The rudder colors, seen often on the aircraft during the war years, were apparently blue and red. (*via R. E. Johnson*)

During the course of a long service life with the company, the Model 75-A was modified and used as a test bed for a variety of engines and equipment. Here, NX-22028 mounts a rather large engine, and a very complicated exhaust system, on either side of the fuselage. Note also the rather large intakes under and on top of the engine cowling. The nature of these tests, carried out at the Wright engine field at Caldwell, NJ, is unknown. (*via Paul Vercammon*)

With yet a different engine installation, but bearing large intakes nearly identical to those visible in the earlier photo, NX-22028 here has a special instrument array on the port outer wing, a truncated anti-glare panel, and doped aluminum rudder. The propeller also seems to have rather wide-chord blades, probably to accommodate the large engine. Unfortunately, the stenciling under the cockpit cannot be read. (*via Paul Vercammon*)

Curtiss also proposed an alternate version, identified as the P-75A,[81] to the same Air Corps Pursuit Circular, identified as a "...*Curtiss P-75 Modified*" on May 2, 1935. This was an estimate only, however, based on what was then the latest "F" form for the P-75, reflecting the then estimated weight and balance, which included about 75% actual weights, the remainder being calculated only.

The 75-C was a proposed version to have been fitted with a Wright SR-1820-G3 *Cyclone* engine; the 75-D was also a proposal only variant with another version of the Wright *Twin Whirlwind* SGR-1670B-5; the 75-E was the Y1P-36, while the 75-F was also a proposed only variant using the Wright SR-1820-G25 *Cyclone*, and the 75-G was again only a planned or studied version using a Wright SGR-1820-G5B *Cyclone*.

A Curtiss preliminary proposal dated August 15, 1935, for a "*Low Wing Monoplane Single Seat Fighter for the U.S. Navy*" was described in some detail as a "...*Design 75 with the Wright R-1670 Direct Drive Engine and an arresting gear.*" It is not clear if it received a definitive suffix letter in the Model 75 series. This design was predicted to have a gross weight of 4,734 pounds with 725hp available at 2,300rpm, with a maximum speed capability at 10,000 feet of 268mph with a service ceiling of 29,000 feet. Interestingly, takeoff into a 25 knot wind was estimated to require 235 feet.

Curtiss Model *Hawk* 75-H, 75-J, 75-K, 75-M, 75-N, 75-O, and 75-P

Curtiss wanted a modern, but less complicated pursuit type for export purposes as an all Curtiss-Wright aircraft, including airframe, engine, and propeller, and to this end produced two prototypes based on the Model 75 design. These had fixed panted landing gear, Wright *Cyclone* engines, and a Curtiss Electric constant speed, variable pitch propeller. Airframe construction was similar to the Y1P-36, except for the landing gear.

It consisted of an all metal semi-monocoque fuselage having stressed skin reinforced with transverse bulkheads, stiffeners, and longitudinal stringers, and a sliding canopy over the cockpit. The wing was an all metal multi-spar type with removable tips and internal structure of longitudinal stiffeners, shear spars, and fore-aft bulkheads riveted to the skin.

Wing halves were joined by bolts on the aircraft centerline. Hydraulically operated split flaps were incorporated. The tail consisted of all metal fixed surfaces, and fabric covered metal framed rudder and elevators, both of which incorporated trim tabs. The main gear, however, was fixed, and the tail wheel was fully swiveling.

Two demonstrator aircraft were built as Model 75-Hs in early 1937. The first D-75H[82] flight took place on May 18, 1937. The first plane, with Restricted U.S. civil registration NR-1276 and MSN

The first of two D-75H aircraft was NR1276, Manufacturers Serial Number 12327. After a spectacular flight demonstration before Madame Chang Kai-shek on August 25, 1937, at Nanking, in quasi-Chinese national markings, she ordered the aircraft purchased and presented to U.S. Air Advisor Claire Channault. It is pictured here at Buffalo prior to shipment already bearing Chinese markings, and very highly polished indeed. (*Dean Collection*)

Although Claire Chennault's D-75H lasted only a few months in China, being lost to a ground loop, the Chinese had been duly impressed with the type, and ordered 30 similar Model 75-Ms with Wright GR-1820-G3 *Cyclones*. This aircraft is believed to have been the first 75-M (MSN 12625), pictured at Buffalo before painting in olive drab, on June 21, 1938. They were the first Model 75 aircraft fitted with four guns from the start. (*Curtiss S-F11184 via Peter M. Bowers*)

12327, was delivered for China from the Curtiss plant on June 8, 1937, on Sales Order No.169. After a flight demonstration at Nanking on August 25, 1937, Madame Chiang Kai-shek bought the aircraft and provided it to American Air Advisor Claire Chennault for his personal use in China. The aircraft was painted olive drab overall, and was equipped with four guns: two in the nose, synchronized to fire through the propeller, and two in the wings. The three .30 caliber guns had 600 rounds each, and the single nose .50 caliber gun, 200 rounds.

The 75H was the fastest pursuit the Chinese had, and its demonstrated performance shortly led to the purchase of more of the type. The demonstrator aircraft lasted several months in China, but was finally destroyed in a vicious ground loop. With a narrow landing gear tread, it was not the easiest aircraft to land.

Characteristics of the 75H, quite typical of all the Model 75 fixed gear pursuits, were as follows: span, length, and height were 37 feet, three inches, 28 feet, seven inches, and nine feet, four inches. Wing area was 236 square feet, with root chord 9 feet, tip chord 3.86 feet, and airfoils NACA 2215 tapering to NACA 2209. Wing incidence was one degree, dihedral six degrees, wing aspect ratio 5.9. Horizontal and vertical tail areas were 48.0 and 20.7 square feet, respectively. Wheel size was 27 inches.

Structural ultimate load factor was 12.1 at 5,305 pounds gross weight, and not-to-exceed limit dive speed was 385mph.

The powerplant was a Wright *Cyclone* GR-1820-G3 with a 6.45 compression ratio, rated at 875hp at 2,200rpm for takeoff at 38.5 inches of mercury manifold pressure, and 840hp at 2,100rpm at 8,700 feet at 35 inches MAP, all on 87 octane fuel. The propeller was a Curtiss Electric constant speed type of 10 feet, six inches in diameter. Fuel tankage consisted of two wing center section tanks each of 60 gallons capacity (part of normal useful load), a wing center section tank of 43 gallons capacity, and a fuselage tank of 57 gallons capacity for a total overload capacity of 220 gallons. Normal and overload oil capacities were 9 gallons and 20 gallons, respectively.

The fixed gear 75H weighed as follows: wing 780 pounds, tail 107 pounds, landing gear 342 pounds, and fuselage 467 pounds for an airframe total of 1,696 pounds. The powerplant weighed 1,893

Believed to be the first Curtiss Model 75-M erected after arrival in China, the aircraft clearly shows evidence that the overall semi-gloss olive drab scheme at delivery was modified only by the Chinese national insignia on four wing positions and the rudder stripes. This aircraft has had a rather crude, white "75" painted on the fuselage as well. (*San Diego Aerospace Museum*)

The first Chinese Model 75-M to receive full serials presentation was 2501, assigned to the 25th Fighter Squadron. Note the racks for light bombs under the starboard wing. The color of the vertical stripe on the rudder is unknown, and is reminiscent of USAAC rudder presentation. (*San Diego Aerospace Museum Courtesy of Ray Wagner*)

pounds, and fixed equipment 386 pounds, giving an empty weight of 3,975 pounds. The normal useful load was 1,330 pounds, composed of a 200 pound pilot, 720 pounds (120 gallons) of fuel, 68 pounds (9 gallons) of oil, 174 pounds of armament (one .50 caliber and one .30 caliber cowl gun with 200 rounds and 600 rounds, respectively), a 100 pound radio, a 15 pound oxygen system, an 8 pound signal pistol and ammunition, and 50 pounds of flares and containers. The normal wing loading was thus 22.48psf, and power loading 6.06 pounds per horse power.

Maximum useful load was 2,443 pounds, comprised of the previous useful load, plus another 600 pounds (100 gallons) of fuel, 82 additional pounds of oil (11 gallons), 111 pounds of wing guns and ammunition (two .30 caliber), and 320 pounds of bombs. In this maximum useful load configuration, the gross weight was 6,418 pounds, and the wing and power loadings were respectively 29.2psf and 7.33 pounds per horse power, while the useful load to gross weight ratio was 0.38.

Performance-wise, the maximum speed was 238.6mph at sea level, 280mph at 10,700 feet, and 270mph at 16,400 feet. Normal cruise speed was 240mph at 10,700 feet, and stall speed 68mph at sea level. Climb times were 3,280 feet in 1.4 minutes, 6,560 feet in 2.77 minutes, 9,840 feet in 4.12 minutes, and 22,960 feet in 12.52 minutes. Service and absolute ceilings were 31,800 feet and 32,800 feet, respectively. Cruising ranges with full fuel tanks were 1,210 miles at 240mph at 10,700 feet, 1,385 miles at 210mph at 10,700 feet, 1,380 miles at 16,400 feet at 240mph, and 1,540 miles at 210mph at 16,400 feet.

The *Hawk* 75-J (proposed Pratt & Whitney R-1830 turbine supercharged *Twin Wasp*) and 75-K (Pratt & Whitney R-2190 *Twin Hornet* powered) were studies only, and were never built.

Another long standing Curtiss customer, Siam selected a specially modified version of the Model 75 in April 1938, known as the 75-N. These were amongst the most heavily armed fighters on earth at the time, with either two 8mm or 12.7mm guns synchronized over the nose and two Madsen 20mm cannon, one in a special housing under each wing. (*Curtiss S-F 11440*)

A further 30 Model 75-M fixed gear *Hawks* (MSN 12625 to 12654) with Wright GR-1820-G3 *Cyclones* were ordered by the Chinese Nationalists on Curtiss-Wright Export Corp. Contract 7773[83] at a unit price of $30,888.66, and these were listed by Curtiss as delivered between May 6 and August 5, 1938. They actually arrived in China later that year, however, but experienced delays in getting into combat. Apparently, many of these aircraft were washed

Here, bearing U.S. Restricted License NR-1277 (MSN 12328), the second D-75H (the so-called *South American Demonstrator*) also wears full Argentine Army markings as of May 11, 1937. Although at first glance it appears a carbon copy of the first, it in fact influenced the subsequent Chinese Model 75-M, including the concave cutouts aft of the cockpit to aid rearward visibility. It was not sold to Argentina, despite many claims to the contrary, and crashed at Mendoza while enroute to be demonstrated in Chile. (*Curtiss 10147*)

The Siamese Model 75-Ns featured a rather bulkier undercarriage fairing, and in service, usually flew without the heavy 20mm guns and detachable pods. This example is seen at Don Muang Aerodrome around 1939, not long after delivery, still natural metal overall with Siamese national markings. (*via Ted Young*)

This Royal Thai Air Force *Hawk 75-N* wears the camouflage and national markings that were in use as of February or March 1942 at Don Muang Aerodrome. Here, the 20mm under wing guns have been mounted. (*via Ted Young*)

The oldest surviving *Hawk 75* series aircraft in existence, this beautifully restored 75-N (MSN 12763, the eighth delivered) resides today in the Royal Thai Air Force Museum at Don Muang in full WW II era markings. The under wing 20mm gun pod fairing does not appear to be structurally correct, however. That is noted aero-historian Ray Wagner in the sweater. (*via Ray Wagner*)

cannon starting in September 1939. These Siamese 75N *Hawks* were well liked by their pilots. In January 1941 they were in action supporting bombers in the invasion of French Indochina, and they fought against the Japanese invasion of Indochina for a short period in 1941 before being overwhelmed. They did not, however, see action on December 7, 1941, against Japanese forces; only *Hawk Type IIIs* got airborne that day. They did, however, see extensive service (though no known air-to-air combat) in northern Thailand in support of the Thai Army's advance into the Shan States of Burma in 1942-43. A small number survived the war to be used as advanced trainers. One example still exists in the Royal Thai Air Force Museum.

Argentina also purchased fixed gear *Hawks*. The second (South American) demonstrator, D-75H civil registration NR-1277 (Curtiss MSN 12328) was delivered very shortly after the China demonstrator on June 14, 1937, headed for Argentina, also on Sales Order No.169.[86] It took some time, but Argentina ended up ordering 30 Model 75-O *Hawks* (MSN 12768 to 12797) costing $30,406.35 each, and these pursuits, with two nose guns and two in each wing, were delivered, according to Curtiss billing records, from November 28, 1938, to December 30, 1938. Upon arrival, the pride of the service were issued to the newly created *Ier Regimiento de Aviación's 1er Grupo de Caza* at El Palomar (alongside the surviving *Hawk IIIs*), and the *IIer Regimiento de Aviación's II° Grupo de Caza* at Los Tamarindos (Mendoza). They received Argentine Army serials 601 to 630. Additionally, for a time, a special *Regimiento Aéreo Escuela* (not to be confused with the *Escuela Militar de Aviación*), a kind of operational training unit, also operated *Hawk 75-Os*, as well as Northrop 8A-2s, Martin 139WAAs, and Focke-Wulfe Fw 44Js, until

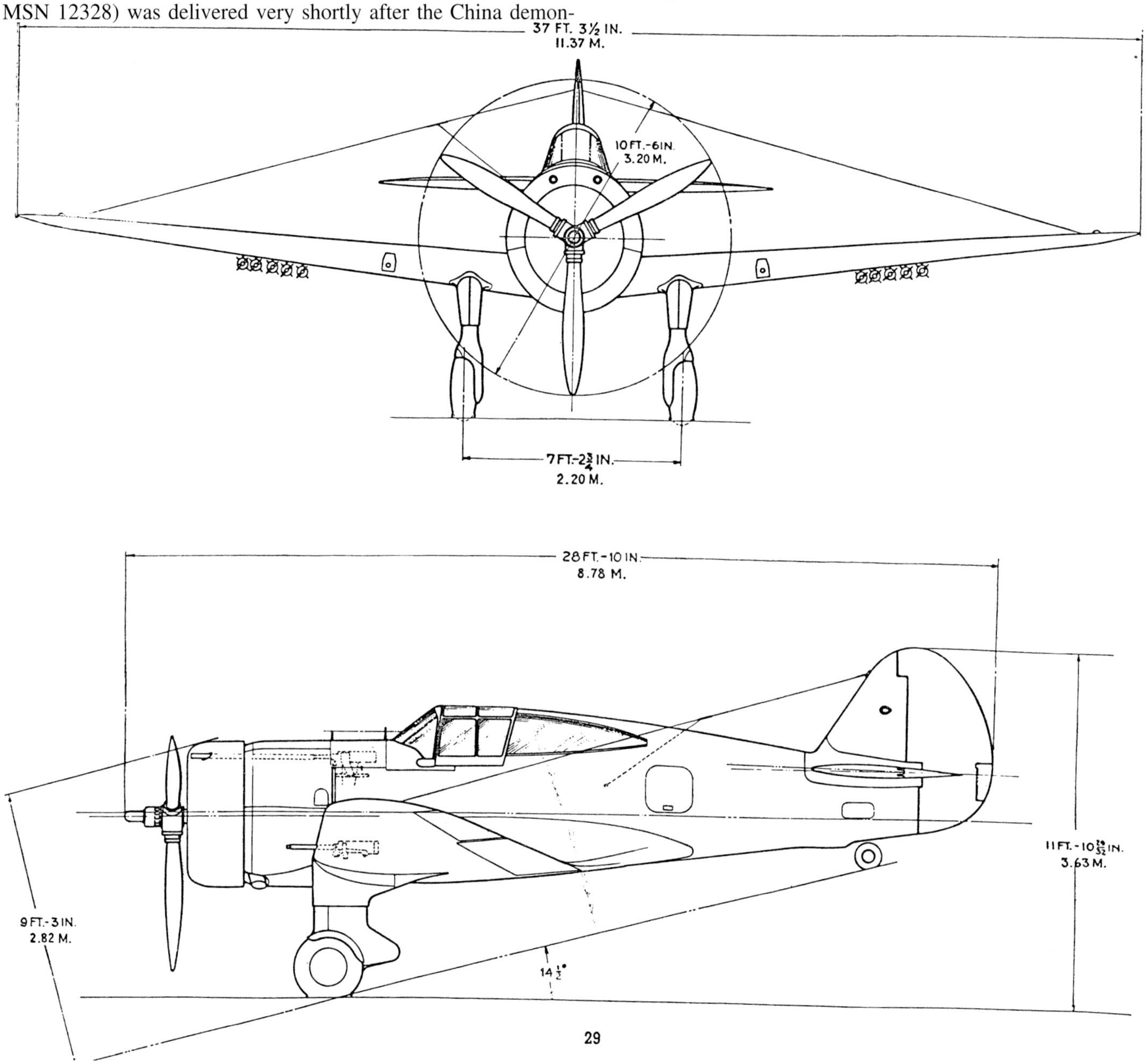

This Curtiss dimensional drawing shows a variant of the *Hawk 75* that appears to be a cross between the Chinese and Argentine *Hawk 75-M* and *75-O*. (*Curtiss*)

Believed to be the first Argentine Army *Hawk 75-O* (MSN 12768), this view shows the slightly modified wheel pant arrangement of this variant. The dual ring-and-bead gun sights atop the cowling in this November 25, 1938, view, just forward of the windscreen, are noteworthy. The Argentine aircraft mounted four guns: two synchronized, and one in each wing. (*Dean Collection*)

out in training Chinese pilots to handle them. Sometimes mud from unprepared airfields would accumulate inside the fixed gear wheel fairings, freeze at altitude, and lock up the wheels upon landing. As a result of Japanese bombing and Chinese training accidents, the number of *Hawks*, the fastest Chinese pursuit at the time, was quickly reduced to ineffectiveness.

It appears there may have been more *Hawks* not officially listed in the Curtiss billing book as airplane exports. An excerpt from a Don Berlin letter of August 17, 1970, to Joe Christy stated:

"*Yesterday I found a list of Hawk 75 type airplanes (fixed landing gear) as follows: 30 H75, China, $896,905.65. One set tools and material $557,540. H75 spares, China $143,132. Probably for (Bill) Pawley's Intercontinent Corp. for manufacture in China.*"

Another communication from Berlin lists 18 additional H75-M*[84] aircraft for China.[85]

Chinese Model 75-Ms are known to have been assigned to the 16th, 18th, and 25th Squadrons, and were assigned four-digit serial numbers, known examples having been in the 2500 range.

Another customer for the fixed gear *Hawk* was Siam (later Thailand), a country already acquainted with Curtiss products via the *Hawk* biplanes that had been acquired in some numbers earlier. The Siamese *Hawk* monoplane variant was the 75-N, of which they placed an order for 12 aircraft in April 1938 (MSN 12756 to 12767). Curtiss billing records show these were delivered from November 11, 1938, to December 9, 1938, at a unit price of $31,074.50. They incorporated under wing racks for 30 or 50 pound light bombs, and a centerline rack for a 500 pound bomb. The aircraft differed from the standard design in having a modified fixed landing gear with increased fairing chord and more wheel coverage. Gun armament consisted of two Vickers 8mm or 12.7mm nose machine guns and, after tests at the Curtiss plant at Buffalo, two 20mm Madsen pod-mounted wing cannon. The aircraft were equipped to Siam with the

A period color presentation of two pre-1941 Argentine Army *Hawk 75-0* fighters, showing the Argentine practice of the day in placing the serial numbers on the wings, top and bottom, in reverse on each wing. The numbers also appeared on the leading edge of each wing. Much later most were camouflaged, and a "C" prefix (for *Caza*) was added. (*Courtesy Aero Espacio*)

In line with most wartime powers, Argentina camouflaged most of her Army tactical aircraft when the world war got underway in earnest. Here, C-628 displays the rather unusual practice of painting the olive drab upper camouflage down the front of the landing gear pants, common on nearly all the aircraft, and details of the stenciling style. *(via Jorge F. Nuñez Padin)*

sufficient cadres had been thoroughly familiarized on these new types. It is interesting to note that a small U.S. Army Air Corps Mission later became involved in this process.

The Argentine *Hawk 75-Os* featured an undercarriage more similar to that of the Siamese 75-Ns, and differed from the demonstrator *Hawk 75-H*. It also featured a redesigned engine exhaust system with a semi-circle of electrically operated gills at the rear of the cowling (which, incidentally, gave considerable problems later on). Armament, contrary to other reports, consisted of four 7.65mm Browning machine guns (two synchronized and one in each wing), and not Madsen 7.62mm guns as widely reported.

The Argentine Army liked the 75-O *Hawk* well enough to obtain a license from Curtiss-Wright to build that model, and turned out 20 more from their own factory in Cordoba starting in 1940.[87] The *Fabrica Militar de Aviones (FMA)* license-built examples were, at first, to have been supervised by Curtiss pilot James H. Gray, who arrived in Buenos Aires around the end of 1938. However, while Gray was an excellent pilot, it was quickly recognized that a seasoned engineer and businessman was needed on the spot to ease *FMA* into the assembly process. In fact, Curtiss supplied many of the complex components for these aircraft, as some of the jigs and tools required were quite beyond the abilities of the *FMA* and its staff at the time.

Finally, the first *FMA* assembled example was declared ready for tests at Cordoba August 6, 1940, the locally built aircraft differing only slightly from the parent company machines, major differences being the *Cyclone* G-5 variant engines. In fact, the first flight did not occur until September 19, 1940, and was reported "completely satisfactory."

The first *FMA* example, Argentine Army serial 631 (MSN 01), was publicly displayed, highly polished, in October 1940, but the factory was in the meantime finding manufacture of the remaining aircraft somewhat more difficult than had been anticipated and, by July 1, 1941, only six in total had been turned over to operating units. However, this quickly accelerated with Curtiss help, and all 20 had been delivered by the end of 1941. Considerable credit was given to *Mayor* Dominguez, Director of the *FMA*, who was described by a Curtiss official as "most capable."

By August 1942, a total of 30 *Hawk 75-Os* were reported in service, the remaining examples being non-airworthy for a variety of reasons. By May 26, 1943, the total on hand and assigned to

Some of the camouflaged Argentine Army *Hawk 75-Os* wore unit insignia on the forward fuselage after being camouflaged. This aircraft (C-639) was one of the 30 assembled in Argentina by the *Fabrica Militar de Aviones (FMA)*. *(via Dr. Atilio Marino)*

This view of one of the first five Argentine Army *Hawk 75-0* aircraft (number 605) shows the location of the wing guns, and the rather narrow stance of the fixed undercarriage. The stubs for the light bomb attachment points are also clearly visible. (*via Dr. Atilio Marino*)

units had increased to 33, but not less than eight of these were unserviceable due to a lack of needed parts. Starting in June 1943, all Argentine Army aircraft were camouflaged in a pattern of dark green and brown (although some *Hawk 75-Os* appear to have been dark green over all upper surfaces, with light gray or light blue undersides), and pre-war national rudder markings were deleted in favor of small Argentine flags on the vertical fin. Likewise, the large pre-war serials (which, in the Argentine fashion, had appeared in large block numerals on both upper and lower wing panels—the numerals on the left upper and lower right wings facing *forward*) had also been reduced in size and location, and were now preceded with a "C" (for *Caza*), these also being worn on the wing leading edges, vertical fin, and cowling in about six inch characters.

As of August 28, 1944, although 40 *Hawk 75-Os* were still shown on contemporary Air Orders of Battle, intelligence observers noted that "*...only about 60% are airworthy, and all are in rather poor condition at the moment*." All were assigned, by this time, to the *Regimiento 2 de Caza* and, within the regiment to two *Grupos* with three subordinate *Escuadrillas* each. Each of these had either six or seven aircraft.

Incredibly, as late as June 1954 not fewer than 20 *Hawk 75-Os* were still in service with the *1° Grupo de Caza, IV Brigada* at El Plumerillo (Mendoza), amongst other types, and the USAF rated them as "*combat ready*!" This was the last report of the *Hawk 75-O* in service, and almost certainly the last examples of the type operational anywhere in the world.

Thus, a total of at least 73 fixed gear *Hawks* were exported to China, Siam, and Argentina in 1937 and 1938, making a tidy export business for Curtiss.

The Design 75-P was to have been a variant designed around a Pratt & Whitney R-180 of 1,000hp at 2,350rpm.

Curtiss Model *Hawk* 75-I

Curtiss issued a Detailed Specification for the Model 75-I on March 15, 1937, which was proposed in response to a combination of two Army Type Specifications: No.98-605 of January 22, 1936, and 98-1800-C of August 6, 1936.

It was to have been essentially a Model 75 with an Allison XV-1710-9 1,000hp (at 2,600rpm) at critical altitude 25,000 feet. See the section on the XP-37.

Curtiss P-36A/P-36B (*Hawk 75-L*)

A little over a year after Seversky obtained the production contract for their 77 P-35s, and after the Army evaluation of the Y1P-36 service test aircraft, Curtiss was finally rewarded for their 1934 to 1936 efforts on the Model 75 pursuit by an Army contract totaling $4,113,550 for 210 Curtiss design 75-L pursuit planes designated as P-36As on July 7, 1937. The contract (W535-ac-10136) was the largest for fighter planes ever given up to that time in the United States, and more than made up for the earlier Curtiss defeat by Seversky. These aircraft were assigned Curtiss MSNs 12415 to 12624, and Air Corps serial numbers 38-1 to 38-210, the very first Army aircraft acquired using Fiscal Year 1938 funding.

The P-36A production aircraft were little different from the Y1P-36s. Propellers were Curtiss Electric constant speed instead of Hamilton Standard hydraulic constant speed, and engine cowl flaps were added to better cool the *Twin Wasps* in certain flight conditions. Machine gun blast tubes were revised. The initial batch

Foreign customers for Curtiss fighters almost invariably specified the armament that they wanted their aircraft to be able to mount. The Argentine Army *Hawk 75-0* aircraft had four 7.65mm Madsen machine guns, and this December 9, 1938, view shows the installation of the starboard gun on one of the aircraft. (*Curtiss S-F 11547 via Museum of Flight PM10538*)

Curtiss Model 75-L covered the 210 P-36As ordered by the U.S. Army Air Corps which, joined by the competitor Seversky P-35s, were certainly the finest fighter aircraft acquired by the AAC to that time. This P-36A is unusual, in having the emblem of the 1st Pursuit Group on the engine cowl and being highly polished, suggesting that it may have been the Group Commander's aircraft. Note also that the cowl guns are devoid of the characteristic muzzle blisters. *(via Gerry Beauchamp)*

of 13 P-36As had R-1830-13 engines operating on 92 octane fuel, while the remainder were fitted with -17[88] engines designed to operate with 100 octane, bestowing increased power and performance.

The first aircraft (serial 38-1) was delivered to Wright Field in Ohio on April 25, 1938, and the final P-36A was delivered on November 4, 1938, less than a year before the start of World War II. The unit price was $17,885 without Government Furnished Equipment (GFE). According to company billing records 101 aircraft were delivered in 1938, and 105 in 1939. These figures have to include most of the P-36C versions. Serial 38-10 was withheld as a P-36B, and delivered on November 4, 1938. The initial aircraft (serial 38-1) now resides in the National Museum of the United States Air Force at Wright-Patterson AFB, OH.

As seen, the P-36As had a slow delivery rate, and left some pursuit Groups bare of operational aircraft for some time. It was found that wing areas around the landing gear were buckling and needed reinforcement, and fuselage skins were wrinkling. In late 1938 and early 1939 there were groundings to apply fixes, or special limits placed on maneuvers and airspeeds. Curtiss, the Army, and Pratt & Whitney worked very hard to provide solutions for early teething problems.

Initial P-36A specifications were: span, length, and height 37 feet, three inches, 28 feet, six inches, and 12 feet, two inches. Wheel tread was eight feet, two inches. Tail span measured 13 feet, two inches. Wing area was 236 square feet, airfoils were root NACA 2215, and tip NACA 2209, wing dihedral six degrees, root incidence 1.5 degrees, root chord 108 inches, and tip chord 46.3 inches.

The powerplant was a Pratt & Whitney R-1830-13 (later -17) rated at 1,050hp at 2,700rpm for takeoff at sea level, and 900hp at 2,550rpm at 10,000 feet. Compression ratio was 6.7:1, blower ratio 7.15:1, and propeller reduction gear ratio 3:2. Fuel specified was 92 and 100 octane, the latter for the -17 engine. The propeller was a three blade Curtiss Electric model of 10 feet diameter. Maximum fuel capacity was 164 gallons. Oil capacity was 54 quarts.

This is the solitary P-36B, subject of experimental camouflage tests at Wright Field, separate and distinct from the temporary camouflage applied during the GHQAF maneuvers, and still reveals elements of its rudder markings and under wing national insignia, as well as U.S. Army titles. *(via Gerry Beauchamp)*

Army Ai Corps P-36As of the 36th Pursuit Group arrived at Ponce Field, Puerto Rico, in early February 1938, and most of them remained in the Caribbean with the Sixth Air Force well into the war years. They are seldom illustrated. (*Cecil R. Wells via Jerry Casius*)

Empty weight was 4,567 pounds, and useful load 1,083 pounds, totaling to a normal gross weight of 5,650 pounds. Maximum gross weight was 6,010 pounds. Normal wing loading was 23.9psf, and normal power loading 5.38 pounds per horse power. Normal useful load to gross weight ratio was 0.192.

Maximum speed was 300mph at 10,000 feet, later increased to 313mph at 2,700rpm at 8,500 feet with the -17 engine and higher rated fuel. Cruise speed was 270mph at 2,230rpm, and landing speed 75mph. Stall speed was 69mph. Climb times were 3,400 feet in one minute and 15,000 feet in 4.8 minutes. Service and absolute ceilings were 32,700 feet and 33,600 feet, respectively. Range was 625 miles at 270mph at 10,000 feet and 860 miles at 200mph.

Armament of the P-36A consisted of one .50 caliber synchronized cowl gun with 200 rounds of ammunition, and one .30 caliber synchronized cowl gun with 500 rounds.

The 1st Pursuit Group at Selfridge Field, Michigan, started receiving P-36A aircraft in November 1938, with the 94th and 27th Pursuit Squadrons receiving those in place of P-35s. Most pilots, including Charles Lindbergh, agreed that the P-36A was easier to fly than the P-35. Other Air Corps groups to receive P-36As were the 20th and 35th at Moffat Field, California, and later Hamilton Field there. P-36s were also at Langley Field, Virginia, with the 8th Pursuit Group.

No.37 of the 29th Pursuit Squadron, 16th Pursuit Group sits the line with her other Group aircraft at a location her designers could hardly have imagined five years previously.The site is Rio Hato, Republic of Panama, a classified airfield forming part of the outlying defensive ring of the strategic Panama Canal. Note the small black diamond on the starboard cowling leading edge. (*via Jim Dias*)

No.37 of the 29th Pursuit Squadron, 16th Pursuit Squadron at Rio Hato, Republic of Panama, viewed from the port (left) side, with a 43rd Pursuit Squadron P-36A (No.61) to the right. Note that the aircraft number is also painted on the left side of the engine cowl, but not on the right, and the small diamond seen on the right on the other photo is also not evident here.The squadron insignia seems to be incomplete on this side. (*via Jim Dias*)

Fine study of the "business end" of a 16th Pursuit Group P-36A (No.33) at Rio Hato, Republic of Panama, in 1939. The bands just visible around the rear fuselage indicate that this was a Squadron Commander's aircraft. AAC fighters, even at this point in time, still only mounted two guns over the nose. *(via Jim Dias)*

A mix of eight P-36As of the 16th Pursuit Group sit the line at Rio Hato, Republic of Panama, in 1939. The nearest two (No.13 and No.59) bear the insignia, respectively, of the 24th and 43rd Pursuit Squadrons. Rio Hato was about 80 air miles west of the Panama Canal on the Pacific coast. *(via Jim Dias)*

This close-up of a 24th Pursuit Squadron, 16th Pursuit Group aircraft (No.15) is A.C.38-52, and is seen being fueled by a tropically kitted crew. This aircraft was wrecked December 30, 1940, at Albrook Field, Canal Zone, when her crew chief, Sgt. L. Linsermacher, taxied into P-36As A.C.38-56 and 38-142. *(via Jim Dias)*

Delivered to the Amy November 4, 1938, A.C.38-20 was originally laid down as a P-36A, but was held back and converted to the single P-36B, involving an engine change to the R-1830-25 with a supercharger blower ratio of 8:1, giving a 13mph speed boost at altitude. It was later reconfigured as a standard P-36A. Like many P-36As, it received temporary, water soluble camouflage paint for the GHQAF maneuvers. (*Aeroplane Photo Supply via Dean Collection*).

Soon, however, these aircraft were to be shipped overseas to Panama, Hawaii, the Philippines, and Alaska, as P-40s started replacing them in the Continental U.S. In September 1939, 30 P-36As went to Albrook Field in the Panama Canal Zone. The next month 20 P-36As went via aircraft carrier to Wheeler Field in Hawaii, and another batch of 31 arrived there in February 1941 for the 15th and 18th Pursuit Groups.

There were 45 P-36As at Wheeler Field in Hawaii on the morning of December 7, 1941, when the Japanese made their attack. They were assigned to the 45th and 46th Pursuit Squadrons of the 15th Pursuit Group. Of these, six P-36As managed to take off about 9:15 in the morning. Two of these aircraft shot down two enemy aircraft, and damaged two more. Six more P-36As took off at 9:30.

After the attack 35 P-36As remained, of which 16 were considered to be serviceable. This was the only war action of World War II in which U.S. Army P-36As participated, in contrast to the Curtiss 75A export models.

In March 1942 10 RP-36A pursuits were turned over to Brazil under Lend Lease—these obtained from American units based in the Panama Canal Zone—and were used by the Brazilians as fighter trainers, three lasting until May 1945, although unserviceable as early as August 1944. Two crashed during training (07 and 08), and one simply never returned to base (probably number 10), and has been officially listed as "missing" ever since. All were well used; one aircraft had almost 12,000 hours on it! These were serialed by the Brazilians as simply FAB 01 to FAB 10, and were based primarily at Fortaleza, Natal, and Recife. Brazil had actually requested 20 P-36As, and the U.S. had in fact allocated 20 for delivery from USAAC assets in the Caribbean Defense Command, but the local commander there protested that these aircraft were needed for the defense of the Panama Canal and Puerto Rico, so the number was reduced to 10.

Ecuador also requested P-36As under Lend Lease, reasoning that the U.S. desire to acquire base rights in the Galapagos and Salinas might give them some leverage, asking for 12 aircraft as late as October 1944. The Munitions Assignment Board wisely denied the requisition, however, stating accurately that the USAAF no longer supported the continued service of the type by that time.

The P-36B designation was given to a single P-36A, serial 38-20 (MSN 12434), held back for an engine change to an R-1830-25 having a supercharger blower gear ratio changed to 8:1, giving a 13 mph higher speed at altitude. It was later revised back to P-36A standard. The -25 engine was rated at 1,100hp, and high speed was 313mph. Delivered on November 4, 1938, the P-36B price without GFE was $17,885. Maximum gross weight was still 6,010 pounds.

One P-36A (AC38-180) was assigned to the Aircraft Laboratory at Wright Field for 10 weeks as of December 30, 1940, to test the drag characteristics of a supercharger exhaust system, and this aircraft has often been pictured, in error, and identified as the P-36B. This same aircraft was being used by March 12, 1942, for tests with skis.

Finally, the very first P-36A, MSN 12415 and formerly USAAC AC38-1, was registered as NX-52203 circa December 1945 to one Harry Porter of Chattanooga, TN. So far as is known, this was the only P-36 to be sold surplus after the war.

Curtiss P-36C, XP-36D, XP-36E, and XP-36F

The P-36C (despite frequent published statements to the contrary, the Army did not call the P-36 aircraft *Hawks*) was a minor revision of the P-36A model, the most notable changes, ordered by the Army on January 26, 1939, outwardly being installation of two additional .30 caliber machine guns with 500 rounds per gun added to the basic armament of the two cowl guns,[89] and slightly higher powered *Twin Wasp* engines. The last 31 of the original 210 plane order (A.C.38-188 onward) were delivered as C types from April 3, 1939, through May. The unit price without GFE was $19,123.21. Dimensions and areas were like the P-36A.

The last 31 aircraft on the original U.S. Army Air Corps order for 210 P-36As were completed as P-36Cs. The principle differences, highly visible in this photo, were the addition of one more .30 caliber machine gun, with the attendant and rather curious underwing fairing to capture shell casings, and a slightly higher powered *Twin Wasp* engine. Deliveries commenced in early April 1939, and No.2, shown here, was one of the first. (*Dean Collection*)

Some P-36Cs also received the rather garish and random temporary camouflage colors that were tested during the pre-war maneuvers. Note that the colors wrapped completely around the aircraft, leaving no traces of national markings, unit codes, etc. (*Edgar Deigan via Dean Collection*)

This P-36C was an exception to the rule while wearing the water-soluble camouflage of the pre-war maneuvers, in having the number-within-unit on the vertical fin, and the 27th Pursuit Squadron unit insignia on the fuselage. All of the P-36Cs thus camouflaged were from that squadron. (*Dean Collection*)

The powerplant was the Pratt & Whitney R-1830-17 (S1C-3G) rated at 1,200hp for takeoff, and 1,050hp at 7,500 feet driving the same 10 foot diameter Curtiss Electric propeller with solid aluminum blades.

Empty weight was 4,620 pounds, normal useful load 1,180 pounds, normal gross weight 5,800 pounds, and maximum gross weight 6,150 pounds. Normal wing loading was 24.58psf, and power loading was 4.83 pounds per horse power. Normal useful load to gross weight ratio was 0.203.

Maximum speed was 311mph at 10,000 feet, and cruise speed 270mph. Climb time was 4.9 minutes to 15,000 feet, service ceiling 33,700 feet, and ranges were 600 miles at 270mph at 10,000 feet, and 820 miles at 200mph.

One of the high points of the P-36C's career was their demonstration by the 27th Pursuit Squadron of the 1st Pursuit Group at the September 1939 National Air Races at Cleveland, Ohio. The 18 P-36C aircraft were painted in camouflage schemes, each aircraft different according to crew chief whims, using green, brown, white, and orange paint. Demonstrations of formation flying and intricate squadron maneuvers were performed every day of the races to the delight of large crowds. It was apparently quite a task to later remove the camouflage paints.

Shortly the aircraft left the 27th, and went to a new group at Maxwell Field, Alabama. With the expansion of the Air Corps as the war in Europe started, P-36Cs, like the A models, were shipped overseas or distributed to new pursuit groups forming in the U.S. for training use. Many went to units in Hawaii and Alaska commencing in February 1941.

With the Japanese attack on Pearl Harbor, the Air Corps directed a nearly nationwide redistribution of combat-worthy aircraft still located in the Continental U.S. Those P-36A and P-36C aircraft still in the Zone of the interior, at least 27 aircraft, were scattered all over the map at the outbreak of war. Two were at Biloxi, Mississippi, four at Chanute Field in Michigan, and eight at Selma, Alabama, while other, smaller concentrations were at Lowry Field, Wichita Falls, Wright Field, Tulsa, and Eglin Field. All of these were consolidated at two locations, with 14 going to Baton Rouge, Louisiana, and 13 to Meridian, Mississippi.

One P-36C (AC38-197) was assigned to NACA between December 10, 1940, and June 5, 1941, for a comparison of aileron control characteristics between it, an early P-40 (q.v.) and, in August 1942, similar tests between it and a Supermarine *Spitfire* and Hawker *Hurricane*.

The XP-36D was a P-36A (serial 38-174) modified, after a September 1939 Army approval, to test heavier armament by installing two .30 caliber guns in each wing with 500 rounds per gun in addition to two .50 caliber nose guns with 200 RPG. Over 400 pounds of weight was added, thus reducing performance.

The engine was an R-1830-13 *Twin Wasp* of 1,050hp for takeoff. Maximum gross weight was 6,429 pounds, and maximum speed 291mph.

Seldom pictured from below, this 27th Pursuit Squadron P-36C not only reveals the configuration of the temporary camouflage on the lower side of the aircraft, but the flaps as arrayed for landing. (*via Gerry Beauchamp*)

Likewise, the upper surfaces of the P-36Cs of the 27th Pursuit Squadron were seldom illustrated, as in this excellent in-air view. The basic idea wasn't so much to hide the aircraft, as it was to confuse what was being seen. *(via Gerry Beauchamp)*

Nearly the entire complement of the 27th Pursuit Squadron at Selfridge Field, Michigan, in September 1939, preparing to exhibit at the National Air Races. Number 69, nearest, was AC38-85. No two aircraft were marked the same. *(NARA RG342FH)*

After the U.S. prepared for war, photos of operational P-36 series aircraft became harder to take, as restrictions were clamped down even on aircrew. This rather shabby P-36C was No.27 of an unidentified unit, the significance of the "23MM" having eluded identification. *(Dean Collection)*

This P-36C was assigned to the 23rd Composite Group, which provided support to the Air Corps Board at Maxwell Field, Alabama. It was painted Olive Drab, with Neutral Gray extending rather high up the fuselage sides. It retained glossy national insignia on the fuselage, but had no wing insignia. The presentation of the data block in white or yellow characters is also noteworthy. (*Dean Collection*)

Photos of P-36C aircraft in wartime colors are rare. Here, A.C.38-191 bears early wartime camouflage and markings, and retains the pre-war national insignia. This aircraft was delivered April 10, 1939, at Selfridge Field, then spent time at Maxwell Field, Orlando, Eglin, and Lake Charles. It was lost on March 18, 1943, when Raymond H. Allen bailed near Eagle Pass, Texas, while assigned to the 826th Single Engine Advanced Flying Squadron. He was killed when his chute failed to function. (*Dean Collection*)

The XP-36F was P-36A A.C.38-172, configured to test a 23mm Madsen cannon housed under each wing in a fairing very similar to those used on the fixed-gear, export Model 75-Ns for Siam. The same mounts were used to test 20mm Hispano-Suiza guns as well, and the over-the-nose armament was retained. (*Dean Collection*)

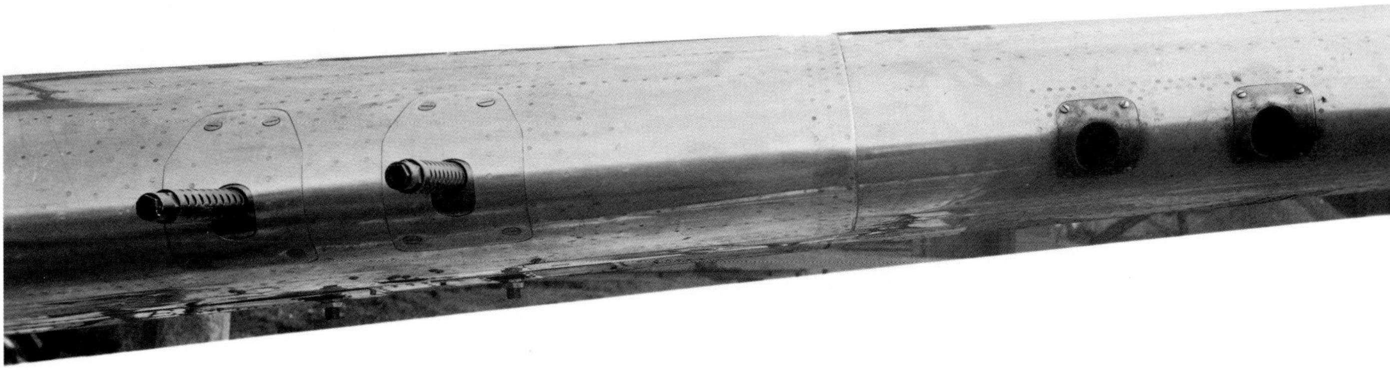

The first American eight-gun fighter was a former P-36A (AC38-147), modified as the single XP-36E in September 1939. This close up of the port (left) wing shows the two inboard .30 caliber guns at left, and the two outboard guns, set far back into the wing, at right. Strictly speaking, the XP-36E was a nine gun fighter, but a single .50 caliber gun left in place over the nose was inoperative. (*Curtiss S-F12470*)

The XP-36E was a P-36A (serial 38-147) employed for another armament test with revised wing panels having either three or four .30 caliber guns in each wing with 500 rounds per gun. A single nose .50 caliber gun was not operative.

The -13 engine was still used, maximum gross weight was 6,576 pounds, and maximum speed was 289mph.

The XP-36F was a P-36A (serial 38-172) employed to test installation of a 23mm Madsen cannon with 100 rounds per gun in an under wing pod on each side. Seldom reported is the fact that, in addition to the Madsen cannon, the aircraft was also tested circa April 16, 1940, with two 20mm Hispano-Suiza cannon as well, and some photos of the aircraft that have been published have mistaken these two different weapons for one another. The nose armament of one each .30 caliber and .50 caliber gun was retained.

The XP-36F was passed to Class 26 status (Instructional Airframe) around July 21, 1944, with but 167 hours total time on the airframe.

The maximum gross weight was 6,850 pounds, and maximum speed was only 265mph.

In addition to the following table, showing USAAC and USAAF units that were issued P-36 series aircraft, see Annex 3 at the end of this volume for the locations, by serial number, of all P-36, YP-37, and P-40 series aircraft on strength with the USAAC as of December 7, 1941.

The Army Air Corps gradually became aware that U.S. fighters were insufficiently armed compared to those of other major nations. One of the first steps towards addressing this was the single XP-36D (A.C. 38-174), formerly a P-36A, modified in September 1939 to accommodate four .30 caliber guns in the wings—much like those that Curtiss had already been preparing for export orders—in addition to the two .50 caliber nose guns. It was otherwise indistinguishable from a P-36A. (*USAF via Walter J. Boyne*)

USAAC/USAAF Units Known to have been Issued P-36 Series Aircraft

Unit	Period	Stations
Panama Interceptor Command (Detachment)	1942	San Jose, Costa Rica
HHS, 6th Interceptor Command	1942	Panama Canal Zone; Caribbean
HHS, 16th Pursuit/Fighter Group	1939-1942	Panama Canal Zone; Caribbean
24th Air Base Group	1941	Borinquen Field, Puerto Rico
HHS, 32nd Pursuit/Fighter Group	1940-1942	Panama Canal Zone; Caribbean
HHS, 36th Pursuit/Fighter Group	1942-1943	Panama Canal Zone
40th Bomb Group	1942	Panama Canal Zone; Caribbean
11TH Pursuit Squadron	1941-1942	Selfridge Field; Alaska (?)
18th Pursuit Squadron	1940-1941	Hamilton Field, CA
20th Pursuit Squadron	1940	Philippines
21st Pursuit Squadron	1940-1941	Philippines
22nd Pursuit Squadron	1940-1942	Langley Field; Puerto Rico; Trinidad
23rd Pursuit/Fighter Squadron	1940-1942	Langley Field; Puerto Rico; St. Thomas
24th Pursuit Squadron	1936-1942	Panama Canal Zone
27th Pursuit Squadron	1939	Selfridge Field, MI
29th Pursuit Squadron	1939-1941	Panama Canal Zone
32nd Pursuit/Fighter Squadron	1940-1943	Langley; Puerto Rico; Curacao; Aruba
33rd Pursuit Squadron	1939-1940	Langley; Mitchel
34th Pursuit Squadron	1940-1941	Kelly; Hamilton; Philippines
35th Pursuit Squadron	1939-1940	Langley; Mitchel
36th Pursuit Squadron	1939-1940	Langley; Mitchel
39th Pursuit Squadron	1940-1941 (unconfirmed)	Selfridge; Baer Field, IN
43rd Pursuit Squadron	1940-1942	Panama Canal Zone
44th Pursuit Squadron	1941	Hawaii
46th Pursuit Squadron	1940-1941	Hawaii
47th Pursuit Squadron	1941-1943	Hawaii
51st Pursuit/Fighter Squadron	1941-1943	Panama Canal Zone
52nd Pursuit/Fighter Squadron	1941-1942	Panama Canal Zone
53rd Pursuit/Fighter Squadron	1941-1942	Panama Canal Zone
54th Pursuit/Fighter Squadron	1941-1942	Hamilton; Washington state; Alaska
55th Pursuit Squadron	1938-1940	Moffett; Hamilton
67th Pursuit Squadron	1941	Baton Rouge, LA
68th Pursuit Squadron	1941	Selfridge; Baton Rouge, LA
69th Pursuit/Fighter Squadron	1941-1942	Selfridge; Louisiana; Florida
70th Pursuit Squadron	1941	Hamilton Field
77th Pursuit Squadron	1938-1940	Moffett; Hamilton
78th Pursuit Squadron	1940-1941	Hawaii
79th Pursuit Squadron	1938-1940	Moffett; Hamilton
94th Pursuit Squadron	1938-1940	Selfridge
108th Reconnaissance Squadron (Special)	1943	Panama Canal Zone

Curtiss *Hawk* H75-R

As noted earlier, Curtiss had built another retractable gear 75 type as a company owned airplane with civil registration NX-22028 (MSN 12931). Utilized for testing and demonstration, the 75-A, as it was designated by the company, was normally equipped with a Wright R-1820 *Cyclone* engine driving a three blade Curtiss Electric propeller, a totally Curtiss Wright product. Most 75-A testing was in the area of experimental power plants, including propeller blade vibration testing using strain gages.

The characteristics of the basic 75-A were: span, length, and height 37 feet, three and 1/2 inches, 28 feet, eight inches, and 9.25 feet. Wing area was 236 square feet, landing gear tread 8.07 feet, and wheel size 27x6 ply.

The powerplant was a Wright *Cyclone* of 1,000hp at sea level. Fuel capacity was 161 gallons.

Empty weight was 4,483 pounds, useful load 1,209 pounds, and gross weight 5,692 pounds. Wing and power loadings were 24.1psf and 7.59 pounds per horse power, respectively.

Maximum speed was 302mph, cruise speed 260mph, service ceiling 33,140 feet, and normal range 677 miles.

Two engine test installations out of many were particularly notable, both involving investigation, with Pratt & Whitney, of su-

Subject of considerable confusion over the years, this is the H75-R (NX-22028), a Curtiss owned aircraft that had a number of incarnations. Bearing full Air Corps markings and national insignia, it was used to test a turbo supercharger installation on the *Twin Wasp* engine. This involved addition of a rather bulbous housing under the cowling, and an intake arrangement under the post wing. Tested at Wright Field in May 1939, it later reverted to H75-A configuration. (*Curtiss via J. Schneider*)

percharging the R-1830 *Twin Wasp* engine used in the P-36A aircraft.

The first, with NX-22028 now called a 75-J, involved installation of a new mechanical supercharger, most probably a two stage system as later used on the Grumman *Wildcat*, to improve altitude performance of the P-36 type.

The other installation of note was a turbo supercharger on the *Twin Wasp* with the same objective. NX-22028 was now labeled a H75-R[90] for the records, and this version was entered into the 1939 pursuit competition with Army wing and rudder markings, even though it was still very much Curtiss property, and delivered to Wright Field for evaluation in late January of that year, and again in late May. The test configuration had the turbo unit in a faired bulge under the engine accessory compartment, and the required intercooler downstream in another protrusion, with an air scoop beneath the fuselage at the wing location. Like the XP-37, the turbo supercharger had problems, including that of control, and the installation was not sufficiently developed to be reliable. In addition, empty and gross weights went up by over 500 pounds.

Characteristics of the H75-R version were: span, length, and height same as the P-36A.

Empty weight was 5,074 pounds, useful load 1,089 pounds, and gross weight 6,163 pounds. Wing and power loadings were 26.1psf and 4.83 pounds per horse power, and useful load to gross weight ratio was 0.177.

The powerplant was a Pratt & Whitney R-1830-SC2-G, rated at 1050hp maximum driving a Curtiss Electric constant speed propeller.

Maximum speed was 330mph at 15,000 feet, and cruise speed 302mph at 15,000 feet. Climb time was 4.75 minutes to 15,000 feet, and normal range was 600 miles.

After failing to obtain an Army contract, NX-22028 was stripped of its military colors and returned to Curtiss, where it resumed its role as a company test bed aircraft. In its later life as an H75-A it was based at the Caldwell Wright Airport in northern New Jersey. It was last seen taking off from that airport in the summer of 1948.

Curtiss *Hawk* 75-S, 75-T, 75-U, and 75-V

Previously seldom noted, Curtiss very nearly completed the alphabet in what seemed a determined effort to build a Model 75 variant for every conceivable customer and requirement with the *Hawk* 75-S, 75-T, and 75-U Detailed Specifications.

The 75-S was to have been a basic aircraft with a Wright R-1820-G111 of between 900 and 775hp at 2,200rpm, and a critical altitude of 6,000 to 16,000 feet, while the 75-T was proposed to take the SGR-1820-G12 of 810 to 860hp at 2,100rpm, with critical altitudes of 3,200 to 10,300 feet. The 75-U was described as a Pratt & Whitney R-1830-9, 850hp at 2,450rpm model with critical altitude of 8,000 feet.

Finally, the 75-V was submitted against Army Air Corps Circular 36-590 of March 12, 1936, and was exactly identical to the D-75-I (XP-37), except that the turbo-supercharger equipment was omitted.

Curtiss *Hawk* H75A-1 to A-4 and *Mohawk I*, *II*, *III*, and *IV*

The *Hawk* 75A type was the export version of the U.S. Army P-36. Curtiss sold far more of these export versions than U.S. Army models. Export 75As ended up fighting nearly all over the world.

France ordered no less than 730[91] of this basic type. After initiating contract negotiations in February 1938, that country, though unhappy about Curtiss pricing, ordered an initial batch of 100 H75A-1 models on Sales Order No.181 (Contract 8875) on May 17, 1938 (Curtiss MSNs 12798 to 12897). These gained French serials H75-C1 No.1 to No.100. After a first flight in November at Curtiss in Buffalo, New York, four aircraft were shipped to France, and tested in late December 1938. In addition, the French took an option on Sales Order No.187 (Contract 9413) on 100 more pursuits as H75A-2 models, Curtiss MSNs 12932 to 13031, and these got French serials H75-C1 No.101 to No.200.

The U.S. Army was not happy about the French orders, feeling they might interfere with P-36 deliveries. After all, the first P-36A was accepted only a month before the French contract, and the final P-36A was delivered only in November 1938, and the final P-

Anxious to expand and equip her fighter arm with the best available aircraft, France ordered not fewer than 730 variants of the H75A commencing in May 1938, just as other foreign nations were also scrambling to acquire the state-of-the-art Curtiss fighters. Here, the Buffalo production line is crowded with eight French H75C-1s (as the H75A-1 was designated), and a Dutch H75A-7 in the foreground.

36C in May 1939. Thus, the Curtiss domestic and export production programs were concurrent.

The export models started in French service in March 1939. Initially a few aircraft were shipped overseas complete, but the remainder were assembled in France. The export *Hawk* had French equipment where required, and a reverse acting throttle movement to meet French convention. The two nose and two wing guns were F.N. built 7.5mm types. Seat armor was provided, but an armored glass windshield was not and, significantly, there were no self sealing fuel tanks. The H75A-1s were powered with a Pratt & Whitney *Twin Wasp* engine rated at 950hp for takeoff, and 900hp at 12,000 feet. Generally, characteristics were similar to the U.S. P-36A. Pratt & Whitney obtained a separate French order for 100 *Twin Wasp* engines, plus about 75 percent spares for the H75A-1s.

The French option for another 100 *Hawks*, the H75A-2 model with two additional F.N. 7.5mm wing guns, was picked up on March 8, 1939, six months before the start of World War II. Many of the earlier H75A-2 aircraft had the same engine model as the A-1, but later aircraft were powered by an R-1830-SC3-G model up rated at takeoff to 1,050hp at 2,700rpm. Deliveries in France of the A-2 commenced in late May 1939, and by the end of September, the first month of war, a total of 97 had arrived, and four French squadrons were equipped. It is interesting to note that one of the French H75A-2s (No.188) was loaned to the British RAF during the winter of 1939 for unspecified trials.

The U.S. Military Intelligence Division was following the French experience with their *Hawk 75As* with great interest, and two detailed reports, compiled in October and December 1939, bear examination. These included a synopsis of conversations that had been held with French pilots who had experienced combat operations in the type, as well as members of the French Air Ministry technical services. They observed that it was essential that fuel tanks receive some form of protective covering, and noted that the French were undertaking measures, as of October 21, 1939, to make this change in the aircraft they had on hand. They pointed out that a number of *Hawk 75As* would have clearly survived if they had benefited from this protection. They also observed that the fuel tank system was regarded as too complicated for combat operations. They recommended a system that permitted simultaneous draining of both main tanks. Failing that, they requested that a system be devised in a position where it could be manipulated without the necessity of the pilot taking his eyes off his gun sights. They further observed that it would be vastly preferable to have a landing gear system capable of being lowered in one operation, and practically begged for as much as 8mm of sheet armor plate to protect the pilot's seat. They also observed that they felt that the gun ammunition capacity was inadequate.

One French commander in particular, *Commandant* Hughes, expanded on these recommended improvements, and made very specific recommendations regarding armor protection, fuel tanks,

The first batch of 100 H75A-1s for France were designated as H75C-1 by the *Armee de l'Air*. Here, No.35 receives attention from ground crew after combat with German forces in 1940. Note the very small size of the wing roundels. (*French Air Force No.276*)

French pilots were delighted with the Curtiss fighters, which soon equipped a number of front-line *Armee de l'Air* units, such as No.8—an H71C-1 (H75A-1) of *GC I/5*—by June 1939. Most were initially operated in bar metal, but this soon gave way to camouflage. *(via Philippe Listemann)*

canopy glazing, the tail wheels and landing gear, and the location of the prop pitch control. He pointed out that at least three aircraft from his *Groupe* had been damaged due to enemy bullets penetrating the hydraulic system for landing gear retraction, and hoped that a second, parallel system for emergencies could be devised. He also criticized the electrically operated landing gear position indicator, which had failed to function on some occasions. He had his own unit engineers design a novel field modification to fix this problem. They devised a simple mechanical method to supplement the original indicator. Through a small mica-covered window located on the wing that they installed, the pilot could see part of the surface of a ball within the wing. This ball rotated, actuated by a lever which moved with the landing gear. The surface of the ball visible when wheels were "down" was painted white, while the remaining surface was painted red.

By January 8, 1940, the head of the French Air Mission in the U.S. was making nearly frantic efforts to purchase 30 spare wings sets for the *Hawk* 75-As acquired to that time for immediate delivery to France. He even tried, with predictable results, to obtain the wings from those then being produced for the USAAC in order to

No.178, seen here with the *Centre d'Essai en Vol (CEV)* at Cazaux in 1940—French equivalent of Wright Field in the U.S.—was designated by the French as an H75-C1, but was built as an H75A-2. *(via Philippe Listemann)*

French No.301, designated as H75-C1, was built as an H75A-3, and is seen here while assigned to *GC I/4* at the remote French colony of Dakar, Senegal, as flown by Deputy Commander *Capitaine* Gautham as of July 1940. *(via Philippe Listemann)*

The final order from France was for 285 H75A-4s, which received the French designation H751C-1. Here, the first machine sits in the snow at Buffalo, awaiting flight testing before being shipped in April 1940. It is believed that fewer than a dozen of this six-gun variant reached France before the armistice with the invading Germans. (*Curtiss*)

When France capitulated to German forces and resistance ceased on June 25, 1940, the *Armee de l'Air* had taken the prudent precaution of re-assigning all remaining *Hawk 75A* equipped units to bases in North Africa. These subsequently adopted the garish markings of the so-called Vichy French Air Force, like those worn by H75C-1 (H75A-2) No.285 of *GI I/4*, pictured here based at Dakar, Senegal, in 1941. (*via Philippe Listemann*)

After the Allied invasion of North Africa in November 1942, *Operation Torch*, during which French units equipped with *Hawk 75As* mounted token resistance to satisfy honor, the surviving aircraft were incorporated into the Free French Air Force, and engaged as fighter trainers, like this lineup in French Morocco in 1943. No.183, in the foreground, was an H75A-2. (*via Philippe Listemann*)

After the occupation of continental France, a substantial number of *Hawk 75A* variants were seized by German forces, including this *H75-C1* (No.261, an H75A-3), which the Germans elected to label with both the French designation and serial number under the swastika. (*Collection of Jan van den Heuvel via Leif Hellström*)

gain quicker delivery. The reasons given for this previously unreported rush order was that, of the *Hawk* 75-As then remaining airworthy in French service, about 30 had been grounded because spare wings were simply not available. France had purchased, in money value, the equivalent of 50 airplanes as spares for the 200 aircraft purchased. A combination of machine gun fire in combat, wing failures due to high landing stresses at poor fields, and in some instances piloting, were cited as the causes of the unusually high consumption of wings. The U.S. Army Air Corps requested that Military Intelligence Division look into these allegations, insomuch as it was feared that the French experience might indicate that the USAAC P-36 wings might not be up to combat stresses as well. The MID replied that:

"*...reliable information indicates that damages to wings due to gunfire has been negligible, and that damage due to high landing stresses caused by wartime airdromes is not a direct cause for this order for wings. Instead, a high rate of landing accidents has been the major cause, in conjunction with an insufficient order for spare parts.*"

An interesting sidelight that made the headlines was the fact of Curtiss test pilot Lloyd Child, diving a French *Hawk* to the then sensational speed of 575 mph on December 9, 1938. Another interesting facet was that one of the later H75A-2 *Hawks* was loaned to Britain, where it was tested against an early *Spitfire*. A very nice handling aircraft with excellent aileron action, even at the higher speeds, the *Hawk* could out-turn the *Spitfire*, and acquitted itself well in a dogfight, but the British aircraft's superior straight-away speed allowed it to enter or break off combat as desired. Cockpit visibility of the *Hawk* was rated better than that of the *Spitfire*, as well.

The next French export *Hawk* was the H75A-3 version, having a further up-rated *Twin Wasp*, with 135 ordered. These machines

Still bearing remnants of its former French *Armee de l'Air* unit badge on the vertical fin, this H75A-1, with rather crude German markings, was probably set out as a decoy for marauding Allied intruders somewhere in France. The fuselage just aft of the cockpit is covered with graffiti. (*Collection of Jan van den Heuvel via Leif Hellström*)

Probably an H75A-3, this ex-French aircraft is fully armed, and bears *Luftwaffe* unit codes, probably those of *II./Tr.Gr.186* (later *III./JG77*) under the starboard wing. The photo was taken in occupied France, although the exact location is not known. (*Collection of Jan van den Heuvel via Leif Hellström*)

were not ordered (on Sales Order No.140) until late 1939, after war had commenced. They were generally similar in characteristics to the U.S. P-36C except for armament[92] and other French oriented equipment. They received French serials H75-C1 No.201 to No.335, and were MSNs 13671 to 13805.

Not all the A-3 models arrived in what was by then wartime France; some got no further than the French West Indies island of Martinique, and some were still at Curtiss when the French collapsed under the German attacks of June 1940. The 40th aircraft on the contract, for instance (MSN 13710), was not weighed at Buffalo until March 22, 1940. The total number of *Hawks* that reached units of the French Air Force was 291, comprising most all the A-1 and A-2 aircraft, but only a portion of the A-3s. About 60 of these reached France or French North Africa. French *Hawks* escaping to England became *Mohawks*, *Mohawk I*, *II*, and *III* for the A-1s, etc.

Technical data for the H75A-3 follows: span 37 feet, three and 1/2 inches, and length 28 feet, seven inches. Wing area was 236 square feet.

Powerplant was a Pratt & Whitney R-1830-S1C3-G, rated at 1,200hp at 2,700rpm for take off at 48 inches Hg. Manifold pressure, and 1,050hp at 2,550rpm at 7,500 feet. Compression ratio was 6.7:1.

Armament was six 7.5 mm Browning guns, two in the fuselage and four in the wings. Empty weight was 4,483 pounds, useful load 1,209 pounds, and gross weight 5,692 pounds. Wing and power loadings were 24.12psf and 4.74 pounds per horse power, respectively. Useful load to gross weight ratio was 0.212.

Maximum speed was 311mph at 10,000 feet, cruise speed 270mph, and landing speed 69mph. Sea level climb rate was 2,340 feet per minute, service ceiling 33,700 feet, and normal range at 200mph cruise speed was 820 miles.

The final French version of the *Hawk* was the H75A-4 (the French designation of which, H751-C1, differed from the earlier three variants), of which no less than 285 were contracted for by France in some desperation. These had Curtiss MSN 13806 onwards, and acceptances started April 8, 1940. Apparently well less than a dozen of this six gun model,[93] powered now by a nine cylinder Wright Cyclone GR-1820-G205A of 1,200hp, maximum, reached French units before the defeat, although 81 had reached French territory. About two dozen A-4s were dumped off at the French West Indies islands of Guadalupe and Martinique, and some were lost when aboard a transport ship that sunk. Only 285 A-4 variants were actually built by Curtiss.[94] The characteristics of this Wright powered final French *Hawk*, labeled *Mohawk IV* by the British, were as follows: span, length, and height 37 feet, three and 1/2 inches, 28 feet, eight inches, and nine feet, six inches. Wing area was 236 square feet.

Powerplant was a Wright GR-1820-G205A *Cyclone*, rated 1,200hp at 2,500rpm for takeoff, 1,100hp at 2,500rpm at 5,100 feet, and 1,000hp at 15,000 feet, with a compression ratio of 6.5:1 driving a three blade Curtiss electric propeller. Normal and maximum fuel capacities were 105 gallons and 168 gallons.

Empty weight was 4,541 pounds, normal useful load 1,209 pounds, and normal gross weight 5,750 pounds. Maximum useful load was 2,121 pounds, and maximum gross weight 6,662 pounds. Normal wing loading was 24.36psf, and normal power loading 4.79 pounds per horse power. Normal useful load to gross weight ratio was 0.21.

Maximum speed was 323mph at 15,700 feet, with maximum cruise speed 262mph, and landing speed 69mph. Climb time was 4.9 minutes to 15,000 feet, and service and absolute ceilings were respectively 32,700 feet and 33,600 feet. Normal range was 603 miles at 248mph, and maximum range was 1,003 miles.

Despite some reports to the contrary, *Hawks* did quite well in combat with German aircraft during the "phony war." In September 1939 alone 37 German planes were shot down, almost all fighters, and most of these by Curtiss *Hawks*. On November 6, in a fight with Bf-109Es, one Hawk went down while French pilots claimed eight of the enemy. During the winter, however, the *Hawks* tried with little success to intercept high flying German reconnaissance aircraft. Their failure, however, appears to have had more to do with poor intelligence and vectoring than with any failure of the aircraft.

With the German spring offensive starting May 10, 1940, about 175 *Hawks* were in action at critical points, and before the Curtiss aircraft operations stopped on June 18th these planes had destroyed

311 German aircraft (233 confirmed and at least 81 probable) out of a grand total for the French Air Force of 935. A total of 29 *Hawks* were lost. An armistice was signed, and fighting stopped on June 25th, at which time half of all French fighters had been evacuated to North Africa, including all *Hawk* units.

French *Hawk 75A* operations ended some time before June 18th but, as noted, by that time they had laid claim to a truly astonishing number of enemy aircraft.[95] The grand total of claims filed by the entire *Armee de l'Air* since the commencement of hostilities was 935 aircraft destroyed, and its total fighter force had consisted during that time of 28 squadrons and six semi-autonomous *escadrilles*. Curtiss *Hawk 75As*, flown by pilots of five *Groupes*, had claimed 311 enemy aircraft, and one of them, *GC III/2*, had flown on only 11 operational days. The four original *Hawk* units had placed, respectively, in first, second, third, and fifth positions amongst the top scoring French units. In order, they were:

GC I/5 - 111 victories credited; nine pilots killed
GC II/4 - 71 victories credited; eight pilots killed
GC II/5 - 70 victories credited; two pilots killed
GC I/4 - 42 victories credited, eight pilots killed
GC III/2 - 17 victories credited; two pilots killed

Starting in July 1940, *Hawks* built for France were diverted to England, with the final total 204 aircraft, all of them H75A-4s. All of these were initially shipped to the U.K. and designated as *Mohawk IVs* (the RAF designations *Mohawk I* to *III* were reserved for earlier H75A-1, etc, versions, had they escaped France). The 204 British H75A-4s were French Numbers 65 to 78, 91, 95, and 98 to 285.[96] These were revised to British standards, stored on arrival for some time, and held in a reserve force.

The British took over a large number of French aircraft contracts when that nation unexpectedly fell to the German *blitzkrieg*, including some early variants that escaped to England and other, later variants that were diverted. RAF serial BT471, designated as a *Mohawk IV* (seen here), was assigned to 155 Squadron in India. (*Dudman via R. L. Ward*)

The decision was made to allocate the ex-French H75A-4s to RAF units in the Middle East (90 aircraft), to South Africa (also 90),[97] and to the RAF fighter squadron at Aden (the remaining 24). Some thought was given to transferring 30 of them to the Greek Air Force at the time of the Italian invasion, but this did not take place due to a shortage of shipping space, and the rapid turn of events there. In the end, a large number were sent to South Africa for training use, and others went to India, where they equipped two RAF fighter squadrons (Nos. 5 and 155), as well as No.151 Operational Training Unit (OTU).

Sixteen *Mohawk IVs* were also offset for Portugal, and these were shipped to the *Força Aérea Portuguese (FAP)* in two batches,

Curiously, while the French had enjoyed considerable success with their *Hawk 75A* variants against the best that the *Luftwaffe* could mount, the RAF quickly ruled that the aircraft they inherited from France were not fit for European conditions. Most were shipped off to India, South Africa, or Portugal. This rare image shows a mix of *Mohawk IVs* in varying markings configurations flying in strength with 155 Squadron in Bengal state, India, as of August 17, 1943. (*Hagedorn Collection*)

one of 10 by sea on August 21, 1941, and five more on October 10th, as encouragement for this semi-neutral nation to continue to favor the Allied cause. In the event, however, only 15 actually entered service, but only 11 of these received FAP serials, numbers 480 to 490.[98] One of the *Mohawks* was apparently damaged beyond repair during the delivery, and eight others modestly damaged, but the aircraft lost was replaced and, by December 16, 1941, the B.A.2 at Ota could count 11 aircraft on strength. While in continental Portugal, the aircraft were assigned to the so-called XY squadron and, besides their FAP serials, received unit codes, such as XY-F (FAP 485) and XY-C (FAP 482). They wore standard RAF camouflage of the time otherwise, plus the Portuguese national insignia in six positions.

On July 14, 1944, the *Esquadrilla Expedicionaria N°.3* (E.E.C.No.3) was formed at Sao Miguel, in the Azores, to replace E.E.C.No.1, which had been stationed there previously with venerable Gloster *Gladiators*. It was equipped with the eight surviving *Mohawks* (s/n 480 to 484, 486, 488, and 490, s/n 489 having been destroyed on April 15, 1942, at Monsanto, Lisbon, with the loss of pilot Sub.Tte. Agostinho Martins, s/n 485 on July 5, 1943, at Samora, Correia, and s/n 487 on October 21, 1943, at Valada do Ribatejo). To bring the unit at Sao Miguel to its statutory strength of 12 aircraft, four of the aircraft that had been damaged earlier—former RAF serials AR642, AR680, AX886, and BS78—were overhauled and repaired by the O.G.MA. work shops, and were flown by the unit without Portuguese roundels, and with their former RAF serials. While in the Azores the unit suffered two more accidents. On December 21, 1944, s/n 483 crash landed, with pilot Tte. Quintela injured and, on August 23, 1945, s/n 484 was destroyed when the commander of the unit, Sub.Tte. Burnay, crashed. By then, the unit had been formally disbanded (effective July 21, 1945), and most of the pilots had returned to the homeland.

Seldom recorded, four captured or escaped French *Hawk 75As* were taken over by the RAF and serialed in the Middle East "local acquisitions" series as HK823 to HK826, and two of these subsequently flew with the South African Air Force.

With the November 1942 Allied invasion of North Africa, rather weary French Curtiss *Hawks* fought briefly against U.S. Navy Grumman *Wildcats* with poor results against the heavy machine guns of the F4Fs, and many *Hawks* were shot down.

Against the German fighters Curtiss *Hawks* were excellent in turning performance, and excelled in a level altitude dogfight, but Bf-109s were faster, and had better climb and dive performance. In addition, Hawk armament was inferior, with only light machine guns that were subject to freezing at high altitude in winter, but French *Hawk* pilots, many of whom were older and more experienced than their adversaries, put up an astonishingly good fight against heavy odds prior to the French-German armistice.

France continued to operate some *Hawks* even after the end of World War II in 1945, using them as fighter trainers. Finally, all were retired in 1951.

Curtiss *Hawk* H75-Q

In 1938, Curtiss saw yet another opportunity to sell additional *Hawk* variants to a well established customer, Nationalist China. The light weight, fixed gear H75 model had had only moderate success, with just 72 aircraft manufactured for China, Thailand, and Argentina, not counting 20 assembled under license in Argentina.

Even before the last fixed gear H75 had come off the production line in December 1938, however, Curtiss had held back the last H75A-1 model to serve as a demonstrator to the Chinese. Designated the 75-Q, the airframe, serial number 12898, was equipped with a Wright R-1820G-105 *Cyclone* of 1,100hp, thus assuring another Curtiss-Wright product would be part of any deal. The actual Detail Specification for the 75-Q was laid down on precisely the same date as the 75-M, 75-N, 75-O, and 75-P: March 15, 1937.

First flight of the 75-Q took place on October 7, 1938, at Buffalo, and this aircraft was the prototype for all the *Cyclone* powered retractable gear *Hawks* to follow. After company tests, the aircraft was made ready in November for shipment to Loiwing (also sometimes cited, concurrently, as Loi Wiang, just inside the Sino-Burmese border), China, where the Central Aircraft Manufacturing Corp. (CAMCO) had relocated, and was being operated. Some sources state that the aircraft arrived at Rangoon on January 14, 1939. Curtiss test pilot Bob Fausel was sent to demonstrate the pursuit ship, which had been designed to accommodate two wing pod mounted 23mm Madsen cannon, in addition to a .50 caliber and a .30 caliber nose gun.

The aircraft was assembled and made ready for test in China in mid-February 1939, after an arduous journey from New York. The

Britain provided considerable numbers of aircraft during the war years to officially neutral Portugal, which had a long standing special relationship with the Empire. These included 16 *Mohawk IVs*, including FAP-482 (coded XY-C), pictured here at the *Base Aèrea No.2* at Ota. It later served with *Esquadrilha Expedicionaria N°.3* at Sao Miguel in the Azores, and survived in Portuguese service into 1945. (*via Mario Canongia Lopes*)

H75-Q, often in company with the Curtiss-Wright (St. Louis Division) Model 21 interceptor, performed demonstration flights before high Chinese officials, including mock combat with Soviet-built Polikarpov I-15 and I-16 types on February 25, 1939, at Chengtu, and also at Kunming and Chungking. On March 5th the Madsen 23mm wing cannon were installed, and two days later a combined demonstration of the H75-Q and the Curtiss-Wright 21 was held, including cannon firing at ground targets, since the basic mission of the *Hawk* was to be ground attack. With the cannons installed, the H75-Q achieved a high speed of 304mph at 20,000 feet and 2,370rpm, and 285mph at 9,100 feet in low blower at 2,370rpm.

Flight demonstrations continued in China, and Chinese pilots were checked out until March 17, 1939, when pilot George Weigle took off in the H75-Q, climbed at a very sharp angle, and spun in after making a turn at 3,000 feet.

Characteristics of the H75-Q follow: span, length, and height 37 feet, three and 1/2 inches, 28 feet, six inches, and 12 feet, 10 inches. Wing area was 236 square feet.

Armament was one .30 caliber and one .50 caliber cowl gun, and two pod mounted wing 23mm cannon. Wing racks for 10 small 30 pound bombs, and a fuselage rack for a 500 pound bomb were fitted.

The powerplant was a Wright *Cyclone* GR-1820-G-105A[99] rated at 1,100hp maximum driving a three blade Curtiss Electric propeller of 10 feet, nine and 1/2 inch diameter.

Empty weight was 4,515 pounds, maximum useful load 2,425 pounds, and maximum gross weight 6,940 pounds. Maximum wing and power loadings were 29.4psf and 6.3 pounds per horse power, respectively. Maximum useful load to gross weight ratio was 0.349.

Maximum speed was 305mph at 20,000 feet, sea level climb rate 3,150fpm, service ceiling 32,800 feet, and normal range 600 miles.

Curtiss *Hawk* H75A-5

The long-standing Curtiss-Wright Corporation relations with China led to the establishment of an American owned aircraft assembly plant there in October 1934, as noted earlier, and this came to be called the Central Aircraft Manufacturing Corporation (CAMCO). The plant was eventually going to be turned over to China. Along with Curtiss aircraft, aircraft acquired by China from other U.S. manufacturers were to be assembled in this plant, as well. After the Japanese bombed CAMCO out of eastern China the plant was moved westward.

Based on successful demonstration of the retractable gear H75-Q pursuit plane before it crashed, and a contract gained thereby, Curtiss in early 1940 fabricated an H75A-5 aircraft at Buffalo (MSN 13655, on Sales Order 195, Contract 478) to be used as an assembly pattern for 54 CAMCO built aircraft in Loiwing, China, from Curtiss supplied parts, including Wright R-1820 engines. This aircraft was billed to the Chinese at a whopping $100,438.16, but this may have included drawings and related engineering materials. However, in late October 1940 the Japanese bombed out the new CAMCO factory, and remaining plant equipment and aircraft parts were moved westward to Hengyang, then Loiwing, and then, again, into India, where William D. Pawley, the American owner of CAMCO, reformed it into Hindustan Aircraft Ltd. (HAL) at Mysore, Bangalore, India. Here the original contract was translated, in April 1941, into one from the British for 48 H75A-5 *Hawks*, again from Curtiss supplied parts, these planes to be used by the Indian Air Force against the Japanese in Burma. The first aircraft was ready in the summer of 1942, and as many as five may have been completed. Indeed, the RAF reserved serial numbers DR761 to DR808 for these aircraft. However, it has also been suggested that these aircraft may have included RAF serials BT470 to BT462, always assumed to have been ex-French aircraft, but known to have served in India.

As it happened, besides the pattern aircraft, only the four H75A-5 types under Curtiss license were constructed before the program was stopped. These planes were integrated into service with the British *Mohawks* obtained from the French contract, and those the British had found in Iran from the Iranian contract. Some of these *Mohawks* fought the Japanese in Burma well into 1943. DR761, at least, served with No.151 OUT, as did AX799, which was the RAF serial issued to the Curtiss-built pattern aircraft.

The H75A-5 aircraft had essentially the same characteristics as the H75-Q demonstrator, however, no Madsen cannon could be obtained, since Denmark had been overrun by Germany. Curtiss documents indicate that the 75A-5 was to be equipped with two Colt .50 caliber synchronized guns and two Madsen 23mm cannon under the wings.

Curtiss *Hawk* H75A-6

As World War II started in September 1939, Norway, with no capability of its own to produce modern pursuit planes, ordered a total of two dozen Curtiss H75A-6 *Hawks* (MSNs 13643 to 13654 on Sales Order 198, Contract 528 and 13659 to 13760 on Sales Order 198 Amendment), powered by Pratt & Whitney R-1830-SC3-G *Twin Wasp* engines of 1,200hp, in late 1939. Costing $31,705.07 each, the Norwegian *Hawks* carried four F.N. 7.9mm machine guns, two in the nose and two in the wings.

These export *Hawks*, according to Curtiss billing records, were shipped from the plant between February 5 and March 19, 1940. The timing could not have been worse, for the Germans attacked Norway just three weeks later on April 9, 1940, with the *Hawks* only in or near process of assembly at the Kjeller depot, and only 19 had arrived in the country. No Curtiss aircraft got off the ground. A few of them were destroyed, but at least 13 were captured by the Germans and became war booty.

The H75A-6 aircraft batch was split up. Thirteen of those captured by Germany were later sold to Finland, arriving in that country in the spring of 1941, where they were shortly employed in the war against Russia.[100] The planes that had not yet left the United States took another path. The Norwegian government in exile, after consultation with the British Air Ministry and the Canadian government, obtained permission to organize and train Norwegian air squadrons in Canada. In November 1940 a training center, dubbed "Little Norway," was established near Toronto, Canada, and it was to this base the remaining A-6 Hawks were delivered, shortly to be joined by some A-8 versions.

Another Portuguese Air Force *Mohawk IV* (FAP-485, coded XY-F) at Ota. The Commander of the *XY Squadron* was Cpt. Machado de Barros, second from the right. This aircraft was lost on July 5, 1943, at Samora Correia when *Sub.Tte.* Quintela bailed out after engine failure. They were painted at this time in RAF style brown/green upper surfaces camouflage and sky undersides. (*via Mario Canongia Lopes*)

Five of the Norwegian H75A-6s were diverted to the United Kingdom after the German invasion, as they were on board the Norwegian-American line ship *SS Idefjord*, which was diverted to Kirkwall, in the Orkney Islands, and RAF serials AR639 to AR634 were issued for them. These, being unarmed, were mostly used as high speed communications aircraft by the RAF. These aircraft became *Mohawk IIIs*.

The characteristics of these A-6 aircraft were very similar to the French A-3 versions.

Curtiss *Hawk* H75A-7

Yet another country to order the Curtiss 75 *Hawk* was the Netherlands when, in 1939, war clouds gathered once again over Europe. Twenty pursuits destined for that country were produced by Curtiss, given the designation H75A-7, and according to Curtiss records were delivered from the factory in Buffalo, New York, between May 6 and May 31, 1940. By this time, the invading Germans forced diversion of these planes to the Netherlands East Indies, where they arrived in May and June 1940. The first example was MSN 14424, and they were built on Sales Order No.199.

The A-7 versions were powered by Wright *Cyclone* R-1820 engines of 1,200hp maximum, and cost $31,676.85 each. Armament consisted of four machine guns, one Colt 12.7mm in the right forward fuselage, with a .303 caliber Colt on the left,[101] and two Colt .303 caliber guns in the wings. These aircraft were fitted with A-3 wing bomb racks.

The Curtiss machines found a varied collection of other U.S. and Dutch aircraft in the East Indies, including Curtiss-Wright Model 21 interceptors and Brewster 339s. As with these other fighters, the *Hawks* were overwhelmed by the Japanese in early 1942, some

The Netherlands were also hastening to equip their modest air force with modern equipment to guard their neutrality, and ordered 20 H75A-7s in 1939. The first of these, with the U.S. experimental test registration NXC1 on the orange (surrounded with black) Dutch rudder insignia, poses for the Curtiss photographer at Buffalo May 16, 1940—six days after German forces invaded their homeland. (*Curtiss S-F1 3070 via Peter M. Bowers*)

Another view of the first Dutch H75A-7, showing the prominent U.S. experimental test registration on the starboard upper wing. The *Hawk 75* series has been rarely pictured from astern, and this angle reveals the streamlining of the planform, as well as the relative size of the engine and cowling. (*Hatfield Collection, The Museum of Flight*)

destroyed on the ground, and others in the air. In one instance, on February 19, 1942, 23 Japanese fighters based in Balikpapan, Borneo, made a fighter sweep over Soerabaja in late morning. In a wild air battle, one Japanese pilot spoke of "Dutch P-36s" being shot down, with at least six of the Curtiss planes being lost.

Initially, the Dutch H75A-7s were bare metal, with the rather large triangular "Neutrality Marking" national insignia, which had been ordered placed on all Dutch aircraft effective September 23, 1939, in four wing positions, and on the fuselage side, plus the orange rudder with black (10cm) outline. Later, they were camouflaged in patterns very similar on each aircraft, and the national insignia was carried only on the rear fuselage, either side.

The Dutch H75A-7s equipped the 1st and 2nd Squadrons of *IV Groep*, and received Dutch serials C-323 to C-342 (although apparently painted on without the hyphens). All but one were lost during the battle for Java and Sumatra, but one was captured by the Japanese and taken to Japan for evaluation.

Finally, the Netherlands East Indies also attempted to acquire 28 French H75A-4s very early in the war, and these were to have been issued the serials 367 to 394, but the purchase was not approved.

Curtiss-Wright Design Proposal P-243

In the midst of the Curtiss-Buffalo surge in orders for variants of the Model 75 and 81, the Curtiss-Wright Corp. St. Louis Airplane Division had not completely given up hopes of entering a winning design for U.S. Army Air Corps acceptance.

On May 12, 1939, they submitted the preliminary model specifications for Design Proposal P-243, an interceptor pursuit, in partial accordance with Type Specification C-616.

The basic design was one of a low-wing, cantilever monoplane with retractable landing gear and, most surprisingly, equipped with an Allison V-1710-F3 engine of 1,000hp (normal), or 1,150hp (take-off). The arrangement was basically conventional, consisting of a

Unlike the French, the Dutch were able to divert all of their H75A-7s to the Netherlands East Indies (present day Indonesia), where they were welcomed, initially bearing only national insignia and codes C 323 to C 342 on bare metal. (*Royal Netherlands Air Force G/02k-23 via Harm Hazewinkel*)

A lineup of nine H75A-7s at Andir, in the Netherlands East Indies, after receiving camouflage, which included deletion of the distinctive black-bordered orange rudder. C 324 is foremost, MSN 14425. (*Royal Netherlands Air Force 6/02K-27 via Harm Hazewinkel*)

A trio of H75A-7s of the Netherlands East Indies *IV Groep* on patrol with C 332 in the lead. The Dutch aircraft were armed with three .303 Caliber Colt machine guns, one in either wing, and one over the nose, with a 12.7mm Colt over the nose as well. (*Royal Netherlands Air Force CDR 5/04 via Harm Hazewinkel*)

Contrary to many accounts, 19 of the initial order for 24 H75A-6s reached the Royal Norwegian Air Force, and apparently 13 of them had been hastily erected before the German invasion, including 445 shown here. *Per Bugge via Cato Guhnfeldt*)

tractor engine installation ahead of the pilot and conventional tail wheel type landing gear. The armament was proposed at two .50 caliber guns and two .30 caliber guns mounted in the fuselage and synchronized, suggesting strongly that the design was basically a re-engined Model 21.

The principal deviation from Type Specification C-616 were the omission of the 37mm cannon, and the substitution of a tail wheel type landing gear for the nose wheel type (as on the successful Bell P-39 series built to the same specification).

Curtiss-Wright hinged their hope in this design on the claim that the benefits obtained by direct weight saving by deleting the cannon, provision for firing through the propeller shaft, and nose wheel installation would result in as much as 500 to 700 pounds. The latter benefit, maximum performance, would be a direct result, plus the advantages derived from a more compact arrangement, which would allow a minimum fuselage cross section. The result, they claimed, would be an aircraft of minimal size, with the highest possible speed and rate of climb for its power, and still be able to accomplish the stated mission.

They estimated the high speed of the P-243 at critical altitude at 470mph, with a 4,500 foot rate of climb per minute at a gross weight of 5,100 pounds with but 100 gallons of fuel.

No documentation could be located recording Wright Field's response to this ambitious but interesting proposal.

Norway came back to Curtiss with a follow-on order for a second batch of not less than 36 H75A-8s, but these could not be delivered before the Germans invaded that country. Consequently, these aircraft were delivered to the Free Norwegian Air Forces that formed at *Little Norway*, near Toronto, Ontario, Canada. These received Norwegian serials between 401 and 471 (using odd numbers only). They were similar to the French H75A-4s. (*Curtiss WRF-200*)

Curtiss *Hawk* H75A-8/P-36G

Not long before the German occupation of Norway, that country ordered from Curtiss a second batch of 36[102] *Hawk* aircraft to supplement the H75A-6 types previously obtained. In this case, Norway was occupied before the new H75A-8 *Hawks* could be delivered. Unit cost was to have been $37,930.66. These aircraft were very similar to the French H75A-4s. These Norwegian aircraft were issued serials 401 to 471 (odd numbers only, Curtiss MSNs 14546 to 14581).

The 75A-8 was powered by a Wright *Cyclone* engine, and armed with two Colt .50 caliber synchronized cowl guns and four Colt .30 caliber wing guns, and had racks under each wing panel for five small caliber and one large caliber bomb; it was the fastest of the *Hawk* 75 variants.

Of the 36 aircraft, at least 18 were delivered on February 4, 1941, to "Little Norway," near Toronto, Canada, a training center for exiled Norwegians established in November 1940. There, they supplemented the H75A-6 aircraft already on hand.

Royal Norwegian Air Force H75A-8 No.453 shows the unique Norwegian national insignia, as well as details of her armament installation and exhaust configuration in this February 1941 view. (*Curtiss WRF-199*)

The distinctive Norwegian national insignia, consisting of two broad bands of red, with a thin blue band bordering two of white, shows to good advantage on No.465 at Toronto's *Little Norway* on the starboard lower wing and rudder in this 1943 view. (*via Peter M. Bowers*)

This very rare color view of four of the Norwegian H87A-8s at *Little Norway* reveals the rather unusual brown color, with the Norwegian national insignia, that the aircraft were painted overall. (*Forsvarsmuseet, Oslo*)

The Norwegian H75A-8s incorporated rather unusual bomb rack installations under either wing, the inboard pair capable of accommodating fairly sizeable bombs, while the five outboard could mount only small caliber, anti-personnel weapons. These were unquestionably the fastest of any *Hawk 75* variants, topping out at 322mph. (*Curtiss S-F 13708*)

In a most unusual scheme, the U.S. purchased at least 30 of the former Free Norwegian H75A-8s starting in January 1942, with the objective of refurbishing these, designating them as P-36Gs, and providing them to Peru under Lend-Lease. These were delivered commencing September 1942. Here, *Sub.Ofc.* Gonzalo Pizarro, maintenance officer for the *Cuerpo de Aeronautica del Peru* (left), poses with LTC Boeker Batterton, USMC, and 1LT Frederick O'Connor, USMC, of the U.S. Mission in April 1943 before a flight in one of the *11° Escuadron de Caza* P-36Gs. (*U.S. Navy AM-MIS-13-42000*)

At least 30 of these aircraft are the examples that were acquired later by the U.S. Army Air Forces, and designated as P-36Gs for a time, in spite of their obsolescence and use of a different engine than the American P-36 types. Indeed, as early as January 19, 1942, Curtiss had actually advised the AAC against the purchase of these Norwegian machines and, for their part, the Norwegians were engaged in intense negotiations to sell the same aircraft to the Free Belgian forces! Peruvian officials had, however, become rather enchanted by the aircraft, and the AAC saw in them a reasonably affordable solution to their diplomatic imbroglio *vis-a-vis* their earlier impoundment of aircraft Peru had acquired commercially. These aircraft gained USAAF serials 42-38305 to 42-38322 and 42-108995 to 42-109006, and were "bought" from the Norwegians in two groups of 18 and 12, respectively. The Materiel Division of the AAF was directed by Headquarters AAF to procure and set up for flight, initially, 18 of the Norwegian aircraft, which, by February 25, 1942, had been stored near Toronto.

In fact, 17 P-36Gs were ferried to Memphis, TN, for modification for Peru, and these were issued USAAF serials 42-38305 to 42-38315 and 42-38317 to 42-38322. Why serial 42-38316 was not used is a mystery. Of these, 42-38321 was wrecked at Memphis and, together with another damaged aircraft (42-38314) were shipped to Patterson Field, Ohio, where they were rebuilt into one complete aircraft.

Characteristics of the H75A-8 variants were: span, length, and height 37 feet, three and 1/2 inches, 28 feet, six inches, and nine feet, three inches. Wing area was 236 square feet.

The powerplant was the nine cylinder Wright *Cyclone* R-1820-G205A/-95 rated at 1,200hp maximum.

Empty weight was 4,675 pounds, useful load 1,205 pounds, and gross weight 5,880 pounds. Wing and power loadings were 24.92psf and 4.9 pounds per horse power, respectively, and useful load to gross weight ratio was 0.205.

Maximum speed was 322mph at 15,000 feet, and cruise speed was 240-262mph.

Climb time to 15,000 feet was six minutes, service ceiling 32,350 feet, and normal and maximum ranges were 650 and 1,000 miles, respectively.

This Peruvian P-36G (coded 11+3-3), a former Norwegian H75A-8, came to grief when it collided with another P-36G while avoiding a *Panagra* DC-3 during landing at Talara, Peru, on February 25, 1944, killing *Ens.* Francisco Cossio and Reynaldo Moran. (*via Ole Griffith*)

By 1944, Peruvian P-36Gs had converted to three-digit serial numbers, dropping to unit codes initially assigned, like FAP-303 (shown here). Peru also adopted, probably with the influence of the U.S. Marine Corp Air Mission, cowling paint codes indicating the section within the operating squadron, and unit insignia on the fuselage sides. Note also the distinctive bulges under each wing between the .30 caliber gun breaches, unique to the P-36Gs. (*Servicio Aerofotografico Nacional, Peru, R-46191*)

The P-36G aircraft, as noted earlier, were destined to be a part of a Lend-Lease shipment to Peru in South America, the first batch of 18[103] heading south between September 1942 and July 1943, and the rest[104] following later. The USAAF had, in essence, "purchased" the first 18 from Norway to settle, at least in part, a Peruvian order—which had been paid for much earlier—for Northrop/Douglas 8A-5 attack aircraft. To say that the resulting aircraft were unique is an understatement. The USAAF engaged the Chicago & Southern Airlines Modification Center in Memphis, TN, to modify and prepare the aircraft for delivery to Peru on Contract AC-13340. This rather extraordinary step was necessary because the aircraft did not have the armament, nor the radios that Peru had specifically specified. The work involved installing two .50 caliber guns in the nose and four .30 caliber guns in the wings, SCR-274-N radios, two M-8 parachute flares and A-8-B oxygen masks, and equipment to be supplied with the aircraft was to include 18 jungle kits, 18 twenty-four foot parachutes, and 18 life jackets. Of the first 18, offset to Peru under Lend-Lease Requisition PU-53, not fewer than six crashed prior to delivery while engaged in a combination of flight tests and Peruvian crew orientation, and could not be repaired. As a consequence, they were used for spares sources, although this is not the full story. One, as noted, had crashed during flight tests (42-38321) on September 1, 1942, and it, together with the remains of 42-38314, which had also crashed, were to have been shipped to the San Antonio Air Depot (SAAD), where they were to have been rebuilt into one complete aircraft. Instead, the hulks were sent to Patterson Field, OH, where this work was accomplished. A subsequent Peruvian requisition for 13 additional aircraft (PU-529) was deleted in favor of PU-529-A1, which covered the second set of 12 aircraft (of which one was cancelled and one crashed prior to final delivery). The first six Peruvian P-36Gs were orchestrated to arrive in dramatic fashion during the closing stages of the annual Peruvian Aviation Day celebrations on September 23, 1942, having departed from Barksdale Field, LA, on September 9th, and were a source of enormous pride to the *Cuerpo de Aeronautica del Peru (CAP)* because, as of that date, of all Latin American nations, Peru and Brazil alone had received "modern" fighter aircraft from the U.S. under Lend-Lease. By December 18, 1943, the *CAP* had integrated the "new" P-36Gs into the force, but not without incident. Four had been damaged in-country, but only one beyond repair,[105] and the U.S. Air Attaché probably correctly attributed this loss rate with pilot inexperience in handling such high performance aircraft, especially in cross-wind landings, common at the primary Peruvian operating base at *Las Palmas*, and a reported excessive use of brakes—a novelty to *CAP* fighter pilots at the time.

By March 1944 the *CAP* could count 24 P-36Gs on strength, of which six were under repair of one form or another. Two of these had only recently arrived by boat from the U.S., where they had earlier been damaged enroute to Peru, the repairs to these completed by the *CAP* arsenal at *Las Palmas*. One P-36G (of the 10 that had been flight delivered to Peru in November 1943) had been damaged at Pito airfield, on the remote Colombian-Panamanian frontier, and was the one repaired at France Field, with some difficulty, as parts were almost impossible to obtain by that time. The aircraft

The Peruvians eventually received a total of 30 P-36Gs under Lend-Lease from the U.S., and were the only air arm to fly this derivative. FAP-287, seen here bearing the unit emblem of unknown derivation, has had all camouflage paint removed, and the remnants of a band around the rear fuselage. The nature of the ordnance on the inboard bomb rack is unknown. (*via Sergio de la Puente*)

One of the last airworthy Peruvian P-36Gs was FAP-296. Peru operated the type until December 1955, by which time some of them were cited, for reasons unknown, as P-36Hs. (*via Amaru Tincopa*)

Last customer for the export *Hawk 75A* series was Persia, which ordered 10 H75A-9s, ostensibly delivered in March and April 1941. In fact, they were never assembled, and were seized by the British in August. Serialed 252 to 261 (the last three digits of their MSNs), they wore their serials on the white mid-section of the rudder markings, and on the rear fuselages. This aircraft, clearly a Persian H75A-9, was photographed at Buffalo during flight tests—but bears an aileron from a Norwegian aircraft! (*The Museum of Flight*)

on hand were assigned to the *11° Escuadron de Caza, 1° Region Aèrea* at Talara (11), and the *21° Escuadron de Caza, 2° Region Aèrea* at the *Limatambo* aerodrome, near the capitol (13). It is worth noting that the *21° Escuadron de Caza* was being run, in effect, by the U.S. Naval Air Mission to Peru at the time, and had been set up in accordance with a standard U.S. Marine Corps fighter squadron.

In fact, the final two P-36Gs were delayed in delivery until postwar in November 1945, after having a long stay in Panama starting in May 1944, for a total of 31 to Peru. There they served as a popular fighter aircraft, some as late as December 31, 1955, when four were still listed as fighter-trainers at *Las Palmas*. For reasons unknown, by this date, the *Fuerza Aérea del Peru* (*FAP*), as the service had been redesignated, was citing the aircraft, invariably, as type P-36H.

Curtiss *Hawk* H75A-9

The last in the H75A retractable gear Curtiss *Hawk* line was the *Cyclone* powered H75A-9, of which 10[106] were ordered by Iran on Sales Order No.202, and delivered to them between March 9 and April 4, 1941. These were Curtiss MSNs 15252 through 15261, and cost Iran $37,689 each. They received Persian Air Force serial numbers 252 to 261 (the last three digits of their MSNs).

One of the Persian Curtiss H75A-9s being test flown near Buffalo in early 1941. The yellow cowl is noteworthy, and the blue cast to some of the metal surfaces was a special coating applied to protect the aluminum during manufacture. The Persian aircraft mounted six 7.92mm guns: four in the wings, and two over the nose. (*The Museum of Flight*)

A Curtiss workman in the paint shop marshals the rudders for five of the Persian H75A-9s, complete with serials applied in Arabic characters. Note the U.S. wing panels in the background, probably for SBC-3s. (*The Museum of Flight*)

One of the Persian H75A-9s being prepared for crating and shipment. It is not clear what color was specified for the aircraft, although the fuselage is clearly painted, and when shipped had the individual serial, and the insignia of the Shah of Persia on the fuselage of each aircraft. (*The Museum of Flight*)

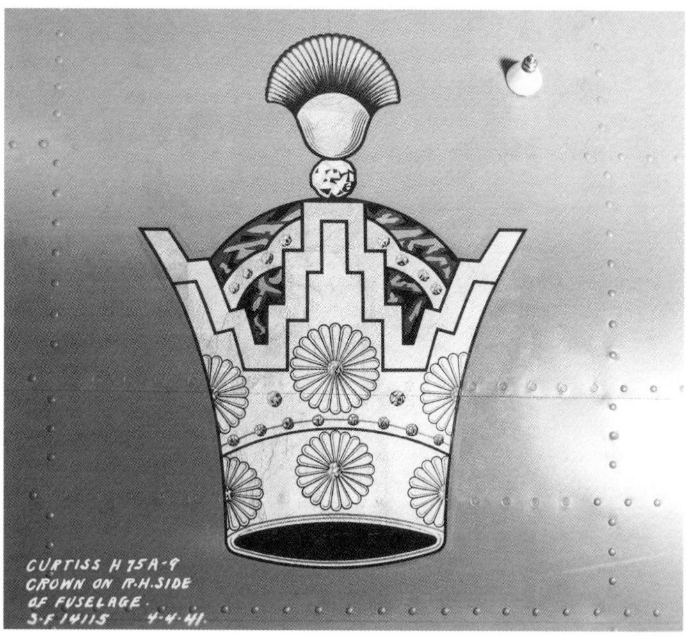

Never illustrated before, the 10 Persian H75A-9s each had the crown of the Shah of Persia painted in color on either side of the mid-fuselage. These aircraft were never erected in Persia, and were all seized by the British in August 1941, becoming RAF *Mohawk IVs*. (*The Museum of Flight*)

In August 1941 the British and Russians occupied that country, and found these aircraft not yet assembled. At least nine of the H75A-9s were shipped to India as *Mohawk IVs*, where they were issued RAF serials LA157 to LA165, and apparently all nine served with No.151 OTU at Risalpur. RAF serial LA166 was issued to the 10th Persian aircraft, but it is not clear what became of this aircraft.

The H75A-9 characteristics were similar to the other *Hawks* with later model Wright Cyclone engines. They had R-1820-G205As rated at 1,200hp at 2,500rpm and 44 inches of manifold pressure for takeoff, and 1,100hp at 2,500rpm at 5,100 feet and 40 inches of manifold pressure.

They were armed with two synchronized Colt MG-40 7.92mm guns with 600rpg and provision for four Colt 7.92mm wing guns, although these were apparently not installed at delivery. They had simple ring-and-bead gun sights, an RCA AVT-12B transmitter, and AVR-7G receiver

The Finnish *Hawks*

As will have been noted from a close examination of the preceding accounts, one country employed Curtiss H75A *Hawk* pursuits without ever ordering any from the manufacturer. At various times during World War II, Germany supplied Finland with *Hawk* variants from war booty stocks captured from France and Norway. Num-

Finland acquired a significant fleet of *Hawk 75A* aircraft via unconventional sources. Most of the 44 aircraft obtained were ex-French *H75A-1*, *H75A-2*, *H75A-3*, and *H75A-4* aircraft, but Finland also received a few ex-Norwegian *H75A-6s*. Most were brought to a standard similar to the *H75A-4*, including CU-502 of *Lentolaivue 12*, pictured here during the summer of 1941. (*via Carl-Frederik Geust*)

Coded CU-553, this Finnish *H75A* was assigned to *Lentolaivue 32* as of July 1943 after nearly a complete overhaul by the state aircraft factory, the *Valtron Lentokonetehdas*. This aircraft appears to have a gun sight inside the windscreen area. (*via Carl-Frederik Geust*)

bers vary slightly on variants, but it appears generally agreed that Finland operated a total of 44 *Hawks*, starting soon after the fall of France at the end of June 1941, and continuing at odd intervals until the last three arrived in January 1944. Several remained in service as late as August 30, 1948, the date of the last flights of aircraft coded CU-560 and CU-578. These came from defeated France, Vichy France, and Norway, and thus were a mixed bag of H75A-1s, A-2s, A-3s, A-4s, and A-6s. The earliest examples, coded CU-501 to 507 in Finnish service, were *Cyclone* powered H75A-4s, while the remainder were all Pratt & Whitney *Twin Wasp* powered examples. Primary operating units for the type were *Lentolaivue 32* and *12*, squadron-size organizations, although at least one served with the *Lentosotakoulu* (Air Force College) in 1947-48 at Kauhava.

Apparently, since most of these aircraft were *Twin Wasp* powered, an attempt was made to standardize by re-engining the *Cyclone* powered A-4s to Pratt & Whitney power plants, and instrumentation and other equipment were standardized as well by the State Aircraft Factory (*Valtion Lentokonetehdas*).

Curtiss-Wright 19R

While the parent firm in Buffalo was heavily engaged in developing the basic *Hawk 75* export and domestic P-36 series, Curtiss-Wright St. Louis Airplane Division had taken their 1935 Design 19-L *Coupe* into the Model 19R, which received U.S. Department of Commerce Approved Type Certificate No.629 on February 19, 1937. This suggests a very lengthy gestation period indeed, as photos of the 19R mockup are dated November 12, 1935, suggesting that it was being considered concurrently with the 19-L.

Billed, perhaps with tongue-in-cheek, as "...*suitable for business or sport*," Curtiss-Wright Export Corporation promptly commenced marketing the aircraft as a two-seat fighter, basic trainer, light attack, and light combat aircraft for small military establishments with limited budgets.

Powered by a Wright R-975-E3 rated at 420hp at 2,200rpms at 1,400 feet (with 450hp available for take-off), the two-seater was compact, with the following dimensions:

Wingspan was 35 feet, length 26 feet, four inches, and height seven feet, six inches. Wing chord at the root was 84 inches, and at

After the end of World War II, Finland adopted a new national insignia, as displayed on this *H75A*, CU-560 of the *Lentosotakoulu* (Air Force College) at Kauhaua circa 1947-1948. (*via Carl-Frederik Geust*)

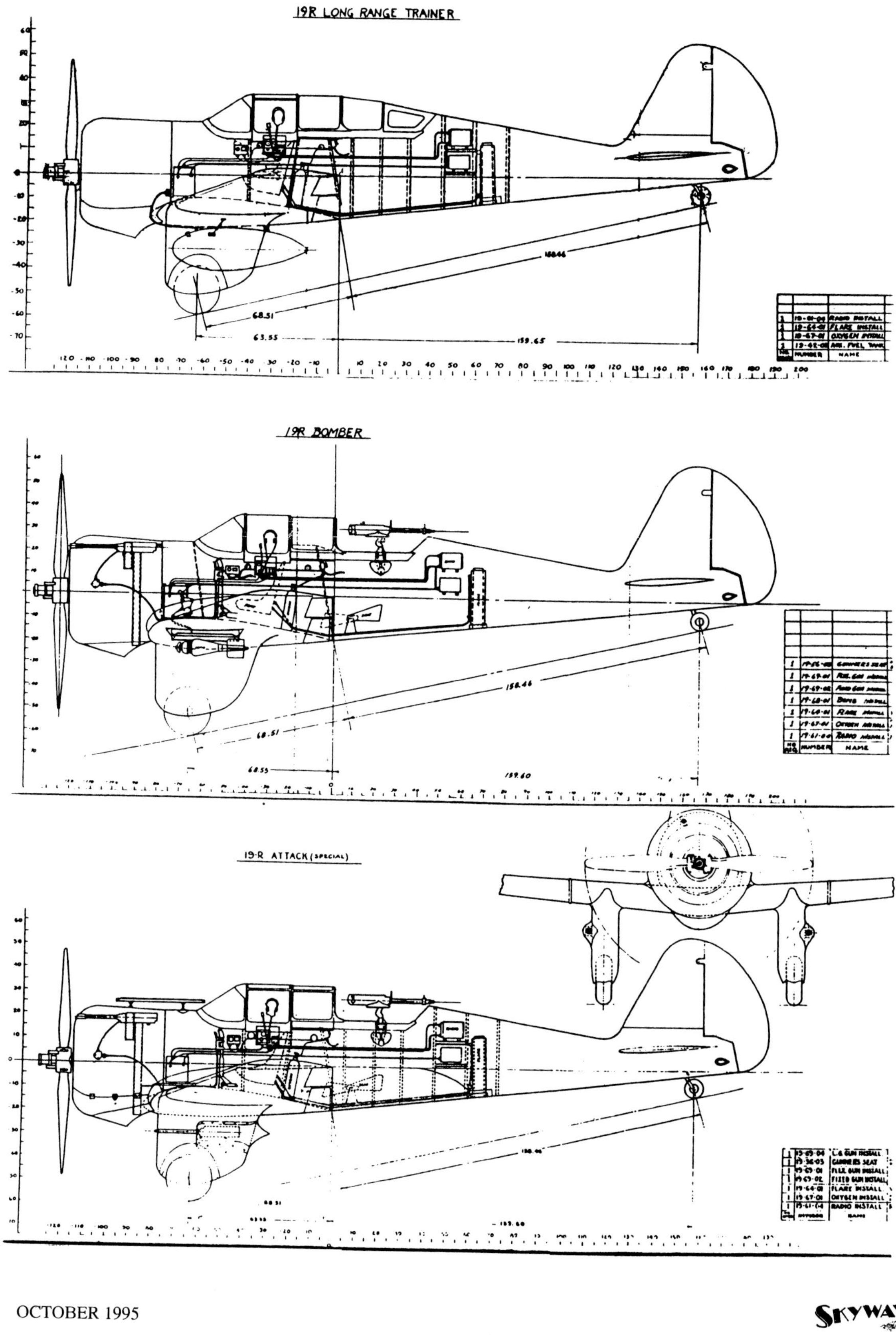

While the Buffalo factory was churning out world-class fighters for major nations in the *Hawk 75* series, the Curtiss-Wright St. Louis Division was marketing a remarkably versatile two-place fighter and multi-purpose combat aircraft known as the Model 19R. These drawings show most of the possible configurations offered. (*Curtiss-Wright via David W. Ostrowski*)

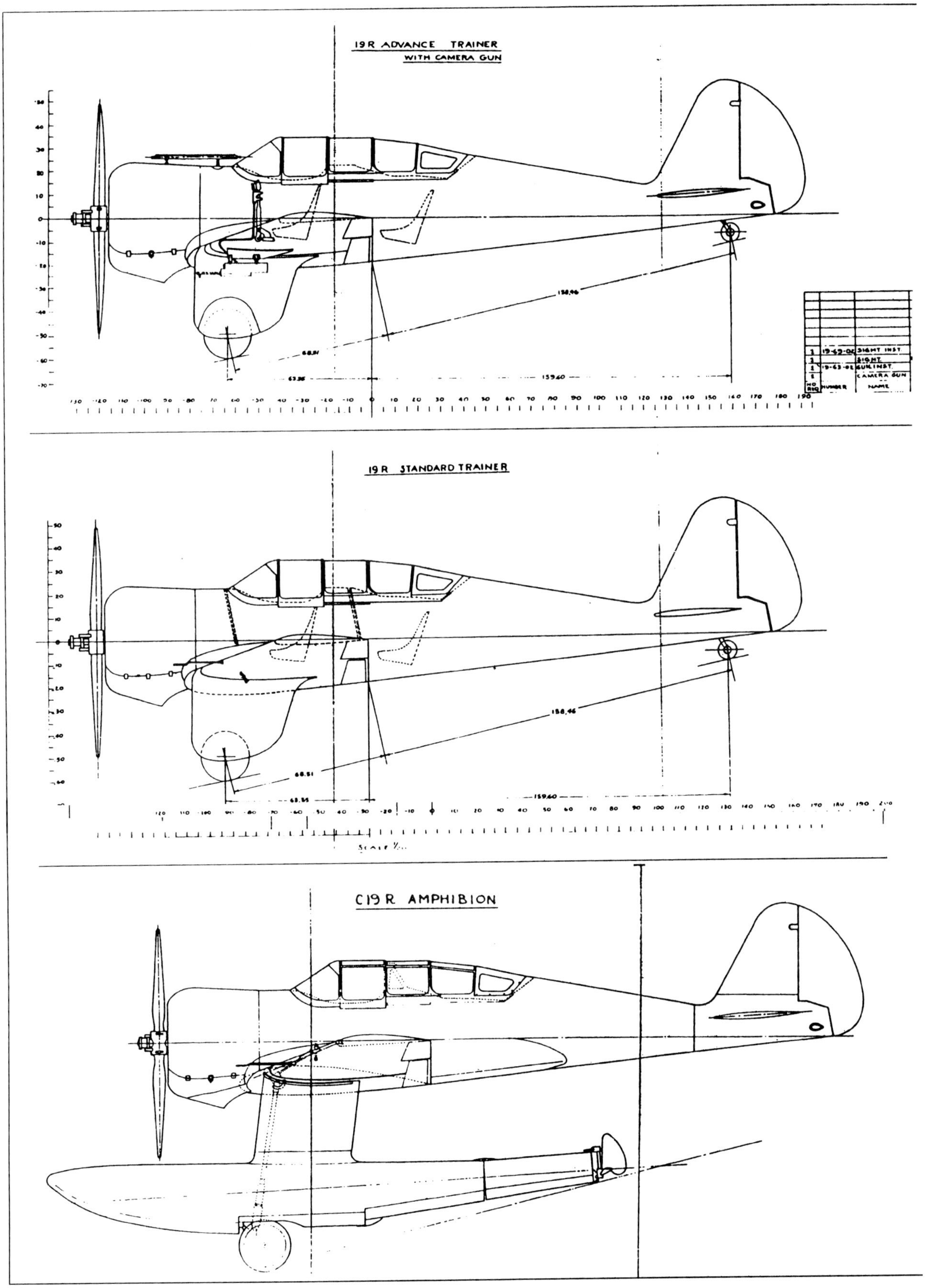

8 OCTOBER 1995

SKYWAYS

Besides being demonstrated in more foreign nations than the more expensive *Hawk 75* series, the Curtiss-Wright 19R was also entered in the U.S. Army Air Corps basic trainer competition in 1937. Here the demonstrator, bearing Department of Commerce Identified Aircraft number 16417, poses at Wright Field. (*USAF 13716AC*)

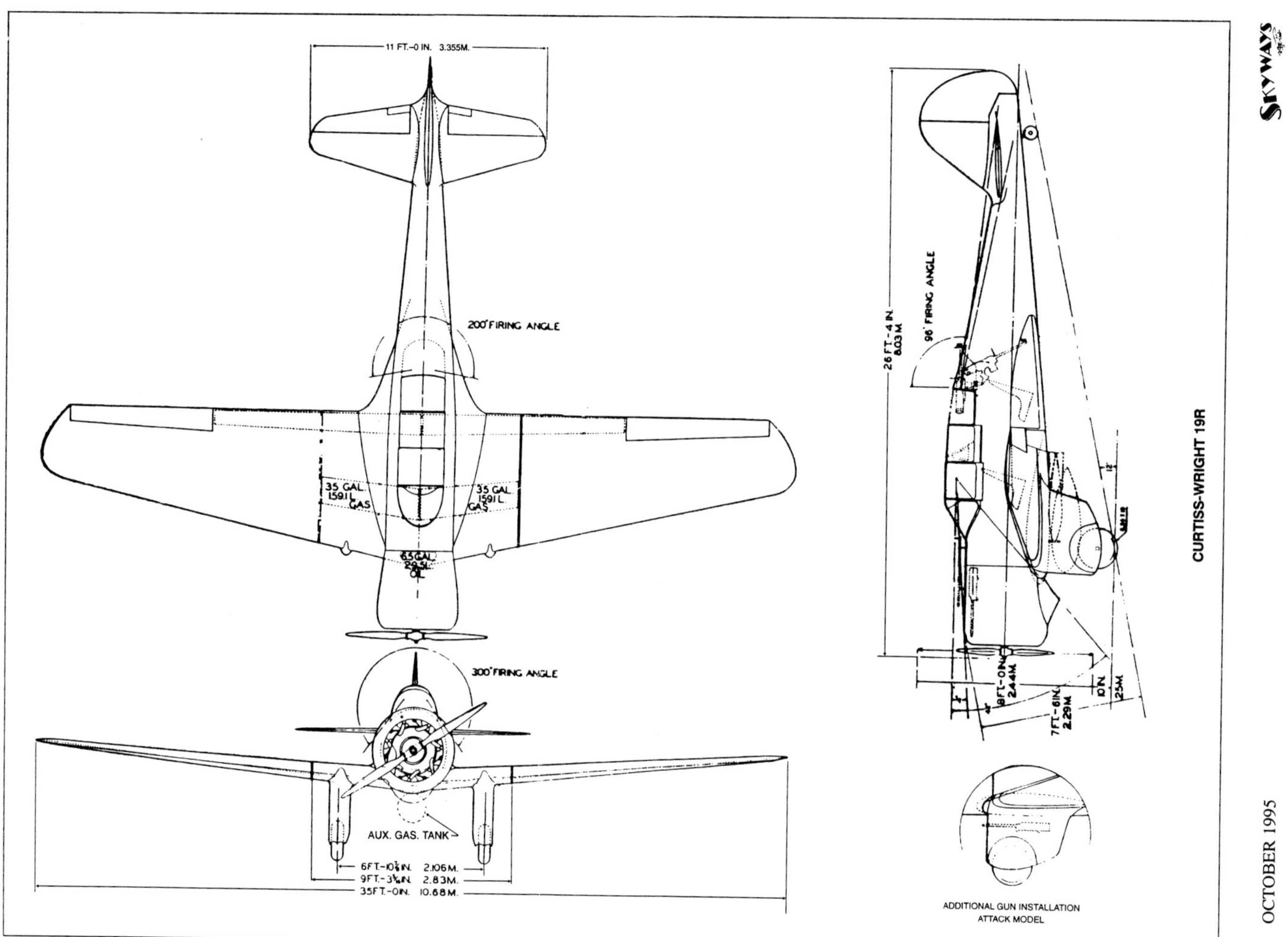

Although diminutive, with a wing span just two feet short of that of the *Hawk 75* series at 35 feet, the Model 19R was a two-place fighter powered with only a 420hp engine. It was exceptionally nimble, however, and marketed specifically to small nations who could not afford the top-of-the-line. (*Curtiss-Wright via David W. Ostrowski*)

The "business end" of the Curtiss-Wright 19R could bring three .30 caliber machine guns to bear. Two of these could be mounted in special blisters on the wheel spats, one was synchronized through the cowl, and a fourth was flexible in the rear pit. It could also mount small caliber bombs. This is 19R-12 as of August 20, 1937, the second of two that went to the Dominican Republic. (*Curtiss CF1073 via Museum of Flight M10536*)

the tip, 41 inches. Total wing area was only 174 square feet, and the airfoil was described as a "CW-19 Special." Empty weight was only 1,980 pounds, with a useful load of 1,220 pounds, thus gross weight was 3,200 pounds.

Maximum speed was a respectable 212mph at 2,000 feet, while cruise was 190mph at 75% power. Landing speed was only 56mph with flaps, and climb to 2,050 feet from sea level could be accomplished in one minute flat. Time to 10,000 feet was 6.45 minutes. Service ceiling was 22,900 feet, and cruise range at 75% power at 23 gallons per hour was a very handy 760 miles.

Billed, and recalled often by user nations, as "The Curtiss All-Metal," the aircraft could be ordered in a variety of configurations. Unusual for the time, if could mount as many as three forward-firing .30 caliber weapons (two of them in unique "cheek" blisters on the main undercarriage spats), plus a free gun in the rear, in addition to bomb racks, auxiliary fuel tank, gun camera, aerial photographic camera, and floats.

Although the Model 19R was modestly successful in the export market, it is seldom recognized that it was an unofficial competitor against the immortal North American NA-16 (which evolved into the AT-6 *Texan* series) in a U.S. Army Air Corps competition in late 1937 for the new, standard basic trainer for that service. In every measurable category, the Model 19R bested the NA-16, with the exception of distance required to clear a 50 foot obstacle while landing and take-off. On December 8, 1937, the Air Corps also provided the British Embassy and the Royal Canadian Air Force with details of the competition between the two types, specifically at their request, which indicates that the Model 19R could well have become the *Harvard* instead of the NA-16! The sole factor in selecting the NA-16 was production capacity and earliest availability, coupled with the fact that the NA-16 had been adopted by the USAAC as the BT-9 and was in production.

It is worth noting that, at the time that Curtiss-Wright started producing 19Rs, the standard USAAC light attack aircraft was the Curtiss A-12 which, with its 690hp Wright R-1820-37 engine, was actually some 37mph *slower* than the 19R (on 420hp), the latter having a cruising speed faster than the A-12. Likewise, while St. Louis employees were polishing the first 19Rs, British workers were just starting to deliver biplane Hawker *Hinds* to the RAF, and there was simply no French or German equivalent.

The aircraft was available in a practically universal series of variants and configurations. These included the 19R Long Range Trainer, 19R Light Bomber, 19R Photographic Reconnaissance Aircraft, 19R Fighter, 19R and 19Q Seaplane, 19R Attack (Spe-

One of two surviving export Curtiss-Wright 19Rs (the other, an ex-Bolivian aircraft, is now owned by a U.S. citizen in California), No.9 is still on display in the Dominican Republic, one of two aircraft. (*Guido Buehlmann*)

The Model 75-B, illustrated earlier in this account, became the Model 75-I by 1937, which was acquired by the Army Air Corps as the exotic XP-37, mounting a V-1710-11 engine. It is pictured here at Buffalo shortly after acceptance. (*The Museum of Flight*)

Next up was the small *Arma de Aviación, Ejército Nacional* of the Dominican Republic, which bought two aircraft (MSN 19R-11 and 19R-12) at a purchase price of $25,000 each, delivered in March and August 1937. One of these aircraft participated in the Columbus Memorial Good Will Flight of December 1937, in company with three Cuban aircraft, through much of Latin America and the Caribbean, and this aircraft still survives today in the Dominican Air Force Museum.

Cuba's *Cuerpo de Aviación Ejército de Cuba (CAEC)* acquired five 19Rs[107] starting in July 1937, apparently built concurrently with the Dominican examples. These were probably 19R-8 and 19R-9, and three others between 19R-13 and 19R-16 not positively identified. They received *CAEC* serials 50 to 54 and, later, survivors were re-serialed as 100 to 102 in a new "advanced trainer" category. One (s/n 102) survived as late as January 1949.

But by far the largest user of the type was Bolivia, where the *Cuerpo de Aviación* acquired no less than 10 examples commencing in October 1938. These were probably issued MSNs 19R-16 and up, and received Bolivian serials 118 to 127. At least four remained on the Order of Battle as late as January 1949, and one survived to return to the United Sates in 1996 and was later, in full Bolivian markings as FAB-120, awarded Grand Champion Warbird at the EAA convention at Oshkosh, WI.

One other 19R, probably 19R-10A (NR-16417), was exported to the Chinese Nationalists in the summer of 1937, but was crashed January 5, 1938, killing U.S. crew members Harold Welsh and Bo Sangster. It is known to have been photographed, identified as the "China Demonstrator" on December 8, 1936. Another demonstrator was washed out while giving a spirited exhibition in Argentina, and has not been identified.

Despite intensive sales demonstrations by the Curtiss-Wright Export Corporation, the 19R enjoyed only a limited market, and the price-per-aircraft probably doomed it to obscurity.

Curtiss XP-37 (Model 75-I)

Curtiss had always been noted for attempting to modify and stretch their aircraft designs. Knowing the Air Corps interest in the then-new Allison liquid cooled V-12 aircraft engine in the 1,000hp class, and its potential to power pursuit aircraft to higher speeds at high altitude, Don Berlin of Curtiss proposed to the Army a P-36/Model 75 airframe modified to use this engine equipped with a General Electric turbo supercharger. The basic airframe was already available. It was that of the Model 75-B company owned prototype, MSN 11923. So modified, the Curtiss designation for the well-traveled aircraft became 75-I.

Curtiss studies showed such a pursuit plane might achieve as much as 340mph at 20,000 feet altitude at a time when the best Army pursuits could barely make 300 mph at altitude. The secret, of course, was to maintain high engine power at high altitude, where air drag of a streamlined V-12 powered machine could be minimized.

Design studies started in late 1936. A contract was signed for $95,858.30 on February 16, 1937, and the Army designated the new aircraft XP-37, with Army serial number 37-375 (MSN 11923). It was delivered, according to the Curtiss billing book, to Wright Field, Ohio, on April 20, 1937. The billing book says "*...but not accepted - damaged - re-shipped June 16, 1937.*" The circumstances of shipment and damage are somewhat speculative, but Wright Field testing restarted in July, with first flight on the 23rd.

The XP-37 was quite a striking aircraft, characterized by a long pointed nose, and a cockpit located well aft of the wing. The 75-B prototype was quite considerably revised. The nose was long because it housed a V-1710 engine over a turbo unit, and behind that,

The XP-37 experienced a number of modifications to the cowling, brought about mainly by the erratic performance of the turbo-supercharger, parts of which can be seen here in good detail. The aircraft suffered a port main landing gear failure at Wright Field on March 10, 1938, while being flown by Captain Harris, but was repaired. (*Wright Field 60168 via Peter M. Bowers*)

By September 1938, the contours of the engine cowling of the XP-37 had been changed once again. Note that the two intakes noted on the March 1938 accident photo had been eliminated, and the Wright Field "arrow head" had been painted on the fuselage. (*Curtiss S-F11299*)

inside the fuselage, the turbo system intercooler, the liquid cooling system radiators, the auxiliary fuel and oil tanks, and an oil cooler. Appropriate scoops were disposed around the nose, and a shuttered slot around the fuselage dumped exit air.

Two problems besetting the XP-37 from the start were the lack of good pilot visibility with the aft cockpit location forced by powerplant items, and erratic performance of the turbo supercharger. Tail buffeting took place unless powerplant air exit shutters were closed upon landing, until wing leading edges inboard were modified. With these problems the XP-37 was in no shape to participate in the Army 1937 Pursuit Competition. After several months of flight testing failures, a Wright Field accident on March 10, 1938, and interim modifications, the XP-37 was returned to Curtiss for some major changes, these to make it more closely conform to the intended arrangement of the YP-37 service test aircraft.

The revised XP-37, with a new V-1710 engine model and other powerplant changes, was again ready for test in mid-1938, and a few flight test hours showed improved characteristics, but in September 1938 the revised aircraft suffered a landing gear failure that laid it up until the end of the year. Again repaired, it was returned to Wright Field in January 1939, where it stayed until late in 1941. At this time the XP-37 was flown to Chanute Field, Illinois, where it served out its time as a maintenance trainer.

Characteristics of the revised XP-37 were as follows: span, length, and height were 37 feet, three and 1/2 inches, 31 feet, and nine feet, six inches. Wing area was 236 square feet.

The powerplant was an Allison V-1710-21 V-12 liquid cooled turbo supercharged type rated at 1,150hp at 2,950rpm for takeoff, 1,100hp at 2,900rpm Military at sea level, and 1,000hp at 20,000 feet driving a three blade Curtiss Electric propeller of 10 feet diameter.

This February 19, 1939, view of the single XP-37 (AC37-375) reveals further changes to the super-charger air intakes, two slightly off-center fairings having been added under the nose. This was one of the last photos taken of the aircraft at Wright Field. (*Wright Field 63247via Peter M. Bowers*)

The Air Corps ordered 13 Curtiss Model 81s for operational evaluation, and designated them as YP-37. Here, the first (AC38-472) poses on a frigid Buffalo taxiway, barely revealing the evidence of her 1920s era armament configuration of only two guns over the nose. (*Curtiss*)

Fuel capacity was 104 gallons normal and 148.5 gallons maximum, all internal.

Empty weight was 5,272 pounds, design useful load 1,078 pounds, design gross weight 6,350 pounds, and maximum gross weight 6,643 pounds. Design wing and power loadings were 26.9psf and 5.52 pounds per horse power. Normal useful load to gross weight ratio was 0.17 (very poor).

High speed (when the supercharger was working properly) was 340mph at 20,000 feet, and 330mph at 2,950rpm at 25,000 feet, and cruise speed was 304mph at 20,000 feet. Landing speed was

Above and following: The advanced YP-37s proved a maintenance challenge for the crews of the 36th Pursuit Group at Langley Field, Virginia, which received most of them initially. Specially prepared manuals, the first of many such detailed "owner's guides" to follow in WW II, were issued to ground crews. (*T.O.01-25CC-2*)

75mph. Climb time to 20,000 feet was recorded variously at 7.1 to 7.9 minutes. Normal and maximum ranges were 485 miles and 625 miles.

Curtiss YP-37

Though the Curtiss XP-37 was clearly not a practical and reliable pursuit aircraft, the Army felt strongly that a type so powered needed further operational evaluation. Thus, on December 11, 1937, a service test order was placed (Contract W535-ac-10535) for 13 Curtiss Model 81 types (MSN 12655 to 12667), labeled by the Army as YP-37s. This order came no more than five months after initial Army flight testing of the XP-37 prototype. Total contract cost was $531,000. The second YP-37 was delivered to the Army, according to Curtiss billing records, on April 29, 1939. This aircraft was serial

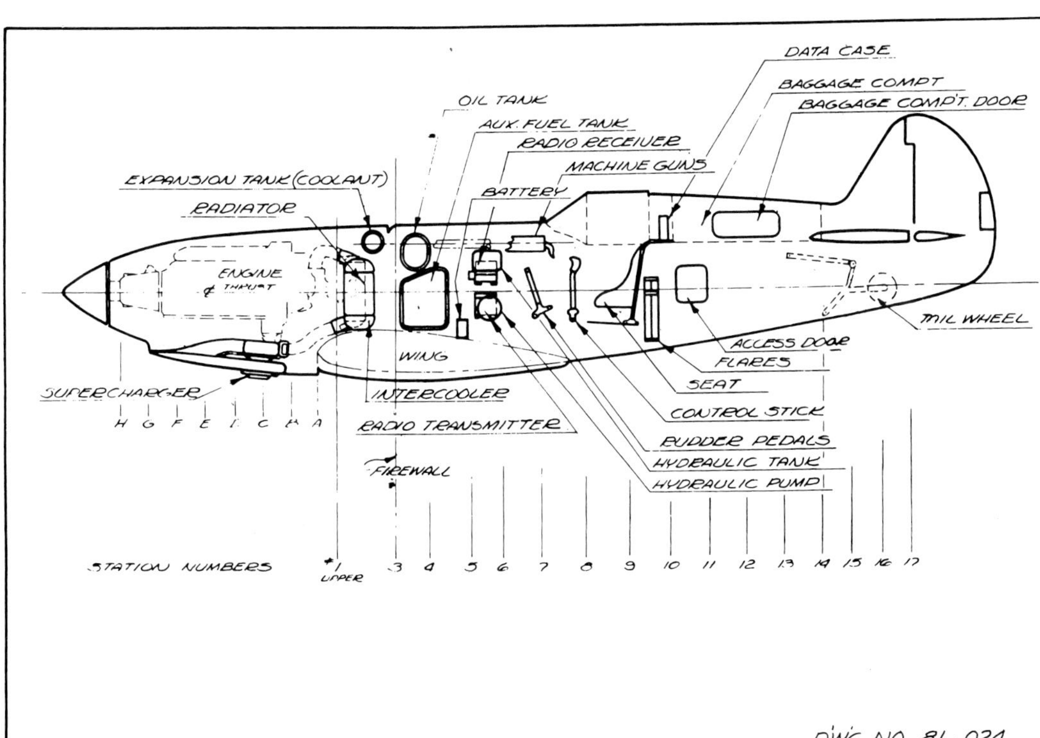

FIG. 3 – FUSELAGE CONTENTS & STATIONS DIAGRAM

38-473 (constructors number 12656), costing $34,481.03. The initial YP-37 was held at the Curtiss plant, and did not get to Wright Field until mid-1941. The remaining 11 pursuits were delivered between November 3 and December 5, 1939, at a unit Curtiss price of $34,852.65

The YP-37s were different from the XP-37 prototype in several ways: principally, the fuselage behind the cockpit was about 20 inches longer, and a new Allison V-1710-21 engine was installed, together with an updated version of the General Electric Type B-2 turbine supercharger. In addition, other powerplant changes were made, including use of a single coolant radiator instead of two.

Most YP-37s were delivered to the 36th Pursuit Group[108] at Langley Field, Virginia, where they stayed until early 1941. Turbo supercharger operation continued to be erratic, according to Don Berlin, with short lived components and turbo regulator problems. In the summer of 1940 two YP-37s were sent to Fairbanks, Alaska, for cold weather testing. One of these aircraft was lost in a ground loop accident late in that year. At one time or another, YP-37s were assigned, in small numbers, to the following USAAF units: 1st Pursuit Squadron (1939-1940 at Maxwell Field, AL); 22nd Pursuit Squadron (1940, Langley Field, VA); 23rd Pursuit Squadron (1940, Langley Field, VA); 32nd Pursuit Squadron (1940, Langley Field, VA); 33rd Pursuit Squadron (1937-1940); and 35th and 36th Pursuit Squadrons (1938-1940).

Another YP-37 was assigned to NACA Langley for testing. The others went to various Army bases, principally as maintenance trainers at Chanute Field, Illinois. The last YP-37 was junked at Biloxi, Mississippi, in February 1942. For the record, the fate of the individual YP-37s, seldom noted, follows:

USAAC Serial	Fate
38-472	Wrecked January 24, 1942
38-473	Wrecked February 9, 1941
38-474	To N.A.C.A. for various tests August 4, 1942
38-475	To Lowry Field November 21, 1941
38-476	To Biloxi as Class 26 (instructional airframe)
38-477	To Ladd Field, Alaska for cold weather tests November 19, 1940, including suitability on skis. Surveyed at Fairbanks May 29, 1941
38-478	Surveyed and condemned at Biloxi February 6, 1942
38-479	To Chanute Field November 7, 1941
38-480	To Chanute Field September 19, 1941
38-481	Ground looped at Ladd Field, Alaska and to Class 26 April 8, 1941

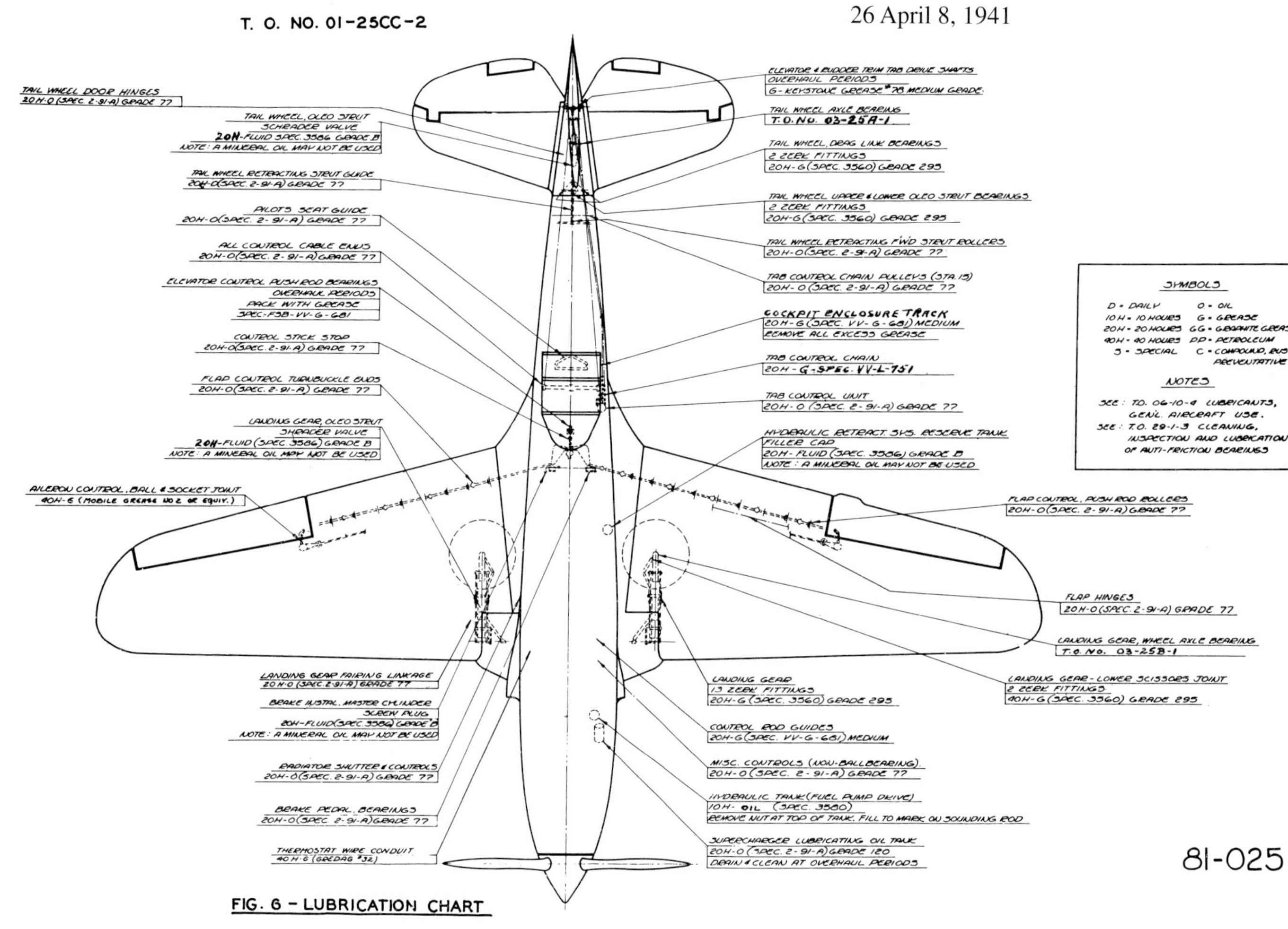

The first hint of the configuration of the legendary P-40 series that would follow can be discerned in this rarely seen overhead view of the YP-37 planform. It also vividly illustrates the challenges that pilots must have faced in dealing with that long, long nose. (*T.O. 01-25CC-2*)

Some of the YP-37s received the temporary, water-based camouflage schemes illustrated so often on other service types during the immediate pre-war years. Somehow, the paint made the troublesome aircraft seem more combat-ready. Note that the blisters over the nose guns, normally in place in most photos, have been removed, and the muzzles are exposed. (*USAF A-19612AC*)

38-482 Wrecked at Gulfport, MS January 5, 1942
38-483 To Class 26 at Chanute November 7, 1941
38-484 To Class 26 at Sheppard Field, TX November 6, 1941

Characteristics of the YP-37 follow: dimensions were as the XP-37, except length was 32 feet, 10 inches.

Powerplant was the Allison V-1710-21 rated at 1,150hp at 2,950rpm for takeoff (later de-rated to 1,000hp), 1,000hp at 2,600rpm at 25,000 feet (later de-rated to 880hp), driving an 11 foot, six inch diameter three blade Curtiss Electric propeller. Fuel capacity was 108 gallons normal and 163.5 gallons maximum, carried in a front main tank in the wing (40.5 gallons), rear main tank in the wing (61.3 gallons), and auxiliary tank in the fuselage (61.7 gallons).

Armament consisted of two fixed synchronized machine guns, one .30 caliber with 500 rounds, and one .50 caliber with 200 rounds.

Empty weight was 5,723 pounds, useful load 1,166 pounds, normal gross weight 6,889 pounds, and maximum gross weight 7,150 to 7,178 pounds. Wing loading and power loading were 29.2psf and 5.99 pounds per horse power, respectively, and the normal useful load to gross weight ratio was 0.17.

High speed was 328mph at 20,000 feet and 346mph at 25,000 feet, with cruise speed 297mph at 2,200rpm at 20,000 feet. Landing speed was 85mph. Climb capability was 2,920fpm at sea level, and 8.5 minutes to 20,000 feet. Service ceiling was 34,000 feet. Normal range was 570-610 miles at 297mph at 2,200rpm at 20,000 feet, and normal endurance 2 hours. Maximum range was 870 miles.

It is interesting to note the flight restrictions imposed on the YP-37s. First and foremost (indeed, it was underlined), the aircraft was not to exceed an indicated airspeed of 397mph. It was also prohibited to be flown in inverted flight, inverted spins, outside loops, snap rolls at more than 166mph indicated, and slow rolls at more than 248mph indicated. It was also prohibited from doing more than three turns in a spin, spins with armament, baggage, auxiliary fuel, or "any overload" on board. Finally, mechanics were urgently cautioned that the aircraft would "*...nose up when on blocks at about one third power*!"

Most YP-37s were eventually farmed out to Air Corps bases across the country, where they in effect became *ad hoc* spokesmen for U.S. preparedness prior to 1941. This aircraft is No.146 of the 10th Air Base Squadron, and has the Air Corps Technical School badge on the rear fuselage. The long anti-glare panel is noteworthy. (*Logan Combs via Warren Bodie*)

Besides cowling, intake, and prop experiments, the XP-42 was also the subject of "all flying" horizontal tail trials. (*NASA 41749*)

the public at the Cleveland Air Races in September 1940, and later that year was pictured in Army olive drab paint with the same intake scoop system; a single inlet was now supplied for the carburetor.

Engine cooling was still not satisfactory, however. Data for the original configuration was as follows: span, length, and height: 37 feet, three and 1/2 inches, 30 feet, seven inches, and 12 feet. Wing area was 236 square feet.

The powerplant was a Pratt & Whitney *Twin Wasp* R-1930-31 rated 1,050hp at 2,550rpm at takeoff and 1,000hp at 2,300rpm at 8,500 feet, and at 2,450rpm at 11,500 feet. Propeller reduction gear ratio was 16:9, supercharger impeller drive gear ratio 8.47:1, and compression ratio 6.7:1.

Empty weight was 4,818 pounds (251 pounds greater than a standard P-36A), normal useful load 1,101 pounds, normal gross weight 5,919 pounds, and maximum gross weight 6,260 pounds. Wing and power loadings were 25.0psf and 5.64 pounds per horse power. Useful load to normal gross weight ratio was 0.186. Normal and maximum fuel capacities were 105 and 161 gallons, respectively.

Maximum speed attained was 315mph at 15,000 feet, cruise speed was 286mph, and normal and maximum ranges were 730 miles and 1,200 miles, respectively.

Clearly, no significant speed gains were measured over the standard P-36A/P-36C pursuits. The XP-42 was sent to the NACA laboratories at Langley Field, Virginia, September 4, 1940, where it sat until more testing started in May 1941, and lasted until December 1942.

NACA made a powerplant cowl/propeller spinner and blade cuff /cooling fan test vehicle of the XP-42 over many months, arranging a systematic variation of front end changes in attempting to find the configuration providing best high speed capability combined with proper radial engine cooling. These tests encompassed long and short noses, high and low inlet velocity air intakes with propeller spinners, and cuffs and no cuffs on propeller blades. With careful design speed increases were obtained; using 1,000hp at 14,500 feet altitude, maximum airspeeds varied from 338mph to 344mph, the latter with a short nose arrangement in no way resembling the original XP-42.

With the Curtiss P-40 development with Allison V-1710 engine well in hand, and greater speed capability, no further work on a long nose radial engine installation took place, though Vultee tried the same thing on their Model 48 fighter with similar results.

NACA then used the XP-42 as a test bed for an all-flying horizontal tail. These tests led to much later use of such an arrangement in other aircraft. It remained at NACA, incredibly, through July 15, 1947, when it was finally scrapped, the last flight having been made in April 1947.

Curtiss-Wright Model 21

In 1938, the St. Louis Division of the Curtiss-Wright Corporation undertook the design of a lightweight interceptor fighter plane intended as an inexpensive, yet high performance type, primarily for the export market. The design was labeled the Model 21, and advantage was taken of the division's previous experience in all metal aircraft design with the civil Model 19 *Coupe*, and the 19R light combat aircraft. In fact, the basic design and size of the Model 19 wing was employed in the interceptor.

There were two versions of the aircraft: the basic CW-21[109] with aft retracting main landing gear housed in bulbous fairings under the wings outside of basic wing structure, and the later CW-21B, with an inward retracting main gear laying flush in a modified wing center section. A version identified in a Curtiss-Wright document as the CW-21A was a variant of the 21B with an Allison engine and flush-fitting landing gear. The company designation of this proposal was later apparently changed to P-248A. The CW-21A has also been identified as the variant sold to China, but this is not correct.

The first flight of the CW-21 at St. Louis has been variously noted as taking place anywhere from September 1938 to January 1939, but a photo exists of the complete aircraft dated October 10, 1938, suggesting the actual date was closer to that time. The prototype (MSN 21-1), bearing U.S. civil experimental license NX-19431,[110] was soon employed as a demonstrator in an attempt to win orders from China, a nation under attack by the Japanese. China desperately needed defensive interceptor aircraft.

Never previously reported is the fact that the Model 21 (NX-19431) was in fact demonstrated to Army Air Corps officials at

While the Curtiss Buffalo Division was busy marketing and developing the Model 75 and P-36 series, Curtiss-Wright St. Louis Airplane Division had taken a slightly different tack, and evolved the Model 21 from the basic Model 19R airframe. A dedicated, point defense interceptor, it was probably the best of its class when introduced in late 1938. NX19431 was the prototype, serial number 21-1. Note the diminutive size of the aircraft compared to the pilot, who was literally "wearing" the airplane. Contrary to many reports, the aircraft was painted overall green at this point, not red, and was *never* named "Demon." (*The Museum of Flight*)

Wright Field November 28, 1938, where it was flown by Major J. P. Richter. Major Richter turned in a rather glowing report on the aircraft, and his observations were that:

a. The aircraft possessed fine handling qualities in all maneuvers
b. Absolutely no adverse aerodynamic characteristics were noted
c. The aircraft possessed outstanding performance and left a highly favorable impression in handling
d. The patented Curtiss-Wright "Tell-Tale" pilot check list was impressive
e. He found the cockpit to be comfortable, but noted that the seat had insufficient adjustment to accommodate a tall pilot
f. He noted that the parking brake cross-over control was subject to compression
g. He stressed that the take-off and climb were exceptionally good
h. He also emphasized that stability was exceptionally good for an interceptor
i. He noted that the aircraft set up severe buffeting from about 10mph above the stall, however.

The chief failing of the Curtiss-Wright Model 21 was its limited range; it was, after all, intended as a point defense interceptor. However, in an attempt to address concerns by potential customers, Curtis-Wright developed these twin auxiliary fuel tanks (not droppable) on 21-3, by March 1940. (*Curtiss CF 2426A via Peter M. Bowers*)

Despite the highly favorable comments by crews at Wright Field, the Air Corps by this time had committed to other interceptor designs, and Curtiss-Wright turned to the export market to sell the Model 21, which had been the intended audience from conception. In February 1939 NX-19431, the CW-21 demonstrator, arrived in Mandalay, Burma, in company with another Curtiss demonstrator (as noted earlier, the H75-Q *Hawk*). Later that month it got to Loiwing, China, where the CAMCO plant was located. The CW-21 was demonstrated by Curtiss pilot Bob Fausel against Russian and French planes then in use in China, and before highly placed Chinese officials. In one instance, the aircraft was actually used to shoot down an intruding Japanese bomber—while apparently still bearing a U.S. civil license! Eventually the Chinese bought, and later crashed, the demonstrator on Sales Order D-5.

The result of this sales work was a Chinese purchase of CW-21s on May 31, 1939, which called for three assembled pattern aircraft (MSN 13656 to 13658 on Sales Order D-8/196, Contract 504),[111] plus 27 ship sets of parts[112] to be assembled at the Central Aircraft Manufacturing Corp. (CAMCO) at Loiwing, China. The three assembled CW-21s purchased by China were built in March 1940, and shipped out via Burma, from where they were to be ferried into China by May. Unfortunately, all three aircraft crashed during bad weather on December 23, 1941, in rough terrain while on the ferry flight, killing one of the pilots. Worse yet, though, before Curtiss parts for assembly of the remaining aircraft arrived in China, the Loiwing CAMCO plant was lost to the invading Japanese in the spring of 1942 before additional CW-21s could get into service. However, at least one CW-21 is known to have been integrated into the American Volunteer Group (AVG), the famous *Flying Tigers*, suggesting that at least a few of the CAMCO aircraft (Chinese sources believe five) must have been assembled. Most sources agree that CAMCO did manage to nearly complete two aircraft but, due to the evacuation to India in 1942, were previously believed not to have flown.

The construction of the CW-21 was as follows: the fuselage was an all metal semi-monocoque, stressed skin structure with longitudinal stringers and transverse bulkheads and former rings, with an armored bulkhead behind the pilot. The wings were of cantilever, multi-cellular, five spar construction, consisting of a center panel integral with the fuselage and two outer panels. The tail group was of all metal multi-cellular construction, with trim tabs on rudder and elevators. The landing gear was hydraulically retractable. Design provision was made to incorporate two .50 caliber and two .30 caliber cowl machine guns, but normally only one .50 caliber (on the left) and one .30 caliber gun (on the right) was carried. All guns were synchronized.

Characteristics of the CW-21 were: span, length, and height were 35 feet, 26 feet, six inches, and eight feet, eight inches. Wing area was 174.3 square feet, and the root airfoil was a NACA 2315 type. Fin, rudder, stabilizer, and elevator area were respectively 8.06, 7.36, 16.98, and 8.58 square feet. Landing gear tread was 83 inches, and wheel size was 7.50x10.

The powerplant was a Wright *Cyclone* R-1820-G5 rated at 1,000hp at 2,200rpm for sea level takeoff, 850hp at 2,100rpm at 6,000 feet, and 750hp at 15,200 feet. It had a Hamilton Standard constant speed three blade propeller of nine feet diameter. Fuel and oil capacities were 96 gallons and 8.5 gallons, respectively.

Empty weight was 3,148 pounds, useful load 1,032 pounds, and gross weight 4,180 pounds. Wing and power loadings were 23.98psf and 4.18 pounds per horse power, respectively. Useful load to gross weight ratio was 0.25.

Maximum speed was 303mph at 17,000 feet, 286mph at 7,500 feet, and 261mph at sea level. Cruise speed was 274mph at 17,000 feet, with a fuel consumption of 58 gallons per hour. Stalling speed was 67mph. Initial climb rate was a high 4,800fpm, and time to 20,000 feet was just six minutes. Service ceiling was 36,200 feet, and normal range 530 miles.

The solitary customer for the basic Model 21 was China, which received the three prototypes from Curtiss-Wright St. Louis as patterns to facilitate assembly of 27 at the CAMCO facilities at Loiwing. Here, one of the three sits next to one of the original Chinese AVG *Hawk H81A-2s*, but has not yet received Chinese markings. Between three and five of these aircraft served briefly with the AVG. (*Ray Wagner via San Diego Aerospace Museum*)

Chinese troops inspect the remains of what is obviously a painted hulk of a Curtiss-Wright Model 21 at the former CAMCO factory, which had been seized by the Japanese earlier in the war. This suggests that the Japanese may have made some attempt to complete the 27 kit aircraft that Curtiss-Wright had shipped in March 1940. (*U.S. Army Signal Corps SC 316699*)

Curtiss-Wright found a customer in the Dutch for the improved Model 21-B, that nation ordering not fewer than 24. Intended originally for shipment to the homeland, they ended up in the Netherlands East Indies when Holland was invaded by Germany in May 1940. Here, the crowded St. Louis plant rushes completion of the order. The third aircraft in line reveals ports for only two nose guns, although the aircraft was designed to accommodate four. (*The Museum of Flight*)

The CW-21B version of the interceptor[113] was modified to reduce landing gear drag, and had increased fuel capacity, but in the main was similar to the CW-21. The prototype of this variant (MSN 21-2) received U.S. Experimental License NX-19441[114] in 1940. However, the earliest known photo of a Model 21B was dated by Curtiss-Wright January 21, 1939, indicating that, instead of being a development, as has so often been quoted, it was actually developed in parallel with the basic Model 21. Like the Model 21 demonstrator, NX-19441 was also evaluated by the USAAC at Wright Field between April 12 and 24, 1940, where the Air Corps noted that the design was now quoted by Curtiss-Wright as the Model CW-21-B *Interceptor Pursuit*. The results of the Air Corps evaluation are quoted, as well:

a. Landing and take-off characteristics were rated, by all six Army pilots who flew the aircraft, as "excellent."
b. Stability was also noted as excellent in all planes
c. Stick forces during maneuvers were noted as being much higher than those found on the P-36A, but "not objectionable." All six Army pilots also rated the rate-of-climb as "outstanding" and noted that it was in excess of 5,000 feet per minute at sea level. However, they also noted that the CW-21B could not escape during a combat by climbing once a P-36A got behind it.
d. While at Wright Field, the following six Army officers flew the aircraft: Captains Benjamin S. Kelsey, E. K. Warburton, George E. Price and M.S. Roth and Lieutenants M. E. Bradley and M. F. Cooper

On July 11, 1940, Curtiss received an order for 24 CW-21B aircraft from the Netherlands on Sales Order D-12, the document identifying the aircraft as Model 21-B *Interceptor Fighters*. When that country was overrun by Germany the order was switched to the Netherlands East Indies. Most of the new interceptors were delivered in the last quarter of that year to the island of Java, but at the

Determined to improve even more on a spectacular interceptor, Curtiss-Wright marketed the Model 21-B, with a still larger engine and flush-retracting undercarriage—and the ability to mount four machine guns in the nose. This fanciful drawing, with fictitious markings, was included in the sales literature. (*Curtiss-Wright*)

The first of the Dutch Curtiss-Wright 21-Bs, coded CW-344, poses at St. Louis on October 10, 1940. The camouflage paint was not, as it appears here, a solid color, but rather a mixed pattern of green and brown over light gray. *(Curtiss-Wright CF-2936)*

outbreak of the Pacific War only 17 were available to enter the fight near Bandoeng. In early February 1942 the Japanese attacked the Dutch islands, and the CW-21Bs were soon decimated by marauding fighters so that two days after the first attack only five of the Curtiss aircraft remained airworthy. At least two were captured by the Japanese, and one CW-21B was found at Singapore at the end of the war. These aircraft received Dutch serials CW-344 to CW-363,[115] and they differed from the basic CW-21 and those sold to China in that they had flush-retracting landing gear and better performance than the Chinese aircraft. It is interesting to note that, on some Curtiss-Wright documents, the Dutch aircraft are cited as type CW-21B-1.

Characteristics of the CW-21B follow: span, length, and height 35 feet, 27 feet, two inches, and eight feet, 11 inches. Wing and tail areas were as the CW-21. Tire size was 27 inches, streamlined.

Powerplant was the same as CW-21, except maximum fuel capacity was 128 gallons, with two 50 gallon main tanks and two 14 gallon auxiliary wing tanks. Oil capacity was 9.5 gallons.

Empty weight was 3,382 pounds, useful load 1,118 pounds, normal gross weight 4,500 pounds, and maximum gross weight 5,000 pounds. Wing and power loadings were respectively 25.8psf and 4.5 pounds per horse power. Useful load to gross weight ratio was 0.248.

Frequently illustrated in pre-war publications, this Dutch Curtiss-Wright 21-B reveals the details of the two-color camouflage scheme used on the upper surfaces—but the white serial number painted on (C-338) in this September 28, 1940, view may have been a left-over from the original Dutch order, as this series was used on fighters in the homeland. *(Curtiss-Wright CF2889)*

The first of three XP-55s built (42-78845), after finally being assembled in secrecy at Scott Field, Illinois, after a very protracted gestation, in October 1943. By then, the operational requirement had passed the aircraft by. (*Curtiss SF-11480 via Harold Andrews*)

for testing this aircraft, known as the CW-24B. The CW-24B was a two place pusher with characteristics (in developed form) as follows: span, length, and height 36 feet, seven inches, 27 feet, four and 1/4 inches, and 10 feet. Wing area was 203.4 square feet, dihedral 4.5 degrees, wing sweep at quarter chord 28.5 degrees, and airfoils Curtiss 6500-0015. Elevator span was 107 inches, and elevator area 12.52 square feet. Elevator trail edge movement 25 degrees up and 17 degrees down. Wheelbase measured 155.78 inches, and tread was 121.1 inches.

The powerplant was a Menasco C6S-5 rated at 275hp driving an eight foot diameter, two bladed controllable pitch propeller.

Empty weight was 3,350 pounds, useful load 649 pounds, and gross weight 3,999 pounds. Wing and power loadings were 19.66psf and 14.54 pounds per horse power, respectively.

Performance is not available, but it was very poor. The primary purpose of the CW-24B was to ascertain stability and control characteristics.

First flight of the CW-24B took place on December 2, 1941, at Muroc Bombing Range in California. A quite comprehensive test

The second XP-55 (42-78846) receiving last minute attention by ground personnel before a flight. This aircraft spent much of her test career at Wright Field, and is now in the collections of the National Air and Space Museum. (*Dean Collection*)

Originally intended to have mounted contra-rotating pusher props, for development purposes a single-rotation prop was settled upon, as well as an interim powerplant (the Allison V-1710), shown here. (*Dean Collection*)

program of 169 flights was conducted, with completion in May 1942. The overall results of the program, wherein many aircraft changes were made, were considered very satisfactory by Curtiss pilots, though there were enough concerns that the CW-24B was later sent to the 40x80 foot NACA Langley wind tunnel in Virginia for further testing.

The CW-24B was considered successful enough to warrant the Army giving Curtiss a July 10, 1942, contract for three XP-55 experimental fighters after a full scale mockup. The contract (AC-15020) was valued at $1,222,894.00. The pursuit aircraft, waggishly dubbed *Ascender*, were given Army Air Corps serial numbers 42-78845, -78846, and -78847 for number 1, 2, and 3 aircraft, respectively. In the interest of saving powerplant development time, they were to be powered by an Allison V-1710 engine driving a single rotation, instead of a dual rotation pusher propeller as originally envisioned. A system was devised wherein the propeller could be jettisoned for an emergency bailout.

The first XP-55 was assembled in some secrecy at Scott Field, Illinois, and after ground tests had a first flight on July 13, 1943. Problems arose, among them an extremely long takeoff run due to the inability to raise the nose easily to achieve the required wing angle of attack, and modifications were made, including increasing the size of the nose elevator. During this time, further wind tunnel model testing was accomplished at both Wright Field and at NACA Ames, in California. Flight #27 of number 1 aircraft was made on November 15, 1943, to test stall/spin characteristics, always a touchy item, and when stalled in "dirty" condition, gear and flaps down, the XP-55 pitched nose down all the way over on its back. After a 16,000 foot drop in that condition, with the engine stalled out, pilot J.H. Gray managed to successfully depart the aircraft, which was of course lost.

After the crash, more model spin testing was done with many variations, one of which was extending wingtips, and another revising the limits of elevator travel. The number 2 aircraft was not immediately reworked, but #3 would incorporate the latest revisions. Flight tests of number 2 were started on January 9, 1944, but flight conditions near stall were carefully avoided. New modifications of #2 came later on, and in late September 1944 official performance tests of 42-78846 were run at St. Louis, with updates to the latest modifications. Tests showed ground handling was good, takeoff distance required was still excessive, on landing the nose wheel would slam down, stability and maneuverability were rated fair only, and stall behavior was unsatisfactory, with no warning, and excessive altitude loss for recovery. Overall, there were just too many problems.

Aircraft #3 was completed in April 1944, with a first flight on the 25th incorporating the latest modifications, including a stick shaker stall warning system. In November 1944 this aircraft went to Eglin Field in Florida for gun firing tests.

Basic characteristics of the XP-55 serial number AC42-78847 follow: span, length, and height 41 feet, 0.06 inches, 29 feet, seven inches, and 11 feet, six and 1/2 inches. Wing area was 217.2 square feet. Wing airfoil selected was the Curtiss 6500-0015. Root and tip chords were 92 inches and 44.77 inches. Wing dihedral 4.5 degrees. Wing sweep at quarter chord 28.5 degrees. Free floating elevator area 21.46 square feet. Elevator span was 134 inches. Normal elevator travel 70 degrees up and 17 degrees down (at trailing edge). Fin area 7.4 square feet. Wheelbase was 173 inches, and tread 142 inches. Main and nose wheel diameters 27 inches and 19 inches, respectively

Powerplant was an Allison V-1710-95 (F23R) rated at 1,275hp at 3,000rpm at sea level, and 1,125hp (Military Power) at 3,000rpm at 15,560 feet. A three blade, 10 foot diameter Curtiss Electric propeller was used. Normal and maximum fuel with drop tanks was 110 and 210 gallons, respectively.

Empty weight was 6,354 pounds normal, with useful load 1,077 pounds, and normal gross weight 7,931 pounds. Maximum overload gross weight was 8,805 pounds. Wing and power loadings were 36.51psf and 7.05 pounds per horse power. Useful load to gross weight ratio was 0.136 (very poor).

Maximum speed was 377.5mph at 16,900 feet, and landing speed was 120 mph (very high!). Maximum climb rate was 2,460fpm. Estimated service and absolute ceilings were 35,800 and 36,800 feet.

The XP-55 armament consisted of four .50 caliber machine guns in the nose with 250 rounds per gun.

On October 25, 1944, #2 aircraft was flown to Wright Field, Ohio, where several pilots flew it, after which it was assigned to the National Air and Space Museum, where it currently resides in storage at the Paul E. Garber Restoration and Storage Facility, Silver Hill, Maryland, awaiting transfer to the new Stephen F. Udvar-Hazy Center near Dulles International Airport.

Number three XP-55 was flown from Eglin Field in Florida to Wright Field in December 1944, where it resided until the next spring. On May 27, 1945, this aircraft was flown at an air show and crashed during a fly-by, killing its pilot and a spectator.

The XP-55 was an unsuccessful design, with excessive time required for development, and displayed performance no better than fighters then in service. The stall/spin characteristics alone would never have been satisfactory for a service fighter.

An expensive and protracted program, it is difficult to understand why the Army continued to fund the XP-55. The "banana peel" cowling arrangement over the pusher engine was little short of a maze, although access, albeit rather lofty, was good. (*Dean Collection*)

10

The P-40, *Hawk 81*, and *Hawk 87* Series

The Curtiss P-40, more readily identified with the house of Curtiss than any other type by generations of aviation enthusiasts, has probably been, in the words of a Curtiss wartime document, "...*doubted, damned, praised, ridiculed and lauded*" more than any other American airplane in aviation history. Yet it and its immediate forbearers fought with distinction on every single Allied battle front, both before and after the entry of the United States into World War II, a claim that no other fighter or warplane can make.

During its four years' aerial service, Curtiss claimed that P-40 series aircraft destroyed more enemy aircraft than any other Allied airplane. While at first glance this may appear an outrageous claim, and though it poses unique research challenges, it may not be far off the mark. On the basis of a study that Curtiss commissioned in-house near the end of the war (admittedly a perhaps biased control group), in 50 known aerial combats in which 457 P-40s engaged 1,257 Axis planes on battle fronts throughout the world, this sturdy craft allegedly destroyed an average of 13.5 enemy planes for every P-40 lost in action.

Whatever the statistics might or might not prove, it is a matter of record that, in those crucial days of 1941 and 1942, when the very foundations of the democratic world were swaying under the terrific trip-hammer of the Axis armed forces, the U.S. had only two fighter aircraft geared into anything near quantity production—the P-40, and Grumman's F4F *Wildcat*, with Bell P-39s just starting to be churned out. Because of this, P-40s and F4Fs were found in the thick of many of the widespread battles fought across the face of the globe, with the P-40 series more widely dispersed than the carrier-based F4Fs. Of course, following the P-40 and F4F and the early, dark days of the war, faster and more powerful fighters, including the Lockheed P-38 *Lightning*, North American P-51 *Mustang*, Republic P-47 *Thunderbolt*, Grumman F6F *Hellcat*, and Vought F4U *Corsair* series aircraft rolled off the production lines—and quickly achieved almost total dominance over Axis airpower in every theater, and clinched eventual victory. But the magnificent "holding" role played by the Curtiss *Tomahawks*, *Kittyhawks*, and P-40s was destined to go down in the pages of World War II history as a distinct and valuable contribution to the Allied cause.

The battle saga of the Curtiss P-40 began almost simultaneously with the outbreak of the conflict in 1939, and in September of that year, a Curtiss *Hawk 75A* shot down the first German plane over French soil. Two months later, on November 7th, a formation of nine French *Hawk 75As* engaged a force of 27 German aircraft and destroyed nine of them without loss to their formation.

Subsequent to the fall of France in June 1940, the P-40s fought with British Commonwealth forces over the far-flung skies of Ethiopia, Iraq, Syria, over the desert wastes of North Africa, and with the famed American Volunteer Group (A.V.G.), the *Flying Tigers*, over Burma, China, and Thailand, with the U.S. Army Air Corps units in Hawaii, the Philippines, the Dutch East Indies, New Guinea, Australia, India, and over the bleak and fog-shrouded snow lands of Alaska, with the Russians before Leningrad and Rostov, and other battle areas over the globe.

The P-40 series contribution towards the Allied victory in Africa is also a matter of record; P-40s, *Tomahawks*, and *Kittyhawks* were in the thick of the battle at El Alamein, when Field Marshall Erwin Rommel, the famed "Desert Fox," and his Italian allies stood only 63 miles from the great naval bastion at Alexandria, and not much further from the vital Suez Canal. For months preceding the turn of the tide at El Alamein, the Curtiss-equipped RAF, Royal Australian, South African, and U.S. squadrons softened up the enemy by pounding away incessantly at German and Italian troop and materiel concentrations and its supply lines, tanks, trucks, and gun emplacements, with such fury and success as fighters and fighter-bombers that previously skeptical Commonwealth crews began to swear by the P-40.

After General Montgomery's famous "crow bar" offensive, when on October 23, 1942, the British theater commander launched his withering offensive against the Axis forces, the P-40s continued to pound the fleeing Axis forces for 1,500 miles across the northern rim of Africa.

When American forces finally entered the fray in Operation "Torch" on November 8, 1942, P-40s, which had been brought to the invasion on U.S. Navy aircraft carriers, took off and went into action as though they were seasoned Naval aviators, and helped

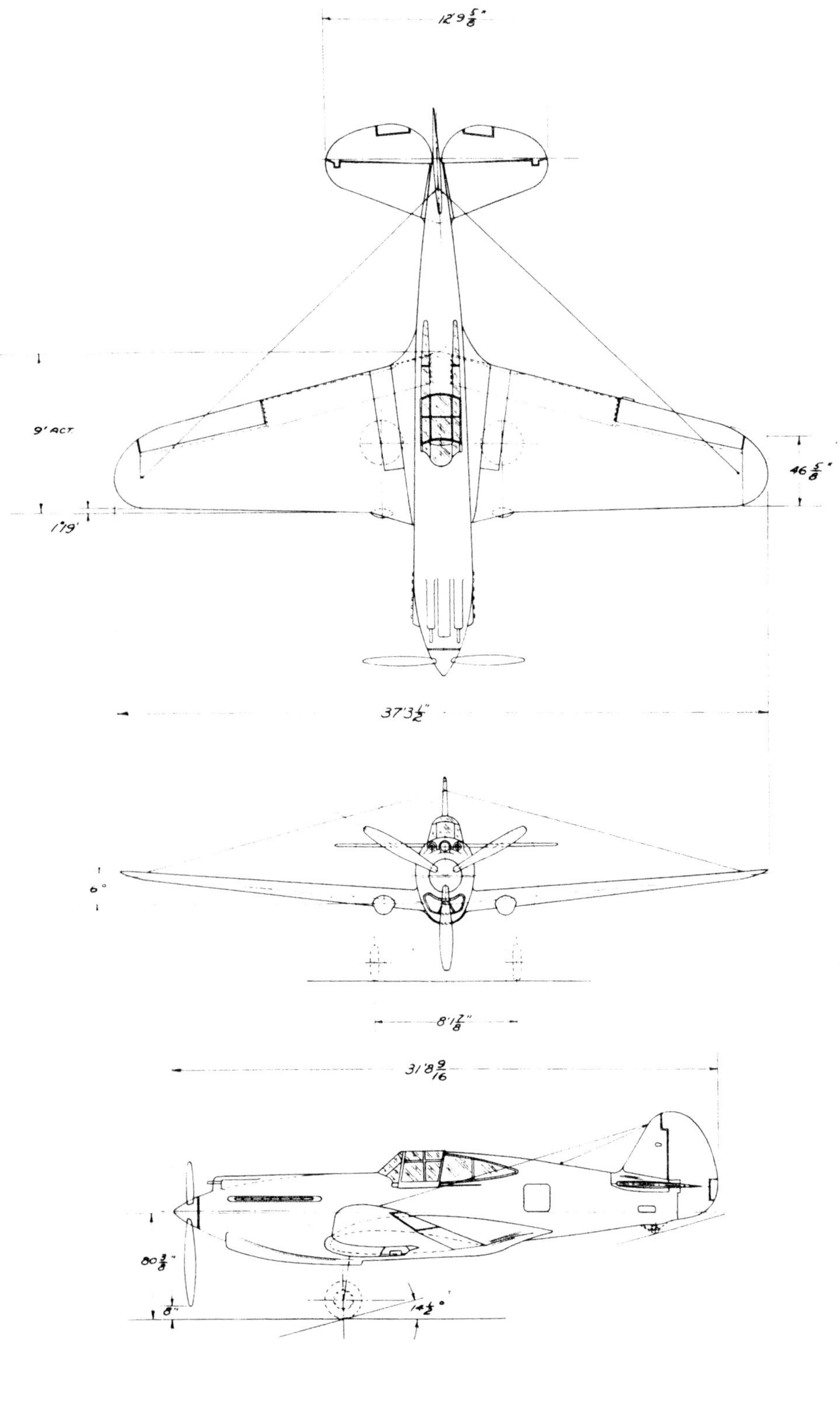

This is the earliest known, Curtiss-originated drawing of the XP-40. (*Curtiss*)

Curtiss XP-40

provide an aerial umbrella for the Allied invasion fleet and counter Vichy French resistance.

When the Commonwealth 8th Army stood within striking distance of Germany's famous Mareth Line, P-40 and British *Hurricane* fighter-bombers, sometimes referred to locally as *Kittybombers* and *Hurribombers*, were called upon to lead the way for the great aerial assault against this powerful assembly area. The hard-pressed Curtiss and Hawker fighters attacked nearly every known enemy gun emplacement and supply dump within 20 miles of the front.

With the reduction of the Mareth Line and Allied drives from all directions, the Axis armies were cornered in Tunisia. A few weeks before the Axis strongholds in Tunisia fell to the victorious Allied forces, the enemy tried repeatedly to evacuate and re-supply by air some of its more important military personnel and equipment.

On Sunday, April 18th, a formation of U.S. P-40s of the 57th Fighter Group, covered by high-flying Supermarine *Spitfires*, struck at a huge German and Italian aerial convoy of more than 100 transports, with escorting fighters. The P-40s decimated the formation and, before it was over, at least 74 troop carriers and escorts littered the beaches off Cape Bon. The U.S. lost six P-40s.

Five days later, a formation of P-40s, flown by the South Africans commanded by Lieutenant Colonel Douglas Loftus, turned in a similar performance when they encountered a large formation of German Messerschmitt Me 323 transports, escorted by German and Italian fighters. Within five minutes they had destroyed 31 enemy aircraft with the loss of four *Kittyhawks*.

After the fall of Axis held areas of North Africa, P-40s contributed their share of destruction heaped upon the faltering Italian island outposts, including Pantelleria and Sardinia, as well as targets on Sicily and the Italian mainland. In one engagement over Sardinia, on July 22, 1943, a formation of P-40s destroyed 17 enemy fighters with no losses to themselves.

Eight days later, over the same targets, another formation of P-40s took on a large number of Axis aircraft that came up to intercept them and, before the engagement was many minutes old, 21 of the Axis aircraft had gone down, at a cost of one *Warhawk*.

North Africa was perhaps the ideal operational environment for the P-40 series, and there was, in fact, a tactical reason for this. The African theater was primarily a battlefield area and, as such, required aircraft that could render service in close cooperation with rapidly moving ground forces. It required almost exclusively low-altitude cooperation by bombers, fighters, and the newly evolved fighter-bomber. Because of its excellent low altitude characteristics, which allegedly disqualified it for service in Europe proper, the well armored and powerfully gunned P-40s were nearly ideal for this assignment.

In China, where the P-40s, depending on whose math you prefer, destroyed as many as 20 Japanese aircraft for every P-40 lost in actual combat, and in the South Pacific, the nimble Japanese Mitsubishi A6M series *Zero* of the Imperial Japanese Navy and its Army counterpart, the Nakajima Ki-43, were the P-40's chief nemesis. Both had superior climbing power, higher ceiling, and better dog-fighting maneuverability, but Allied crews eventually learned how to master these characteristics through use of the P-40's terrific diving power, greater speed in level flight at its best altitudes, heavier concentrated firepower, and much better construction. The great combat pilot and leader, Lieutenant Colonel John R. Alison of the Fourteenth Air Force in China, said flatly that "*...I wouldn't trade the wing-tips of a P-40 for a Zero*." Similarly, Lieutenant Colonel Phillip Cochran, upon his return to the U.S. from leading the 33rd Fighter Group in Tunisia, stated that "*...the P-40 is my idea of a fighter plane*." Colonel Robert L. Scott, former Commander of the 23rd Fighter Group in China, carried his admiration for the P-40 one step further when he said:

In the Curtiss tradition, the prototype XP-40 was a modified P-36A (AC38-10) designated by Curtiss as their Model 75-P, and it was flown to Wright Field as such on October 16, 1938. Contrary to popular belief, it underwent a number of modifications. It is pictured here with the aft, under-slung radiator arrangement, just five days earlier. (*Dean Collection*)

With this configuration, and the radiator air scoop moved up under the nose, the XP-40 won the 1939 USAAC Fighter Competition, powered by the Allison V-1710-19. (*Dean Collection*)

"...we have used the P-40s in China for everything except submarines, and by the Gods, if you put a periscope in the canopy, we'll use it with torpedoes."

But in the beginning, before the world conflict had reached stretches of the earth's surface that few could have imagined, the P-40 was undergoing a difficult birth, and survival of this, the designated standard U.S. Army fighter at the dawning of the decade of the 1940s, was very much in doubt.

P-40 series aircraft saw extremely widespread service with Army units, and certainly more units were issued aircraft from this series during the war than any other pursuit series aircraft. A preliminary survey of known squadron-size units issued P-40s is appended at the end of this account.

Curtiss XP-40

It was clear to Curtiss and the Army that the XP-37/YP-37 and the XP-42 were not solid candidates to win the 1938 Pursuit Competition, delayed, as it happened, until January 1939. A new candidate design was needed, faster than the P-36, more reliable than the turbo supercharged P-37, and more practical than the XP-42. Don Berlin of Curtiss wanted an "altitude rated" Allison V-1710 inline V-12 for a powerplant, and that company came through with a single-stage, single speed integral mechanically supercharged version with an impeller geared 8.77:1 and rated at 10,000 feet. In March 1938, Curtiss proposed that a P-36 be modified to take the V-1710 engine, and envisioned this type as their Pursuit Competition contender. The Army accepted the proposal, and the 10th production P-36A, serial 38-10 (MSN 12424), was defined as Curtiss Model 75-

The XP-40 was tested extensively at the NACA wind tunnel facility at Langley. The prop blades have been removed, and a dummy spinner installed, and the national insignia on the upper wings are interesting, in that they are of different size. (*NASA L-17472*)

The heart and soul of the initial production P-40 series was the in-line Allison V-1710 engine, a pristine example of which is shown here at Buffalo. (*The Museum of Flight*)

Final configuration of the XP-40 essentially established the shape of the aircraft that started issuing forth from the Buffalo production lines to meet USAAC and Allied demands. Incredibly, even at this stage, the aircraft was to be equipped with only two forward-firing guns. (*Aeroplane Photo Supply via Dean Collection*)

P and Air Corps model XP-40 (Curtiss Specification 98-605-1) in an Army official order of April 1938.[117]. By October 14th of that year, the XP-40 had made a first flight, with Curtiss test pilot Ed Elliot at the controls. Almost immediately thereafter, on October 16th, the aircraft was flown to Wright Field for Air Corps tests.

The initial prototype configuration had the radiator for the V-1710 beneath the fuselage aft of the wing, the oil cooler scoop low under the engine compartment, and carburetor air taken from a wide flat inlet atop the nose. Shortly the configuration was modified after tests at NACA Langley showed cooling drag was less with a radiator located up front under the engine. In addition, the far aft radiator was particularly sensitive to foreign object damage, and involved long vulnerable coolant lines to and from the engine. The new arrangement had the forward radiator with an oval inlet, the oil cooler fed from wing root leading edge inlets, and carburetor air fed around the blast tubes of the two .50 caliber nose guns, all this done in the 1938-1939 winter.

In early 1939 the XP-40, so revised, won the January 1939 Pursuit Competition using the Allison V-1710-19 (C13) engine rated at 1,090hp at 2,950rpm at 10,000 feet. On April 26, 1939, Curtiss won the big prize; the Air Corps awarded production contract W535-ac-12414 for 524 P-40 aircraft at a total cost of $12,872,898.00. These aircraft were assigned Curtiss MSNs 13033 to 13556. However, only 200 were delivered as P-40s, and these were assigned Air Corps serials 39-156 to 39-289 (134) and 40-292 to 40-357 (66).

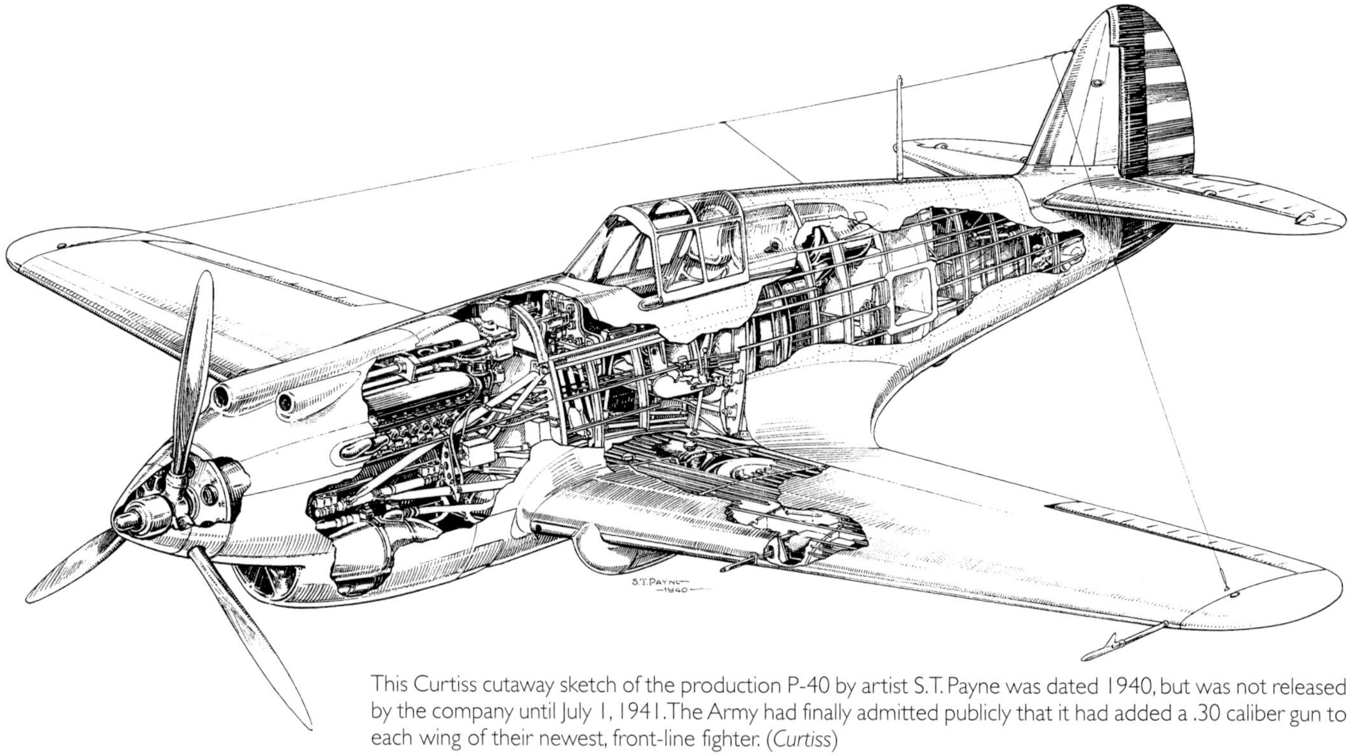

This Curtiss cutaway sketch of the production P-40 by artist S.T. Payne was dated 1940, but was not released by the company until July 1, 1941. The Army had finally admitted publicly that it had added a .30 caliber gun to each wing of their newest, front-line fighter. (*Curtiss*)

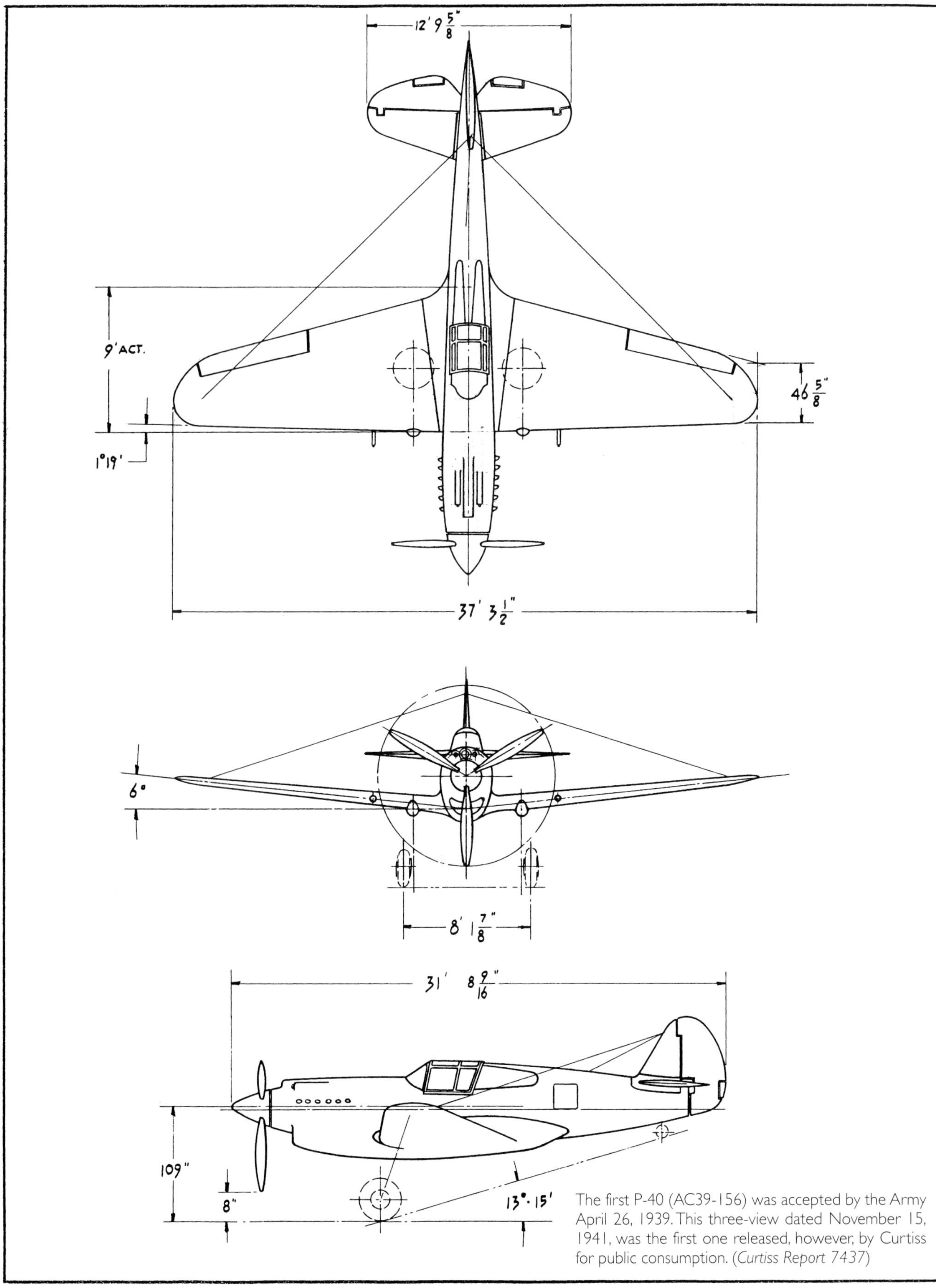

The first P-40 (AC39-156) was accepted by the Army April 26, 1939. This three-view dated November 15, 1941, was the first one released, however, by Curtiss for public consumption. (*Curtiss Report 7437*)

Specifications for the XP-40 in its modified form follow: span, length, and height were 37 feet, three and 1/2 inches, 31 feet, one inch, and 12 feet, four inches. Wing area was 236 square feet.

The powerplant was an Allison V-1710-19 (C13) rated at 1,150hp (Military) at 1,000 feet and 1,000hp at 2,950rpm at 13,500 feet driving a Curtiss Electric three blade propeller. Normal and maximum fuel capacities were 100 gallons and 158 gallons.

Empty weight was 5,417 pounds, normal useful load 843 pounds, normal gross weight 6,260 pounds, and maximum gross weight 6,870 pounds. Normal and maximum useful load to gross weight ratios were 0.135 and 0.21.

Maximum speed was 342mph at 12,200 feet, and maximum cruise speed 299mph, with economical cruise speed 210mph. Landing speed was 72mph. Normal and maximum ranges were 460 miles at 299mph, and 1,180 miles at 210mph with maximum fuel.

Armament was two cowl guns, one .50 caliber, and one .30 caliber, or both .50 caliber, which was the preferred Air Corps combination.

The XP-40 survived far longer than might be expected for the prototype of a major production aircraft, and was not salvaged by the Air Corps until August 31, 1944, by which time it had amassed a total time of 611 hours. The letter requesting that the XP-40 be reclassified as Class 26 (ground instructional airframe) noted that it was "*...in bad condition.*" The aircraft was shipped to the Casey Jones School of Aeronautics in Newark, NJ, where it apparently ended its days. The AAC truly got its money's worth from the XP-40 airframe. Amongst the many tests that it was subjected to, perhaps that which commenced on May 12, 1943, was the most interesting. It was sent to Wright Field for 20 days to test a tracked type landing gear system for use on crude airfields.

By the time P-40 production started at Buffalo, Curtiss was nearly overwhelmed with contracts from both the U.S. armed forces and foreign export orders. As a result, much of the final assembly of America's newest first-line fighter took place outdoors. Notice that two of the aircraft in this crowded ramp shot have engines running, even though the one at right is still unbuttoned. (*Dean Collection*)

The earliest known color image of a "straight" P-40 was taken in 1940 at an open house, featuring this 20th Pursuit Group aircraft beside the monstrous Douglas XB-19. (*Courtesy U.S. Ordnance Co.*)

The P-40s (Model C-39-7)

The Army and Curtiss formally announced the order for production P-40s on April 27, 1939, a bit more than five months before Germany invaded Poland.

The $12,872,398.00 order called for 560 aircraft at a unit cost of $22,929.30, or a total of $12,480,408.00, comprising 524 complete aircraft and 36 as spare parts. Seldom noted, the contract also included one "skeleton" aircraft at $19,489.92, drawings, and a detailed parts list (at .15 cents per square foot!), complete stress analysis and weight data, various manuals and handbooks, and parts catalogs.

Curtiss further modified the production P-40s (no suffix) in the powerplant, landing gear, and armament areas, along with some flush riveting of skins for production. For production, the radiator intake was increased in area, and the lower ducting contained three cooler cores: two outboard for the engine cooling radiator, and the center one for the oil cooler. A new single round inlet was provided atop the cowl near the propeller for carburetor air. In addition, individual exhaust stacks were used. The first three production aircraft were kept in bare aluminum; those coming later were painted in Army olive drab over gray undersurfaces, the first Army aircraft so camouflaged. The initial production P-40 took to the air on April 4, 1940, piloted by H. Lloyd Child. This plane was the first of 200 production P-40s delivered to the U.S. Army, with the first few accepted the next month. The P-40s were operated by three Pursuit Groups, the 31st, 20th, and 8th. They were now armed with two .50 caliber nose guns and two .30 caliber wing guns.

P-40 number 1, MSN 13033 and Army serial number AC39-156, had a base price of $22,921.30, and was accepted by the Army on April 26, 1939. P-40 number 2, MSN 13034 and Army 39-157, was priced at $24,830.59. The 200th P-40, MSN 13232 and AC40-357, was priced as #1, and was delivered October 16, 1940, all according to Curtiss billing records.[118] Of the first 200 aircraft, however, 18 planes were assigned to the U.S. Army, but delivered to the British or Russia under the new Defense Aid program (predecessor to Lend-Lease), these not in any sequence, with delivery dates noted as from July 1 to October 5, 1940. These became some of the little-known P-40Gs (q.v.). Although there have been repeated published reports that some of these aircraft were converted to "reconnaissance" configuration and redesignated as "RP-40s," these have been misrepresentations. The "R" prefix at this juncture did not indicate "Reconnaissance"; instead, it was a prefix to indicate that the aircraft were regarded as obsolescent and second line. Another assertion that has been repeated suggests that the designation P-40A was never formally assigned. This, too, is incorrect. One aircraft, serial 40-326, was so formally designated March 2, 1942 (q.v.).

P-40 airframes and Allison V-1710 engines were not without initial production problems. Temporary limitations on use of engine power were put in place, and in mid-1940 several aircraft were assigned to an accelerated service test program to get bugs worked out as quickly as possible. In October 1940 another interesting test of P-40s took place when two dozen of them from the 8th Pursuit Group were hoisted aboard the aircraft carrier USS *Wasp* and taken off at sea, flying back successfully to Langley Field, Virginia.

In view of the perceived need that prevailed by August 1940 to possibly reinforce, by air, U.S. garrisons in the Caribbean and Latin America, a serious study was initiated at the time by Wright Field that looked at the possibility of installing Edo Model 6560 twin floats on P-40s to expedite such deployments. So far as can be determined no actual installation took place, however.

Finally, it would be naÔve to expect that the introduction of an aircraft system as radical as the P-40 into Army Air Corps line units would proceed without incident. The Commanding Officer of the 20th Pursuit Group at Hamilton Field, CA, none other than (then) Colonel Ira Eaker, reported in a blistering document dated May 9, 1941, addressed to the Chief of Staff, General Headquarters Air Force, on the trauma being experienced by pilots of his command, and this extraordinary document is quoted here in its entirety:

"The P-40 type aircraft with which this Group is equipped is considered by the Group flying personnel to be unsuited for modern combat operations. Exhaustive tests establish that, below 15,000 feet, it is definitely inferior in all tactical respects to the P-36A. The P-36A will out-climb the P-40. The P-40 has so little excess speed over the P-36A that, once committed to combat, any hope of escaping the P-36A by the use of speed differential is useless. The P-40 will not dive away from the P-36A from a 15,000 foot altitude and in following the P-40 in a dive, the P-36A must be throttled back to prevent overshooting its target. It is at a great disadvantage against the P-36A in close combat."

Additionally, both Curtiss and the Army were very concerned by the number of ground loop accidents that were being experienced as the P-40 entered squadron service. So serious and frequent were these that AC39-165 was detailed to NACA Langley between June 18 and July 15, 1940, to evaluate this phenomenon and recommend solutions. Another early P-40 aircraft, AC39-160, was also detailed to NACA between September 3 and December 20, 1940, for flight test comparisons of the aileron characteristics between the service P-36A, the P-40 and, by August 1942, the Supermarine *Spitfire* and Hawker *Hurricane*.

Even with its teething problems and inevitable difficulties associated with entry into service use of a new and radically different design, it is illuminating to visualize the prominence that Curtiss held in fighter aircraft production in the United States in the 12 months of that crucial year 1940. Following is a breakout of all U.S. fighter production, by designation, for 1940.

This USAAC P-40—No.32 of the 33rd Pursuit Squadron, 8th Pursuit Group stationed at Langley Field, Virginia—is making history in this view. This was the first recorded take off of a U.S. Army aircraft (certainly a monoplane) from a carrier, in this instance the USS *Wasp* on October 14, 1940. The pilot was Major Moffett, and note that no flaps were used! (*NARA RG80G #64700*)

This P-40 (No.11 of the 35th Pursuit Group) appears to have a two-tone olive drab scheme, and the gun muzzles protruding from the distinctive fairings are shorter than on earlier aircraft. (*Roger Besecker*)

MODEL	**JAN**	**FEB**	**MAR**	**APR**	**MAY**	**JUN**	**JUL**	**AUG**	**SEP**	**OCT**	**NOV**	**DEC**	**TOTAL 1940**
YP-39	—	—	—	—	—	—	—	—	1	2	—	10	13
H75/P-36	—	29	77	83	76	95	91	14	—	—	—	16	481
H81A, P-40, P-40G	—	—	—	—	11	25	56	104	114	135	168	165	778
YP-37	—	—	—	—	—	—	1	—	—	—	—	—	1
CW-21, CW-21B	—	—	—	—	—	3	—	—	—	6	14	4	27
NA-50/P-64	—	—	—	—	—	—	—	—	—	—	6	—	6
EP-1/P-35A	4	8	12	13	11	—	15	5	11	9	5	9	102
YP-43	—	—	—	—	—	—	—	—	1	—	—	1	2
YFM-1. YFM-1A,YFM-1B	—	—	2	—	—	5	2	—	—	2	—	—	11
YP-38	—	—	—	—	—	—	—	—	1	—	—	—	1
F2A, 239, 339	24	14	—	1	8	22	9	—	6	20	16	40	160
F4F/ G-36A	—	—	—	—	—	—	1	32	29	21	1	19	103
TOTAL	28	51	91	97	106	150	175	155	163	195	210	264	1,685

As can be seen by doing a bit of math, of the 1,685 fighter type aircraft produced during 1940 by all U.S. manufacturers, Curtiss and Curtiss-Wright accounted for not less than 1,287 of them for both domestic and export customers.

The Air Corps, however, had by this point irrevocably staked its immediate future on the in-line, liquid cooled product from Buffalo, for better or for worse and, as they say, the rest is history.

Specifications for the P-40 follow: span, length, and height 37 feet, three and 1/2 inches, 31 feet, eight and 3/4 inches, and 12 feet, four inches. Wing area was 236 square feet, horizontal tail area 48 square feet, and wing airfoils (root) were NACA 2215 and tip NACA 2209. Wing root and tip chords were nine feet and 3.88 feet, and wing incidence +1.0 degree. Stabilizer incidence +2 degrees, wing dihedral 6 degrees, wing aspect ratio 5.89, and twist 0 degrees.

The powerplant was an Allison V-1710-33 (C15) rated 1,090hp (Military) at 3,000rpm at 15,000 feet, and 960hp at 2,600rpm at 12,000 feet. The supercharger gear ratio was .77:1, and the propeller reduction gear ratio was 2:1. The propeller was a Curtiss Electric constant speed model with three aluminum blades in 11 feet diameter, with blade high and low angles of 24 degrees and 49 degrees, respectively.

Images of early series P-40s in the war years are rare. Here, P-40 AC39-280 sports the AVG popularized shark's mouth, seemingly tailor made for the P-40, and an unidentified unit insignia on the rear fuselage. This aircraft suffered three accidents during its career, being initially assigned to Hamilton Field, California, and later Everett Field, Washington, and finally Victoria Field and Randolph Field, Texas. Incredibly, it survived to be scrapped in May 1945. (*Dean Collection*)

As they were replaced by later variants, early series P-40s, including in this view what was probably AC39-165, were detailed to various test duties. Photographed at NACA Langley July 6, 1940, this aircraft has large leading edge "blisters" installed, although the nature of these installations has not been located. (*NACA 20422*)

Weights for P-40 number 5 were: (this plane was 66 pounds under guaranteed empty weight): empty weight 5,367 pounds, consisting of 2,453 pounds of airframe, 2,387 pounds of powerplant (including 1,345 pounds of installed V-1710 engine), and 527 pounds of fixed equipment. Normal useful load was 1,440 pounds, consisting of a 200 pound pilot, 720 pounds (120 gallons) of fuel, 135 pounds (18 gallons) of oil, 365 pounds of armament (2 .50 caliber guns with 400 rounds of ammunition, and 2 .30 caliber guns with 1,000 rounds of ammunition), and a 20 pound oxygen cylinder. Normal gross weight was 6,807 pounds. The maximum useful load with 1,086 pounds (181 gallons) of fuel was 1,806 pounds, giving a maximum gross weight of 7,173 pounds. Normal and maximum wing loadings were 28.84 and 30.39psf, and normal and maximum power loadings were 6.24 and 6.58 pounds per horse power. Normal and maximum useful to gross weight ratios were 0.21 and 0.251.

Maximum speed was 357mph at 15,000 feet, and maximum cruise speed was 277mph. Landing speed was 80mph. Service and absolute ceilings were 32,750 feet and 33,800 feet, respectively. Climb in one minute was 3,080 feet, and time to 15,000 feet was 5.3 minutes. Normal range was 650 miles, 950 miles at 250mph, and 1,400 miles at 181mph at maximum gross weight.

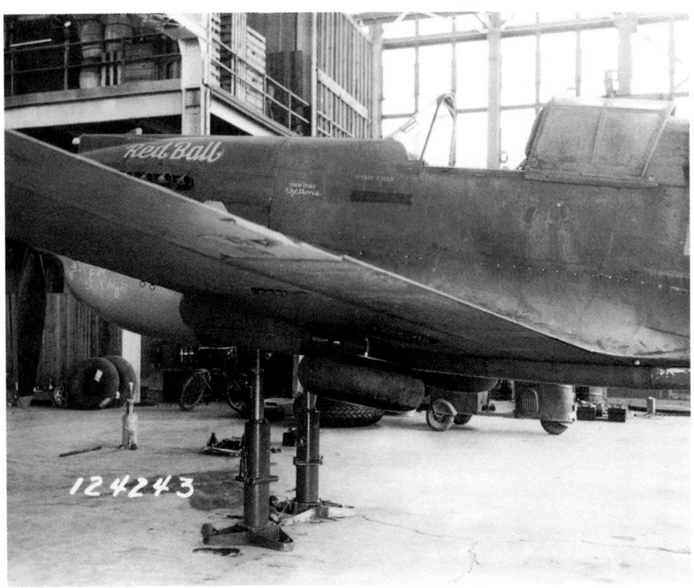

This P-40 (AC40-3020, by September 14, 1943, had been reclassified as an RP-40, indicating second-line, restricted use) nicknamed *Red Ball*, and was engaged in tests of a unique dual-wheel undercarriage installation at Spence Field. Her Crew Chief was S/Sgt. Parris. Note that the inboard wheels have no tread. This aircraft spent nearly its entire service life at Hamilton Field, California, and suffered three accidents until assigned to Wright Field as Class 26. (*Wright Field 124243 and 124241*)

These first two production batches of basic P-40s, only 200 of which were actually completed as such (AC39-156 to 39-289 and AC40-292 to 40-357, MSNs 13033 to 13232), have received little attention. In September 1940, the remaining 324 aircraft of the originally configured order were deferred so that Curtiss could expedite the delivery of the first large block of 140 French-ordered H81As. Of the first batch (39-156 to 39-289), at least 46 were lost to accidents in service, while 48 ended up classified as Class 26 airframes (instructional airframes). One (AC39-159) had the distinction of being exhibited at the New York World's Fair in June 1940, and another (AC39-165) went to NACA Langley for intensive tests June 2, 1940. One other, interestingly (AC40-324), was assigned for the exclusive use of Colonel Jimmie Doolittle effective February 24, 1942.

The last RP-40 in the Army Air Force's inventory was AC39-280, last assigned to Victoria, Texas, where it was scrapped in May 1945 with a total of 735 hours on the airframe. Of the second batch (AC40-292 to 40-357), 21 were lost to accidents, and 21 also ended up as Class 26 airframes.

The next-to-last RP-40 in the inventory, however (AC40-302), which had amassed 1,078 hours total time by May 16, 1944, although recommended to go to Class 26 status (instructional airframe), was actually transferred to the Public Relation staff at Wright Field, OH, which promptly put the airframe on a tour of six Ohio cities to aid in Women's Army Corps (WAC) recruiting, specifically for service at the Materiel Command. The final two displays were in Cincinnati, Ohio, and Wheeling, West Virgnia.

Curtiss P-40A

As noted earlier, a single P-40 was redesignated as P-40A on March 2, 1942, while stationed at Bolling Field, DC (AC40-326). Most sources attribute this redesignation of a single airframe to the fact that it was configured to carry a camera, but this has eluded verification to date. It became RP-40A, and later served at both Orlando Army Air Field, FL, and Maxwell Field, AL, but was transferred to Class 26 on October 13, 1942.

Curtiss P-40G

After initial production as P-40s, not fewer than 46 aircraft were taken from initial service or repossessed from British shipments and updated to make them combat-worthy, and redesignated as P-40Gs. Most of these conversions took place between August 14, 1941, and September 25, 1941.[119]

Changes included armament and armor additions to bring them up to near a P-40C standard, except for the ability to carry a belly fuel drop tank. Wings of the type for export H81A-2 aircraft incorporating four .30 caliber guns, two on each side, were employed. Indeed, one AAC document dated September 10, 1941, stated that the "standard" P-40 wings were replaced with *Tomahawk* wings, and one was flown to Wright Field to determine whether or not the change affected the functioning of the gunnery equipment. These tests were followed by extensive gunnery trials at Selfridge Field, MI, with 40-338, possibly the same aircraft flown to Wright Field. Armor plate, a bullet proof windshield, and self sealing fuel tanks were added, along with other lesser modifications, including elimination of gun round counters. All this added over 500 pounds to the gross weight of the fighter.

At least 21 of these P-40Gs were exported to England, and some then on to Russia under Defense Aid.[120] Interestingly, of those designated for Defense Aid, at least three were returned to USAAC custody before departing and, of these, two received "new" Air Corps serials, as apparently the original serials had been stricken from the Air Corps books as going to a foreign user. These were 39-182 (became 42-14269) and 40-338 (became 42-14261). Most others that survived were transferred to Class 26 (ground instructional airframes), although several were specifically assigned to coastal patrol duty early in the war. One was returned to Curtiss October 31, 1941, for unspecified duties. At least four were redesignated

Photographs of genuine and poorly documented P-40Gs have rarely surfaced. This image, taken at the Russian Bureau of New Technologies at the Zhukovsky aerodrome, reveals a most interesting lineup, consisting of a Bell P-39D at left, a North American P-51B center, and a Curtiss P-40G at right—all still bearing their USAAC markings. (*via Hans-Heri Stapfer*)

back to straight P-40s late in their careers. The designation P-40G was used because the D, E, and F variants of the P-40 were already in being at the time, as the F model first flew in June 1941.

The last P-40G (39-288, recovered from Defense Aid) was stricken from the AAF inventory to Class 26 at March Field on March 12, 1944.

These redesignations of early P-40s were not the end of the P-40G story, however. AAF Individual Aircraft Record Cards confirm that at least 17 of these same aircraft were issued "new" USAAF serials in the range 42-14262 to 42-14281, but of these, there were no cards for 42-14273, 42-14275, 42-14276, 42-14279, and 42-14280, which is inexplicable. This range of Army serials had originally been issued for a batch of P-40L-30-CUs that were cancelled. The earliest of these was picked up on the Air Corps budget on December 26, 1941, suggesting that the Japanese attack may have precipitated a rush order to Curtiss for additional aircraft, possibly some that had been laid down for France. To add to the confusion, of these 17 aircraft, two (42-14265 and 42-14272) were redesignated as "straight" P-40s on June 2, 1942, and July 26, 1942, respectively, five were wrecked in accidents, and eight went to Class 26.

These aircraft obviously confound any attempt to establish a grand total for all P-40 variants built and, what is worse, the Manufacturers Serial Numbers for these aircraft remain, in most instances, unknown.

Curtiss P-40B

It became clear in 1940 that a standard combat worthy version of the P-40 for both the U.S. Army and Britain was required where only minor equipment differences would be involved. A September 1940 meeting at Curtiss of the Joint Aircraft Committee (JAC) provided agreement wherein the U.S. version would be the P-40B (Curtiss Specification 98-610-5A), and the export version the H81A-2, with the British designation being *Tomahawk IIA*. Suitability for modern combat meant self sealing fuel tanks and pilot armor protection.

In September 1940, the U.S. Army ordered 131 P-40Bs with a Curtiss unit price of $33,439, and these gained AAC serials 41-5205 to 41-5304 and 41-13297 to 41-13327 (MSNs 15973 to 16103). Although most sources state that deliveries of this version commenced in January 1941, this is incorrect, since the first aircraft (41-5205) wasn't formally accepted from Curtiss until May 5, 1941, after an initial test flight by H. Lloyd Child of Curtiss on March 13th.[121] Actually service delivery thus commenced in March 1941. These planes were equipped with two .50 caliber M-2 cowl guns with a total of 760 rounds, and four .30 caliber M-2 wing guns with 1,960 rounds total. In addition, fuel tanks were externally self sealed, and windshield armor glass was provided, along with 93 pounds of armor plate, a 9.5 mm thick plate ahead of the pilot, a 9.5 mm upper plate aft of the pilot, and a lower aft plate 7.5 mm thick.

Characteristics of the P-40B follow: span and height were 37 feet, three and 1/2 inches, and eight feet, two inches. Wing area was 236 square feet, and wheel treads eight feet, two inches.

The powerplant was an Allison V-1710-C15 (-33), rated at 1,090hp (Military) at 3,000rpm at 15,000 feet, and 960hp (Normal) at 2,600rpm at 12,600 feet. The single stage, single speed mechanical supercharger impeller was geared 8.77:1, and propeller reduction gear ratio was 2:1. The propeller was a Curtiss Electric constant speed model with three blades in 11 feet diameter, and low and high blade angles of 24.5 and 54.5 degrees, respectively. Fuel capacity was 120 gallons normal and 160 gallons maximum. There was no external fuel tank. Oil capacity was 16.5 gallons.

The weights for P-40B number 11 were: empty weight 5,615 pounds (consisting of airframe 2,514 pounds, powerplant 2,517 pounds, and fixed equipment 584 pounds). Normal useful load was 1,737 pounds (consisting of a 200 pound pilot, 720 pounds of fuel, 124 pounds of oil, 600 pounds of armament, and 93 pounds of armor). Normal gross weight was 7,352 pounds. Alternate useful load

The P-40B was the first true combat-ready variant of the series to reach Air Corps units in significant numbers. This production line view reveals the curious blue coating used to protect the duralumin surface during manufacture. The P-40B was the first true six-gun fighter in the U.S. inventory. (*The Museum of Flight*)

As Curtiss struggled to cope with the seemingly endless rush of orders for domestic and foreign customers, the Buffalo plants went on an overtime schedule, often working seven days a week, around the clock. Here, warmly dressed assembly crews test the fresh mating of a V-1710 to a still unfinished airframe in the wee hours. (*Dean Collection*)

with extra internal fuel was 2,009 pounds, and alternate gross weight was 7,624 pounds. Normal wing and power loadings were 31.15psf and 6.74 pounds per horse power. Normal useful load to gross weight ratio was 0.236.

For performance, maximum speed was 352mph at 15,000 feet at 1090hp. High cruise speed was 273mph, and landing speed 80mph. Initial climb rate was 2,860fpm, and time to climb to 15,000 feet was 5.1 minutes. Takeoff over a 50 foot obstacle was 1,350 feet, and landing over the same obstacle was 1,400 feet. Service ceiling was 32,400 feet, and ranges were 1,230 miles at 188mph at 5,000 feet with 160 gallons of fuel, 940 miles at 280mph at 15,000 feet with 160 gallons of fuel, and 730 miles at 280mph at 15,000 feet with 120 gallons of fuel. Demonstration dive speed was 485mph.

Curtiss P-40B fighters were sorely needed for the defense of U.S. bases overseas. It was initially considered that some would be delivered to Midway and Wake Islands in the Pacific in late November via aircraft carrier, but the Navy reminded the planners the planes would be stuck there with no means of return, because they could not land back on a carrier. Most P-40Bs were carrier-delivered and flown off to Wheeler Field in Hawaii, and 55 were on hand there at the end of April 1941 with the 15th and 18th Pursuit Groups. Eventually, 93 P-40Bs were transferred to Hawaii, the first of which (41-5206) arrived March 25, 1941. A total of 30[122] were shipped by freighter to the Philippines for the 20th Pursuit Squadron at Clark Field, arriving May 16, 1941, and six P-40Bs were among the fighters shipped to the Panama Canal Zone, the above account-

These P-40Bs—the one on left already wearing USAAC olive drab, while the one in the foreground still awaits open-air installation of key cowling panels and gun fairings in natural and anodized metal—reflect the urgency with which Curtiss hustled to meet the demand for their newest pursuit. (*Dean Collection*)

As Curtiss employees gained experience on the line, the apparently chaotic scene in the final assembly areas became the norm. This October 1941 view shows a mix of British Commonwealth *Tomahawks*, late P-40Bs, and early P-40Cs. (*Curtiss #15209 via Harold Andrews*)

As delivery pressures mounted, a shortage of both service and contract pilots to fly the aircraft to their destinations resulted in resorting to trucking completed P-40Bs to USAAC stations within a reasonable distance of Buffalo. Once unloaded, it was simply a matter of mating the wings to the fuselage. The aircraft were test-flown prior to shipment at Buffalo. (*The Museum of Flight*)

P-40Bs were issued to nearly every one of the premier USAAC pursuit groups in existence as of delivery. No.54 was assigned to the 8th Pursuit Group at Langley Field, Virginia, and the squadron insignia, probably the 33rd Pursuit, is not yet complete. The fuselage surface already shows signs of heavy use in this 1941 view. (*via Art Krieger*)

P-40Bs were amongst the first modern USAAC pursuit aircraft dispatched in significant numbers to America's distant overseas bastions, including the Philippines, Hawaii, Puerto Rico, and the Panama Canal Zone. This 16th Pursuit Group aircraft (No.61) shows evidence of an auxiliary fuel tank installation and tropically eroded camouflage. The Sixth Air Force retained some P-40Bs until the end of the war. (*Jim Dias*)

ing for practically all production. It is interesting to note that two of the P-40Bs assigned to the Sixth Air Force in the Panama Canal Zone region were formally redesignated as P-40Cs as early as December 4, 1942, these having been 41-5283 and 41-13327.

In the Japanese attack on Hawaii, 37 P-40B aircraft were either destroyed or damaged, with only 25 in commission after the attack. At least 25 of the Hawaiian based P-40Bs were lost in accidents between the time of initial assignment and their retirement. After the initial Japanese attack on Clark Field in the Philippines little more than a half dozen survived, though a few managed to get into the air and shot down four Japanese aircraft. The remaining P-40Bs were all lost by April 1942.

The very few remaining P-40B types on strength were put in the restricted category as RP-40Bs in late 1942, as later aircraft came into use to replace them as first line types.

Curtiss P-40C

The original contract of Curtiss with the U.S. Army for the P-40 type was completed by the manufacture of 193 P-40C (Curtiss Specification 98-610-11) versions, with delivery from March 31, 1941, through May 20, 1941. The unit price was $33,429.71. First flight of this model took place on April 10, 1941. Interestingly, one Curtiss billing sheet reported a total of only 192 aircraft. These aircraft received USAAC serials AC41-13328 to AC41-13520 (MSN 16104 to 16296). In fact, these aircraft had been ordered as P-40Bs on AC-15802, but were modified under Change Order No.8 and redesignated as P-40Cs.

The P-40C was thus very like the P-40B, the major changes being a redesigned fuel system with internal self sealing of the fuel tanks in place of the external sealing of the P-40B, new radios, and the capability of carrying an external fuel tank under the belly, probably the only external distinguishing feature with respect to the B model. The Curtiss designation for the P-40C was H81B.

Some references indicate that 38 P-40C aircraft were shipped to Russia, and 10 went to Britain's RAF. However, this is an oversimplification of what actually happened. In fact, the Air Corps had decided, starting July 20, 1941, to reinforce the Army defenses in the Caribbean, after the fall of France, and dispatched no less than 41 P-40Cs to Borinquen Field, Puerto Rico, for assignment to the 35th Pursuit Squadron of the 36th Pursuit Group, along with some P-40Bs. There at least seven of these were wrecked. Nearly all of the surviving 34 aircraft were returned to Curtiss in Buffalo in September 1941, refurbished, crated, and shipped to Russia, together with 27 others as brand new aircraft, which had departed as early as June 11, 1941. Like the P-40Gs that went to Russia described elsewhere, these aircraft were covered by Curtiss Sales Order 7198. Therefore, a total of at least 61 P-40Cs went to Russia.[123] Some of these may have been offset, enroute, to the British. Of the P-40Cs bound for Russia, the first 30 (at least) received special treatment by Curtiss at Buffalo before shipment. Curtiss was instructed to obliterate all external markings and insignia, paint the props identical to those on the *Kittyhawk* series, install ring-and-bead gun sights, and install rear view mirrors on each aircraft. An additional 14 P-40Cs were to be similarly treated.

After Curtiss had completed 131 P-40Bs, the remainder of most of the initial contract for 193 additional aircraft were completed as P-40Cs. The P-40C was armored, had self-sealing fuel tanks, a centerline drop tank (retrofitted to some P-40Bs), and was rather heavier, maximum speed on a good day falling to 340mph. The AAC serial number was probably painted on the vertical fin of this aircraft, but has been carefully airbrushed out by the censor in this publicity still. (*Curtiss*)

Factory fresh, this P-40C poses for the camera while receiving fuel, ostensibly for its delivery flight to an operational unit. The centerline drop tank was first installed as standard equipment of the "C" variant. Note the highly polished prop blades and taped over wing gun ports (if installed, the .30 caliber gun barrels would have been evident) and cartridge chutes. The nose guns are not installed either. (*Curtiss*)

U.S. forces defending the Panama Canal received 80 P-40Cs, with the first (41-13335) arriving at Albrook Field, Canal Zone, on July 14, 1941. By the end of their service in Panama, 32 had been lost to accidents in the difficult conditions there. Then, on July 25, 1941, 32 P-40Cs were hoisted aboard the aircraft carrier *Wasp*, these from the 33rd Pursuit Squadron of the 8th Pursuit Group, and all aircraft were flown off the carrier to Iceland for defense purposes by August 30th. This squadron stayed in Iceland for the duration of the European war, and nine were lost to accidents there. At least 13 P-40Cs got to Hawaii by April 26, 1941 (the first was 41-13328, the first P-40C), and the 15th and 18th Pursuit Groups had 13 C models to go along with their P-40Bs. At least four were lost during the Japanese attack, and four others were lost to accidents during their assignment in the islands. No C models went to the Philippines. Of the remaining P-40Cs, all remained in the Continental United States, with nine lost to accidents, and not less than 16 going to Class 26 instructional airframes.

On December 7, 1941, when the Japanese attacked Pearl Harbor, the 13 P-40C fighters on hand were assigned as follows: three to the 19th Pursuit Squadron, seven to the 41st, two to the 47th, and one to the 5th Pursuit Squadron. The rest of the P-40s in the islands were B models. Nine of the P-40Cs were still on hand after the air raids, but only two were in useable condition. Two P-40Cs of the 47th Pursuit Squadron at Haleiwa managed to get into the air, and accounted for four Japanese aircraft. The P-40Cs at Bellows Field had no luck at all; two of these were shot down in takeoff attempts, and the remaining planes were destroyed on the ground.

P-40C AC41-13385 was loaned to the Armament Laboratory at Wright Field for a week in September 1941 for an interesting experiment. The aircraft was fitted with a device in its tail for holding and controlling a special flare capable of propelling small pyrotechnic pellets, with a view towards assessing the feasibility of using this method for disengaging an enemy in pursuit!

Characteristics of the P-40C follow: span, length, and height 37 feet, three and 1/2 inches, 31 feet, nine inches, and 12 feet, four inches. Wing area was 236 square feet, and wing dihedral 6 degrees. Wheel tread was 8 feet 2 inches.

The powerplant was an Allison V-1710-33, rated at 1,040hp for takeoff, 1,040hp (Military) at 3,000rpm at 14,300 feet, and 930hp (Normal) at 3,000rpm at 12,600 feet. Single stage supercharger impeller was geared 8.77:1, and propeller reduction gear ratio was 2:1. The Curtiss Electric constant speed propeller was 11 feet in diameter, and blade angles were 24.5 degrees low and 54.5 degrees high. Internal fuel capacity was 134 gallons, and maximum fuel, including external tankage, was 186 gallons.

Weights for the #1 P-40C were: empty weight 5,767 pounds, composed of airframe 1,494 pounds, powerplant groups 2,689 pounds, and fixed equipment 584 pounds. Normal useful load totaled 1,737 pounds, comprised of a 200 pound pilot, 720 pounds (120 gallons) of fuel, 124 pounds of oil (16.5 gallons), 600 pounds of armament, and 93 pounds of armor plate. Gross weight was thus 7,504 pounds. The alternate useful load consisted of fuel 1,185 pounds (including external belly tank with 52 gallons of fuel), flares totaling 33 pounds, and a mooring kit of 11 pounds for a total of 2,246 pounds, and an alternate gross weight of 8,013 pounds. Normal and alternate wing loadings were 31.8 and 33.95psf, and normal and alternate power loading were 7.22 and 7 70 pounds per horse power. Normal and alternate useful load to gross weight ratios were 0.231 and 0.28.

Maximum speed was 345mph at 15,000 feet, cruise speed 270mph, and landing speed 86mph. Sea level climb was 2,690fpm, and service and absolute ceilings were 29,500 feet and 30,500 feet,

By the time production had switched to the P-40C, Curtiss employees in final assembly accepted the apparently chaotic conditions as the norm. The nearest aircraft, chalked with number 285 on the vertical fin, identifies herself as P-40C 41-13481. This aircraft was assigned to the Sixth Air Force at Albrook Field, Canal Zone, and ended her days a long way from Buffalo with the 16th Fighter Group at Salinas, Ecuador (APO 661), when Major Marion Foster wrecked her in a landing accident. (*Curtiss*)

respectively. Ranges were 800 miles at 260mph at 15,000 feet, and 1,250 miles at 195mph at 5,000 feet.

Armament consisted of two .50 caliber cowl synchronized guns with 380 rounds per gun, and four .30 caliber wing machine guns with 490 rounds per gun.

Export Curtiss H81s

Curtiss produced far more export H81 variants of the early type than of early P-40 aircraft for the U.S. Army. These fighters were produced for France (where they were to have been designated H81-C1), England, and China, but other countries also ended up with the type through transfers from British orders. Many were on cash-and-carry contracts before the Lend-Lease Program went into effect.

For a time, the production of the U.S. Army P-40 was held up to allow export orders to be filled; these planes were called *Tomahawks* by the British, and there were three basic variants: the 81-A/81A-1[124], 81A-2, and 81A-3, respectively called *Tomahawk I*—the equivalent of the P-40—*Tomahawk IIA*, like the P-40B, and *Tomahawk IIB*, essentially as the P-40C.

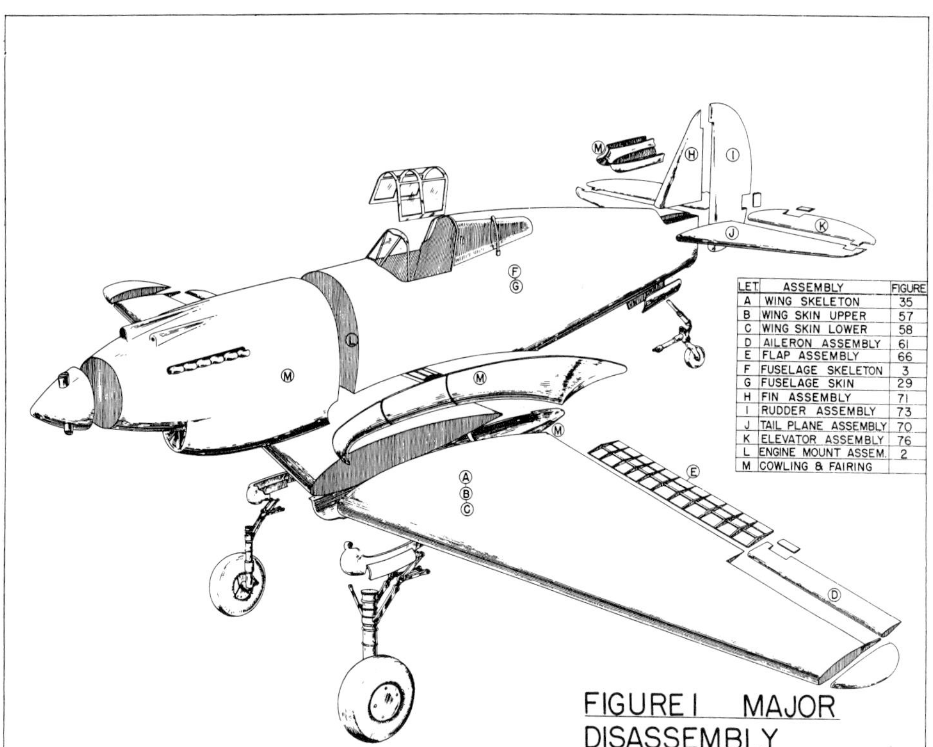

As Curtiss rolled out the large order for Army Air Corps P-40Bs and P-40Cs, large orders for export *Hawk 81A*, *H-81A-1*, and *H81A-2* variants were being produced alongside them. This exploded view shows the major component assemblies of these export variants. (*Curtiss*)

Although France placed an order for no less than 280 *H81As* in early October 1939, prior commitments precluded Curtiss from fulfilling the order before it was too late, and the aircraft eventually went to the British. One aircraft, bearing the French designation H81-C1, did receive French markings at Buffalo, however, including an oddly truncated anti-glare panel ahead of the windscreen. This is almost certainly serial number 14446 as she appeared in mid-June 1940. Inexplicably, the entry for this aircraft is stricken through in the Curtiss Billing Book. (*Curtiss*)

A total of 1,183 of these export aircraft were produced, this according to Curtiss billing records. Some sources cite 1,180, but the difference can be accounted for in the records of three aircraft delivered to "airport," probably locally for test, and not exported, since no price or delivery date is cited for one each H81A, H81A-1, and H81A-2. All of these fighters were delivered between September 18, 1940, and August 21, 1941. Those for China (the 100 American Volunteer Group/*Flying Tigers* aircraft, broken out from British orders) were delivered between January 15 and March 13, 1941. Unit prices for these fighters varied between $35,841 and $38,888. Planes received by the British were a mix of *Tomahawk I*, *IIA*, and *IIB*; those going to the AVG in China are listed as H81A-2 (P-40B equivalent, although some sources claim, incorrectly, that these aircraft were designated H81A-3).

The French ordered 230 81A versions[125] as early as October 9, 1939, equipped with French radios and instruments, throttle movements in reverse of U.S. sense, and with provisions for French armament to be installed. First flight of a French aircraft took place only on June 6, 1940, and thus no French aircraft could be delivered prior to the French collapse that year. In the meantime, the Anglo-French Purchasing Commission had been established, and had organized a combined program of new purchases. Among these was the placement of Letters of Intent for the purchase of a further 500 *Hawk 81As*. The intended allocation was for 285 aircraft to Britain and 215 to France. With the collapse of France in June 1940, all French contracts and Letters of Intent were assumed by the British. As a result, the first 100 of these aircraft that came off the production line were effectively transferred to British Contract F-273 (MSNs 14446 to 14545, which became *Tomahawk Is*, RAF serials AH741 to AH840). As these aircraft—P-40 equivalents—had no self sealing fuel tanks or pilot armor, they were not considered combat worthy. Some were used in an Army cooperation role for a time, but later were placed in reserve, or used as instructional airframes. Armament, according to Curtiss, for part of the order (apparently the former French aircraft) consisted of two synchronized Colt .50 caliber guns and four British Browning .303 caliber wing guns, while others had two Colt .50 caliber synchronized guns and four Colt .30 caliber wing guns.

Characteristics of the 81A/81A-1 aircraft were essentially the same as those for the P-40.

The H81A-2 *Tomahawk IIA* ordered by the British as the result of the September 1940 meeting of the Joint Aircraft Committee at Curtiss in Buffalo to effect maximum possible standardization was considered combat worthy, but not for the European Theatre. This determination has often been repeated, and has been almost universally accepted without question. Your scribes decided to investigate the genesis of this conclusion.

As early as February 25, 1941, the Military Air Attaché of the U.S. in Britain, Brigadier General Martin F. Scanlon, met with the British Deputy Chief of Air Staff to specifically learn how the *Tomahawk* was fairing in RAF service, amongst other topics. The British official quoted to Scanlon the substance of a telegram that the Ministry had sent to their forces in the Middle East which, essentially, gave RAF officials there the Ministry's opinion of the aircraft series thus far received. As this is a most revealing document, the essential components are quoted in full as follows:

"We have been trying out some non-operational Tomahawks *(i.e., lacking some operational equipment) in a non-operational squadron, to see how they compare with our own fighters. The reports so far received indicate that the aircraft has no vices on the ground or in the air. The pilots find it easy and responsive, while the visibility from the operational point of view is excellent. It is a very good aircraft for formation flying, and seems to have no difficulty in keeping up with some of our most modern fighters, and even to have a bit of speed in hand. It has a better climb than, for instance, the* Spitfire I, *and a high maneuverability, which renders it an excellent aerobatic aircraft. We are taking steps to have the fully modified operational type cleared and tried in action as soon as possible, and we are confident that it will give an excellent account of itself, as soon as certain difficulties with the armament, of which you are aware, have been straightened out."*

Three months later, a U.S. Military Intelligence Division-Office of Naval Intelligence (MID-ONI) report dated May 21, 1941, quoting from British sources, stated that "*...the* Tomahawk *is faster, climbs better and is more maneuverable than the Hurricane*."

That same month (May 1941), none other than Dr. Don R. Berlin, in company with G. B. Clark and Rod Molloy, traveled to England to conduct their own investigation into the entry of the Curtiss aircraft into service. Their detailed report included a visit to an RAF *Tomahawk* unit stationed at Baginton, Coventry, and commanded by a Squadron Leader Morris at the time. This was 403 Squadron, RCAF, which had formed at Baginton on March 1, 1941. In meeting with the RAF officer, they requested that he be perfectly frank with them regarding the relative merits of the aircraft, as they very much wanted to institute any corrective actions immediately. Squadron Leader Morris obliged them by admitting that, at first, the *Tomahawk* had not been liked, mainly because of the many differences that the crews found between the American aircraft and those they had been used to, which was not surprising. He continued, however, by saying that the unit had soon gotten used to these differences, and that they liked them very much indeed, although they still preferred the British brake system (brake handle, as opposed to the *Tomahawk's* toe brakes). He further confided the flying characteristics of the aircraft were "*...as good as the Hurricane I but not quite as good as the Spitfire I...*" and that "*...the* Tomahawk *could out-maneuver either of the other airplanes*." Features that the RAF pilots did not like included the lack of an automatic boost control for the engine, and the need to watch the manifold pressure gauge; they had also had some difficulty with ground loops when they first received the Curtiss fighters, but with revised training, this problem all but ceased. They also craved armor plate aft of the fuselage fuel and oil tanks, and thought that the landing gear retraction operation took too long.

Barely two months later, none other than Army Air Corps Lt. Hubert Zemke, seconded at the time with the RAF station Old Sarum, Wilts., reported on July 28, 1941, in great detail on the RAF experience on the type to that date. He very candidly observed that, since the P-40 variants had arrived in the UK, a vain attempt had been made to bring them into operational service. At first, the RAF had fully intended to use them as first-line fighters, but rated the *Tomahawks* inferior on the following detailed grounds:

(1) The fire power, compared to the standard eight-gun armament of most RAF fighters at the time, was rated as considerably less. However, it should be noted that this was largely because the RAF had been having endless trouble adapting to the .50 caliber Colt machine guns with which the aircraft were equipped, and thus were left with only the rifle caliber guns (two or four, depending on the Mark). Had the .50 caliber guns been fully accepted and operational, this critical judgment might have been very different, and the killing power and rate of fire of those two guns might have been devastating to the relatively low flying German bombers and intruders.
(2) High altitude performance was lacking and, at home, the RAF fighter force was still very much an interceptor organization—and had to be able to engage the *Luftwaffe* at those altitudes.
(3) In a test against the *Hurricane Mk.I*, the *Tomahawk*, however, was officially found to have a superior climb rate to 20,000 feet (although thereafter it fell away from the *Hurricane*); it had a 20mph superior speed at 18,000 feet, and 30mph at 13,000 feet; maneuverability was very close, with a slight edge given the *Tomahawk* and, finally, the *Tomahawk* readily out-dived the *Hurricane*.

Thus, the RAF officially acknowledged that the *Tomahawk* was superior at low altitudes than the *Hurricane Mk.I*, save for fire power, which was problematical, and based solely on the poor adaptability of the RAF to these large caliber guns, with which they had little or no experience.

A factory-fresh *Tomahawk I* in full RAF European style camouflage and markings. Had the British been able to overcome armament problems with these aircraft, the oft-repeated legend that they were found "*...unsuitable for European conditions*" might never have been coined. (Curtiss)

To satisfy himself, Zemke asked if he could engage in a mock dog fight with a skilled RAF pilot in a *Hurricane Mk.I*. This took place at Debden on June 27, 1941, and Zemke concluded that he found the RAF figures "*...somewhat high, though the Tomahawk airplane did have the advantage*." However, he also admitted that his impromptu test did not go over 10,000 feet, and acknowledged that, since at that time most of the aerial combats were being fought at considerably higher altitudes, that the *Tomahawk* was "*...definitely not up to the standards of British line fighters at altitudes above 15,000 feet or the British standards in fire power*." Thus, it would appear the gross conclusions reached about the suitability of the aircraft for "European operations" at the time are upheld, although with the caveat that the RAF wisely recognized the utility of the aircraft below 15,000 feet, and quickly dispatched the majority of them to North Africa, where they excelled. When Zemke arrived in the UK there were at least 515 *Tomahawks* in the home islands, but by the middle of June 1941, this had dwindled rapidly to 280, as many were shipped to Africa and Russia.

These aircraft, taken all together, were the result of a combination of the earlier Letter of Intent, with the outstanding French contract for 130 H81A-2s to cover no less than 630 aircraft, and was initially designated as Contract F-1328. However, by the time it was signed, it had become Contract A-84, the designation of an earlier British contract drafted in 1939, that had been in abeyance while the Anglo-French Commission was arranging a combined procurement program. The aircraft that resulted were Curtiss MSNs 14091 to 14220 (RAF AH841 to AH970), and MSN 14582 and onwards (RAF AH971 to AH880, all *Tomahawk Is* as well). Production then continued from RAF serial AH881 to AH990 as *Tomahawk IIAs*. They incorporated armor, self sealing fuel tanks, British radios, two .50 caliber cowl guns, and four Colt .303 caliber wing guns. About two dozen of these were transferred to Russia,[126] while the others were used for training.

With deliveries starting in late 1940, the H81A-3, or *Tomahawk IIB*, was the final version of the early export P-40 type. RAF serials commenced from AH991, together with RAF serials AH971 to AH999 and AK100 to AK570 which, together with the earlier *Tomahawk IIAs*, made up the 730 aircraft. There is confusion as to the Curtiss MSNs of the *IIBs*. Logically, they might have been expected to run from 14582 to 15081, but available records have not

Of the 100 *H81A-2s* offset on a priority basis for specific delivery to the legendary American Volunteer Group (AVG) fighting for China, only 99 were actually erected—one having been damaged during off-shipping. These two views show the last of these, and the rather curious camouflage pattern shortly after erection—and the fact that the primary Chinese serial number (P-8191) had also been painted on at this early stage. (*San Diego Aerospace Museum*)

Something of a mystery aircraft, this British *Tomahawk*, donated to the Empire by the contractors who built Camp Edwards on Cape Cod, Massachusetts, had the name of the donors and recipient painted on a quasi-British style roundel in rather large size on the rear fuselage. The stain aft of the cockpit is unexplained as well. (*Howard Levy*)

been located to confirm this. Further orders were placed by the extension of Contract A-84, first for a further 150 aircraft (RAF AM370 to AM519), and then 300 more (AN218 to AN517[127]). Corresponding to the U.S. P-40C, the *IIB* had a completely revised fuel system with internally self sealing tanks, and the capability of carrying in addition an external centerline tank of 52 gallon capacity, and had U.S. made .30 caliber wing guns. This version equipped RAF Army Cooperation home squadrons for a time, and about three hundred were sent to fight in the North African desert war with RAF, RAAF, RNZAF, South African Air Force, and the Royal Egyptian Air Force (which received 20) units in the spring of 1941. They served with distinction through 1941 and beyond, and were particularly effective against most Italian aircraft, but less so against the German Bf-109s. The shark mouths painted on some *Tomahawks* originated with RAF and RAAF squadrons in the desert war. A total of at least 171 mixed *Tomahawk IIA* and *IIB* variants were dispatched to Russia as well, with the first 48 of these having arrived by September 1, 1941. Once again, none other than Lt. Hubert Zemke, in company with Lt. John R. Alison and five RAF mechanics, was dispatched to northern Russia to oversee the arrival, erection, and conversion of Russian crews to these aircraft, which was accomplished under extremely trying conditions. These were the so-called "pre-Protocol" aircraft; that is, they were delivered on Prime Minister Winston Churchill's personal authority prior to the first Anglo-American aid Protocol, which came into effect late in 1941. Subsequently, RAF serials AN469 to AN517, inclusive, were shipped direct from Curtiss to Russia as part of the same arrangement. These deliveries were accounted for as 190 "pre-Protocol" and 30 "1st Protocol" aircraft and, consequently, never served a day with the RAF. Requisition BSC-1016, which came after the German invasion of Russia, were also shipped to Russia on British instructions "pre-Protocol." These had in fact been packed, ready to sail from Baltimore, when the invasion of Yugoslavia took place. They were USAAC serials 41-13389, -13390, 13396 to -13401, -13406, and -13407.

At least four early *Tomahawk* series aircraft also found their way into service with the Royal Canadian Air Force (AH793, AH840, AH774, and AH938), becoming A314 to A317 in the RCAF's ground instructional airframe serial series. These had been damaged during shipment from the UK to Takoradi, West Africa, and were trans-shipped back across the Atlantic once again (there was lots of deck space going west) back to the U.S., where the RCAF somehow claimed them.

Mr. C. B. Williams, a Curtiss Service Representative, in a very candid and detailed report of his visit to England between Novem-

Most of the *Tomahawk IIAs* to reach the RAF, including AH925 seen here, had been amongst the mix of early British and French contracts, and lacked certain items of equipment that were deemed essential for combat conditions in England by the time of delivery, although certainly existing British aircraft lacked the same equipment. This aircraft served nearly a year, from April 17, 1941, with the Central Flying School (CFS) at Boscombe Down, and later with No.30 OUT at Hixon, and survived until December 31, 1944. (*RAF*)

ber 1941 and June 1942, observed that the RAF still had eight Army Cooperation squadrons equipped with *Tomahawks*, but they were being replaced with early *Mustangs* as rapidly as possible. He visited each of these units, and found nothing but praise for the airframes, no doubt influenced by the fact that most of the same units, as late as June 1941, had been equipped with Westland *Lysanders*. The Allison engines, on the other hand:

"*...saw many of the pilots leery or actually afraid of the engines. While none of them would name anything specific in support of this feeling, it seemed to me to be due mostly to the fact that first of all, in the early use of this engine, there had been a number of unfortunate accidents; and secondly, many of them had previously been accustomed to flying with the Rolls Royce Merlin engine. However, most of them agreed that the Allison was a smoother running engine than the Merlin.*"

Most of the *Tomahawks* issued to the Army Cooperation Squadrons had been modified to accommodate cameras with automatic mechanisms, which required them to cruise at not more than 150mph when taking aerial reconnaissance images.

A few *Tomahawks IIBs* were also sent to Turkey (some sources cite 42, but only 29 RAF serials can be accounted for), but perhaps the most famous export models were the 100 H81A-2 fighters diverted from British orders and sent to China in early 1941 for the American Volunteer Group (AVG). These planes, assembled in China starting in the summer of 1941, were divided into three "*Flying Tiger*" squadrons (Adam and Eve, Panda Bears, and Hells Angels). The AVG went into combat against the Japanese on December 20, 1941, and was officially disbanded on July 4, 1942. In that time they were credited with downing 286 Japanese aircraft.

These aircraft were delivered to China on the direct orders of President Roosevelt, and came from British Contract A-84 (see above), somewhat to the annoyance of the British. These received the Chinese Nationalist Air Force serials P-8101 to P-8200, and all were assembled at Rangoon between August and November 1941. Some sources claim these were in fact H81A-3s, and that P-8101 to P-8136 were in the range of MSN 15337 to 15522 (RAF serials range AK466 to AK570), with P-8137 to P-8169 in the range MSN 15828 to 15926 (RAF serials range AM375 to AM473), allotted in February, and arriving in June 1941, and P-8170 to P-8200 in the range MSN 15928 to 15972 (RAF serials range AM475 to AM519) allotted in March, and actually arrived in Rangoon in July 1941.

It is seldom noted that the arrival and assembly of these aircraft was not the result of magic. None other than William D. Pawley, the U.S. Curtiss-Wright Export Corp. mover and shaker who had formed the CAMCO facility to produce *Hawk IIIs* and other U.S. aircraft at Loiwing (known amongst the small U.S. staff there as Pawleyville), nearly 1,000 miles north of Rangoon. According to his own account, Pawley was called to see British General Archibald Wavell, who was a great friend of his, who informed him in no uncertain terms that U.S. General George Brett wanted to see him urgently. Brett was well aware of the highly successful CAMCO enterprise, which by this time was employing nearly 3,500 personnel. Apparently acting on orders from Washington, Brett essentially demanded that Pawley move the entire CAMCO enterprise from Loiwing to Rangoon immediately, mainly to help expedite Allied aid to the Chinese and, in particular, to facilitate the arrival and erection of the *Tomahawks*. Although he protested the impossibility of such a move, Japanese rapid advances in the direction of Loiwing convinced him of the necessity and, as only the Chinese could, the entire operation was moved to Rangoon via sampan and light river vessels.

The first order of business, while actually engaged in reestablishing the CAMCO enterprise at Rangoon, was to erect and deliver the *Tomahawks* to the AVG, which was accomplished in amazing fashion. However, the aircraft had been delivered without spares, which very quickly became a major issue. Pawley was once again called upon to work a miracle. He was aware, via his Curtiss connections, that the USAAC had by then shipped significant numbers

Identified by Curtiss as an *H81A-2*, RAF serial AH979, pictured here at Buffalo on November 14, 1940, was designated by the British as a *Tomahawk IIA*. This aircraft was passed on to the Soviet Union by the British, via Cunliffe-Owen Aircraft, on August 12, 1941. (*Curtiss S-F13624*)

Both the Axis and Allies attempted to woo neutral Turkey into the war, and provided her air force with a large number of capable service aircraft. These included a number of *Tomahawk IIBs*, including serial 3838 pictured here. (*The Museum of Flight*)

of similar P-40 variants to U.S. units in the Philippines, and Pawley reasoned that he should be able to "liberate" some of these to service the AVG aircraft. Pawley allegedly flew to Manila via *Pan American Clipper* and, upon arrival, called General Douglas MacArthur's quarters, but reached the General's wife. She made an appointment for him for 0900 the following morning to meet with the legendary U.S. patriarch, but in the meantime, the night before, had dinner with a number of ranking U.S. Navy officers who, upon learning of the nature of the challenge—and the connections that Pawley enjoyed—offered him the use of U.S. Navy Consolidated PBY-5 *Catalina* flying boats to ferry the spares (if he could shake them loose from the USAAC) to Singapore. When he presented himself at MacArthur's office the next morning, Generals Brereton and Sutherland were also present, as well as Wainwright and General Magruder, who had been sent to the Far East on the express orders of General Marshall to investigate first hand whether or not the U.S. should disengage itself from the AVG. Magruder had apparently, according to Pawley, already recommended that it ought to be disbanded. Pawley then presented this august body with his list of spares needed and MacArthur, pacing up and down his office, pleaded that, although he had a significant number of P-40s on hand, with a large stock of spares, he was "*...going to need them.*" He had also, according to Pawley's account, been briefed by Magruder and Brett that the AVG was not worth supporting. That night, another dinner party was organized and, by then, Pawley had apparently had time to organize his clout, and the Philippines Department supply office, Colonel Harold George, essentially agreed to give him what he needed. The next morning, three U.S. Navy PBYs were made available, and Pawley, his small staff, and the spares that the AVG sorely needed were flown to Singapore, and the rest is history.

Pratt & Whitney R-1830-SSC7-G Powered H81A *Special*

In September 1940, the Pratt & Whitney Aircraft Division of the United Aircraft Corporation took the unusual action of purchasing from Curtiss a complete H81A-1 airframe, minus engine, with the intention of using the airframe to exhaustively test their 1,100hp R-1830-SSC7-G, 14-cylinder, two-stage, twin row *Twin Wasp* radial engine. The resulting aircraft looked like nothing less than a P-36 on steroids.

By November 10, 1942, Pratt & Whitney's T. E. Tillinghast was reporting to one and all that the hybrid aircraft had been flown "*...considerably in mock combats with P-40F aircraft stationed at our airfield, and in both climb and high speed, is very much better than the P-40F.*" Pratt & Whitney also observed that the R-1830-SSC7-G weighed less than the Rolls Royce *Merlin*, and had been flying routinely at a gross weight of 7,107 pounds, but of course minus armament (it had provisions only for four .30 caliber wing guns). They reported that the hybrid had a high speed of 380mph at 24,000 feet, with a calculated decrease to 370mph at the same altitude when corrected to a military service aircraft with standard equipment and armament installed at 8,300 pounds gross weight.

While Curtiss was frantically trying to meet the demands of the Allies during the first three years of the new World War, a very strange commercial transaction took place. Pratt & Whitney Aircraft Division purchased an *H81A* airframe (MSN 17816) in September 1940, for the express purpose of mounting a 1,100hp R-1830-SSC7-G engine. The resulting aircraft, issued an experimental license as NX28990, looked like a P-36 on steroids. (*United Technologies courtesy John Connors*)

At first glance, the so-called *H81A Special* re-engined by Pratt & Whitney looked more like a Grumman or Republic product than the spawn of Curtiss. The fairing on the R-1830-SSC7-G engine was exceptionally smooth all the way back to the firewall. Note the unusual antenna mast, offset to starboard, ahead of the windscreen. *(United Technologies courtesy John Connors)*

A Pratt & Whitney Report (No.120A) reported additional flight tests were conducted with this aircraft, to establish maximum airspeed, between July 1, 1943, and October 22, 1943. These revealed that the aircraft achieved 315mph at sea level at 1,200bhp, and 388mph at military power at 25,000 feet at 1,015bhp.

This aircraft is something of a mystery. Approved for Experimental License NX-28990, the Manufacturers Serial Number was 17816, which makes it the aircraft just before a major block of RAF *Tomahawk IIBs* commencing with MSN 17817 (*AN218). It had been registered to Pratt & Whitney September 29, 1940.

By November 25, 1942, Army Air Forces officials had met with Pratt & Whitney, and were particularly intrigued by the unique exhaust system that the firm had developed for the aircraft, which included a jet propulsion effect. Passed along to the Aircraft Lab at Wright Field by December 29th, however, after considerable thought, the Air Materiel Command ruled that "*...putting the R-1830 engine into the latest type P-40 aircraft is viewed as not worth the trouble and engineering time*," and opted instead to stay with the mix of liquid-cooled engines that equipped all subsequent P-40 variants.

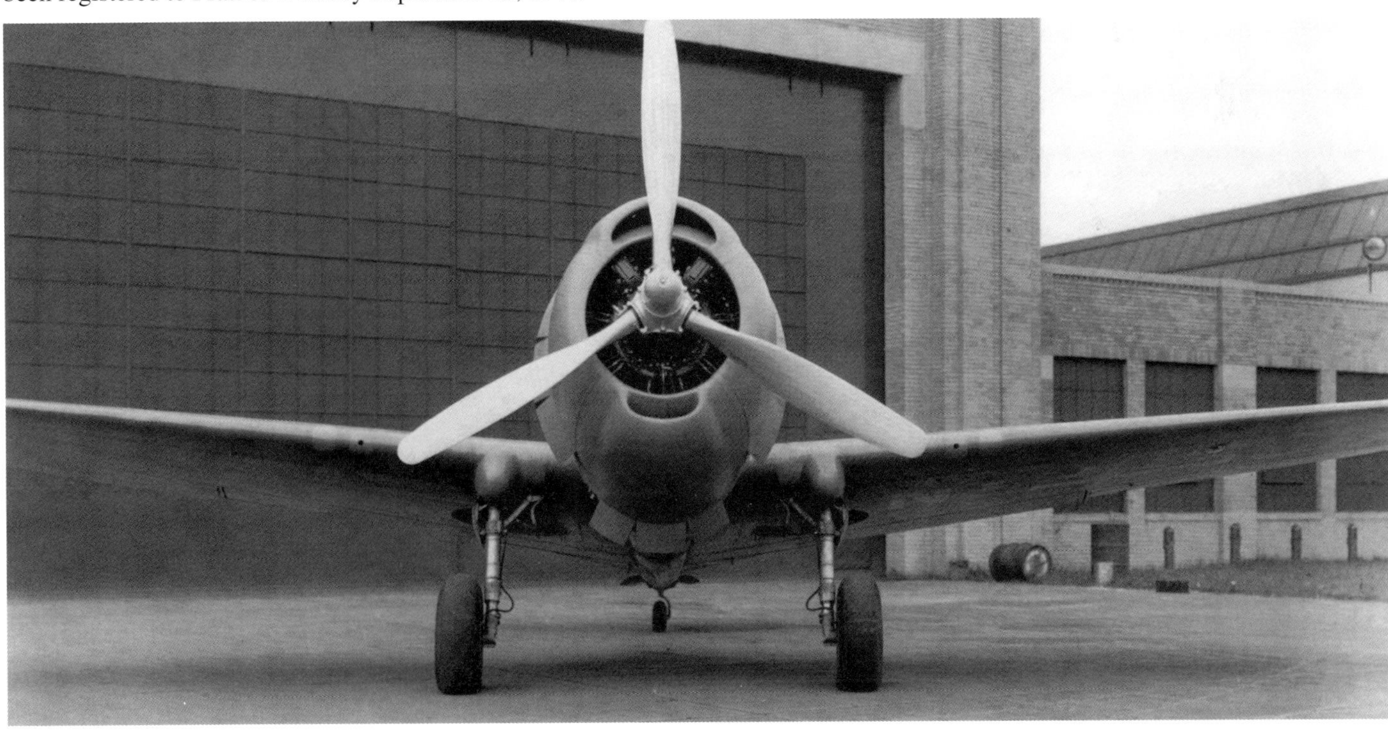

Viewed nose-on, with the cowl flaps open, the Pratt & Whitney owned *H81A Special* had the wing gun ports faired over but, curiously, the two inboard apertures had holes for some reason. Pratt & Whitney tests revealed that the hybrid could achieve 388mph at 2,500 feet. *(United Technologies courtesy of John Connors)*

Pratt & Whitney officials went out of their way to inform the Army Air Forces leadership that their *H81A Special* was routinely "cleaning the clocks" of regular AAF units stationed nearby equipped with Curtiss P-40F-1-CUs, such as 41-14182, seen in this interesting nose-to-nose view. The P-40F was wrecked January 24, 1943, at Mitchel Field, NY, when it hit a power line during low altitude flight. (*United Technologies courtesy of John Connors*)

Curtiss XP-46, CP-39-13A *(Hawk 86)*

The XP-46 was the first of hoped-for replacements for the P-40 fighter on the Curtiss production lines, and was originally called CP-39-13 (later CP-39-13A) at Curtiss, referring to the 13th Circular Proposal of 1939. The initial plan was to provide accelerated pursuit plane development to allow procurement of 195 aircraft by Fiscal Year 1941.

It was desired to take advantage of lessons learned by the French in the war using the export *Hawk* 75A. Desired high speed was 425mph at 15,000 feet. Actually, Curtiss came in third in the original design competition. On September 13, 1939, the Army authorized procurement of two Curtiss fighters, one XP-46 (AC40-3053, MSN 14444), and one XP-46A (AC40-3054, MSN 14445), the latter being a stripped aircraft to obtain early flight characteristics, meaning no armament or armor on board. Official procurement started on September 29, 1939, and the Air Corps assigned their designation XP-46 to Curtiss Design CP-39-13A on October 10th. The official contract of $416,644 was approved on January 17, 1940, and covered one each XP-46 and XP-46A with Allison V-1710 engines, drawings, and reports, a wind tunnel model, and a spin test model. In October 1939 reports of actual French war experience dictated addition of more armament and armor, and the resulting weight increase dictated adding an additional 30 square feet to the wing area, and decreased target high speed to 403mph at 15,000 feet. In February 1940 armament requirements changed again. Mockup inspection of the XP-46 was completed on March 4, 1940, with minor changes requested. A full engineering inspection took place later that month.

In June 1940, Curtiss was allowed to delay the project a month to devote time to the P-40D model that had more immediate production possibilities, and in September more delay time was granted the contractor on account of the P-40D. Because of these and other delays in the pressure of the times, the first flight of the XP-46A did not take place until February 15, 1941.

Initial testing showed the need for a larger oil cooler because of engine overheating. More changes were also made. Official contractor tests on the aircraft were performed at Curtiss to the Army's satisfaction between September 9th and 16th, and both planes were delivered to Wright Field, Ohio, one on September 11th, and the other September 22, 1941. Since they had not met Curtiss performance guarantees, the contract value was reduced by $14,995.

Even as Curtiss was gearing up for large scale production of the P-40 and *H81A* series, the engineering staff were hard at work on what was hoped would be the next generation. Laid down as the company designation CP-39-13A and *Hawk 86*, the full-scale, initially 12-gun mockup configuration clearly owed its heritage to the *Hawk 75* and *Hawk 81* predecessors. (*Curtiss*)

This August 4, 1939, side-view of the Curtiss CP-39-13 mock-up reveals the differences between the original concept and the CP-39-13A. Exactly how the engine was to be cooled in this arrangement isn't clear. (*Curtiss S-F12403*)

Delays in testing were encountered at Wright Field due to required modifications needed by the Army, and getting in line for official weighing by very busy Army personnel. Wing leading edge slats on the planes were wired shut because they were deemed of little value, and pilots were worried about possible asymmetrical deployment. Near the end of October it was found impossible to properly ballast the XP-46A, since no place could be found for fastening the required weight.

First flight of the XP-46 at Wright Field finally took place on November 17, 1941, but testing proceeded slowly, and was not completed until late March 1942. Problems occurred with wing flaps. Other problems encountered included a spare parts shortage, higher priority of other aircraft needing testing, and bad weather.

Shortly after the wing flaps were reworked, the two aircraft were flown to Chanute Field, Illinois, to be used for ground school instruction, since the XP-46 and XP-46A still did not cool satisfactorily in the warmer weather, and no spare parts were available to keep them in commission. In addition, performance characteristics were no better than those of the P-40D model.

Characteristics of the XP-46 follow: span, length, and height 34 feet, 3 1/2 inches, 30 feet, two inches, and 10 feet, one inch. Wing area was 208 square feet. Wing root and tip chords were 100 inches and 43 inches. Wing incidence 1 degree, dihedral 6 degrees, and sweep 4.75 degrees. Root and tip airfoils were the NACA 23018 and NACA 23009, respectively. Wheel tread was nine feet, nine and 1/2 inches.

The powerplant was an Allison V-1710-39(F3R) rated 1,150hp at 2,600rpm at 46.8 inches of mercury for sea level takeoff, 1,150hp (Military) at 3,000rpm at 9,600 feet, and 1,000hp (Normal) at 2,600rpm at 9,000 feet, with a geared single stage supercharger having a blower ratio of 8.80:1. The propeller was a Curtiss Electric three blade constant speed type with low and high blade angles of 19 degrees and 50 degrees, respectively. Propeller reduction gear ratio was 2:1. Maximum internal fuel capacity was 156 gallons, and oil capacity was 22 gallons maximum.

Empty weight was 5,625 pounds, design useful load was 1,807 pounds (consisting of a 185 pound pilot, 936 pounds of fuel, 168 pounds of oil, 510 pounds of armament, and eight pounds of miscellaneous equipment.). Gross weight was thus 7,432 pounds.

Wing and power loadings were 35.73psf, and power loading had to be 0.46 pounds per horse power. The useful load to gross weight ratio was 0.243.

Performance at 7,081 pounds gross weight was: maximum speed 355mph at 12,200 feet, 348.5mph with bullet proof glass

By March 12, 1940, the XP-46 mock-up configuration had changed once again. Although the aircraft appears huge, based on the diminutive person in the cockpit, the wing span was actually more than three feet less than the P-40. (*David W. Ostrowski Collection*)

The actual configuration of the XP-46, in this August 26, 1941, view, differed only in minor respects from the CP-39-13A mock-up. (*Curtiss S-F14846*)

Never before published view of the XP-46 being run up at Buffalo on a frigid ramp. Curtiss had high hopes for the aircraft, but wartime demands on the severely taxed engineering department pushed it repeatedly to the back burner. (*The Museum of Flight*)

windshield installed and wing gun holes open for firing. Cruising speed was 305mph at 75 percent (Normal) power. Climb times 2.1 minutes to 5,000 feet, 4.0 minutes to 10,000 feet, 6.5 minutes to 15,200 feet, and 33.8 minutes to 29,500 feet. Sea level climb rate was 2,240fpm. Service and absolute ceilings were 29,500 feet and 30,500 feet, respectively. Cruising range was 717 miles at 4.6 miles per gallon with 156 gallons of fuel.

Armament was two Browning synchronized machine guns of .50 caliber with 200 rounds per gun, one each side of the fuselage nose, and four browning M2 .30 caliber machine guns in the wings with 500 rounds per gun.

It is seldom noted that the Anglo-French Purchasing Commission placed a Letter of Intent with Curtiss for a quantity of *Hawk H86s* early in 1940, with the intention that these would be built by

Besides the basic XP-46, the Air Corps also authorized Curtiss to construct a single XP-46A, shown here in February 1941. The two aircraft were dimensionally smaller overall than the P-40, and had in-ward retracting main gear. The XP-46 was actually tested with 10 guns (two .50 caliber guns firing under the nose, and eight .30 caliber guns in the wings), but the XP-46A was never fitted with guns. It suffered from engine cooling and balance problems that were shoved aside as other aircraft stood up for the war effort. (*Curtiss S-F13911*)

Curtiss hedged its bets on the XP-46 by proposing to the Army a modified P-40 series aircraft with the new 1,150hp Allison engine, known initially as the *H87A-1*, and given the Army designation P-40D. These 22 aircraft were all delivered in July 1941, and are the rarest of the breed to illustrate. They dispensed with the synchronized nose guns of earlier variants, and introduced the heaviest U.S. armament on a Army fighter to that time, four .50cal. wing guns. *(Aeroplane Photo Supply via Dean Collection)*

both Curtiss and North American Aviation, to follow-on from *Hawk 81A* orders. In the event, the *Hawk 87A (Kittyhawk)* was substituted, and the intended North American connection resulted in the design of the NA-51 *Mustang* for the British.

After conclusion of exhaustive tests at Wright Field, including considerable work with the Propeller Lab by the XP-46A as late as February 16, 1942, both aircraft were shipped to Chanute Field, and assigned as Class 26 as instructional airframes circa May 22, 1942.

Besides the basic XP-46, the Air Corps also authorized Curtiss to construct a single XP-46A, shown here in February 1941. The two aircraft were dimensionally smaller overall than the P-40, and had in-ward retracting main gear. The XP-46 was actually tested with 10 guns (two .50 caliber guns firing under the nose, and eight .30 caliber guns in the wings), but the XP-46A was never fitted with guns. It suffered from engine cooling and balance problems that were shoved aside as other aircraft stood up for the war effort. *(Curtiss S-F13911)*

Curtiss P-40D

Curtiss had second thoughts about the XP-46, and in late May 1940 suggested to the Army that the new Allison 1,150hp engine in the XP-46 be used instead in a revised P-40 type, thereby keeping more continuity in company production. On June 10, 1940, the P-46 plans were shelved, and the Army approved a P-40D model (Curtiss Specification 98-610-3A), officially ordered in September. This design was Curtiss Model 87A-1, sufficiently different from the H81A type to warrant a new design number. The first aircraft (AC40-359) was delivered by Curtiss to Patterson Field, OH, May 7, 1941, and was assigned to "Project X" on December 28, 1941. It survived as late as November 22, 1944, when it was finally condemned due to age.

Initial P-40D delivery took place in May 1941, the first of 22 aircraft (the second, 40-360, was designated as the single XP-40F from the start, thus resulting in a total of 22, rather than 23 P-40Ds), and all were delivered by July 23, 1941. Major changes from earlier models included incorporation of the Allison V-1710-39 (F3R) engine of increased power using an external spur propeller reduction gear drive in place of the internal gear drive of the earlier -33 engine. This change raised the propeller thrust line and, together with other powerplant changes, much modified the P-40 nose lines, as well as allowing a shorter landing gear. Other major changes were elimination of fuselage machine guns, and incorporation of two .50 caliber guns, with 246 rounds per gun in each wing firing outside the propeller arc. About 175 pounds of armor and self sealing fuel tanks were included, and cockpit canopy changes made. Provision was also made for carrying a 500 pound bomb under the fuselage as an alternate to a 51 gallon centerline auxiliary fuel tank. Additionally, a July 1942 Army document states that the aircraft had provision for one 20mm cannon in each wing as well, although this option was apparently never exercised.

Characteristics of the P-40D version follow: span, length, and height 37 feet, three and 1/2 inches, 31 feet, two inches, and 12 feet, four inches. Wing area was 236 square feet.

Powerplant was an Allison V-1710-39 (F3R), rated 1,150hp at 2,800rpm at 46.2 inches of mercury manifold pressure at sea level takeoff with fuel flow of 125gph, 1,150hp at 3,000rpm (Military) at 15,000 feet at 43.9 inches of HG, and 1,000hp at 2,600rpm (Normal) at 15,000 feet at 38.7 inches of HG manifold pressure with 103gph. Propeller gear ratio was 2:1, and supercharger gear ratio 8.80:1. The propeller was a Curtiss Electric constant speed three blade model of 11 feet in diameter. Low and high blade angles were 24.5 degrees and 54.5 degrees. Fuel capacities were 197.5 gallons, total (front main wing tank 32 gallons, rear main wing tank 51.0 gallons, auxiliary fuselage tank 62.5 gallons, and external belly tank 52 gallons). Normal fuel load was 120 gallons (included 34.5 gallons in auxiliary tank). Normal oil capacity was 18 gallons, with alternate load 21 gallons.

Empty weight was 5,970 pounds, normal useful load 1,817 pounds, and normal gross weight was 7,787 pounds. Maximum useful load was 2,700 pounds, and maximum gross weight 8,670 pounds. Normal and maximum wing loadings were 32.99 and 36.74psf, and normal and maximum power loadings were 6.77 and 7.54 pounds per horse power. Normal and maximum useful load to gross weight ratios were 0.23 and 0.31.

Maximum speed was 359mph at 15,000 feet (no belly tank), and 330mph at 15,000 feet (with belly tank) at Military power. Maximum speed at (Normal) power with 1,000hp was 345mph at 15,000 feet with no belly tank, and 324mph with a belly tank. Desirable cruise speed at 60 percent (Normal) power, 600hp at 2,190rpm, at 27.1 inches of mercury at 15,000 feet with no belly tank was 285mph, and 266mph with a belly tank. Sea level rate of climb was 2,580fpm at 7,787 pounds weight. Best climb speed was 140mph at low altitude. Service and absolute ceilings were 30,600 feet and 31,600 feet, respectively. Takeoff speed was 93mph, and takeoff ground run 1,125 feet. To clear a 50 foot obstacle the run was 1,650 feet. Landing speed was 85mph with a ground run of 860 feet. Landing over a 50 foot obstacle took 1,500 feet. Normal and maximum ranges were 800 miles and 1,150 miles, the latter at 195mph. The indicated "do not exceed" speed was 485mph.

The Curtiss price for each of the P-40D fighters was $25,007.56 without GFE. The P-40Ds received USAAC serials 40-359 to 40-

The smallest of all wartime Curtiss production batches, the 22 P-40D aircraft were pushed through the factory in record time. Note the O-52 *Owl* in the background in this Buffalo ramp shot. (*Dean Collection*)

381. These were (from 40-361) MSN 13236 to 13256, or 21 aircraft. The MSNs for 40-359 and 40-360 can only be assumed.

Although it has frequently been reported that the small number of P-40Ds built were all assigned to duty with the Sixth Air Force in the Caribbean, this is completely incorrect. None served in the Caribbean. The first aircraft (40-359) was bailed to Allison in Indianapolis on January 6, 1943, after extensive service at Patterson and Wright Field (Allison finally returned it to storage at Wright Field on August 30, 1944), and at least eight were designated for rush delivery to the Philippines—but were diverted to Hawaii instead, where they joined 12 others specifically intended for Hawaii, and 13 more designated for Foreign Destination Code COPPER (also Hawaii). One (40-361) was assigned to Elmendorf Field in Alaska on June 25, 1942, and one (40-362) was specifically assigned to the 99th Fighter Squadron (the Tuskegee based unit) April 7, 1942, very possibly that all black units' first tactical aircraft. Oddly, two (40-368 and 40-371) were redesignated as P-40Es on November 24, 1941, and 40-368 is noted as having been based on Midway Island as of July 12, 1942, with the 18th Fighter Group. This was probably one of the COPPER aircraft. At least one other was wrecked in the Continental United States, and two became Class 26 instrumental airframes.

At least 14 completed P-40E fuselages await movement on their own, individual carriages to be mated with the wing assemblies at Buffalo in 1941. *(The Museum of Flight)*

Curtiss P-40E

Curtiss went ahead with a modified version of the P-40D as the P-40E (Curtiss Specification 98-610-7A), and this version, characterized ordinarily with installation of six .50 caliber wing guns instead of the four on the P-40D, went into high rate production for a total of 820 aircraft. Curtiss billing records show 649 delivered in 1941 and 171 delivered in 1942 at a unit price of $34,809. These were all U.S. Army models exclusive of any export versions, and carried the Curtiss Model 87B-2. A decision of February 18, 1941, started P-40E/H87B-2 production commencing August 29th. Army serials were AC40-358 (MSN 13233), AC40-382 to 40-681 (MSN 13257 to 13356), AC41-5305 to 41-5744, and AC41-13521 to 41-13599 (MSN 16737 to 16815).

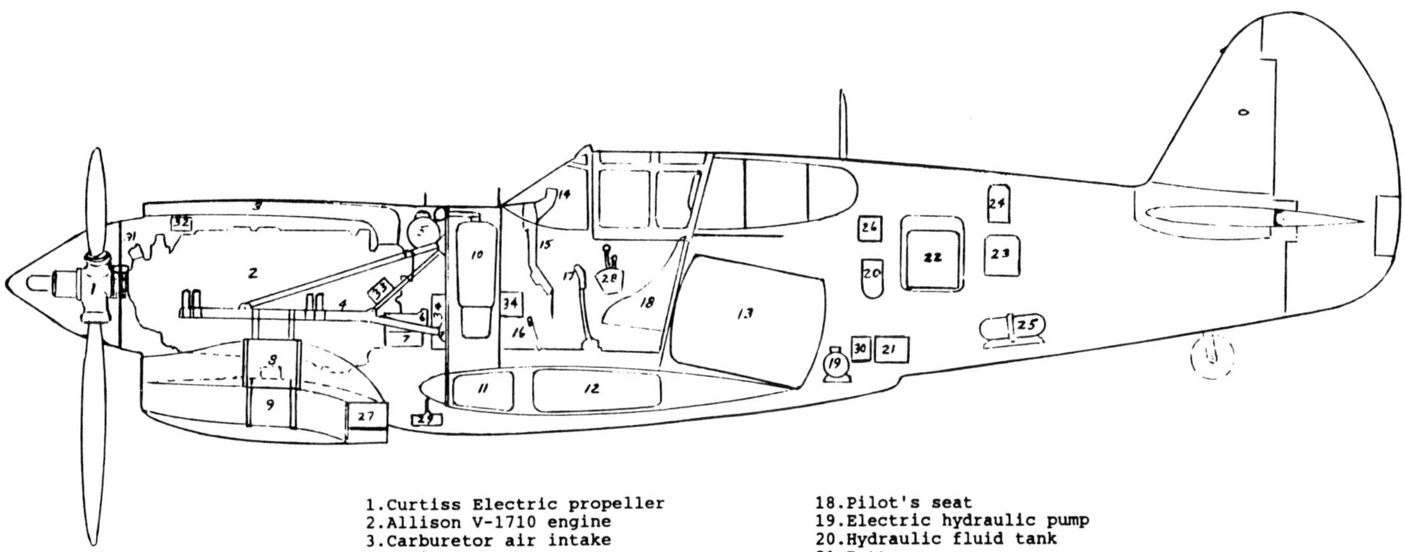

1.Curtiss Electric propeller
2.Allison V-1710 engine
3.Carburetor air intake
4.Engine mount
5.Coolant expansion tank
6.Electric generator
7.Engine starter
8.Coolant radiator (2)
9.Oil cooling radiator
10.Oil tank
11.Wing reserve fuel tank
12.Wing main fuel tank
13.Fuselage fuel tank
14.Gunsight
15.Instrument panel
16.Rudder pedals
17.Pilot's control stick

18.Pilot's seat
19.Electric hydraulic pump
20.Hydraulic fluid tank
21.Battery
22.Radio
23.Radio
24.Hydraulic reserve tank
25.Oxygen bottle
26.Data case
27.Cooling air exit gills
28.Throttle quadrant
29.Fuel selector valve
30.Battery junction box
31.Propeller governor
32.Propeller relay box
33.Booster coil
34.Electrical junction boxes

The first true mass-production version of the P-40 was the P-40E and associated British *Kittyhawk* variants. This in-board profile shows the typical equipment integral to the fuselage of most of these. *(USAAF)*

The first P-40E (40-358) was delivered to Patterson Field, OH, August 20, 1941, and after use there, was assigned to Alaska on October 11th, but crashed enroute, and was returned to the U.S. Of the first block between AC40-382 and 40-681, a total of 88 were shipped, 50 direct from the factory to the Philippines commencing August 19, 1941, with AC40-462, and all but two, which had crashed in training, were on hand when the Japanese made their attack. The Philippine P-40Es were hastily assembled for use by the 24th Pursuit Group squadrons not long before the attack. The first American ace of World War II, Lt. Buzz Wagner, flew a P-40E against the Japanese there. By early May 1942, the last five P-40Es were destroyed by U.S. forces to prevent capture by the enemy. One of the P-40Es in this batch (40-582) was assigned to the Photo Laboratory at Wright Field as of October 7, 1942, for the installation of an experimental camera for aerial reconnaissance, one of the first such conversions of a service fighter during the war. Another (40-431) was sent to Wright Field for the installation of special cold weather equipment and, following this work, was dispatched to Project X (Fourth Air Force), along with eight others similarly modified.[128]

A total of 50 P-40Es had also been allocated to the American Volunteer Group in China in January 1942.[129] These were the aircraft destined for Foreign Destination Code OLIVE which, early on, was defined simply as "Asia." About 30 of these got to the AVG in March 1942, flying in by way of Africa and India. At least 51 P-40Es on Project X (Foreign Destination Code SUMAC) also reached Australia, and in late January 1942 a dozen were sent to Java, followed by more later for defense against the marauding Japanese, but to no avail. By mid-March 1942 337 early P-40s had reached Australia, some of which were turned over to the Australians. At least two P-40Es have been identified as going to Russia by February 25, 1942 (41-5347 and 41-5529).

Although seldom noted, 50 P-40Es were fitted in the field with two Q-2 bomb racks by the Sacramento Air Depot around February 11, 1942, apparently as a stopgap measure to equip units on the west coast for repelling any Japanese landings that might ensue.

Finally, although the exact model is not known (and can only be assumed to have been P-40Es), the Commanding General of the AAF Materiel Command was notified on September 18, 1943, in a rather indignant teletype message that "*...since December 7, 1941, two P-40 type aircraft, fully loaded with ammo, have been kept ready for immediate take off at the Curtiss plant at Buffalo. Five Army test pilots are stationed there*," and the implication was, of

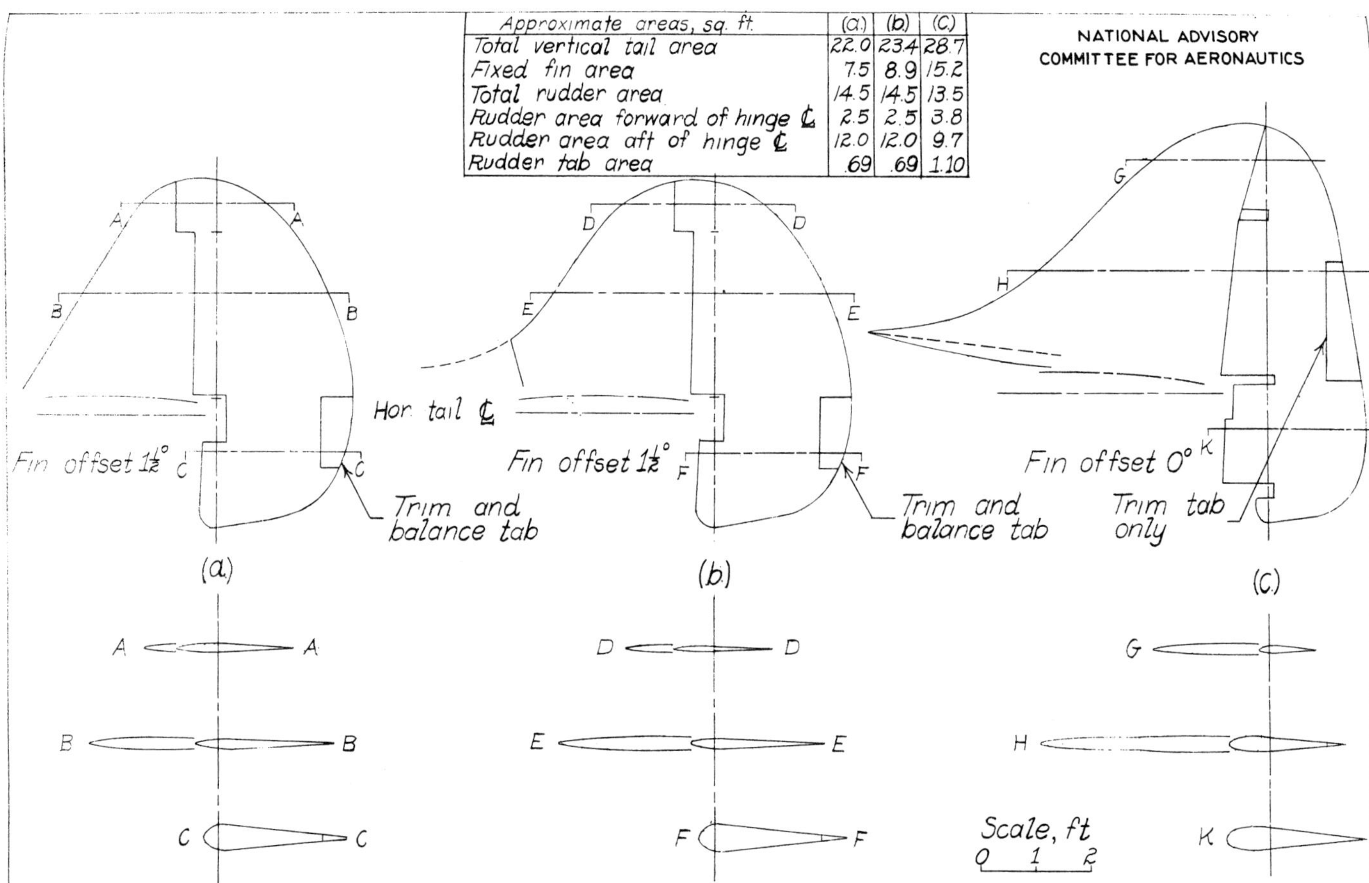

Figure 7a. - Vertical tails tested on P-40E airplane: (a) original P-40E vertical tail; (b) fin extension no. 1 on original vertical tail; (c) fin extension no. 6 on tall fin (Curtiss dwg. SK-5524) and rudder (Curtiss dwg. SK-5676).

One of the nagging criticisms reported to Curtiss from the field was the longitudinal instability of the entire series in certain flight regimes. Curtiss and the NACA used two aircraft (P-40E 41-5534 and P-40K-1-CU 42-45801) to address these issues, and tried any number of vertical fin and rudder fixes. These comparative drawings show the trials on the P-40E. (*Curtiss*)

Curtiss Buffalo engineers, one in a quite jolly ball cap, try one of a number of fin filets on P-40E 41-5534 in an attempt to address longitudinal stability concerns. (*The Museum of Flight*)

course, that they would have served as point-defense interceptors had Axis aircraft made an attempt on the Curtiss facilities, although civilian test pilots were also allegedly flying the aircraft!

One P-40E, the 75th production example, was accepted by the AAF on April 7, 1942, but was not delivered, as it was authorized to be retained at Curtiss for tests.

Japanese P-40Es

Ironically, when the Japanese conquered the Netherlands East Indies and Java, in particular, they apparently captured a sizeable number of the virtually brand new P-40Es that had been shipped there in such haste, intact. One Japanese source, in fact, claims that sufficient numbers of the aircraft—as many as 38—were available to equip a Japanese Army Air Force *Sentai*, and this unit actually operated the aircraft for a time. It is not clear if Allied intelligence was aware of this development, as it certainly would have posed unique challenges for the already hard-pressed defenders in the region. To this number must also be added at least five P-40E series aircraft that the Japanese captured intact in China on May 31, 1943, at least one of which was used by the *25th Sentai* for aerial combat training, and still another P-40E acquired somehow by the *44th Sentai* (equipped with *Sonias*).

On February 6, 1943, the headquarters of the Japanese Army's *5th Hiko Shidan* (Air Division) ordered the *50th Sentai* to organize a temporary interceptor unit equipped with captured P-40Es for the aerial defense of Rangoon, because the Japanese regarded the P-40E as having firepower and speed superior to that of the *Oscar*. The local command apparently took this decision independently, and without consultation with Tokyo. The *50th Sentai* selected four pilots, led by Lt. Akira Takano, and two experienced mechanics, and then moved to Seletar Aerodrome at Singapore, together with other *Sentai* personnel, who were going to be transitioned from the

This P-40E cockpit close up view reveals not only fuselage stenciling, but a new gun sight being tested by this AAC Lieutenant. This is almost certainly 41-5521, but only the last three digits of the serial are visible on the data block. This aircraft was assigned to the 57th Fighter Group at Windsor Locks, CT. (*Curtiss 81757*)

Some of the early block P-40Es shipped to the Army Air Corps garrison in the Philippines and Java were seized by the marauding Japanese early in the war, and sufficient numbers of them were assembled to form an operational unit at Rangoon. This image was found by a U.S. serviceman in Yokota in September 1945. (*via W. S. Shawm 58th Bomb Squadron*)

Ki-43-I to the Ki-43-II at Sungei Petani, in Malaya. Takano and his crew started training on two of the P-40Es that were enroute from Java to Japan and, on February 13th, four more pilots were transported to Clark Field, in the Philippines, for further flight training and receipt of the four additional P-40Es, and they returned to Tengah Aerodrome with these on the 27th. Upon completing transition training and re-equipment with Ki-43-IIs, the *50th Sentai* members, together with the so-called *Rangoon Special Interceptor Unit*, left Tengah for Mingaladon, Burma, on March 11th.

On May 13, 1943, the *Rangoon Special Interceptor Unit* moved to Meiktila Airfield, in central Burma, to continue the same duties, but soon lost its operational status due to a complete lack of spares. It was formally disbanded on May 26th.

But this was not the end of Japanese involvement with the P-40E. The Imperial Japanese Navy also reportedly had two examples, one airworthy and one grounded, assigned to the Flight Experimental Department of the Yokosuka *Kokutai* at Oppama until nearly the end of the war.

Although widely held to be outclassed by the leading Japanese and German fighters, the P-40E's six .50 caliber machine guns often proved decisive in the hands of an experienced pilot. Here, they are being test fired in a gun bunker with the access cover hanging open. Often overlooked by modelers, the gun muzzles were mounted rather low on the leading edge of the wing. (*Curtiss*)

Besides 12 *Kittyhawk IAs* acquired directly, the Royal Canadian Air Force (RCAF) also acquired some offset from the RAF, including AK803 seen here, coded RE+K with No. 118 Squadron. This unit flew from Toronto to Annette Island, Alaska, in June 1942 to reinforce USAAF units there when it was thought that the Japanese might try to consolidate their landings in the Aleutians. (*RCAF*)

P-40Es for Other Foreign Destinations

By April 1942, 30 winterized P-40Es were starting operations in the Aleutian Islands. Also in that month, 68 P-40Es were flown to Quonset Point, Rhode Island, and with their crews loaded aboard the aircraft carrier USS *Ranger*. They were thus transported to Accra, in West Africa, and from there ferried across Africa to the Middle East and India. Eventually, 58 of these fighters reached the Tenth Air Force in India. At least 31 early P-40Es also went to Hawaii (COPPER), followed by 92 more from the batch AC41-5305 to 41-5744 (of which some were diverted from Project XYZ for Russia to Project X for Australia) and, by July 12, 1942, five were also shipped to Midway, including AC40-398. This shipment was followed by 14 more to Midway, diverted from Projects X and XYZ, from the second batch. Seldom reported, 21 early P-40Es were shipped to the Soviet Union on Project XYZ, commencing October 14, 1941, under Defense Aid.[130] These were followed by 204 more from the batch AC41-5305 to 41-5744 (of which some had originally been intended for Britain) on Project XYZ. The Caribbean Defense Command, and the Sixth Air Force, also received 46 early P-40Es, and these were distributed throughout the region, from Puerto Rico to Salinas, Ecuador. Alaska got 24 P-40Es from the batch AC41-5305 to 41-5744. Not fewer than 42 early P-40Es were lost to training accidents in the U.S., and at least 33 became instructional airframes as Class 26.

Of the final major batch of P-40Es (AC41-13521 to 41-13599), at least seven went to Australia on Project X starting with 41-13521, delivered from Curtiss on January 16, 1942, while not less than 72 went to the Soviet Union under Defense Aid commencing January 17, 1942.

A number of P-40Es were assigned to special projects during the war, including AC40-582, which was sent to Aberdeen Proving Ground, MD, in July 1942 to serve as the platform to test a rocket gun installation, and AC40-633, which was used to test the "Brownscope" rear vision periscope circa July 7, 1942.

Characteristics of the P-40E follow: span, length, and height 37 feet, three and 1/2 inches, 31 feet, eight and 1/2 inches, and 10 feet, eight inches. Wing area was 236 square feet. Wing sweep one degree, 19 minutes, incidence -1 degree, dihedral six degrees, root chord 108 inches, and tip chord 54 inches at wing station 197. Mean aerodynamic chord measured 81.6 inches, and airfoils were the NACA 2215 at root and 2209 at the tip. Wing aspect ratio was 5.9. The ultimate load factors were +8 and -4. Horizontal tail area was 48 square feet, vertical tail area 20.74 square feet, elevator area 19.2 square feet, and rudder area 13.74 square feet.

The powerplant was an Allison V-1710-39 (F3R) rated 1,150hp at 3,000rpm at takeoff, 1,150hp (Military) at 3,000rpm at 12,000 feet, 1,000hp (Normal) at 2,600rpm at 10,800 feet, and 880hp at 2,600rpm at sea level. The supercharger drive gear ratio was 8.8:1, and propeller reduction gear ratio 2:1. Fuel capacity was 120 gallons normal, and 200 gallons maximum. The propeller was a Curtiss Electric constant speed three blade model of 11 feet diameter with low and high blade pitch angles of 23 degrees and 53 degrees.

Weights for P-40E #29 were: empty weight 6,069 pounds (comprised of airframe 2,744 pounds, powerplant 2,645 pounds, and fixed equipment 680 pounds). Normal useful load was 2,030 pounds (made up of a 180 pound pilot, 720 pounds of fuel, 120 pounds of oil, 901 pounds of guns and ammunition, and 109 pounds of equipment.). Normal gross weight was 7,952 pounds. Normal wing and power loadings were 33.69psf and 6.91 pounds per horse power. Normal useful load to gross weight ratio was 0.255. Maximum fuel useful load was 2,593 pounds (a 180 pound pilot, 1,200 pounds of fuel, 150 pounds of oil, 901 pounds of guns and ammunition, a 53 pound belly fuel tank installation, and 109 pounds of miscellaneous equipment.). Maximum gross weight was then 8,575 pounds, and maximum wing and power loadings were 36.33psf and 7.46 pounds per horse power, respectively, with maximum useful load to gross weight 0.302.

Speed capabilities were 366mph at 1,150hp (Military) at 3,000rpm at 15,000 feet, 344mph at 920hp (Normal) at 2,600rpm at 15,000 feet, 302mph at 940hp (Normal) at 2,600rpm at 5,000 feet, and 308mph at 75% (Normal) at 2,600rpm at 15,000 feet. Stall speed was 81mph at sea level. Climb to 15,000 feet took 6.25 minutes, and service ceiling was 29,100 feet. Endurance at 920hp at 2,600rpm at 15,000 feet was 3.32 hours with 148 gallons of fuel. Range at the same condition was 716 miles with 148 gallons. Sea level takeoff over a 50 foot obstacle was 2,075 feet, and landing over a 50 foot obstacle was 1,760 feet.

See Annex 3 at the end of this volume for a detailed description of the location of all USAAC P-40 series aircraft on strength with the USAAC as of December 7, 1941.

Curtiss P-40E-1

Most sources state that the 1,500 aircraft built as variants of the P-40E with a "block" number, known as the P-40E-1 (Curtiss Specification 98-610-9A), were intended exclusively for use by British Commonwealth air forces. Although built with British equipment, and thus not exactly equivalent to the P-40Es that had been built previously (they were H87A-4s), they were nevertheless assigned USAAC serials AC41-24776 to 41-25195 (MSN 18795 to 19214) and AC41-35874 to 41-36953 (MSN 19395 to 19474), and the very first one was indeed assigned to Britain, and delivered February 21, 1942. There, and elsewhere in British Commonwealth service, the vast majority of these aircraft became known as *Kittyhawk IAs*.

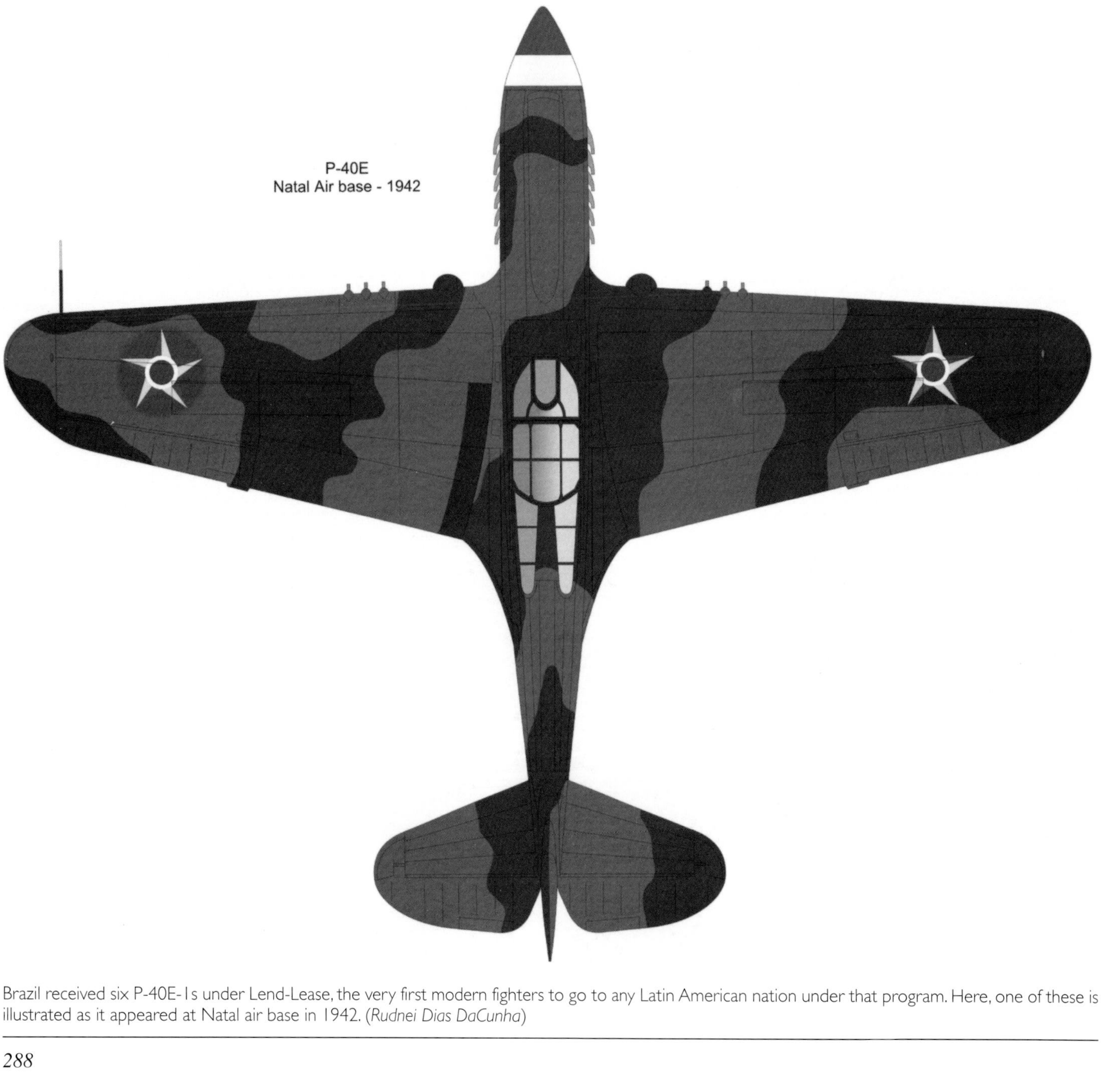

Brazil received six P-40E-1s under Lend-Lease, the very first modern fighters to go to any Latin American nation under that program. Here, one of these is illustrated as it appeared at Natal air base in 1942. (*Rudnei Dias DaCunha*)

Although most sources state that all, or nearly all, of the P-40E-1 aircraft were delivered to the British Commonwealth, this was not the case. Here 41-25094, in full USAAC markings, is being used to test two 225 gallon auxiliary fuel tanks on August 18, 1942. This aircraft was bailed to Curtiss by the AAF until June 20, 1943, when it was transferred to Moore Field, Eagle Pass, TX, where it was wrecked on July 15, 1943. (*Curtiss 1658*)

The difficulty in tracking the ultimate destinations of combat aircraft at this juncture in the war was, at least in part, due to the rapidly shifting tactical situation world wide, and conflicts in shipping schedules, losses at sea to submarines and other causes, and communications difficulties between the agencies charged with directing the flow of this massive operation. A typical exchange involving Wright Field (Air Materiel Command, or AMC) and the British Air Commission and a large batch of *Kittyhawks* and P-40E-1s is a prime example. AMC, in trying to bring order to this particular shipment, on December 23, 1941, sent the following message:

"*Reference previous instructions regarding the release of 174* Kittyhawk *P-40s and 76 P-40E-1s released December 19th without specific allocation between British Air Commission (BAC) and Russia, the following modification of previous instructions is furnished: 150* Kittyhawk *aircraft released to BAC, 26 to Russia; 10 P-40E-1s, now at Mitchel Field and one at Windsor Locks, to Russia; 64 P-40E-1s now at Buffalo released to Russia.*"

By May 23, 1942, 544 of the P-40E-1s had been delivered to Russia, against the 780 allocated under the original Arnold-Portal Protocol, leaving a balance of 236 still due them. The Munitions Assignment Board (MAB) Case No.56 allocated 48 more to the Russians, leaving 284 more still to be delivered. There were only 241 aircraft remaining on the original contract with Curtiss, however, all of which were already covered by shipping instructions for delivery to Russia. Therefore, at the end of the P-40E-1 production run, the Russians were short 43 of the aircraft promised. The numbers were slightly skewed even further when P-40E-1 41-25066 crashed circa April 4, 1942, prior to delivery while being flown "unofficially" by a USAAF pilot, reducing the total by at least one.

P-40E-1 41-25084 again on August 22, 1942, this time with a 150 gallon production plastic belly tank with a No.1 fairing. (*Curtiss 1691*)

However, while the Commonwealth (and the Soviet Union) did indeed receive the bulk of the P-40E-1s built, a small number were retained for USAAC and USAAF service, as well. At least 18 were assigned to the 50th Pursuit Group at Meridian, MS, and Orlando, FL, two went to Eglin Field—also in Florida—for armament trials, 11 went to Alaska, 30 to China (commencing with 41-36252 on April 4, 1942), and 19 were assigned to the 57th Pursuit Group at Boston, MA. Others went to the 33rd Pursuit Group.

Seven P-40E-1s[131] were provided to Brazil under Defense Aid and, retrospectively, Lend-Lease, and were flown down direct from Bolling Field, DC, in a rush delivery at the direct order of President Roosevelt. Initially marked as simply FAB 01 to 06, these retrospectively became FAB 4020 to 4025, and were the first of at least 85 P-40 variants to reach Brazil during the war. Most sources report only six going to Brazil, and apparently only six were taken up, suggesting that the seventh aircraft may have been lost in transit.

The Royal Canadian Air Force received 12 *Kittyhawk IAs* from RAF deliveries, and these gained RCAF serials 720 to 731, most seeing service with 132(F) Squadron. Two survived in RCAF service as late as August 23, 1946.

The Netherlands were also identified as receiving 36 P-40E-1s on Curtiss records, but these may have been diverted to other destinations at the fall of the East Indies, or possibly to the Netherlands' training establishment in the U.S.

From an engineering standpoint, the P-40E-1 series marked a significant, but seldom recognized development in the service life of the P-40 series. The fin extension that was finally worked out by Curtiss and Wright Field engineers became effective on aircraft serial number AC41-36463 and subsequent new-build aircraft. Additionally, effective April 28, 1942, AMC ordered that the extension be retroactively installed on all surviving P-40D, P-40E, and P-40E-1 aircraft then in USAAC service in the Continental United States. Exactly how many aircraft were actually so modified in the field remains an open question, and may account for the obviously modified appearance noted in so many photos that have surfaced over the years.

The British named their P-40E-1s *Kittyhawk IAs*, and this example, with the chalked ship number 1332 on the nose, was 41-35785 in this April 2, 1942 photo. Oddly, no national markings or serial had yet been applied. (*Curtiss S-F16354*)

Taken on June 30, 1942, this interesting photo affords a direct comparison of the P-40E-1 (41-25026) to a captured German Messerschmitt Bf 109E and a Bell P-39D *Airacobra*. This aircraft was assigned to the 50th Pursuit Group at Orlando AAF, FL, where it served until March 20, 1943, when it was surveyed following an accident. (*via Peter M. Bowers*)

This aircraft, built as an *H87A-3* (MSN 18796) for the British Commonwealth as AL152—a *Kittyhawk I*—went to the Royal Canadian Air Force, becoming RCAF 1082 December 3, 1941. It served with both 115 and 118 Squadron. It survived the war to become N1207V in the U.S. in 1948, and was photographed at Santa Ana, California, in April 1968. (*Hagedorn Collection*)

Very rare photo of one of the two P-40ES aircraft modified by Bristol Aeronautical Corp. (40-582). This aircraft ended up at Luke Field, AZ, where it remained in service as late as 1944, although it was at Wright Field from the time it was delivered until then. (*via Craig "Buz" Busby*)

The USAAF authorized an unusual offset, from its own stocks, of 47 specially modified Allison V-1710-73 engines, fitted with a unique oil line connection to the breather cap, and a special adaptor for the oil pump inlet mounting pad for installation on RAF P-40E and P-40E-1

Kittyhawk aircraft in the Middle East on August 11, 1942, the original engines and equipment having suffered badly in the hot and dusty environs of the region.

Finally, one P-40E-1 was retained at the Curtiss Buffalo plant, and nominally assigned to the 3525th Air Base Unit there for training ferry crews. This was the 1,580th example built, formally accepted by the AAF April 28, 1942, and cited as being "at the Auditorium."

Curtiss P-40ES

Alarmed by the high number of training accidents being experienced as Air Force cadets entered the fighter stream from advanced training bases, the AAF issued an urgent requirement for study of a "Two-Place P-40" under CTI-1106, dated January 7, 1943.

This initiative was attributed by Wright Field to a suggestion made by Lieutenant Colonel James Ferguson, Commander of the 337th Fighter Group at Drew Field, Tampa, FL, on November 21, 1942.

Moving with an "A-1" priority assigned to the issue by none other than General "Hap" Arnold, Chief of the AAF, bids were solicited from contractors who felt that they had the excess capacity

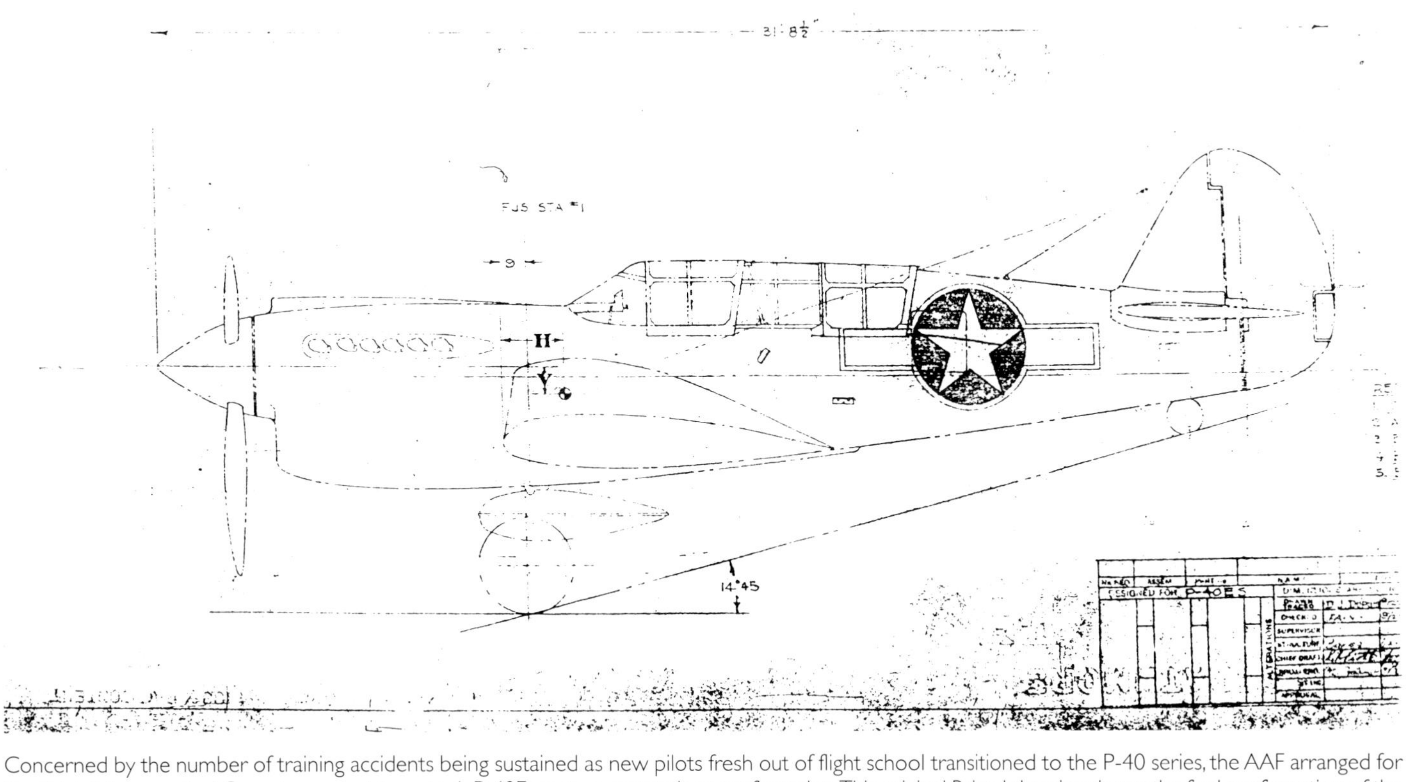

Concerned by the number of training accidents being sustained as new pilots fresh out of flight school transitioned to the P-40 series, the AAF arranged for the Bristol Aeronautical Corp. to convert two stock P-40Es to two-seat trainer configuration. This original Bristol drawing shows the final configuration of the canopy arrangement. (*USAAF*)

to address the question, and the first of these—and the winner of the bid—was the Bristol Aeronautical Corporation of New Haven, CT, which submitted a detailed proposal to the Chief of the Engineering Division at Wright Field on January 28, 1943. Bristol was given the go-ahead to commence the conversion on February 12th, and a second conversion was authorized on March 23rd, at a unit cost of around $5,000. Wright Field advised that these two conversions were to be designated as P-40ES aircraft. The aircraft converted were AC40-582 and AC40-633. In the meantime, Bristol had submitted yet another proposal to the AAF to provide a similar conversion of a P-40D, but when the Army received the proposal, they ruled the costs too high.

The conversion of the P-40Es took rather longer than had been anticipated, however, mainly due to shortages of required materials during that period of the war, and the first item was completed June 17, 1943, followed by the second July 2nd. They were delivered to Wright Field on July 21, 1943. The first aircraft was later flown to Washington's National Airport, for first hand examination by high officials of the AAF (including Arnold himself), on September 24, 1943.

During flight tests of the aircraft at Wright Field, concluded by September 16, 1943, test pilots reported "*...no difference in flying characteristics of the subject aircraft as compared to conventional P-40s.*"

By October 16, 1943, both of the P-40ES aircraft had been assigned to Luke Field, AZ, where they underwent extensive service tests and evaluation. AC40-633 was later tested at MacDill Field, FL, with a unique dual gun sight system in early May 1944.

Decoy P-40E Aircraft

It is not known with any precision exactly how many decoy, or "dummy" P-40s were created by units of the Army Air Forces during the war. However, a measure of how extensive this effort must

The British conducted a number of tests on the U.S. built Curtiss *Kittyhawks* at the world-renowned Aeroplane and Armament Experimental Establishment (A&AEE) at Boscombe Down, in England. This included extensive tests on the flame damping qualities of the U.S. designed "fishtail" exhaust stacks on *Kittyhawk I* AK579. They concluded that this was the best such damper system noted to date, and recommended that the same design be fitted to all *Mustangs* and *Airacobras* in service, as well as Merlin engined aircraft. *(A&AEE AM9965)*

have been can be gained by observing that the Engineering Division of the Panama Air Depot in the Canal Zone had made not fewer than 150 dummy P-40 aircraft by July 15, 1943, and these were distributed to fields occupied by Panama Interceptor Command units to be deployed as decoys.

Curtiss Export Model 87A *Kittyhawks*

The first British *Kittyhawks* were export versions of the U.S. Army P-40D and P-40E fighters. The initial British order was placed in May 1940 for 20 Model 87A-2, *Kittyhawk Mark I* aircraft, starting with British serial AK571.[132] The first flight of this type took place

The British Commonwealth acquired a large number of *H87A-2* and *H87A-3* aircraft, some as direct purchases, and some via Lend-Lease. These served widely throughout combat areas where Commonwealth forces engaged Axis elements. This overhead view shows that, even with camouflage applied, wear-and-tear from crews entering and servicing the aircraft eroded the paint near the wing root aft of the cockpit, creating a glare from the sun overhead. *(Dean Collection)*

Curtiss prepared this schematic to aid in the training of British Commonwealth aircrews in the care and feeding of the *H87A-2*. (*Curtiss*)

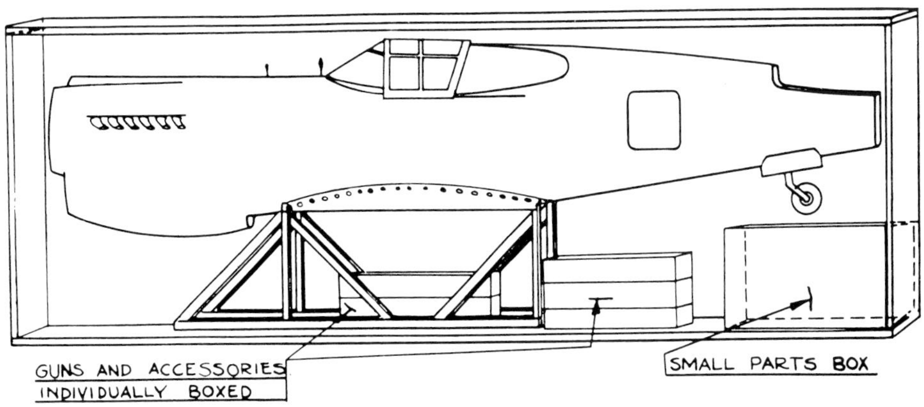

The vast majority of *H87A-2* and *H87A-3 Kittyhawk* variants provided to British Commonwealth forces were crated for shipment via surface vessel, and erected in a phenomenal number of distant places by relatively untrained crews. This is how the fuselage and accessories were boxed. (*Curtiss*)

Yet another ex-Royal Canadian Air Force *Kittyhawk I* that survived to be sold surplus into the U.S. was AK979 (RCAF 1064), MSN 18723, which eventually became N5672N with a much modified canopy. It had entered service in Canada in April 23, 1942, and served with 132 Squadron. It is pictured here at Lambert Field, in St. Louis, on May 27, 1958. (*Hagedorn Collection*)

One of the P-40Ds (AC40-360) was modified by June 30, 1942, to become the XP-40F with a British *Merlin 28* engine. Tested as such only briefly, it had passed to Class 26 (instructional airframe) at Lincoln, Nebraska, by September 16th. (*Aeroplane Photo Supply via Dean Collection*)

on May 22, 1941, piloted by Curtiss test pilot Lloyd Child, and production deliveries were initiated in August 1941. These initial 20 export *Kittyhawks*, like the U.S. P-40D, had four Colt .50 caliber wing guns instead of the six of later aircraft. Belly fittings were included for attachment of either a 52 gallon external drop tank or a 500 pound bomb. Characteristics of these fighters were similar to those of the U.S. P-40D.

An additional 540 aircraft were again bought directly by Britain (before Lend-Lease took effect) as 87A-3 models on Contract A-1835, commencing with MSN 14972 as AK591. They were still labeled *Kittyhawk Mark I*, even though they differed from the A-2s in being six gun fighters. These 540 planes were generally like the U.S. P-40E aircraft. Hard on the heels of these *Kittyhawks* came the first Lend-Lease model designated as 87A-4, 1,500 of which were completed by Curtiss. The first 420 aircraft had been ordered on May 7, 1941, and the second batch of 1,080 ordered June 30, 1941. The planes were accepted by the U.S. Army under the designation P-40E-1 (q.v.), and then transferred to the United Kingdom under Lend-Lease provisions, where they were labeled *Kittyhawk Mk.IA*. So important were these aircraft in the RAF at the time that a so-called *Tomahawk School* had been established at the firm of Cunliffe-Owen Aircraft Ltd. and, by November 1941, were largely responsible for repairs to most RAF *Tomahawks*, as well as Bristol *Blenheims* and Lockheed *Hudsons*, with *Kittyhawks* added, as well. The school operated under rather severe wartime conditions. For instance, at the start of a course they conducted, they had no literature whatsoever on Curtiss Electric props, until by accident, one of the instructors found a small bulletin in the Southampton Public Library and reprinted it! The manuals that had been shipped with the aircraft has disappeared somewhere in the wartime confusion, and never arrived at depot levels.

Another British firm intimately involved in the introduction of *Kittyhawks* into the RAF Order of Battle was Scottish Aviation, Ltd., of Prestwick, which assembled and modified many of the aircraft, commencing with AK751 and AK764. Another important *Kittyhawk* modification center was the Air Service Training Center (A.S.T.) Hamble, near Southampton, which also handled early RAF *Airacobras* and *Mustangs*.

Curtiss had really gotten into mass production by this point, because these planes were all delivered by mid-1942. Some of the *Kittyhawks* (at least 691 P-40Es) went to Russia, where it appears they were not as well liked as the Bell P-39. Deliveries of the P-40E-1 began in September 1941, with most going to North Africa, the first arriving in Egypt in October. Some *Kittyhawks* got to the Southwest Pacific; in December 1942 the Royal New Zealand Air Force had one squadron. On January 1, 1942, Royal Air Force *Kittyhawks* went into action in North Africa. Deliveries of an eventual total of 72 *Kittyhawk Mk.Is* were made to Canada, commencing October 9, 1941 (initially with RAF serials, but issued RCAF serials 1028 to 1099, these served with 11, 14, 111, 115, 118, 130, 132, and 133 Squadrons), and also in March Royal Australian Air Force *Kittyhawks* of three squadrons were in action from New Guinea, in the Southwest Pacific, against the Japanese. That same month the British in North Africa started using their *Kittyhawks* as fighter-bombers, and in April initiated replacing Curtiss *Tomahawks* with the later models. In April 1942 six P-40E-1s went to Brazil under Lend-Lease. By mid-May RAF 112 Squadron was converted

Often cited as a "YP-40F," but never officially cited as such in Army records, the third production P-40F was modified by moving the radiator system aft to align with the wing leading edge, but this aircraft was returned to conventional configuration. (*via Peter M. Bowers*)

P-40F 41-13600, marked only as "148" on the vertical fin, was assigned to the NACA between July and September 1942 to investigate solutions to the continuing directional stability problems of the type. Compare the location of the horizontal tail surfaces relative to the vertical fin in this image to the next view. (*Dean Collection*)

to the First Fighter-Bomber Squadron in the British Desert Air Force, and other squadrons followed. In June 1942, the Royal Canadian Air Force sent 15 *Kittyhawks* to assist in the defense of Alaska. The next month, in New Guinea, RAAF *Kittyhawks* started to use 500 pound bombs against Japanese installations. In September, two RCAF *Kittyhawk* squadrons returned to Canada after fighting alongside USAAF squadrons in the Aleutians.

Somewhat strangely, perhaps, USAAF P-40F fighters with British-designed Rolls Royce *Merlin* engines were fighting in North Africa attached to British RAF squadrons who were using *Kittyhawks* powered with American-designed Allison engines.

Typical characteristics for the *Kittyhawk MkIA* were: span, length, and height 37 feet, three and 1/2 inches, 31 feet, two inches, and eight feet, two inches.

Areas, dimensions, and powerplant were the same as the U.S. P-40E.

Empty weight was 6,350 pounds, normal useful load 1,750 pounds, maximum useful load 2,950 pounds, normal gross weight 8,100 pounds, and maximum gross weight 9,200 pounds. Normal gross weight, wing, and power loadings were 39.32psf and 7.04 pounds per horse power. Normal useful load to gross weight ratio was 0.216.

Maximum speed was 354mph at 15,000 feet. Cruise speed was 300mph, and landing speed 84mph. Initial climb rate 2,050fpm, service ceiling 29,000 feet, and normal and ferry ranges 700 miles and 1,500 miles, respectively.

There were also some *Merlin* powered P-40F models delivered to Britain in mid-1942 via Lend-Lease, about 230 to 250 aircraft labeled by Curtiss as Model H87B-3, and by the British as *Kittyhawk Mk.II*. Later, since the U.S. was operating *Merlin*-engined P-40Fs in North Africa, a few were returned to U.S. service there; the numbers are uncertain.

Curtiss received a copy of the RAF's 150 hour Intensive Flying Test on the *Kittyhawk* dated May 1, 1942, and, based on the language of the report, the aircraft tested must have been one of the second batch of 540 *Mk.Is*. Although the complaints seemed minor, they reflected the difficulties encountered during the war in fielding large numbers of U.S. designed aircraft to a foreign operator.

For example, the report pointed out that "*...all pipeline joints on all systems are secured with American type clips. An appreciable number of these showed a tendency to work loose, and the checking and tightening of them was a prominent item of dail inspection.*" There was also comment on the lack of any throttle control friction device, common on British designs, and something that British Commonwealth trained pilots expected. Other comments involved the fuel selector cocks, the ignition harness, and the emergency hydraulic system to the tail wheel. All in all, however, it observed that, in spite of these points, maintenance of the aircraft had been accomplished with "reasonable ease," and that, in this respect, the aircraft appeared generally to be more accessible than most American fighter aircraft and, in view of the duration of the tests, had emerged "*...in a very satisfactory manner.*"

Curtiss P-40F *Warhawk*

Curtiss badly wanted improvement in the altitude performance of the P-40, and to this end designed a modification using a Packard-manufactured Rolls Royce *Merlin 20* Series engine. This was not the two stage supercharged engine later employed in the P-51 *Merlin* powered Mustang, but rather a single stage, two speed *Merlin* variant similar to that used in the British Hawker *Hurricane* fighter. The *Merlin* engined version was designated by Curtiss as H87B-3 (Specification 98-610-8A), and as P-40F by the U.S. Army. The P-40F series was the first to be officially given a popular name by the Air Corps.

This is P-40F 41-13600 again, now marked on the vertical fin as "F-1" in chalk, as of September 10, 1942, at the NACA. Compare the empennage arrangement with the earlier photo. A 20-inch fuselage extension was been inserted, and is difficult to discern. Note that the red "dot" in the national insignia has now been roughly painted over with white. (*NACA via Dean Collection*)

Curtiss and the AAC had, however, by January 17, 1942, initially attempted to mount a *Merlin 61* series engine in a P-40F, but with nearly disastrous results for Curtiss. None other than the Chief of the Technical Staff Section at Wright Field, LTC H. Z. Bogert, weighed in on the aircraft by saying that:

"...*based on the reported speed of 375mph at 21,000 feet, this airplane, equipped with the Merlin 61 without additional cooling, should go about 392mph. The Production Engineering Section feels it is wrong to continue to develop the P-40 type airplane as a new model on the basis of increased speed alone. This is apparently the only improvement gained by changing the engine. Rate of climb, maneuverability, and other factors making up good performance all suffer. They are not opposed to putting a Merlin 61 engine in existing P-40Fs, providing it does not interfere with the production schedule. They are very much opposed, however, to extending the production schedule of this type airplane by Curtiss.*"

Even more damning was an endorsement to these comments by LTC F. O. Carroll, Chief of the Experimental Engineering Section at Wright, dated January 19th, in which he stated that "...*it is wrong to continue development about the P-40 type airplane on any basis whatsoever.*"

In spite of these very pointed comments by officers in key positions, an experimental aircraft, fashioned as the XP-40F (Curtiss Specification 7437A), was modified from a P-40D airframe (Serial 40-360)[133] on Change Order No.12 to AC-12414, but using instead a British *Merlin 28* engine. This aircraft was formally handed over to the Air Corps June 30, 1942, and went immediately to Wright Field. Oddly, it did not survive long, becoming Class 26 (instructional airframe) at Lincoln, NE, by September 16th. Nose lines were modified, and the upper cowl scoop for the downdraft carburetor of Allison models was eliminated, since the Merlin used an updraft carburetor. The airscoop for this was combined with the lower cowl scoop used for the oil cooler and the cooling radiator intake air.

Even as the P-40F was under development for production, however, the AAF, by September 2, 1942, recorded a "...*immediate requirement for a maneuverable interceptor with a high rate of climb,*" and felt that the installation of an R-2600 engine in a P-40 airframe might supply the answer. They proposed that such an aircraft would have only four .50 caliber guns and "...*a minimum of gadgetry,*" and the ubiquitous Captain Ben Kelsey had, in addition, been pressing hard, at the same time, for the idea of even installing an R-2800 in a P-40 airframe.

Other, perhaps more practical configurations were tried instead, however. A single YP-40F[134] (Curtiss Specification 7437A) was the third production P-40F (41-13602) airframe tested with revised cooling, the radiator system being aft and aligned with the wing leading edge, an arrangement not put into production. In addition, various tail configurations were tested to eliminate stability problems that had cropped up starting with the P-40D model, and relating to the destabilizing effect of the large scoop up front.

Curtiss records indicate 1,302 aircraft of the P-40F type were delivered at a unit price of $38,695 less GFE: 1,255 in 1942, and 27 in 1943. Other records indicate that 1,311 aircraft P-40Fs were built. Deliveries of the "F" model stared on January 3, 1942, using Packard-built *Merlin* V-1650-1 engines. The P-40F was the first to use a production block number system.

The basic P-40F was produced into August 1942, and totaled 699 aircraft.[135] Next production switched to the P-40F-5 version, with a 20 inch longer fuselage, with 123 aircraft manufactured starting in August, this change to alleviate the stability problems previously encountered.[136] Then, 177 P-40F-10 fighters came off the lines using manual instead of electric cowl flap operation. A total of 200 P-40F-15 variants with electrical and oxygen system changes followed, and 112 P-40F-20-CUs ended production. USAAF serials were 41-13600 to 41-13695 (P-40F-CU, 96 aircraft), with the first being accepted April 3, 1942, all of which remained in the U.S.; 41-13696, a serial often inexplicably deleted from most references, was in fact manufactured and delivered on March 31, 1942, but was employed only as a static test article and never flew; 41-13697 to 41-14299 (P-40F-1-CU, 603 aircraft); 41-14300 to 41-14422 (P-40F-5-CU, 123 aircraft); 41-14423 to 41-14599 (P-40F-10-CU, 177 aircraft); 41-19733 (delivered November 26, 1942) to 41-19932 (P-40F-15-CU, 200 aircraft); and 41-19933 to 41-20044 (P-40F-20-CU, 112 aircraft).

Characteristics of the P-40F were as follows: span, length, and height were 37 feet, three and 1/2 inches, 31 feet, seven and 23/32 inches, and 10 feet, seven and 25/32 inches. Wing area was 236 square feet, and horizontal and vertical tail areas 48 square feet and 21.74 square feet, respectively.

The powerplant was a Packard *Merlin* V-1650-1 rated 1300hp at 3,000rpm at sea level takeoff, 1,240hp (Military) at 3,000rpm at 11,800 feet, and 1,122hp (Military) at 3,000rpm at 19,000 feet. Supercharger gear ratio was 8.151:1, and propeller reduction gear ratio was 21:44. Fuel capacities were 120 gallons normal and 200 gallons maximum. The propeller was a Curtiss Electric constant speed 11 foot diameter three blade model with Design 614 blades. High and low blade pitch settings were 54 degrees and 26.5 degrees, respectively.

Weights calculated August 23, 1941, in Curtiss Report 7437A were: empty weight 6,190 pounds, normal useful load 1,921 pounds (a 180 pound pilot, 720 pounds of fuel, 120 pounds of oil, and 901 pounds of armament), maximum ammunition useful load 2,004 pounds (83 pounds of ammunition added), and maximum ammunition gross weight 8,194 pounds. Maximum fuel useful load was 2,484 pounds (comprised of a 180 pound pilot, 1,200 pounds of fuel, 150 pounds of oil, and 901 pounds of armament). Maximum fuel gross weight was 8,674 pounds.

Actual weights of P-40F #400 from Curtiss Report 8763 dated June 24, 1942 (where the aircraft was over Curtiss guaranteed weight by 109 pounds), were: empty weight 6,576 pounds, useful load with normal fuel 1,933 pounds (pilot 180 pounds, 120 gallons of fuel at 720 pounds, 98 pounds of engine oil, trapped fluids 37 pounds, and armament 898 pounds), and normal fuel gross weight 8,509 pounds.

Curtiss guaranteed performance as of August 23, 1941, was: maximum speed 370mph at 3,000rpm at 1,105hp at 22,000 feet; 346mph at 2,650rpm at 996hp at 18,500 feet, 318mph at 3,000rpm at 1,180hp at 5,000 feet; 303mph at 2,650rpm at 1,050hp at 5,000 feet; and 300mph at 2,490rpm at 752hp (75 percent of maximum

This P-40F was a "presentation aircraft" funded by the Brotherhood of Railroad Trainmen, and named *The Iron Eagle*, at least as of the time she departed the U.S. for North Africa. (*The Museum of Flight*)

power) at 15,000 feet. Stall speed was 82mph. Time to climb at (Normal) power at 2,850rpm was 6.9 minutes to 15,000 feet. Service ceiling was 32,000 feet. Endurance was 2.56 hours at 752hp at 2,490rpm at 15,000 feet at 300mph. Takeoff distance over a 50 foot obstacle was 2,300 feet at 1,300hp at 3,000rpm at sea level. Landing distance over a 50 foot obstacle was 1,800 feet at sea level.

Later, actual performance was recorded as follows: maximum speed was measured at 364mph at 20,000 feet, 352mph at 15,000 feet, 340mph at 10,000 feet, 320mph at 5,000 feet, and 300mph at sea level. Cruise speed was 290mph, and landing speed 82mph. Climb to 15,000 feet took 7.6 minutes, and service ceiling was 34,400 feet. Maximum range with normal fuel was 700 miles at 10.000 feet.

Armament consisted of six .50 caliber wing mounted unsynchronized machine guns with 281 rounds per gun. The P-40F could carry a 500 pound bomb under the fuselage, plus two 100 pound bombs under the wings.

On July 1, 1942, the 57th Fighter Group, with P-40Fs, went aboard the carrier *Ranger* for North Africa, and then flew across Africa to join the Western Desert Air Force. Indeed, none other than a direct order from General Henry H. "Hap" Arnold himself, dated June 24, 1942, had directed that the 57th be equipped with 77 factory-fresh P-40Fs then at Buffalo, and that they be fully equipped for combat and ready to fly. He further instructed that, if necessary, aircraft from British production could be "acquired" to arrive at the total of 77 aircraft. This may explain why some 57th FG aircraft have been noted wearing RAF style camouflage and fin flashes early in the North African campaign that followed.

As the 57th FG P-40Fs were to be launched from U.S. Navy aircraft carriers, the subject of precisely how to do this became a pressing issue. On August 10, 1942, a Memo was issued giving basic instructions of how to accomplish such a launch.

First, the carrier speed was to be increased to more than 25 knots, with the wind crossing the port bow. Flaps on the P-40Fs were to then be set at about 25°, and maximum manifold pressure of 54" hg and 3,000rpm with full brakes were to be selected. The maximum safe launch distance was established at 350 but, in actual practice, this distance was not required. The pilots were instructed to leave their undercarriages fully extended until the deck was cleared, and then execute a right turn, and not the conventional left turn.

Reinforcement of the British in North Africa saw P-40Fs of the 33rd Fighter Group fly off the USS *Ranger* much earlier than the celebrated *Operation Torch* launches January 1943. Here No.12 (*Jo*) prepares to launch on July 19, 1942, with a gaggle of skeptical sailors looking on from the gun pits on the port side. (*USAF*)

A first P-40F victory was scored on August 9th over a German Bf-109. After training with Royal Air Force *Kittyhawk* squadrons, the 57th flew its first official combat mission for the U.S. Ninth Air Force in North Africa on August 31, 1942. The 57th P-40Fs scored a significant victory over Axis aircraft on October 27, 1942, and by early November had claimed its 20th victory.

On November 11, 1942, in conjunction with *Operation Torch*, the 33rd Fighter Group with P-40Fs launched 78 fighters off two aircraft carriers for the North African invasion. A day later, the 79th Fighter Group with P-40Fs reached Egypt. In January 1943, the final P-40F-20 was delivered from the Curtiss plant. That same month on the 9th, the U.S. forces donated 25 long-fuselage P-40Fs to equip a French unit in North Africa, and their first victories came on the 10th, but only five were left by mid-March.

On the 19th, 72 P-40F and P-40L aircraft were successfully flown off the carrier *Ranger* to Casablanca, in French Morocco. On March 14, 1943, the P-40Fs of the 57th Fighter Group joined the fray in Tunisia, North Africa. In that month the Free French unit, having lost most of their P-40Fs, received new P-40L aircraft. To ease the American logistics problem, the U.S. Groups in North Africa used *Merlin* engined P-40F and P-40L aircraft, the only U.S. P-40 versions so powered.

Some, but very few, P-40Fs were employed in the Southwest Pacific area in 1943. The 44th Fighter Squadron of the 18th Fighter Group received the P-40F model on Oahu about October 1942, and went to Guadalcanal in January 1943.

Official Army assignments of the P-40F series are illuminating, but must be viewed with caution, as inter-theater transfers were often not noted accurately on Aircraft Record Cards, from which this data was extracted raw. With the foregoing paragraphs in mind, this snapshot summary may give the reader a more concise appreciation for the breadth of deployment of this, the first truly mass produced P-40 variant:

From Block AC41-13697 to 41-14599
• Many of the initial deliveries were dispatched for use by the 33rd and 56th Pursuit Groups
• Three aircraft (41-13751, 41-13894, and 41-13797) were retained and assigned to "Camp Curtissaire" for instructional purposes near Buffalo as late as August 28, 1943, but were later reassigned to the Air Forces Training Command (AFTC)
• At least 76 were wrecked in the U.S. during training
• At least 36 eventually reached Class 26 (instructional airframe) status in the U.S.
• At least 146 were offset for British Commonwealth forces under Lend-Lease. These were to be FL219 to FL448, and of these, FL219 to FL243 have been perfectly matched to USAAF serials 41-13751 to 41-13775.
• At least 14 were diverted to Free French Forces
• Not fewer than 295 were destined for Foreign Destination Code **HEATH** (Africa, Cairo, Middle-East, including 64 on the so-called "MK" Projects in batches of 16 each, MK-33, MK-34, MK-35, and MK-36). A further 59 were destined for Foreign Destination Code **GLEN** (Oran, Algeria), obviously in connection with the Allied invasion there. Of these aircraft, 30 are identified as DEA (Flak) (Destroyed by Enemy Action, Flak), one as DEA (usually as the result of aerial combat), and 12 as MIA (Missing in Action).
• At least 58 were assigned to Hawaii under Foreign Destination Codes **IRON** and **MAESTRO**. Of these, at least 25 were reassigned to Destination Code **EPIC** (Noumea, New Caledonia), also designated as **POPPY**. Another two were designated for **BEVY** (Guadalcanal, Solomon's), and a solitary example was designated for merely **ACID** (Southwest Pacific area, also given as **ROSES**).
• At least 115 were designated for Foreign Destination Code **WILDFLOWER**, which was originally the Eighth Air Force in England. However, nearly all of these were diverted to **BLOT**, which was Morocco, and thus probably part of Operation TORCH. Of these, six were noted as Missing in Action.

From Block AC41-19733 to 41-20044
• At least 120 aircraft from this batch went to Foreign Destination Code **BLOT** (see above), of which at least seven were lost to flak, and six were Missing in Action. Interestingly, some of these aircraft were returned to the U.S., and at least three went to Class 26 instructional airframe duties after return.
• At least 88 went to Foreign Destination Code **HEATH**, and 30 to **GLEN**, of which 10 were lost to flak, three Missing in Action, and one lost to Enemy Action (aerial combat).
• At least 45 went to Foreign Destination Code **ACHE**, which was an alternate code for Cairo, Egypt. Of these, 14 passed to **GLEN** and, of the total, six were lost to flak, two to enemy action, and two missing in action.
• At least 30 were designated for shipment to Foreign Destination Code **POPPY** (Noumea, New Caledonia), of which nine went on to **BEVY** (Guadalcanal), and six to **ROSES**.

Factory-fresh, the 78 P-40Fs provided to the 33rd Fighter Group for the invasion of North Africa had been directed by none other than General "Hap" Arnold himself. Here, 41-20002 is parked amidst Navy Grumman TBF-1 *Avengers* while enroute to the invasion in January 1943 on CV-4, the USS *Ranger*. This aircraft survived the North African campaign, and was stricken as war-weary on January 30, 1945. (*NARA RG-80G #34279*)

Much earlier than *Operation Torch* in July 1942, the 57th Fighter Group had been transported to North Africa, also on the USS *Ranger*, and had then flown across Africa to join the Allied Desert Air Force. By December 8, 1943, the Group was in Italy supporting the northern movement of the Eighth Army. This aircraft, adorned with the emblem of the 64th Fighter Squadron, appears to have seen very hard use. (*H. Farrell*)

• One aircraft from this batch was offset for the Free French Forces which, taken together with the total of 14 from the earlier batch, is the first accurate accounting of *Warhawks* clearly intended for French use.
• Two aircraft from this batch were assigned to Ladd Field, Alaska, and a significant number never left the Continental United States, with at least five lost to accidents in the U.S.

Finally, no fewer than six P-40F aircraft were formally accepted by the AAF, but not delivered. These included the 1st production aircraft, retained from April 30, 1942, for tests; the 152nd, 198th, and 295th examples, retained by Curtiss, and described as being "at the auditorium," a euphemism meaning they were being used locally for various purposes; the 538th example from July 25, 1942, also for tests; and the 593rd example for unspecified purposes. These may have been amongst the aircraft Curtiss retained for plant defense, flown by Army and Curtiss test pilots.

The U.S. Navy's Curtiss P-40F

On June 6, 1942, the Army Air Force transferred P-40F 41-13701, then on the strength of the 60th Fighter Squadron at Bolling Field, to the U.S. Navy at Anacostia Naval Air Station, DC, for comparative tests against the Grumman F4F-4 *Wildcat*, at the time the standard U.S. Navy production fighter.

These two P-40Fs of the 79th Fighter Group's 86th Fighter Squadron were almost unique in USAAF service, in having "tail art" instead of the more conventional "nose art." (*The Museum of Flight*)

USAAF P-40Fs in the Pacific Theater made landings via surface vessel—rather less glamorous than their Mediterranean brethren. Here, P-40F-1-CU 41-14210 is being sent to shore via lighter off, appropriately, the USS *Kittyhawk* (APV-1), near Palmyra Island at Pallikulo Bay, in the New Hebrides, sometime after November 1942. This aircraft, delivered to the AAF August 18, 1942, survived until October 31, 1944, when it was stricken as war weary. (*NARA RG-80G #72795*)

With this aircraft, the Navy performed standard performance and stability trials with the aircraft loaded as a normal fighter. The results were candid, and rather surprising.

At normal power settings, the P-40F and F4F-4 were found to have nearly the same average power up to 16,000 feet, with a temporary advantage zigzagging between the two as altitude was increased. Above 19,500 feet, the F4F-4 was found to have an advantage of about 100bhp at normal rating. However, above the critical altitude for both aircraft, the increase for the P-40F was 150bhp, and the F4F-4 just 50bhp.

The Navy found also that the P-40F was superior below 20,000 feet in climb and speed, while the F4F-4 was superior above that altitude. However, it also noted that, above 24,000 feet, at either power rating, the F4F-4's advantage in speed and climb was marked. The P-40F, however, could easily dive away from the F4F-4.

Fuel capacity of the two was almost identical, with 148 gallons for the P-40F, and 144 for the F4F. The Navy admired the 52 gallon belly tank the P-40 could sport, and observed that the F4F-4 had two 50 gallon under wing tanks under test, but apparently these were never employed operationally.

Visibility for the pilot was rated as markedly superior in the F4F-4, as the pilot sat higher, and the aircraft had a much shorter nose. The P-40F's gun sight was appreciated, but the Navy rated the F4F-4 as a far superior gun platform, due mainly to the poor visibility over the nose of the P-40F, high rudder forces, and tendency to abrupt high speed stalling, which made close-range, full-deflection shooting extremely difficult.

The Navy admired the quiet of the P-40F cockpit compared to the F4F, as well as the cockpit temperature control and ventilation, but noted that the cockpit of the P-40 was cramped compared to the F4F. They also noted that the P-40F had a much higher rate of roll than the F4F-4.

This experiment was followed, later that same month, on June 21, 1942, by an extraordinary Memorandum from the Navy Department to the Operations and Plans Division (OPD) of the War Department (Navy Message 210317), originating with none other than the CinCPAC, in which he stated:

"*...it is believed that providing P-40 planes for all Marine fighting squadron assigned to outlying bases of high importance is imperative, if the P-40 can be modified for carrier operations.*"

The fate of the "Navy P-40" is not clear, but at this point in the war, it is noteworthy that the Navy took the time to conduct such an evaluation.

Curtiss Tail Forward - Pusher Pursuit/Interceptor

On January 30, 1942, the Curtiss Engineering Department committed to paper a proposal for what was described as a Tail Forward-Purchaser Type Airplane, Pursuit-Interceptor. It was described briefly as a single-engine, single place aircraft with a Pratt & Whitney R-2800-29 1,675hp engine (at 2,550rpm at sea level) engine with remote propeller gear reduction, and was apparently in-

The "office" of a standard P-40F as of April 24, 1943. Notice the reflection of the instruments of this very functional instrument panel on the side windscreen glass. (*Wright Field 113516 via Peter M. Bowers*)

Although often cited as being able to heft a 500 pound bomb slung on a rack under the fuselage, it is often overlooked that the P-40F could also load two 100 pound bombs under each wing. (*Curtiss S-F15674*)

tended for Army consideration at a very dark moment in the war for the U.S.

By March 23rd, the exact same design was detailed in Report No.8718, but for the Navy. Neither design was developed and, so far as can be determined, no Design Numbers were assigned.

Curtiss 3-Place Fighter

On January 13, 1942, the Curtiss Engineering Department proposed a radical design, described as a 3-place fighter, consisting of a crew of a pilot and two gunners (one of them firing to the rear) with four .50 caliber guns. It was to have mounted a single Wright *Tornado* engine with *Acrotorque* propeller drive, and two Allison engines. It did not proceed beyond the concept stage.

Curtiss P-40J

According to several sources, the designation P-40J was assigned to a projected version of the P-40E, which was to incorporate a turbo supercharged engine. The project was reportedly abandoned in May 1942 without reaching hardware stages. Independent confirmation of this project in Curtiss records has not been located, nor have any AAF documents been identified confirming the project. An official Army document, "*Model Designations Army Aircraft*" dated July 1942, noted that designation P-40J had not been assigned.

Curtiss P-40K *Warhawk*

The P-40K was the 1942 version of the Allison powered P-40 *Warhawk* fighter, Curtiss Specification 98-610-13. The initial order for 600 P-40K aircraft came on October 30, 1941. The remaining P-40Ks (700 planes) were ordered (along with some P-40L and P-40M models) on June 11, 1942, in place of the Curtiss P-60, after the decision had been made by the Army Air Forces not to interrupt current P-40 production for a new Curtiss type. An order for an additional 1,299 P-40K fighters was cancelled. All P-40K fighters were delivered in 1942 at a unit price of $42,490. The original 600 aircraft had been ordered in October 1941 for China under the Lend-Lease program, though as it happened few were delivered there, and these only in June 1943.

A big change was the up-rated Allison engine with a sea level takeoff rating of 1,325hp, and a War Emergency rating was added for the first time. Also, automatic manifold pressure regulation was finally added. The P-40Ks were built in four variations according to block numbers. The P-40K-1 (Curtiss Specification 7437A) was the most produced, with 600 aircraft delivered (USAAF serials 42-9727 to 42-9729—three aircraft—were cancelled, and serials 42-45722 to 42-46321 were assigned to the production batch). The first of these (42-45722) was MSN 18520, and was retained at Curtiss for tests from May 19, 1942. It was a "short fuselage" model,

Although frequently cited as an "XP-40K" (42-10219), the aircraft bailed to Allison for development work for six months in 1942 retained a straight P-40K-10 designation throughout a number of modifications. It is seen here at the Allison Test Section on June 10, 1944, and was written off there during tests. (*NARA RG342*)

Basically a P-40E with an Allison V-1710-73 (F4R), the P-40K series could heft up to 1,500 pounds of bombs on ventral and under wing racks. 42-9987 is pictured on November 4, 1942, at Buffalo, having been retained by Curtiss after delivery on September 28th.. This is the very same aircraft that became the XP-40Q-2 later on. (*Curtiss via Harold Andrews*)

with a large fillet added on the vertical fin, and these were delivered in May through August 1942. Some sources claim that one aircraft (P-40K-10 42-10219) was redesignated as an XP-40K while undergoing development work with Allison in Indianapolis. However, this is not correct. Although the aircraft went to Allison on a bailment about six months after delivery, it retained the normal designation P-40K, and was eventually passed to Class 26 (instructional airframe) duties on June 12, 1944, after a very serious crash. The P-40K-5 came next, with 200 aircraft delivered in September 1942 (USAAF serials 42-9730 to 42-9929, with 42-9730 accepted from the manufacturer on August 31, 1942); except for slight powerplant changes, it hardly differed from the earlier version. From September into November 1942 a P-40K-10 came off the lines, of which 335 were produced (USAAF serials 42-9930 to 42-10264). This version was the first "long fuselage" K, with the vertical tail moved aft. The fuselage length increase was about 20 inches. Some of these were winterized for northern service. The K-10 production ended in November, and a final version (the P-40K-15), of which 165 were manufactured (USAAF serials 42-10265 to 42-10429), had the emergency hydraulic system eliminated, and the battery relocated. The last K was delivered on November 7, 1942.

Some P-40Ks went to the 57th Fighter Group in Palestine in August 1942. Many Ks were sent to the North African desert in September 1942, and some were ferried from there to reinforce China Air Task Force squadrons. Only a few P-40K fighters went to Britain; 21 were used by the Royal Air Force as *Kittyhawk Mark III* and, somewhat oddly, nine were used, with their USAAF serial numbers, by the Royal Canadian Air Force between November 26, 1942, and June 23, 1943, when the survivors were returned to U.S. custody.[137]

In December 1942, P-40K-1 *Warhawks* were with the U.S. Ninth Air Force, and P-40K-10s were with the 79th Fighter Group in North Africa in 1943. In December 1942, P-40K models were in India with the 51st Fighter Group of the Tenth Air Force. In March 1943 P-40Ks started arriving in quantity in China, and the Chinese-American Composite Group was formed with eight squadrons of P-40Ks.

This P-40K-1 (42-46178) is shown taking off from the USS *Breton* (CVE-23), a very small escort carrier, on December 10, 1943. It was flying off to Wheeler Field, in the Hawaiian Islands, where it remained until returned to the U.S. mainland on May 3, 1944. (*NARA RG-80G #212783*)

There were two groups, each with four squadrons. In addition, the 23rd Fighter Group in China operated P-40Ks, as did the 51st Fighter Group, by then in Burma. The 49th Fighter Group also operated P-40Ks, along with E models, and in March 1943 was located partly at Horn Island, off Queensland, Australia, and partly at Port Darwin. In October1943 P-40Ks flew their last combat mission in Alaska,[138] but in January 1944 P-40Ks of the 344th Fighter Group were based at Shemya, Alaska, on patrol trying to cope with the bad weather, and just plain boredom. In late 1943 P-40Ks were also assigned to units in Hawaii, so this version was well spread over the Pacific area.

The Soviet Union was allocated 30 P-40K-1s as of August 21, 1942 (the first batch of a total of 313 P-40Ks they received), and these were to be fitted, on a rush basis, with long-range auxiliary fuel tanks, and be ready for departure no later than August 24, 1942.

Brazil received 31 P-40K-1s, the first 10 in November 1942, 17 more in January-March 1943 and, in October 1944, two more, all under Lend-Lease.[139] The first five of these apparently were serialed as 07 to 09, and 01 and 05, but were later retrospectively issued the serials, through the P-40Ks remaining, of FAB 4026 to 4050, 4148 and 4149, and 4101 and 4102. Chile came very close to receiving 12 P-40s in mid-1943, and these would probably have been P-40Ks. Indeed 10 Chilean pilots, trained by the Navy at Corpus Christi NAS, had been selected by name to be trained on the aircraft, but the requisition was changed instead to Douglas A-24B *Dauntless* attack bombers, as it was felt that these would more closely meet Chilean requirements at that point in the war. Likewise, Colombia had submitted a Lend-Lease requisition for six P-40s, but the Munitions Assignment Board disapproved this request. Finally, the Munitions Assignment Board reluctantly approved an allocation of 18 unidentified P-40 variants (but probably P-40Ks) for the Mexican Air Force, for delivery between August and December 1943. This was wisely converted to a requisition for twin-engine Beech AT-11 "bombers" instead. Arrangements had reached the point where Mexican mechanics had been sent for training on maintaining the engines.

By April 1944 the P-40K aircraft in the China-Burma-India Theatre were being exchanged for new North American P-51B fighters, and the variant's place on the stage rapidly faded into the background.

Characteristics of the P-40K follow: span, length, and height 37 feet, three and 1/2 inches, 31 feet, eight and 1/2 inches (short fuselage), 33 feet, four inches (long fuselage), and eight feet, two inches. Wing area was 236 square feet, and wheel treads eight feet, two inches.

The powerplant was an Allison V-1710-73 (F4R) model with a single stage, single speed mechanical supercharger, rated 1,325hp at 3,000rpm at sea level takeoff (War Emergency), 1,550hp at 3,000rpm at sea level (rammed), 1,150hp (Military) at 3,000rpm at 11,800 feet, and 1,000hp (Normal) at 2,600hp at 11,000 feet. Fuel capacity was 157 gallons.

Weights (for P-40K #700) were: empty weight 6,367 pounds (comprised of 2,578 pounds of airframe, 2,731 pounds of powerplant, and 1,058 pounds of fixed equipment), useful load 1,933 pounds (composed of a 180 pound pilot, 720 pounds of fuel, 135 pounds of oil, and 898 pounds of armament). Design gross weight was 8,300 pounds. Passive defense items included 36 pounds of bullet proof glass, and 136 pounds of armor plate.

Maximum speed was 320mph at 5,000 feet, 343mph at 10,000 feet, and 362mph at 15,000 feet. Cruise speed was 290mph, and landing speed 85mph. Climb capability was 2,160fpm at 5,000 feet and 1,650fpm at 15,000 feet. Climb times were 4.9 minutes to 10,000

This P-40K-5 (42-9768) for some reason has the number "255" on the vertical fin, and is unusual in having the short-lived red outline to the national insignia, authorized only between June and August 1943. The RDF loop is of interest. It as shipped b=via Charleston, SC to the CBI, and was finally handed over to China on December 28, 1945. (*Pima Air and Space Museum*)

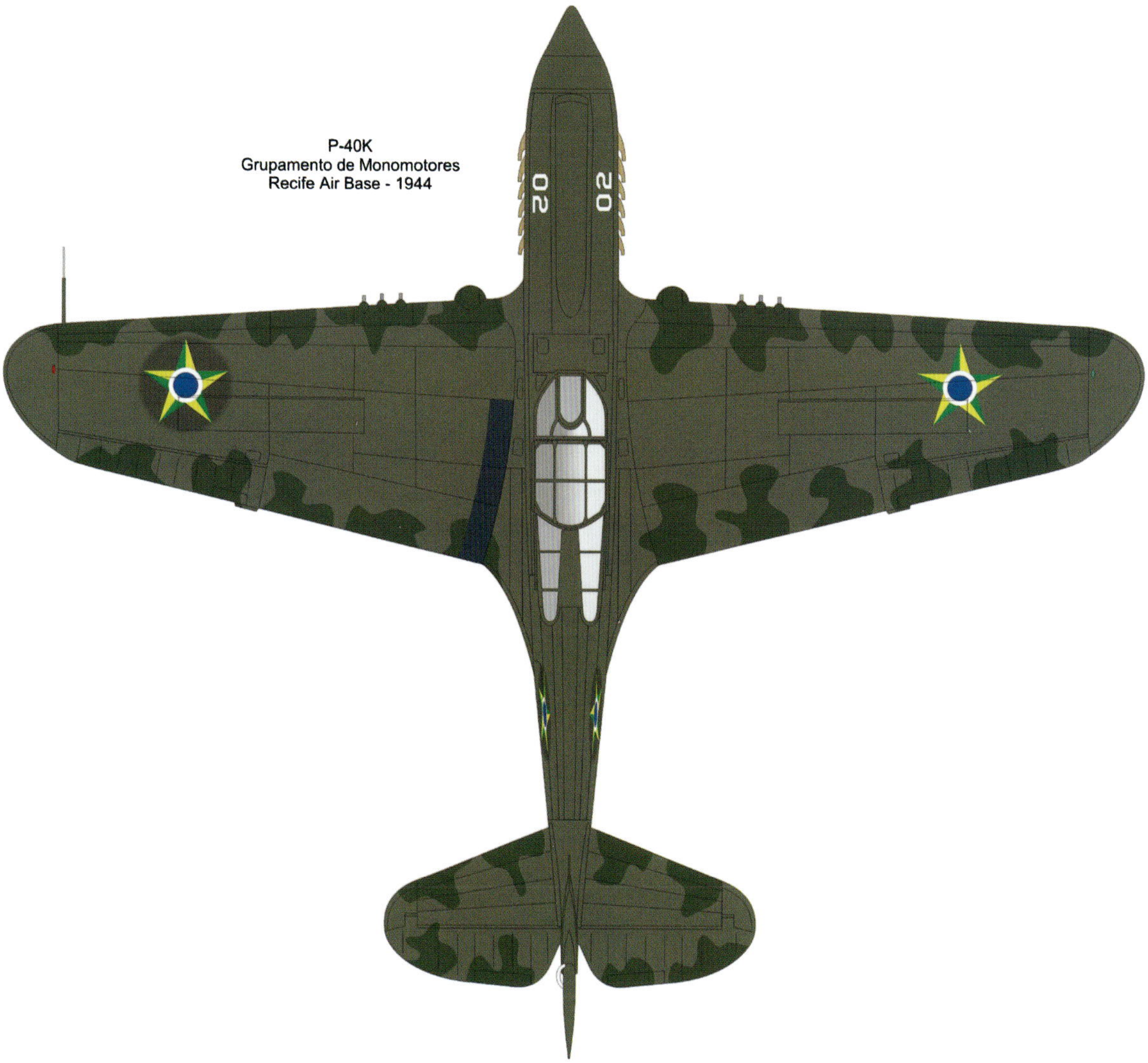

Brazil received a total of 31 P-40Ks under the Lend-Lease program beginning in November 1942. This example, No.210 and coded 02, was assigned to the *Grupamento de Monomotores* at the Recife base by 1944. (*Rudnei Dias DaCunha*)

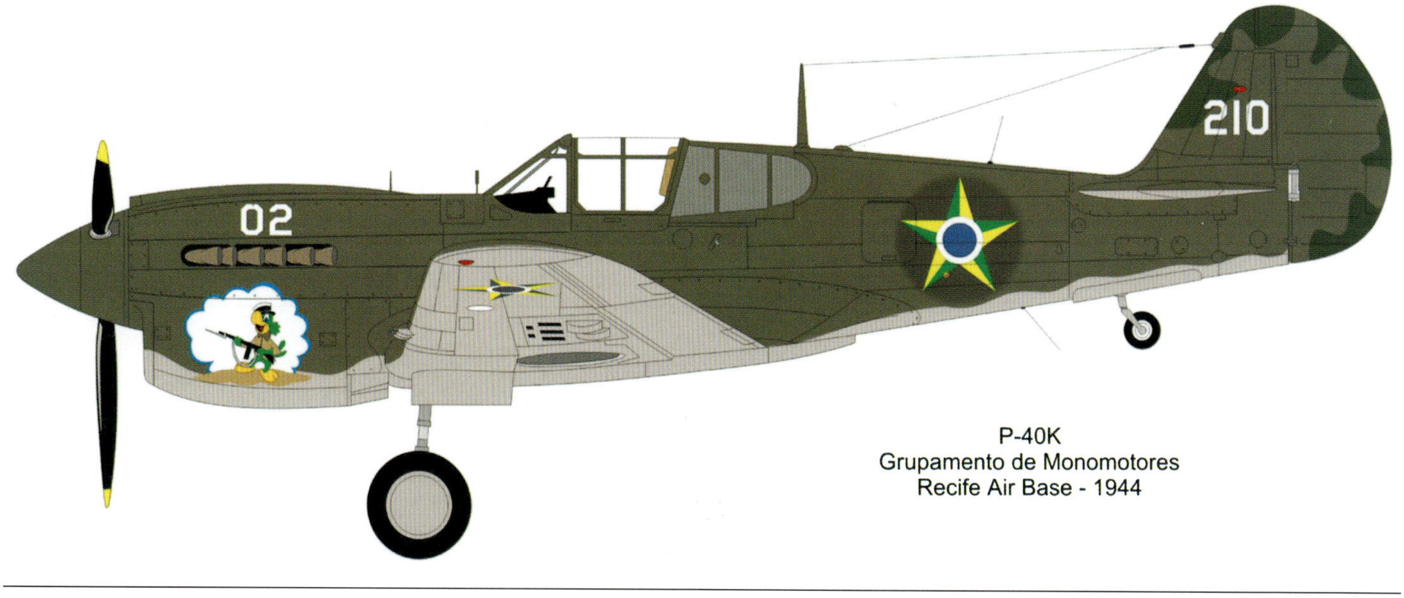

feet, 7.5 minutes to 15,000 feet, and 11.2 minutes to 20,000 feet. Range capability, clean, was 700 miles; range with a 500 pound bomb was 350 miles.

Armament consisted of six .50 caliber wing machine guns. Normal bomb load was 700 pounds, with a 500 pound bomb under the fuselage, and two 100 pound bombs under the wings. There were times in the combat areas where two 500 pound bombs were carried, however.

Following are details of the major production blocks of the P-40K series:

From Block AC42-9730 to 42-10429
• Although almost universally identified as P-40K-5-CUs (42-9730 to 42-9929), P-40K-10-CUs (42-9930 to 42-10264), and P-40K-15-CUs (42-10265 to 10429), not a solitary Aircraft History Card for any aircraft in this block carried such block identifiers in the type block.
• At least 236 of these aircraft were offset, direct from the factory, for the Soviet Union.
• At last 162 (most sources say 192) were offset direct from the factory for the British Commonwealth, where they became *Kittyhawk IIIs* (q.v.). An additional 42 aircraft were designated for Australia (Foreign Destination Code **SUMAC**), direct from Curtiss, and 10 more direct for New Zealand (Foreign Destination Code **FULCRUM**), the latter commencing with 42-10153 on October 25, 1942. Canada received 15 of these on January 26, 1943, serialed RCAF 831 to 845, most serving in the Western Air Command.
• Three aircraft were specifically identified for Lend-Lease delivery to China (by way of Foreign Destination Code **PACT**).
• Brazil received 30 aircraft, commencing with 42-10089 on December 3, 1942.
• USAAF forces retained at least 45 aircraft, shipped direct to Foreign Destination Coe **PACT** (Chungking, China), of which three were diverted to Chinese forces, as noted, with an additional 62 designated independently or onwards from **PACT** to Destination Code **CHEROKE** (India). One of these aircraft was coded as lost to Enemy Action. Some of these aircraft were apparently transferred, in theater, to British Commonwealth forces.
• At least 48 aircraft were shipped to Foreign Destination Code **BRONZE** (Alaska, Eleventh Air Force).
• A sizeable number of aircraft from these batches never left the U.S.; at least 37 were lost to training accidents in the U.S., and three became Class 26 (instructional airframes).
• P-40K 42-9987 was retained by Curtiss to become the XP-40Q-2 (q.v.).

From Block AC42-45722 to 42-46321 (P-40K-1-CU)
• The first aircraft from this block (P-40K-1-CU 42-45722) was accepted from the manufacturer May 20, 1942.
• British Commonwealth forces received at least 182 aircraft from this batch.
• The Soviet Union received at least 87 aircraft, new from the factory, from this batch.
• At least 86 aircraft were shipped direct to Foreign Destination Code **CHEROKE** (India), while some of the 64 aircraft shipped to Destination Code **HAZEL** (unknown) were diverted to India, as well. Between Codes **CHEROKE** and **HAZEL**, at least 74 aircraft were further diverted to Destination Code **PACT** (Chungking, China).
• Hawaii received at least 92 aircraft new from the factory. At least 24 of these passed on to Destination Code **BALSA** (Midway Island). For reasons unknown, 57 of the aircraft were specifically identified as bound for Hawaii by name, while 28 were designated for Destination Code **IRON**, which was also Hawaii (Oahu). Ten more went to Destination Code **VERB**, another code for Midway Island. Some numbers of these aircraft were later returned to the Continental United States.
• Foreign Destination Code **BRONZE** (Alaska, Eleventh Air Force) received 47 brand new aircraft from this batch.
• Destination Code **PEWTER** (Iceland, also given as **OILY**) received 11 new aircraft from this batch. Some of these aircraft were returned to the U.S.
• Destination Code **HEATH** (Special Project 473, Africa/Middle East) received 59 aircraft from this batch, of which 13 moved on to **ACHE** (Cairo, Egypt), 31 to **PACT** (Chunking, China), and 15 to the Chinese direct. Of the aircraft for **HEATH**, 22[140] of which arrived at Takoradi, West Africa (in company with 16 P-40Fs), by October 19, 1942, were found to have factory originated defects, which resulted in a furious exchange of teletype messages to the highest levels of the AAF and Curtiss for immediate correction.
• Foreign Destination Code **SUMAC** (Southwest Pacific, Australia) received 41, of which 12 passed on to **TEAK** (Port Moresby, New Guinea), and 10 to **LEFT** (Brisbane, Australia). Surprisingly, some of these aircraft returned to the U.S.
• Eight aircraft were intended for **POPPY** (Nouemea, New Caledonia), but almost immediately moved on to **ROSES** (Thirteenth Air Force), then **EPIC** (another code for Noumea), and finally, **LEFT**. These assignments undoubtedly attested to the rapidly changing strategy and enemy situation in the region.
• Three aircraft were designated for Destination Code **BLECHER** (Central Pacific, Seventh Air Force), but this was changed to **ARCH** for the same area.
• Brazil received two aircraft from this batch (42-46213 and 42-46294) for a Mechanical Training School between July and October 1944. They became FAB 4101 and 4102.

Finally, one P-40K-1, the 580th item, was retained at Curtiss for winterization from August 31, 1942.

Curtiss P-40X

By October 27, 1942, it had become clear to the Army Air Forces that, although the P-40E, the first really major production version of the series to enter service, possessed a number of qualities that were prized by fighter pilots, the chief complaint reaching both Curtiss and the Army leadership was that the aircraft was simply too heavy to deal with the light Japanese fighters it was facing in the Pacific and Asia.

Consequently, a P-40E was assigned to Wright Field for the express purpose of drastically lightening the aircraft, while leaving it with the minimum necessary equipment and armament.

It was to form the basis for what both Curtiss and Wright Field officials were terming the "*...production P-40X version*." Indeed, Wright Field specifically requested that the series be designated as the P-40X, and noted in official correspondence that it was in fact being cited as such both at Curtiss and at Wright Field.

The AFRAD (Research and Development) section at Wright Field, however, after rather lengthy correspondence on the subject, insisted that the aircraft, if entered into production, should bear the designation P-40H. However, when official performance tests of the aircraft commenced at Buffalo on December 9, 1942, the Allison-powered aircraft was still being quoted as type P-40X. Curtiss advised Wright Field that the results of these tests, and tests with a Packard *Merlin* engine as well, would be forwarded as soon as possible. These apparently followed on December 30, 1942. The calculated performance had apparently been sufficiently promising to prompt a proposal to order as many as 2,000 of the stripped P-40Xs as early as November 9, 1942, even before the actual performance tests had been started.

The identity of this aircraft has not surfaced, but it unquestionably led to the definitive, lightweight P-40N series.

Curtiss P-40L *Warhawk*

The P-40L series was the second of the *Warhawk* type using the Packard/Rolls Royce V-1650-1 *Merlin* engine with a single stage, two speed supercharger, the first being the P-40F. The L variants were produced from January 1943 through April of that year for a total of 600 aircraft in five block numbers (-1 through -20). All these fighters had the long fuselage, except the initial fifty P-40L-1 aircraft (USAAF serials 42-10430 to 42-10479). These first fifty had the same fuel capacity and six gun armament as the P-40F models.

The next block number variants (-5, -10, -15, and –20), of which 220 (42-10480 to 42-10699), 148 (42-10700 to 42-10847), 112 (42-10848 to 42-10959), and 170 (42-10960 to 42-11129) were produced, respectively, were the so-called stripped, or "Gypsy Rose Lee" versions. Two wing guns were removed, leaving four, fuel capacity was reduced by 37 gallons, ammunition capacity was reduced to 201 rounds per gun, some armor was removed, and other equipment reduced in an effort to get weight down and pep up performance. Fittings for rockets were applied on some aircraft. Differences in block numbers -5 through -20 were minor, involving powerplant item and subsystem changes.

Characteristics of the P-40L were as follows: span, length, and height: 37 feet, three and 1/2 inches, 31 feet, eight and 1/2 inches (short fuselage, apparently the first 50 aircraft built as P-40L), 33 feet, four inches (long fuselage), and eight feet, two inches. Wing area was 236 square feet.

The powerplant was a Packard *Merlin* V-1650-1, rated 1300hp at 3,000rpm at sea level takeoff, 1,240hp (Military) at 3,000rpm at 11,800 feet, and 1,122hp (Military) at 3,000rpm at 19,000 feet. Supercharger gear ratio was 8.151:1, and propeller reduction gear ratio was 21:44. Maximum internal fuel capacity was 127 gallons. The propeller was a Curtiss Electric constant speed three blade model of 11 feet diameter.

Weights for P-40L #66, a P-40L-5 long fuselage model, were: empty weight was 6,485 pounds (comprised of 2,614 pounds of airframe, 2,786 pounds of powerplant, and 1,085 pounds of fixed equipment), normal useful load was 1,635 pounds (a 180 pound

P-40K-10-CU 42-10181 was converted into a TP-40K in a most unusual manner for use not by pilots, but by mechanics at the AAF Technical Training School at Camp Curtissair, at Buffalo. Nicknamed *Susie Q*, it was used by April 1943 to train ground crews to taxi the aircraft safely, and never left the ground. The "crew" in this view were Bob Mitchell and Reilly Osborne. It had initially been assigned to Drew Field, Sarasota, FL, but following an accident was reclassified to Class 26 for use at Buffalo. Oddly, it was scrapped on August 5, 1945, and described at the time as a RP-40N. (*Curtiss #3160 via Harold Andrews and SDASM*).

pilot, 120 gallons of fuel at 720 pounds, 18 gallons of oil at 135 pounds, four .50 caliber guns at 318 pounds, and 203 rounds per gun of ammunition at 282 pounds), and normal gross weight was thus 8,120 pounds. Wing and power loading were 34.41psf and 6.25 pounds per horse power, respectively. Normal useful load to gross weight ratio was 0.20.

Maximum speed was 370mph at 20,000 feet, and cruise speed 295mph. Landing speed was 80mph. Initial climb rate was 3,300fpm, and service ceiling was 36,000 feet. Normal range was only 295 miles.

The P-40L served primarily in the North African campaign, along with the P-40F, where commonality of the *Merlin* engine installation was helpful logistics-wise. A total of 260 P-40L fighters went to Britain as both *Kittyhawk II* and *III* models. In March 1943 the Free French got 49 P-40L-10 *Warhawks* as replacements for the earlier P-40Fs. In late June the 99th Fighter Squadron (with all black pilots, the noted "Tuskegee Airmen") of the 325th Fighter Group arrived in North Africa using P-40L-1 aircraft.

At least one of the RAF *Kittyhawk IIs* (FS490) serving in the Mediterranean was converted in the field to a quasi-two-seater configuration, apparently while assigned to No.3 Squadron, and became known as the *Eton Hawk* after the officer who adopted it, Group Captain Eton.

The French used some of both long and short fuselage P-40L aircraft even after the end of World War II in southwestern France. At the main French test base, there were still some flyable *Warhawks* as late as 1946 and 1947. Following are some assignment specifics for the P-40L series:

From Block 42-10430 to 42-10647
- Although often cited as P-40L-1-CUs, none of the aircraft in this series were designated as such on Individual Aircraft Record Cards. The first aircraft (42-10430) was accepted on January 4, 1943. This is because the "Block" system was not introduced officially in the P-40 series until a directive was issued by Wright Field January 28, 1943, commencing with the P-40M-5-CU and P-40L-5-CU and subsequent aircraft. Wright Field at the same time issued a detailed list to the field, instructing them how to identify aircraft in this system that had already been delivered.
- The largest batch from this block—100 aircraft—were designated for Foreign Destination Code **GLEN** (Oran, Algeria), of which eight were noted as Missing in Action, two lost to enemy action, and two ditched. Some were later returned to the U.S.
- At least 63 were destined for Foreign Code **BLOT** (Morocco), with 16 others for **ACHE** (Cairo, Egypt), and one other for **HEATH** (also Cairo). Of this second lot, one is noted on the History Card as going to Yugoslavia, which is very strange and, of the **BLOT** aircraft, 18 were turned over to Free French Forces, along with some of 56 aircraft specifically designated for Britain.
- At least eight aircraft from this batch were designated for Destination Code **PACT** (Chungking, China), of which two were noted lost to flak, and two moved on to Destination Code **ELMS** (Algiers!), apparently through some shipping mix up.
- At least two aircraft were relegated to Class 26 instructional airframe duties in the U.S.

From Block 42-10648 to 42-10699 (P-40L-5-CU)
- The first aircraft from this batch (42-10648) was accepted from Curtiss on February 13, 1943.
- At least 33 aircraft went to Destination Code **BLOT** (see above). Of these, eight passed on to **GLEN**, of which one was lost to enemy action, and one went missing. At least 15 of the **BLOT** aircraft later passed to Free French Forces.
- Five aircraft were destined for **ACHE**, of which four moved on to **GLEN**.
- At least two aircraft went to Class 26 instructional airframes in the U.S.

From Block 42-10700 to 42-10863; 42-10865 to 42-10872; 42-10874 to 42-10893; 42-10904 to 42-10922; 42-10924 to 42-10933; 42-10935 to 42-10953; 42-10955 to 42-10963; 42-10965 to 42-10972; 42-10974 to 42-10982; 42-10984 to 42-10990; 42-10992 to

The P-40L series was the second to use the 1,350hp Packard/Rolls-Royce V-1650-1 *Merlin*, and P-40L-10-CU 42-11125, pictured here with an Air Transport Command emblem on the rear fuselage, was a typical example. A total of 600 were built between January and April 1943, and all but the first 50 had the "long fuselage," and only four guns. In a block that most sources cite as being P-40L-20-CUs, AAF documents state it was redesignated as a P-40L-10. It was last assigned to the 5th Fighter Group at Dallas, TX, and then went to Class 26 September 12, 1943. (*via Peter M. Bowers*)

41-11002; and 42-11005 to 42-11009 (all specifically identified as P-40-L-10-CUs)
• The first aircraft from this batch (42-10700) was accepted from Curtiss on February 27, 1943.

A quick study of the above cited serials will quickly reveal that there are a number of "missing" serials. The missing numbers were almost all P-40L-15-Cus (q.v.), and it has become readily apparent that the oft quoted sequences are not accurate for these two series.

• At least 145 aircraft from this batch were designated for Destination Code **BLOT** (see above), of which nine were noted lost to flak, 12 were missing in action, and five lost as a direct result of enemy action. Six moved on to Destination Code **GLEN**, and three to Free French Forces. Some later returned to the U.S.
• At least 135 aircraft went to Destination Code **ACHE** (Cairo, Egypt), of which one moved on to **ELMS** (Algiers), and at least 13 to Free French Forces. Of the total assigned to **ACHE**, 66 went on to **GLEN**, and between these assignments, five aircraft were lost to enemy action, 14 to flak, and no less than 18 went missing.
• At least 42 aircraft from this batch were specifically identified for Britain.
• At least five aircraft from this batch became Class 26 instructional airframes in the U.S.

Serials 42-10864, 42-10873, 42-10894, 42-10903, 42-10923, 42-10934, and 42-10954 (P-40L-15-CU)
• Based on Aircraft History Cards, these were the only aircraft specifically designated as P-40L-15-CU series aircraft by the USAAF. The first (42-10864) was accepted from the manufacturer March 19, 1943. All remained in the U.S., and one became a Class 26 instructional airframe

Serials 42-10964, 42-10973, 42-10983, 42-10991, 42-11003 and -11004, 42-11010, 42-11026, 42-11060, 42-11062, 42-11064 to 42-11067, 42-11072, 42-11074 to 42-11076, 42-11078 to 42-11080, 42-11082 to 42-11084, 42-11086, 42-11092, and 42-11100 P-40L-20-CU

Curtiss P-40R-1 and P-40R-2 conversions were P-40F and P-40L aircraft based in the U.S. that had their high-priority *Merlin* engines replaced with Allison V-1710s, which were regarded as more than adequate for training purposes. 41-13659, built as a P-40F-CU, was a typical Training Command conversion. It spent most of its service life with the 369th FS/GP at DeRidder Field, Louisiana. (*Dean Collection*)

• Based on Aircraft History Cards, these 27 aircraft were all built as P-40L-10-Cus, but were redesignated as P-40L-20-CUs on May 1, 1943. They were the only aircraft designated as such by the USAAF according to the cards.

Serials 42-11130 to 42-11676 were to have been a batch of P-40L-25-CU aircraft, but this order was cancelled

Curtiss P-40R-1 and P-40R-2

The P-40L was the final version to use the *Merlin* engine. Although the *Merlins* in P-40s were a different version than that used in the North American P-51 *Mustang*, having only a single stage supercharger, instead of the two stage type in the P-51, Packard later needed all their production capacity for the two stage *Merlins*. When a *Merlin* P-40 engine replacement was needed, in many cases an Allison V-1710 was used instead, and the re-engined aircraft were labeled as P-40R-1-CU for the revised P-40F (51 identified), and P-40R-2-CU for the modified P-40L, P-40L-5, P-40L-10, and P-40L-20 conversions (49 aircraft).

The first known order to accomplish such work was a Memo dated February 2, 1944, from the Air Materiel Command (AMC) to the Commanding General, Air Services Command (ASC).

The number of P-40s so converted was thus at least 100,[141] but the total is uncertain, as other modifications may have been made in the field that were not dutifully entered onto the History Cards. These aircraft were used as trainers in the US. Some also used the designation TP-40F. For the record, based on aircraft identified on Aircraft History Cards, the P-40R-1s and P-40R-2s were assigned in sizeable groups to the following stations and organizations after conversion:

DeRidder Army Air Field, DeRidder, LA (369th FS/GP): 41-13659, 41-13822, 41-13825, 41-13830, 41-13842, 41-13916, 41-14150, 41-14190, 41-14383, 41-14387, 41-19939, 42-10864, 42-10903, 42-10913, 42-10924, 42-11055, 42-11059, 42-11070, 42-11075 and 42-11085 (19 aircraft)

DeRidder Army Air Field, DeRidder, LA and Lafayette, LA (74th RCT GP): 41-13747, 41-14124, 41-14132, 41-11561, 41-19733, 42-10873, 42-11076, 42-11090 and 42-11114 (nine aircraft)

Laredo Army Air Field, Laredo, TX:
41-18715, 41-14046, 41-14051, 41-14293 (had been returned to the U.S. from Morocco), 41-19786, 41-19845 (returned to the U.S. from overseas), 41-19880, 41-19971, and 42-10676 (nine aircraft)

Spence Field, Moultrie, GA: 41-13722, 41-13853, 41-14071, 41-19990, 41-20039 (returned to the U.S. from overseas), and 42-10513 (had been returned to the U.S. from Oran, Algeria) (six aircraft).

Drew Field, Tampa, FL: 41-13794 (one aircraft)

Lawson Field, Columbus, GA and Napier Field, Dothan AL (3rd Composite Squadron): 41-13818, 41-14167, 41-14382, and 42-10642 (four aircraft)

El Paso Municipal Airport, El Paso, TX: 41-13834 (one aircraft)

Pollock Airport, Pollock, LA, Avon Park Army Air Field, Avon Park, FL, Gulfport Army Air Field, Gulfport, MS, Esler Field, Alexandria, LA, Campbell Army Air Field, Hopkinsville, KY and Luke Field, Phoenix, AZ (69th RCT GP): 41-13976, 41-13982, 41-14335, 41-14500, 42-10669, 42-10712, 42-10874, 42-10883, 42-10953, 42-10954, 42-10974, 42-10983, 42-11010, 42-11037, 42-11053, 42-11065, 42-11068, 42-11092, 42-11105, 42-11109 and 42-11116 (21 aircraft)

Olmsted Field, Middletown, PA (369th FB GP): 41-13992, 41-14168, 42-10616, and 42-10992 (four aircraft)

Foster Field, Victoria, TX: 41-14078, 41-14499, 41-19782, 41-19783, 41-19784 and, 41-19889 (six aircraft)

Moore Field, Mission, TX: 41-14129, 41-14189, 41-14304,

Morris Field (probably Charlotte, NC, 74th Tactical Reconnaissance Group): 41-14334 (one aircraft)

Pope Field, NC, Olmsted Field, Middletown, PA and Pollock Airport, Pollock, LA (372nd FS GP): 41-19886, 42-10944, 42-10964, 42-10991, 42-11060, 42-11064, 42-11069, 42-11078, 42-11080, 42-11083, 42-11091, 42-11110, 42-11113, and 42-11115 (14 aircraft)

Unknown Station: 42-11120

Curtiss P-40M *Warhawk*

The next Lend-Lease *Warhawk* model was the P-40M, a total of 600 being manufactured after a June 11, 1942, order. Deliveries ran from November 25, 1942, to February 13, 1943, with 287 being manufactured in 1942, and 313 made in 1943. The British Commonwealth Air Forces took over no less than 595 of these P-40M models, these being known as *Kittyhawk Mark IIIs*. Based on Aircraft History Card entries, however, the quantities designated for specific recipients is at odds with known data. For example, the cards show the following breakdown: Royal Air Force (94), South African (a mix of 90 *Kittyhawk IIIs* and *IVs*), Royal New Zealand (36), and Royal Australian Air Forces (97) as the principal users of these machines. However, at least 220 others were designated for "British Russia," indicating that Great Britain shipped at least that number of aircraft allocated to them on to Russia on their accounts. However, the RAF allocated serials for 264 *Kittyhawk IIIs* (FR779 to FR872 and FS100 to FS269), while known Royal Australian Air Force serials account for 168 aircraft (A29-300 to A29-389, A29-400 to A29-414, A29-420 to A29-434, A29-442 to A29-460, and A29-473 to A29-502). The number quoted for New Zealand on the cards was close to the reality, however, with 34 known, as NZ3066 to NZ3073, NZ3075 to NZ3089, NZ3109 to NZ3119, and NZ3180. No.5 Squadron of the South African Air Force was also known equipped with *Kittyhawk IIIs* while serving in Italy, and these were probably drawn from theater RAF stocks. Unit price for a P-40M without GFE was $36,157. North Africa, Italy, and the Far East were the deployment locales for their air war.

Powered by a new version of the Allison V-1710 engine with a War Emergency rating, the P-40M *Warhawk* went back to a six wing gun armament, and was designed to carry a 500 pound bomb under the fuselage, and a 250 pound bomb under each wing.

According to most sources, P-40M production was divided into three major blocks: P-40M-1, -5, and -10, with 60 (43-5403 to 43-5462, with 43-5403 being MSN 27091 and used only for static tests), 260 (43-5463 to 43-5722), and 280 (43-5723 to 43-6002) aircraft, respectively, delivered from Curtiss. This model was the first to

Intended primarily, at first, for Lend-Lease obligations, Curtiss built 600 P-40Ms after receipt of a June 1942 order, with deliveries commencing in November. 43-5418 was in the first block of 60 P-40M-1-CUs. It was assigned to the 50th Fighter Group at Leesburg as of May 1943, and spent the remainder of its service life at Training Command installations in Florida and Louisiana. It survived to be surplused March 24, 1945. (*via Roger Besecker*)

Lend-Lease P-40Ms for the British Commonwealth were designated as *Kittyhawk III* and *Kittyhawk IV*, and FR241, pictured here on July 9, 1942, although labeled by Curtiss as a P-40K, was in fact built as a P-40M *Kittyhawk III*, and was one of 152 in this block shipped directly to the middle east. (*Curtiss B8-17043-SD*)

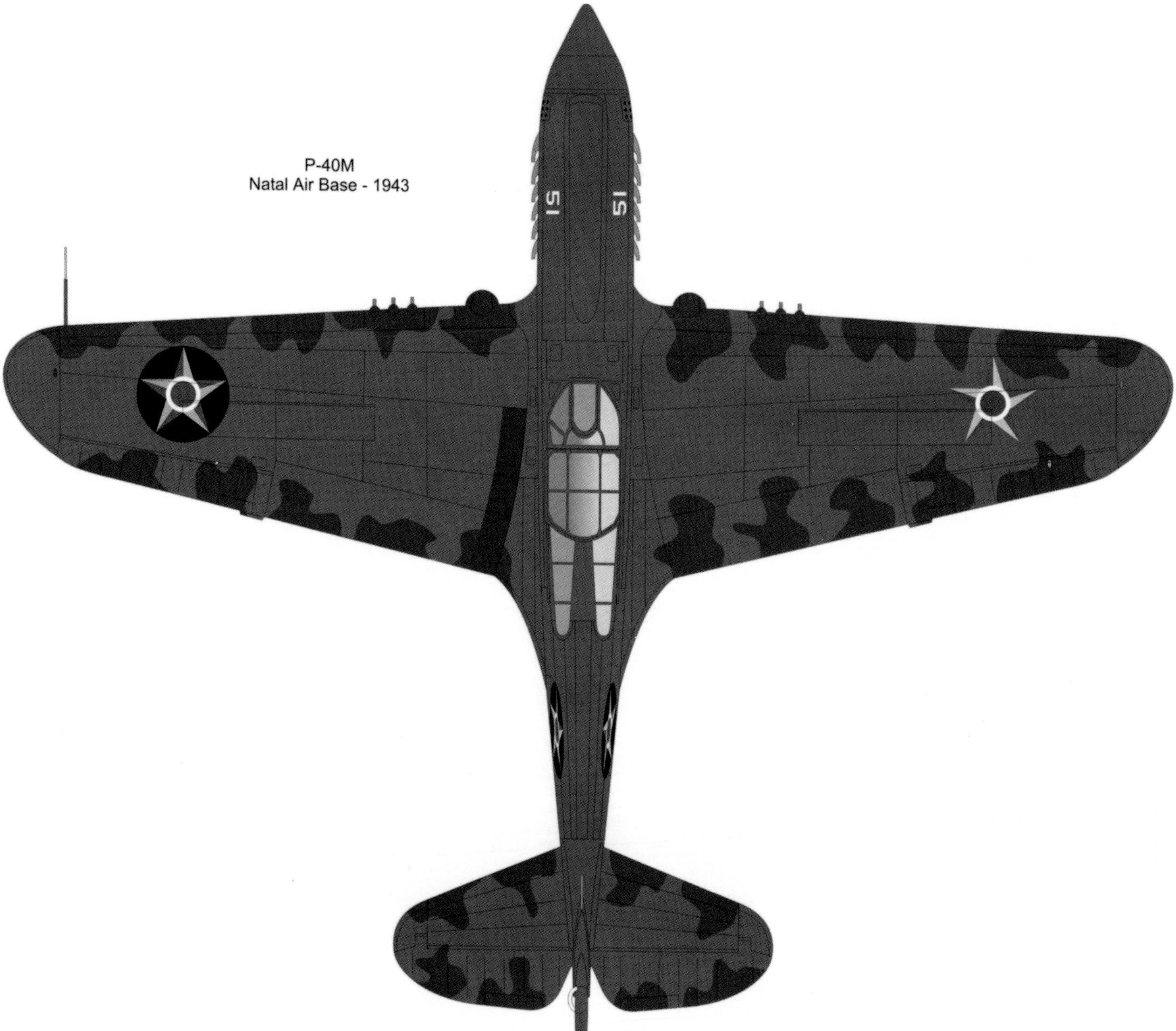

Although many sources claim that Brazil received 19 P-40Ms under Lend-Lease, in fact only 10 were allocated, one of which was lost enroute. No.51 served at the Natal Air Base after February 1943. (*Rudnei Dias DaCunha*)

Oddly, only one P-40M is known to have been converted, apparently in the field, to two-seat TP-40M configuration. Built as a P-40M-5-CU, 43-5487 was assigned to 372nd Fighter Squadron at Pollock Field, a satellite of Orlando. Although a similar view has been published before, it did not have the distinctive *Short Snorter* nose art! Note also that the aircraft has 1943-44 era national insignia on the fuselage, but 1942 era insignia under the starboard wing, as well as the large "U.S." lettering of late pre-war aircraft. *(Dean Collection)*

make use of alternate air intake grills located between the propeller spinner and the engine exhaust stacks. All of the aircraft were long fuselage models; the short fuselage had disappeared from the assembly lines. Changes between block numbers were minor, mainly with ailerons, a new landing gear position warning system, and powerplant revisions.

Characteristics of the P-40M follow: span, length, and height 37 feet, three and 1/2 inches, 33 feet, four inches, and 12 feet, four inches. Wing area was 236 square feet, with root and tip chords nine feet and three feet, 10 and 5/16 inches, respectively.

The powerplant was an Allison V-1710-81 (F20R), rated 1410hp (War Emergency) at 9,500 feet at 57.0 inches MAP; sea level takeoff rating 1,200hp; and 1,125hp at 15,500 feet at 44 inches MAP. Propeller reduction gear ratio was 2:1, and supercharger gear ratio 9.6:1. The engine was equipped with an integral carburetor air filter. The propeller was a Curtiss Electric three blade model, constant speed, with an 11 foot diameter. Fuel capacity was 120 gallons normal and 157 gallons maximum.

The weights for P-40M-5 #300, USAAF Serial 43-5702, as of January 4, 1943, were: empty weight 6,386 pounds, comprised of 2,580 pounds of airframe, 2,756 pounds of powerplant, and 1,050 pounds of fixed equipment. Normal useful load was 1,933 pounds, composed of six .50 caliber guns at 475 pounds, .50 caliber ammunition at 423 pounds, fuel at 720 pounds, oil at 135 pounds, and the pilot at 180 pounds. Normal gross weight was thus 8,319 pounds. At this weight wing and power loadings were respectively 35.25psf and 6.93 pounds per horse power. Normal useful load to gross weight was 0.232. Maximum gross weight was 9,100 pounds.

Maximum speed was 360mph at 20,000 feet, and 346mph at 5,000 feet. Cruise and landing speeds were 272mph and 82mph. Climb rate at sea level was 2,050fpm; 15,000 feet could be attained in 7.2 minutes. Service ceiling was 30,000 feet. Normal range, clean, was 810 miles, and with a 500 pound bomb 350 miles. Ferry range was 1,600 miles maximum.

Most P-40Ms, as noted earlier, went overseas in Lend-Lease packages. In addition to those noted for Great Britain, Commonwealth Forces, and Russia, 15 went to Canada, and nine[142] were obtained by Brazil in February 1943 to add to the P-40Es and P-40Ks already there. These were assigned Brazilian serials 4051 to 4059, although at least one was serialed "113," suggesting that they may have, in fact, in some instances received serials in an earlier series used by Brazil.[143]

USAAF units also operated P-40Ms, although this service is seldom cited. At least 36 were shipped to Foreign Destination Code **CHEROKE** (Karachi, India), and at least 20 of these moved on to Destination Code **PACT** (Chungking, China). At least 15 others were shipped to Destination Code **OBEY** (Thirteenth Air Force), nine to **POPPY** (Noumea, New Caledonia), 21 to **ROSES** (Efate, New Hebrides), and, from this last batch, seven moved on to **ACID** (Southwest Pacific, Thirteenth Air Force area). Destination Code **BENT** (Calcutta, India) received 31, of which 15 were diverted to the Chinese.

Of these assigned to **POPPY**, and subsequently based at Espiritu Santo as of April 26, 1943, a series of interesting experiments were carried out in-theater, and the results of these reported back to Wright Field. The AAF operating unit there had stripped a number of the P-40Ms assigned to them to only essential equipment, and had flown them in mock dogfights against standard P-40Fs, P-40Ms, P-40K-1s, P-39Ks, and U.S. Marine Corps Grumman F4F series *Wildcats* stationed there. They reported to the AAF Production Branch and on to AMC that "*...the combat comparisons, including speed, rate of climb, and turning radius demonstrated conclusively the superiority of stripped P-40Ms*," and concluded by reporting that these modified aircraft could climb to 20,000 feet in 10 minutes.

By August 28, 1943, the Thirteenth Air Force's 18th Fighter Group took the unusual action of forwarding, through channels, what was little short of a glowing report on the actual combat success of the so called "stripped" P-40s over that of the standard P-40

Compare the canopy framing on this TP-40M, probably the port side of 43-5487, with views of TP-40Ns elsewhere in this volume. While the starboard side of the nose cowling had the nose art for *Short Snorter*, the port side had the name *Noir*, probably someone's girlfriend. This photo was taken at the AAF Tactical Center at Orlando AAF, Florida, March 24, 1944, while engaged in training Brazilian pilots. (*Hagedorn Collection*)

series aircraft they had been issued. They recorded that the aircraft (which had been reduced to just a four gun armament) had scored continuously, without loss, in the hands of relatively inexperienced pilots, from the date of their first engagement on August 7, 1943, and recorded the following victories:

- 1st Lt. G. R. Smith downed a *Zeke* over Munda August 4, 1943.
- Flight Officer J. M. Cosgrove downed a *Zeke* over Munda the same date.
- 1st Lt. F. J. Radzuikinas claimed a half claim for a *Zeke* off the west coast of New Georgia August 7, 1943.
- 1st Lt. H. M. Shafer down a *Zeke* August 7, 1943, off the west coast of New Georgia.
- 1st Lt. B. H. Macklin claimed a half claim for a *Zeke* August 7, 1943, off the west coast of New Georgia.
- 1st Lt. L. B. Shuler claimed a *Zeke* August 19, 1943, also off the west coast of New Georgia.

Finally, although the block numbers for the various batches of P-40Ms have been published frequently, the Aircraft History Cards suggest a disagreement with these. For example, the first P-40M-5-CU specifically identified as such on the cards was 43-5469 circa January 28, 1943, while most published sources cite the first P-40M-5 as 43-5463. At least one P-40M-5-CU (43-5487) was apparently converted to TP-40M status with the 372nd Fighter Group at Pollock Field, LA. This is the only P-40M known to have been so converted. It was also briefly described in official records as an XP-40M and, according to one source, was not a true dual control aircraft. Instead, it was used as a "hack" by the unit, and was sometimes referred to as a "C-40." The aircraft survived the war.

Curtiss P-40N and P-40P *Warhawk*

The final production version of the P-40 type, and the most extensively produced, were assigned to series P-40N, which were first described as of November 28, 1942, as "base fighters." Ordered in

Although this aircraft was officially designated as an XP-40N, and is believed to have been 42-45722, formerly the first P-40K-1-CU in the batch 42-45722 to 42-46321, it bears no serial, and only the characters "XM-1" on the upper vertical fin. It became the XP-40Q-2A, and survived until surplused May 27, 1947, becoming NX300B. (*Dean Collection*)

By far the most numerous variant of the series, at least 5,210 P-40Ns were manufactured. This aircraft (42-106174) was a P-40N-15-CU, and is believed to have been one of the aircraft converted to photoreconnaissance training. Note the camera port in the forward area of the national insignia on the fuselage side. This aircraft was assigned to the 74th RCT at DeRidder, Louisiana (later the 74th RC GP), and survived the war to be surplused on September 20, 1945. *(via Craig "Buz" Busby)*

This Chinese Nationalist-bound P-40N-20-CU had some shipping instructions chalked on the lower cowling (the number cited was *not* the USAAF serial), and has both a radio antenna mast and RDF loop on the rear fuselage. The wing pylons, distinct to this and later variants, were slightly different in location under each wing, the starboard pylon being further outboard. *(Curtiss via Dean Collection)*

Little Jo was P-40N-5-CU 42-104924, pictured here at Yunnanyi, China, in May 1944, with the 25th Fighter Squadron. Note the assorted shark's mouth versions in the lineup, and that *Little Jo* mounts rocket tubes. This aircraft had been accepted May 25, 1943, and was apparently lost to AA fire on or about December 22, 1944. *(Ken Hoylman)*

This detail view of rocket rails installed on a 25th FS P-40N in China also reveals the rather odd bombs and sway-braces under the wing and fuselage. The rocket tubes were made by Firestone and were 10 feet long and 4 1/2 inches in diameter. The three tubes, in a cluster, were made from either magnesium or plastic-hardened paper. They were discharged electrically, and during combat maneuvering, had the unfortunate habit of bending—with often spectacular results. *(via William B. Johnson)*

late January 1943, and first appearing in March of that year, the P-40N was powered by an Allison engine, rather than a Packard *Merlin*, on the basis of available engine production.

The first actually designated as a P-40N[144] was apparently P-40L 42-11126, stripped down in accordance with guidance provided on October 12, 1942. This included addition of aluminum alloy radiators, aluminum alloy oil coolers, removal of the front wing fuel tank, addition of rear wing fuel tank, prop increase, removal of the vacuum system, 27 inch magnesium wheels and eight-ply tires, *Fabreeka* type engine mounting, a turn-over structure, boost controls, reduction in the pilot's front armor plate, and a radio change.

The total production numbers for P-40Ns differ slightly according to source; one Curtiss company reference says 5,222 (3,218 in 1943 and 2,004 in 1944), and other sources, including the Army Air Forces, indicate 5,219. Possibly three were held back by Curtiss for test or modification, and were never officially delivered as P-40Ns. One of them may well have been an XP-40Q.

Again, a major effort was made to reduce fighter empty weight and improve performance in the P-40N-1 block, where 400 aircraft were manufactured (42-104429 to 42-104828, MSN 28191 to

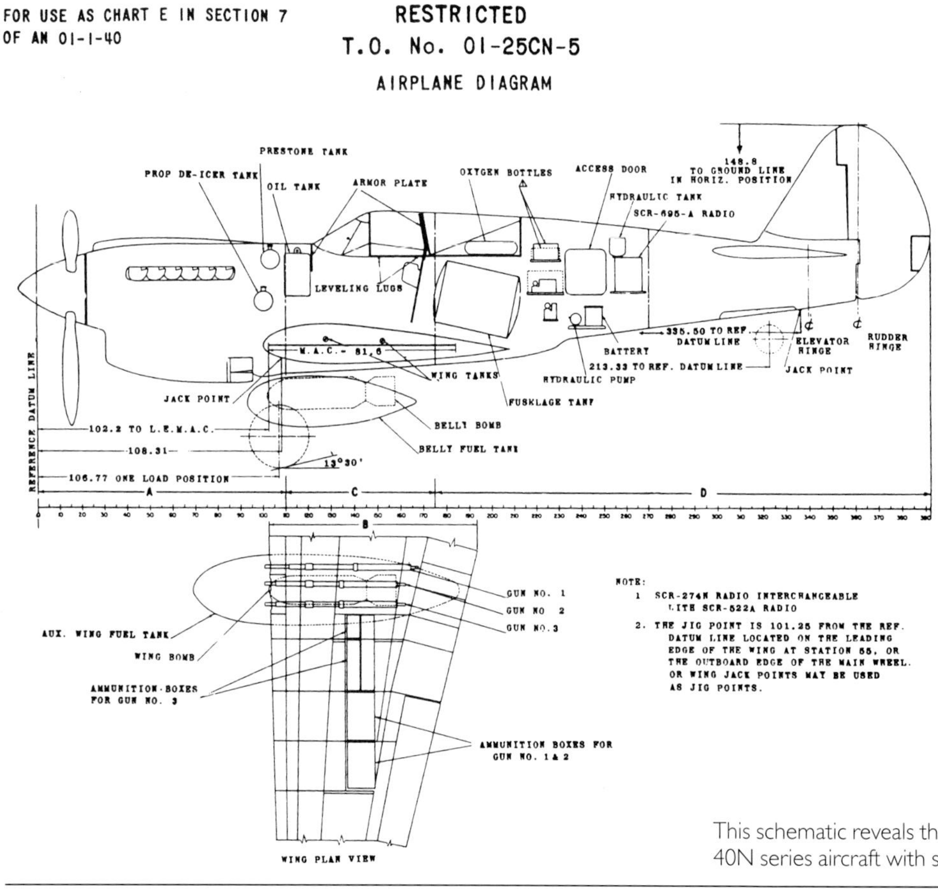

This schematic reveals the standard equipment mix and location on most P-40N series aircraft with six guns. *(USAAF T.O. 01-25CN-5)*

This P-40N, although appearing to be a new arrival, is in fact a used aircraft that had previously been painted olive drab on the upper surfaces. Note the wing root area and the lower cowling at left, which had large letters on it, starting with "N." The aircraft was obviously being prepared for shipment, but the circumstances are unknown. *(Dean Collection)*

28590), and the first of this block was accepted on March 13, 1943. Two of the normal .50 caliber guns were removed, aluminum radiators and oil coolers were used, new design magnesium landing gear wheels fitted, changes in armor made, and other weight reductions, including fuel tank changes, were effected. Even the battery and starter were removed for a total weight savings of 464 pounds. (In service, a good part of the weight went back in!) The stripped empty weight got down to about 6,000 pounds based on these efforts.

Characteristics of the P-40N-1 follow: dimensions and areas were like those of the P-40M. Similarly, the powerplant was an Allison V-1710-81. Normal fuel capacity was 122 gallons, with maximum capacity 292 gallons.

Empty weight was 6,000 pounds, useful load 1,740 pounds, normal gross weight 7,740 pounds, and maximum gross weight 8,850 pounds. Normal wing and power loadings were 32.8psf and 6.45 pounds per horse power, respectively. Useful load to gross weight ratio was 0.225.

By late October 1944, P-40N-40-CU production was winding down, and new aircraft were being rolled out *sans* camouflage. This aircraft (44-47860) was accepted October 27th, and spent the war at Napier Field with the 2116th Air Base Squadron, and was converted to a TP-40N. It was surplused at Walnut Ridge November 14, 1945. *(Curtiss via Harold Andrews)*

Brazil received 41 P-40N-1-CUs under Lend-Lease starting in September 1944, and this lineup shows a mix of schemes, including three with the unit insignia of the *3°GAvCa*. Some of these remained in front-line service into June 1954. *(Museo Aeroespacial via Rudnei Dias DaCunha)*

This immaculate Brazilian P-40N (FAB 4064) is probably the most perfectly preserved P-40 in original condition in existence. Delivered in September 1944 and formerly 44-7700, it was last operated by the *1°/14°GAvCa.* (*Museo Aeroespacial*)

The P-40N-1 was the fastest of the whole series, with a maximum speed of 378mph at 10,500 feet at 7,700 pounds gross weight. Normal cruise and landing speeds were 288mph and 82mph, respectively. Climb time at 7,700 pounds weight was 6.7 minutes to 15,000 feet. Takeoff and landing distance over a 50 foot obstacle were both 1,300 feet. Service ceiling was 38,000 feet. Normal range was 260 miles at 288mph at 10,000 feet, or 240 miles at 263mph at 10,000 feet with a 500 pound bomb under the fuselage. Ferry range capability was 1,400 miles at 187mph at 10,000 feet.

The four .50 caliber wing guns had 200 rounds per gun. Maximum bomb load was 700 pounds: one 500 pounder under the fuselage, and two 100 pound bombs under the wings. In service, much more was sometimes carried. Kits could be added for carrying rockets under the wings.

The P-40N entered Mediterranean area fighting in June 1943, flown by the 99th Fighter Squadron with black pilots. In July, the 18th Fighter Group of the Fifth Air Force in the Southwest Pacific was operating P-40Ns around the Guadalcanal area with considerable success, and in September the 80th Fighter Group took the N-1 into action in Burma, with the 88th, 89th, and 90th Fighter Squadrons. Brazil received 41 P-40N-1s commencing in September 1944, and these were almost all assigned to the *3° GavCa.*[145] Brazilian P-40s remained in unit strength and first-line as late as June 30, 1954.

An unknown number of P-40N-1s were modified for the exclusive use of Tactical Reconnaissance Squadrons under CTI-1366, and involved the installation of the following mission essential equipment:

- one left-oblique K-24 camera (a substitute until such time as the K-28 became available)
- remote camera controls for the pilot
- sight aiming point marks on the canopy
- installation of SCR-274, SCR-522 radios and Detrola 438 receivers, as well as SCR-595 or 596 radios

One P-40N-1 (AAF 42-104528, MSN 28290) was delivered to Allison for test purposes in April 1943, while another (42-104824, MSN 28591) was retained by Curtiss for unspecified tests, but was re-delivered to the 3rd Fighter Command at Tampa, FL, on October 12, 1943.

The second version was the P-40N-5, of which no less than 1,100 were built (42-104829 to 42-105928, MSN 28591 to 29690). The -5 block models introduced the new cockpit canopy, where the transparency was extended aft and squared off. This configuration was used on all subsequent models. The six gun armament was also restored. In addition, a new maximum bomb load capacity was provided for. The total allowable load was increased to 1,500 pounds by increasing the capacity of the wing bomb racks to carry 500 pounds. The same Allison -81 engine was used, but fuel capacity went back to 161 gallons, and the pilot seat design was improved. Noteworthy is the fact that four P-40N-5s were modified for dive bomber units on Project DOM-852 for specific assignment to the

Besides Brazil, Russia, the Netherlands East Indies, China, New Zealand, Canada, and Australia received variants of the P-40N. In British Commonwealth service they were known as *Kittyhawk IVs*, and A29-652 (a P-40N-20-CU) was one of at least 450 received by the Royal Australian Air Force December 1, 1943. It served with No.80 and 82 Squadron, and was stricken after August 15, 1945. (*via Gene Sommerich*)

Chinese Nationalist Air Forces received a large number of P-40Ns, including one coded 2214 (the "P" serial number on the vertical fin is illegible), sitting alongside another at a dusty field somewhere in China. (*San Diego Aerospace Museum*)

48th Bomb Group at Key Field, Meridian, MS. Additionally, 10 P-40N-5s were winterized for service in Alaska on Project 92197R, preceding the P-40N-10 block (q.v.), all of which were intended for service there.[146] At least three (42-105063, 42-105073, and 42-105088) were retained by Curtiss for test purpose by June 5, 1943.

The P-40N-10 block of fighters, as noted above, were winterized exclusively for service in Alaska. A total of 100 aircraft (42-105929 to 42-106028, MSN 29691 to 29790) were produced starting in August 1943. These planes equipped the 343rd Fighter Group.

The next block of P-40N-15s were a little different, with electrical system changes, and 377 fighters rolled off the Curtiss lines (42-106029 to 42-106405, MSN 29791 to 30167).

The most produced version of the *Warhawk* was the P-40N-20, with 1,523 aircraft turned out (42-106406 to 42-106428, MSN 30168 to 30190, and 43-22752 to 43-24251, MSN 30681 to 32180). They used an Allison V-1710-99 engine, the major change being the installation of an automatic engine control. At least 49 aircraft from this block were assigned to the Netherlands East Indies Air Force commencing in December 1943, and coded as C3-500 to C3-548, assigned for the most part to 120 Squadron, NEIAF, attached to the Royal Australian Air Force, and operated from Merauke and Biak, New Guinea, and Soerabaja and Andir, on Java.

The remainder of the P-40N model *Warhawks*—blocks N-25, -30, -35, and -40, of which 499 (43-24252 to 43-24751, MSN 32181 to 32680), 500 (44-7001 to 44-7500), 500 (44-7501 to 44-8000),[147] and 220 (44-47749 to 44-47968) aircraft were built, respectively—were similar enough that the Air force lists only one set of major characteristics. Changes were limited to subsystems details. For example, 13 Block -35 aircraft were fitted with Bendix Radio Compass equipment, and these were all intended for assignment to Foreign Destination Code **BIRD** (USAAF units in China). Altogether, 45 P-40N-5s were to eventually receive the Bendix Radio Compass installation, and were identified as Blocks -37F, -37G, and -45A. At least 200 P-40N series aircraft were also modified for "reconnaissance training" duties commencing June 26, 1943, but the exact nature of these modifications has not been determined. One P-40N-40-CU (44-47922) was bailed to Curtiss in March 1945 to serve as a mount for test pilot training. Curtiss had requested a TP-40N, but none were available.

Some, but very few, P-40N models were modified for photographic duties; these were designated P-40N-6, -16, -26, and -37C. Of the latter, not fewer than 71 "P-40N reconnaissance airplanes" were included in Block 37C for delivery during August 1943. These aircraft were not built as such by Curtiss but, rather, were converted by post-production Modification Centers, and 20 had been so converted by September 21, 1943. At least 34 of the 71 recon conversions were accomplished by the Bell-Niagara Falls, New York, Modification Center. Others were revised as two place trainers (q.v.), including 22 N-30s changed to P-40N-31s.

An interesting note by the Air Force indicated that P-40N-5s had provisions for trans-Atlantic towing by B–17 bombers, though it is doubted this was ever done.

The Lend-Lease P-40Ns were labeled as *Kittyhawk IV* by the British, and many went overseas for use by other countries. A few RAF squadrons operated these *Warhawks*, including one that finished the war so equipped. Russia received at least 130 aircraft; well over 450 went to Australia, and almost 200 to New Zealand. A few were sent to the Netherlands East Indies, and 35 went to Canada, where they gained RCAF serials 846 to 880 (serving for the most

The relative abundance of brand new P-40Ns enabled the USAAF to offset some to various test programs, rather than war-weary aircraft. This early block P-40N was used to test some truly remarkable land range tanks, with rather stout sway-braces by June 20, 1943. (*Dean Collection*)

Only a handful of P-40Ns survived the war to be sold surplus to the civil market. NL1226N had been registered August 12, 1947, and was owned by the Confederate Air Force as of March 1970, and wearing a rather unimaginative color scheme at Kelly Air Force Base. It was delivered to the Royal Canadian Air Force as a *Kittyhawk IV* September 17, 1943, and served with 132 Squadron. (*Hagedorn*)

The advent of the P-40N also enabled the Curtiss employees in Buffalo to elect *Miss Warhawk*, pretty Margaret Gilbert, a tool crib clerk at Plant No. 1, by April 18, 1944, as a GI makes the inevitable approach. (*Curtiss*)

part in the Western Air Command, many surviving into August 1946), and 41 P-40Ns were sent to Brazil in the period September 1944 to March 1945. Some of the NEI aircraft were flown until early 1949, while some of the Brazilian machines were operated until 1954. The last production P-40, an N-40 model, left the Curtiss plant on November 30, 1944.

During the war P-40Ns operated in the Pacific, South East Pacific, and China-Burma-India (CBI) theatres.

In September 1943 P-40N-5s of the 45th Fighter Squadron, Seventh Air Force flew from Hawaii to Bakers Island, in the Pacific. New Zealand P-40Ns were attacking the big Japanese base at Rabaul with 500 pound bombs in March 1944, and the same month the 23rd Fighter Group in China got new P-40N-20s. The first thing they did was to reinstall the electric starters. In October 1944 the 82nd Reconnaissance Squadron, flying P-40Ns, arrived on Morotai just prior to the invasion of the Philippines in Leyte Gulf. But by December 1944, there were no P-40s on the Far East Air Force fighter lists, though in the Central Pacific one fighter group was still operating P-40Ns in July 1945 just before war's end.

General specifications for the P-40N-5 through -40 were as follows: dimensions and areas were like the P-40N-1. Powerplant was either an Allison V-1710 -81, -99, or -115, rated at 1,200hp for sea level takeoff, 1,125hp (Military) at 14,600 feet, 1,000hp (Normal) at 13,800 feet, and War Emergency of 1,350hp at sea level. The propeller was a Curtiss electric three blade constant speed type of 11 feet in diameter. Maximum internal fuel capacity was 159 gallons, and maximum total fuel 609 gallons.

Weights were (for P-40N-25, Aircraft #3901): empty weight 6,206 pounds (consisting of 2,528 pounds of airframe, 2,616 pounds of powerplant, and 1,062 pounds of fixed equipment), and useful load was 2,148 pounds (made up of a 200 pound pilot, 954 pounds (159 gallons) of fuel, 97 pounds of oil, six .50 caliber guns at 474 pounds, and 423 pounds (1410 rounds) of ammunition.). Gross weight was 8,354 pounds. Included in the empty weight were 130 pounds of armor plate and 34 pounds of bullet proof glass. Wing and power loadings were 35.4psf and 6.96 pounds per horse power. Useful load to gross weight ratio was 0.257.

Maximum speeds were 350mph at 16,400 feet, 343mph at 15,000 feet, 325mph at 25,000 feet, 325mph at 25,000 feet, and 308mph at 5,000 feet. Cruise speed was 290mph. Landing speed was 82mph. Initial climb rate was 2,120fpm; rate at 25,000 feet was 900 fpm. It took 7.3 minutes to achieve 14,000 feet. Service ceiling was 30,800 feet. Ranges were normally 750 miles at 10,000 feet, and with a 500 pound bomb 340 miles. Ferry range was 3,100 miles at 198mph and 2,800 miles at 10,000 feet. At combat weight takeoff distance over a 50 foot obstacle was 2,700 feet; while landing over a 50 foot obstacle took 1,850 feet.

Curtiss attempted to sell a quantity of two-seat P-40N models as advanced trainers after the war but was not successful. It is unclear who the intended customers were.

Seldom cited, Curtiss documents dated December 12, 1942, described both the P-40N and P-40P "Base Fighters," noting that the P-40P was to have the SCR-522 radio and 52 pound battery aft of the baggage compartment, and forward of the baggage compartment on the P-40N. The SCR-522 was, however, replaced with the stripped SCR-274N radio, for the most forward C.G. condition. The aircraft were to have wide-blade (89303-24A) dural propellers installed, and armor plate on the P-40P was to have been the same as on the P-40N, but with pilot's head armor added to both types. Rear wing tank and fuselage tanks were to be installed with 120 gallons of fuel. Apparently one aircraft was in fact configured as a P-40P, this having formerly been P-40F No.538, and was converted on November 23, 1942. The aircraft had four .50 caliber guns with 940 rounds total, and an optical sight with a total fuel capacity of 54 gallons (rear wing tanks) and 66 gallons (fuselage tank).

The so-called P-40P-1—to have used the V-1650-1 engine—was cancelled, and 1,500 aircraft were built instead as P-40N-1 and P-40N-5 with the V-1710-81.

The very last production P-40 series aircraft—44-47968, a P-40N-40-CU—was delivered to the AAF at Buffalo on November 27, 1944. It was flown almost immediately to DeRidder Army Air Base in Louisiana, where it was assigned to the 369th Fighter Training Group. It was surplused at Walnut Ridge, Arkansas, on August 21, 1945, as an RP-40N.

Like the P-40E, Japan also acquired at least one P-40N series aircraft when, in June 1944, a Chinese Nationalist pilot defected and landed at an airfield in China occupied at the time by the *44th* (*Sonia* equipped) and *48th* (*Oscar* equipped) *Sentais*. This aircraft was later shipped back to the home islands to the Akeno Flying School for tests, where it was flown by Warrant Officer Tamotsu Homma of the *48th Sentai*.

Annex 4, at the end of this volume, outlines the initial assignments of the large P-40N production run, as shipped from Curtiss.

Curtiss TP-40N

According to a USAAF document cited by Eric H. Hart in a letter to the American Aviation Historical Society in their Autumn 1967 issue, three P-40N-25s, 22 P-40N-30s, and five P-40N-40s, for a total of 30 aircraft, were factory modified to TP-40Ns, becoming P-40N-26s, P-40N-31s, and P-40N-41s, respectively. It is not clear, from Individual Aircraft History Cards, if these aircraft were ever officially redesignated as "TP" or not. Additionally, an unknown number of P-40 variants had been converted to two-seat configuration unofficially in the field,[148] leading Curtiss to issue an official factory modification kit with a service memo issued by Ed Kellogg, Walt Arakelian, and Miss Barbara Hilldritch, with art work describing the conversion by a Mr. Mackenzie. Miss Hilldritch is of historical significance, as she was the first female engineer so rated by Curtiss, and may well qualify as the first female American engineer to work on a fighter type aircraft.

In fact, the story of this, the major batch of two-seat P-40 variants—the first official conversions since the two P-40ES aircraft (q.v.) of 1942—is rather more complex than has previously been reported.

First formal mention of a large scale conversion program for P-40s to two-seat configuration was on April 8, 1944, when Wright Field advised that 196 aircraft would be so configured and, initially, redesignated as RP-40Ns. By October 9, 1944, however, the aircraft were being cited as TP-40Ns, the first mention of this designation. A formal requirement for 200 modified aircraft, originally described in a document dated November 2, 1944, as "*Two-Seater Piggy-Back P-40 Airplanes*," was put on hold at that time pending the completion of similar work on the last two of four similar P-47 conversions. All 200 conversions, apparently raised slightly from the first mention in April 1944, were to come from P-40N-5 and later block series aircraft.

After considerable debate, however, the total number of formal conversions consisted of a total of 115 aircraft, but this was reduced to 112 by June 7, 1945, and, of these, only 107 required the 195 conversion kits assembled by Curtiss (the balance of 78 kits were held in reserve). In the listing shown below, however, by AAF serial number and Curtiss MSN, only 99 have been positively identified. These were distributed as follows:

The subject of much confusion, a total of around 107 P-40Ns were converted to two-seat TP-40Ns, although 195 kits were manufactured. This aircraft (44-7068), with Field Number 708Y, was laid down as a P-40N-30-CU, but converted to a TP-40N-35-CU. It had been assigned to the 53rd Fighter Group at Venice, Florida. It is pictured here at Kingman, Arizona, awaiting disposal in 1947 after going to storage there December 15, 1945. (*William T. Larkins*)

Possibly the last TP-40N conversion, Ship Number 5176 (note placard aft of the canopy) was 44-47924, accepted by the AAF November 2, 1944, and photographed here at Buffalo on January 5, 1945. Note that the aircraft had provision for all six wing guns. It was assigned to the 345th Air Base Squadron at Waycross, Georgia, until stored at Walnut Ridge in September 1945. (*Curtiss B4-33418-TH*)

Project Number	Total Assigned	Receiving Command
DOM-864	5 (Curtiss factory mod.)	Third Air Force
DOM-864	6	First Air Force
DOM-864	14	Air Training Command
DOM-865	62	Air Training Command
DOM-866	24	First Air Force
DOM-867	1	Air Technical Services Command (ATSC)

In addition to these deployments, the Sixth Air Force, headquartered in the Panama Canal Zone, received word in April 1944 that the Command would be receiving four of these aircraft, to be specifically assigned for use by the unit engaged in training Brazilian crews. So far as can be determined, these were the only TP-40Ns deployed overseas, although they have not been identified by serial number.

Finally, two AAF Technical Orders bear recording in this connection. T.O. 01-25C-155, dated June 20, 1944, and T.O. 01-025C-155, dated April 18, 1945, covered the removal of armor plate and wing guns from nearly every P-40E, P-40E-1, P-40F, P-40K, P-40L, P-40M, and P-40N still extant in Air Training Command hands as of that date. When this work was completed, the T.O. specifically stated that "*....these aircraft will be given the auxiliary prefix "T."* The T.O. did not mean that all guns would be removed; instead, it directed that they be removed in pairs, and that the number of guns removed would depend on the type of training for which the aircraft was employed. The T.O. did, however, recommend that all guns be removed, if practicable, and that at most only two guns be retained, with emphasis on the two innermost guns. The order was specific to the following aircraft, as noted:

P-40E - all remaining aircraft (all six guns)
P-40E-1 - all remaining aircraft (all six guns)
P-40F - all remaining aircraft (all six guns)
P-40K - 42-45722 to 42-46321 (removal of two, four or six guns)
P-40K - 42-9730 to 42-10364 (removal of two, four or six guns)
P-40K - 42-10365 to 42-10429 (removal of two, four or six guns)
P-40L - all remaining aircraft (all four guns)
P-40M - all remaining aircraft (all six guns)
P-40N - 42-104429 to 42-106028 (removal of two, four or six guns)
P-40N - 42-106029 to 42-106248 (removal of two, four or six guns)
P-40N - 43-22752 to 43-24751 (removal of two, four or six guns)
P-40N - 44-7001 to 44-7500 (removal of two, four or six guns)
P-40N - 44-7501 to 44-8000 (removal of two, four or six guns)
P-40N - 44-47749 to 44-47968 (removal of two, four or six guns)

The following aircraft have been positively identified as having been designated as TP-40Ns and, in nearly all instances, are confirmed as having been converted to two-seat configuration. Most of these conversions were carried out by the Curtiss-Wright Modification Center. Since some of the assignment dates predate the first known formal modifications of TP-40Ns, they may be assumed to have been amongst those converted in the field.

AAF Serial	MSN	Date	Assignment	Notes
42-105473	29235		Project DOM-853, Romulus, MI (Fry)	To San Antonio
42-105475	29237	7/1/43	Romulus, MI (Fry)	To Third AF
42-105484	29246	7/3/43	Romulus, MI (Fry)	
42-105486	29248		Project DOM-853, Romulus, MI (Fry)	To Third AF
42-105493	29255		Project DOM-853	10th Tac Rcn, Esler Field, Third AF
42-105495	29257		Project DOM-853, Romulus, MI (Fry)	74th Tac Rcn, Third AF
42-105505	29267		Project DOM-853, Romulus, MI (Fry)	74th Tac Rcn, Third AF
42-105514	29276		Project DOM-853	75th Tac Rcn Grp, Third AF
42-105530	29292		Project DOM-853, Romulus, MI (Fry)	Key Field, Meridian, MS, Third AF
42-105532	29294		Project DOM-853, Romulus, MI (Fry)	69th Group, Third AF
42-105543	29305		Project DOM-854	Third AF
42-105545	29307		Project DOM	Third AF, 76th Rcn Grp
42-105547	29309		Project DOM	10th Tcn Rcn, Esler Field, Third AF
42-105560	29322		Project DOM-854	
42-105562	29324		Project DOM	Third AF
42-105573	29335		Project DOM-853	Third AF
42-105575	29337		Project DOM-854	74th Rcn Grp
42-105588	29350			Esler Field, Third AF
42-105596	29358			Esler Field, Third AF
42-105600	29362		Project DOM-853	DeRidder Field
42-105604	29366		Project DOM-855	DeRidder Field
42-105657	29419		Project DOM	74th Rcn Grp
42-105927	29689			
42-105968	29730			
42-105974	29736			Sherman Field, TX
42-106004	29766		Project DOM-857	Esler Field
42-106006	29768			
42-106019	29781			Esler Field
42-106021	29783			Esler Field
42-106028	29790			Key Field, Meridian, MS, Third AF
42-106030	29792			Key Field, Meridian, MS, Third AF
42-106036	29798			Sherman Field, TX
42-106045	29807			Columbia, SC
42-106049	29811			Key Field, Meridian, MS, Third AF
42-106058	29820			Marianna Field, FL
42-106066	29828			Key Field, Meridian, MS, Third AF
42-106073	29835			Key Field, Meridian, MS, Third AF
42-106079	29841			Esler Field
42-106088	29850			DeRidder Field, LA
42-106090	29852			Esler Field
42-106092	29854			Marianna Field, FL
42-106094	29856			Esler Field
42-106104	29866			Key Field, Meridian, MS, Third AF
42-106108	29870			Craig Field, CO
42-106110	29872			Barksdale Field, LA
42-106112	29874			Craig Field, CO
42-106136	29898			Greenville, TX
42-106140	29902		Modified by Bell Mod Ctr, DOM-857	Barksdale Field, LA
42-106142	29904		Modified by Bell Mod Ctr, DOM-857	Esler Field
42-106144	29906		DOM-857	Craig Field, CO
42-106158	29920		Modified by Bell Mod Ctr, DOM-857	74th Rcn Grp, DeRidder, LA
42-106168	29930			Lake Charles, LA
42-106170	29932		Modified by Bell Mod Ctr, DOM- 857	69th Rcn Grp, Esler Field
42-106172	29934		Modified by Bell Mod Ctr, DOM-857	Key Field

42-106176	29938		Modified by Bell Mod Ctr, Project 96175R	Drew Field, Tampa, FL
42-106184	29946			Napier Field, Dothan, AL
42-106186	29948		DOM-857	Foster Field, TX
42-106188	29950			Suffolk Field, NY
43-24080	32019	4/17/44	Omaha Mod Center	Barksdale Field, LA
43-24382	32321	4/10/44		Punta Gorda, FL, Third AF
43-24542	32481	4/10/44		Dale Mabry Field, Third AF
43-24568	32507	4/17/44	Omaha Mod Center	Barksdale Field, FL
43-24609	32548	4/21/44	Omaha Mod Center	Avon Park, FL
43-24602	32541	4/13/44	Omaha Mod Center	Drew Field, Tampa, FL
43-24615	32554	4/21/44	Omaha Mod Center	Drew Field, Tampa, FL
43-24733	32672	4/21/44	Omaha Mod Center	Lakeland, FL, 2nd Air Commando Group
44-7032	22199	4/13/44	Omaha Mod Center	Page Field, Fort Meyers, FL
44-7055	22222	4/17/44	Omaha Mod Center	MacDill Field, FL
44-7066	22233	4/15/44	Omaha Mod Center	Lake Charles, LA
44-7092	22259	4/21/44	Omaha Mod Center	Punta Gorda, FL
44-7093	22260	4/17/44	Omaha Mod Center	Greenville, TX
44-7098	22265	4/11/44		Bartow Field, FL
44-7103	22270	4/13/44	Omaha Mod Center	Thomasville, GA
44-7124	22291	4/13/44	Omaha Mod Center	Page Field, Fort Meyers, FL
44-7125	22292	4/11/44		Perry Field, FL
44-7129	22296	4/13/44	Omaha Mod Center	Foster Field, TX
44-7130	22297	4/13/44	Omaha Mod Center	Key Field
44-7135	22302	4/21/44	Omaha Mod Center	Lake Charles, LA
44-7137	22304	4/17/44	Omaha Mod Center	Thomasville, GA
44-7139	22306	4/13/44	Omaha Mod Center	Napier Field, Dothan, AL
44-7140	22307	4/19/44	Omaha Mod Center	Lake Charles, LA
44-7143	22310	4/17/44	Omaha Mod Center	MacDill Field, FL
44-7149	22316	4/13/44	Omaha Mod Center	Sarasota, FL
44-7151	22318	4/17/44	Omaha Mod Center	Punta Gorda, FL
44-7152	22319	4/19/44	Omaha Mod Center	Greenville, TX
44-7155	22322	4/13/44	Omaha Mod Center	Drew Field, Tampa, FL
44-7156	22323	4/13/44	Omaha Mod Center	
44-7161	22328	4/17/44	Omaha Mod Center	Pinellas Field, St. Petersburg, FL
44-7162	22329	4/17/44	Omaha Mod Center	Columbia, SC
44-7165	22332	4/17/44	Omaha Mod Center	Spence Field, Moultrie, GA
44-7168	22335	4/15/44	Omaha Mod Center	Drew Field, Tampa, FL
44-7173	22340	4/19/44	Omaha Mod Center	Venice, FL
44-7175	22342	4/13/44	Omaha Mod Center	Albuquerque, NM
44-7178	22345	4/17/44	Omaha Mod Center	Barksdale Field, LA
44-7191	22358	4/19/44	Omaha Mod Center	Venice, FL
44-7192	22377	4/19/44	Omaha Mod Center	Barksdale Field, LA
44-7210	22377	4/19/44	Omaha Mod Center	Columbia, SC
44-7218	22385	4/19/44	Omaha Mod Center	Woodward Field, OK, Second AF

Although some of the single-seat P-40 series aircraft that survived the war to become "warbirds" have since been converted to two-seaters, a few of them were genuine wartime conversions, like N923, noted here at Santa Ana, California, on May 22, 1963. It had been delivered to the AAF November 2, 1944, as 44-47923, and served for the duration of the war with the 2539th Air Base Squadron at Venice, Florida, and later Foster Field, Texas. The vivid scheme, although colorful, was a fiction. *(Hagedorn Collection)*

The three aircraft that received the basic designation XP-40Q have been widely misunderstood. The first of these, 42-9987, was a conversion of a P-40K, with a two-stage Allison V-1710-121 (F27R) with water injection, and a four-blade Curtiss Electric prop, shown here. Erroneously labeled the XP-40Q-1, it was in fact the XP-40Q-2. It was wrecked at Buffalo January 27, 1943, while being flown by Wing Commander C. Clarkson as a P-40K, and rebuilt as the XP-40Q-2. (*Curtiss via Peter M. Bowers*)

Curtiss XP-40Q

The XP-40Q aircraft were the result of one of Curtiss' efforts to affect a quantum jump in P-40 performance to compete with the more modern fighters then being operated by both friend and foe. Often cited as a purely Curtiss-originated concept, this was in fact far from how the aircraft actually evolved.

As early as December 4, 1943, the Air Materiel Command issued a document that marked the genesis and justification for the entire XP-40Q program. It read as follows:

"In order to alleviate the shortage of fighter aircraft and to assure availability of P-40 aircraft to the Army Air Forces in 1944, it is desired that P-40 production be maintained at a higher level than previously contemplated. Preliminary indications are that the XP-40Q has performance characteristics justifying its consideration as a combat aircraft which might be placed in quantity production should shortages in this category become critical. It is therefore desired that action be taken to:

a. Establish and maintain a production rate of not less than 200 P-40s [see P-40N series] *per month for 1944*

The second aircraft designated an XP-40Q was the first production P-40K-1 (42-45722), and was designated as the XP-40Q-2A. It used the same engine as the XP-40Q-2. The aircraft suffered continuous problems during tests, and was unserviceable 40 of the 70 days it was under test. It survived the war, however, and became a racer as NX300B. (*Dean Collection*)

Although it suffered constant engine problems during service tests, the XP-40Q-2A (42-45722) survived the war to be purchased surplus as a racer and registered NX300B. Note the stylized bird emblem on the fuselage just under the windscreen holding an ace of spades in its beak, seldom noted in most illustrations of this handsome aircraft. (*Dean Collection*)

b. Convert at least two additional P-40Ns to P-40Qs for test purposes
c. Investigate practicability and desirability of converting all scheduled P-40N production to P-40Q without any drop in 1944."

Consequently, there were three aircraft in the XP-40Q development program spanning the years 1943, 1944, and 1945 and, as can be discerned from the foregoing, Curtiss had every right to believe that this would be the next major production series. Two development aircraft were conversions of P-40K airframes. These stayed in Air Force records initially as P-40Ks, even though much modified, and only the third, a modified P-40N, was listed from the start, after changes, as an XP-40Q, thus accounting for some confusion in later years.

The improvements made in the basic P-40 included, primarily, an Allison engine with a two stage mechanical supercharger to gain much better altitude performance, four blade propellers to absorb the additional altitude power available, revised cooling systems for the same reason, and bubble canopies with cut down aft fuselage turtledecks. The fuselage was extended both forward and aft to provide the space for the longer powerplant with the two stages of supercharging up front, and to counter the destabilizing effect of this extension by adding to the tail arm. All the aircraft were limited to four wing guns for weight reduction purposes. Reportedly one or more aircraft were fitted with a new wing having laminar flow airfoil sections, though this is not clear. In some cases wingtips were clipped and windshields revised.

The three aircraft involved were defined by Curtiss and the Flight Test Engineering Branch at Wright Field as the XP-40Q-2, -2A, and -3.

The so-called XP-40Q-2[149] was a P-40K-10, USAAF serial 42-9987, with the least overall modifications, but with installation of the two-stage Allison V-1710-121 (F27R) with water injection where the carburetor was located between the two supercharger stages. There were no intercoolers, and the engine drove a four-blade, Curtiss Electric controllable prop. There was probably ballast in the back end. This aircraft did not have the bubble canopy, and had

The XP-40Q-2A made a better looking racer than it did an Army Air Forces fighter, in many observers' eyes. Race Number 82 was entered in the 1947 Thompson Trophy Race, and was in fourth place piloted by Joe Ziegler when the temperamental engine once again let the airplane down. Ziegler bailed out, and the aircraft was destroyed. (*Dean Collection*)

The last hope of Curtiss for a contender was the seldom illustrated XP-40Q-3 (43-24571). Often mistaken for the externally similar XP-40Q-2A, it was a modified P-40N-25, and was accepted in April 1944.The aircraft was written off in a forced landing a few days after tests began, again due to engine failure. *(Dean Collection)*

the standard wing, but with only four guns. It had crashed as a P-40K January 27, 1943, while being flown by Wing Commander C. Clarkson at Buffalo, and was rebuilt as the XP-40Q-2. After Curtiss testing it went to Wright Field in mid-1944, and shortly incurred extensive damage in a landing accident on July 31, 1944, while being flown by Captain Charles R. Able. Flight tests at Curtiss were conducted by AAF Lt. Robert M. Edholm between March 8 and 24, 1944, during which time 20 flights were made for a total flying time of about 25 hours. Edholm suffered an accident with the aircraft on March 24th at Buffalo when the tail of the aircraft, lightened by a long flight and use of most of the fuel, was caught by the wind, and nosed the running engine and prop onto the runway. On this aircraft the wing tips were squared or clipped, the coolant system moved into the wing section, and an early "bubble" type canopy was installed.

In general, the performance and handling characteristics of the XP-40Q-2 were reported as very good, and it was a decided improvement over previous versions of the P-40 series. At war emergency power with water injection, a high speed of 420mph at 15,000 feet, and a maximum rate of climb of 4,410 feet per minute at 5,000

Army Air Force evaluators praised the new canopy of the XP-40Q-3, comparing it favorably to the visibility afforded by the P-51D and P-47D fighters then being mass produced. Overall performance, however, was slightly less than these production aircraft, and the last "stretch" of the legendary P-40 airframe ended, too little, too late. *(USAAF)*

feet were achieved. It was finally surveyed after the accident noted on October 8, 1944.

The XP-40Q-2A was the initial production P-40K-1, USAAF serial 42-45722, very much modified. It was so radically modified, as early as March 28, 1944, as to be almost unrecognizable as a regular P-40, with fuselage and clipped wing redone. Again, the two stage Allison V-1710-121 engine was used, with the long slim fuselage and a slightly different bubble canopy, along with a much revised radiator and oil cooler cowling.

Persistent power plant maintenance difficulties plagued the XP-40Q-2A, and the loss to a crash on September 1, 1944, of the major test item resulted in very little test information from the aircraft. It was noted, repeatedly, that the regulation of maximum available engine power was completely unsatisfactory, however, during the entire test period, and the aircraft suffered two previous forced landings. Indeed, the aircraft was reported out of commission for maintenance work approximately 40 out of the 70 days it was under test. As a result, testing was abandoned in favor of the newer XP-40Q-3, the converted P-40N (USAAF serial 43-24571).

In 1946, after performance testing, Allison wished to bail the aircraft, but it was declared surplus by the Army into the commercial second hand market. Bought and groomed as experimental civil registration NX 300B for racing, it was entered in the 1947 Thompson Trophy Race as Race No.82, though not qualified. It was in fourth place when on the 13th lap the engine quit. Pilot Joe Ziegler pulled up and bailed out, breaking a leg, and quickly ended the racing career of the aircraft.

The XP-40Q-3 was a modified P-40N-25 airframe, USAAF serial 43-24571, and was officially delivered to the USAAF and accepted in April 1944 under Contract AC-34423. This aircraft was powered by an Allison V-1710-121 (F28R) two stage engine, and except for minor changes was quite similar to the -2 aircraft. Oil coolers in this machine were moved to inboard wing panels. The AAF noted that visibility from the cockpit of the XP-40Q-3 was much better than in the XP-40Q-2A, mainly due to changes in the nose contour and gun sight location. Unfortunately, the XP-40Q-3 was destroyed in a forced landing a few days after testing was begun due, again, to engine failure early in the test regimen.

The following characteristics pertain to the XP-40Q-3: span was 35 feet, three inches, and length was 35 feet, four inches.

Powerplant was the Allison V-1710-121 (F28R) two stage engine rated 1,425hp at sea level takeoff, 1,800 War Emergency horse power at sea level, 1,100hp (Military) at 25,000 feet, and 1,000hp (Normal) at 21,000 feet driving a four bladed propeller. Gross weight was 9,000 pounds.

Maximum speed was 422mph using 1,700hp at 20,500 feet. Climb to 20,000 feet took 4.8 minutes. Service ceiling was 39,000 feet.

Armament consisted of four wing .50 caliber guns with a total of 1,208 rounds of ammunition.

The Curtiss "Twin" P-40

A solitary photo exists of what appears, upon careful examination, to be a rather elaborate hoax.

Marked with an actual P-40C series serial number, and bearing pre-June 1942 U.S. national insignia, the aircraft looks like a short-tailed H87 series aircraft with crude twin engine nacelles mounted, one on each wing, a truncated forward fuselage, and absolutely no provenance. The wing of the aircraft appears to be a standard P-40 series wing which, if true, would hardly support the weight and stresses of two fully faired, operating engines. The canopy appears to be from a P-40D series aircraft, and the engines, on close examination, look like P-40F type *Merlins*. Under close scrutiny, the starboard (right) engine seems to have a shark's or tiger's mouth painted on. The setting appears to be a well-established airfield, but the precise location has not been determined, which could well be a clue to the origins of the contraption.

In consultations with aeronautical engineers specializing in structures, all agreed that they did not believe that a standard P-40 wing would support the weight or stresses of a *Merlin* engine, or

The crash of the XP-40Q-3 effectively ended the production development of the P-40 series. This never before published view reveals that the aircraft had a stenciled, large format number "12" on the lower engine cowl. (*USAAF*)

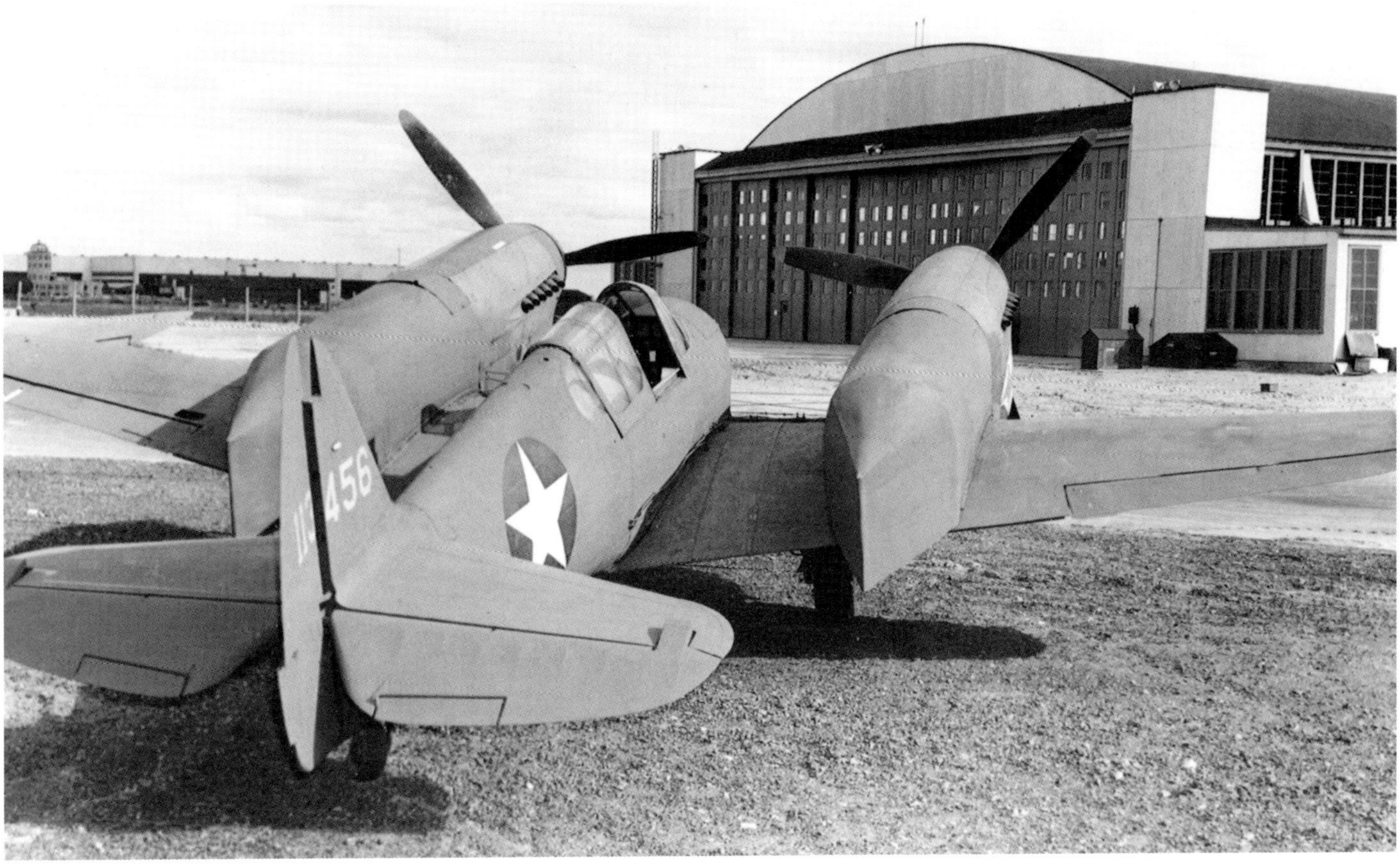

The P-40 series ends with a mystery. The so-called "Twin P-40," even though emblazoned with a bogus (but correct) P-40C serial number, has eluded identification. Perhaps a reader can provide details of what was apparently, at the least, a very elaborate hoax. *(via Peter M. Bowers)*

that the undercarriage would support the weight of two engines and attendant fuel required. Any armament would have had to be grouped in the truncated nose and, in order to have been capable, would have had to be at least four guns.

Historians of the aircraft have, to date, been completely baffled by this apparition, and the consensus seems to be that it may have been assembled as a decoy or intelligence misinformation token.

11

Final Experiments and Decline

Curtiss XP-53

Curtiss and the Army were anxious to develop a worthy successor to the P-40, and it was becoming clear the XP-46 was not the answer. The hoped for answer was thus to be the XP-53; larger and heavier than the XP-48, employing a wing with laminar flow airfoil sections, and a new two stage supercharged engine with intercooler under development by Continental—the XIV-1430-3, 12 cylinder liquid cooled inverted "V" model. The XP-53 was the Curtiss Model 88 (Specification XC-622-3), and two aircraft, often quoted as Air Corps Serials 41-140 and 41-19508,[150] were to be built under Contract AC-15581 of October 28, 1940. This contract was a "no cost" arrangement and, at the outset, was for but one aircraft and engineering data, and resulted from Army AFP No.165269 dated August 3, 1940.

Characteristics, and optimistically predicted performance were as follows: span, length, and height were 41 feet, five inches, 35 feet, three inches, and 12 feet, five inches. Wheel tread was 10 feet, three inches, and wing area 275 square feet.

Believed by many at Curtiss to be the designated replacement for the P-40, a *Merlin XXVIII* powered *Hawk 90* was initially ordered as the XP-53, but before completion was redesignated, with changes, as the XP-60 (AC41-19508). This November 3, 1941, view shows the six gun armament. The aircraft had first flown on September 18th. (*Dean Collection*)

The powerplant was a Continental XIV-1430-3 rated at 1,250hp at sea level takeoff, 1,600hp (Military) at 15,000 feet, and 1,300hp (Normal) at 18,500 feet. The propeller was a Curtiss Electric constant speed design of 11 feet, two inches diameter. Design fuel capacity was 204 gallons.

Empty weight was estimated at 7,650 pounds, design useful load was 2,325 pounds, and design gross weight 9,975 pounds. Maximum ferry gross weight was 10,693 pounds. Design wing and power loadings were 36.27psf and 7.98 pounds per sea level horse power, respectively. Useful load to gross weight ratio was 0.233.

Armament was to consist of eight .50 caliber wing guns with a total of 2,000 rounds of ammunition.

Maximum speed was estimated as 430mph at 18,000 feet. Climb capability was calculated at 6.4 minutes to 15,000 feet, and service ceiling 30,500 feet. Endurance was estimated as 2 hours at 975hp. Takeoff distance over a 50 foot obstacle and landing distance over 50 feet were estimated, respectively, as 2,800 feet and 2,200 feet.

The development of the hoped for Continental engine was lagging, however, and a few weeks after the XP-53 contract was signed the Army decided the contract with Curtiss was to be changed, such that one of the two aircraft would be revised to use the license-built Packard/Rolls Royce V-1650-1 *Merlin* engine as used in the Curtiss P-40F. The other aircraft would continue with the Continental engine. The *Merlin* powered aircraft would now be the Curtiss Model 90, sometimes called the "*Hawk 90*" at Curtiss, and labeled by the Army as the initial XP-60, because of the engine change. An XP-53 was never completed for flight test, serving only for structural testing, and as a source for XP-60 spare parts and static test article for same. An Army document also stated that it contributed its "combat protection equipment" (assumed to mean armor plating, and possibly self-sealing fuel tanks) and guns to the XP-60. Wright Field also referred to the XP-53 as the Project MX-4.

A Foreign Release Agreement was entered into by Curtiss and the Anglo-French Purchasing Committee for the XP-53 but, because of the loss of interest in the type by the USAAC, this never went forward.

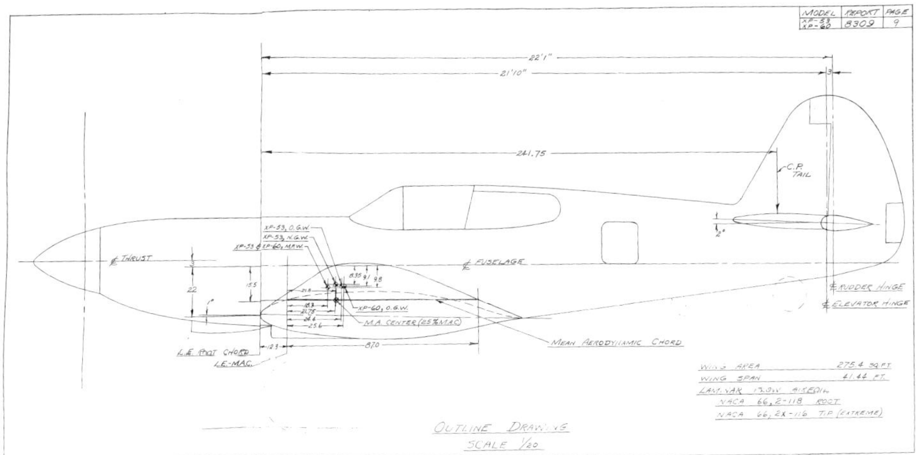

Although of low quality, these are the only known drawings showing the plan form of the XP-53 and XP-60, both being superimposed on the other, and having but a three inch difference in length.

Curtiss XP-60 *Hawk 90* and P-60A

To begin, the reader may find the convoluted history of the various aircraft with a common root designation, P-60, rather confusing, as indeed it was. Seemingly out of sequence, they are presented here in chronological, rather than designation sequence, since these aircraft in actuality had little else in common.

The original design that received the USAAC designation XP-60 was procured on Contract AC-18551, and was basically an improved P-40 designed around the Packard V-1650-1—a license-built Rolls Royce *Merlin* engine—a modified P-40D fuselage, and a new, laminar flow wing. The XP-53 (q.v.), it should be recognized, was structurally identical, aft of the firewall, to the original XP-60, with the exception of the engine and associated cooling installations. The XP-60 was assigned the Wright Field, Materiel Command Project Number MX-69.

The Packard-built Rolls Royce *Merlin XXVIII* powerplant designated for the XP-60 was a proven type with a single stage two speed mechanical supercharger, and in early 1941 work was preceding on an aircraft much like the XP-53, but re-engined and with, initially, an eight gun armament, but later reduced to six .50 caliber guns with 2,000 rounds total. Indeed, an Army document dated March 15, 1941, covering the AFP for purchase of the XP-60s had actually been issued, but the contract not written, as such. It went so far as to state that if the *Merlin* was installed, the aircraft would be called XP-60 (Curtiss Specification XC-627-1A); if the Continental engine was used, as a substitute, it would automatically be designated XP-53.

This side view of the XP-60, taken November 19, 1941, shows the rather unusual application of the USAAC rudder markings. The aircraft suffered from a number of problems, and had several minor accidents, but survived to eventually became the XP-60D. (*Curtiss*)

In late 1941, it was decided to use the other XP-53 airframe (42-19508) as a static test model for the XP-60, since there was structural similarity, and the Army was ready to abandon the development of the Continental engine for the Curtiss fighter. The XP-60 in original form had the aft fuselage and tail of a P-40D, and the larger laminar flow section wing of the XP-53. With this new wing was an inward retracting landing gear, as opposed to that of the P-40 series. The new plan was to borrow any parts needed, such as armor and armament, from the static test aircraft for use in the XP-60.

Construction of the "*Hawk 90*" was completed, and a first flight made three weeks before America was thrown into World War II by the Japanese attack. The XP-60 was procured, as a direct consequence, as a rapid development project to make possible the delivery of a production type airplane incorporating the laminar flow wing and the *Merlin XXVIII* engine at the earliest possible date. In order to accomplish quick delivery, it was originally planned to eliminate the armament installation, self-sealing fuel tanks, armor plate protection, and other minor items not essential for determining flight characteristics. Curtiss was even allowed to deviate from standard practice, which normally required that a complete set of drawings and reports be submitted to the Air Corps Engineering Division. As might be expected, performance of the XP-60 did not reach that estimated for the XP-53. Reasons put forth included poor manufacture of the new laminar flow wing, and less than expected engine performance. But the V-1650-1 *Merlin* did not have the amount of supercharging calculated for the ultimate Continental two stage engine, and disappointing results from early laminar flow type airfoil wings were not uncommon.

Taxi tests of the XP-60 started September 16, 1941, and the first flight followed on the 18th. On November 18th, following protracted discussions in connection with the XP-53 and XP-60, a plan

By January 1943 Curtiss engineers working on the XP-60D, the reworked second XP-53, and original XP-60, must have been thoroughly discouraged. The radiator intake under the nose had been redesigned a number of times and, in this view, appears to have an under bite, and the vertical tail surfaces had been significantly increased in area, but all to no avail. (*USAAF 15581*)

was submitted by Curtiss to convert the XP-53 into a static test article for the production P-60, and to make the installation of bullet-proof windscreen, self-sealing fuel tanks, and gun installation in the XP-60 in lieu of the XP-53. An official demonstration flight followed in March 1942, and official Army performance tests were in April and May. The aircraft was officially accepted by the Army July 11, 1942, but invoiced in March. The aircraft was returned to Curtiss in August 1941 for installation of the *Merlin 61* engine. It is interesting to note that, as of the date of acceptance, Curtiss records do not reflect either an Army or Curtiss serial number for the aircraft. The aircraft became the XP-60D (q.v.).

Characteristics of the XP-60 were as follows: span, length, and height were 41 feet, five and 1/4 inches, 33 feet, four inches, and 10 feet, nine inches. Wing area was 275.4 square feet.

The powerplant was a Packard-built *Merlin* V-1650-1 two speed, single stage, supercharged engine rated 1,300hp at sea level takeoff, 1,120hp (Military) at 19,000 feet, and 1,080hp (Normal) at 9,500 feet, driving a Curtiss Electric constant speed three bladed propeller of 11 feet diameter. Internal fuel capacity was 228 gallons.

Empty weight was 7,060 pounds, normal useful load 2,290 pounds, and normal gross weight 9,350 pounds. Wing and power loadings were 34psf and 7.19 pounds per horse power. Normal useful load to gross weight ratio was 0.245.

Maximum speed was 380mph at 1,120hp at 20,000 feet, and landing speed was 85mph. Climb capability was 7.3 minutes to 15,000 feet, and service ceiling was 29,000 feet. Range capability was 800 miles at 365mph at 16,500 feet, and 1,100 miles at 314mph at 15,000 feet. Takeoff distance over a 50 foot obstacle was 2,550 feet, and landing distance over a 50 foot obstacle was 1,925 feet.

In addition to disappointing performance, the XP-60 had stability problems, resulting in the requirement for an increase in area and aspect ratio of the vertical tail. Don Berlin's opinion, though he was on his way to Fisher Body Division of General Motors, was that, like some P-40 versions, the front airscoop was poorly designed, and much too destabilizing, making a large tail necessary. In addition, the XP-60 encountered several minor accidents during testing. It was subsequently modified to the XP-60D version.

The P-60A was to have been the production version of the XP-60, and in fact, production engineering for this aircraft had been started in the summer of 1941, by which time it appeared that the airplane would weigh a little over 9,000 pounds. On October 25, 1941, Curtiss submitted a quote to the Army for the construction of 1,950 P-60As to be built in accordance with Curtiss Specification X8509, dated March 1, 1941. A contract (W535-ac-22714) was actually issued and approved but, by November 17, 1941, the Project Officer, on nothing more than an Inter Office Memo, advised the Assistant Chief of the Materiel Division that it had been concluded that the P-60A would be underpowered. Wisely, a conference between Curtiss and Army officials, which was chaired on the Army side by none other than Brigadier General George C. Kenny, was convened on January 2, 1942, to discuss the future of the P-60A contract. This meeting proved to be a pivotal event in the history of Curtiss fighter evolution because, as a direct result of this meeting, the P-60A contract was essentially set aside when Curtiss could not guarantee the performance, and Curtiss was essentially compelled, at that dark moment of the war, to undertake the construction of 2,400 Republic P-47G *Thunderbolts*, 700 P-40Fs, 700 P-40Es, 100 P-62s, and only one each of the P-60A, P-60B, and P-60C variants it had pinned such hopes on. Needless to say, most of these production figures, for various reasons, were never realized and, instead, Curtiss spent the war building yet more variants of the basic P-40.

After all of these exertions, the Army finally accepted the one-and-only XP-60A (42-79423, MSN 15523) on October 13, 1943, at Buffalo.

Curtiss XP-60D

The XP-60D was the same airframe as the XP-60 with a significant improvement incorporated.

The powerplant was changed in August 1942 to a two stage, supercharged V-1650-3 *Merlin* engine in place of the earlier single stage version in the XP-60, driving a four-blade prop. The XP-60D emerged later in 1942, but had a relatively short life of much less than a year. It crashed and was destroyed on May 6, 1943, at Rome Air Depot, NY.

Specifications of the XP-60D were: span, length, and wing area 41 feet, five inches, 33 feet, seven inches, and 375 square feet. Wheel tread was 11 feet, nine inches.

With the new, two-stage *Merlin* engine installed in August 1942 and enormous wheel covers, from this aspect the XP-60D almost appears a cousin of the British Boulton Paul *Defiant*. The aircraft crashed and was destroyed on May 6, 1943. (*USAAF 15581*)

Ironically, the XP-60A (42-79423), with a supercharged V-1710-75 engine of 1,425hp, looked more like a product of the Republic or Grumman line than an evolution of the P-40 and XP-53. This October 14, 1942, view shows the aircraft incomplete in several respects, and the fact that it bore little resemblance to the XP-60 or XP-60D, which actually preceded it. (*Curtiss BB-17772DS*)

Powerplant was a Packard *Merlin* V-1570-3 with a two stage supercharger rated 1,380hp at 3,000rpm for sea level takeoff, and 1,210hp at 3,000rpm at 25,800 feet, driving a four blade Curtiss Electric propeller of 11 feet diameter. Fuel capacity was 228 gallons.

Normal gross weight was 9,980 pounds. Wing and power loadings were 36.3psf and 7.23 pounds per horse power, respectively. Maximum speed was 390mph at altitude.

Curtiss XP-60A and XP-60B

The search for a greatly improved successor to the P-40 fighter continued with the advent of the XP-60A (Curtiss Specification 8509) as a hopeful combination of a new laminar airfoil wing and the proper powerplant. In this case it was the Allison V-1710-75 with a turbo supercharger to achieve high speed at altitude. There would thus be no interference with production by Packard of the V-1650 *Merlin* engine needed for other fighters.

It looked for a while that Curtiss would be on its way with a new production fighter when, on October 31, 1941, the company was awarded a contract for no less than 1,950 P-60As (Curtiss Model 95A) with the turbo supercharged Allison, even though the P-60A was a particularly inelegant looking aircraft with a new, redesigned fuselage.

But little more than a month after the big production order, the Japanese struck at Pearl Harbor. Official doubts that were expressed even before this event about the advisability of interfering with current P-40 production at a time of national emergency came to the fore, and in late December 1941, P-60A production planning was held up. In early January Curtiss was handed a bitter blow. The P-60 program was to continue only as a series of prototype developments; a single model each of an XP-60A with the General Electric turbo supercharged Allison engine, an XP-60B like the XP-60A, except with a Wright SU-504-2 turbo supercharged Allison, and an XP-60C using a new engine starting into development by Chrysler. The Materiel Center at Wright Field took action on October 31, 1942, however, to change the designation of the XP-60B to XP-60E which, in turn, was described as being "*...identical to the XP-60C with the exception of the reduction gearing and propeller.*" It is little wonder that the Curtiss engineering staff was reeling under the pressure to improve the P-40 design, while at the same time having to struggle to make sense of the design changes being issued rapid-fire by the Army. As an added blow, Curtiss was obliged, at nearly the same juncture, to build Republic P-47 *Thunderbolt* fighters under license instead of a production P-60A. As it turned out, the XP-60B was never built, as such.

In October 1942, tests on the XP-60A prototype (USAAF serial 42-79423, MSN 15523) commenced, with powerplant difficulties quickly surfacing, resulting in the removal of the turbo supercharging system, with a first flight on November 11, 1942. Later, a revised system was incorporated, and the aircraft test flown. The aircraft was not officially accepted by the Army until October 13, 1943, and passed to Class 26 (Instructional Airframe) at Wright Field April 15, 1944.

The Army gave the following specifications for the XP-60A: span, length, and height 41 feet, four inches, 33 feet, 11 inches, and 10 feet, nine inches. Wheel tread was a broad 12 feet. Wing area measured 275 square feet.

The powerplant was an Allison V-1710-75, turbo supercharged, rated 1,425hp at sea level takeoff, 1,425hp (Military) at 25,000 feet, and 1,100hp (Normal) at 25,000 feet driving a 11 foot, eight inch

Chronologically, the next player in the epic of the XP-60 series was the XP-60C, which had been planned to be fitted with the monster 2,300hp Chrysler XV-2220, 16-cylinder engine. When this had endless development problems, it received a Pratt & Whitney R-2800 instead. This image was taken shortly before the first flight in January 1943 at Buffalo. AAF serial 42-79424 also featured contra-rotating props, but only four .50 caliber guns. (*Dean Collection*)

diameter Curtiss Electric constant speed four blade propeller. Internal fuel capacity was 200 gallons.

Empty weight was 7,800 pounds, normal useful load 1,818 pounds, normal gross weight 9,616 pounds, and maximum gross weight 10,160 pounds. Normal wing and power loadings were respectively 34.97psf and 6.75 pounds per horse power. Normal useful load to gross weight ratio was 0.19—quite poor.

Maximum speed was 420mph at 25,000 feet, and climb capability 6.5 minutes to 15,000 feet. Service ceiling was 32,500 feet. Normal range was 375 miles at 375mph. Takeoff and landing distances over a 50 foot obstacle were respectively 2,200 feet and 2,100 feet.

Armament consisted of six .50 caliber wing guns with 1,200 rounds of ammunition total.

It was decided that, although P-60A performance would be sufficient for production, early Republic P-47 variants' performance was just about as good. Consideration had been given to a possible production order for 500 P-60A-1 fighters, but it never happened. Parts of the XP-60A were used in later XP-60 series variants, and it was not formally accepted by the resident Army representative at the factory until October 13, 1943, on S.O. 460.

Curtiss XP-60C

The XP-60C, in an early 1942 Curtiss study, was to have used a new 2,300HP Chrysler engine under early development, the XV-2220 with 16 cylinders in an inverted "V" configuration, and much later tested on the Republic XP-47H. At the time, however, this engine was not ready.

In the early fall of 1942, Curtiss and the Army agreed that the prototype would instead be powered by a Pratt & Whitney R-2800-53 18-cylinder radial engine with a two stage mechanical supercharger in place of the Chrysler engine. The powerplant installation would be unusual, in that the XP-60C (Curtiss Model 95C) would have a dual rotation (counter-rotating) propeller, presumably to zero out the large torque reaction resulting from a high powered single rotation propeller. There was extra weight and mechanical complexity also to be considered, however, and a special R-2800 engine model with reduction gearing to accommodate this propeller had to be provided, of course.

The XP-60C (42-79424) first flew on January 27, 1943. Characteristics of this fighter were as follows: span length and height were 41 feet, four inches, 33 feet, eight inches, and 10 feet, nine inches. Wheel tread was 12 feet, and wing area 275 square feet.

The powerplant was a Pratt & Whitney R-2800-53 twin row, 18 cylinder mechanically supercharged air cooled model rated at 2,000hp for sea level takeoff, 2,015hp War Emergency Power at 20,000 feet, and 1,550hp (Normal) at 21,500 feet driving a Curtiss Electric constant speed six blade (two threes) dual rotation propeller of 12 feet, two inches in diameter. Fuel capacity was 225 gallons.

Empty weight was 8,600 pounds, useful load 1,925 pounds, and gross weight 10,525 pounds. Overload gross weight was 11,835 pounds. Normal wing and power loadings were 38.27psf and 5.26 pounds per horse power. Normal useful load to gross weight ratio was 0.183.

Rarely illustrated showing full national markings and the AAF serial number, XP-60C (42-79424), although possessing some of the most advanced features available to the designers, still possessed archaic canopy features. (*Dean Collection*)

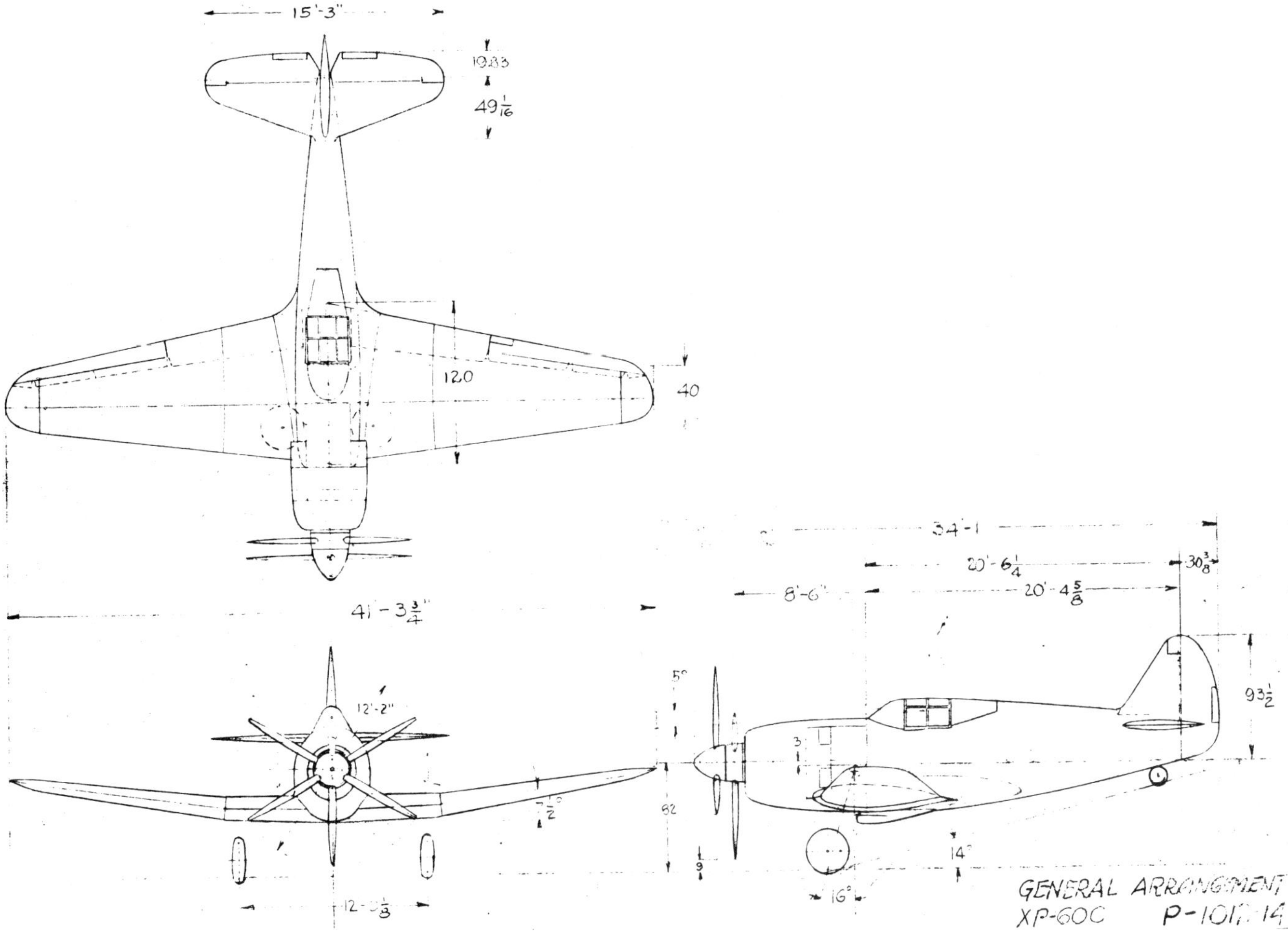

With a cranked wing planform and nearly three feet more span than the P-40 series, the XP-60C was a hefty aircraft. This never before published three-view suggests that, even if the aircraft had reached production and squadron service, a recognition problem may have resulted, as the overhead view showed a striking resemblance to the German Focke-Wulfe Fw 190 and the Japanese Kawasaki Ki 100. (*Curtiss P-1012-14*)

Maximum speeds were 414mph at 2,000hp at 20,350 feet and 324mph at sea level. Landing speed was 89mph. Initial climb rate was 3,890 feet per minute and climb to 30,000 feet took 6.0 minutes. Service ceiling was 35,000 feet and normal range 315 miles. Takeoff distance over a 50 foot obstacle was 1,325 feet.

Armament consisted of four .50 caliber wing machine guns.

Initial flight tests of the XP-60C provided generally favorable results, though accidents did occur, such as loss of a piece of powerplant cowling. In early 1943 the Army Air Force desired to flight test available U.S. fighter prototypes, and Curtiss submitted the XP-60C; the XP-60E was not yet ready. Problems were experienced during the tests at Patterson Field in Ohio, including poor powerplant performance and surface roughness of the laminar flow wing, resulting in poor performance of the Curtiss prototype. It was finally accepted by the AAF June 5, 1944, but oddly is not reflected by serial number in the Curtiss Billing Book, only in the summary at the end of the summary for that month. The aircraft was eventually stored at Robins AAF, where it was salvaged April 27, 1945.

These test results pretty much doomed Curtiss chances for a production contract, and a contract gained earlier for 500 P-60A models using R-2900 engines and dual rotation propellers gained in November 1942 was cancelled after pilot production had been initiated, this in June 1943. Only two fighters were to be built.

Curtiss YP-60E

The final Curtiss P-60 series version was the YP-60E. In May 1944, Curtiss informed the Army that they wished to discontinue any development of the P-60 type. By this time, it was clear there was to be no production contract, and the variants so far had little if any advantages over U.S. fighters already in production by other manufacturers.

It was agreed, however, that Curtiss would finish one of the aircraft started as YP-60A-1s, and it would be designated YP-60E, since it most resembled the XP-60E. Differences involved use of a more powerful Pratt & Whitney *Double Wasp* engine, a bubble canopy, and six .50 caliber wing guns with 267 rounds per gun instead of four guns.

First flight of the YP-60E prototype (43-32763, MSN 27691), which looked, ironically, somewhat like a P-47 *Thunderbolt*, took place on July 13, 1944. It was taken on only one subsequent test

By May 1944, Curtiss had all but given up on the seemingly endless morphing of the P-60 series, and informed the Army that they wished to discontinue the development. They agreed, however, to complete an aircraft started as one of the YP-60A-1s as the single YP-60E, since it most resembled the XP-60E then under development. 43-32763, MSN 27691 was formally accepted on September 16, 1944. (*Dean Collection*)

flight at Curtiss, and then delivered to the Army Air Force at Wright Field in Ohio, officially, on September 16, 1944, where it was promptly set aside, and later sold as surplus.

Characteristics of the YP-60E were: span, length, and height 41 feet, four inches, 33 feet, 11 inches, and 12 feet, six inches. Wing area was 275 square feet.

The powerplant was a Pratt & Whitney R-2800-18 rated at 2,100hp for sea level takeoff driving a four blade, single rotation Curtiss electric single rotation propeller of 12 feet, two inches diameter. Internal fuel capacity was 225 gallons.

Empty weight was 8,285 pounds, useful load 1,985 pounds, and normal and maximum gross weights 10,270 pounds and 11,520 pounds respectively. Wing and power loadings at normal gross weight were 37.35psf and 4.89 pounds per horse power. Normal useful load to gross weight ratio was 0.193.

Maximum speed was 405mph at 24,500 feet. Climb time was 4.8 minutes to 14,000 feet, and service ceiling was 34,000 feet.

Postwar the aircraft was sold to James DeSanto, the owner of a flying school at Cleveland, Ohio. Mr. DeSanto intended to race the aircraft in the 1947 Thompson Trophy Race at the National Air Races. For this purpose the plane was considerably modified. One spectator called it "*...big, fat, and ugly*." The R-2800 engine was boosted to put out 2,440hp, and it was equipped with a water injection system. The wing was cut down to a span of only 31 feet, two inches, or about 10 feet total lopped off. All military equipment was stripped out. Issued the Experimental License NX 21979 (given as MSN 27691), the name "*Connie II*" was painted on the engine cowl, and the race number 80 was applied. DeSanto took the YP-60E racer up for a test flight over Cleveland airport prior to qualifying for the race, and put on a spectacular display of the aircraft's flight qualities, but in the process parts of the tail started leaving the aircraft. Out of control, the plane crashed into a local cornfield. DeSanto managed to depart the aircraft and parachuted safely. This was the ignominious end of the Curtiss P-60 fighter series.

Seldom in the history of fighter development have experimental aircraft with the same root design number, in this instance P-60, been so different in nearly every respect. The YP-60E was completed before the XP-60E, but accepted nearly six months later. It survived the war to become a racer, but crashed while being tested prior to the 1947 Thompson Trophy Race as NX21979. (*Dean Collection*)

The Curtiss XP-60E (AAF 42-79425, MSN 15525) was formally accepted by the Army May 13, 1944, although it had been tested in Florida as early as January. It was the XP-60B airframe with a Pratt & Whitney R-2800-10. It was written off in a landing accident. *(Dean Collection)*

Curtiss XP-60E

The XP-60E (42-79425, MSN 15525) was the XP-60B airframe originally slated to be fitted with an Allison V-1710-75 engine turbo supercharged by a Wright turbo unit. The XP-60B installation never came about, and the airframe became the XP-60E on Contract AC-28113, powered with a Pratt & Whitney R-2800-10 engine driving a four blade single rotation propeller of less weight than a dual type, which resulted in moving the engine forward by a few inches for proper balance. Otherwise the aircraft was similar to the XP-60C, and was the prototype aircraft desired by the Air force to be tested at Patterson Field, in Ohio.

Because the XP-60E was not ready (it had not yet even flown), the XP-60C was substituted with the results noted.

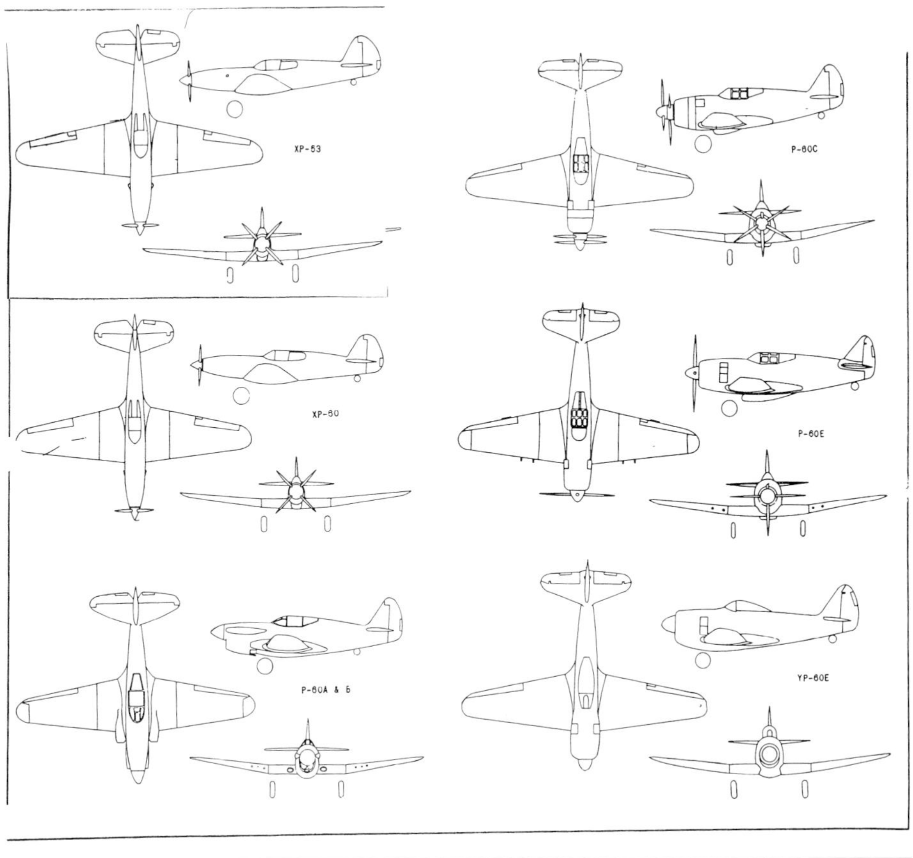

This Army produced series of line drawings reflects the evolution of the complex P-60 series, commencing with the XP-53, and ending with the YP-60E. *(USAAF)*

In January 1944 the XP-60E was delivered to Eglin Field, Florida, where a fighter conference was being held, with many fighter types on hand for testing by pilots from various manufacturing companies and U.S. and Allied military services who attended. One of the pilots was Charles Lindbergh. In spite of the fact that the XP-60E lost a radio mast in a dive at about 380mph indicated airspeed, Lindbergh called it "*...an interesting plane with many good characteristics, but still experimental.*" Generally, the speed performance was not as good as some of the other fighters; however, the initial climb rate of 4,200 feet per minute was considered very good. A more negative factor was that the armament consisted of only four .50 caliber machine guns, whereas the P-47 had eight.

Characteristics of the XP-60E prototype follow: span, length, and height 41 feet, four inches, 33 feet, 11 inches, and 10 feet, nine inches. Wheel tread was 12 feet, and wing area 275 square feet.

The powerplant was a Pratt & Whitney R-2800-10, rated at 2,000hp at sea level takeoff, 2,000hp War Emergency Power at 19,000 feet, and 1,550hp (Military) at 22,500 feet driving a four blade 12 foot, 11 inch diameter single rotation Curtiss Electric constant speed propeller. Internal fuel capacity was 225 gallons.

Empty weight was 8,574 pounds, useful load 1,746 pounds, and normal and maximum gross weights 10,320 pounds and 10,667 pounds, respectively. Normal wing and power loadings were 37.53psf and 5.16 pounds per horse power. Normal useful load to gross weight ratio was 0.17.

Maximum speed was 410mph at 20,200 feet, and 391mph at 24,200 feet, with cruise speed 348mph. Initial climb rate was 4,200fpm, and the aircraft could reach 10,000 feet in 2.5 minutes. Service ceiling was 38,000 feet.

The aircraft was formally accepted from Curtiss by the AAF representative on May 13, 1944; it later had a serious landing accident, and was then written off.

Curtiss XP-60F

Almost completely ignored in the strange odyssey of the P-60 series, the Army Air Force assigned the designation XP-60F to a proposed YP-60A reworked to accommodate an R-2800 series engine. The project was cancelled by the Army, however, who by this point had had quite enough of the P-60!

Curtiss-Wright XP-71

The XP-71 was a proposed design laid down by the St. Louis Division of Curtiss-Wright as the CW-26 (Specification 26-Z-51), but is interesting to note here because of its great size. Conceived as an escort fighter plane for bombers over long ranges, and concurrently as a destroyer against invading enemy bomber formations, the two-place XP-71 was proposed to the Army on November 2, 1941, and two aircraft were ordered. The project got only as far as partial mockups and wind tunnel models, and was cancelled in 1942 due to the pressure of other projects, with no aircraft actually built.

The XP-71 was ahead of its time. It was to feature counter-rotating propellers, have a gross weight of 40,000 pounds with a wing loading of 44.3, a span of 83 feet, and a length of 78 feet. It was to have been powered by two Pratt & Whitney R-4360 engines of 3,000hp, equipped with turbo-superchargers. Critical altitude was estimated from 27,000 to 33,000 feet and, at 25,000 feet, high speed was expected to have been 430mph. Tests were in fact accomplished with a 1/19th scale model.

By December 3, 1942, the concept still had some life left in it, and AAF planners, by then completely disenchanted with the "convoy fighter," were speculating as to whether or not the aircraft might be useful as a photo reconnaissance type. They reasoned that it could easily accommodate three K-17 cameras, while retaining, oddly, the massive 75mm cannon, with the cameras being arrayed behind the gun in left and right oblique positions. They may not have given

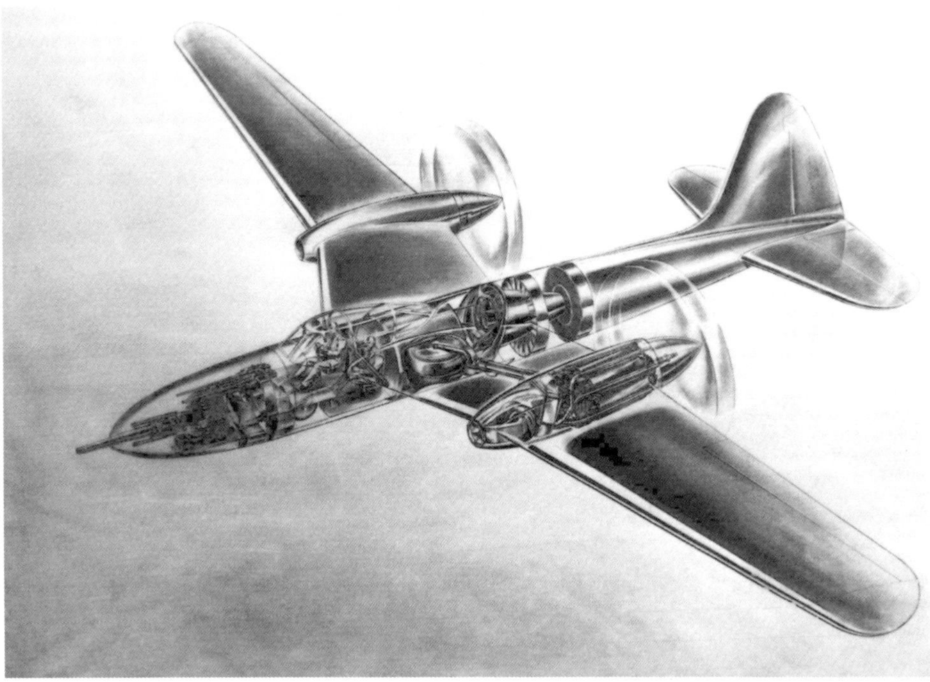

Although never actually completed, both the Army Air Force and the Curtiss-Wright St. Louis organization exerted enormous energy and substantial development costs in the proposed XP-71. Intended as either an escort fighter or bomber destroyer, it was to have employed a number of very advanced systems. Note that in this artist's concept, the inboard wing sections are cranked, and the outboard panels have a straight leading edge. (*Curtiss-Wright via J. Schneider*)

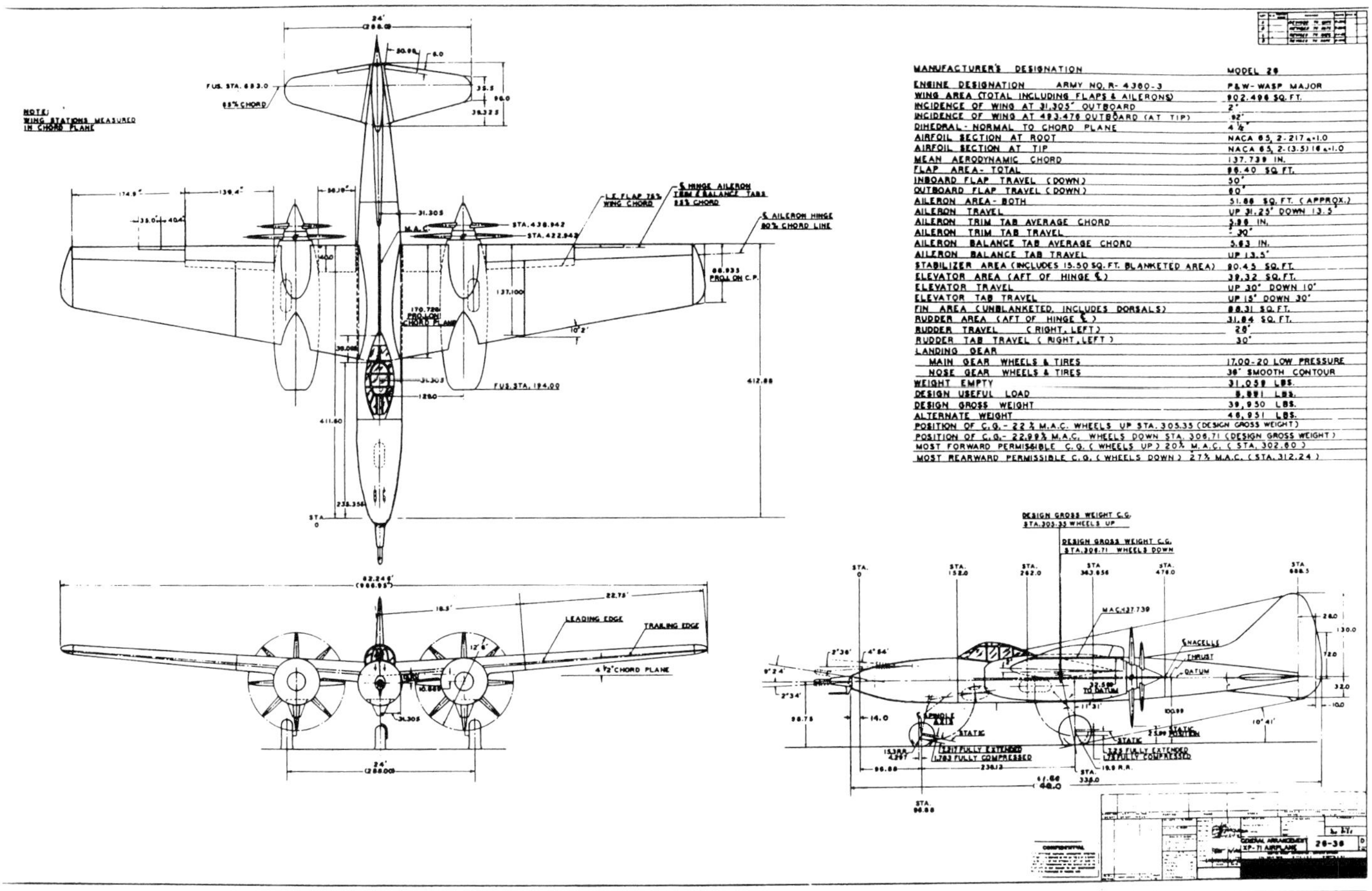

This June 1, 1943, drawing shows what would have been the final configuration of the XP-71. With a wing span of 82.3 feet, a comparison with the Northrop P-61A *Black Widow* at 66 feet span gives some idea of the size of this large aircraft. (*Curtiss-Wright via David W. Ostrowski*)

Curtiss-Wright tested a number of wing configurations for the XP-71. On this configuration model, the wing section is shoulder-high and straight through, and the contra-rotating pusher props have enormous spinners. (*Curtiss-Wright*)

Believed to have been the final wing configuration for the proposed XP-71, the entire wing has been lowered from shoulder height to a near mid-wing section, and the outboard panels have been dramatically swept. (*Curtiss-Wright via J. Schneider*)

This January 26, 1943, view of the full-scale mock-up of the massive XP-71 shows the 75mm cannon on the traversing mount that would have been in the extreme nose, flanked by two 37mm cannon. (*Curtiss-Wright via David W. Ostrowski*)

The XP-71 would have been a handful for the one-man crew, the pilot, and this mockup of the cockpit as it appeared in January 1943 included indicators of the gun laying switches at top center. *(Curtiss-Wright via David W. Ostrowski)*

too much thought to the impact of the gun on the sensitive cameras in such an arrangement.

The gestation of the XP-71 dragged on for an inordinate length of time, however. By February 11, 1943, the design itself was more or less complete, and was awaiting only the fire control equipment, which was to be built by the United Shoe Machinery Corporation. When finally completed and tested earlier that month, the nose section failed catastrophically. Curtiss-Wright had originally intended to use an optical range finder, known as the T-12, to lay the 75mm gun but, by June 12, 1942, this had been changed to the experimental AN/APG-5 radio-type range finder.

Seldom mentioned is the fact that a representative of the British Purchasing Commission visited Curtiss-Wright on August 5, 1942, to discuss possible RAF acquisition of the type.

By October 14, 1943, the AAF and Curtiss-Wright finally reached agreement that the entire XP-71 program should be dropped. The AAF wanted Curtiss-Wright to shift their engineering talent to other projects which, by this point in the war, were enormously higher in priority, particularly the C-46 cargo transport. Curtiss-Wright, in spite of the agreement, however, as late as October 20th was still promoting a modification of the requirement so as to produce the aircraft as a high-altitude photo-reconnaissance aircraft.

The estimated characteristics of the XP-71, which differed slightly from the initial specification, were: span, length, and height 82 feet, 61 feet, 10 inches, and 19 feet. Wing area was 902 square feet.

The power plants (2) were to have been Pratt & Whitney R-4360-13 *Wasp Major*, 28 cylinder, four-row radial turbo supercharged engines mounted as pushers, each rated at 3,450hp at sea level takeoff. Engines were located in the wings, each driving counter-rotating dual pusher propellers behind the wing trailing edge.

Empty weight was proposed to be 31,060 pounds, useful load 8,890 pounds, and design gross weight 39,950 pounds, with overload gross weight 46,951 pounds. Wing loading and power loading were 44.29psf and 5.79 pounds per horse power, respectively. Design useful load to gross weight ratio was 0.223.

Estimated maximum speed was 428mph at 25,000 feet, with cruise speed 270mph. Climb to 25,000 feet was estimated to take 12.5 minutes. Service ceiling was to be 40,000 feet, and maximum range 3,000 miles.

The very heavy armament was to be one 75mm cannon with 20 rounds fixed in the fuselage nose, plus two 37mm cannon with 60 rounds per gun, also fixed in the nose. The 75mm gun installation, covered by Project MX-391 (the aircraft itself was Project MX-147), was identical to that intended for the XP-58. The little-known trials of a 75mm gun in a Douglas B-18 at Aberdeen Proving Ground, MD, in October 1941, were in fact incident to the development of the XP-71 fire control system. It is interesting to note that the AAF requested that Curtiss-Wright pass its rather extensive knowledge of the 75mm gun installation and fire control system on to Beech, in Wichita, on April 1, 1942, "*...without specifically mentioning the XP-71*." Undoubtedly, the AAF desired to see Beech use this experience in the development of the Beech XA-38 *Grizzly*.

Luckily, this escort fighter project was abandoned early by the Air Force.

Seldom viewed nose-on, this wind tunnel model of the final configuration of the XP-71 reveals the air intakes for the radiators, which almost make it appear jet powered. *(Curtiss-Wright via David W. Ostrowski)*

Curtiss was obliged, grudgingly, to undertake license production of the Republic P-47 *Thunderbolt* alongside their own designs at Buffalo as the P-47G. The April 1944 production line view shows P-40Ns at right, led by 42-104582, parallel to the P-47G production line, probably including 42-21837 and up. Note the camouflage pattern on the wing of the P-40N, and the relative numbers of workmen on the two lines. (*Curtiss B8-24839*)

Republic (Curtiss) P-47G *Thunderbolt*

Curtiss suffered what was for many a singular indignity to a premier U.S. fighter manufacturer by the cancellation of their October 1941 contract for 1,950 P-60As so they could continue volume production of P-40s, but also so as to produce Republic P-47 *Thunderbolt* fighters in Buffalo, New York, as ordered by the Army.

After notification in January 1942 Curtiss was able to deliver the first P-47G in December of that year.

The first 20 P-47G-CU models (42-24920 to 42-24939, commencing MSN 21814 although, for some reason, the second aircraft, MSN 21815, was also given as 42-24920) out of the Curtiss plant duplicated the P-47C, and the first was accepted on Septem-

Between January 17 and 29, 1944, the *Buffalo Evening News* sponsored an air power show to raise money for war bonds. Late model P-40Ns and a P-47G were on display, plastered with currency in multiple denominations pasted on by factory workers. (*Curtiss 1817-X*)

Two of the Curtiss-built P-47G-15s were converted to two-seat trainer configuration as TP-47Gs, including 42-25266 (MSN 22160, the other was apparently 42-25267), which was accepted February 26, 1944. It was apparently converted to two-seat configuration at the Evansville, IN, Republic plant. This aircraft was initially assigned to the 53rd Fighter Group, Third Air Force at Fort Myers, Florida, prior to conversion, and then to Mitchel Field. It went to storage at Walnut Ridge October 11, 1945. (*Dean Collection*)

ber 24, 1942; the remaining aircraft—P-47G-1-CU (40 aircraft, 42-24940 to 42-24979), P-47G-5-CU (60 aircraft, 42-24980 to 42-25039), P-47G-10-CU (80 aircraft, 42-25040 to 42-25119), and P-47G-15-CU (154 aircraft, 42-25120 to 42-25273)—versions were similar to the P-47D "razor-back" version. Production of Curtiss *Thunderbolts* was slow. In the approximately fifteen months of their production the rate averaged less than 24 aircraft a month, and orders were cancelled in March 1944.

Curtiss XP-62

The single XP-62, Curtiss Specification XC-627-2A, Army Serial 41-35873 (MSN 20787), was intended as a high altitude interceptor fighter project for the Army initiated in January 1941. The concept was for a fast, heavy hitting aircraft, incorporating a pressure cabin for the pilot, and a turbo supercharged version of the most powerful engine available. Curtiss-Wright selected the Wright 18 cylinder GR-3350 *Duplex Cyclone* radial of 2,250hp for the job, and planned on a fixed armament of either eight 20mm cannon, or not less than 12, .50 caliber machine guns, and a combination of requirements certain to make the XP-62 a very large and heavy machine. The goal for high speed was set at 468mph at 27,000 feet (a Mach number close to .70, or near the drag divergent Mach number for most wartime wing airfoils, leaving little or no reserve for diving, but at the time little was known about compressibility).

The initial Curtiss proposal, received on April 29, 1941, called for two aircraft—one XP-62 and one XP-62A—with delivery optimistically within 15 and 18 months, respectively. Army authority for such a purchase was gained on May 16, 1941, and Contract AC-19440 was signed dated June 27, 1941. Further study resulted in contractor changes submitted August 2, 1941, covering a new high speed of 448mph, and an increase in gross weight of 1,537 pounds. In December 1941, a mockup inspection of the XP-62 was held at Curtiss that resulted in about 90 changes, and on January 1, 1942, it was recommended that gross weight be reduced from 15,568 pounds to 14,000 pounds by reduction of structural weight, elimination of four of the cannon, and elimination of the propeller deicing system.

Looking like little more than a single-seat version of the SB2C-1 *Helldiver* for the Navy, the XP-62, Army serial number 41-35873 (MSN 20787), was actually a high-altitude interceptor project for the Army dating from January 1941. To have mounted, initially, an astounding eight 20mm cannon or 12 .50 caliber machine guns, the prospects for production looked good—until July 1942, when the project was suddenly terminated at Curtiss produced P-47G instead. This aircraft was finally accepted on June 29, 1944. (*Dean Collection*)

Originally projected to have a top speed of more than 460mph, the XP-62, with a Wright R-3350-17, 18-cylinder *Duplex Cyclone*, was estimated to be capable of 448mph but, for reasons unknown, was never officially tested for this performance number. Final armament settled upon was only four 20mm cannon. This photo was taken June 19, 1942, when hopes for production were still high. (*Dean Collection*)

The aircraft was fitted with a six blade dual rotation Curtiss propeller.

On January 13, 1942, Curtiss submitted a proposal for a production lot of 100 P-62 fighters, the initial aircraft to be delivered in May 1943, and production of 30 planes per month by October1943. On May 27, 1942, a contract for 100 aircraft was approved. This was the high point of the P-62 program, because shortly afterward, on July 27, 1942, this contract was suddenly terminated. It had been decided that the P-62 program would hurt the desired production by Curtiss of Republic P-47 *Thunderbolts*. In addition, it would be a drag on Wright Aeronautical Corp. production of their R-3350 engines needed for the high priority Boeing B-29 program.

At production cancellation time, the XP-62 prototype was 75 percent complete, and was allowed to go forward; first flight was scheduled for April 1943. But this event was delayed due to powerplant installation changes, as well as delays in the cabin pressurization system installation. It finally took place on July 21, 1943. The second aircraft (XP-62A) was cancelled on September 21, 1943, however.

The prototype program lagged due to other priorities, with Curtiss personnel stretched thin. A limited amount of XP-62 flight testing had been accomplished by February 1944, still without the pressure cabin system installed.

Time caught up with the P-62 development program. The operational requirement for the fighter had vanished, and no more test work took place. The aircraft was formally accepted by the AAF September 5, 1944. It was dropped to Class 26 (instructional airframe) on March 2, 1945, and was scrapped September 26, 1945.

Specifications for the big XP-62 follow, however, the performance figures are Curtiss estimates shown in Army documents: span, length, and height 53 feet, seven and 3/4 inches, 39 feet, six inches, and 16 feet, three inches. Wing area was 420 square feet.

The powerplant was a Wright R-3350-17, 18 cylinder *Duplex Cyclone*, turbo supercharged, rated at 2,250hp (Military) at 25,000 feet, and 2100hp (Normal) at 25,000 feet driving a 13 foot, two inch diameter Curtiss Electric constant speed six blade dual rotation propeller. Normal and maximum fuel capacities were 245 gallons and 384 gallons, respectively.

Empty weight was 11,773 pounds, normal useful load was 2,887 pounds, and normal and maximum gross weights were 14,660 pounds and 16,651 pounds, respectively. Normal wing and power loadings were 34.9psf and 6.5 pounds per horse power. The normal useful load to gross weight ratio was 0.197.

Maximum speed was estimated at 448mph at 27,000 feet, and 358mph at 5,000 feet. Cruise speed was 340mph, and landing speed 85mph. Landing distance over a 50 foot obstacle was 2,150 feet. Service ceiling was 35,700 feet, and range capabilities with 245 gallons of fuel were 900 miles at 340mph at 25,000 feet, and with 384 gallons of fuel 1,300 miles at 340mph at 25,000 feet; with ferry fuel of 384 gallons 1,500 miles at 290mph at 25,000 feet.

Armament consisted of four 20mm cannon in the wings with 600 rounds of ammunition total.

Production P-62A-1-CUs (Curtiss Specification 8560) were cancelled July 17, 1942.

Curtiss XF14C-1 and XF14C-2 (Model 94A)

This fighter was envisioned as a shipboard based type for high altitude operations, and a contract was placed with Curtiss on June 30, 1941, for two XF14C-1 prototype aircraft. The company designation was Model 94A. Interestingly, the Navy agreed to use of the

Originally laid down as early as June 1941 for the Navy as the XF14C-1—a dedicated high-altitude, carrier fighter with an experimental Lycoming XH-2470 engine—development ceased in 1943 when this engine failed to develop. Curtiss managed to wring small contracts from the Navy to continue work on an XR-3350-16 powered XF14C-2 to be armed with four 20mm cannon, BuA 03183 (MSN 27087). (*Dean Collection*)

Not accepted formally by the Navy until September 2, 1944, the single XF14C-2 was a stocky aircraft, with certain characteristics reminiscent of the failed XP-60 series for the Army, including the large wheel covers. (*Dean Collection*)

experimental liquid cooled Lycoming XH-2470 engine for the prototypes, going against their aircooled radial engine practice.

The estimated characteristics of this aircraft were as follows: span, length, and height 46 feet, 38 feet, four inches, and 14 feet, six inches. Wing area was calculated at 375 square feet.

The powerplant was to be a Lycoming XH-2470-4, rated at 2,200hp (Military) at sea level takeoff, and 2,000hp (Normal) at 4,500 feet.

Empty weight was estimated at 9,868 pounds, useful load 2,823 pounds, and normal and overload gross weights 12,691 pounds and 13,868 pounds. The overload gross weight included 800 rounds of 20mm ammunition, and 191.5 imperial gallons of fuel. Wing and power loadings were 33.84psf and 5.77 pounds per horse power, respectively. Useful load to gross weight ratio was 0.22.

Estimated performance was 374mph at 17,000 feet at normal gross weight, 344mph at 3,500 feet, and 327mph at 27,000 feet. Initial climb rate was to be 2,810fpm, and service ceiling 30,500 feet. Time to climb to 10,000 feet was estimated as 3.7 minutes. Cruise range was 1,080 miles at 176mph at 4,500 feet, and with auxiliary fuel tanks 1,520 miles at 164mph at 4,500 feet.

Armament was to consist of four 20mm wing mounted cannon with a total of 664 rounds of ammunition.

Shortly, it was realized the Lycoming engine would not be available to meet the set time schedules, and though the airframe was well along in construction, all work was stopped on the XF14C–1 by the end of 1943.

The decision was made to change the power plant to a turbo supercharged Wright 18 cylinder R-3350 *Duplex Cyclone* engine driving a dual rotation propeller, and the second of the two contracted aircraft was continued in development with the new engine.

In addition, some design study work was done by Curtiss on an XF14C-3 variant with a pressurized cockpit, and an estimated 400mph high speed at altitude, but no -3 was built, and the study work was cancelled in 1945.

By March 9, 1944, Curtiss had come to the realization that their agreement to continue P-40N production in large numbers, with encouragement from the AAF for the XP-40Q, and license-production of the P-47G *Thunderbolt*, had placed their role as a world-class producer of fighter aircraft in jeopardy. This was further aggravated by the extremely high priority that the AAF had assigned to the Curtiss C-46 transport program, and that the Navy assigned to the SB2C *Helldiver* program, both of which further taxed the Curtiss engineering department. As a result, a rather contentious conference with AAF officials was held in March, and the following conclusions were reached:

(1) continued development of the XF14C would continue to be handled in Buffalo
(2) continued development of the XP-62 would be handled in Buffalo as well, with a view towards having the work completed by May 1, 1944
(3) continued development of the XP-60E would also be continued in Buffalo, with every effort expended to conclude this by June 1, 1944. However, it was felt that, in order to offer some relief to both the Experimental Hangar and the Experimental Department in Plant 1, that these aircraft should be racked in railroad cars in an "as is" condition, and the entire project moved to St. Louis, where completion and flight testing would be performed.

Army Colonel Walter E. Richards, the AAF Resident Representative at Buffalo at the time, in a confidential Memo to the Commander of the AAF Materiel Command, however, put the situation at Curtiss bluntly, when he reported that:

"*...it is the opinion of this office that, for the immediate future, the Curtiss-Wright Corporation, Airplane Division, Buffalo, can no longer be considered as a reliable nor enthusiastic member of the Army's experimental program. This contractor no longer views his Army experimental obligations with zeal nor interest in their conclusion, except that the quicker all Army experimental projects are terminated, the quicker the contractor will have his experimental facilities available for development of a proposed Navy fighter* [the XF14C]."

The development program on the single XF14C-2 prototype (BuA 03183, MSN 27087) remaining was continued, but was protracted because other programs had priority, and the XF14C-2 did not have a first flight until July 1944, although photos of an essentially complete aircraft are dated as early as September 7, 1943. With R-3350 engines badly needed for the very high priority Boeing B-29 bomber program, and the Navy's need for a special high altitude fighter disappearing, plus the prototype's performance being no better than fighters in service, further development was stopped. The XF14C-2 was formally accepted by the Navy on September 2, 1944.

Specifications for the XF14C-2 aircraft follow: span, length, and height 46 feet, 37 feet, nine inches, and 12 feet, four inches. Wing area was 375 square feet.

The powerplant was a Wright XR-3350-16, turbo supercharged, rated at 2,300hp at sea level takeoff and 2,250hp at 32,000 feet driving a Curtiss dual rotation propeller. Normal and maximum fuel capacities were 230 gallons and 480 gallons.

Empty weight was 10,582 pounds, useful load 2,823 pounds, and normal and maximum gross weights 13,405 pounds and 14,582 pounds, respectively. Normal wing and power loadings were 35.7psf and 5.83 pounds per horse power, respectively. Normal useful load to gross weight ratio was 0.21.

Estimated maximum speed was 424mph at 32,000 feet (apparently the actual maximum speed reached during testing was 398mph), 386mph at 20,000 feet, and 317mph at sea level. Cruise speed was 296mph. Initial climb rate at sea level was 2,700fpm. Climb times were 3.8 minutes to 10,000 feet, and 7.9 minutes to 20,000 feet. Service ceiling was 39,500 feet. Normal range was 950 miles at 172mph at 2,500 feet, and ferry range 1,355 miles at 162mph at 2,500 feet.

Armament consisted of four 20mm cannon mounted in the wings with 166 rounds per gun.

Curtiss XF15C-1

Early in the history of jet powered aircraft, the U.S. Navy realized their future carrier planes must use jet power to keep up with the times. There were problems in adapting jet fighters to carriers, however. The early jet engines did not develop enough thrust, sometimes even with a catapult assist, to allow the fighter to take off from a carrier deck. A temporary "solution" to the problem was the "composite" powered fighter, according to its proponents. This arrangement involved combining a piston engine and propeller powerplant with a jet engine. The high thrust at low speed of the propeller would aid jet engine thrust to enable carrier takeoffs, and in high speed dash conditions the jet thrust would add to the conventional propeller thrust enabling higher maximum speeds. Also, since the jet engine alone had high fuel consumption, it would be shut down during long range cruise flight on the piston engine and propeller powerplant only.

This philosophy was implemented by the Navy in two fighter types, one being the Ryan FR-1 *Fireball*, and the other a higher performance Curtiss Model 99 designated by the Navy as the XF15C-1. As it happened, the aircraft would be the final fighter type built for the Navy by Curtiss.

Three XF15C-1 composite high altitude fighters were ordered from Curtiss on April 7, 1944. In a particularly good Curtiss development performance, the three were delivered to the Navy in March 1945 after a first flight of the type, without the jet engine installed, on February 27, 1945. The three aircraft were serialed BuA 01213, 01214, and 01215.

The plane had a conventional Pratt & Whitney R-2800 piston engine up front driving a four blade Hamilton Standard propeller, and the jet engine, of British design, was fitted low in the fuselage aft with a short tailpipe and wing root intakes. The two engines were designed to run off the same aviation gasoline fuel system. The original prototype configuration had a low set horizontal tail.

The first aircraft (BuA 01213) crashed during Curtiss flight testing prior to being turned over to the Navy, reportedly because of the failure of the piston engine. The second fighter flew first on July 9, 1945, and testing continued through late 1946. The second and third aircraft were fully equipped for carrier operation, and had tail hooks and catapult fittings. Initial Navy testing showed instability at low landing speeds, and the aircraft were returned to Curtiss for modifications, wherein the vertical tail surfaces were enlarged and a "T" tail fitted, bringing the horizontal surfaces far above the jet blast. The third aircraft was also tested by the Army Air Force.

Major problems continued to occur during testing. In addition, jet engines of greater thrust were being developed, leading to the eventual solution of the carrier takeoff problem without the relative complexity of a composite powerplant arrangement. As a result, the contract with Curtiss was terminated by the Navy on October 10, 1946.

Specifications for the XF15C-1 follow: span, length, and height 48 feet, 44 feet, and 15 feet, three inches. Wing area was 400 square feet.

The engines consisted of a Pratt & Whitney R-2800-34W *Double Wasp* rated 2,100hp at sea level takeoff, plus an Allis Chalmers J36 (deHavilland Halford H-18) jet engine rated 2,700 pounds maximum jet thrust. The propeller was a Hamilton Standard four blade constant speed model. Normal and maximum fuel capacities were 376 gallons and 526 gallons.

The final Curtiss fighter design to mount a propeller was the composite XF15C-1 high altitude fighter, three of which were ordered from Curtiss in early April 1944. The result was a rather large aircraft with a conventional Pratt & Whitney R-2800-34W *Double Wasp* , and a U.S. developed deHavilland *Halford* H-18 jet engine, the Allis Chalmers J36 exhausting under the rear fuselage. This is one of the earliest known photos, dated July 18, 1946, as the first jet unit was not installed until April. (*Curtiss 18312 via Harold Andrews*)

The XF15C-1 was a large aircraft for a carrier fighter, with a wing span of 48 feet and a gross weight of 18,698 pounds. (*Dean Collection*)

Empty weight was 12,648 pounds, normal useful load 3,982 pounds, normal gross weight 16,630 pounds, and maximum gross weight 18,698 pounds. Wing loading was 41.6psf, and power loading, based only on the piston engine, was 7.9 pounds per horse power. Useful load to gross weight ratio was 0.239.

Maximum speed with both engines operating was 469mph at 25,300 mph, and 432mph at sea level; maximum speed with the piston engine only was 373mph at 25,300 feet, and 322mph at sea level. Service ceiling was 41,000 feet, and initial climb rate, both engines operating, was 5,020fpm. Normal range was 635 miles, and maximum range 1,385 miles at 163mph.

The armament consisted of four 20mm cannon in the wings.

Curtiss XP-87 *Blackhawk*

The XP-87 jet fighter was a final case of frustration for Curtiss-Wright. The advent of the jet age was upon them, and in March 1945 the company made a proposal to the Air Force for a large twin jet fighter, at an estimated cost of $7,628,475. The most interesting features of the proposal, in the view of the Army's ATSC, was the incorporation of tandem main wheel and dive brakes (controlled by the pilot with the ground brake foot pedals while in flight) mounted on the engine nacelles. The proposal was rejected on April 26, 1945, because there was no requirement for such an aircraft, according to Air Force Headquarters and, additionally, ATSC opined that the aircraft was too heavy and too large for a fighter type.

Contrary to many previously published accounts, however, the aircraft proposed by Curtiss was not, initially, a night fighter, nor was it at that time as yet named *Blackhawk*. An AAF Memo dated April 9, 1945, identified the aircraft as the Curtiss entry to meet the military characteristics of a *day* fighter. Curtiss proposed, however, that the aircraft be fitted with all necessary equipment for instrument flying as well as heated wing design, with the result that Curtiss styled the aircraft as an "All Weather Fighter," perhaps the first use of this term, which gained wide acceptance during the 1950s.

Shortly, however, in a turn of events, Curtiss was given a $5.8 million contract for work to start on an XA-43 jet attack plane, and some work was accomplished in 1945, all this at the Columbus, Ohio, plant then designated for all future Curtiss airframe construction. In November, a modified proposal was made for what the Air Force now called a "*...vitally needed night and inclement weather*

Exhaust temperatures from the R-2800-34W conventional engine in the nose were a recurrent problem on the XF15C-1s, as evidenced by the additional plating installed just aft of the exhaust, and the discoloration on the fuselage. Here the number 2 aircraft, probably BuA 01214, flies on jet power alone. (*Dean Collection*)

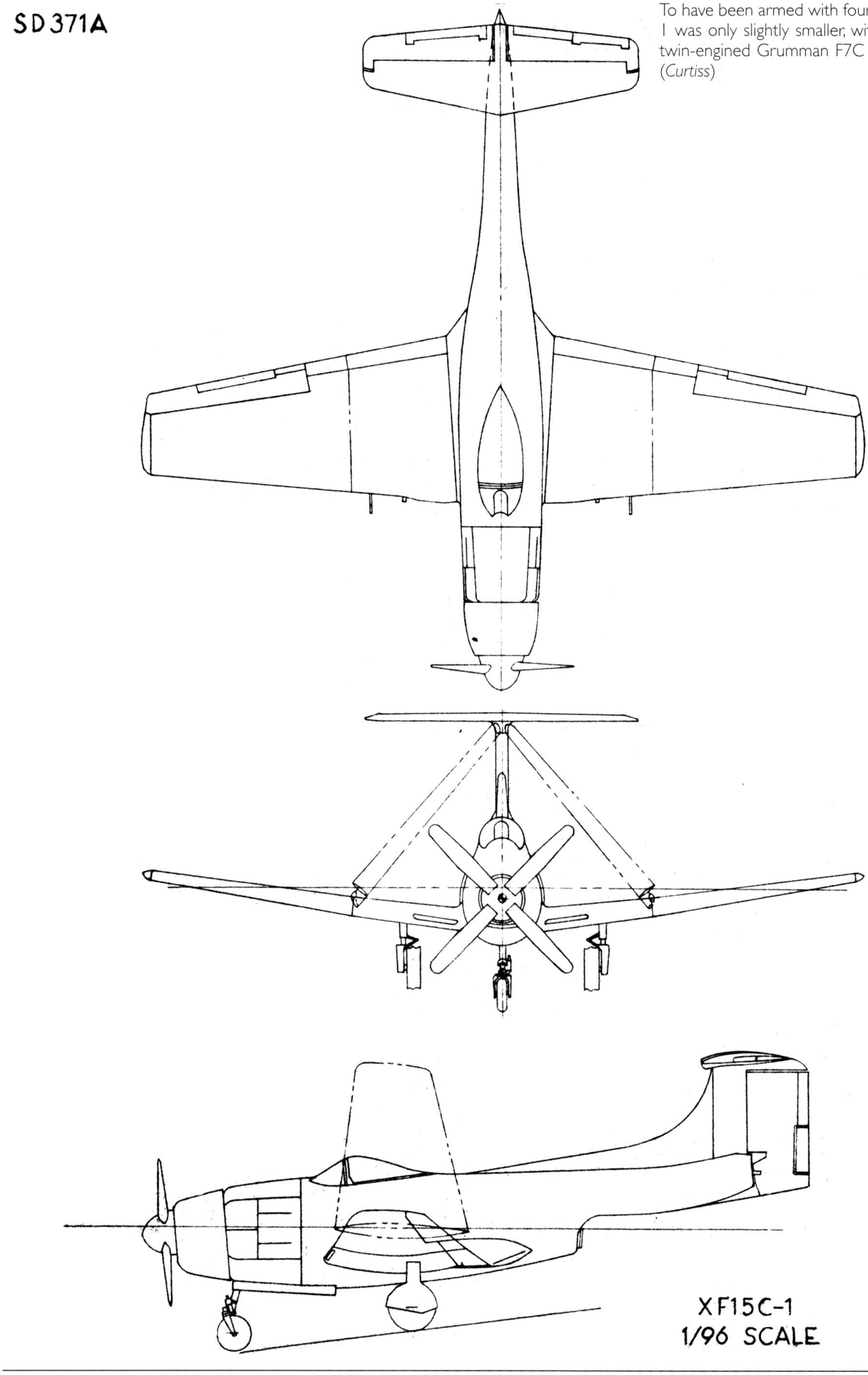

To have been armed with four 20mm cannon, the XF15C-1 was only slightly smaller, with wings extended, than the twin-engined Grumman F7C *Tigercat*, but weighed more. (*Curtiss*)

The final frustration for Curtiss, and last hope of remaining a player in the military aircraft market, was the XP-87 *Blackhawk*, being hopefully announced in this view by a pretty Curtiss employee during final assembly. (*Curtiss via J. Schneider*)

fighter," and on December 26th they approved procurement of a Curtiss XP-87 design to be started with the unused funds from the XA-43 program. This involved two prototype aircraft, plus a mockup, models, and data at an added cost of slightly over $9.0 million, with the aircraft to be delivered in mid-1947 for testing.

The XP-87 *Blackhawk*, as it was named, was much different from the aborted XA-43 with four Westinghouse 24C engines, a side by side crew of two, a gross weight of about 20 tons, and a 60 foot wing span. It was to have a large bay in the belly for stores, a flexible Martin turret with four 20mm cannon in the nose, and .50 caliber tail guns, along with considerable armor. High speed was to be about 600mph. It was described at the time as a two-place, side-by-side, mid-wing, high performance night and inclement weather fighter.

There was competition for the mission from three other manufacturers. Northrop was working on a twin jet XP-89; Douglas had a twin jet XF3D-1 under way for the Navy; and Lockheed was preparing a much modified, stretched P-80 variant as a single jet night fighter known as the XP-94.

There were soon modifications to the XP-87 design. The nose armament was changed to four fixed 20mm cannon, and the rear firing tail guns were eliminated.

A full size mockup was constructed, and Air Force mockup inspections were held in mid-July and early October 1947 at Curtiss, where criticisms of instrument layout and weapons installation were made. The first aircraft was to have test instrumentation instead of armament. Wind tunnel testing was conducted, though the Air Force funding did not cover the full extent desired by Curtiss.

By November 1947, the first prototype was completed, with only taxi tests conducted at Curtiss and, in spite of a couple of mishaps along the way, the aircraft was shipped west by road to Muroc Dry Lake, California (later Edwards AFB), arriving on December 1, 1947, for Phase I testing. A first accident occurred February 25, 1948, when landing gear tires blew out during high speed taxi tests. But by March 1, 1948, the XP-87 had a fairly successful 57 minute first flight at a 42,000 pound takeoff gross weight. A landing gear door failed to fully close, and speed was limited to 365mph at 13,000 feet due to buffeting, this to be a continuing problem.

On the 15th test flight in late April 1948 a landing gear failed to extend, and a belly landing resulted. In addition, tail buffet continued; one fix was to use a bullet shaped fairing at the intersection of the horizontal and vertical tail surfaces.

Phase I flight testing by Curtiss resulted in a total of 55 flights, and a total flight time of 47 hours. On July 21st, a nose landing gear accident dropped the XP-87 down on its nose, and repairs took a month.

The first prototype XP-87 (46-522—the second, 45-59600, was never completed) was rolled out for taxi tests in November 1947, and the activities in this image appear to suggest that the engines were about to be started for the first time in the airframe. (*Curtiss*)

Symbolically bowing to the inevitable, the solitary XP-87, and the very last Curtiss fighter (46-522), suffered a nose gear failure late in development, not long after the news that the production contract for 58 F-87C fighters and 30 RF-87C reconnaissance versions was terminated on October 14, 1948. (*Curtiss*)

Phase II flight tests by the Air Force took place from September 24, 1948, to October 2, 1948, with 19 flights taking place involving 12.58 hours of flight time in total.

On October 14, 1948, Flight 84 took the XP-87 back to Wright Field in Ohio.

Flight test criticisms included the Westinghouse jets not putting out advertised thrust, and it was proposed that the design of the plane be revised to use two General Electric jet engines, and that a large change in wing area—from 600 to 740 square feet—be made in any production vehicle. These were of course very major changes. Other problems included the continuing buffet, particularly under G loading, touchy stall performance, a high landing speed, and slow takeoff acceleration. Also nose wheel steering was desired, and the ejection seat system design was criticized. Flight and ground visibility was considered good only if there were two in the cockpit.

The high point of the program for Curtiss was reached on September 7, 1948, when the company was finally authorized by the Air Force to build 58 F-87C fighters and 30 RF-87C reconnaissance versions at a cost of $55,413, 891.00, with production to climb to 12 aircraft per month by June 1951. The production aircraft would have the new, larger wing and J33 engines. It looked like Curtiss might still be in the aircraft business!

Joy at Columbus was short lived, however. On October 14, 1948, both the experimental and production programs were ordered terminated by the Air Force, based on comparative flight test results at Muroc by veteran Air Force test pilots covering the XP-87, the XF3D-1, and the XP-89. An Air Force committee unanimously agreed to cut the XP-87 and XF3D-1, and go with the Northrop aircraft, with the Lockheed F-94 jet used as an interim night and inclement weather fighter. On October 19th, Curtiss was ordered to cease all work on the XF-87. The second prototype was to be used as a source of spare parts for the first for limited testing at Wright Field. Both prototypes were accepted by the Air Force on December 14, 1948 (45-59600 and 46-522). The demise of the program marked the end of the Curtiss fighter line after approximately 30 years.

Characteristics of the XP-87 were: span, length, and height were 60 feet, 62 feet 10 inches, and 20 feet, five inches.

Propulsion consisted of four Westinghouse 24C (J34) jet engines each of 3,000 pounds thrust maximum. Maximum fuel capacity was 2,600 gallons.

Empty weight was 27,935 pounds, useful load 11,940 pounds, and design gross weight 39,875 pounds. Wing loading was 66.5psf. Useful load to gross weight ratio was 0.299.

Maximum speed was 582mph at sea level at 39,200 pounds gross weight at 12,500rpm, 572mph at 8,500 feet, 548mph at 17,600 feet, and 532mph at 29,300 feet. Takeoff distance over a 50 foot obstacle was 4,245 feet. Initial climb rate was 5,500fpm, and service ceiling 45,000 feet. Absolute ceiling was 47,000 feet. Maximum range with 3,100 gallons of fuel using two wingtip tanks was 1,891 miles.

Annex 1: Curtiss-Wright Airplane Model Designations

When the late Peter M. Bowers published his great standard, ***Curtiss Aircraft 1907-1947*** in 1979 (Putnam & Co., Ltd, ISBN 0-370-10029-8), he included in the text the first concerted attempt to make sense of the complex series of Curtiss internal designations, Army, Navy and export designations which have come to be associated with Curtiss aircraft over the years. Often, as noted throughout this book, these have been found to be utterly without foundation in primary Curtiss originated documents, and the authors of this book have endeavored to use them only when they found clear and irrefutable proof that they were in fact used and applied. In many other instances, Curtiss designations have been found in primary documents, and presented in this book, that were not represented at all in Pete's book, nor in the Curtiss document cited herein.

In mid-2005, co-author Hagedorn was afforded the opportunity to examine part of Pete Bowers Collection and, to his astonishment, found a 29 page document dated September 25, 1945, entitled as shown above, and revised to January 15, 1946. A subsequent examination of this document quickly established that it was the source of Pete's application of Curtiss "designations" as used in his classic book. Unfortunately, as will be seen, the document was clearly a retrospective effort by officials at Curtiss, which they based, in part, on a document that they cited as *"C-W Report 5789,"* plus *"miscellaneous correspondence and records."*

In spite of its shortcomings, however, it has been decided that it should be included as an annex to this work, so that readers can make their own comparisons against the data that Pete presented in his book, what is presented in this volume, and what Curtiss was saying as of January 1946. By doing so, we hope that it will serve as a point of departure for further research, but illustrating the many obviously open questions that Curtiss officials had after barely 36 years of existence.

It is interesting to note that the listing commences only in 1916 with the JN-4A, even though Curtiss produced many aircraft prior to that time. In every instance, we have endeavored to present the list exactly as Curtiss prepared it, even where there are clearly erroneous entries and unknown abbreviations and presentations.

Note: This document is reproduced here precisely as prepared by Curtiss-Wright in 1945 and 1946. It is clearly a retrospective attempt by this company to rationalize their aircraft designations system and production, and has been used as a source for nearly every historical work on Curtiss aircraft since. It is the hope of the authors of this book that an analysis of this document, in contrast to the designations and details noted in the text of this book, will aid in the understanding of some of the historical anomalies that have resulted. Many readers will quickly recognize errors in this listing, but these have been, nonetheless, faithfully reproduced just as Curtiss recorded them, so that the evolution of some of these elements might be better understood. Even with the warts and blemishes, however, the listing provides details, puzzles and clarifications found nowhere else in extant Curtiss documentation, and must therefore be regarded as a significant historical document.

Curtiss-Wright Airplane Model Designations

Revised to: 25 Sept., 1945
15 Jan., 1946

Each different design is given a designating number. Subsequent variations or developments of the design are given a dash letter.
(References: C-W Report 5789 plus miscellaneous correspondence and record)

Design numbers noted in ( ) represent St. Louis (Curtiss-Robertson Airplane Mfg. Co. or Curtiss-Wright Airplane Corporation), Travel Air, and Moth airplanes for which numbers of a different series were assigned before establishment of the present master numbering system. They are inserted in their approximately correct chronological order.

Design	Type	Model	Year	Qty.	S.O.	Customer	Model	Built At	Engine	Description
1	Trainer	Jenny JN4A	1916	-	-	-	-	-	OX-5	Army
1A	Trainer	Jenny JN4B	1916	-	-	Army	-	-	-	-
1B	Trainer Mil	JN Twin	1917	-	-	Army	-	-	OX	2 motors;ldg.Pont.
1C	Trainer	Jenny JN 4D	1917	4	-	Export	-	-	C-6	Bi-plane
1D	Trainer FB	N-8	1916	-	-	-	-	-	-	Tr. LP
1E	Trainer Adv	4H	1918	-	-	-	-	-	Hispano	Tr. LP Hisso
1F	Trainer Adv	6HB	1918	-	-	-	-	-	Hispano	Tr.LP
2	Military Tr	R2	1916/17	-	-	Army	-	-	-	Tr.LP
2A	Trainer	R6 (TH)	1917	3	-	Army	-	-	OX	Tr.LP
2B	Mail (1st)	R2A	1917	-	-	-	-	-	-	Tr.LP First Mailplane
2C	Mail	R-4LM	1918	-	-	-	-	-	-	Tr.LP
3	Night Mail Model T	Canada	1916	-	-	U.S.Mail	-	Buffalo	-	-
4	Trainer	K Boats L-1	1915/16/17	-	-	Navy	-	-	OX	Triplane-Tractor
5	Trainer	N-8G	1917	-	-	Army	-	-	OX	Pusher biplane
6	Patrol Boat	H-4,6,7,8,H-10	1916/17	-	-	-	-	Buffalo	-	2 Eng.Tr.Boat
6A	Patrol Boat	12	1917	-	-	-	-	-	-	2 Eng.Tr.Boat
6B	Patrol Boar	12A	1917	-	-	-	-	-	-	2 Eng.Tr.Boat
6C	Channel	16	1917/18	-	-	-	-	-	-	2 Eng.Boat
6D	Boat	12B	1918	-	-	-	-	-	-	Twin motor
7	Sport Boat	FL	1917	-	-	Mr.Judson	-	-	-	Tri-plane
8	Channel Patrol Military	HS-1	1917	-	-	-	-	-	-	Pusher-1 eng.Boat
8A	Coast Patrol	2L	1918	-	-	-	-	-	Liberty	Pusher
9	(no entry)	-	-	-	-	-	-	-	-	-
10	(no entry)	-	-	-	-	-	-	-	-	-
10A	-	S-4	1917							
10B	Fighter	5	1917	-	-	-	-	-	OX	-
10C	-	6	1917	-	-	-	-	-	-	TR.LP
11	Auto Land Plane	F	1917	-	-	-	-	-	-	1st Aero Show
12	Patrol	NC-1	1918							
		NC-2	1918							
		NC-3	1919							
		NC-4	1917	-	-	Navy	-	Garden City	Liberty	1st Transatlantic
13	Trainer	BA	1918	-	-	-	-	-	OXX	Bi-plane
14	Trainer	BPA	1918	-	-	-	-	-	OXX	Bi-plane
15	Triplane	18-T	1919	4	-	Navy (1) Bolivia	-	Garden City	Wasp	World Alt. Record
15A	Biplane	18-B	-	-	-	-	-	-	-	Wasp
16	-	HA	1919	3	-	-	-	-	OX-5	Tr. Bi-plane
17	Comm'l	Oriole Specials	1919	3	-	-	-	-	OX-5	Wing Radiator Comm.
18	Trainer	Seagull M.F.	1920	16 (200 Over 2 or 3 Years)	-	Navy	-	-	OX-6	Bi-plane modified F
19	Transport	Eagle	1920	1 or more		-	Army	-	-	K-63-eng.comm'l
-	-	Crane M.F.	1924	1	-	Comm'l	-	-	-	Amphibian
20	-	Seagull M.F.	1920	50	-	-	-	-	C-6	-
21	Night Pursuit	-	1920	2	-	Army	-	-	K-6	-
22	Racer	Wild Cat L-19-1	1921	1	-	Cox Navy	-	Garden City	D-12	Bi-plane
23	Racer	CR1 L-17-1	1921	1	-	Navy	-	Garden City	D-12	World Record bip.
23A	Hydro Racer	CR3	1923	1	-	Navy	-	Garden City	D-12	SP(Float) Record

24	Torpedo Mono-Seap.	C.T.	1921	1	-	Navy	-	-	Hispano/D-12	B1
25	Boat	Seagull M.F.	1921	-	-	-	-	-	-	Comm'l MF
26	Pursuit	Orenco	1921	50	-	Army	-	-	Hisso	Not C-W design
27	Racer (Navy)	CR2 L-17-3	1922	1	-	Navy	-	Garden City	D-12	Biplane
-	Army Racer	R-6	1922	-	-	-	-	-	D-12	World Record
28	Landplane	TS-1	1923	-	-	-	-	-	J-1	-
-	Biplane Seaplane	TS	1923	33	-	Navy	-	-	J-1	-
29	Boat Glider	SX4-1	1922	1	-	G.H.Curtiss	-	-	-	-
30	Bomber	Martin L85-1 NBS-1	1923	50	-	Army	-	Kenmore	Liberty 12	Biplane
31	Torpedo SB	CS-1 H-510-1	1923	5	-	Navy	-	Garden City	T-2	S.P.
-	Torpedo	CS 1 H-510-1	1923	-	-	Navy	-	-	T-3	L.P.
31A	-	2	1923	3	-	Navy	-	-	-	-
32	Land Racer	R2C1	1923	2	-	Navy	-	Garden City	D-12A	World Record Bip.
32A	Racer Hydro	2	1924	2	-	Navy	-	Garden City	D-12A	TR Twin Floar
33	(First Pursuit)	Hawk XPW8	1923/24	4	-	Army	-	-	D-12	-
33A	Pursuit	PW8	1924	25	-	Japan(1)	-	-	-	-
34	Navy Pursuit	F4C-1	1924	1	-	Navy	-	-	S-3	1st Alum.Alloy
-	Pursuit	XPW8A	1924	-	-	Army	-	-	D-12	-
34A	Pursuit	Hawk P-1	1925/26	15	-	Army	-	-	D-12	Tap.Wing
34B	Pursuit	Hawk P-2	1925/26	5	-	Army	-	-	V-1400	-
34C	Pursuit	Sea Hawk F6C-1	1925-32	16	-	Navy Colombia Bolivia	-	-	D-12	-
34D	Pursuit	F6C2	1925-32	1	-	Navy	-	-	D-12	-
34E	Pursuit	F6C3	1925-26	1	-		SD-105-36	Garden City	D-12	-
34F	Pursuit	Hawk XP3	1926	1	-	Army	-	-	-	-
34G	Pursuit	Hawk P-1A	1926	23	-	Army	-	-	D-12C	-
34H	Pursuit	Hawk F6C4	1926/27	31	-	Navy	SD-105-4	-	R-1300	Wasp
34I	Pursuit	Hawk P-1B	1927-28	25	-	Army	-	-	D-12C	-
34J	Adv.Tr.	Hawk AT4 (P-1D)	1927	40	-	Army	-	-	Wright E	-
34K	Pursuit	Hawk P-1E	1927	5	-	Army	-	-	-	-
34L	Pursuit	Hawk P5	1928	5	-	Army	-	-	DRF	Sup.chgd.
34M	Adv.Tr.	Hawk AT5A (P-1F)	1928	31	-	Army	-	-	J-E	-
34N	Pursuit	Hawk P3A	1928-29	5	-	Army	-	-	R-1340	-
34O	Pursuit	Hawk P-1C	1929-30	33	-	Army	-	-	D-12E	-
34P	Pursuit	Hawk P6	1927-29	11	-	Army	-	Garden City	V-1570	Tr. BP.
34Q	Racer	P6A	1927-29	-	-	Army	-	Garden City	V-1570	H.C.
35	Pursuit	Hawk AT-5/P-6E	1927	-	-	-	-	-	J-5	-
			1932-32	45	-	Army	-	-	V-1570	-
35A	Pursuit	Hawk Type I	-	-	-	-	-	-	-	-
35B	Pursuit	Cuba Hawk	1932	4	-	Cuba	-	-	-	-
35C	Pursuit	Hawk XP6F	1933-34	1	-	Army	-	Buffalo	V-1570B	-
35D	Pursuit	XP-6H	1933-34	1	-	Army	-	-	V-1570	-
36	Night	Condor	1922-24	2	-	Army	-	-	Liberty	Tr.BP.(2 motors)
-	Bomber	Martin XII NBS-4	1921-22	50	-	Army	-	-	Liberty	-
37	Observ.	Falcon XO-1	1924	1	-	Army Corps	-	Garden City	M-1500	-
-	Observ.	Falcon XO1	1924	1	-	Army Corps	-	Garden City	Liberty	Tractor biplane
37A	Observ.	Falcon O1	1926	10	-	Army	-	Garden City	D-12	2 P Landplane
-	Night Bomb.	Condor XB-2	1929	-	-	-	-	Garden City	GV-1570	TR.BP Twin
-	-	Hawk	1932	24	-	Turkey	-	-	-	-
-	-	PW-8	-	-	-	-	-	-	D-12	L.C.
-	-	PW-8	-	-	-	-	-	-	D-12	H.C.
-	-	PW-8	-	-	-	-	-	-	D-12	L.C.
-	Coast-to-Coast	PW-8	-	-	-	-	-	-	D-12	L.C.
-	-	Hawk PW-8	-	-	-	-	-	-	D-12	L..C.Supercharged
-	-	Hawk PW-8A	1924	-	-	-	-	-	D-12	St.wings L.C.
-	-	Hawk PW-8A	1924	-	-	-	-	-	D-12	St.wings H.C.
-	-	Hawk YP-6E	1931	-	-	-	-	-	V-1570	St.wings H.D.
-	-	Hawk YP-6E	1932	-	-	-	-	-	V-1560	C
-	Pursuit	Hawk P6-D	1931	10	-	-	-	-	-	-
-	-	Hawk P6-G	1933	-	-	-	-	-	V-1590F	19173
-	Observ.	Falcon O-1A	1926	1	-	Army	-	Garden City	Liberty	2 P. landplane
37B	Observ.	Falcon O1B	1927-28	25	-	Army	-	Garden City	D-12	2 P. landplane
37C	Observ.	Falcon O-11	1927-28	66	-	Army	-	Garden City	Liberty	TR. 2P. landplane
37D	Observ.	F8C-1	1928	6	-	Navy	-	-	-	-
-	-	Falcon	1929	-	-	-	-	-	Wasp	-
37E	Observ.	F8C-3 OC-2	1928	-	-	-	-	-	-	-
-	-	Falcon	1929	21	-	Navy	-	-	Wasp	-

37F	Observ.	Colombia Falcon	1929	15(2)	-	Colombia	-	-	D-12	SP Single Float
37G	Observ.	Falcon XO16	1929-30	6	-	Army	-	Garden City	V-1570	TR. 2 PLP
37H	Attack	Falcon A3B	1929-30	96	-	Chile, Army	-	-	D-12	-
37I	Observ.	Falcon O-1E	1930	57	-	Army	-	Garden City	D-12	TR 2 PLP
37J	Observ.	Falcon O-1F	1930	1	-	Army	-	Buffalo	-	-
37K	Spec.	Falcon O-13C	1930	3	-	Army	-	Garden City	V-1570	TR. 1PLP
37L	Observ.	Falcon O-26	1930	1	-	Army	-	Garden City	GV-1570	TR. 1PLP
38	Observ.	Falcon XO-1G	1930	1	-	Corps	-	Garden City	D-12	TR. 1PLP
-	Observ.	Falcon O-1G	1930	30	-	Army	-	Garden City	D-12	TR. 1PLP
38A	Observ.	Falcon O-39	1931	10	-	Army	-	Garden City	V-1570	TR.1PLP
39	Light Fighter	Hall F4C1	1924	-	-	Navy	-	-	J-3	-
40	Mailplane	Carrier Pigeon	1925-26	11	-	NAT	-	-	Liberty	-
41	-	Lark	1925	3	-	Commercial	-	-	C-6	-
42	Racer	Lark R3C1	1925	3	-	Navy	-	Garden City	V-1400	LB
42A	Racer	Lark 2	1925	1	-	Army	-	Garden City	V-1400	LB Twin pontoon
43	Racer	Lark 4	1926-27	1	-	Navy	-	Garden City	V-1570	TR. BP (seaplane)
-	Fighter	Hawk XF7C-1	1927	1	-	Navy	-	-	Wasp	-
43A	Fighter	F7C-1	1929	18	-	Navy	-	-	R-1500	-
44	Attack	Falcon A-3	1928	76	-	Army	-	-	D-12	-
45	Special	Lindbergh A-3B	1930	1	-	Army/Lindbergh		-	-	D-12E/ -
									GV-1570	
46	Trainer	Falcon XBT-4	1930	1	-	Army	-	-	D-12	-
-	Special	Flying Ser ice XBT-4	-	-	-	Flying Service	-	-	-	-
-	Merrill-Ronne	Falcon	1928	13	-	NAT	-	-	D-12D	Mail plane
47	Special	Doolittle Hawk	1928	-	-	Doolittle	-	-	-	-
48	Trainer Com.	Fledgling N2C	1929	100	-	Flying Service	-	-	Challenger	-
-	Trainer	Fledgling N2C1	1926&29	33	-	Navy	SD113	-	J-5	-
48A	Trainer	Fledgling N2C2	1929-30	30	-	Export Navy CA&C	SD-124-B	-	(R-600)	J-6 7 Cyl.2B
-	-	Falcon XA-4	1928	1	-	Army	-	-	Wasp	Rebuilt from A-3
-	Special	Falcon	1928	-	-	Wilson	-	-	-	2 P
-	-	Fledgling XN2C-1	1928	-	-	-	-	-	J-5	Land plane
-	-	Fledgling XN2C-1	1928	-	-	-	-	-	J-5	Sea plane
-	-	Short Span N2C-1	1930	-	-	-	-	-	J-5	Land plane
-	-	Short Span N2C-1	1930	-	-	-	-	-	J-5	Sea Plane
-	-	Falcon	-	-	-	-	-	-	-	-
-	-	Chieftan XOC-3	1930	-	-	-	-	-	-	-
-	Observ.	Falcon XO-12	1929	-	-	Army	-	-	Wasp	TR 2PLP
-	Observ.	Falcon XO-13	1929	-	-	Army	-	-	V-1570	TR 2PLP
-	Observ.	Falcon XO-18	1928	-	-	Army	-	-	Chieftain	TR 2PLP
-	Racer	Falcon XO-13	1927	-	-	Army	-	Garden City	V-1570	BP LP
-	Racer	Falcon XO-13A	1927	-	-	Army	-	Garden City	V-1570H.C.	BP LP
-	-	Falcon	1934	14	-	Bolivia	-	-	-	-
-	Navy Racer	R3C-3	1926	-	-	-	-	-	Conqueror	-
-	Observ.	XO-11	1927	1	-	Army	-	-	Liberty	-
-	Observ.	O1-A	1926-27	-	-	Army	-	-	D-12	-
-	Observ.	XO-13	1927	1	-	Army	-	-	Conqueror	-
-	Observ.	XO-13A	1927	1	-	Army (Spec)	-	-	Conqueror	-
-	Observ.	XO-13B	1929	1	-	Army	-	-	Conqueror	Sec.Davidson Spec.
-	Observ.	XO-12	1928	1	-	Army	-	-	Chieftain	Rebuilt from O-11
-	Pursuit	XO-18	1929	1	-	Army	-	-	Chieftain	-
-	Observ.	O1-C	1928	-	-	Army	-	-	D-12	Special
-	Observ.	O-11A	1928	-	-	Army	-	-	Liberty	-
-	Observ.	O1-B	1927-28	25	-	Army	-	-	D-12	-
-	Observ.	O1-C	1928	4	-	Army	-	-	D-12	-
-	Trainer	Fledgling XN2C-1	1928	3	-	Navy	-	-	J-5	9 cyl.
-	Challenger	Guardsmen Fledgling	-	-	-	-	-	-	-	2P
-	3 BLT.	Fledgling	-	-	-	Colombia	-	-	J-6	7 cyl. 2P
-	Observ.	Fledgling O-13D	1929-30	-	-	Army	-	-	Conqueror	(Super Charged)
-	Fighter	XO2C-2	1931	-	-	Navy	-	-	Cyclone	(Special)
-	Observ.	Falcon	1928	18	-	Chile	-	-	D-12	-
-	Observ.	XOC-3	1929	1	-	Navy	-	-	Chieftain	rebuilt from OC-1
-	-	Falcon	1930	1	-	Pan American	-	-	Cyclone	Mail plane for S.A.
-	Observ.	O-39	1931	10	-	Army	-	-	Conqueror	-
-	-	Hawk XP-10	1930	-	-	-	-	-	V-1520	(supercharged)
-	-	Hawk YP-20	1931	-	-	-	-	-	R-2820E	-

-	-	Hawk YP-22	1931	-	-	-	-	-	R-1570	H.C.
-	-	Hawk F6C-5	1928	-	-	-	-	-	Hornet	-
-	Racer	XF6C-6 (from F6C-3)	1930	-	-	-	-	-	Conqueror	TR. MP
-	Trainer	XPT-5	1929	-	-	Army	-	Consolidated	R-600	TR. BLP
-	-	"Courier"	1929	-	-	-	-	-	J-5A	Single Bay BP
-	Pursuit	Hawk	1933	3	-	Peru	-	-	-	-
-	Pursuit	Hawk	1933-34	35	-	Colombia	-	-	-	-
-	Pursuit	Hawk	1933	1	-	CA&M Co.	-	-	-	-
-	-	(Demons)	-	-	-	(For sale to Chile 1935)	-	-	-	-
-	Pursuit	Hawk	1933-34	3	-	Bolivia	-	-	-	-
	Pursuit	Hawk	1933	2	-	Udet	-	-	-	-
-	Type III	Hawk	1934	1	-	Commercial	-	-	-	Demonstrator
-	-	Hawk BF2C-1	1934	27	-	Navy	-	-	-	-
-	Type III	Hawk	1935	1	-	Turkey	-	-	-	Demonstrator
-	Adv.Trainer	XAT-4	1926	-	-	Army	-	-	-	-
-	Fighter	XF6C-3	1926	-	-	Navy	-	-	D-12	-
-	Fighter	XF6C-4	1927	-	-	Navy	-	-	Wasp	-
-	Fighter	XF6C-5	1927	-	-	Navy	-	-	Hornet	-
-	Pursuit (Spec.)	XF6C-6	1930	-	-	Navy	-	-	Conqueror	-
-	Pursuit	XP-3A	1927	-	-	Army	-	-	Wasp	-
-	Pursuit	XP-6	1927	-	-	Army	-	-	Conqueror	-
-	Pursuit	XP-6A	1927	-	-	Army	-	-	Conqueror	-
-	Pursuit	XP-6B	1928	-	-	Army	-	-	Conqueror	-
-	-	Hornet	1919	-	-	Army	-	-	-	Bi-plane
		N	1916	1	-	-	-	Buffalo	-	-
		N-7	1916	-	-	-	-	-	-	-
49	Dive Bomber	XF8C-2 Helldiver	1928	1	K-6430	-	-	Garden City	Wasp	original 2PBLP
49A	Dive Bomber	Helldiver 4	1930	1	K-8777	Navy	SD-125-4A	Garden City	R-1340C	-
49B	Dive Bomber	Helldiver 5	1930	18	-	Navy	-	Garden City	Wasp	-
49C	Dive Bomber	Command Helldiver 7	1930-31	1	-	Navy	SD-125-5B	-	R-1340D	-
49D	Dive Bomber	Carrier O2C1	1930-31	82	-	Navy	SD-125-5B	-	R-1340D	Contract 22592
49E	Dive Bomber	O2C2-8	1931	3	-	Navy	-	-	R-1820E	-
-	Scout	O2C-2	1933	-	-	Navy	-	-	R-1510	-
50	-	Robin OX	1928-29	-	-	-	-	Garden City	OX-5/OXX-6	3PCLM
50A		Challenger Robin	1928-29	1	-	-	-	St. Louis	R-600	3PCLM
( )	-	Robin OX-5	1928-30	2	-	-	-	St. Louis	OX-5/OXX-6	3PCLM 90hp or 102hp
( )	-	Robin CR	1929	-	-	-	-	St. Louis	R-600	3PCLM 185hp
( )	-	Robin	1928	-	-	-	-	St. Louis	Hispano	3PCLM 150hp
50C*	-	Robin C-1	1929-31	-	-	-	-	St. Louis	-	-
50D*	-	Robin C-2	1929	-	-	-	-	St. Louis	R-600	3PCLM 185hp
50E*	-	Robin 4C	1929	-	-	-	-	St. Louis	R-600	4PCLM 185hp
50F*	-	Robin 4C-1	1930	-	-	-	-	St. Louis	R-600	3PCLM 185hp
50G*	-	Robin 4C-1A	1930	-	-	-	-	St. Louis	R-600	4PCLM 185hp
50H*	-	Robin J-1	1929-31 1935	25	Export	-	-	St. Louis	R-540	3PCLM-SM 165hp
-	-	J-1 Deluxe	1929-31 1935	-	-	-	-	St. Louis	R-540	3PCLM-SM 165hp
50I*	-	Robin J-2	1930	-	-	-	-	St. Louis	R-540	3PCLM 165hp
50J*	-	Robin W	1929	-	-	-	-	St. Louis	Warner Scarab	125hp

[*Assigned to St. Louis unofficially]

-	Commercial	N-2	1928	-	-	Ireland	-	Garden City	J-5	Amphibian Pusher
-	Commercial	N-2B	1929	-	-	Ireland	-	Garden City	J-6	Amphibian Pusher
-	Fighter	Vought X4-U1	1931	-	-	-	-	Garden City	Wasp	2P BP
-	Observ.	Vought O3U-1	1930	-	-	Navy	SD-156	Garden City	Wasp	TR. BLP.
-	Convertible	Vought O3U-1	1929	-	-	Navy	SD-156	Garden City	Wasp	TR. BLP.
-	Flying Boat	Rodgers X9735	-	-	-	Commercial	-	Garden City	J-6-7	Pusher BP
-	-	Martin T4M	-	-	-	-	-	-	Hornet	-
???	Fighter	Boeing XF7B-1	1934	-	-	-	-	-	Wasp	1P
-	Fighter	XF8C-2A	1929	1	K8760	Navy	-	-	Wasp	Replacement XF8C-2

-	Fighter	XF8C-4	1930	-	-	Navy	-	-	Wasp	-
-	Fighter	F8C-4	1930	27	-	Navy	-	-	Wasp	-
-	Fighter	F8C-5	1930	9	-	Navy	-	-	Wasp	Larger gas capacity
-	Pursuit	YP-20	1930	-	-	Army	-	-	Cyclone	-
-	Pursuit	YP-10	1930	-	-	Army	-	-	Conqueror	(Supr. Chg.)
-	Trainer	AT-5	1927	-	-	Army	-	-	J-5	-
-	Attack	A-3	1928	-	-	Army	-	-	D-12	-
-	Pursuit	XP-6E	1931	-	-	Army	-	-	Conqueror	-
-	Pursuit	XP-60?	1932	-	-	Army	-	-	Conqueror	-
( )	Sport Trainer	4-D	1929	-	-	-	-	St. Louis	R-760	3POLB 240hp
( )	Land & Seaplane	4-D	1929-30	-	-	-	-	St. Louis	R-760	3POL-SB 240hp
( )	Sport Trainer	D-4D	1928-30	-	-	-	-	St. Louis	R-760	3POLB 240hp
( )	Sport Plane	4-P	1929	-	-	-	-	St. Louis	Ace LA-1	3POLB 170hp
( )	Sport Plane	Reid Rambler	1926	-	-	-	-	St. Louis	Cirrus III	2POLB 80hp
( )	Sport Plane	Moth 60GM	1928-30	-	-	-	-	St. Louis	Gipsy II	85hp
51	Trainer	Fledgling N2C Flying Service	1929	100	-	-	-	-	R-600	-
( )	Sport Plane	60 GMC	1930	-	-	-	-	St. Louis	Gipsy	2POLB 90hp
52	Bomber	"Condor" B2	1929-30	10	-	Army	-	Garden City Buffalo	GV-1570	Twin TW. LB
53	Transport	Condor B20	1929-30	6	-	E.A.T.	-	-	GV-1570	-
54	Special	Tanager	1929	1	-	Commercial	-	-	Challenger	-
55	Feeder Transport	Kingbird	1929-30	3	-	Commercial	-	Garden City	R-600	-
-	Transport	Kingbird D-1	1930	-	-	-	-	St. Louis	2xR-760	8PCLM 300hp
-	Transport (Cargo)	Kingbird D-2	1931	-	-	-	-	St. Louis	2xR-975	4PCLM 300hp
-	Mail, Passenger	Kingbird D-2	1931	-	-	-	-	St. Louis	2xR-975	7PCLM
-	Passenger	Kingbird D-2	1931	-	-	-	-	-	-	8PCLM
-	Transport	Kingbird D-3	1931	-	-	-	-	-	2xR-975	6PCLM 300hp
-	Bomber	"Condor" XB-2	1927	-	-	Army	-	-	Conqueror	-
56	-	Thrush	1929-30	3	-	Commercial	-	Garden City	J-6, J-6-9	R-600
57	-	Teal	1930	2	-	Commercial	-	Garden City	J-6-5	-
(CW-1)	Trainer	Junior	1931	-	-	-	-	St. Louis	Szekely	2PCLM, 45hp
(CA-1)	Amphibian	-	1935	-	-	-	-	St. Louis	R-975E-1	5PCAmB 365hp
(CW-2)	Coupe	-	1931	-	-	-	-	St. Louis	Kinner	2PCLM, 100hp
(CW-3W)	Amphibian	Junior	1931	-	-	-	-	St. Louis	-	-
(CW-3L)	-	Junior	1931	-	-	-	-	St. Louis	Lambert	POAmM 90hp
58	Fighter	Sparrow	1930	-	-	-	-	-	-	-
		Hawk	1931	-	-	-	-	-	J-6	-
		Dirigible XF9C1	1932	7	-	Navy	-	Kenmore	J-6/R-975E	-
58A	Fighter	2	1931/32	1	-	Navy	-	Kenmore	R-975E	-
58B	Carrier	Sparrow Hawk	1932	8	-	Navy	SD-169-2	Kenmore	R-975E-3	-
-	-	Shrike Y1A-8 Service Test	1932	-	-	Army	-	-	GV-1570	-
59	Ground Attack	XA-8	1931-32	14	-	Army	-	Garden City	V-1570C	-
59A	-	Shrike YA-8	1932	11	-	Army	-	Kenmore	V-1570E	-
59B	Attack	Shrike YA10	1932	1	-	Army	-	Kenmore	R-1690	-
60	Attack	Shrike A-14	1934-35	-	-	Army	-	-	SGR-1670-A5	
	Attack	Shrike A-12	1933-34	46	-	Army	-	Kenmore	R-1820-F1	-
60A	Commercial	Shrike	-	-	157	-	-	Kenmore	-	-
61	Scout Dive Bomber	XS3C1	1932	1	-	Navy	-	Kenmore	R-1820E	-
62	Observation	Raven YO-40	1932	1	-	Army	-	Kenmore	R-1820E	Sesquiplane, tractor
62A	Observation	Raven YO-40A	1933	1	-	Army	-	Kenmore	Y1R-1820F	Sesquiplane, tractor
62B	Observation	Raven Y1O-40B	1933/34	4	-	Army	-	Kenmore	Y1R-1820F	Tr. Monoplane
-	Observation	Raven O-40C	1934	-	-	-	-	Kenmore	GR-1820F-2	Tr. LMP
(CW-4)	Transport	Condor XT-32	1933	-	-	-	-	St. Louis	GR-1920F-1	-
(CW-4G)	Transport	Condor T-32	1933	-	-	-	-	St. Louis	2xCyclones	17PCLB, 690hp
(CW-4G)	Transport	Condor AT-32	1934	-	-	-	-	St. Louis	2xCyclones	15PCLB, 720hp
(CW-4G)	Transport	(Converted Condor T-32-C)	1933	-	-	-	-	St. Louis	2xCyclones	18PCLB, 720hp
-	-	Y1A-18	1937	-	-	Army	-	-	Cyclone 639	-
-	-	XP-23	1932	1	-	Army	-	-	Conqueror	Monoque.
(CW-4G)	Cargo	Condor (Expt.)	1937	-	-	-	-	St. Louis	-	-

(CW-4G)	Bomber	CT-32 Condor (Expt.) BT-32	1935	-	-	-	-	St. Louis	-	-
(CW-5)	Freighter	Pegasus (proposed)	-	-	-	-	-	-	-	-
(CW-6B)	Commercial	Travel Air 6000-B	1930	-	-	-	-	St. Louis	J-6-9	6PCLM, 330hp
(CW-7)	(Probably reserved for Travel Air 7000)			-	-	-	-	-	-	-
(CW-8)	(Probably reserved for Travel Air 8000)			-	-	-	-	-	-	-
(CW-9)	(Probably reserved for Travel Air 9000)			-	-	-	-	-	-	-
(CW-10D)	Commercial	Travel Air	1929-30	-	-	-	-	St. Louis	J-6-7	4PCLM, 250hp
(CW-11)	-	Travel Air	1929	-	-	-	-	St. Louis	-	1POLB, 250hp
(CW-12)	Sport Trainer	Travel Air 12-Q	1930-31	-	-	-	-	St. Louis	Gipsy	2POLB, 90hp
-	Sport Trainer	Travel Air 12-K	1931		-	-	-	St. Louis	Kinner	2POLB, 125hp
-	-	Travel Air 12-W	1931	-	-	-	-	St. Louis	Scarab	2POLB, 125hp
(CW-13)	(Unassigned)	-	-	-	-	-	-	-	-	-
(CW-14)	Sport Trainer	Travel Air 14	1930	-	-	-	-	St. Louis	J-6-7	3P 132 LP
(CW-14C)	-	Travel Air 14-C (Osprey)	1931	-	-	-	-	St. Louis	Challenger	3POLB, 185hp
-	-	Travel Air B-14B (Sportsman)	1932	-	-	-	-	St. Louis	R-975	3POLB
-	-	Travel Air B-14-D (Speedwing-fabric covered)	1931	-	-	-	-	St. Louis	R-760	3POLB, 240hp
(CW-15C)	-	Sedan (Executive)	1931	-	-	-	-	-	Challenger	4PCLM, 185hp
	-	Sedan 15-D (Executive)	1931	-	-	-	-	St. Louis	R-760	4PCLM, 240hp
	-	Sedan 15-N (Short-Line)	1931	-	-	-	-	St. Louis	Kinner	4PCLM, 125hp
	-	Optr. or Executive	-	-	-	-	-	-	C-5	210hp
(CW-16)	Trainer	Travel Air 16-E	1930-33	-	-	-	-	St. Louis	R-540	3POLB, 175hp
	(Com)	Travel Air 16-K	1931	-	-	-	-	St. Louis	Kinner	3POLB, 125hp
	-	Travel Air 16-W	1931	-	-	-	-	St. Louis	Scarab	3POLB, 110hp
(CW-17R)	Pursuit	Osprey (metal)	1932	-	-	-	-	-	Whirlwind	420hp
(CW-18)	Army trainer	(not built)	-	-	-	-	-	-	-	-
-	Passenger Transport	Keystone K-78D Patrician 2 pilots	1930	-	-	-	-	Garden City	3xCyclone	or Hornet, 525hp
-	Pursuit	XP-22	1931	-	-	Army	-	-	Conqueror	-
63	Pursuit	XP-23	1931	1	-	-	-	Kenmore	G1V-1570	-
64	Fighter	XF11C-1	1932	1	-	Navy	SD-189-1	Kenmore	R-1510	-
64A	Fighter	Goshawk XF11C-2	1932-33	27	-	Navy	SD-189-24	Kenmore	R-1820	Cont. 26480
64B	Fighter	Goshawk F11C-2	1933	28	-	Navy	SD-189-2A	Kenmore	R-1820F	-
65	-	Hawk Type 2	-	-	-	-	-	Kenmore	-	-
65A	Demonstrator	Hawk	-	-	-	-	-	Kenmore	-	-
66	Pursuit	P-31 XP-934	1931	1	-	Army	-	-	GIV-1570	Slots & Flaps
67	Fighter	Hawk (115) XF11C-3	1933	1	-	Navy	SD-184-4	Kenmore	R-1820-F3	-
67A	Fighter	Hawk BF2C-1	1935	-	-	-	SD-121-1	Kenmore	R-1820-04	Landplane sgl.seat
68	Pursuit	Hawk Type 3 (#1 demonstra.)	-	-	-	-	-	Kenmore	-	-
-	-	Keystone B-6A	1931	-	-	Army	-	Kenmore	1820-E	-
-	-	P-31 XP-934	1933	-	-	Army	-	Kenmore	GIV-1570	Slots & Flaps
68A	Pursuit	Hawk (#2 demonstra.)	-	-	-	-	-	-	-	-
68B	-	Siam Hawk	-	-	-	-	-	-	-	-
68C	Demonstra.	China	1933	51	-	China	-	-	R-1820-F3	-
69	Scout	Shrike XS2C-1	1932-33	1	-	Navy	-	Kenmore	R-1510	-
70	Fighter	XF13C-1	1934	1	-	Navy	SD-201B	Kenmore	SGR-1510-2	Single seat monopl.
-	-	XF13C-2	1934	-	-	Navy	-	Kenmore	SGR-1510-2	-
-	-	XF13C-3	1935	-	-	-	-	Kenmore	SGR-1510-2	-
71	SB (Amphib)	XO3C-1	1935	1	-	Navy	SD-208	Kenmore	R-1340-12	(Wasp)
71A	S.O.	SOC-1	1935-36	175	-	Navy	SD-230	Kenmore	R-1340-18	-
71B	S.O.	SOC-2	-	-	-	Navy	SD-230-1	Kenmore	R-1340-22	-
71C	Convertible	XSO2C-1	1936 & 1939	2	-	Navy	SD-244	Kenmore	R-1340-36	-
71D	S.O.	XSO3C-1	-	-	-	-	SD-257A	-	V-770-4	single eng. VSO class
71E	Obs.	SOC-3	1937	87	-	Navy	-	-	-	-

71F	Obs.	SOC-4	1937	3	-	Coast Guard	-	-	R-1340-36	-
72	Single Strut	Falcon	1934	1	-	National	-	Kenmore	-	-
73	-	XF12C-1	1934-35	1	-	Navy	SD-197	Kenmore	SGR-1510	2-seat air cooled end.
-	Fighter	XSBC-1	1934	1	-	Navy	-	Kenmore	SR-1820-80	Tractor land mono.
-	SB	XSBC-2	1935-36	1	-	Navy	-	Kenmore	XR-1510-12	-
74	Army Observation Type II	Falcon	1934	-	-	-	-	Kenmore	-	-
75	Pursuit	-	1935	1	-	-	-	-	GR-1670-5	Army single seat
75A	As finally submitted for Army test			-	-	-	-	-	-	-
75B	Pursuit	SGR-1820-G5	1936	-	-	-	-	-	-	-
75C	Pursuit	SR-1820-G3	-	-	-	-	-	-	-	-
75D	Pursuit	SGR-1670-G5	-	-	-	-	-	-	-	-
75E	Pursuit	Y1P-36	1936	3	-	Army	-	-	-	-
75F	Pursuit	SR-1820-G25	-	-	-	-	-	-	-	-
75G	Pursuit	SGR-1820-G5B	-	-	-	-	-	-	-	-
75H	Pursuit (demonstrators)	Hawk 75	-	2	-	-	-	-	-	-
75I	Pursuit	XP-37	1937	1	-	-	-	-	GV-1710	-
-	-	YP-37	-	13	-	-	-	-	GV-1710-11	-
75J	Pursuit	-	-	-	-	-	-	-	R-1830	Turbo supercharged
75K	Pursuit	-	-	-	-	-	-	-	R-2180	-
75L	Pursuit	P-36A	1937	210	-	Army	-	-	R-1830-13 R-1830-17	-
-	Pursuit	P-36B	-	(#20 of above)	-	-	-	-	R-1830-23	8:1 blower PD12 carb.
-	Pursuit	P-36C	1939	(#85 of above)	-	-	-	-	R-1830-17	2x30cal M-2 wing gun
75M	Pursuit	Hawk 75 III	1937-39	112	-	China	-	-	-	-
75N	-	Hawk 75	1938 1934 1935	25	-	Siam	-	-	-	-
75O	Pursuit	Hawk 75	1933 1934 1938	- - 30	- - -	- - Argentina	- - -	- - -	- - -	- - -
75P	Pursuit	XP-40	1939	-	-	-	-	-	V-1710-19	P-36A with Allison Dwg. P-1142
75Q	Pursuit (Export Demonstrator)	Hawk 75A	1936	2	-	-	-	-	Cyclone	-
75R	Physical Article for Pursuit proposal (Similar to the P-36A) (Opening date 1/10/39)			-	-	-	-	-	R-1830-19	2 stage supercharger
75S	Pursuit	XP-42 (No.4 airplane On P-36A Contra)	-	-	-	-	-	-	R-1830-31	Long nose cowl in a P-36A
-	-	Hawk 75A	-	-	-	-	-	-	-	Retractable landing Gear Dwg. P-1083
-	Pursuit	Hawk 75A-1	1939	100	181	France	-	-	P & W	-
-	Pursuit	Hawk 75A-2	1939	100	187	France	-	-	P & W	-
-	Pursuit	Hawk 75A-3	1939	136	140-148	France	-	-	SC3-G	about same as 75A-2
-	Pursuit	Hawk 75A-4	-	395	-	-	-	-	G205	Same as A-3
-	-	Hawk 75A-5	-	1 & parts	195	China	-	-	-	-
-	-	Hawk 75A-6	-	24	198	Norway	-	-	R-1830	-
-	-	Hawk 75A-7	-	20	199	N.E.I.	-	-	G205A	-
-	-	Hawk 75A-8	-	36	201	Norway	-	-	G205B	-
-	-	Hawk 75A-9	-	10	202	Iran	-	-	G205A	-
76	Attack	A-14	-	1	-	-	-	-	-	-
76A	Attack	Shrike Y1A-18	1931-2-3-6	13	-	Army	-	-	Conqueror	-
-	-	XP-36D	1939	-	-	-	-	-	R-1830-17	-
-	-	XP-36E	1939	-	-	-	-	-	R-1830-17	
76B	Attack	Y1A-18	-	-	-	-	-	-	R-1830	-
76C	Attack	Y1A-18	-	-	-	-	-	-	R-1535	-
76D	Attack (Export)	A-18	-	-	-	-	-	-	R-1830	Modified
76E	-	Y1A-18	-	-	-	-	-	-	P&W	-
77	Navy Scout Bomber	XSBC-2 XSBC-3	1936	1	400	Navy	SD-268-1A	Columbus	R-2600-20	changed to XSBC-3
77A	Navy Scout Bomber	Helldiver 77 (Export XSBC-3) SBC-3	1937	83	-	Navy	-	Kenmore	R-1535-94	Dwg.95729
77B	Navy Scout	Helldiver SBC-4	1939-40	124	-	Navy	SD-213-3A	Kenmore	R-1830-34	Hydraulic landing gear & flap control

78	Pursuit	(Proposal only)	-	-	-	-	-	-	-	Single seat midwing
79	-	Type 4 Hawk	-	1	-	-	-	-	-	Hawk 3 with special Power plan & cabin
80	Interceptor	Fighter proposal	-	-	-	-	-	-	-	With extension shaft
80A	Interceptor	Fighter proposal	-	-	-	-	-	-	-	-\
81	Pursuit	P-40	1939	200	100-109	Army	-	Buffalo	V-1710-33	Proposed CP-37-7
-	Pursuit	P-40B	-	131	300	Army	-	Buffalo	-	Con. W535-ac-12414
-	-	(H-81B)	-	-	-	-	-	-	-	Con.W535-ac-12414
-	Pursuit	P-40C	-	193	300-	Army	7437	Buffalo	V-1710-33	Con.W535-ac-13802
-	-	(H-81B)	-	-	309	-	Append. IIG	Buffalo	-	-
-	-	P-40G	-	50	7186	-	-	-	-	H-81A-2 wing panels To convert 50 P-40 Airplanes into P-40G
-	-	H-81A	-	100	150-159	France	-	-	-	-
-	-	H-81A-1	-	130	121-123	France	-	Buffalo	-	-
-	-	H-81A-1	-	85	125-127	France	-	Buffalo	-	-
-	-	H-81A-2	-	315	130-134	British	-	Buffalo	-	-
-	-	H-81A-2	-	100	320-329	British	-	Buffalo	-	-
81	-	H-81A-2	-	150	340-349	British	-	Buffalo	-	-
-	-	H-81A-2	-	300	360-369	British	-	Buffalo	-	-
-	-	H-81A-3	-	100	-	British	-	Buffalo	-	Diverted from British S.O.130,320,340 to
-	-	H-81A-C	-	40	7198	British	-	Buffalo	-	converted P-40C
-	-	H-81A-G	-	44	7198	British	-	Buffalo	-	converted P-40G
-	-	H-81B	-	-	-	-	-	-	-	see P-40B, C above
(19)	Trainer	19L	1935	1	C-ZO	D.O.C.	19-Z8	St. Louis	R-266	2P side-by-side all Metal
-	Trainer	19R	1936-37	23	-	S.America, Cuba, China	19-Z8	St. Louis	R-975E-3	2P tandem fighter trainer
-	-	A-19-R	1937	1	C-37	St. Louis Lambert	-	Kenmore	R-266/ R-975E-3	Commercial version of 19R
82	-	Seagull XSO3C-1	1938	1	177	Navy	SD57B	Columbus	XV-770-4	Con.60516 Drawing P-1008
82A	Scout Observation	Seagull SO3C-1	1942	150	330	Navy	SD257-1B	Columbus	V-770-6	no provision for carrier operation
82B	Scout Observation	Seagull SO3C-2 SO3C-2C	1942 1943	150 300	330	Navy Britain	SD257-2	Columbus	V-770-6	Provision for carrier operation
82C	-	Seagull SO3C-3	1943-44	200	330	Navy	SD257-2	Columbus	V-770-6	basically similar to 82B but with Redesigned center Panel, fuel system Revisions, protected Tanks, etc.
83	Attack Bomber	-	-	-	-	-	-	-	R-1830	-
83A	Attack Bomber	Proposal	10/25/38	-	-	-	-	-	2xR-2600	-
84	Dive Bomber Scout	Helldiver XSB2C-1	1939	1	188	Navy	SD-268A	Buffalo	XR-2600-B	Dwg.P-1676 3-view Hawk 84A, Shrike for Export. Contract
	S.B.	SB2C-1	1942	200	350	Navy	SD2681B	Columbus	R-2600-B	66638 Con. Noa(S) 1609
84A	Scout Bomber	Helldiver SB2C-1C	1943	778	350	Navy	SD2681B	Columbus	R-2600-8	Con.Noa(3)1609
84B	Scout Bomber	Helldiver SB2C-1A	-	1	350	Navy	SD2681B	Columbus	R-2600-8	Con.Noa(3)1609
84C	-	Helldiver XSB2C-2	-	1	100	Navy	SD268-1A	Columbus	R-2600-8	Con.93691 Marine
84D	-	Helldiver SB2C-2	Canc.	-	350	Navy	-	Columbus	R-2600-8	Con.79082 Marine
84E	Scout Bomber	Helldiver SB2C-3	1943	1112	40	Navy	SD-268-3	Columbus	R-2600-20	Con.Noa(s)1609 same as 84B except Engine
84F	Scout Bomber	Helldiver SB2C-4	1944	2045	40	Navy	SD-268-4	Columbus	R-2600-20	Con.Noa(s)1609 Same as 84E except Perforated dive & Landing flaps
84G	Scout Bomber	Helldiver SB2C-5	1945	970	50	Navy	SD-268-5	Columbus	R-2600-20	Con.Noa(s)1609 Same as 84F except Beefed up, with new Cockpit

84H	Scout Bomber	Helldiver XSB2C-6	1944	2	17	Navy	None	St. Louis	R-2800-	Con. Noa(s)1609 Converted from 84E Longer fuselage and Engine mount
84I	Dive-Bomber	XBT2C-1	1945	10	20	Navy	SD-394	Columbus	R-3350-24W	Con. Noa(s)6263 single place with Jump seat, internal Torpedo
S-84	Attack Bomber	A-25A	1942	700	D-31 D-34	Army	S84-252	St. Louis	R-2600-8	Army version of SB2C-1A. W535-ac-3834B
85	Observation	O-52	1940	203	110	Army	-	-	R-1340-H1	W535-ac-13362
86	Pursuit	XP-46	1940	2	-	Army	-	Buffalo	V-1710	(CP-39-13) W535-ac-13447
21	Pursuit	(Demons)	1938	1	D-5	China	-	St. Louis	R-1820-65	-
(21)	Pursuit	-	1939	3 & 32 Sets material & 1 set tools & drawings	D-8	China D-9 D-10	21-Z4 & -	St. Louis 7737	- -	- - -
(21A)	Pursuit	-	-	-	-	-	-	-	-	Proposal of 21B (flush ldg gear) Designation later changed to P-248A (The Chinese 21 is Sometimes erroneously referred to as 21A)
(21B)	Pursuit	21B	1940	24	D-12	N.E.I.	21-Z5 21-Z51	St. Louis	R-1820-G5	Performs better than 21 due to Flush-retracting Landing gear
(A-22)	Trainer	-	1939	1	D-4	St. Louis Lambert	-	St. Louis	R-975E-3	Development of A-19R; has Retractable ldg. Gear Of the type on 21
(22)	Trainer	Falcon 22	1939	-	194	Turkey	22-Z4	Buffalo	R-975E-3	No detail spec. other than contained in S.O.194
(22)	Trainer	CW22	1940	36	D-14	N.E.I.	22-Z4 & 22-Z52	St. Louis	R-975E-3	Similar to A22 & Turkish 22s with exception of special equipment installed at buyers request
(22B)	Trainer	-	1941	50 25	D-25 D-24 (D-28 (D-29 (D-32	Turkey N.E.I. Spanish Speaking Countries	22-Z5 22-Z53 22-Z54 22-Z55	St. Louis	R-975E-3	Export version of 22N (SNC-1) to which it is almost identical. No. 3604 built for demons. General spec. is first listed; others are de-Tail specs. for each customer.
(22N)	Trainer	SNC-1	1942	335	D-19	Navy	SD-279B	St. Louis	R-975-28	Two place scout Trainer VSN class
(23)	Trainer	-	1939	1	-	Army	23-Z2	St. Louis	S3H1	Submitted under C.P.39-100. Built for USAAC Basic Combat Competition. Plane Has been scrapped
(23A)	Trainer	-	-	0	-	-	23A-Z1	St. Louis	S3H1	2P advanced trainer similar to 23 submitted under C.P. 39-750.
(23B)	Trainer	-	-	0	-	-	23A	-	Cyclone G-5	2P advanced trainer. No extensive Development
(23C)	Pursuit	-	-	0	-	-	23C-Z1	-	-	1P interceptor fighter similar to 21B but has door type rather than sliding type enclosure. No development.

(23D)	Trainer	-	-	0	-	-	-	-	Cyclone G-5	2P advanced trainer similar to 23B but with more extensive armament. No development.
(24)	Pursuit	XP-55	1942-44	3	D-35	Army	24-Z51	St. Louis	V-1710-F23R	Originally designated P-249C. (At one time A proposal for a 4 engine transport was inadvertently design-ated as the Model 24 but this was corrected to P-240. Tail first pusher type with swept back wings)
(24B)	Full scale Flying Model	XP-55	1941	-	D-26	Army	24-Z52	St. Louis	C68-5	Built to test XP-55 de-sign arrangement. steel tube, wood & fabric construction. has gross weight of approx. 3000 lbs. & engine power of 300
(25)	Training	AT-9	1940	491	D-13 D-16 D-18	Army	25-Z51	St. Louis	R-680-9	Twin engine trans-ition trainer submitted as Proposal P-253
(25)	-	AT-9	-	300	D-30	Army	25-Z52	St. Louis	R-680-13	-
(25A)	Training	-	-	0	-	-	25-Z2	St. Louis	R-680E-3B	Export or commercial Version of 25.
(26)	Fighter-Pursuit	XP-71	1941-43	2	D-27	Army	26-Z51	St. Louis	R-4360-3	2P twin engine. Outgrowth of P-259 & P-264. High performance & forward firing power. Cancelled.
(27)	Cargo-Transport	Caravan YC-76	1943	25	D-33	Army	27-Z51	St. Louis Louisville	R-1830-92	2 engine; constructed principally of wood & non-strategic mats., utilizing parts and installations already in production on other planes.
87	Pursuit	P-40D	-	22	170	Army	7436-A Rev. 5/24/40	Buffalo	V-1710-39	(CP-40-4) W535-ac-12141
-	Pursuit	P-40E (H87-B2)	-	301	170	Army	7438-A & Appendix II-3	Buffalo	-	W535-ac-12141
-	Pursuit	P-40E (H87-B2)	-	519	310	Army	7437-A & II-E.O.	Buffalo	-	W535-ac-15802
-	Pursuit	P-40E-1 (H87A-4)	-	420	420	Lend-Lease	8291	Buffalo	-	DAW 535 AC-3
-	Pursuit	P-40E-1 (H87A-5)	-	1080	390	Lend-Lease	8291	Buffalo	-	Has now been made a part of the P-40E-1 (H-87A-4)
-	Pursuit	XP-40F	-	1	170	Army	7437-A & Appendix II-F	-	-	W535-ac-12414
-	Pursuit	P-40F (H87B-3)	-	1000	400	Army	"	-	V-1650-1	Contract 15802
-	Pursuit	P-40F (H87B-3)	-	312	410	Army	"	-	V-1650-1	AC-18685
-	Pursuit	P-40G (H-81A-2 Panels)	-	50	-	Army	-	-	V-1710-C15	Original P-40 24 volt system
-	Pursuit	P-40H	-	(never built)		-	-	-	-	- -
-	Pursuit	P-40K	1943	1300 700	480	Army	7437-KF	Buffalo	F4E	changed engine to incorporate automatic pressure regulator. Contract 22614
-	Pursuit	P-40L	1943	700	490	Army	7437-L	Buffalo	RR/Packard	Continuation of P-40F Contract 22714
-	Pursuit	P-40M	1943	600	530	Army	7437-M	Buffalo	F20R	Contract 30491
-	Pursuit	YP-40F-5CU	-	-	-	-	-	-	Merlin 61	-
87V	Pursuit	P-40N	-	5000	550	Army	-	Buffalo	-	Contract 34423

87W	Pursuit	P-40N	-	1000	640	Army	-	Buffalo	-	Contract 34423
87X	Pursuit	P-40Q	-	3	10207	Army	-	Buffalo	-	W535-038AC-1526
-	-	H87A-1	-	-	-	-	-	-	C-15	Was French airplane But none mfg'd. 4x.50 cal. wing guns
-	-	H87A-2	-	20	160-169	British	7910A Rev. 4/10/41	Buffalo	-	-
-	-	H87A-3	-	540	160-169	British	"	Buffalo	-	-
-	-	H87A-4	-	-	-	-	-	-	-	(P-40E-1)
-	-	H87A-5	-	-	-	-	-	-	-	Made part of H87A-4
-	-	H87A-6	-	(proposal)		-	-	-	-	- -
(20A)	Transport	C-55	1941	1	D-22	Army	20-Z51	St. Louis	R-2600-17A	Personnel transport converted from CW-20 prototype
(20B)	Transport	Commando C-46A	1942	1000	440,500, 510,590	Army	20-Z16	Louisville Buffalo	R-2800-51	Transport cargo, troop & task force
(20C)	Transport	-	-	-	-	-	20C-F1& 20-Z20	Buffalo	-	Export or commercial cargo version of 20B
(20D)	Transport	-	-	-	-	-	20-Z24	Buffalo	R-2800	airline day transport Revision and improvement of 20B. Not built. Superseded by 20E.
(20E)	Transport	-	-	-	-	-	20-Z27	Buffalo	-	Commercial airliner converted from 20B Not built.
(20-E-1)	Transport	CW-20E	-	-	-	-	20-Z55	Buffalo	R-2800-C	3-blade props
(20-E-1A)	Transport	-	-	-	-	-	-	-	-	same as 20E-1 but 4-blade props
(20-E-1B)	Transport	-	-	-	-	-	-	Buffalo	R-2800-H20 injection	Same as 20E-2A Except engine
(20-E-2)	Transport	-	-	-	-	-	-	-	R-3350	3-blade 830 props
(20-E-2A)	Transport	-	-	-	-	-	-	-	R-3350	20E-2 but with 834 Prop blades
(20-F)	Transport	(changed to 20-E-2)		-	-	-	-	-	-	-
(20-G)	Transport	XC-113	1945	1	-	Army	P-291-22	St. Louis	TG-100	on 3/2/45 wire
(CW-20H)	Transport	CW-20H	1945	-	-	-	-	-	R-3350	See ltr. of 5/2/45
(CW-20I)	Transport	CW-20I	1945	-	-	-	-	-	R-3350	See ltr. of 5/2/45
(20B-1)	Transport	Commando XC-46B	1945	1	-	Army	P299-Z1	St. Louis	R-2800-34W	C-46R converted by engine change. Incorporated mockup Of C-46D, E, F
20B-2	Transport & Troop Carrier	Commando C-46D	1944	1412	600, 620	Army	9501	Buffalo	R-2800-51	W535-ac-24581 Troop carrier version of C-46A
(20B-3)	Transport	Commando C-46E	1945	17	-	Army	20-Z62	St. Louis	R-2800-75	Same as C-46F with flat glass windshield
20B-4	Transport & Troop Carrier	Commando C-46F	1945	400	620	Army	9164	Buffalo	R-2800-75	Same as C-46D but with Hamilton Standard props. Hydraulic boosters Eliminated on Aileron, rudder & Elevators
88	Pursuit	XP-53	-	1	204	-	7853A	Buffalo	IV-1430-3	(CP-40-2) W535-ac-15581
89	Observation	-	-	0	-	-	-	-	-	Twin engine proposal Never built
90	Pursuit	Hawk 90 XP-60	-	1	206	Army	-	Buffalo	Rolls Royce	W535-ac-18551
90A	Pursuit	XP-60	-	1	206	Army	-	Buffalo	V-1650-1	Contract 18551
90B	Pursuit	XP-60D	-	1	16064	Army	-	Buffalo	V-1650-3	Contract 15581
91	Pursuit	XP-62	-	2	430	Army	8343	Buffalo	R-3350	AC-19440
91A	Pursuit	XP-62	-	2	430	Army	8343	Buffalo	R-3340	AC-19440 G.E. C.M. Turbo
92	Scout Bomber	Helldiver XSB2C-2	Canc.	1	400	Navy	SD-268-1	Columbus	R-2600-8	Marine seaplane (twin float) replaced By Design 84C, 84D
92	Attack	XA-43	-	-	200	Army	-	Buffalo	TG-180	2P W33038 AC6266
93	Scout Bomber	Helldiver XSB3C-1	Canc.	2	110	Navy	-	Columbus	R-3350-8	Contract 88659 VSB carrier

94A	Fighter	XF14C-1	*	**	380	Navy	SD-284A	Buffalo	XH-2470-4	Contract 88194 Terminated before Delivery. **changed To XF14C-2
94B	Fighter	XF14C-2	1944	2*	380	Navy	SD-284-2	Buffalo	R-3350-6	Birman Turbo in engine compartment *Only 1 completed and delivered.
94C	Fighter	XF14C-3	*	1	380	Navy	SD-284-3	Buffalo	R-3350-6	Pressure cabin added Contract terminated
95	Pursuit	-	-	-	-	-	-	-	-	Single engine
95A	Pursuit	XP-60A	1941	1	460	Army	8509	Buffalo	V-1710-F15R	Contract 28113
95B	Pursuit	XP-60B	1942	1	460	Army	8509	Buffalo	"	Contract 28113
95C	Pursuit	XP-60C	1942	1	460	Army	8509	Buffalo	-	no engine decided on. Contract 28113
-	-	XP-60E	1943	1	460	Army	8509	Buffalo	R-2800-10	-
96	Dive Bomber & Torpedo	-	-	-	-	-	-	-	-	VBTC series, 1P
96A	Dive Bomber & Torpedo	XBTC-1	1943	Canc.	120	Navy	SD-239	Columbus	R-3350-8	VBT single seat
97	Scout	-	-	-	-	-	-	-	-	VSO series
97A	Scout	XSC-1	1944	2	130	Navy	SD-332	Columbus	XR-1820	1P, equipped with Wright Turbo-Super Charger
97B	Scout	Seahawk SC-1	1944	566	14	Navy	SD-332-1	Columbus	R-1820-62	Contract NOa(s)231
97C	Scout	Seahawk XSC-2	1946	1	25	Navy	-	Columbus	R-1820-76	Contract NOa(s)6685 No turbo, jump seat with sea rescue provisions
97D	Scout	Seahawk SC-2	1946	10	30	Navy	SD-332-2	Columbus	R-1820-76	Contract NOa(s)6749 First "functional" cockpit
98	Dive Bomber & Torpedo	-	-	-	-	-	-	-	-	VBT series, 1P
98A	Dive Bomber & Torpedo	XBTC-2	1944	2	120	Navy	SD-329-2	Columbus	XR-4360-8	1P
99	Fighter	XF15C-1	1945	3	650-	Navy	SD-371	Buffalo	R-2800 & Halford H1B	Contract NOa(s)3245
(1)28	Transport	CW-28 P307 P309A P309B	-	-	-	American Airlines (Proposal)	P307-Z1 P309-Z1 P309-Z3	-	C18B6 CE15	Low wing, 2 engine DC-3 replacement
(1)29	Pursuit	-	-	-	-	-	-	-	-	4 engine, two place All-weather fighter
(1)29A	Pursuit	XP-87	1947	1	62	Army	9566	Columbus	24C	jet-powered, all Weather fighter

Annex 2:
U.S. Army Air Corps and Army Air Forces Squadron Size Units Issued P-40 Aircraft

Unit	Period of Service	Station or Theater
HHS, 12th Pursuit Wing	1941	Panama Canal Zone
Chinese American Composite Wing	1942-	China
13th Fighter Command (Detachment)	1943-	Guadalcanal (including elements of the 12th FS, a Detachment of the 70th FS and the 6th FS) with P-40Fs
HHS, XXVI Fighter Command	1944	Panama Canal Zone
8th Pursuit/Fighter Group	1940-	U.S., Southwest Pacific, Fifth Air Force
13th Fighter Group		
HHS, 16th Pursuit Group	1941	Panama Canal Zone
15th Pursuit/Fighter Group	1941-	Hawaii, Seventh Air Force
18th Pursuit/Fighter Group	1941-	Hawaii; Australia, Thirteenth Air Force
20th Pursuit Group	1941-	Hamilton Field, CA etc
23rd Fighter Group	1942-April 1944	CBI
24th Pursuit Group	1941-	Philippines
28th Composite Group	Feb.1942-Sept.1942	Alaska
31st Pursuit Group	1940-	U.S.
33rd Pursuit/Fighter Group	1941-	North Africa (TORCH)
HHS, 36th Pursuit Group	1942-1943	Panama Canal Zone
HHS, 37th Pursuit Group	1942	Panama Canal Zone
48th Fighter Group	1944-	New Britain, Southwest Pacific, Fifth Air Force
49th Fighter Group	1942-1943	P-40Es, P-40Ks, P-40Ls, Southwest Pacific, Fifth Air Force
50th Fighter Group	November 1942-	P-40Ms
51st Fighter Group	1942-	CBI, Tenth Air Force
54th Pursuit/Fighter Group	1942-	Eleventh Air Force
57th Fighter Group	1942-	North Africa, Ninth Air Force
79th Fighter Group	1942-	Egypt, North Africa, Ninth Air Force
80th Fighter Group	1943-	CBI
312th Light Bomb Group	1942-	Southwest Pacific, Fifth Air Force
318th Fighter Group	1942-	Hawaii, Seventh Air Force
324th Fighter Group	1942-	North Africa
325th Fighter Group	Jul.1942-	North Africa (TORCH), Italy
343rd Fighter Group	Sept.1942-	Alaska, Eleventh Air Force
347th Fighter Group	1942-	Southwest Pacific, Fifth Air Force
369th Fighter Group	1944-45	Stations in California, Louisiana, Arkansas
1st Pursuit Squadron	1941-1942	Eglin Field, FL
2nd Composite Squadron	1944-1945	Marshall Field, KS
2nd Pursuit/Fighter Squadron	1941-1942	Selfridge Field, MI
3rd Composite Squadron	1944-1945	Lawson Field, GA
3rd Fighter Squadron (Commando)	1944	Lakeland AAF, FL
3rd Pursuit Squadron	1941-1942	Philippines; Australia; Java
4th Pursuit Squadron	1941-1942	Langley Field, VA; Selfridge Field, MI
4th Fighter (Commando) Squadron	1944	Lakeland AAF, FL
5th Pursuit Squadron	1941-1942	Selfridge Field, MI
6th Pursuit/Fighter Squadron	1941-1943	Hawaii, Guadalcanal by July 1943 with P-40Fs
7th Pursuit/Fighter Squadron	1942-1944	Australia; New Guinea
8th Pursuit/Fighter Squadron	1942-1944	Australia; New Guinea
8th Tactical Reconnaissance Squadron	1945	Stuttgart AAF, AR
9th Pursuit/Fighter Squadron	1941-1943	Australia; New Guinea
10th Pursuit/Fighter Squadron	1942-1943	Various fields in Florida
10th Tactical Reconnaissance Squadron	1943-1945	Various fields in Texas and Louisiana
11th Pursuit/Fighter Squadron	1941-1945	Alaska
11th Tactical Reconnaissance Squadron	1943-1944	Various fields in North Carolina and Kentucky
12th Fighter Squadron	1943	Element of 13th Fighter Command Detachment on Guadalcanal as of July 1943 with P-40Fs
13th Pursuit Squadron	1941	Tallahassee, FL
13th Tactical Reconnaissance Squadron	1944-1945	Deridder AAF, LA

Annex 2: Squadron Size Units Issued P-40 Aircraft

Unit	Years	Location
14th Pursuit Squadron	1941	MacDill Field, FL
15th Pursuit Squadron	1941	MacDill Field, FL
15th Reconnaissance Squadron (Fighter)	1942-1943	Various fields in Kentucky and Mississippi
16th Pursuit/Fighter Squadron	1941-1944	India, China
16th Reconnaissance Squadron	1942-1943	Langley Field, VA; Morocco, North Africa
17th Pursuit Squadron	1942-1942	Philippines; Australia; Java
17th Reconnaissance Squadron	1942-1943	Salinas AAF, CA and fields in Louisiana
18th Pursuit/Fighter Squadron	1941-1945	Alaska
19th Pursuit/Fighter Squadron	1941-1943	Hawaii
20th Pursuit/Fighter Squadron	1941-1942	Philippines; Australia; Java
20th Tactical Reconnaissance Squadron	1942-1945	Various fields in Missouri, Mississippi and India
21st Pursuit Squadron	1941-1942	Philippines
21st Tactical Reconnaissance Squadron	1942-1943	Various fields in Oklahoma, Tennessee and Mississippi
22nd Pursuit/Fighter Squadron	1941-1943	Puerto Rico, Trinidad and Curacao
22nd Tactical Reconnaissance Squadron	1943-1945	Campbell AAF, KY and Deridder AAF, LA
23rd Pursuit/Fighter Squadron	1941-1943	Puerto Rico, St. Thomas and Mitchel Field, NY
23rd Tactical Reconnaissance Squadron	Uncertain	Various fields in North Carolina, Missouri, North Carolina, Georgia and California
24th Pursuit/Fighter Squadron	1943-1944	Panama Canal Zone, Caribbean
25th Pursuit/Fighter Squadron	1941-1945	Various stations in California and CBI
25th Liaison/Observation Squadron	1942-1943	Various stations in Mississippi
28th Pursuit/Fighter Squadron	1941-1942	Panama Canal Zone
28th Tactical Reconnaissance Squadron	-	(see 36th Photo Mapping Squadron)
29th Pursuit/Fighter Squadron	1941-1944	Panama Canal Zone
30th Pursuit/Fighter Squadron	1940-1945	Panama Canal Zone
30th Tactical Reconnaissance Squadron	1943-1944	Various fields in Mississippi
31st Pursuit/Fighter Squadron	1941-1944	Panama Canal Zone
31st Tactical Reconnaissance Squadron	1943	Deridder Field, LA and Abilene, TX
32nd Pursuit/Fighter Squadron	1942-1944	Puerto Rico, Curacao, Aruba and Panama Canal Zone
33rd Pursuit/Fighter Squadron	1940; 1944	Mitchel Field, NY; Iceland
35th Pursuit/Fighter Squadron	1940-1944	Mitchel Field, NY; Australia, New Britain and New Guinea
36th Pursuit/Fighter Squadron	1940-1941	Mitchel Field, NY
36th Photo Mapping Squadron	1943-1944	Camp Campbell, KY, Muskogee, OK
43rd Pursuit/Fighter Squadron	1941-1944	Panama Canal Zone
44th Pursuit/Fighter Squadron	1941-1944	Hawaii; Efate, Guadalcanal with P-40F, P-40K, P-40M
45th Fighter Squadron	1942-1944	Hawaii; Guadalcanal; Baker Island
46th Pursuit/Fighter Squadron	1941-1943	Hawaii
47th Pursuit/Fighter Squadron	1941-1943	Hawaii
48th Pursuit Squadron	1941	Hamilton Field, CA; March Field, CA
49th Pursuit Squadron	1941	Hamilton Field, CA; March Field, CA
50th Pursuit/Fighter Squadron	1941-1942	Hamilton Field, CA; March Field, CA
51st Pursuit/Fighter Squadron	1942-1944	Panama Canal Zone
52nd Pursuit/Fighter Squadron	1942-1944	Panama Canal Zone
53rd Pursuit/Fighter Squadron	1942-1943	Panama Canal Zone
54th Pursuit/Fighter Squadron	1941-1942	Hamilton Field, CA; various fields in Washington state and Alaska
55th Pursuit/Fighter Squadron	1940-1942	Hamilton Field, CA and various fields in North Carolina and Florida
57th Reconnaissance Squadron	1944-1945	Deridder AAF, LA
58th Pursuit/Fighter Squadron	1941-1944	Langley Field, VA and North Africa (TORCH)
58th Reconnaissance Squadron	1944-1945	Deridder AAF, LA and various fields in Arkansas and Oklahoma
59th Fighter Squadron	1941-1944	Organized in the US but served principally in North Africa (TORCH), Italy and on to the CBI
60th Fighter Squadron	1941-1944	Organized in the US but served principally in North Africa (TORCH) and later the CBI
61st Fighter Squadron	1941-1942	Various stations in North Carolina, South Carolina, Connecticut and Georgia
62nd Fighter Squadron	1941-1942	Various stations in Georgia, North Carolina, South Carolina and New Jersey
63rd Fighter Squadron	1941-1942	Various stations in Georgia, North Carolina, New York and Connecticut
64th Fighter Squadron	1941-1944	Various stations in New York, Connecticut, Massachusetts and then to the Middle East and Italy
65th Fighter Squadron	1941-1944	Various stations in New York, Connecticut then to the Middle East, North Africa and Italy
66th Fighter Squadron	1941-1944	Various stations in New York, Connecticut, Rhode Island then to the Middle East, North Africa and Italy
68th Fighter Squadron	1941-1943	Baton Rouge, LA, California, Australia and New Caledonia
68th Observation Squadron	February 1942-	Mainly P-40Fs
69th Fighter Squadron	1942-1943	Various stations in Florida, Virginia, Connecticut, Massachusetts and New Hampshire
70th Fighter Squadron	1943	Guadalcanal, P-40Fs (Detachment)
72nd Fighter Squadron	1941-1943	Hawaii
73rd Fighter Squadron	1941-1943	Hawaii

74th Fighter Squadron	1942-1944	China
75th Fighter Squadron	1942-1944	China
76th Fighter Squadron	1942-1944	China
77th Pursuit/Fighter Squadron	1940-1942	Hamilton Field, CA and various fields in North Carolina
78th Pursuit/Fighter Squadron	1941-1944	Hawaii, Midway and back to Hawaii
79th Pursuit/Fighter Squadron	1940-1942	Hamilton Field, CA and various fields in North Carolina
81st Fighter Squadron	1942-1943	Various fields in Mississippi and Florida
82nd Reconnaissance Squadron (Fighter)	1942-1945	Various fields in California, Louisiana, Mississippi and then to New Guinea, Biak
85th Fighter Squadron	1942-1944	Various fields in Florida, North Carolina, Massachusetts then to North Africa, Malta and Italy
86th Fighter Squadron	1942-1944	Various fields in Florida, North Carolina, Rhode Island then to Egypt, North Africa and Italy
87th Fighter Squadron	1942-1944	Various fields in Florida, North Carolina, Connecticut, then to Egypt, North Africa, Sicily and Italy
88th Bomb Squadron (Light)	-	Redesignated as the 495th Fighter Bomber Squadron (q.v.)
88th Fighter Squadron	1943-1944	Stations in New York then to India and Burma
89th Fighter Squadron	1943-1944	Stations in New York then to India and Burma
90th Fighter Squadron	1943-1944	Stations in New York then to India and Burma
91st Fighter Squadron	1944	India and China
91st Tactical Reconnaissance Squadron	1942-1943	Stations in Kentucky and Pennsylvania
92nd Fighter Squadron	1944-1945	Italy then on to India and China
93rd Fighter Squadron	1944	Italy then on to India and China
94th Pursuit Squadron	1939-1941	Selfridge Field, MI
97th Reconnaissance Squadron (Fighter)	1942-1943	Stations in Georgia, Tennessee and North Carolina
98th Fighter Squadron	1942-1944	Stations in North Carolina and Florida
99th Fighter Squadron	1943-1944	Tuskegee, AL then to Morocco, North Africa and Italy
100th Fighter Squadron	1943-1944	Stations in Michigan and then Italy
101st Tactical Reconnaissance Squadron	1943	Reading AAF, PA
102nd Tactical Reconnaissance Squadron	1943-1944	Stations in Louisiana, Texas and California
103rd Tactical Reconnaissance Squadron/Reconnaissance Squadron (Fighter)	1943-1944	Reading AAF, PA
106th Observation Squadron	1941-1942	Stations in Florida and Georgia
110th Tactical Reconnaissance Squadron	1944-1945	New Guinea and the Philippines
115th Liaison Squadron	1943	Stations in Louisiana and Texas
118th Reconnaissance Squadron (Fighter)/Tactical Reconnaissance Squadron	1942-1945	Stations in South Carolina, Tennessee, North Carolina, Kentucky, Georgia
120th Reconnaissance Squadron (Fighter)	1942-1943	Deridder AAF, LA then to stations in Texas, and Alabama
124th Reconnaissance Squadron (Fighter)	1943-1944	Stations in Tennessee and Mississippi
127th Observation Squadron	1942	Stations in Tennessee
301st Fighter Squadron	1943-1944	Selfridge Field, MI then to Italy
302nd Fighter Squadron	1943-1944	Selfridge Field, MI then to Italy
303rd Fighter Squadron	1943-1944	Stations in Florida
304th Fighter Squadron	1942-1944	Stations in North Carolina, South Carolina and Florida
305th Fighter Squadron	1944	Stations in Florida
306th Fighter Squadron	1942-1943	Stations in Florida
307th Fighter Squadron	1942	North Africa
308th Fighter Squadron	1942	North Africa
309th Fighter Squadron	1942	North Africa
310th Fighter Squadron	1942-1943	Stations in Florida, Virginia, Pennsylvania, Connecticut, Rhode Island and New Hampshire
311th Fighter Squadron	1942-1943	Stations in Louisiana, Florida, Virginia, District of Columbia, Connecticut, Rhode Island and New Hampshire
312th Fighter Squadron	1944	Perry AAF and Florida
313th Fighter Squadron	1942-1943	Stations in Mississippi and Florida
314th Fighter Squadron	1942-1944	Stations in New York, Maryland, then to Egypt, North Africa and Italy
315th Fighter Squadron	1942-1944	Stations in New York, New Hampshire then to Egypt, North Africa and Italy
316th Fighter Squadron	1942-1944	Stations in New York and Virginia then to Egypt, North Africa and Italy
317th Fighter Squadron	1942-1943	Stations in New York and Rhode Island then to Algeria and Italy
318th Fighter Squadron	1942-1943	Stations in New York, Massachusetts, New Hampshire then to Algeria and Italy
319th Fighter Squadron	1942-1943	Stations in New York, Connecticut, Rhode Island then to Algeria and Italy
323rd Fighter Squadron	1942-1943	Stations in New York, Pennsylvania and Virginia
324th Fighter Squadron	1942-1943	Stations in New York, District of Columbia and Virginia

325th Fighter Squadron	1942-1943	Stations in New York, Virginia and New Jersey
339th Fighter Squadron	1943-	SOPAC at TRUCULENCE by June 1943 with one P-40, 13 P-38s and 45 P-39s
344th Fighter Squadron	1942-1945	Alaska
350th Fighter Squadron	1942-1943	Stations in New York, Virginia and Maryland
351st Fighter Squadron	1942-1943	Stations in New York, Virginia and New Jersey
352nd Fighter Squadron	1942-1943	Stations in New York, Virginia, New Jersey and Virginia
365th Fighter Squadron	1943	Stations in Virginia, Maryland, New Jersey
366th Fighter Squadron	1943	Stations in Virginia, Maryland, Pennsylvania
367th Fighter Squadron	1943	Stations in Virginia, Maryland, New Jersey, and Pennsylvania
386th Bomb Squadron (Dive)(Light)	1943-1944	Stations in Louisiana, California and then to New Guinea
387th Bomb Squadron (Dive)(Light)	1943-1944	Stations in Louisiana, California then to New Guinea
388th Bomb Squadron (Dive)(Light)	1943-1944	Stations in Louisiana and California, then to New Guinea
389th Bomb Squadron (Dive)(Light)	1943-1944	Stations in Louisiana and California, then to New Guinea
398th Fighter Squadron	1944-1945	Stations in California, Louisiana, Arkansas
399th Fighter-Bomber Squadron	-	(Redesignated as the 57th Reconnaissance Squadron, q.v.)
400th Fighter Squadron	-	(Redesignated as the 58th Reconnaissance Squadron, q.v.)
403rd Fighter Squadron	1943	Stations in Michigan
407th Fighter Squadron	1944-1945	Stations in Louisiana
408th Fighter Squadron	1944-1945	Stations in Louisiana
409th Fighter Squadron	1944-1945	Stations in Louisiana
436th Fighter Squadron	1943-1944	Stations in California
439th Base HQS and Air Base Squadron	1943-	Ladd Field, AK had one P-40 for cold weather experiments as of 28 April 1943
440th Fighter Squadron	1943-1944	Stations in California and Florida
441st Fighter Squadron	1944	Stations in Florida
443rd Fighter Squadron	1943	Stations in Virginia
445th Fighter Squadron	1943-1944	Stations in Florida and California
447th Fighter Squadron	1944	Stations in Georgia
488th Fighter Squadron	1944	Stations in Georgia
492nd Fighter Bomber Squadron	1943	Stations in Tennessee
493rd Fighter Bomber Squadron	1943	Stations in Tennessee
494th Fighter Bomber Squadron	1942-1943	Stations in Georgia, Mississippi and Tennessee
495th Fighter Bomber Squadron	1942-1944	Stations in Georgia, Mississippi, Tennessee and Texas (formerly 88th Bomb Squadron (L)
499th Fighter Bomber Squadron	1944	Stations in Georgia
500th Fighter Bomber Squadron	1944	Stations in Georgia
501st Fighter Bomber Squadron	1944	Stations in Georgia
502nd Fighter Bomber Squadron	1943-1944	Stations in Georgia and Florida
512th Fighter Bomber Squadron	1943	Stations in Mississippi and South Carolina
513th Fighter Bomber Squadron	1943	Stations in Mississippi and South Carolina
514th Fighter Bomber Squadron	1943	Stations in Mississippi and South Carolina
518th Fighter Bomber Squadron	1943-1944	Stations in Mississippi, Florida, Texas, Louisiana and Oklahoma
519th Fighter Bomber Squadron	1943-1944	Stations in Mississippi, Florida, Texas, Louisiana and Oklahoma
520th Fighter Bomber Squadron	1943-1944	Stations in Mississippi, Florida, Texas, Louisiana and Oklahoma
522nd Fighter Bomber Squadron	1944	Italy
523rd Fighter Squadron	1944	Italy
524th Fighter Squadron	1944	Italy
525th Fighter Squadron	1944	Italy
526th Fighter Squadron	1944	Italy
527th Fighter Squadron	1944	Italy

Annex 3: Locations of Aircraft

Curtiss "X" & "Y" Pursuits, December 7, 1941

X1P-36: 37-068: Wright Field, LOST 9-22-40 near Fairfield , Kentucky. Complete Wreck, pilot killed. (YP-36) 315.9 hours

YP-36: 37-069: Wright Field, DAM 12-41, flew until 6-24-42 at Chanute F, Class 26 with 703.6 hours.
YP-36: 37-070: Wright Field, Retired 10-29-40 to Class 26 at Chanute F, Fair Wear & Tear, with 474 hours,

==

1 ops YP-36: 37-069DAM

==

XP-37: 37-375: Chanute F, Retired 11-13-41 after spending entire career at Wright F, with 162 hours

YP-37: 13 Aircraft built, 38-472-484: 2 lost, 5 retired to Class 26 = 6 A/C remaining on December 7, 1941

YP-37: LOST = 38-477: Ladd F, Alaska, Wrecked 11-19-40, nosed over in snow. Career at Langley 11-39 to 9-40 before being shipped to Alaska for Cold Weather tests. 129.7 hours
LOST = 38-480: Chanute F, Wrecked 9-19-41, engine overheated. Spent most of career at Langley F, before sent to Chanute 6-41. 165.8 hours.

Recently Retired = 11-41 = 5 YP-37 A/C:
38-473 at Chanute F, Retired 11-7-41 to Class 26 at Chanute F, after spending most of career at Wright F and Langley F. 181.6 hours
38-475 at Lowry F, Retired 11-21-41 to Class 26, after spending most of career at Langley F before being sent to Lowry 3-41. 212 hours.
38-379 at Chanute F, Retired 11-7-41 to Class 26, after spending most of career at Langley F before being sent to Chanute 3-41. 196.1 hours.
38-483 at Chanute F, Retired 11-7-41 to Class 26, after spending most of career at Langley F before being sent to Chanute 3 -41. 116.8 hours.
38-484 at Sheppard F, Wichita Falls, Texas, Retired 11-6-41to Class 26, after spending most of career at Langley F, then Chanute, before being sent to Sheppard 10-41. 88.1 hours.

Operational 12-7-41 = 6 YP-37 A/C:
38-472 at Chanute F, Spent career at Curtiss Wright Corp and Chanute.
To Class 26 on 3-4-42 with 168.5 hours, after engine fire due to overheating 1-24-42.
38-474 at NACA/Langley F. Spent career at Langley until 2-41.
To Class 26 in 2-43 with 180.3 hours.
38-476 at Biloxi, MS. Spent career at Langly, and Chanute, until Biloxi 10-41.
To Class 26 on 1-2-42 with 98.7 hours.
38-478 at Chanute F, Spent career at Langley, and Chanute, until Biloxi 1-42.
To Class 26 on 1-28-42 with 182.7 hours.
38-481 at Ladd F, Spent career at Langely. Sent to Ladd 10-4-40 with Cold Weather detachment.
To Class 26 on 2-3-42 with 279.3 hours. Did not fly in December 1941.
38-482 at Biloxi MS, Spent career at Langley and Chanute, until Biloxi 10-41.
To Class 26 1-2-42 with 182.4 hours.

==

6 Ops YP-37: 38-472, -474, -476, -478, -481, -482

==

XP-40: 38-010 at Wright F, converted P-36A. Entire career at Wright until survey 8-31-44 with 433.2 hrs.
XP-42: 38-004 at NACA/Langley, converted P-36A. Career at Wright until 9-40. Retired 8-4-42 with 132.6 Hours.

==

2 Ops XP-40: 38-010
XP-42: 38-004

==

XP-46 : 40-3053 at Wright F, delivered 9-41 and tests at Wright. To Chanute 5-19-42.
XP-46A: 40-3054 at Wright F, delivered 9-41, 1st flight Feb 15, 41. To Chanute 5-19-42. Survived till end of War to be surplused by Reclamation Finance Corporation, RFC.

==

2 Ops XP-46 & -46A: 40-3053, -3054

==

YP-36, P-36A, & P-36C in USAAC, December 7, 1941

	YP-36	**P-36A**	**P-36C**	
1st Air Force, Northeast				
Selfridge F, MI	0	2	0	P-36A: 38-115DAM, -147DAM (became XP-36E)
Chanute, IL	0	4	0	P-36A: 38-001, -003DAM, -016, -178
Wright F, OH	1	3	0	YP-36: 37-069DAM P-36A: 38-020, -180 XP-40: 38-010 (ex-P-36A)
Fairborn Air Depot, FAD, OH	0	2	0	P-36A: 38-101DAM (ex-Selfridge), back 12-8-41 38-138DAM (ex-Selma), back 6-42
Middletown Air Depot MAD, OH	0	1	0	P-36A: 38-044 (ex Charlotte)DAM, back 1-42
NACA/Langley VA	0	1	0	XP-42: 38-004 (ex P-36A
	1	13	0	YP-36: 1 A/C, of which 1 DAM P-36A: 11 A/C, of which 5 DAM XP-40: 1 A/C XP-42: 1 A/C
2nd Air Force, Northwest				
Lowry F, CO	0	2	0	P-36A: 38-007, -099
Paine F, WA	0	2	0	P-36A: 38-024 DAM, -088
Portland, OR	0	1	0	P-36A: 38-096
	0	5	0	P-36A: 5 A/C, of which 1 DAM
3rd Air Force, Southeast				
Baton Rouge, LA	0	2	0	P-36A: 38-006, -153
Meridian, MS	0	1	1	P-36A: 38-113 P-36C: 38-204
Biloxi, MS	0	2	0	P-36A: 38-156, -177
Selma, AL	0	4	2	P-36A: 38-126, -137, -139, -143DAM P-36C: 38-195, -202
Eglin AAB, FL	0	2	15	P-36A: 38-085, -172(tested asXP-36F) P-36C: 38-182DAM, -183DAM, -186, -188, -189DAM, -191, -193, -194, -197, -199, -200, -207, -208DAM, -209, -210
Orlando, FL	0	0	1	P-36C: 38-187DAM
Charlotte, NC	0	6	3	P-36A: 38-119DAM, -135, -136, -162, -164, -174(was ex-P-36D) P-36C: 38-181, -185, -190
	0	17	22	P-36A: 17 A/C, of which 2 DAM P-36C: 22 A/C, of which 5 DAM
4th Air Force, Southwest				
Shepperd F, TX	0	2	0	P-36A: 38-009, -157
Tulsa, OK	0	1	0	P-36A: 38-132
Luke F, AZ	0	0	4	P-36C: 38-184, -192, -196, -206
March F, CA	0	3	0	P-36A: 38-065, -072, -091
Hamilton F, CA	0	1	0	P-36A: 38-094
Sacramento Air Depot SAD, CA	0	2	0	P-36A: 38-035DAM(ex-Hamilton), back 2-42 38-087DAM(ex-Hamilton), back 3-42
	0	9	4	P-36A: 9A/C, of which 2 DAM P-36C: 4 A/C
TOTAL	1	44	26	= 71 P-36 Total in U.S.
DAM	-1	-10	5	= -14DAM
12-7-41 TOTAL OPS	0	34	21	= 55 Ops in Continental U.S.

Overseas Locations of P-36, December 7, 1941

	YP-36	P-36A	P-36C	
Hawaii				
Wheeler F, TH	0	39	0	P-36A: 38-002DAM, -011DAM, -021, -022 -027, -031, -032, -036DAM & L, -045DAM, -055, -057, -063L, -073, -076L, -078DAM(condemned as L but then fixed), -082, -086, -090, -092, -093, -098, -102, -109, -110, -111L, -118L, -121DAM, -124, -125L, -128L, -133DAM, - 145DAM (condemned as L but then fixed), -149DAM, - 160L, -161DAM, -167DAM, -169, -171, -176DAM & L
Hawaiian Air Depot, HAD, TH	0	2	0	P-36A: 38-127, Lost on 12-7-41 38-152, Lost on 12-7-41
	0	41	0	P-36A: 41 A/C, of which 14 DAM

L= Lost on 12-7-41
= 9 lost at Wheeler + 2 lost at HAD = 11 P-36A lost,
+ 2 condemned as LOST at Wheeler, but later repaired

2 of the 9 lost were shot down in aerial combat to Zero & to AA, and the pilots KIA
1 of the 9 was DBR in aerial combat 38-086 and LOST
3 were damaged in the air
6 lost on the ground

Known A/C that flew sorties that day were: 38-092, —057, -090, -169 (and 38-086)

	YP-36	P-36A	P-36C	
Elmendorf, Alaska				
Elmendorf F	0	19	0	P-36A: 38-013, -014DAM, -017, -019DAM, -025, -026, -028, -030, -033, 034, -061, -066, -068, -069DAM. -071, -074, -089, -095, -097DAM
	0	19	0	P-36A: 19 A/C, of which 4 DAM
Panama				
Albrook F	0	9	0	P-36A: 38-005, -051DAM, -054, -060, -105, -106, -142, -159, -175
Rio Hato F	0	6	0	P-36A: 38-037DAM, -039, -043, -050, -053, -158
	0	15	0	P-36A: 15 A/C, of which 2 DAM
Puerto Rico				
Borniquen F	0	5	0	P-36A: 38-100, -104, -107DAM, -141, -151
Losey F, Ponce	0	8	0	P-36A: 38-112, -114DAM, -120DAM, -122, -123, -144DAM, -163DAM, -173DAM
	0	13	0	P-36A: 13 A/C, of which 6 DAM
TOTAL OVERSEAS	0	88	0	= 88 A/C Overseas
DAM	0	-26	-0	= -26 DAM

12-7-41 TOTAL Ops 0 62 0 = 62 A/C P-36 Ops Overseas

P-36 TOTALS: TOTAL BUILT:

3 YP-36	-	2 LOST	=	1 YP-36	-	1 DAM	=	0 YP-36 Ops
180 P-36A	-	48 LOST	=	130 P-36A	-	36 DAM	=	94 P-36A Ops
1 XP-40	-	0 DAM	=	1 XP-40 Ops				
1 XP-42	-	0 DAM	=	1 XP-42 Ops				
30 P-30C	-	4 LOST	=	26 P-36C	-	5 DAM	=	21 P-36C Ops
213 P-36	-	54 LOST	=	159 P-36	-	42 DAM	=	117 P-36 Ops
		71 CONUS		-		16 DAM		= 55 CONUS Ops
		88 Overseas		-		26 DAM		= 62 Overseas Ops

**DAM means actually documented damage from the Record Cards for a significant period of time where no or little flight time is recorded, OR when there is a period of 2 months or more near the 12-7-41 time where little or no flight time is recorded. It is assumed that there was a major maintenance reason why the aircraft did not fly, and hence was unavailable. LOST means that an aircraft was actually written off, or did not fly again after an accident. It is assumed that the aircraft was LOST at that time, and it is NOT based on Survey or Condemned bureaucratic paper dates, nor if the aircraft went to a school or CL-26 and never flew again. It is considered LOST at the actual date of the accident.

P-40 Locations, December 7, 1941 in Continental U.S.

Location	P-40	P-40G	P-40B	P-40C	P-40D	P-40E	Serial #'s
1st Air Force, NE							
Mitchel F, Long Island, NY	34	2	0	9	0	2	P-40: 39-161, -163, -164DAM, -165DAM, -168, -169, -170DAM, -172, -173DAM, -174, -175, -181DAM, -184, -189, -192, -205, -208, -210DAM, -215, -216, -218DAM, -219, -222DAM, -223DAM -227, -230, -232DAM, -233, -261, -281(lost 12-7-41), -283, 40-296, -330DAM, -339, -350 P-40G: 39-176DAM, 39-206DAM P-40C: 41-13338, -13347, -13379, -13380, -13387, -13393DAM, -13456DAM, -13500 P-40E: 40-383, -487
Groton, CT	0	0	0	0	0	1	P-40E: 40-520
Windsor Locks, CT	0	0	0	1	0	0	P-40C: 41-13365
Selfridge F, MI	3	4	0	0	0	2	P-40: 40-324, -345DAM, -350 P-40G: 40-323, -331, -337DAM -340DAM P-40E: 40-492, -513
Chanute F, IL	1	0	0	0	0	0	P-40: 39-158
Bolling F, DC	1	0	0	0	0	0	P-40: 39-188
Langley F, VA	1	0	0	0	0	0	P-40: 39-225DAM
Wright F. OH	1 3	0	1	1	0	2	XP-40: 38-10 (ex P-36A) P-40: 39-259. 40-351, 40-353 P-40B: 41-5205 P-40C: 41-13385 P-40E: 40-584, -5521
Patterson F, OH	0	0	0	2	1	11	P-40C: 41-13339DAM, -13501DAM P-40D: 40-361DAM P-40E: 41-385DAM, -412, -582, -600, -607, -627, -628, -629DAM, 633 P-40E: 41-5449, -5455
FAD, OH	1	1	0	0	0	0	P-40: 40-334DAM P-40G: 40-348DAM
MAD, PA	1	2	0	8	0	4	P-40: 39-156DAM P-40G: 39-204DAM, 39-220DAM P-40C: 41-13343DAM, -133368DAM, -13377DAM, -13382DAM, -13386DAM, -13391DAM, -13394DAM, -13449DAM P-40E: 40-389DAM, -392DAM, -401DAM, -428DAM
Allison Engine, IN	0	0	0	0	1	0	P-40D: 40-359
Curtiss A/C, Buffalo, NY	1	23 (1)	0 (26)	0	1	4	P-40: 40-327DAM P-40G: 7 of these a/c kept their original #'s, and 6 of these were Taken back by US on 12-26-41 at March F, & stayed in the Continental US: 39-243, -248, -275, -279, -288, -300 However, 39-221 kept its number & went to USSR in 1943. A further 17 of these a/c were somehow taken off the official Record for export to USSR, but then taken back by AAF at March F on 12-26-41, so they had to be issued new serial #'s while they stayed in the Continental US under their new #'s and were never sent to USSR. OLD #'s: 39-162, -182, -191, -196, -209, -217, -238, -297, -301, -303, -309, -318, -320, -332, -335, -336, -338 All of these went through MAD and Curtiss, and were Assigned new Serial #'s with no pattern: NEW #'s: 42-14261 thru -14274, -14277, -14277, -14281 Only 2 assigned #'s are definitely known: 39-182 became 41-14269 and 40-338 became 41-14261 P-40C: 10 a/c were pulled for shipment to Yugoslavia 6-11-41, But then diverted to UK and USSR: 41-13389, -13390, -13396, -13397, -13398, -13399, -13400, -13401, -13406, -13407. Apparently all were exported at some time. —Another 32 a/c were taken from service in Puerto Rico, refurbished by Curtiss. 16 a/c were sent on Defense Aid directly to USSR from 10-27-41 to 11-3-41: 41-13351, -13353, -13354, -13355, -13356, -13357,

							-13358, -13369, -13370, -13371, -13373, -13374, -13395, -13450, -13451, -13469 The other 16 a/c were kept in the U.S. by the U.S. P-40D: 40-362DAM P-40E: 40-386, -405DAM, -432, -599
TOTAL	46 +1 XP40	32 (1)	1 + (26)	21	3	26	P-40 = 48 A/C, of which 15 DAM P-40G = 32 A/C, of which 5 DAM, + 1 for export export export P-40B = 1 A/C P-40C = 21 A/C, of which 12 DAM, + 26 for export P-40D = 3 A/C, of which 2 DAM P-40E = 27 A/C, of which 7 DAM
2nd Air Force, NW							
Lowry F, CO	1	0	0	0	1	0	P-40: 39-157DAM P-40D: 40-376DAM
Everett F, WA	5	0	0	0	0	0	P-40: 39-246, -254, -274, -277, -280
TOTAL	6	0	0	0	1	0	P-40: 6 A/C, of which 1 DAM P-40D: 1 A/C
3rd Air Force, SE							
Jackson, MS	1	0	0	0	0	0	P-40: 40-352DAM
Maxwell F, AL	1	0	0	0	0	0	P-40: 40-326, became P-40A, 3-2-42
Palm Beach, FL	3	0	0	0	0	0	P-40: 39-160DAM, -195DAM, -229
Tallahassee, FL	4	0	0	0	0	0	P-40: 39-185, -186DAM, -211DAM, 40-357
Eglin F, FL	0	0	0	0	0	4	P-40E: 40-521, -603, -605, -606
Macon, GA	0	0	0	1	0	0	P-40C: 41-13416
TOTAL	9	0	0	1	0	4	P-40: 9 A/C, 3 of which DAM P-40C: 1 A/C P-40E: 4 A/C
4th Air Force, SW							
March F, CA	21	2	1	0	0	2	P-40: 39-234, -237DAM, -244, -245, -249, -251DAM, -271, -286, -289, 40-293, -298, -302DAM, -306, -307, -313, -314, -316, -317, -321, -328DAM, -355 P-40G: 39-257, 39-292 P-40B: 41-5238 P-40E: 40-399, -404
Hamilton F, CA	3	0	0	4	3	50	P-40: 39-269, 40-322, -349 P-40C: 41-13381, -13383, -13384, -13459 P-40D: 40-363, -365DAM, -374 P-40E: 40-387, -390, -395, -396, -402, -406, -407, -410, -411, -413, -415, -417, -418, -419, -420, -422, -423, -424, -425, -427, -430, -434, -435, -437, -438DAM, -440DAM, -444DAM, -446, -447, -449, -452DAM, -455, -456, -460, -484, -486, -494, -497, -498, -499, -500, -501, -502, -510, -511, - 525, -526, -528, -532, -539
Long Beach, CA	5	0	0	0	0	0	P-40: 39-268DAM, -270DAM, 40-304, -308, -347
SAD, CA	1	0	0	0	15	52	P-40: 40-319DAM P-40D: 40-365DAM Other 14 a/c in transit to reinforce Philippines and then Hawaii 1-7-42: 40-364DAM, -366DAM, -367DAM, -368, -369, -370, -371DAM, -372, -373, -377, -378, -379, -380, -381DAM P-40E: 40-358, -384, -431DAM, -433DAM All 25 a/c assigned to prep to reinforce Hawaii 1-7-42: 40-388, -394, -398M, -400, 408, -409, -436, -439M, -441, -443, -445, -450M, -451, -457, -458M, -459, -461, -493, -512, -518M, -519, -527, -533, -535, -542 All 23 a/c assigned to winterize & prep for Elmendorf, Alaska 1-17-42 40-549, -583, -585, -586, -587, -588, -589, -590, -591, -592, -593, -594, -595, -596, -597, -598, -601, -602, -608, -609, -610, -611, -612

SAAD, San Antonio, TX							
TX	1	0	0	0	0	5	P-40: 39-284DAM P-40E: 40-414DAM, -421DAM, -426DAM, -454DAM, -495DAM
TOTAL	30	2	1	4	18	108	P-40: 31 A/C, 5 of which DAM P-40G: 2 A/C P-40B: 1 A/C P-40C: 4 A/C P-40D: 18 A/C , 1 DAM, 14 in transit to Hawaii P-40E: 108 A/C, 10 of which DAM 25 prep for Hawaii
TOTAL IN CONTINENTAL U.S. 23 prep for Alaska							
1st AF	47	32	1	21	3	26	
2nd AF	6	0	0	0	0	0	
3rd AF	9	0	0	1	1	4	
4th AF	31	2	1	4	18	109	
	93	34	2	26	22	139	(62 prepping for transit)= 316 TOTAL + 27 export not counted
DAM	-29	-12	-0	-12	-10	- 15	- 80
OPS	64	22	2	14	12	124	= 256 Ops in Continental US

IN CONTINENTAL U.S., FRESH FROM THE FACTORY, DESIGNATED AS REINFORCEMENTS FOR SW PACIFIC

ALL designated “X”, “XYZ” or “Project X” upon delivery. All delivered before 12-7-41 to unknown location location in U.S. Probably at Curtiss in Buffalo or at SAD. All designated for SW Pacific, but all might not have ended up there from this group. It is known that 111 P-40E arrived by convoy in Australia on 2-4-42, most likely from this group.	0	0	0	0	0	131	P-40E: 41-5307, -5311, -5315, -5319, -5323, -5327, -5331, -5332, -5333, -5335, -5336, -5337, -5338, -5339, -5344, -5345, -5346, -5348, -5349, -5350, -5351, -5352, -5353, -5355, -5356, -5357, -5358, -5359, -5360, -5361, -5362, -5363UK, -5364UK, -5365UK, -5366UK, -5367UK, -5368UK, -5369UK, -5370UK, -5371UK, -5372UK, -5373UK, -5374UK, -5376UK, -5377UK -5378UK, -5379UK, -5380UK, -5381UK, -5382UK, -5384UK, -5386UK, -5392UK, -5394UK, -5395UK, -5397UK, -5398UK, -5399UK, -5400UK, -5401UK, -5402UK, -5403, -5404, -5405 -5406, -5407, -5409, -5413UK, -5414, -5415UK, -5416, -5417, -5418UK, -5419, -5420, -5423, -5424UK, -5425UK, -5426UK, -5427, -5428UK, -5432UK, -5434, -5436UK, -5437UK, -5438, -5439, -5440, -5441, -5442, -5443UK, -5444UK, -5445UK, -5446UK, -5447UK, -5448UK, -5450UK, -5451UK, -5452, -5454UK, -5456UK, -5457, -5458UK, -5460UK, -5461UK, -5462UK, -5463UK, -5465UK, -5468, -5470UK, -5475UK, -5477UK, -5479UK, -5480UK, -5481UK, -5485UK, -5486UK, -5488UK, -5490UK, -5494UK, -5496UK, -5497UK, -5498UK, -5499UK, -5503UK, -5504UK, -5506UK, -5507UK, -5523UK, -5524, -5527UK
Some alternate Deliver YDestinations given. Many A/C alread Yin U.S. also targeted for “XYZ” delivery “UK “ means repossessed from UK allocation, 12-24-41 to 1-11-42						46	To Wheeler F: 41-5375UK-M, -5383UK, -5385UK-M, -5387UK, -5388UK-M, -5389UK, -5390UK, -5391UK, -5393UK, -5396UK, -5408, -5410UK, -5411UK-M, -5412UK, -5421UK, -5422UK, -5429UK, -5430UK, -5431UK-M, -5433UK, -5435UK-M, -5453UK, -5459UK-M, -5464UK, -5466UK-M, -5467UK-M, -5469UK, -5471UK, -5472UK, -5473UK, -5474UK, -5476UK-M, -5478UK, -5482UK, -5483UK, -5484UK-M, -5487UK, -5489UK-M, -5491UK-M -5492UK, -5493UK-M, 5495UK, -5500UK, -5501UK, -5502UK-M, -5505UK
77 A/C + 46 A/C = at least 123 A/C repossessed from UK contract						2 25	To Hamilton F, 1-29-41: 41-5347, 5354UK To Defense Aid to Russia, 12-41: 41-5340, -5341, -5342, -5343, 40-613, -636, -641, -644, -645, -648, -649, -652, -653, -656, -657, -660, -661, -664, -665, -668, -669, -672, -673, -676, -680

"-M" means sent to reinforce Midwa
Yafter the Battle of
Midway on USS
Saratoga, 14 A/C

204 P-40E fresh from factory, assigned to "XYZ ", SW Pacific

TOTAL BUILT BY 12-7-41 -	LOST	- EXPORT	=	TOTAL 12 -7-41	
XP-40 = 1	- 0	- 0	=	1 = XP-40	
P-40 = 154	- 62	- 0	=	92 = P-40	
P-40G = 46	- 11	- 1	=	34 = P-40G	
P-40B = 131	- 13	- 0	=	118 = P-40B	
P-40C = 193	- 23	- 26	=	144 = P-40C	
P-40D = 23	- 1	- 0	=	22 = P-40D	
P-40E = 301	- 14	- 0	=	493 = P-40E	
TOTAL = 1055	- 124	- 27	=	904 in U.S. Service =	316 Continental U.S.
					349 Overseas
					35 P-40E in transit to Philippines
					204 P-40E Committed to "XYZ" SW Pacific
				Total	904 A/C

***"DAM" Means that the a/c was documented as damaged and out of service for a prolonged period over the 12-7-41 date, due to major damage, such as 2nd or 3rd Echelon maintenance. It also includes a/c with no hours recorded for 2 months or more, with the assumption that there was some type of damage or maintenance issue with the aircraft. Aircraft were also counted as LOST if they were not flown operationally (no recorded hours), regardless if they were at a Depot or notÖ.if they were not flown again and put back into flyable service, they were counted as LOST as of the actual date of the accident. There was sometimes a tremendous lead time after an accident before an aircraft was surveyed or condemned or sent to a maintenance school or Class 26. Even if the airframe or pieces may have existed, if it was not flown again, then it was effectively LOST as of the date of the accident, rather than relying on the whims of the bureaucracy of official paperwork.

P-40 Locations Overseas, December 7, 1941

HAWAII

Location							Aircraft
Wheeler F	0	0	56	0	0	0	P-40B: 41-5207DAM, -5210DAM, -5211L, -5212L, -5213DAM, -5214L, -5215L, -5216L, -5217L, -5218L, -5219L, -5220L, -5221, -5222DAM & L, -5223, -5224, -5225L, -5226L, -5227L, -5228L, -5229L, -5230, -5231, -5232L, -5233L, -5234, -5235L, -5236DAM, -5237DAM, -5239, -5241,
	0						-5242L, -5243DAM, -5244L, -5245, -5246L, -5247DAM & L, -5248, -5249, -5250DAM, -5251
	0						-5252L, -5253, -5254, -5255, -5257L, -5286, -5291L, -5293, -5294, -5295, -5298, -5299L, -5301, -5303DAM, -5304DAM
	0	0	23	0	0	0	41-13297DAM, -13299DAM, -13300L -13302DAM,, -13303L, -13304DAM, -13305, -13306, -13307, -13308, -13310DAM & L, -13312L, -13313, -13314DAM, -13316DAM, -13317L, -13318, -13320DAM & L, -13321DAM, -13322DAM, -13324L, -13325, -13326
	0	0	0	3	0	0	P-40C: 41-13331DAM & L, -13349, -13366
Bellows F	0	0	6	0	0	0	P-40B: 41-5206, -5208L, -5209L 41-13315, -13319, -13323 P-40C: 41-13328L, -13329, -13330L, -13332, -13336, -13337L, -13340DAM, -13344, -13367
HAD, Hickam	0	0	1	0	0	0	P-40B: 41-5330L (damaged 10-10-41), LOST PH
	0	0	86	12	0	0	P-40B: 86 A/C, of which 21DAM, L=36 P-40B a/c lost at PH (+ 5 P-40B A/C originally condemned and listed as LOST at PH, but later repaired: 41-5231, -5237, -5250, -5251, -5304) P-40C: 12 A/C, of which 2 DAM L= 4 P-40C a/c lost at PH

PHILIPPINES							
Clark F.	0	0	25	0	0	0	P-40B: 41-5258, -5259, -5260, -5261DAM, -5263DAM, -5264, -5265, -5266DAM, -5267, -5268, -5270, -5271, -5272, -5273, -5274, -5275DAM, -5277, - 5279, -5281, -5282,. 5285, -5287, -5288, -5289, -5290
Clark F (all assigned here but stationed at: Nichols F, 17 PS = 21a/c	0	0	0	0	0	47	P-40E: 40-462, -464, -465, -466, -467, -468, -469,-470, -471, -472, -474, -475, -476, -477, -478, -479, -480, -481, -482, -483, -488, -489, -490, -491, -496, -503, -504, -505, -507, -508, -509, -514, -515, -516, -517, -522, -523, -524, -529, -530, -531, -536, -537, -538, -543, -544, -545 (2 of these DAMAGED)
Iba F, 3 PS = = 24 a/c Nichols F, 21PS Received last of 24 a/c, 12-8-41	0	0	0	0	0	24	P-40E: 40-616, -617, -618, -619, -620, -621, -622, -623, -624, -625, -626, -634, -635, -638, -639, -642, -643, -646, -647, -650, -651, -654, -655, -659
	0	0	25	0	0	71	P-40B: 25 A/C, of which 4 damaged P-40E: 71 A/C, of which 2 damaged
EN ROUTE TO PHILIPPINES, Part I							
Likely on Freighter SS Blomfontein, Arrived in Australia In a convoy, 12-22-42. 18 a/c crated and likely from this list	0	0	0	0	0	14	P-40E: 40-646, -658 ,-662, -663, -666, -667, -670, -671, -674, -675, -677, -678, -679, -681, ASSIGNED TO PHAD IN THE PHILIPPINES
	0	0	0	0	0	14	P-40E: 14 A/C in Transit
ENROUTE TO PHILIPPINES, PART II							
Likely on Freighter SS Luddington, 20 a/c likely from this list already crated and loaded.	0	0	0	0	0	21	P-40E: 41-5305, -5306, -5308, -5309, -5310, -5312, -5313, -5314, -5316, -5317, 5318, -5320, -5321, -5322, -5324, -5325, -5326 -5328, -5329, -5330, -5334 (One of these #'s, unknown, belongs in the above shipment in Part I) ASSIGNED TO PHAD IN THE PHILIPPINES
	0	0	0	0	0	21	P-40E: 21 A/C in transit
ICELAND							
Reykjavik	0	0	0	30	0	0	P-40C: 41-13341DAM, -13345DAM, -13346DAM, -13350, -13419DAM, -13420, -13421, -13423, -13424DAM, -13426, -13427, -13429DAM, -13431, -13433, -13436, -13437DAM, -13438DAM, -13439DAM, -13440DAM, -13444DAM, -13445DAM, -13446, -13452DAM, -13455, -13458, -13460, -13462DAM, -13463, -13464DAM, -13465
	0	0	0	30	0	0	P-40C: 30 A/C, of which 15 DAM
PANAMA	P-40	P-40G	P-40B	P-40C	P-40D	P-40E	
Albrook F	0	0	5	50	0	15	P-40B: 41-5283, -5292, -5297, - 41-13298DAM, -13327 P-40C: 41-13335, -13402, -13405DAM, -13413, -13415, -13417 -13418, -13430, -13434, -13435, -13441, -13442DAM, -13443, -13448, -13453, -13461, -13466, -13467, -13468, -13470, -13473, -13474, -13475, -13476, -13477, -13478DAM, -13479, -13481DAM, -13482, -13483DAM, -13484, -13485, -13486,-13487DAM, -13488 -13489, -13490, -13491, -13492, -13494, -13495, -13496DAM, -13497DAM, -13498, -13499, -13502, -13503, -13506, -13507DAM, -13508 P-40E: 40-448, -574, -575, -577, -578, -579, -580, -581, -604, -614, -630, -631, -632, -637, -640,
	0	0	5	50	0	15	P-40B: 5 A/C, of which 1 DAM P-40C: 50 A/C, of which 9 DAM P-40E: 15 A/C

PUERTO RICO							
LoseyF, Ponce	0	0	0	17	0	29	P-40C: 41-13359, -13360, -13361, -13362, -13363DAM, -13372, -13376, -13378, -13447DAM, -13457DAM, -13509, -13511, -13512, -13513, -13514, -13516, -13519 P-40E: 40-382, -534, -540, -541, -546, -547, -548, -550, -551, -552DAM, -553, -554, -555, -556, -557, -558, -559, -560DAM, -561, -562,-563, -564, -566, -567, -568, -569, -570, -571, -572
	0	0	0	17	0	29	P-40C: 17 A/C, of which 3 DAM P-40E: 29 A/C, of which 2 DAM
TRINIDAD							
Waller F	0	0	0	8	0	0	P-40C: 41-13408, -13409, -13410DAM, -13411, -13412, -13414, -13432, -13505
	0	0	0	8	0	0	P-40C: 8 A/C, of which 1 DAM
VIRGIN ISLANDS							
Benedict F	0	0	0	1	0	0	P-40C: 41-13388
	0	0	0	1	0	0	P-40C: 1 A/C
OVERSEAS TOTALS							
Hawaii =	0	0	86	12	0	0	
Philippines =	0	0	25	0	0	71	
Panama =	0	0	5	50	0	15	
Puerto Rico =	0	0	0	17	0	29	
Trinidad & V.I. =	0	0	0	9	0	0	
Iceland =	0	0	0	30	0	0	
TOTAL	0	0	116	118	0	115	= 349 Total Overseas + 35 P-40E enroute + 204 in U.S. designated
DAM -	0	0	- 26	- 30	0	- 4	- 60 for "XYZ"
TOTAL OPS 12-7-41	0	0	90	88	0	111	= 289 Ops Overseas, 12-7-41
En route =	0	0	0	0	0	35	
XYZ =	0	0	0	0	0	204	

Annex 4: P-40N and *Kittyhawk IV* Series Aircraft Initial Assignments Factory New

Not less than 5,678 P-40N and *Kittyhawk IV* series aircraft were produced by the Curtiss factories in Buffalo between March 1943 and November 1944, when production finally came to an end.

These, the definitive versions of the P-40 series, have been largely ignored by historians, and some published works have gone so far as to record that the entire P-40N series did nothing more than equip "second line" and school units. While it is true that many of these aircraft did in fact serve in the vital training system in the Continental United States, a significant number were shipped to active overseas combat theaters, where they were gratefully received.

Curtiss company records note the initial, intended destination for nearly all of the P-40Ns, from the time they left the factory or were flown to the seldom cited Curtiss-Wright and Bell Modification Centers. Based on a comparison of the Curtiss data with U.S. Army Air Forces History Cards, these shipping details are reliable in nearly all instances. It is interesting to note, however, that a number of P-40Ns had no listed destination whatsoever in Curtiss records, indicating that they were flown away from the factory by ATC ferry crews and probable U.S. assignments, since equipment and markings were often linked to the destination.

The destination codes and USAAF organizational titles shown in this Annex are precisely as listed in Curtiss records and, in a number of instances, conflict with more common usage

AIR MATERIEL COMMAND, USAAF	**NUMBER**
Unspecified Air Materiel Command activities, Continental U.S	2
AMC, Dover Army Air Field, Delaware	1
AMC for redelivery to Destination Code	
GOAT (Canada)	1
Wright Field, Ohio	6

AIR TRANSPORT COMMAND, USAAF	**NUMBER**
Unspecified Air Transport Command activities	10
ATC from Buffalo **"DOM" Project 1869A**	1
ATC from Buffalo **"SEA" (Brazil)** .	1
ATC Palm Springs Army Air Field, Palm Springs, California	5
ATC San Antonio, Texas (unspecified location there)	22

ALASKA	**NUMBER**
Project 92131R*	6
Elmendorf Field, Alaska	6
Via Curtiss-Wright Modification Center (probably winterization) for Elmendorf Field, Alaska	22
Via Great Falls, Montana for Elmendorf Field, Alaska **Project 96310R**	2
Via Wayne County Airport **Project 92150R****	5
Via Wright Field, Ohio	
Project 92198R .	1

*Project 92131R actually totaled 30 P-40Ns for Destination Code **GOOSEWING** as flight delivered replacements for units in the Alaskan theater.
Project 92150R actually totaled 10 P-40Ns for Destination Code **GOOSEWING as flight delivered replacements for units in the Alaskan theater

BALTIMORE, MARYLAND PORT OF EMBARKATION	**NUMBER**
Unspecified destination from Baltimore ..	1

BRITISH FOR RUSSIA	**NUMBER**
Via unspecified Port of Embarkation	141

CURTISS-WRIGHT MODIFICATION CENTER	**NUMBER**
For unspecified modifications and unknown subsequent destination ..	14
For **Project DOM-857** .	

FLYING TRAINING COMMAND*, USAAF	**NUMBER**
Unspecified activity .	119
Abilene Army Air Field, Abilene, Texas .	13
Dothan, Alabama .	9
Eagle Pass, Texas .	21
Marianna, Florida .	22
Mission, Texas .	4
Phoenix, Arizona ..	10

Romulus, Michigan ..	3
Selma, Alabama	5
Victoria, Texas .	8

*At least 62 of these aircraft were flight delivered to Flying Training Command activities commencing as early as May 26, 1943, some of the very earliest P-40N deliveries.

DESTINATION CODE "BADE" (SIXTH AIR FORCE, CANAL ZONE AND CARIBBEAN REGION)	**NUMBER**
Including **Projects 94050R, 94066R**	24
Via Romulus, Michigan Port of Embarkation **Project 94050R** .	1
Via Sarasota, Florida **Project 94050R**	1
Via Tampa, Florida Port of Embarkation **Project 94066R** .	1
Via Wayne County Airport Port of Embarkation **Projects 94022, 94023** and **94037R***	15

*Project 94037R covered 10 P-40Ns flight delivered as replacements for units in the Sixth Air Force

DESTINATION CODE "BASS" (NEW ZEALAND)	**NUMBER**
Via unspecified Port of Embarkation	9
Via Galveston, Texas Port of Embarkation ..	80
Via New York City, New York Port of Embarkation ..	64
Via Oakland, California Port of Embarkation ..	10
Via Vancouver, British Columbia, Canada Port of Embarkation	20

DESTINATION CODE "BAX" (NETHERLANDS EAST INDIES)	**NUMBER**
Via Newark, New Jersey Port of Embarkation	12

DESTINATION CODE "BENT" (CALCUTTA, INDIA, TENTH AIR FORCE)	**NUMBER**
Including Projects 90103R, 90333R, 90335R .	69
Via Curtiss-Wright Modification Center for unspecified modifications prior to shipment	36
Via Newark, New Jersey Port of Embarkation **Project 90238R** .	15
Via Rome Army Air Field, New York **Project 90245R** ..	1

DESTINATION CODE "BIRD" (CHINA)	**NUMBER**
Via unspecified Port of Embarkation	52
Via Montreal, Quebec, Canada Port of Embarkation ..	20
Via New York, New York Port of Embarkation .	2
Via Newark, New Jersey Port of Embarkation	200
Via Philadelphia, Pennsylvania Port of Embarkation ..	22
Via St. Johns, New Brunswick, Canada Port of Embarkation .	28

DESTINATION CODE "DAUB" (KARACHI, INDIA, TENTH AIR FORCE)	**NUMBER**
Project 90416R .	9
Via Charleston, South Carolina Port of Embarkation **Project 6128-Air**	83
Via Curtiss-Wright Modification Center for unspecified modifications prior to shipment on **Project 90338R** and **90464R** ..	43
Via unspecified Port of Embarkation **Project 90103R**	4
Via Detroit, Michigan Port of Embarkation **Project 90337R** ..	3
Via Long Beach, California Port of Embarkation **Projects 90337R, 90416R**	12

DESTINATION CODE "GOAT" (CANADA)	**NUMBER**
Via unspecified means ..	15
After "Curtiss for Test"	1
Rockliffe Field .	10
Via Romulus, Michigan "U.N." ..	1
Vancouver, British Columbia	7
Via Wayne County Airport Port of Embarkation .	9

DESTINATION CODE "HARE" (NETHERLANDS EAST INDIES)	**NUMBER**
Via Long Beach, California Port of Embarkation	12
Via New York, New York Port of Embarkation ..	12
Via Newark, New Jersey Port of Embarkation	28

DESTINATION CODE "IRON" (HAWAII, SEVENTH AIR FORCE)	NUMBER
Via Stockton, California Port of Embarkation, **Projects 96015R** and **96046R** ..	21

DESTINATION CODE "LEFT" (BRISBANE, AUSTRALIA, FIFTH AIR FORCE	NUMBER
Via Alameda, California Port of Embarkation including **Projects 96152R*, 96176R** and **"Export"**	32
Via ATC Buffalo including **Projects 96687R, 96720R, 96768R** ..	81
Via Curtiss-Wright Modification Center **Project 96175R** for unspecified modifications before shipment	1
Via Long Beach, California Port of Embarkation **Project 96175R**	14
Via Oakland, California Port of Embarkation **Project 96159R** .	39
Via Stockton, California Port of Embarkation **Project 96159R**	88

*Project 96152R covered 15 P-40Ns shipped by surface vessel to Destination Code **SPAVIN** as replacements for units in the theater. Project 96151R was also for 15 for the same destination, but has not been linked with specific serials.

DESTINATION CODE "LYNX" (AUSTRALIA)	NUMBER
Via unspecified Port of Embarkation .	21
Via New Orleans, Louisiana Port of Embarkation .	1
Via New York, New York Port of Embarkation .	257
Via Oakland, California Port of Embarkation .	1

DESTINATION CODE "MINK" (GREAT BRITAIN)	NUMBER
Via Baltimore, Maryland Port of Embarkation	44
Via New York, New York Port of Embarkation ..	265
Via Newark, New Jersey Port of Embarkation	25
Via Newport News, Virginia Port of Embarkation .	81
Via Philadelphia, Pennsylvania Port of Embarkation .	90
Via U.N. Depot No.4, Buffalo, New York ..	7

DESTINATION CODE "MINK" (GREAT BRITAIN) FOR FURTHER SHIPMENT TO "MOTH" (RUSSIA)	NUMBER
Via Newark, New Jersey Port of Embarkation	19

DESTINATION CODE "MOTH" (RUSSIA)	NUMBER
Via New York, New York and Philadelphia, Pennsylvania Ports of Embarkation .	343
Via Newark, New Jersey Port of Embarkation	234
Via Philadelphia, Pennsylvania Port of Embarkation ..	247
Via Romulus, Michigan	1

DESTINATION CODE "PACT" (CHUNGKING, CHINA, FOURTEENTH AIR FORCE)	NUMBER
Via Curtiss-Wright Modification Center prior to shipment for unspecified modifications including **Projects 90246R** and **90334R** ..	49
Via Detroit, Michigan Port of Embarkation for **Project 90336R**	2
Via Long Beach, California Port of Embarkation including **Projects 90105R, 90106R, 90239R, 90332R, 90334R** and **90336R**	118
Via Newark, New Jersey Port of Embarkation for **Project 90239R**	17
Via Wayne County Airport Port of Embarkation **Project 90218R** .	5
Via Wilmington, Delaware Port of Embarkation **Projects 90197R, 90218R** and **90224R** ..	6

DESTINATION CODE "PEWTER" (REYKJAVIK, ICELAND) OR "OILY"	NUMBER
Via Curtiss-Wright Modification Center (probably for winterization) for Iceland (two of these aircraft were redesignated as type **P-40NT** for reasons unknown) ..	11

DESTINATION CODE "TAX" (AUSTRALIA)	NUMBER
Via New Brunswick, Canada Port of Embarkation .	8
Via New York, New York Port of Embarkation ..	64
Via Oakland, California Port of Embarkation ..	129
Via San Francisco, California Port of Embarkation .	9

NEWARK, NEW JERSEY PORT OF EMBARKATION	NUMBER
Unspecified destination beyond Newark ..	4

OMAHA MODIFICATION CENTER	NUMBER
For 2nd **Air Commando Group** (possibly **TP-40N** conversions)	4

PROJECT 90108R (DESTINATION UNKNOWN)	NUMBER
	26

PROJECT 96015R (DESTINATION UNKNOWN)	**NUMBER**
	2

ROME ARMY AIR FIELD DEPOT, NEW YORK	**NUMBER**
By truck for repair, modification, salvage and/or redelivery to unspecified destinations	6

ROYAL NETHERLANDS FLYING TRAINING SCHOOL	**NUMBER**
Jackson, Mississippi .	10

SAN FRANCISCO, CALIFORNIA	**NUMBER**
Assumed for shipment, but destination not specified ..	12

SECOND AIR FORCE	**NUMBER**
(Unspecified Second Air Force activities)	154

STOCKTON, CALIFORNIA PORT OF EMBARKATION	**NUMBER**
Unspecified final destination	12

THIRD AIR FORCE, USAAF	**NUMBER**
(Unspecified Third Air Force activities) ..	658*
Bell Modification Center for **Project DOM-857, 10th Tac Rcn Sq, Esler Field**	3
Bell Modification Center for **Project DOM-857, 69th Rcn Grp**	4
Curtiss-Wright Modification Center, Romulus, (Fry), MI to unspecified Third AF activity	16
Curtiss-Wright Modification Center to San Antonio then Key Field, **347th BAS** .	1
Curtiss-Wright Modification Center to **Project 853** then **22nd Tac Rcn Sq, Morris Field, NC** .	1
Curtiss-Wright Modification Center to San Antonio, **Project 853** and **857** then to **74th Tac Rcn Gp**, **DeRidder, LA** and **Morris Field** ..	15
Curtiss-Wright Modification Center to **Project 854**	6
Curtiss-Wright Modification Center to **Project 854** then **10th Tac Rcn Sq, Esler Field**	1
Curtiss-Wright Modification Center to **Project 854** then **385th BAS, Tuskegee, AL**	1
Curtiss-Wright Modification Center or Bell Modification Center to **Project 857** then **3d Composite Squadron, Lawson Field** ..	4
Curtiss-Wright Modification Center to San Antonio, **31st Sub Depot, Esler Field** then **75th Tac Rcn,** Key Field	6
Dallas, Texas	2
DeRidder Army Air Base, Louisiana **408th Fighter Bomber Group** .	6
Eglin Field, Florida ..	1
Esler Field, Alexandria, Louisiana ..	41
Fairfield, Ohio .	1
Fort Meyers, Florida .	42
Long Beach Army Air Field, Long Beach, California .	2
Meridian, Mississippi **"DOM"**	1
Niagara Falls, New York ..	2
Patterson Field, Ohio	1
Perry, Florida	1
Philadelphia, Pennsylvania ..	1
Sarasota Army Air Field, Florida .	39
Sarasota Army Air Field, Florida **337th Fighter Group** ..	2
Selfridge Field, Michigan .	16
Sherman Field, Fort Leavenworth, Kansas **335th Base Unit**	4
Thomasville, Georgia	10
Tullahoma, Tennessee (William Northern Field) and **74th Rcn Grp** ..	46
Venice, Florida .	57
Waycross, Georgia	9
Wayne County Airport .	122
Wayne County Airport, **332nd Fighter Group**	5

*At least 75 of the P-40Ns flight delivered from Curtiss to Third Air Force activities commencing May 26, 1943, had unspecified modifications to adapt them for dive bombing training. Ten others were replacements for fighter replacement training units from the same date and at least 100 others were flight delivered new commencing the same date throughout the command.

THIRD FIGHTER COMMAND, THIRD AIR FORCE	**NUMBER**
Tampa, Florida	8

Annex 5:
British Commonwealth Units Equipped with Curtiss *Tomahawk* and *Kittyhawk* Variants

This listing, prepared by Craig "Buz" Busby, reflects Commonwealth units that flew variants of these two principle aircraft in whole or in part, in an operational status. At least 30 to 40 additional miscellaneous units, such as Operational Training Units (OTUs) and the like, also had *Tomahawks* or *Kittyhawks* assigned at one time or another, but a definitive listing of these may never be accomplished.

South African Air Force

Squadron	Theater of Operations	Variants Flown
No.2 Squadron	With RAF in Middle East	*Tomahawk, Kittyhawk* (RAF aircraft)
No.4 Squadron	With RAF in Middle East	*Tomahawk, Kittyhawk* (RAF aircraft)
No.5 Squadron	With RAF in Middle East	*Tomahawk, Kittyhawk* (RAF aircraft)
No.7 Squadron		*Kittyhawk*
No.10 Squadron	South Africa only	*Kittyhawk I* with SAAF serials transferred from RAF
No.11 Squadron* (RAF aircraft)	With RAF in Italy	*Kittyhawk*
No.40 Squadron	With RAF in Middle East	*Tomahawk* (RAF aircraft, only partially equipped)

* One of only three Commonwealth Squadrons to still be flying *Kittyhawks* at the end of the war.

Royal Australian Air Force

Squadron	Theater of Operations	Variants Flown
No.3 Squadron	With RAF in Middle East and Italy	*Tomahawk, Kittyhawk* (RAF aircraft, one of two units to fly *Kittyhawk IIs)*
No.4 Squadron	Southwest Pacific Area	*Kittyhawks* (partially reequipped)
No.5 Squadron	Southwest Pacific Area	*Kittyhawks* (partially reequipped)
No.75 Squadron	Southwest Pacific Area	*Kittyhawks*
No.76 Squadron	Southwest Pacific Area	*Kittyhawks*
No.77 Squadron	Southwest Pacific Area	*Kittyhawks*
No.78 Squadron	Southwest Pacific Area	*Kittyhawks*
No.80 Squadron	Southwest Pacific Area	*Kittyhawks*
No.82 Squadron	Southwest Pacific Area	*Kittyhawks*
No.84 Squadron	Southwest Pacific Area	*Kittyhawks*
No.86 Squadron	Southwest Pacific Area	*Kittyhawks*

Royal Canadian Air Force

Squadron	Theater of Operations	Variants Flown
No.14 Squadron	Alaska	*Kittyhawk*
No.111 Squadron	Alaska	*Kittyhawk*
No.118 Squadron		*Kittyhawk*
No.130 Squadron		*Kittyhawk*
No.132 Squadron		*Kittyhawk*
No.133 Squadron		*Kittyhawk*
No.135 Squadron		*Kittyhawk*
No.163 Squadron		*Kittyhawk*

Royal New Zealand Air Force

Squadron	Theater of Operations	Variants Flown
No.14 Squadron		*Kittyhawk*
No.15 Squadron		*Kittyhawk*
No.16 Squadron		*Kittyhawk*
No.17 Squadron		*Kittyhawk*
No.18 Squadron		*Kittyhawk*
No.19 Squadron		*Kittyhawk*
No.20 Squadron		*Kittyhawk*
No.488 Squadron*		*Kittyhawk*

* Renumbered as No.14 Squadron above

Royal Air Force

Squadron	**Theater of Operations**	**Variants Flown**
No.2 Squadron	British Isles	*Tomahawk* (non-operational). First RAF unit equipped with *Tomahawks,* superseded by *Lysanders*
No.4 Squadron		*Tomahawk* (non-operational)
No.13 Squadron	British Isles	*Tomahawk*
No.16 Squadron		*Tomahawk* (non-operational)
No.26 Squadron	Europe (operational)	*Tomahawk*
No.73 Squadron	Middle East	*Tomahawk* (only partially equipped)
No.94 Squadron	Middle East (training only)	*Tomahawk* (non-operational); later *Kittyhawks*
No.112 Squadron	Middle East (Desert Air Force), Italy	*Tomahawk, Kittyhawk.* First RAF unit in the ME to be equipped with *Tomahawks,* June 1941. Credited with introduction of the "Sharks's Tooth" nose.
No.136 Squadron	British Isles	*Tomahawk*
No.168 Squadron	British Isles	*Tomahawk* (non-operational)
No.171 Squadron	British Isles	*Tomahawk* (non-operational)
No.208 Squadron	Middle East	*Tomahawk* (only partially equipped)
No.231 Squadron	British Isles	*Tomahawk* (non-operational)
No.239 Squadron	Europe (operational)	*Tomahawk*
No.241 Squadron	British Isles	*Tomahawk* (non-operational)
No.250 Squadron*	Middle East, Italy	*Tomahawk, Kittyhawk*
No.260 Squadron	Middle East, Italy	*Tomahawk* (non-operational); 2nd unit to fly *Kittyhawk IIs* in Middle East and Italy
No.268 Squadron	Europe (operational)	*Tomahawk*
No.349 Squadron (Belgian)	British Isles	*Tomahawk* (non-operational)
No.369 Squadron	British Isles	*Tomahawk*
No.400 Squadron (RCAF)	Europe (operational)	*Tomahawk*
No.403 Squadron (RCAF)	British Isles	*Tomahawk* (non-operational)
No.414 Squadron (RCAF) (non-operational)	British Isles	*Tomahawk*
No.430 Squadron (RCAF) (non-operational)	British Isles	*Tomahawk*
No.450 Squadron (RAAF)*	Middle East and Italy	*Kittyhawk*
No.613 Squadron	British Isles	*Tomahawk* (not clear if operational)

* These two units, with No. 11 Squadron, SAAF, were the only Commonwealth units to still be flying *Kittyhawks* at the end of the war.

Notes

[1] Also identified in a Curtiss document dated July 10, 1916 as the Curtiss Model S-2 Tractor Aeroplane *Speed Scout,* a marketing name usually linked in many recent sources with the S-1.
[2] Peter M. Bowers, in his landmark *Curtiss Aircraft 1907-1947* (Putnam, London, 1979 ISBN 0-370-10029-8) stated that the S-3 also carried the Curtiss Model Number 10 while the following S-4, S-5 and S-6 were, respectively, the Model 10A, 10B and 10C. No original period Curtiss documents have been located which substantiate this, and the source of his data was apparently the 1946 retrospective Curtiss-Wright document, appended to the end of this volume, which attempted to reconcile the Curtiss designation schemes. The Army, for its part, described the four Model S-3s obtained under contract by August 16, 1917 as *Triplane Speed Scouts.*
[3] *Flight* magazine for November 9, 1916, however, reported that the S-3 had a Curtiss OXX-2 engine.
[4] The Army is known to have placed three separate orders for what were termed Curtiss *Triplanes.* Besides No.6814 (see the S-6), which, rather confusingly, were identified on some Army documents as Model "L" *Pursuit Triplanes,* S.C.5947, dated July 4, 1917, was a contract for at least one *Triplane "...which had larger wings"* and S.C.6619.
[5] An official Army document entitled *"Report on Plane and Engine Production"* dated August 2, 1918, however, shows that only 24 had been shipped from Curtiss "domestically" by July 19, 1918.
[6] The 15 aircraft shipped to Curtiss were S.C.34234, 34235, 34237-34241, 34243, 34246, 34249-34252, 34254 and 34256, with 34233, 34242 and 34244 to follow. All did in fact have *Liberty* engines installed.
[7] A detailed discussion of the ill-fated American Bristol *Fighter* program can be found in the Summer 1972 issue of the *Journal* of the American Aviation Historical Society.
[8] Also cited in several publications as the Curtiss CB *Liberty Battler,* this was apparently a moniker invented by the press of the day.
[9] The Army document entitled *"Report on Plane and Engine Production"* dated August 2, 1918, however, shows that Curtiss was to have delivered *two* SE-5s by September 13, 1918.
[10] Some Curtiss records cite the aircraft as the Curtiss H-A, while one document dated July 8, 1918, identified it as the *HA Two Place Liberty Motor Fighter.* The Navy, however, apparently never used this designation to describe the first aircraft, which is given on the Aircraft History Card as a Curtiss *Fighting Seaplane (Trainer).* Further, a Navy document dated March 23, 1918 cites the type as the Curtiss *Fighter (H.A.)*
[11] Again, this and HA-2 were purely Curtiss designations, as the Navy gave them on the Aircraft History Cards as type Curtiss *Experimental Fighter Seaplanes.* A December 23, 1918 photo of the HA-1, Curtiss also assigned the aircraft the designator Experiment 506. This aircraft gained Navy Bureau of Aeronautics serial number A-4110.
[12] Kirkham himself is usually credited with the design, although this may not be accurate, as the aircraft configuration clearly owed much to the earlier Curtiss HA series.
[13] Peter M. Bowers reported that, although the name *Wasp* was created for marketing purposes, the Model 18 was also referred to at Garden City as the *Whistling Benny* for the distinctive sound the brace wires made when the aircraft approached during landings.
[14] During the trials, all flights by this aircraft were cited as "Experiment 105".
[15] In a letter to the Army dated December 5, 1918, Curtiss himself; in describing these aircraft, said that *"...the first triplane and biplane recently turned out under Mr. Kirkham, are to be known as "Curtiss, Type 18".*
[16] A-3325 was converted to a seaplane on November 28, 1919.
[17] In Curtiss correspondence, they invariably referred to this aircraft as the Model 105.
[18] However, an Army document dated July 8, 1919, reporting on the testing of one of these aircraft, cited it as a "Curtiss B-18" with no mention of the popular name *Hornet.* Originally, as of September 11, 1918, Contract No.106 had covered a total of four aircraft: two biplanes and two triplanes. On September 21, 1918, a triplane built for the Navy was transferred to Contract 106 and received at McCook. The first triplane constructed under Contract 106 was to have been delivered in October and the first biplane near the end of the same month. This triplane was clearly A-3325 and was cited, for the first time, as type *Kirkham Triplane.* Although formally tested by the Navy on September 20th, after the Army was finished evaluating it, it was apparently then returned to the Navy, further confusing the issue.
[19] Another aircraft, clearly an 18B, was identified as Experiment 502.
[20] Tom Foxworth, in a spring 1976 article in the *Journal* of the American Aviation Historical Society, suggested that this aircraft was the un-delivered U.S. Army S.C.40066, a Model 18T-2.
[21] Peter M. Bowers, however, cited the serial for this aircraft as A.S.63276. See the remaining text, however.
[22] It was also cited, apparently in error, as of August 17, 1921 as test number P-190.
[23] A USAAS photo dated August 17, 1921, interestingly, identified the aircraft as the "PW-1 *Nighthawk,"* the only known instance in which this 'popular' name was cited, and the very first use of the name *Hawk* in any form in conjunction with a Curtiss aircraft. The aircraft was also cited on Contract 223 dated July 27, 1921, as the Curtiss Night Pursuit, Type II.
[24] It should be noted, however, that initially, the Navy listed these on the Aircraft History Cards as merely Curtiss TS aircraft, "TS-1" being added, as a pencil entry to some cards, retrospectively. On many period Navy documents, the designation is also given as T.S.-1.
[25] Although contemporary Curtiss documents record only 33, MSNs 10392 to 10424
[26] Although a 1924 Curtiss list of parts for the F4C-1 identified it as the *F4C-1 – Hall All Metal (1700).*
[27] A Curtiss document gives this Navy officers name as Cuddihy, while the other two members of the Navy Trial Board testing the F4C-1 were Lts. McKenna and Ofatie.
[28] Oddly, the Navy History Cards for the two aircraft show the engine type as the J-1. Similarly, they cite the manufacturer plainly as Curtiss, not Curtiss-Hall, as has often been reported.
[29] This may have been the first Curtiss fighter to have a "popular" name. Army History Cards for these aircraft invariably show them in the Model block as type Curtiss PW-8 "Pursuit".
[30] However, period photos of these aircraft do not show an "X" prefix to the designation, merely PW-8. Peter M. Bowers reported that these aircraft were ordered as straight PW-8s, and the "X" prefix was assigned when it was adopted by the Army in March 1924 to distinguish them from the normal production aircraft.
[31] Often cited as an "unofficial conversion," it was very much sanctioned by the Army hierarchy.
[32] PW-8 A.S.24-201, while at McCook Field as P-357, mounted a Boeing designed X-47511 metal prop of eight feet, two inch diameter.
[33] This aircraft was identified in a Curtiss report dated Jun 12, 1924 as both the *PW-8 (L-18-2) Coast-to-Coast Ship* and as the *1924 Coast-to-Coast Pursuit.*
[34] Curtiss documents seem to cast doubt on this long-held belief, as they show that the single XPW-8A was MSN 10496, while the third XPW-8, A.S.23-1203, was MSN 10495.
[35] Some Army documents give the aircraft as P-354 as of January 6, 1925.
[36] Originally, all 15 aircraft were to have been P-1s, but Deviation W-255 redesignated the last five as P-2s.
[37] However, Curtiss documents show that the Army acquired 14 P-1s with MSNs 10535 to 10548 and four P-2s with MSNs 10549 to 10552, with one additional P-1, MSN 10611 following in 1926. The discrepancy cannot be explained.
[38] These performance figures were based on Curtiss tests conducted on August 6 and 7, 1925.
[39] This engine was also cited, in a May 27, 1930 Army document as type V-1460, possibly a typographical error. Another Army document gives it as the V-1470, rated at 480hp at 2,000rpm!
[40] The U.S. Army Air Service was redesignated as the U.S. Army Air Corps in July 1926, and hence the change in serial number prefixes from A.S. to A.C.
[41] Where it apparently gained Project Number XP-537 equipped with a Liberty L12-A engine circa February 2, 1929. The same aircraft was re-engined with a Curtiss D-12E by July 3, 1929.
[42] This was almost certainly *Hawk* MSN 10876, a Curtiss demonstrator, identified in Curtiss records as ...*"built for Doolittle."*
[43] Oddly, the existing Curtiss sales records and Manufacturers Serial Numbers do not reflect these aircraft whatsoever, although they clearly were built and delivered.
[44] Once again, Curtiss records introduce confusion regarding these five aircraft. They are known to have been redesignated as P-1Es when re-engined with V-1150-3 engines, but Curtiss shows these five aircraft *built* as P-1Es as MSN 10758 to 10762, and *not* the final five aircraft of the original AT-4 order.
[45] The attribution of this popular name appears to have originated with the aviation press of the day, and was completely unofficial.
[46] By August 19, 1929, XP-524, with a Pratt & Whitney R-1340, was being tested by the Air Corps, flown by Captain Gail Breene, and designated as type XP-6A.
[47] This was apparently XP-451, tested as such circa November 28, 1927.
[48] Both of the XP-21s were configured as such from the XP-3A (A.C.26-300) and P-3A (28-189) by the Engineering Division itself in December 1930.

[49] The reason behind the oft cited confusion about the total number of F6C-1s acquired by the Navy may be found in the fact that BuA 6973, 6974, 6975 and 6976 were originally noted on their Individual Aircraft Records as F6C-1s. This was stricken through in pencil at some point, however, and changed to F6C-2 "Arresting Gear". Thus, strictly speaking, the original contract had called for a total of nine F6C-1s.
[50] Oddly, there is no mention of this conversion on the Aircraft Record Card for A-6968 or A-6972 whatsoever.
[51] Curtiss did, however, demonstrate both a later *Hawk I* and *Hawk II* to the Brazilian Army's 1st Aviation Regiment around November 13, 1934, and one Curtiss document cites one of these as having been sold to Brazil, but this has completely escaped verification and cannot be accounted for from production figures.
[52] This unit was briefly designated as VB-1B, a dive bomb test unit, and several of the F6C-3s carried codes for a bombing unit as a result. Unlike Air Corps units, Navy units retained "popular" names while changing function identifiers.
[53] Curtiss records, however, show a total of 18 F7C-1s, MSNs 11214 to 11231, following in sequence directly after the Army P-1Cs. BuA serial numbers, however, 7654 to 7670, account for only 17 aircraft!
[54] An Army document dated November 17, 1930, cited the XP-6A as having a Curtiss V-1570A engine at that time, but gives the serial number as 29-263, q.v.. This was obviously not the same aircraft and seems to indicate that the designation XP-6A was used twice.
[55] The aircraft was cited officially as of October 30, 1929 as simply a P-6, XP-590, the only known instance in which this test/project identification was used.
[56] Again, Curtiss records reflect a discrepancy. MSNs 11240 to 11250 were assigned to 11 P-6s, while 11251 to 11259 were assigned to nine P-6As. Oddly, the P-6A Air Corps serial numbers come in sequence *before* those for the P-6s, having been 29-260 to 29-268. The discrepancy can be explained by the fact that these aircraft were originally planned as Prestone-cooled aircraft, but 11 were changed to water-cooling to facilitate delivery. The Prestone equipped balance were then given the designation P-6A (q.v.)
[57] These eight aircraft have frequently been confused with six additional aircraft of the same basic configuration built under license by Aviolanda in the Netherlands for the NEIAAF. Thus, a total of 14 aircraft, serialed C-307 to C-320 were used in the Netherlands East Indies – with C-315 to C-320 having been the Aviolanda-built machines. The first of these flew with a temporary marking, H-1 in Holland, which was the Aviolanda manufacturer's serial number.
[58] This aircraft is alleged by at least one source to have previously been assigned Restricted License NR-9W, but this has eluded verification.
[59] At least one authoritative source has suggested that Cuba acquired four P-6S aircraft and, as noted, serial numbers reported seem to support this. However, these aircraft do not appear on Curtiss Manufacturer Serial Number listings and thus cannot be confirmed. Cuban Governmental Decree No.2005, dated December 4, 1929, authorized the purchase of three *Hawks,* so if a fourth was indeed acquired, it may have been a replacement for one lost. Photos exist of aircraft marked with serials 15, 16, 17 and 18, leading obviously to the suggestion that either one was reserialed or a fourth replacement aircraft acquired at some point. The small USAAC mission to Cuba recommended against the purchase and had, instead, suggested that Boeing P-12 types might be more suitable.
[60] However, co-author Hagedorn, after conducting an individual search of every Individual Aircraft History Card, can only account for 12 P-6Ds based on the actual Individual Aircraft History Cards entries. Air Corps records indicate that the aircraft converted were A.C.29-269 to 29-273; 29-363 to 29-368; 29-262 to 29-266 and 29-268.
[61] Besides the straightforward Curtiss MSN assigned each aircraft, there is evidence that Curtiss also assigned the P-6Es an "in sequence" number for each aircraft. For instance, A.C.32-242 was also cited as Mfg.No.10 as of January 24, 1932.
[62] A Curtiss-Wright Export Corporation document states that Panama acquired *four* of these aircraft, for a total of $32,400, including two guns each and two A-3 bomb racks each. This total has escaped verification.
[63] For full details of the employment of the Bolivian *Osprey's,* readers are recommended to see another Schiffer book, ***Aircraft of the Chaco War 1928-1935*** by Dan Hagedorn and Antonio Sapienza.
[64] This was also cited, for internal purposes, as the Curtiss L-18-37 as of February 3, 1932.
[65] An official USAAC photo, dated September 10, 1934, identified the aircraft as the "XYP-23"!
[66] This may account for an aircraft listed on the September 1945 "Curtiss-Wright Airplane Model Designations" publication as an "XF8C-2A", a designation that is not found anywhere else.
[67] This mount has invariably been incorrectly identified as the old Type A ("Scarffe") Ring Mount.
[68] Some sources claim a total of 91, but identified Navy Bureau of Aeronautics serials account for only 63 in three batches: BuA 8446 to 8456 (11), A-8589 to 8597 (nine) and A-8748 to 8790 (43).
[69] Which was given as Curtiss Project Number L-20-2 as of January 27, 1932.
[70] This is often cited, erroneously, as NX-986M. At the time, the "N" prefix was optional, and only required if the aircraft was going to be flown or demonstrated outside of the U.S. On the Department of Commerce Application for registration, Curtiss gave the manufacturing date for this aircraft as September 28, 1931 and engine type as a supercharged 420hp Wright J-6-9 *Whirlwind.* The experimental license was issued to expire April 1, 1932 and extended to expire October 1, 1932. It suffered an unspecified accident at Amherst, NY (near Buffalo) on September 30, 1931.
[71] At this time, being flown as a Curtiss-owned aircraft, the aircraft would have required issuance of a Department of Commerce experimental license, but there is no record of such an assignment. Further, as XF11C-1 is clearly a Navy designation, if the aircraft was flown and tested by Curtiss prior to acquisition by the Navy, it would have used some other designator, which has also eluded identification. These two facts, taken together, strongly suggests that Navy involvement in the evolution of the aircraft may have been more discreet than has heretofore been reported. Some historians have suggested that the DoC simply winked at such operations but, in fact, there is ample evidence that Curtiss followed the rules in a number of similar instances. Some sources claim that the XF11C-1 was "completed" after the XF11C-2, but according to Curtiss records, this is clearly not the case, as both were flown for the first time the same day and accepted by the Navy the same day.
[72] These MSNs, however, account for only 27 aircraft. This is because the final aircraft on the contract, MSN 11729, became the XF11C-3 (XBF2C-1) BuA 9269.
[73] There is a conflict in Curtiss documents regarding the total number of aircraft sold to China on S.O.116. One document shows 18, and is supported by the known MSNs, while another, the Curtiss Billing Book assembled by Louis Kessler, reflects a total of not less than 44 without supporting MSNs.
[74] Although this is the date of delivery given in Curtiss documents, an "Actual Weight and Balance Report" for this aircraft, done at Buffalo, was dated October 22, 1934!
[75] Many sources cite China as receiving 112 *Hawk IIIs,* but this has been attributed to a simple administrative error made at some point in the so-called "Curtiss Order Book" and related documents.
[76] One other Curtiss document gives the S.O. as 139, which is more likely correct.
[77] This is contrary to an otherwise excellent monograph on the *Hawks* in Argentina by Jorge Nunez Padin, which stipulated that they were serialed in straight numeric order by MSN. Curtiss records dispute this.
[78] Some sources claim a total of 70 or 71, but this cannot be substantiated, and is believed to include rebuilds of aircraft that were damaged.
[79] For the record, the other contestants in this competition were the Northrop 3A, the Vought V-141, the Seversky SEV-1XP mentioned, and the Consolidated PB-2A.
[80] It is interesting to note that, as of September 4, 1936, Curtiss was referring to the aircraft as the D-75-B.
[81] A Curtiss designation, not to be confused with the much later Fisher P-75A built for the USAAF.
[82] Often cited in many references as type "H75H" for reasons unknown, Curtiss, as of April 23, 1937, invariable referred to MSN 12327 NR-1276 as type D-75H. However, the actual Curtiss Detailed Specifications for these designs gave them as Designs 75-H, 75-M, 75-N, 75-O and 75-P, all dated the same date – March 15, 1937.
[83] These are also cited on Curtiss documents dated October 12, 1937, as merely "China Hawk 75s" with Wright GR-1820-G3 engines on Sales Order 175.
[84] The appearance in some correspondence of the "H" prefix to the 75M designation was apparently an unofficial, short-hand way of expressing *Hawk* 75M.
[85] For an excellent discussion of the Chinese *Hawk* programs, see Gerry Beauchamp's article "*Hawks of the Eastern Skies*" which commenced in Part 1, *Air Classics.*
[86] Although most sources state that this aircraft was sold to Argentina, this is incorrect. Although demonstrated to the Argentine Army bearing Argentine markings during 1937, it was destroyed while enroute to neighboring Chile for demonstrations there at Mendoza, Argentina on March 3, 1938.
[87] The provisions of the License agreement enabled the *FMA* to build up to 200 of these aircraft, and stipulated the fixed-gear *Hawk 75-O* variant, however, at one point it was changed to read "*...Hawk 75-A with retractable undercarriages and other improvements.*" However, this was quickly altered back to the fixed gear variant as it was realized that the *FMA* was not yet up to the task and, further, that the locally built examples should have as much in common as possible with the Curtiss-built examples.
[88] The Air Corps ordered the grounding of P-36As 38-1, 38-2, 38-4, 38-5 and 38-6 effective September 20, 1938, pending modification of their engines to R-1830-17s.
[89] These wing guns necessitated the installation of the distinctive cartridge retainer housing under the wings, often the subject of speculation by observers noting them for the first time.

[90] However, the Detailed Specification for the 75-R dated March 15, 1937, called for an Allison XV-1710-11 of 1,000hp at 2,600rpm. The Air Corps also described the H75-R demonstrated to the Army between May 8th and 26th, 1939, for some reason, as Contractor Model 7434.

[91] Some Curtiss documents cite a total of only 530, to have been covered by Sales Orders 140 to 147, with MSNs 13671 to 14200.

[92] Interestingly, the armament consisted of a mix of two nose, synchronized F.N. 7.5mm guns and four wing-mounted Colt 7.5mm guns.

[93] The vast majority, which went to the British, had six British Browning .303 caliber guns, two synchronized and four wing guns.

[94] There is evidence that France had contracted for about 100 more H75A-4s that were never built.

[95] For an excellent summary of French operational use of their *Hawk 75As,* see Jean Cuny's article in the spring 1966 issue of the *Journal* of the American Aviation Historical Society (AAHS), commencing page 13.

[96] The RAF serials issued to these aircraft were AR630 to AR694 (65 aircraft, a mix of *Mohawk IIIs* and *IVs*), AX880 to AX898 (19 aircraft, *Mohawks*), BB918 to BB937 and BB974 to BB979 (26 aircraft, *Mohawk IVs*), BJ434 to BJ453 (20 aircraft, *Mohawk IVs*), BJ531 to BJ550 (20 aircraft, *Mohawk IVs*), BK574 to BK588 (15 aircraft, *Mohawk IVs*), BK876 to BK879 (four aircraft, *Mohawks*), BL220 to BL223 (four aircraft, *Mohawks*), BS730 to BS738 and BS744 to BS747 (13 aircraft, *Mohawk IVs*), BS784 to BS798 (15 aircraft, *Mohawk IVs*) and BT470 to BT472 (three aircraft, *Mohawk IVs*).

[97] Of these, only 80 serials were issued by the South African Air Force, SAAF 2501 to 2580, nearly all of which were from ex-French contracts, while three others were captured or escaped *Vichy* French aircraft. The SAAF aircraft actually in South Africa were all grounded effective June 11, 1943 due to continual failures of the master rod bearings in the engines, but most were eventually returned to service after considerable exertions by the engine manufacturer.

[98] The 16 aircraft acquired by Portugal were ex-RAF AR636, 642, 652, 668, 679, 680, AX882, 886, BB927, BJ531, 547, 548, BK582, BL220, BS732 and BS789.

[99] The original Detailed Specification had called for a Wright R-1820-G107.

[100] The aircraft which reached Finland were MSNs 13643 to 13654 and 13659 to 13670 with Finnish serials 437 to 473 (odd numbers only).

[101] Most sources state that these aircraft had two 12.7mm guns in the nose, while other claim all four guns were 12.7mm.

[102] These were Curtiss MSNs 14546 to 14581.

[103] These were USAAF serials 42-38305 to 42-38322; one of these was delayed enroute due to damage and wasn't repaired, at France Field, Panama Canal Zone, with Peruvian code 21-1-2, until March 21, 1944!

[104] The second batch, oddly, had an entirely different serials of USAAF serials and included 42-108995 to 42-109006.

[105] This was given as MSN 14549, which was 42-108998, which was damaged beyond repair at Had. San Nicolas on May 10, 1943.

[106] One Curtiss document states that Iran acquired only nine H75A-9's on their contract.

[107] There is evidence that the total actually received by Cuba was only three, and that the other two aircraft are the ones that went to the Dominican Republic.

[108] Some sources cite the 8th Pursuit Group.

[109] The "CW-" prefix to Curtiss-Wright, St. Louis Division designs has gained currency in recent years, and is used here for the sake of brevity only; the convention was apparently rarely used internally by the company, and never officially.

[110] Photos of the aircraft as NX-19431 exist with the date October 10, 1938, thus establishing that the aircraft definitely existed as such at that date.

[111] For reasons unknown, Curtiss started assigning Manufacturers Serial Numbers in the Buffalo series to St. Louis built aircraft commencing in 1939 with 50 export Curtiss-Wright Model 22 *Falcons,* all of which apparently also had St. Louis assigned MSNs as well!

[112] One Curtiss-Wright document states that the order involved 32 sets of material and one complete set of tools and drawings for assembling the aircraft on Sales Order D-9 and D-10.

[113] Often cited in late 1940s and wartime publications by the popular name *Demon,* no corroborating Curtiss-Wright documents could be located authenticating this as an "official", company-authorized type name. Indeed, the origins of this oft-repeated "popular" name may be ridiculously simple: the Curtiss-Wright 1946 document cited elsewhere in this work, which retrospectively attempted to identify all company aircraft projects, listed, in the "Model Designations" block for the original CW-21, the term (Demons). This was, of course, a reference to the fact that the aircraft was a Demonstrator. It is believed that this reference was subsequently perverted by some hasty conclusion to read "Demons".

[114] The earliest known photos of NX-19441 are dated March 15, 1940. At least two other CW-21s apparently were issued U.S. civil Identification Marks as 19442 (MSN 21-3) and 19443 (MSN 21-4), but these may have been test registrations used to satisfy Dutch acceptance team members. One source claims these were amongst three aircraft sent to China, but this is incorrect.

[115] Photos of Dutch aircraft, apparently while being tested in the U.S. in September 1940, have surfaced with what appear to be Dutch type codes as C-338 and C-339, which were MSN 2852 and 2853. Since the aircraft were initially ordered for service in the homeland, the Royal Netherlands Air Force codes would have been in the 300 series as well, but even at that, numbers 338 and 339 don't fit well. The Dutch East Indies serials as shown in the text, however, were definitely used in the East Indies, as MSN 2852 was CW-343 and MSN 2853 was CW-344. The Ministry of the Colonies took over the homeland order for CW-21s when Holland was overrun and, as that Ministry administered the Royal Netherlands East Indies Army, which was completely separate from the home Army, they utilized a similar but distinct system of their own for serialing aircraft.

[116] A full account of the use of the Dutch Model 22 by Dan Hagedorn appeared in ***Skyways: The Journal of the Airplane 1920-1940*** No.63 for July 2002.

[117] This was, officially, Change Order No.2954 to Contract AC-10136.

[118] It is interesting to note that the Final Specification for the P-40, No.7437, dated January 3, 1939 and revised November 15, 1941, referred to the aircraft as the Curtiss Model C-39-7.

[119] For the record, the aircraft which became P-40Gs were USAAC serials 39-162, -176, -182, -187, -190, -191, -196, -197, -204, -206, -209, -217, -220, -221, -226, -235, -238, -243, -248, -257, -263, -267, -275, -276, -279, -288, 40-292, -297, -299, -300, -301, -303, -309, -315, -318, -320, -323, -331, -332, -333, -335, -336, -337, -338, -340 and 40-348. Additionally, there were at least 17 of these same aircraft, as noted in the text, re-serialed later in the range 42-14261 to 42-14281 designated as P-40Gs, and these were all issued on or around December 26, 1941 and most were assigned to either March Field or Middletown Air Depot originally. At least two of these were repossessed from British acquired aircraft. The designation P-40H was proposed to be assigned to the lightweight aircraft initially known as the P-40X (q.v.), which led to the P-40N series.

[120] However, a Wright Field accounting, done on April 14, 1942, positively identified only *one* P-40G as actually having gone to the Soviet Union prior to the so-called Arnold-Portal Protocol, AC39-221. However, Curtiss Billing Book entries reflect that Sales Order 7198, dated between October 25, 1941 and November 1941, covered P-40Gs for Russia including 39-196, 39-209, 39-217, 39-238, 39-243, 29-248, 39-275, 39-288, 40-297, 40-300, 40-301, 40-303, 40-309, 40-318, 40-320, 40-332, 40-335, 40-336 and 40-338 in addition to 39-221 for a total of 20.

[121] It is worth noting that the very first comment made by the pilot after his first 10 minute flight was that "*...it was determined on landing that this plane has very definite ground looping tendencies.*" This was of course fixed by correcting the contours of the wing fillets and extending the tail wheel so as to reduce the angle of attack of the aircraft on the ground.

[122] However, only 23 have been positively identified. Those shipped by April 1, 1941 were 41-5265 to 4105282, 41-5284 and 41-5285 and 41-5287 to 41-5290.

[123] A total of 16 P-40Cs went to Russia *prior to* the so-called Arnold Portal Protocol, and a Wright Field accounting of these, dated April 14, 1942, informed that they were 41-13351, -13353 to 13358, -13369 to 13371, 13373, -13374, -13395, -13450, -13451 and 41-13469.

[124] The actual Contract, No. A-84, between Curtiss and the British Air Commission, cited the aircraft type involved as the *Hawk* 81-A. Significantly, this same contract, which called out 780 such aircraft, stated that "*...the seller has diverted 100 of these airplanes for sale to others and has made full settlement of all moneys owing the purchaser by reason of such diversion*" should establish, once and for all, the source of the aircraft that went to the AVG. For the first time, these aircraft can be positively identified. They were in fact H81A-2s as follows:

Curtiss Man. Serial	Chinese Sequence Number	Former Assigned RAF Serial	Curtiss Man. Serial	Chinese Sequence Number	Former Assigned RAF Serial
15337	1	AK466	15894	51	AM441
15338	2	AK467	15896	52	AM443
15339	3	AK468	15898	53	AM445
15423	4	AK471	15900	54	AM447
15424	5	AK472	15902	55	AM449
15425	6	AK473	15904	56	AM451
15430	7	AK478	15906	57	AM453
15431	8	AK479	15908	58	AM455
15432	9	AK480	15910	59	AM457
15433	10	AK481	15911	60	AM458
15438	11	AK486	15913	61	AM460
15439	12	AK487	15915	62	AM462
15444	13	AK492	15916	63	AM463
15445	14	AK493	15918	64	AM465
15457	15	AK500	15920	65	AM467
15452	16	AK501	15921	66	AM468
15459	17	AK507	15923	67	AM470

15460	18	AK508	15925	68	AM472
15466	19	AK514	15926	69	AM473
15467	20	AK515	15928	70	AM475
15473	21	AK521	15930	71	AM477
15474	22	AK522	15931	72	AM478
15480	23	AK528	15933	73	AM480
15481	24	AK529	15935	74	AM482
15487	25	AK535	15937	75	AM484
15488	26	AK536	15939	76	AM486
15494	27	AK542	15940	77	AM487
15495	28	AK543	15942	78	AM489
15501	29	AK549	15944	79	AM491
15502	30	AK550	15945	80	AM492
15508	31	AK556	15947	81	AM494
15509	32	AK557	15949	82	AM496
15514	33	AK562	15950	83	AM497
15515	34	AK563	15952	84	AM499
15521	35	AK569	15954	85	AM501
15522	36	AK570	15955	86	AM502
15828	37	AM375	15957	87	AM504
15834	38	AM381	15959	88	AM506
15841	39	AM388	15961	89	AM508
15848	40	AM395	15962	90	AM509
15855	41	AM402	15963	91	AM510
15862	42	AM409	15964	92	AM511
15869	43	AM416	15965	93	AM512
15876	44	AM423	15966	94	AM513
15882	45	AM429	15967	95	AM514
15884	46	AM431	15968	96	AM515
15886	47	AM433	15969	97	AM516
15887	48	AM435	15970	98	AM517
15890	49	AM437	15971	99	AM518
15892	50	AM439	15972	100	AM519

[125] Indeed, the first 100 H81A-1s were tacked on to the end of the last order for H75A-4s and may account for the numeric discrepancy in the total of H75A-4s ordered. They would have been French H81A-1 Nos.1 to 100, MSNs 14446 to 14545. These would have had Allison V-1710-C15 engines with single-stage, gear driven superchargers, as standardized for French orders, identical to the engines specified for the French orders for Lockheed 322s and Bell 14s. Following the placement of this contract, the last 130 H75A-4s were cancelled and reinstated as 130 H81A-1s, intended to become French serials H81A-1 Nos. 101 to 230. They assumed the Curtiss MSNs for the cancelled H75A-4s, 14091 to 14220.

[126] The following aircraft for Russia have been positively identified: AH936, AH952, AH965 to AH971, AH974 to AH985, AH987, AH989 and AH990 for a total of 24 aircraft.

[127] Curtiss records show this batch as type H81A-2, however, commencing with MSN 17817 and accepted starting April 30th.

[128] The other eight winterized P-40Es were 40-384, -391, -594, -596, -598, -608, -609 and -612.

[129] These aircraft were U.S. serials AC41-5654, 41-5655, 41-5657, 41-5659 to -5662, 41-5664 to -5674, 41-5678 to -5682, 41-5686 to -5690, 41-5694 to -5697, 41-5698, 41-5702 to -5704 to -5706, 41-5710 to -5713, 41-5718, 41-5718 to -5720, 41-5656, 41-5658, 41-5663, 41-5721 and 41-5728.

[130] These 21 aircraft, delivered prior to the Arnold-Portal Protocol, were AC40-613, -636, -641, -644, -645, -648, -649, -652, -653, -656, -657, -660, -661, -664, -665, -668, -669, -672, -673, -676 and -680/

[131] These were USAAC serials 41-36096, -36132, (-36133), -36134, -36135, -36136 and -36139, all delivered commencing April 30, 1942.

[132] However, the lowest Curtiss MSN for an H87A-2 that could be located was 14953, which was AK572, accepted August 25th.

[133] Contrary to popular report, this aircraft was never formally designated as a P-40D; the Aircraft History Card designated it as XP-40F from the very beginning.

[134] There is no indication of this designation on the Aircraft History Card.

[135] However, an AAF document dated September 7, 1942 stated that the following P-40F-5-CU block should commence "*...with the 701st P-40F on Contract AC-15802, the starting ship for the fuselage extension.*" Significantly, the same document stated that Curtiss would "*...try to redesignate all P-40K aircraft as P-40F-5-CU and try to pick up P-40F aircraft back to AC41-14300 in lieu of the serial numbers originally assigned,*" although exactly what these were to have been was not cited.

[136] P-40F 41-13600, the very first aircraft, had been assigned to NACA at Langley, VA between July 23 and September 1, 1942 specifically to be used for development testing to improve the directional stability of the aircraft. Revisions to the fin shape and lengthening of the fuselage were areas that were investigated.

[137] These nine aircraft were 42-45921, -45944, -45945, -45951, -45952, -45954, -45977, -46003 and -46004, all assigned within Western Air Command.

[138] The first P-40Ks to go to Alaska were apparently 42-10265 and 42-10266, which were assigned to Ladd Field November 15, 1942, for winterization trials.

[139] These were USAAF 42-10089-10091, 42-10099-10101, 42-10109-10111 and 42-10119; 42-10389-10390, 42-10396, 42-10398, 42-10399, 42-10401, 42-10406-10408, 42-10410, 42-10411, 42-10416-10421 and 42-46213 and 42-46296. For reasons unknown, three additional unidentified aircraft on the March 1943 batch were not delivered, and may have been lost enroute.

[140] These aircraft were 42-45987 to 42-45991, 42-45993, 42-45996 to 42-45998, 42-46000 to 42-46002, 42-46005 to 42-46011, 42-46016, 42-46017 and 42-46019, which had Squadron Numbers 266 to 270, 272, 275 to 277, 279 to 281, 284 to 290, 295, 296 and 298, respectively.

[141] Some sources, including Army documents such as Army Aircraft Characteristics, TSEST-A2 dated April 1, 1946 and the 1945 AAF Model Designation Handbook, quote between 300 and as many as 600 such conversions, although exactly how this figure was arrived at is unknown. These totals are not supported by the Aircraft Record Cards and available aircraft. Peter M. Bowers, in his classic Curtiss book by Putnam, listed 71 P-40R-1s and 53 P-40R-2s, which he stated were "confirmed by serial number". Other historians of the P-40, including Craig "Buz" Busby, through very painstaking research, have arrived at 62 P-40R-1s and 51 P-40R-2s, for a total of not more than 113 aircraft.

[142] Some sources state that Brazil received 19 P-40Ms under Lend-Lease, but this is not correct. Ten were allocated, but only nine delivered.

[143] The USAAF serials for the Brazilian aircraft were 43-5651, -5658, -5659, -5666, -5667. -5674, -5675, -5682, -5690 and a 10th aircraft, unidentified, not taken up and probably lost in transit.

[144] There was an aircraft designated as an XP-40N, USAAF serial 42-45722. However, the relationship of this aircraft to the evolution of the P-40N variant is not clear.

[145] These aircraft were USAAF serials 44-7696-7715; 44-47764-47773; 44-47866-47876.

[146] These aircraft were USAAF serials 42-105346, -105348, -105430, -105443, -105445, -105456, -10565, -105469, -105619, and -105628

[147] 18 aircraft from these two blocks were issued under Lend-Lease to the Netherlands East Indies Air Force and coded C3-549 to C3-566. By V-J Day, 37 Dutch P-40Ns remained on strength with 120 Squadron and 1t least 11 soldiered on as late as May 1, 1949, by which time the survivors had been coded with a "J" prefix, e.g., J-311, J-316, J-322 etc.

[148] At least one of these was a semi-official conversion of an unidentified aircraft completed by the Omaha Nebraska Modification Center.

[149] Many sources over the years have incorrectly labeled this aircraft as the XP-40Q-1, which is incorrect.

[150] In fact, AC41-140 was apparently not actually assigned to an XP-53. There is no Individual Aircraft History Card for any aircraft with this serial, and the official USAF Report of Serial Numbers Assigned to Aircraft simply shows 41-140 as "Windtunnel". Serial 41-19508 was, in fact, the XP-60, and there is no mention of the designation XP-53 whatsoever on the Individual Aircraft History Card for this serial number. It appears, therefore, that if in fact 41-140 was assigned, it was never officially applied to a completed aircraft.